W9-BRU-719

FISHING

Books by the Author

An Outdoor Life Book

FISHING

**An encyclopedic guide to tackle and tactics
for fresh and salt water**

by JOSEPH D. BATES, JR.

Drawings by TED BURWELL

OUTDOOR LIFE

Sunrise Books / E. P. Dutton & Company, Inc.
New York

Library of Congress Number: 73-80714
SBN: 0-87690-109-7

Designed by Jeff Fitschen

Manufactured in the United States of America

To our members
of the younger generation—

PAMELA BATES BIRD
and
BRUCE ELLIS BATES—

and all the others
who bother to notice
the glory of God
in a little patch of
damp green moss

Contents

Part I—FRESHWATER FISHING

Introduction

If you're a fisherman and were lucky, you had a father or an older friend to teach you the sport when you were very young. This may have started innocently enough by dunking a worm off a dock for pumpkinseeds or perch. When you hooked a fish it's a safe bet that you were hooked, too—on a sport that can remain simple or that can lead into fascinating complications and unexplored byroads without end. Fishing, for example, can lure one into fly tying and tackle making. It can lead one into the kindred explorations of limnology, ichthyology, entomology and several other 'ologies, as well as tempting one to collect a library of angling books and perhaps to travel to distant corners of the world to catch the biggest or more elusive tackle busters on the lightest and finest of equipment.

Why does the fishing bug bite so many people so hard? Mainly, because it gets them outdoors and provides something interesting to do when they get there. To a fisherman, the outdoors means beauty, clean water, solitude or companionship; time to experiment, relax and reflect, and to pit one's skill against an adversary he may never have seen. As former President Herbert Hoover once said:

"Fishing is a chance to wash one's soul with pure air, with the rush of a brook, or with the shimmer of the sun on blue water. It brings meekness and inspiration from the scenery of nature, charity toward tackle makers, patience toward fish, a mockery of profits and egos, a quieting of hate, a rejoicing that you do not have to decide a darned thing until next week—and it is discipline in the equality of man, for all men are equal before fish.''

Perhaps part of the lure of fishing is that its addicts can play the game exactly as they want, subject of course to a few rules laid down by the fish and game department. You can start with only a hook or two and a few yards of line, cutting your own pole and finding your own bait. Part of your reward is the excitement of a sharp tug; perhaps a few vigorous runs and jumps, and the thrill of seeing your quarry flopping safely on the bank. You are rewarded again when the quarry has been prepared for the table and served fragrantly hot.

Lazy fishermen can toss out a bait and then sit down and doze while waiting for something to happen. More energetic ones can cruise in boats or wade in streams and cast or troll with a wide array of tackle. Knowing how to cast, where to cast, which lure to use, and how to fish it becomes part of the game—a game that can be developed and continued indefinitely. Active fishermen with an urge for competition can seek the "big ones" and pit their skill against wary trout, giant muskies, leaping tarpon, slashing sailfish and countless other species, even using light fly rods and small artificial flies to catch prizes weighing up to a hundred pounds or more. There is no end to it, and the beckoning endless road is part of the lure of fishing!

When winter comes, or there's a rainy evening or two, the fun of fishing isn't over. Fishing through the ice claims addicts by the millions, and warmer regions offer variety year-round. Indoors, one can tie flies. This is a bug that bites hard, too, because every fly is lovingly and painstakingly assembled to the best of one's ability, and it doesn't take much ability to fashion a fly that will take fish. But this also is an endless road; a road toward the perfection few fly tyers ever reach. Fly tying can become a very fine art, and perhaps the peak of fishing is to catch a trophy on a fly one has tied himself.

If that isn't your cup of tea, or if you want a respite from it, there's always something to do when the weather is bad. There's tackle to mend or to play with, leaders to make, lures to polish and repair, angling books to read, or theories to discuss with friends before the fire.

Some say, "Why bother with fishing any more? Our streams are polluted, our fish are getting smaller and fewer, good waters often are posted, and one has to travel farther and farther for his sport." While this is true to a degree, the tide is being turned. At long last even our politicians have been made to realize that each one must do his utmost to reverse the rape of our environment. Farm ponds are being built and are being stocked. Clubs and state and federal agencies are cleaning up our waters and are planting them with fish. Many attempts are very successful, such as the bonanza of salmon fishing in some of the Great Lakes, where no salmon lived before in the memory of man. Impoundments made for flood control or water conservation may have ruined a few streams, but the resulting lakes and reservoirs often teem with more and bigger fish than the regions ever knew. Fishermen are aiding these efforts by joining together in organized and vocal groups so great in number that they now have a resounding voice in environmental decisions. The stuff which litters our streams and lakesides rarely is left there by fishermen. Usually they are the sort of people who enjoy the outdoors and who want to keep it clean. To quote again from angler Hoover, "All fishermen and fisherladies are by nature friendly and righteous persons. No one of them ever went to jail while fishing—unless he forgot to buy a license."

With the increase of fishermen and the decrease of fish, thoughtful anglers realize added action is necessary to maintain the sport at highest productivity. So "fishing for fun" areas are increasing on many streams. Catch all you want, but keep no more than one. In most places bringing home a creel-full of small fish isn't praiseworthy. Returning with one or two big ones deserves congratulations because probably they should be harvested anyway. Thus, in "fishing for fun" areas, many fish are hooked many times. Of course they get smarter, but that increases the challenge. And, by the same token, reduced bag limits usually are accepted in good grace. The general idea is to cull the big ones and to release the others to grow up.

Thousands of books have been written about fishing, and many have become rare and cherished classics. One of my publishers said, "Why not put everything under one cover—everything a fisherman should know about where to find fish and how to catch them. Include all the new information and make it the *complete* book for both fresh and salt water." The idea seemed to be a good one, and this is the result.

Although I am supposed to know a thing or two about fishing, I would be the first to admit that no one knows everything about it. Thus, some of the information in this book was obtained by passing the hat among my fishing buddies. They came to my rescue, and my thanks to all of them.

JOSEPH D. BATES, JR.
Longmeadow, Massachusetts

FISHING

1

Spinning

In the 1940s, fishermen were startled to see a few rugged individualists using an underslung reel attached to a light rod with outsize guides which could accurately cast even the tiniest of weighted lures amazing distances. They derisively called the reel a "coffee grinder."

As time went on, however, the principle proved so practical that it has become a major angling method, perhaps more popular than any other. Its secret is in the open-faced reel from which the line uncoils from a stationary spool with negligible friction, thus permitting longer casts with much lighter lures. We can compare this with the principle of the much older baitcasting reel where, in casting, the reel spool must revolve. This causes considerable friction, which decreases the distance of the cast unless much heavier lures are used. Also, if the baitcasting reel is not properly "thumbed," or controlled, its spool may revolve so fast as to overrun the line and cause backlash.

Following the advent of the open-faced spinning reel, manufacturers developed another reel which is a compromise between spinning and baitcasting. This is properly called a spincasting reel and should not be confused with either of the other two. Spincasting calls for a closed-faced instead of an open-faced reel spool. It virtually eliminates the backlashes so common to beginners in baitcasting, but, owing to increased friction, it requires stronger lines and heavier lures to cast as far as the open-faced

1

Spinning tackle finds service on lake and stream, for all kinds of gamefish. Grinning with satisfaction, a veteran bass fisherman boats a lunker taken on his rugged spinning outfit; a youngster coolly plays a northern pike in the shallows; a wader reaps thrills tussling with a smallmouth on a light spin rig.

spinning reel. The next chapters will discuss spincasting and baitcasting, their advantages and disadvantages. Here, we are concerned only with spinning.

Since writers about spinning have stressed the ease of learning the method, anglers generally have assumed there's nothing to it. They have fallen into unnecessary trouble by thinking they can buy any kind of tackle and start without instruction. They should realize that there are numerous tricks which, when learned, will make spinning more productive and enjoyable.

When choosing spinning tackle, beginners should avoid low-cost "bargains" in unknown brands. Bargains or discounts are all right if one can get them, but many bargains should be viewed with suspicion. Why the lower price? We all know who the firmly established tackle manufacturers are because our friends use and like the equipment, and we have seen it advertised consistently in outdoor publications. Select current (rather than discontinued) rods and reels made by the firmly established manufacturers because they wouldn't have remained in business so long by offering inferior merchandise. True, we find occasionally excellent imports which may not be well known but, generally, the vast volumes sold by the big and well-known makers assure obtaining the best equipment for your money.

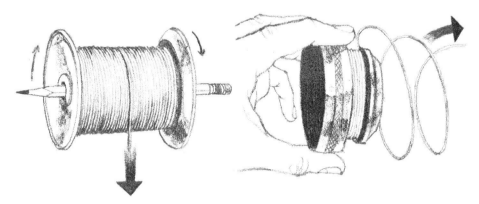

Principle of the spinning reel as opposed to the baitcasting reel. During cast, the weight of the lure pulls line from the baitcasting reel like thread from a spool (*left*). The revolving spool creates friction, and may overrun the line and cause a backlash. Spinning reel has a stationary spool (*right*), from which the line uncoils as it is pulled by the weight of the cast lure.

ASSEMBLING A SPINNING OUTFIT

Although one angler in many still may want a spinning rod made of split bamboo, the most sensible choice is one made of glass fiber. For average freshwater fishing the rod will be 6½ or 7 feet long, with a large butt (or gathering) guide and five or six smaller ring guides properly spaced and graduated in size to the tiptop. The grip may be all cork, or it may have a built-in locking reel seat. While the beginner may prefer the latter, some experienced fishermen using rods in the lighter weight ranges prefer the all-cork reel seat with sliding rings because they consider it more comfortable and it allows the reel to be properly positioned for the best balance.

Sometimes a reel doesn't fit the reel seat on a rod, thus causing it to wobble. Take along a piece of inner-tube rubber and cut part of it to the shape of the reel's foot. Putting this between reel foot and reel seat should prevent wobble.

In cold weather the metal on fixed reel seats may be uncomfortable to handle, or the rings on sliding reel seats may tend to work loose. These difficulties can be eliminated by binding the reel seat with plastic adhesive tape. It's not very pretty, but it can solve the problem!

In buying rods offered by established manufacturers one need not be concerned very much with rod action. Most manufacturers standardize the action that provides greatest casting efficiency. However, the action should be felt well down into the butt of the rod; the tip, when oscillated, should come to rest without excessive wobble.

The average freshwater (or light saltwater) spinning rod should handle lures of about ¼ ounce. When the outfit is assembled and the lure hangs a foot or so below the rod tip, the lure should depress the forward part of the rod only slightly. If the lure hardly depresses the rod tip, it is too light for the rod. If it depresses the tip excessively, it is too heavy. Remember that, in spinning, the monofilament line has negligible weight, and it is the power of the rod combined with the weight of the lure that carries the lure to its target. Lures that are too heavy or too light for the rod won't cast properly.

Spinning reels may be divided roughly into four sizes. The smallest reel normally is used with light tackle, which is lighter than that now being discussed. The next-larger size is for medium freshwater (or light saltwater) fishing. The next-to-largest reel would be used for heavy freshwater or medium saltwater fishing. The largest reel mainly is for heavy saltwater fishing, although it has freshwater uses, primarily for very large fish, especially in fast currents or deep in lakes.

The medium-sized reel should hold at least 200 yards of 6-pound-test monofilament line; a bit more or less, perhaps, when lighter or heavier lines are used. We used to think that 3- or 4-pound-test monofilament was about

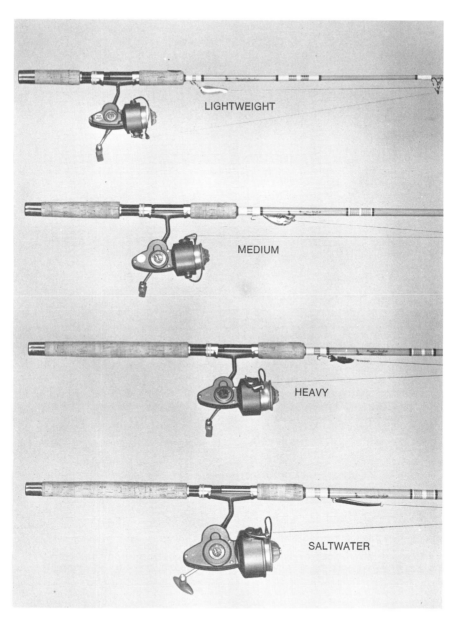

LIGHTWEIGHT

MEDIUM

HEAVY

SALTWATER

Four sizes of spinning reels and rods. Rod lengths range from 6½ feet for lightweight rig to 8 feet or over for heavy saltwater outfit.

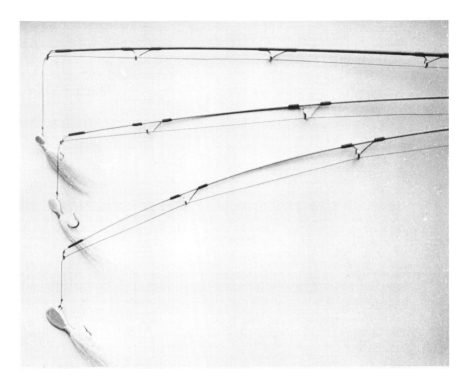

Lure should match rod for maximum casting efficiency. Too light a lure (*top*) fails to arc rod when hung from tip; too heavy a lure (*bottom*) depresses tip too much. Properly weighted lure (*center*) puts just a slight bend in rod.

the right strength for medium freshwater tackle; that lines of 2- or 3-pound test, or perhaps less, were proper for light gear; that 6- or 8-pound test worked best with reels in the next-to-largest class, and that 10 or 12 pounds was as strong as one should go, even with heaviest equipment. However, modern monofilament is strong and limp for its diameter so many fishermen now find 6- or even 8-pound test suitable for medium tackle, even with lures as light as ¼ ounce.

You should use as light a line as possible, considering the weight of lures to be used and whether or not you'll be fishing in open water or in water with snags, weeds or other obstructions where an entangled fish could break a light line. Remember, the lighter the line (the smaller its diameter), the farther you can cast with it. For extra-long casts, use the finest lines consistent with safety and with the tackle.

Thus, except for ultralight tackle (which will be discussed later) we can work out a table of tackle combinations. We should, however, agree that these are generalities; that there can be intermediate sizes; that lure weights are influenced by their size and streamlining, that rod lengths are influenced by their power, and that line strengths depend upon the type of monofilament used and its degree of limpness.

Reel	Line Test	Lure Weight	Rod Length
Light	4–8 lbs.	$1/8$ oz.	$6^{1}/_2$ ft.
Medium	6–10 lbs.	$1/4$–$3/8$ oz.	7 ft.
Heavy	10–15 lbs.	$1/2$–$1^{1}/_2$ oz.	$7^{1}/_2$ ft. (or more)
Extra-heavy	12–20 lbs.	2–4 oz.	8 ft. (or more)

The main point is that spinning tackle should not be assembled in a haphazard manner. If each element is matched with the others, the tackle should function efficiently. The final test is in using the tackle itself. Then we can determine the ideal combination of line and lure weight that functions best with the rod and reel.

We note that there is a line strength range which should be used with each size of tackle. When buying the reel it is very helpful to order at least one extra reel spool for it, and to put on the extra spool(s) lines of various strengths in the appropriate range. Thus, with the medium-sized outfit, we can have spools containing 4- and 8-pound-test line, or even 4, 6 and 8. We would use the lighter line for longest casts and the stronger line for fishing near obstructions or for casting lures which may be somewhat heavier than normal.

MORE ABOUT REELS

Unlike the early days of spinning, modern reels now are so efficient that one can make his selection from those offered by established manufacturers almost on the basis of how much a reel's appearance appeals to him. Modern reels usually have a rate of lure retrieve of between $3^{1}/_2$ and 5 revolutions of the pickup for each turn of the reel handle. While the lower ratio usually is very satisfactory, a higher one provides better lure control, especially in upstream fishing. If one casts out slack line, the fast retrieve picks it up quicker. One may need to retrieve very fast to get strikes from certain species of fish. And, even if the reel has a very fast retrieve, one doesn't have to use it. He can crank in the line as slowly as he wishes.

Antireverse Lever

This device prevents the reel from backwinding when a fish is taking out line. It is conveniently located and easy to engage. But check the reel you propose to buy to be sure the lever is convenient for you.

The antireverse lever should be disengaged when casting for greater ease in handling the tackle. It is engaged at the option of the angler: sometimes as soon as a cast is made; sometimes only when one has a big fish on which starts to make a run. The antireverse is especially valuable in trolling, and always should be engaged to prevent the reel's backwinding on a strike. If one enjoys stillfishing, the bait can be cast out and slack line taken in. Then the antireverse is engaged and the rod can be set in a Y-shaped stick, or otherwise. The device also is useful to keep the tackle tight when not in use. Hook the lure into a rod guide, reel up slack, and engage the antireverse.

The Brake, or Drag

This mechanism is very important. A brake without wide latitude of adjustment, or one that is jumpy, is often the cause of lost fish. This, in part, can be tested at the dealer by screwing down the brake knob until the spool is almost locked. Then back it off until the spool revolves almost freely. One should be able to make at least two complete turns of the brake knob between these two positions, and at least three turns are even better.

Principal parts of a spinning reel.

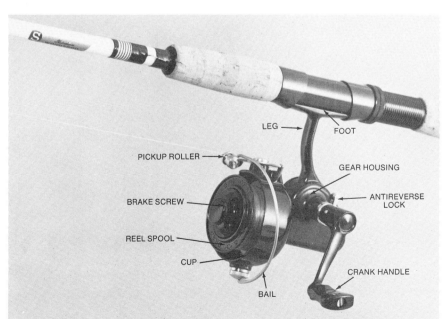

Wide latitude of brake adjustment is necessary in setting the drag of the reel spool easily and properly.

The second element of brake examination is to determine how smooth it is. A good way to do this is by assembling the tackle, setting the brake to moderate tension, hooking the lure to a stump or something similar, and then walking backward with the tackle and allowing the reel to pay out line. By doing this it is easy to find out whether the brake operates smoothly or whether it is jumpy. If it is jumpy, this may be due to lack of lubrication, but a smoothly operating brake is of major importance.

This testing method also is important in learning how to set the brake to proper tension, because beginners invariably set it too tight. The proper adjustment should put a moderate bend in the rod when line is being payed out. (We'll learn of auxiliary braking methods later.) Secondly, doing this before fishing pulls out the coils which are common when monofilament line has been stored on the reel for a length of time. Stretching the line to remove coils is an important aid in easy casting; also in testing the line for weakness.

Old hands at the game can determine proper brake adjustment merely by pulling some line from the reel. Beginners are advised to do this more exactly and then to pull out some line to become familiar with the amount of tension the brake should have.

Method for setting exact brake adjustment on spinning reel.

Spring scale provides the most precise brake adjustment.

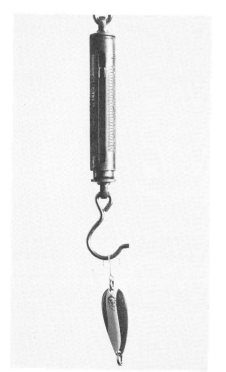

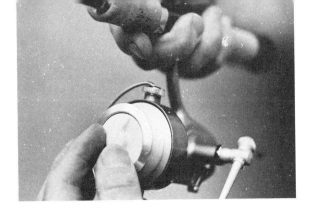

Turning screw on face of the reel spool adjusts the brake (*left*). Once you have learned the correct brake adjustment by the method described below, you can pull line directly from the spool and feel the proper degree of tension (*right*).

If the strength of the line used is commensurate with the power of the rod, a fairly exact method of brake adjustment can be made by hooking the assembled tackle to something solid, as before. Back away, releasing line from the reel until you stand three rod lengths from where the lure is hooked. Tighten the brake screw nearly to a locked position. Hold the rod at an angle of about 55 degrees above the horizontal (a bit more for an unusually limber rod and a bit less for a stiff one) and regain line (with the antireverse lock of the reel engaged) until the rod tip is arced sufficiently to form a continuation of the line. Holding the tackle in this position, release the brake screw gradually until the reel pays out line when you walk backward, but not when you are standing still. This should be the proper brake setting when the line is of proper strength for the rod, or even stronger. If the line is abnormally light, set the brake correspondingly lighter than this method calls for.

If one can obtain a spring scale, a more exact method is recommended. Anchor the scale and tie the lure's end to it. At the same distance as above, and with the rod held similarly, slowly release the brake until the scale reads one-third of the line's published strength. For example, in using a line of 6-pound test, the brake should hold at 2 pounds when you hold the rod as described above, but should start releasing line when you walk backward.

Why not set the brake stronger than this? Because when a spunky sport fish hits a lure he increases the strain on the tackle for an instant or two before the reel gives out line. This temporary strain often is double that at which the brake is set, or two-thirds of the line's strength. By setting the brake in the above way we eliminate the danger of a fish snapping the line on a strike. We also have the insurance of about a third of the line's strength in reserve, which is good for two reasons: there may be a weak spot where the line has been rubbed or scratched; also, the knot which fastens the lure to the line may be weaker than the line itself.

Once the brake is set properly, do not change it under any circumstances. If you need temporary added braking pressure, there are two additional ways of applying it, as discussed later in this chapter.

Line Pickup Devices

Another thing to decide is the kind of pickup desired. This is the device on the revolving cup which collects the line and winds it back on the stationary reel spool. The most common is the bail type, which you open before casting and which flips back into position when the reel handle is turned. This type is recommended for beginners and it often is preferred by experts.

The second type is the hook pickup, which is opened outward before casting and which is engaged (flips closed) when the reel handle is turned. If the hook (sometimes called a "finger") is sturdy, this is an excellent device, although some fishermen complain about it because line can snub around it, or its point may catch on clothing.

The third type is the manual pickup, which is similar to the hook type with the hook removed. Since there is no hook or bail to catch and engage the line, this must be done with the angler's forefinger. After casting, he

Three types of line pickup devices: bail (*above*), hook and manual. Bail pickup is simplest to use and is recommended for beginners.

stops the outflowing line by catching a coil in front of his forefinger and by slipping it over the roller. Since there is a bit of a knack to this, it is not recommended for beginners. Experts who are adept at line handling often prefer it because it is the simplest type and therefore the one least inclined to get out of order.

These various types usually contain a small roller (or "line guide") which is supposed to revolve when a fish is taking out line. Since the roller doesn't always roll, or at least not very much, we should be sure it is made of very hard metal. If the roller should become grooved by the line (which may happen in time) it will fray the line—a point which may be noticed by a roughening of the line or by a small collection of monofilament dust near the roller. In this case the roller should be replaced, and perhaps the roughened part of the line should be cut back, or a new line put on.

Fill the Spool Properly

A rule often ignored is that the line spool should be filled to the lip only. If it is only partially filled, it penalizes us on casting distance. If it is over-filled, too many coils may be cast off prematurely, causing snarls.

Probably the most frequent mistake of beginners is in allowing line to spool too loosely on the reel. This often is caused by bucktailing a lure; that is, by not respooling the line under equal tension. If loose coils are combined with tight coils on the reel, the tight coils may pull off several loose coils, causing a snarl. Proponents of spinning often say one can't get backlashes with the equipment, but one can get them this way, and they are an infernal nuisance. Avoid them by retrieving line under equal tension. This doesn't mean that we can't do a bit of bucktailing if we want to but, if we do, we should notice whether the line has been respooled loosely. If so, make the next cast a short and easy one, regaining line under even tension. If loose coils still are on the reel, a longer, easy cast and the proper retrieve should pack the line tightly and evenly on the spool. We stress the point that the line always must be packed tightly on the spool.

In buying a new spinning outfit, reels often can be purchased with line already on them. If lines aren't on the spools, dealers usually will put them on with line spooling equipment for doing the job quickly. If the angler has to put his own line on a spool, an easy way is to assemble rod and reel and to remove the reel spool. Run some line off the manufacturer's spool and thread it down the rod guides, then fasten it to the reel spool. Open the bail (pickup) and seat the spool on the reel, setting the brake rather tightly. Have someone hold the manufacturer's spool(s) on a pencil or dowel so the line can be reeled off without twist. By cranking the reel, the line can be spooled on it under moderate tension. There are many obvious ways of spooling the

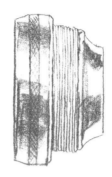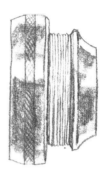

Insufficiently filled reel spool (*left*) prevents line from uncoiling smoothly and cuts casting distance. Overfilled spool (*center*) can cause snarls. Spool should be filled so line is just below the lip (*right*).

line under tension. One way is to let it pass from the manufacturer's spool between the pages of a telephone book, on which a weight may be put, if necessary. The idea is to spool it on the reel tightly and evenly, without line twist.

Since monofilament line often comes on 100-yard spools, we may need two connected spools to fill the reel. These can be taped together until the first spool is used. Of course we could save money by using only one line spool and by filling the base of the reel spool with string, but this is not recommended. Spinning line is inexpensive and reels are made with ample

Best way to wind line onto a spinning reel is to insert a pencil through the hole in the new spool. Have someone hold the pencil and spool as shown, exerting pressure on each side of the spool, while you wind line onto reel.

line capacity because, in many types of fishing, over 100 yards occasionally will be needed. If the forward part of the line should become frayed, or some of it should be lost, it can be repaired by removing the frayed part and by properly filling the spool with an added length of monofilament tied to it with a Blood Knot, as shown in Chapter 12. Also, the line can be reversed by reeling it on an extra reel spool, as described above.

People often ask how much an undamaged monofilament line decreases in strength after a year or more of storage. If kept from sunlight a fairly strong line should remain strong enough over several years of use, but probably some brands of line deteriorate somewhat more rapidly than others. Lines should be tested at the start of each season to be sure they are strong enough, because they do lose strength in time. Particular attention should be paid to fine lines in the lower strength tests. Losing 2 pounds of strength in a 10-pound-test line may not be important, but losing it in a 4-pound-test line could be disastrous!

Reel Lubrication and Care

When buying a reel, if printed instructions don't come with it, the buyer should ask the dealer how it should be lubricated. Tubes of lubrication jelly are cheap, and it's well to carry one. When the reel spool is removed the spindle on which it sets should be greased lightly. Other lubrication points vary from one reel to another, but most of the places which need occasional oiling are marked on the reel, or are obvious.

Spinning reels are sturdy mechanisms which need very little care. The pickup device can be bent by careless use or transportation, which of course should be avoided. It should be opened carefully when in the proper position and should be flipped closed by turning the reel handle without trying to slam it closed. If damaged, it may not spool the line evenly, piling it up on the front or back of the spool. We need not add that reels should be kept clean and dry, particularly after fishing in the rain. If used in salt water, the spool should be removed as soon as possible and the reel and spool rinsed in warm water, then dried carefully. Salt sets up a chemical reaction with the metals of the reel which can bind the reel spool to the spindle and ruin the reel in a matter of hours.

Lures for Spinning

Any lure or bait of the proper weight can be used with spinning gear. These include weighted spinners, wobbling spoons, all sorts of plugs, weighted plastic worms, live or dead minnows and natural baits of many kinds. Some, which are too light to be cast properly, can have additional

Weighted spinners (*above*) are most effective in streams and shallow lakes; the revolving blade tends to keep the lure near the surface. For deep fishing in lakes, wobbling spoons (*below*) are preferred.

weight applied by using split-shot or strip-lead on the line at a suitable distance above the bait. While lures and baits are discussed in other chapters, there are a few tips especially applicable to their uses in spinning.

Weighted spinners work best in ponds and lakes and in streams where currents are from slow to moderate. In fast water they may be inclined to spin, and thus twist the line. This is more true of some types than of others. The revolving spinner blades tend to keep the lure near the surface, so they are less desirable for deep fishing than wobblers and other baits which sink more readily. Every spinner has its own ideal speed of retrieve, when the blades spin most efficiently. Try them nearby to decide the speed which works best. Spinners require a steady retrieve at their ideal speeds. Bucktailing them is less effective.

On the other hand, wobbling spoons can be bucktailed and can be allowed to sink for deep fishing. One often gets strikes while the lure is fluttering to the bottom. When on or near the bottom, it can be jigged. Wobbling spoons are less inclined to twist lines in fast currents, but they may do so if the current is very fast.

Some wobblers are large and thin; others are smaller and thicker. The small, thick ones can be cast the farthest. Bright lures usually work best in high or discolored water; darker ones in thinner and clearer water. You can let the lures corrode, if they will, and polish them to the desired degree of brilliance with crocus cloth or something similar.

When fishing over a shallow, weedy bottom, lures that sink readily of course will become snagged. Here, spinners work better than wobblers, and it may be preferable to use floating-diving plugs that come to the surface at rest but which can be pulled under on the retrieve, or to use surface plugs such as wigglers or poppers.

Plastic Floats

Lures and baits (principally the latter) also can be used with floats of various kinds to keep the bait off the bottom and also to provide casting weight. Four typical rigs are shown in the accompanying illustration. If obtainable, colorless plastic bubble floats are very useful.

Water usually is put into the plastic bubble float to provide the desired amount of casting weight. If not filled full, the bubble will float. If filled full, being about the same density as water, it will drift slightly below the surface, the depth being influenced by current strength and the amount of pull on the line.

In using the bubble with bait, such as a worm or a grub, the trick is to add just enough water or mineral oil (with an eye dropper) so that it will barely float. Thus, when a fish takes the bait, it feels little or no resistance, and is less prone to mouth the bait and to refuse it. This is particularly true

Baits and flies can be fished with a spinning outfit by using a plastic float. Filled with water (or mineral oil), the float provides weight for casting.

in quiet-water fishing, such as in lakes and ponds. Artificial unweighted flies and nymphs can be used on a short leader above or below the bubble, but the author has found it difficult to feel the strike and to hook the fish, especially when using a long line. This can be helped by watching the float. Any unusual motion is a signal for an immediate strike.

SHOCK TIPPETS

Many experienced fishermen enjoy using lines as light as possible because of the longer casts obtainable and because light tackle is sportier and more fun anyway. But it is disconcerting to put on a heavy lure; to make a beautiful cast; and to watch the lure sail out, completely separated from the end of the line.

If one is using lures that are too heavy for the line, a shock tippet, sometimes called a "bumper line," may be necessary, although its use is more common in saltwater fishing than in fresh. This, essentially, is a level leader of much stronger monofilament than the line. It is long enough to allow a few turns around the reel spool when the tackle is in casting position. Thus one casts with the stronger but short tippet but still enjoys the advantages of the finer line for distance casting.

In addition to insuring that lures won't be snapped off, the shock tippet has other advantages. In landing fish the heavy tip section is helpful in preventing them from breaking off at the last minute; particularly when fishing from boats where the deck is a few feet above the water line. Many species of fish have sharp teeth which would bite through the fine line but can't sever the stronger one. In the case of bluefish and others with sharp teeth, even the shock tippet may not be strong enough. So a foot or two of even heavier monofilament is added to the tippet—even 50-pound test. An alternative to this heavier short tippet of course is to use a short single-strand wire leader or a plastic coated "Sevenstrand" twisted wire leader. These may be preferable in some cases, although some fishermen avoid them due to their tendency to kink or because they think the fish can see them more easily. Both types have advantages in certain cases, so the choice is the angler's.

When monofilaments which do not vary greatly in diameters are tied together, the Blood Knot is used most frequently. But, if the monofilaments do vary widely in diameter, the Blood Knot isn't strong enough, so we would use the Surgeon's Knot or the Double Strand Blood Knot. The latter (preferred by the author) is the familiar Blood Knot except that the finer strand is doubled before the knot is tied. All knots are described and illustrated in Chapter 12.

GETTING HUNG UP

All good anglers become hooked up occasionally. When it happens, violently jerking the rod rarely does any good. If the lure won't come free after a twitch or two or a moderate pull, avoid getting hooked up more securely. Go in the opposite direction, if possible, and often the lure will pull free. If one is hooked up securely and can't get to the lure, reel in as much as possible and then keep the spool locked by finger or hand pressure. Walk backward slowly with the rod pointed down the line. When the line is rigid, pull back some more, and something will have to give! Usually the lure will pull out with no more damage than a bent hook. If the line snaps, the lure was too solidly snagged, and nothing more could have been done about it anyway.

When a reel spool is filled with the manufacturer's line, usually part of a spool of it is left over. Take it along when you go fishing. It is valuable for piecing a broken line; for making leaders and droppers, and for other purposes.

TWISTED LINE

Although being watchful should avoid it, many fishermen have trouble with twisted lines, especially when trolling with spinning tackle. Using swivels may help, but probably not enough. Let out a moderate amount of line and check it for twisting after a few minutes. In trolling, the trick is to use lures that don't twist. If it is necessary to use a lure that twists, alternate a pair of them; one that revolves to the left and one that twists to the right. If one twists the line, put on the other to remove the twist.

Another method of lessening or preventing line twist in trolling is by using a plastic or metal keel put on the line just ahead of a swivel. Metal keels are for deeper trolling and usually are cut from sheet lead, often in the form of a heart. The heart is scored along the center line and crimped around the trolling line. Although such keels can be purchased, they are rather easy to make (see Chapter 16).

Angling writers sometimes recommend towing a twisted line behind a boat (with the lure removed), or letting it trail downstream. This may help a little, but not very much. If a line is not too badly twisted perhaps the twists can be stroked out, even though it takes patience. Probably the best answer is to discard the twisted part of the line and to tie in a fresh length. But burn up the twisted part, or take it home. Don't throw it overboard for somebody else to have trouble with.

ULTRALIGHT SPINNING

The French call it *lancer léger* (light casting) or *ultra léger* (extremely light casting). Of course the term is relative because all the tackle we have discussed previously could be called ultralight if the fish are big enough and the conditions sufficiently challenging. Here, let's refer to ultralight as tackle which uses monofilament lines of 2-pound test or less—and they can be obtained very much less!

The reel is a tiny one, with a spool about the size of a half-dollar, or not much bigger. Rods are tiny wands 5 feet long, or so, and rather whippy, to cast lures about 1/8 ounce or less. Needless to say, the tackle is precision-built, and only can be obtained from a few of the quality manufacturers.

This form of spinning is exciting and challenging; somewhat similar to using a trout-size fly rod for Atlantic salmon. One has to pay extra attention to the smallest details of brake setting, knot strength, and so forth. Except for its diminutive size, the tackle is similar to stronger gear, but the angler is challenged to play his fish on the upstream side, and to keep it away from trouble. The name of the game, if there is one, is to land a fish weighing ten times the line's breaking strength. This means a fish of 10 pounds or more on 1-pound-test line, or one of 50 pounds or more on 5-pound-test line. Either could be classed as ultralight in anybody's language!

CASTING WITH
SPINNING TACKLE

PREPARATION

Before actually casting a lure with a spinning rod and reel, there are a few preparatory actions that you must perform. When you have practiced sufficient time with a spinning outfit, these moves become automatic.

The spinning rod is normally held with two fingers ahead of the reel's leg and two behind it. But if it's easier to place the forefinger tip firmly against the front face of the reel spool, for control, one or even three fingers can be placed ahead of the leg.

With the rod held in a comfortable position, reel in the lure until it hangs about a foot from the rod tip. This distance between lure and rod tip is needed for accurate casting. With fingers of the left hand, turn the cup of the reel to bring the bail nearest to the rod. Pick up the line with the forefinger of the rod hand, holding the line on the pad of the finger's first joint, not in the cleft, as shown in photo at right.

APPROX. 12"

Preparing to Cast

1. Turn cup of reel to bring bail pickup roller nearest to the rod. Pick up line on tip of forefinger, not in the cleft.

2. Grasp bail with thumb and fingers of left hand.

The next step is to grasp the bail with the thumb and fingers of the left hand, and flip it across the face of the spool, locking it in position. This opens the spool to allow the line to uncoil freely during the cast.

(If the reel has a hook type of pickup, turn it so the roller is nearest the forefinger and hook the finger under the line. Then turn the pickup counterclockwise to the lower part of the reel so it is out of the way and comletely disengaged from the line. Open it by pulling down at its base, if there is no opening lever on the reel.)

3. With thumb, flip bail across face of spool to lock it in position.

SIDE CAST

The side cast is the easiest one unless nearby bushes or other obstructions make some other type of cast necessary. The advantage of the side cast is that the lure travels in a low trajectory and the line is not caught as much by the wind as in the overhead cast. The photos show casting instructor Tom Stouffer performing this and other casts.

Lower the rod to the right below a horizontal position. Snap it back slightly and *immediately* sweep it upward and forward until it points over the target

(continued on page 26)

1. Lower rod to the right below a horizontal position.

3. And immediately sweep it upward and forward until it points toward the target at an angle of about 45 degrees above horizontal.

2. Snap rod tip back slightly...

4. The instant the rod tip points toward the target, point the forefinger holding the line toward it also, releasing the line and sending the lure through the air.

RELEASE
LINE

at an angle of about 45 degrees above horizontal. At the instant the rod points toward the target, point the forefinger toward it also. This releases the line from the forefinger and allows the lure to soar toward the target.

The forefinger is the key to accurate control of the lure, so let's forget to engage the bail or automatic pickup for the present. Remember how important the forefinger is! It is pointing toward the target as the lure sails through the air. To slow down the lure, merely move the forefinger toward the front face of the reel spool. This will cause the uncoiling line to slap against it, thus slowing down the lure. The lure can be stopped instantly by touching the reel spool with the forefinger. The forefinger controls the line, slowing down the travel of the lure at will or stopping it instantly if it comes too close to any obstruction. As the lure reaches the target, bring the forefinger slowly into contact with the reel spool. If you do it right, the lure can be stopped within a few inches of where you want it to land.

An important advantage of forefinger control is in being able to stop the lure accurately. Slowing down the lure as it nears its target and stopping it as it reaches the target takes all unnecessary slack from the line. Thus, if a fish strikes as the lure lands, you're in control of your tackle and can hook him instantly. You can also keep your lure on the surface if you wish, instead of fumbling with slack line while it sinks. In comparison to this method of forefinger control, stopping the lure by closing the bail or

TOUCH SPOOL TO STOP LINE

5. As the lure nears the target, bring the forefinger slowly into contact with the leading edge of the reel spool, stopping the lure.

pickup arm with the reel handle is much less desirable.

After the lure strikes the water, you can put the line under control of the bail or pickup arm by turning the reel handle counterclockwise. The first partial turn closes the pickup, which thus engages the line by taking it away from the forefinger. Pausing before turning the reel handle allows the lure to sink as much as is desirable.

Now begin to retrieve the line. The speed of turning the reel handle brings it in as fast or as slowly as you wish. By working the rod tip you can give any type of motion to the lure that you desire.

I am often shocked to see fishermen using a spinning rod as if they were beating a balky mule. My advice is to take it easy, because nothing is gained by excess effort.

When reeling in a fish, you should pump it in, if it's a big one. Raise the rod nearly to the vertical and reel in under steady tension as the rod is lowered nearly to the horizontal. Keep repeating this action, as necessary. This is the most comfortable and the easiest way to bring in a big fish. It uses the rod's action to the utmost and prevents twisting the line by cranking against the drag when little or no line is being recovered.

To slow down the lure in its flight, move forefinger toward the face of the reel spool. This will cause the uncoiling line to slap against it.

EXTEND FINGER
TO FEATHER LINE

OVERHEAD CAST

This cast is made in the same manner except that the rod is held pointing vertically. It is snapped back and immediately forward in the same manner as the side cast, and the line is released when the rod is stopped and pointing over the target. The overhead cast has the advantage of greater accuracy because you are casting in a single plane. The variation in direction which often plagues the beginner when side casting, because he does not release the line at the right instant, is largely eliminated. The overhead cast has the disadvantage of a high trajectory, which puts a good deal of belly in the line.

BACKHAND CAST

A cast from the left can be made by crossing the forearm across the body below the chin and pointing the rod downward, casting forward. This cast is handy when there are bushes or other obstructions to the right and above.

FLIP CAST

This cast will deliver a lure accurately, but only a short distance. It is useful for fishing nearby spots in small streams or on ponds and lakes where the lure must land between obstructions and where a long cast is not needed.

The cast must be made slowly. At the start, the lure should be about a foot from the rod tip. Point the rod toward the target and slightly downward. From this position, snap the rod upward through a very small arc and then immediately downward again, to put a bend in it. Using this bend, snap the rod upward again, releasing the lure as this last upward sweep directs it toward the target. This cast requires a bit of practice in timing, but it is a handy one to use. With it, you can poke a rod through a hole in the bushes and send a lure 50 feet or more from the most difficult of casting positions.

1. Point the rod tip slightly downward and toward the target. Then snap the rod tip upward through a short arc.

2. Snap the rod tip downward to put a bend in the rod.

3. Using the bend, snap the rod upward again, releasing the lure at the same time and sending it toward the target.

RELEASE LINE

ARROW CAST

This is more or less a trick cast. It is useful for shooting a lure into an opening in the bushes. Be sure to hold the lure carefully lest a hook become embedded in your finger.

Let out about as much line as the length of the rod and hold the line with the forefinger of the rod hand, the bail open and ready to cast. Hold the lure by the bend of the hook between the thumb and forefinger of the reel hand, and pull the lure back to form a bend in the rod. Aim the butt of the rod directly at the target. Quickly release the lure and, an instant later, release the line from the forefinger. If you do it right the lure will shoot toward the target, although not a great distance.

2
Spincasting

The two types of reels—spinning and spincasting—both have advantages and disadvantages. We have seen that the principal advantage of spinning largely consists of the openfaced spool which allows the line to peel off with a minimum of friction. This permits longer casts with finer lines and lighter lures. Forefinger control has both good and bad points. It's a very easy method when you become familiar with it and then it can provide extreme accuracy. But, to some, forefinger control seems cumbersome and unnecessary when they can obtain another type of reel that doesn't require it. Extreme accuracy isn't always necessary when the degree of it obtainable with spincasting gear may seem good enough. Added to this, in spinning you must be watchful always to see that the line is regained tightly coiled on the spool. With a combination of tight and loose coils a tight one may pull off a few loose ones prematurely. These then spew out in a bunch and become snarled in the rod's gathering guide. This is a nuisance to untangle, particularly during moments when the fishing is good. We have seen that these disadvantages are easy to overcome, but they should be mentioned in comparing the two methods.

The spincasting reel is closed-faced, having a hood, or cone, clamped over the reel spool. This requires the line to be pulled over the front flange of the spool and then to be led downward and out of a small opening (usually called a line guide), in the nose of the hood. This appreciably increases fric-

Spincasting excels in tough fishing situations, where submerged brush and weeds pose hangup hazards, and large lures must be cast on strong line. Spincaster at left nets a large catfish at night in brush-infested stream; southern bass angler, above, lifts a prize from a mass of lily pads.

tion, thus requiring heavier lures (which require stronger lines) to come anywhere near the long casts so easily made with properly matched spinning equipment. In spite of this, the hood of the spincasting reel offers a decided advantage in that it almost completely eliminates casting loose coils prematurely. You rarely get snarls with spincasting gear, even if you bucktail or jig your lure and thus wind the line unevenly on the spool.

A spincasting reel has a pushbutton, or lever, which controls the outgoing line. Even reasonable accuracy requires split-second operation of the pushbutton. The spinning reel always is held in one hand (usually the right hand) and is cranked with the other. Spincasting requires casting with one hand (usually the right hand) and then transferring the tackle to the other hand for reeling.

In summary, if one enjoys making long casts with extremely light lures plus maximum accuracy he probably would favor the spinning method. He would favor it for light or ultralight casting using lines of 4-pound test or less, because these finer lines can become caught inside the spincast reel and because the lighter lures used with these fine lines cast better with spinning gear. If he prefers rugged casting with reasonable accuracy, if he usually jigs or bucktails his lures, or if he fishes near submerged brush or other obstructions frequently, the spincasting method should be more useful to him. Spincasting employs monofilament lines ranging from 4- to 20-pound test, depending somewhat on the size of the reel, so we can be rougher with the equipment. In saltwater fishing, from boats or from the beach, spinning tackle excels mainly because of its ability to make long casts. Both types are suitable for piers and bridges, where long casts are unnecessary.

SELECTING THE TACKLE

Although some may disagree, it seems sensible to narrow reel selection first to those made to accommodate the strength of lines we plan to use. If we're usually going out for small trout or panfish, the line range can be in the lower strengths. If we're planning to go bottom-bumping for bass around weeds or brush piles, the line range should be stronger. If we plan to fish for muskies or for northern pike, which lie near obstructions, the line range may need to be stronger still. Tackle catalogs recommend definite line strength ranges for specific reels shown. A few of these are (in pound-test range) 4–17, 6–10, 6–15, 8–10, 8–15 and 10–20.

Lure weight also is a consideration. Fishermen usually are most comfortable with a certain weight range, possibly favoring lures weighing about 1/4 or 1/2 ounce, or a bit heavier. Naturally, the heavier the lure, the stronger must be the line. This line strength range can be varied by buying an extra reel spool or two of line in different strengths, the lighter to be used in open water with lighter lures, the heavier to be used in obstructed water, perhaps with heavier lures. We remember that the lighter the line is the farther we can cast with it. Thus, if we select a reel made for 6- to 10-pound-test lines, for example, we could use 8-pound test on the reel and have extra spools of 6- and 10-pound test for use when advisable. Extra line spools for spincast reels usually can be bought with the desired strengths of lines already spooled on them. It is a simple matter to remove the hood and to change spools on the reel.

Having decided on the line strength range we want we inspect the various reels available for this range. In doing so we find out how easy it is to change spools; how easy and quick it is to adjust the drag or brake; how wide its range of settings is; how smooth and steady and jerk-free it is, and how easy it is to reach and depress the pushbutton. Spincast reels usually have about a 4 to 1 retrieve ratio to bring line in fast. Some have a permanently nonreversing reel handle, so the drag is in operation even if you take your hand off the handle. Stopping the retrieve puts the drag into use. Others have a nonreverse lever, which has to be engaged when playing a fish.

Principal parts of a spincasting reel, mounted on an offset-handle rod.

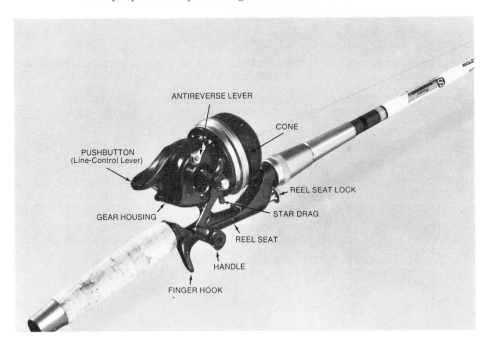

In addition to the drag being efficient, it should be handy to reach. Some reels have star drags set beside the reel handle where they can be easily reached and delicately adjusted. With the stronger lines used in spincasting the drag can be safely readjusted while playing a fish, but care should be taken that it is not screwed down too tight because this could cause a break or a pull-out.

When the thumb-release button of a spincasting reel is pushed it causes the line spool to move forward a fraction of an inch inside the reel housing to put the spool in casting position. Line then can flow out when the cast is made. On the retrieve, the turning of the reel handle retracts the line spool to its former position, at the same time pushing out a small pickup pin, or nub, on the edge of the spool. If the line is retrieved under moderate tension it will respool neatly and firmly. If line should become snarled due to loose spooling or because the spool has been overfilled, remove the reel cover to free the line, and cut some of it back, if necessary.

When you have selected the proper reel for your needs, you can then turn to the matter of selecting a matching rod. While the majority of anglers seem to prefer a plugcasting rod, some like spinning rods better. The main thing is to be sure how well the rod fits the reel, and how comfortable the

Adjusting the brake, or drag, on a spincasting reel with a knob adjustment.

tackle is to operate. For freshwater fishing, spincasting rods usually are between 6 and 7 feet long; experienced fishermen often preferring the longer length especially for use with light lures. A light- or medium-action rod with a softly flexing tip will handle light lures better than a rod with a stiff tip. The answer here is to try the average lure weight which will be used most often. If this weight depresses the tip moderately, it should be correct. If it depresses the tip hardly at all, or if it seems to strain the rod, the rod is too strong or too light.

Within the capability of the strength of the rod, the following table should aid in assembling spincasting tackle and in selecting the proper weight range of lures to go with it:

Reel	Rod Action and Length	Line Lb. Test	Lure Weight
Light	Extra light or soft taper 6'0" to 7'0"	4 to 8	$1/4$ oz. best $1/8$ to $1/2$ oz. good
Medium	Light or stiff taper 6'0" to 7'0"	8 to 10	$3/8$ oz. best $1/4$ to $5/8$ oz. good
Heavy	All-purpose or stiff taper 6'0" to 6'6"	12 to 20	$5/8$ oz. best $3/8$ to 1 oz. good

MONOFILAMENT LINES

We hear too much argument about the relative properties of one brand of spinning line as compared to another. Such arguments may be valid for the super-expert but they should be of little or no concern to the average angler. Monofilament lines are extruded somewhat like very fine spaghetti from a mixture of melted synthetic resins according to the formula of the manufacturer. There are fifty or more varieties of synthetic resins, each of which has a specific range of properties which include visibility, strength, knot strength, abrasion resistance, stretch, limpness and shock resistance. It may be of interest to discuss these briefly:

Visibility includes both how clearly the angler sees the line looking down at it and how clearly the fish sees it when looking up. Usually there is little or no difference, and the line is so fine and translucent that, regardless of color, it doesn't seem to bother fish.

Strength is defined as break load per diameter. The higher the break load per diameter, the greater is the tensile strength.

Knot strength is the ability of the monofilament to resist weakness caused by knots. The type of knot which is used has a decided effect on the breaking strength of the knotted line. For example, we have noted that a simple overhand knot reduces strength in ordinary monofilament by 50 percent.

Abrasion resistance is the ability of the line to resist weakening from being pulled over rocks, sand and other obstacles.

Stretch is the degree to which a line can be elongated by pulling it; for example, a wire compared to a rubber band. Limp lines have too much stretch and too little shock resistance. They fail to spring off the reel spool easily. Their elasticity makes it difficult to set the hook. On the other hand, extremely stiff lines are too wiry and do not absorb the shock of a heavy strike. So the amount of stretch must be controlled carefully to provide desirable qualities in the maximum degrees.

Limpness is the degree of bending ability. Too limp a line won't cast well, since it would act like string, and would have other undesirable characteristics as mentioned above. A line which is too stiff would balloon off the reel in coils which would result in snarls and tangles. Thus the degree of limpness also has to be controlled.

Shock resistance, or impact resistance, is the ability of the line to withstand sudden shock. If too much stretch is removed from the line, its impact resistance would be decreased.

So we have seven characteristics in monofilament, all of which must be balanced properly to provide ideal spinning and spincasting lines and leaders. The fact is that we can't have all of these characteristics to the ideal degree. There must be a compromise. Major manufacturers have been very successful in effecting an ideal compromise, but it is plain that their lines will differ. All this suggests that the average angler can accept brands offered by major manufacturers, but that he should question unknown brands (some of which may be very good ones). The expert angler may insist on an unusually limp line, or an abnormally stiff line, for one reason or another, but he should realize that in getting more of one quality he has to accept less of another.

Monofilament line strengths usually are measured when the line is wet because dry strength is about 20 percent greater than wet strength. When monofilament absorbs water it becomes limper, and more nearly of the strength certified by the label. Lines almost never are of less strength than the labels indicate, but they may be somewhat stronger. In competition, the line's wet strength is measured to avoid variation between one line and another which supposedly are of the same strength. Proper knots make a great difference in the strength of the tackle, as we shall see in Chapter 12.

While monofilament lines are standard for spincasting, braided lines may be appropriate for certain purposes. But, lacking a reason to the contrary, it is safe to use monofilament lines sold by established manufacturers.

CASTING WITH
SPINCASTING TACKLE

Casting methods with spincasting tackle are essentially the same as with spinning tackle, so review the previous chapter for information common to both methods. Since stronger lines are usually used in spincasting, the brake setting need not be as critical. One can test the drag by pulling some line from the spool, setting the brake a bit lighter for fishing in open water and perhaps a bit stronger for casting near obstructions. In doing this, however, remember that additional drag is included due to the resistance caused by the line being pulled through the guides of the curved rod. Also, drag is increased somewhat as more line is taken from the spool. For these reasons the testing methods recommended for spinning should be tried until correct manual methods become instinctive.

If you are a right-handed caster, stand with your right shoulder toward the target, feet spread comfortably apart. Properly used, the spincast outfit is handled the same way that the plug (or bait) casting outfit is; that is, with the wrist cocked slightly so that the palm of the hand faces downward and the back of the hand upward. This provides ideal wrist action, which is necessary for good casting.

1. Grasp rod grip with thumb resting lightly on pushbutton, forefinger curled around finger hook. Depress pushbutton with thumb to prevent the line from uncoiling. Rotate the wrist so V of thumb and forefinger is up.

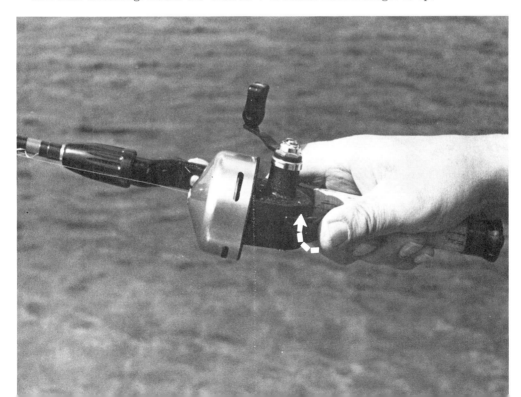

OVERHEAD CAST

This is the most accurate cast with spincasting tackle; use it unless there is reason to the contrary. Reel in the lure to within a few inches of the rod tip and quickly depress the pushbutton with the thumb to prevent line from leaving the spool until you want it to. Point the rod toward the target with it elevated about 45 degrees above the horizontal. You can sight at the target with the right eye by looking at it through the lower (butt) guide of the rod.

As shown in the photos of casting instructor Tom Stouffer, raise the rod to the vertical (but not beyond it) briskly with an accelerating motion to put a bend in it. When this backstroke is stopped at the vertical the power will put an additional bend in the rod. Utilizing this bend, immediately snap the rod forward, using wrist and forearm. This forward part of the cast is stopped between 10 and 11 o'clock. On the instant that the forward part of the cast is stopped, release the lure by raising the thumb from the reel's pushbutton. The lure should shoot toward the target in a fairly flat trajectory.

With the lure shooting toward the target, you must now stop it directly over the target. Too powerful a cast can be slowed down by very lightly pressing the pushbutton with the thumb. Firm

2. Point rod toward target with the tip elevated 45 degrees above horizontal.

3. Briskly accelerate the rod tip to the vertical position.

pressure on the pushbutton will stop the lure completely. This combination should drop the lure directly on target. It also is possible when using some reels to slow down the lure by lightly touching the line with the forefinger (usually of the left hand) as the line streams out of the reel's line guide.

Since most spincasting reels are made for cranking with the right hand, the tackle is transferred to the left hand for retrieving the line. This is done quickly to avoid loose line and to control the lure. Grasp the tackle in the left palm and grasp the reel handle with the right hand immediately upon releasing the pushbutton. You can retrieve line with most reels comfortably by cradling or palming the reel in the left hand so that the line can be passed between thumb and index finger as it is being retrieved. This helps to put even tension on the line and also helps to strike a fish solidly with a tight line.

4. Then snap the rod forward, using wrist and forearm.

5. Stop forward-moving rod at 10 or 11 o'clock for a cast of normal distance. For a short cast, a lower finish point may be required. The instant the forward casting motion is stopped, release the lure by raising the thumb from the pushbutton.

LEASE LINE OVER TARGET

3

Baitcasting

Some call it "baitcasting," others "plugcasting," the latter perhaps being more appropriate because artificial lures now are used more than bait.

When spinning swooped in after World War II, baitcasting (or plugcasting) sharply declined. The advent and constant improvement of monofilament made it practical to cast lighter lures (of about $1/4$ ounce or less) longer distances with lighter lines, adding up to more fun and more fish.

However, when heavy lures are to be cast in fresh water, when fish must be dragged from weeds and undergrowth, and when the constant bucktailing necessary to fish some lures properly winds lines on reels with unequal tension, the baitcasting method usually is superior. Its practicability has been enhanced by the competitive necessity of improving the tackle, resulting in innovations in antibacklash devices, drags and level-wind mechanisms on reels.

Baitcasting addicts have been faithful to their favorite method during these phases of tackle development, and now their number is increasing again due to the availability of better gear. These fishermen prefer this tackle under conditions which they often encounter. They contend that a baitcasting reel gives them lighter and more delicate control at certain times, such as when feeling the soft suck of a bass as he inhales a plastic worm retrieved slowly along the bottom.

Baitcasting tackle still has many adherents among anglers who like the control and power it provides. The fisherman at left thumbs his reel firmly to keep a taut line on the leaping largemouth, while baitcaster below leads his husky pike over the waiting net.

MATCHING TACKLE

As in other methods, tackle of various sizes or strengths is available for various purposes. The choice depends on the size of lures you will cast and the extent of obstructional hazards in the waters you will fish. Obviously, light gear is no good when fish must be horsed from weeds, pads and roots. Heavy equipment can spoil fun and reduce success in open water. If you intend to select only one outfit, a light- or medium-weight rod and reel would be appropriate for most requirements.

Although baitcasting tackle may not fall exactly into one category or another, we won't go far wrong if it is divided into the five which follow. Properly balanced equipment is just as necessary for baitcasting as for any other method. This balance is an adjustment of reel size and rod length (or power) to lure weight and line strength. These factors are all related to the fishing conditions you will encounter: the size of the fish and kind of water where they are found.

Extra Light

This equipment is suitable for small bass and pondfish in fairly open water. One should decide whether or not spinning or spincasting gear would be more appropriate.

ROD: 6 ft. to 6½ ft., very light action
REEL: Extra light
LINES: 6 lb. to 10 lb. (see notes on types of line which follow)
LURES: ¼ oz. to ⅜ oz.
(Lighter lines cast light lures more effectively than heavier ones.)

Light

This is suitable for medium-sized bass, walleyed pike or pickerel in fairly open water; also for smaller fish in weeds.

ROD: About 6 ft., light action
REEL: Light action
LINES: 8 lb. to 15 lb.
LURES: ⅜ oz. to ½ oz.

(A heavier leader slightly longer than the rod, such as a 15-pound leader on a 10-pound line, often is used to insure against lures snapping off in casting and to help in landing fish.)

Medium

This is a good all-purpose outfit, ideal for large bass, walleyed pike, northern pike and small salmon. It is excellent for bait fishing and freshwater trolling.

ROD: 5½ ft. to 6 ft., fairly light action
REEL: Normal size, with antibacklash and adjustable drag
LINES: 15 lb. to 18 lb.
LURES: ½ oz. to ⅝ oz.

Heavy

This tackle is excellent for walleyed pike, northern pike, muskellunge, and for all but the largest saltwater fish. It is ideal for freshwater trolling and for saltwater casting.

ROD: 5½ ft. to 6 ft.
REEL: All purpose
LINES: 15 lb. to 20 lb.
LURES: ⅝ oz. to ¾ oz.

Extra Heavy

This equipment is suitable for the largest freshwater fish and for all but the very biggest saltwater ones. It is used for freshwater trolling for Pacific salmon, large lake trout, big striped bass; and for saltwater casting and trolling.

ROD: 4½ ft. to 5½ ft.
REEL: Heavy duty
LINES: 15 lb. to 30 lb.
LURES: ¾ oz. to 1½ oz., or perhaps larger.

Rods

Usually, baitcasting rods are of medium action. The action should extend down into the butt. In certain kinds of fishing, such as for steelhead or with plastic worms on the bottom, a softer tip may help to feel what is going on. In some cases a stiffer butt may be desirable to sink the hook's barb into the fish. Thus, in bottom bumping for steelhead, for example, we may need a stiff rod with a fairly light tip.

Most baitcasting rods have offset handles whose locking reel seats may vary somewhat in effectiveness. Be sure the reel can be locked to the reel

Two types of baitcasting rods: offset handle (*top*) and straight handle.
Offset rod is better for light casting, the straight handle for heavy duty.

seat tightly, and that it will stay that way. Some baitcasting rods have straight handles with sturdy locking reel seats. These can be tiresome when one is doing a lot of casting. Shorter rods may be advisable when casting in constricted places. The extremely short ones no longer have many advocates. Trolling information will be left for that chapter except to say that, when metal lines are to be used, rods should be equipped with guide rings of the hardest metal to help prevent their being scored by the line. Very hard guide rings are a good investment in any event.

Reels

Free-spooling reels without antibacklash and level-wind features are excellent in the hands of experts for long casts with light lures, fast lure recovery, and delicate contact with plug or bait. They are not as good for short casts and when using heavy plugs. Beginners would find that they invite frustrating backlashes until one has learned to thumb them properly.

Experts often prefer reels without the level-wind mechanism because they prefer to guide the line back on the reel with the thumb. Beginners will find it very useful. In some reels the level-wind disengages when casting. Only the spool moves; not the gears or the crank handle.

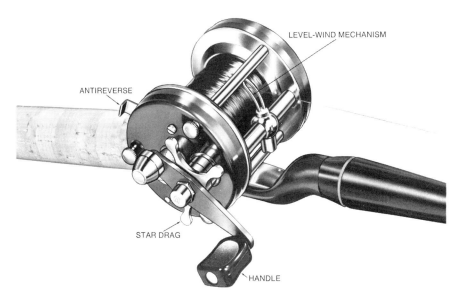

Principal parts of a baitcasting reel.

Reels of different makes have different types of antibacklash mechanisms. As an example, the Shakespeare Company features a reel with "Hydro-film" spoolbraking control. At the start of the cast, where half the backlashes occur, the braking is greater to prevent the spool from over-speeding. The spool runs free during the flight of the lure. When the lure starts to slow down (when the rest of the backlashes occur), the braking mechanism takes over again to equalize the speed of the reel spool and the lure. The manufacturer states that this reel can be cast without thumbing.

Baitcasting reels are equipped with either a star drag or a cap screw for adjusting drag and backlash control.

Lines

Leaving the subject of weighted lines until trolling is discussed in Chapter 16, let us consider the difference between braided line and monofilament. Braided line is first choice for beginners because it is easier to handle. While soft monofilament is preferred by many, it requires more careful thumbing in casting, and tends to become wiry in the stronger sizes. Braided line should be limp enough not to spring off the spool. While slight adhesion of outer coils to under coils is desirable, coils should not stick so much as to cause the revolving spool to jerk and cause a backlash. If braided line carries the name of a reputable manufacturer, this should not be a problem.

In deciding on the proper line strength for your kind of fishing a compromise is usually inevitable. The line must be strong enough to hold the fish, and perhaps to work them out of brush and weeds. But it should be no stronger than necessary because the lighter the line is, the longer are the casts which can be made with it. "The lighter the lure, the lighter the line" is a good rule to go by.

Leaders

A shock leader, also called a bumper line, is a leader which is stronger than the line. It should be long enough so it is in the rod's tiptop when you are casting. For some purposes, it may be long enough to allow a turn or two around the reel.

Under repeated casting the part of the line near the rod's tiptop is sure to become frayed and weakened. A shock leader prevents this.

Sharp-toothed fish like pickerel and pike can bite through a braided casting line, but rarely through a strong monofilament. For added safety, you can use an extra-heavy tippet; for example, with a 15-pound shock leader on a 12-pound line use a foot or so of 20-pound tippet. This eliminates the need for short wire leaders, which are less desirable because they are more visible.

Another use for shock leaders is to provide a stronger terminal section to protect the line's end when handling fish in brush or weeds, or something stronger to hold when bringing fish to boat. If the sections being joined vary only slightly in diameter, the Blood Knot usually is used. If they vary considerably, the Stu Apte Improved Blood Knot is safer. Both are described in Chapter 12.

Obviously a shock leader permits the use of lighter lines for longer casts. It makes little or no difference in strikes because fish that are usually caught with this equipment (with the exception of trout) are not leader-shy.

Level or knotted tapered shock leaders are easy to tie. Knotless tapered ones can be purchased in various lengths graduated from one diameter to another, such as from 10 to 40 pounds. The finer end of this size would be tied to an 8- or 10-pound monofilament line, thus providing a smooth knot for easier passage through rod guides. Fly fishermen who also use baitcasting tackle can get an idea from this. Use heavy knotless tapered fly leaders in reverse, with the tippet end tied to the line. When tying a monofilament shock leader to braided line, use the Nail Knot or the Leader Whip Knot (preferably the latter), described in Chapter 12.

CASTING WITH BAITCASTING TACKLE

With the tackle rigged properly, make two quick adjustments. Adjust the reel's tension so the lure or bait barely fails to drop when you remove thumb pressure from the spool. While expert casters prefer no tension, using thumb pressure only, most casters find that a little helps to prevent backlashes. Experiment with reel tension to discover the degree which best suits you. Using varied thumb pressure and slightly varied adjustments, pull some line off the spool to see how it works.

The plug or bait should not be reeled tightly to the tiptop. The amount of line or leader between lure and tiptop varies with the lure's weight. A heavy plug should be reeled up fairly close. A very light one of a quarter of an ounce or so should be reeled to a distance of about 8 inches.

For greatest distance and accuracy, and to avoid backlashes, proper thumb control of the line on the reel is very important. Apply pressure at the start of the cast; relax pressure while the lure is in flight; re-apply with increasing intensity as the lure slows down to stop it over the target. Thumb pressure also is useful for tight spooling while retrieving line, and it is used as a brake (with a thumb stall—a thumb protector—if necessary) to control the run of a fish.

This suggests practicing with the tackle before fishing with it. Beginners should not be discouraged if they get a few backlashes. These are avoidable and merely are signals that you are doing something wrong.

HOLDING THE TACKLE

The forefinger is comfortably curled around the trigger-like hook just forward of the grip. The thumb rests lightly against the reel spool. The wrist is not bent, but it and the forearm are canted so the palm faces *downward* and the reel's handle *upward*. In raising the rod for casting the action is with the forearm rather than with the wrist. All motions are deliberate and fluid. Jerky casting encourages backlashes.

OVERHEAD CAST

Hold the rod so the tip is about at eye level and is aimed toward the target, with rod, wrist and forearm straight. The pressure of the thumb prevents the reel spool from turning.

Raise the rod with an accelerating motion of the forearm to the vertical position, but not beyond it. This will put a bend in the rod. Immediately begin the forward part of the cast, including some downward motion of the wrist for added power, stopping the rod at an angle of about 45 degrees over the target. As you stop the rod, release pressure on the reel spool to allow the power of the cast to shoot the lure toward the target. Keep pressure off the spool while the lure is in flight, but gradually increase pressure as it slows down. When the lure is over the target, firmer pressure will stop the revolving spool and allow the lure to land on the desired spot. While the lure is in flight, gradually lower the rod to its original position, which is nearly horizontal. Thus the rod always is pointed toward the lure while it is in flight, allowing line to pay out through the rod guides with a minimum of friction.

To retrieve the lure, transfer the tackle to the left hand and cradle the reel in the left palm so thumb and forefinger are against the forward part of the rod grip. Reel in with the right hand, at the same time jerking the rod tip as much as necessary to give desired action to the lure. The thumb is placed on the line against the forward part of the grip to provide enough tension to spool the line back on the reel evenly. If a fish takes the lure the rod quickly can be returned to casting position in the right hand so the thumb can be used as a brake against the run of the fish.

Now, let's see what we've been doing. In raising the rod to the vertical we have put a bend in it. All the power of this bend should be transferred to the forward part of the cast, so this must be started immediately. Did the lure sail up too high in the air, putting a big belly in the line? If so, thumb pressure was released too soon. Did the lure splash down in front, without shooting out properly? If so, thumb pressure was released too late. Did the line snarl into

1. Adjust reel's tension (*see text*), then grasp rod grip with thumb resting lightly on edge of spool. Back of reel hand should be upward.

a "bird's nest"? If so, the cast was jerky, rather than smooth. Avoid forcing the rod, but let it do the work. We are trying to cast with a rhythmic, relaxed swing, at the same time seeking exact timing in releasing the lure.

As the lure lands, transfer the rod from right to left hand, the left hand starting to cradle the reel while the right hand retains hold of the grip. At this point the rod can be raised to about 45 degrees, and can be pulled back a little, which should remove slack from the line. Fish often hit a freshly landed lure immediately. When this happens, you are ready for it because slack has been removed from the line; the rod is at an angle where its spring can take the shock of a strike, and both hands are on the tackle, ready to strike the fish.

Since the Overhead Cast covers all situations except casting from confined places, it is by far the most important one. The two which follow should be ignored until it is mastered completely. It helps to experiment with flexing the rod to see how maximum power can be obtained from it with minimum exertion. The best casters are the most relaxed ones.

2. With lure at proper distance from rod tip, point the rod toward the target with the tip at eye level.

3. Raise the rod with an accelerating movement to the vertical position. Immediately begin the forward cast, stopping the rod about 45 degrees above the target and releasing thumb pressure. When lure is over target, apply thumb pressure gradually, to slow the lure and then stop it.

SIDE CAST

This differs from the previous one in that it is made in a horizontal plane rather than in a vertical one. Hold the rod, pointing forward, at or just below belt level with the palm facing leftward so the reel handles are toward the right. Snap the forearm to the right in a horizontal plane without bending the wrist. Utilizing the bend this puts into the rod, instantly sweep it forward in the same path, accelerating the sweep with a forward bend of the wrist. Withdraw thumb pressure to release the lure as the rod points toward the target. The sweep covers an angle of about 90 degrees from the front to the side.

The first time you try this the lure usually shoots to your left. It is impossible to explain exactly when to release the lure because this only can be learned through practice. In the Overhead Cast the action all is in a vertical plane, so a release made an instant too soon or too late may not make too much difference. The accuracy of the Side Cast, made in a horizontal plane, depends entirely on the instant of release. Try it slowly and easily, without trying to get distance, until this instant of release becomes instinctive. It should prove no more difficult than making the similar cast with spinning or spincasting tackle. Nevertheless, don't use the Side Cast in a boat with other people or anywhere else where anyone could be hit with the lure.

The side cast, caught by the camera just before the lure is swept forward, then to be released by relaxing thumb pressure on the reel spool.

1. With the rod at waist level, pointing slightly toward the left, give it a slight leftward flip and then cast forward.

FLIP CAST

This one also is made when obstructions prevent using the Overhead Cast. It also is used for dropping a lure under overhanging branches where very little distance is needed. Holding the rod at about waist level, horizontal, and pointing somewhat to the left, give it a slight leftward flip and then cast forward. The motion is all in the wrist; little, if any, forearm action is needed. Since the cast occupies a very small arc, the proper timing of the release of the lure can make it very accurate.

The Side Cast and the Flip Cast are easy when the Overhead Cast has been learned. After becoming proficient with all three, some variations will become instinctive. For example, we may not want to make the Overhead Cast in exactly a vertical plane, or the Side Cast in exactly a horizontal one. The Flip Cast can be turned into more or less of an Underhand Cast by holding the rod downward and flipping it upward.

2. As the rod comes up, release thumb pressure on the reel, allowing the lure to shoot toward the target.

RELEASE LINE

UNSNARLING BACKLASHES

Even experts get backlashes occasionally, both in baitcasting and in spinning, although in the latter case they usually are called snarls. They are an avoidable nuisance, but can be worked loose easily with a bit of patience. The tendency is to tug at them, which makes it worse. Instead of this, start at the heart of the snarl and carefully work the parts of it away from the center to open it up. The loop, or loops, which are causing the trouble then can be located easily and pulled out. This done, the snarl will fall apart so the loose line can be respooled on the reel.

Backlashes when casting are caused more by forcing the tackle than by improper thumbing. In other words, we forget to use the rhythm of a relaxed swing and apply too much power instead of letting the rod do the work. Applying excess power jerks the tackle, which causes the reel spool to revolve too fast for the amount of line going out. Thus the reel spool overruns the line, winding it back on itself, or "backlashing."

Lures for Freshwater Fishing

Who can blame beginners for being bewildered when viewing the myriad lures offered by tackle dealers? Millions, bought on impulse rather than for reason, clutter tackleboxes from coast to coast. Of course there are some beauties in every bunch, and a few hot innovations make their debuts every year, but many that still are the best were old standbys when this author was a boy. We don't need as many as we might think, and no one can provide a list of essentials that will hold up everywhere. However, there are plenty of rules to go by, so let's look at the principal types and see why they are effective. This can save money and increase fishing success.

WOBBLING SPOONS

The story is that the wobbling spoon, or "wobbler," was invented by a man who dropped a teaspoon overboard and saw a fish rise to take it. The man sawed off the handle of another spoon and bored holes in both ends of the bowl. He put a split ring into the rear hole, with a treble hook on it, and added a snap swivel to the forward one. He then had a wobbling spoon, and all modern wobblers descend from this idea.

If any readers should try this, do the same thing to the handle. Such a lure may be too big for small fish, but it's a killer for larger ones such as striped bass and pike. Experiment with bending the handle into various degrees of curve until the desired action is obtained. Effectiveness usually can be improved by tying small bunches of dyed bucktail around the shank of the treble hook, or by using a large bucktail fly tied on a ringed-eye hook (which is one having an eye bent neither up nor down).

If we ignore color for the moment, wobblers fall into four basic types: heavy and light (which means thick or thin in proportion to size) and slim or wide, or somewhere in between. Of course they come in various sizes, with proportionately larger and smaller hooks, selected according to the sizes of fish to be caught. If in doubt, the smaller sizes usually are better.

Heavy, or thick, wobblers have two purposes. Since they are compact they offer less wind resistance and so can be cast greater distances. Being heavy, they sink faster, and usually are used for fishing deep. Quite obviously a fast-sinking wobbler will give trouble when used in shallow water or over weeds.

WOBBLING SPOONS

 **Mr. Champ.** For casting, jigging, trolling for trout, salmon and warmwater species.

 **Limper.** Darting, shallow-running spoon that doesn't twist line. For all species of gamefish.

 **Al's Goldfish.** Effective when retrieved at slow speeds. Noted for trout and salmon.

 **Tony Accetta Pet.** Comes in weedless models, often fished with pork strip for bass.

 **Sidewinder.** Has a fluttering, side-to-side action that won't twist line. Good in fast water.

 **Phantom Wobbler.** Popular for trout, salmon in New England—another nontwister of lines.

WOBBLING SPOONS

Cop-e-Cat. Large version of Dare-devle; tops for salmon, pike, muskie, sea-run trout.

Abu-Toby. Fins give it a darting action. Good for trout, salmon and warm-water gamefish.

Abu-Kostar. Trolling spoon that is effective for large fish in deep lakes.

Red Eye Wiggler. Good action on slow or fast retrieves. For all gamefish in appropriate sizes.

Johnson's Silver Minnow. Single weedless hook; good for warm-water species in brush and weeds.

Light wobblers are not intended for long casts. On windy days their lack of weight in proportion to size inclines them to "kite," or to be blown off course during the cast. They work best in relatively shallow water where the heavy ones might snag bottom. They are excellent when worked downstream in shallow, fast currents, and they usually are preferred for trolling.

Wobblers work best with a slow, fluttering motion in imitation of baitfish whose sides flash occasionally as they dart about in search of food. They are much less effective when fished too fast and then are inclined to spin, which twists the line. In slow, deep water an ideal use is to cast them out and to let them sink on a tight line. As they flutter toward the bottom, fish may flash in to take them. If not, let them sink to, or near, bottom and then jig them up a few feet, repeating the process during the retrieve so they cover different depths. In faster, shallower water, try to keep them drifting and flashing with the speed of the current. They are much less effective when the line, swept into a bag by a stream's flow, causes them to be pulled so fast that they will "whip."

In these many sizes and thicknesses wobblers vary in shape from the familiar teardrop design (like the famous Dardevle) to oval patterns (like the Johnson Spoon) and to irregular patterns cut into the outlines of bait-fish. Readers who are inclined to be technical might say (correctly) that size and general shape should resemble those of the baitfish where they are being used. The author would add that the amount of flash of the lure, and its action, are even more important.

The pressure of water on the concave surface of a wobbler is what throws it from side to side. A deeply dished one will fish more erratically than a shallow cupped one. Many wobblers (like the Dardevle) are dished more deeply toward their wider rear and have an additional slightly bent planing surface at their front to increase erratic action.

In general, fish take lures because of their lifelike form, flash and action. In selecting wobblers, size is more important than form. Flash and action are of major importance and color (except for flash) may be overrated. Since manufacturers want to sell as many lures as possible, it is natural for them to provide the widest range of color combinations.

Flash is what attracts (or repels) gamefish, since it is the simulation of the shimmering sides of baitfish. It is easy for fishermen to use lures with too much or too little flash, but this shouldn't be a problem because we know what we are trying to represent. The relative brightness of the day influences the amount of flash of a lure in the water, so it must be considered. If one uses a bright, new lure on a sunny day the lure's flash (like a mirror reflecting the sun's rays) may be so great that fish will be repelled by it. Conversely, fish may not see a dull lure from very far on a dark day or in discolored water. Give them reasonable flash to suit conditions; brighter on a dull day, and duller on a bright one.

The water's depth also enters into it. When fishing a wobbler deep, especially when the water is somewhat discolored, select a brighter lure. Many experienced anglers allow their wobblers and spinner blades to tarnish. They may use them that way on bright days, and they may use a polishing cloth (like crocus cloth) to burnish them to the desired flash when need be. Lacking a polishing material, a bit of mud will do. Metal lures usually are lacquered to preserve their brilliance. This mainly is to keep them looking new in the stores. The lacquer will wear off in time, or it can be removed with preparations like nail polish remover.

As for when to use what finish—nickel, brass, or copper—nickel is probably the best for dull days and brass for brighter conditions. Painted-on colors are of doubtful value. The oft-imitated Dardevle sells best in red, with white stripe. Some prefer colors like green or black, but many will say it makes little or no difference. The underside of the lure is bright metal, and its degree of brightness seems to be what counts most.

A tip on luminous or fluorescent finishes may be helpful. It has been proved (to the author's satisfaction, at least) that a bit of fluorescent material on a fly (such as its tag) attracts strikes. If wobbling spoons don't come that way, a stripe of fluorescence can be painted on. The intensity of fluorescence decreases as sunlight decreases. It is easy to put on too much. Little or none is needed on bright days, but more can be used on dull days or when fishing deep.

An advantage of wobblers of the right size and weight is that they can be fished erratically. They can be jigged deep as described above. They can be fished upstream in deep pools to dredge bottom. They can be fished downstream and, by letting out a bit of line from time to time, can be worked around rocks and other obstructions which provide resting places for fish. They can be cast cross-stream and allowed to swing with the current, bringing them in or letting them out a bit during this process to reach good runs and holding water. Learning how to select and use wobbling spoons properly is an important key to catching fish! If in doubt as to size, use the smaller one.

SPINNERS FOR CASTING

Spinners for casting have a revolving blade attached by a clevis to a springy wire on which are strung a few colored beads or a weight, or both, and a hook. Since this rig is an attractor in itself it usually is not baited. It can be baited (normally with a worm), or a bucktail or streamer fly can be attached to it. Flies used on spinners shouldn't have a wide wing because the purpose of a spinner and fly combination is to imitate a baitfish. They should, however, have pronounced hackles to give added pulsating action.

Spinners differ from wobblers in several ways. They should be fished at constant speed, perhaps with an occasional short pause, rather than very erratically, as a wobbler should be. This speed must be enough to make the blade revolve actively. They can be cast cross-stream and allowed to swing with the current. They can be cast downstream and allowed to hang in the current where, by letting out and taking in line, they can be worked around holding positions for fish. Unlike wobblers, spinners essentially are top-water lures although there are weighted ones which can be fished deep. They are excellent for near-surface fishing in lakes and streams. Another advantage is that they can be cast in to the shoreline where fish often lie and where a wobbler would be more likely to become snagged in the shallow water. In fishing upstream and across stream, hold the rod high to keep as much line as possible out of the water to prevent the lure from whipping, an important point in fishing both wobblers and spinners. A pause in retrieve after casting allows the lure to sink.

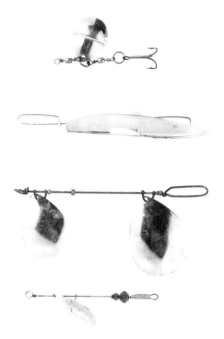

Basic blade shapes of spinning lures (*from top*): Colorado Spinner; Willow Leaf Spinner; Indiana Spinner; June Bug Spinner. These are trolling spinners, but the same blade shapes are found on casting spinners.

In fishing a pool, it usually is better to cover its tail and lower sides before fishing the inlet because hooked fish can be coaxed downstream for playing and netting probably without disturbing those farther up. In fishing deep water a few split shot can be pinched on a foot or more above the lure where they won't interfere with its action. A few small split shot are better than one or two bigger ones.

Spinners are equipped with a wide variety of blades, usually attached to a clevis which is strung on the wire shaft to make them spin easily. Some of the blade designs are the Figure-4, Willow Leaf, Kidney, Indiana, Colorado, June Bug and Fluted. Some spinners are fitted with small propellers rather than blades. All of these fall into four basic types. The standard type, such as the Kidney and Indiana, is attached to the shaft by a clevis which helps it to revolve freely. The Colorado often is hitched to a ring which is attached to a swivel and perhaps also to a second trailing swivel holding a dressed or undressed hook so that the swivel(s) allow rotating action. In spinners of the Figure-4 and June Bug type the shaft passes through the eye and also through a brace extending from underneath to hold the blade at a fixed distance from the wire. The fourth type is the propeller, which obviously is double-bladed to rotate around its center on a shaft. Every spinner addict has his own preference in blades, but there are definite rules for guidance.

Since fish are sensitive to underwater vibrations, the amount of vibration emitted by a spinner can be an attractor for them, as it has been proved to be with other lures such as "sonic" plugs. As proof of this, we know that fish can locate, and will strike at, spinners in complete darkness. (This could be a tip for fishing in very discolored water.)

The shapes and thicknesses of spinner blades have effects on their actions which are of interest. Roundish patterns (like the Colorado) rotate nearly at a right angle from the shaft; more elongated ones more or less at a 45-degree angle from it, and long, narrow ones (like the Willow Leaf) very close to the shaft. The heavier or thicker the blade is, the slower it will spin. Some heavy blades of poor design may drag and have to be twitched into motion. A good spinner starts revolving the instant one begins to fish it. Roundish blades provide more water resistance and so are better in slow currents and in lakes and ponds. Long narrow ones provide minimum resistance and can be used in fast water without usually causing the lure to spin. Thus there are times when slow spinners should be used, and others for faster ones. Sometimes spinners are productive when wobblers aren't, and vice versa. Certain ones may be favorites one season and nearly forgotten the next.

When either spinners or wobblers don't seem as productive as they should be, action often can be increased by adding one of various kinds of

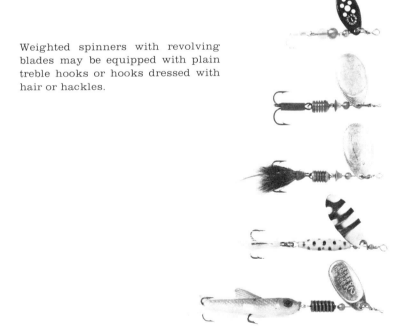

Weighted spinners with revolving blades may be equipped with plain treble hooks or hooks dressed with hair or hackles.

embellishments to the hook. Try a bright worm or nightcrawler, or part of a plastic worm with the cut-off end strung on to cover the shank but to expose the bend and barb. Preserved pork strips work well, either cut into a "V" or any sort of single strip not too long or too big for the hook. Even strips of red balloon rubber cut into a fluttering skirt, or strips cut from a discarded white kid glove, will add action to the lure.

SPINNERS FOR TROLLING

So far, we have discussed spinners which are intended to be cast, although they also can be trolled. Another type, usually unweighted, is fastened to the line's end and a streamer fly or bucktail, or a baited hook, is attached to it for trolling only. These rigs come in all sizes, with one or more revolving blades. Glass beads often are strung on the wire on which they are rigged. The flashing of these spinner combinations attracts fish to the lure, very often with great success. Fish never seem to strike at the blades, even though the lure may be very close to them.

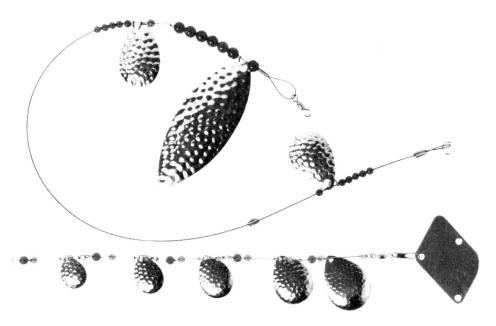

Typical trolling rigs for lake trout and other deep-running gamefish: the Dave Davis Spinner (*top*) and the Webertroll.

Some spinner rigs for trolling have as many as six large revolving blades; these usually being trolled very deep in summer for cold-water species such as lake trout. An advantage of all such rigs is that they work well near surface or at any depth. Keel leads help them to run deeper while lead-cored or wire lines can take them even farther down. Two tips may contribute to success. Troll the rigs slowly; probably more slowly than may seem correct. If in doubt between selecting a larger or a smaller rig, use the smaller one. Fish can see these slowly flashing blades even in very murky water, and they usually will be attracted to whatever lure is offered.

Do-it-yourselfers need little equipment or ability to make their own spinners or to refashion and rebuild those they find. Ways of doing this are described later in this chapter.

PLUGS FOR EVERY PURPOSE

Many fishermen, especially bass addicts, treasure voluminous tackleboxes fitted with several cantilever trays and a well bulging with hundreds of plugs. These are fun to own and to paw over, and some of them are useful to fish with. The trouble is that most of these collections are so mixed up that, when one type of lure is needed, the whole business has to be inventoried to find it, and in the search an even more suitable goodie may be missed. The suggestion is to put all plugs of a type together for easy finding, which would include the four types we will discuss. If we want a plug of the floating-diving type, for example, then we merely look in the appropriate compartment.

How many plugs or similar lures does a fisherman need? If we agree there are four principal types, perhaps three varieties of each type should suffice, which makes a dozen. Probably we'll want each one in a light and a dark color, which makes two dozen. Perhaps we'll want each in two sizes, which adds up to forty-eight. That should be enough. But we'll also include some spinners, jigs, wobblers and so forth, and we'll acquire extra plugs in various sizes, types and colors. Hence a fisherman who owns a tacklebox containing about a hundred lures doesn't think he has too many.

Obviously anyone just starting in can use some advice about the sequence of his acquisition schedule before he buys an excess of this and perhaps none of that. If we divide plugs into four types they will include surface plugs (or floaters), floating-diving plugs, sinking plugs and bottom-bumpers. Let's discuss some of those in each class to decide what may be needed:

Surface Plugs

Since these stay on the surface they are the favorites of many because the smashing strike can be seen when a fish boils up and hits. Many have

SURFACE PLUGS

Chugger Spook. Bass lure, rests on water at a slant, makes a splashing, popping sound when jerked.

Hula Popper. Hollow-faced bass plug makes loud popping, splashing sound when retrieved; rubber skirt adds enticement.

Sputterbug. Head spinner creates surface commotion at high speed. Makes paddling sound on slow retrieve. Bass, pickerel.

Crazy Crawler. Crawling action produced by two arms which paddle the water. Small sizes used for bass, large for muskie.

Dylite Spinning Frog. Swimming animal lure, can be cast on bank and hopped into water like a frog. Bass, pickerel.

concave heads which pop a scoop of water when a quick twitch is given to them. These poppers, of which Arbogast's Hula Popper is a good example, have heads of various sizes, with shallow or deep cups, to provide a variety of popping noises and splashes. Some, like the one mentioned, are equipped with plastic skirts for added motion. Others, like Arbogast's Jitterbug, have wide cheeks providing both a spluttering and wiggling effect. Some of these "splutterers" are minnow-shaped, with fore or aft propellers, or both. Other minnow-shaped plugs have small lips which provide seductive wriggling motions. Many simulate frogs and other fish foods, as well as minnows. These are merely examples, and most are used for bass. In addition to wood and hard plastic models, many of the newer ones like Burke's Pop Top and Flex-Plug are offered in colorful soft plastic. The idea here, which is a good one, is that fish will hold them longer, thus increasing chances of being

SURFACE PLUGS

Jitterbug. Bass lure with gurgling side-to-side action. Also good for pickerel and muskie.

Mirrolure. Torpedo lure, floats on top, runs under surface when retrieved. For bass, pike, muskie.

LeBoeuf Creeper. Swimming animal lure, for warm-water species, that has paddling, creeping action.

Tiny Torpedo. Wounded winnow lure for warm-water gamefish; propeller on tail creates enticing action on retrieve.

Zara Spook. Torpedo lure, darts and dives when rod tip is jerked. Popular for bass, pike, muskie.

hooked. All these are in such a profusion of varieties that the fisherman feels like a kid in a candy store; hard put to decide among them if he limits himself to an initial three. Of course he will want more than that, but three should do for a start.

Floating-Diving Plugs

This is the type which floats at rest but which dives when being retrieved and which rises to the surface when the retrieve is stopped. Good examples are Creek Chub's Pikie Minnow, Bomber's Speed Shad and the expensive balsa-wood Rapala, which has been widely imitated by excellent lower-priced plugs such as the Rebel. All these accurately imitate baitfish in their long, slim shapes and lifelike silvery surface markings. Some feature the ability to give off underwater vibrations which tempt strikes by sound as well as sight. These may be called "sonic" plugs. Sonic plugs usually have no lips, and the attachment eye is on top of the front of the body. This gives them an intensive wiggle that throws off sound vibrations. These lures should be fished fast.

Floating-divers come in two basic types. One is the shallow diver, usually identified by a small lip. The other is a deep diver, equipped with a long scooped lip. The latter, on retrieve, can go down as far as 10 feet.

Thus, if we are to be limited to an initial three, a shallow diver, a deep diver and one of the sonic type would provide the widest variety.

FLOATING-DIVING PLUGS

Creek Chub Darter. Shallow-running plug for warm-water gamefish, darts erratically from side to side.

Bomber. Floats at rest, dives deep on the retrieve. Good deep-water bass lure for casting or trolling.

Rebel Shiner. Dives deep, wobbles on the retrieve. Usually used for warm-water fish; can be trolled for salmon.

Thinfin Silver Shad. Wobbling, darting action when retrieved. For all warm-water gamefish.

Creek Chub Pikie. An old-timer that dives and wobbles from side to side; all-round plug for warm-water fish.

Flatfish. In small sizes, for trout and panfish; in large, for pike, muskie, lakers, salmon. Has rapid wiggle.

SINKING PLUGS

Arbogaster. Deep-running plug primarily used for bass. Has a fast wiggle when retrieved.

Hula Pikie. Sinking, deep-diving plug with jointed body that gives it a side-to-side wiggle. For bass, walleyes, pike.

River Runt. Deep-water lure for bass, walleyes, pike. Faster it is retrieved, the deeper it dives.

Tru-Shad. Vibrating lure for bass, walleyes, pike. Small sizes for medium depth, large for deep running.

Sinking Plugs

These sink after being cast, and thus are used to reach depths in excess of a few feet, but they are not intended to strike bottom. They include wobblers and weighted spinners, as well as plugs. Many, like some of the famous Johnson spoons, have hooks equipped with weed guards because they often encounter obstructions. Others, like Bomber's Bushwhacker, are made to run over logs and brush and through weeds.

Some of the sinking plugs are of the "countdown" type, made to sink at known depths per second. For example, if our testing of water temperatures indicates that the ideal depth is 20 feet, we would cast the lure out and count the seconds as it sinks. If it sinks at one foot per second, we would count 20 seconds before starting the retrieve.

Plugs are provided in a bewildering multiplicity of colors. Pale ones, often in exact baitlike coloration, do well in clear water and on bright days. Red-headed models with white bodies usually are successful when visibility is only moderate. Black or dark colors do well on dark days or late in the evening. Admitting that color preferences from year to year are as fickle as fashions, the redhead with white body is most popular as this is being written. The other three most popular colors or combinations are natural scale, yellow and black. A rule is to use darker colors the deeper plugs are being fished, with black or purple on the bottom.

Plugs with white bellies don't have as much going for them as one might think. Divers in World War II observed that the bottoms of ships most difficult to see from below were the white ones. Probably fish looking up at plugs can see the darker bellied ones more clearly.

Finally, let's give a word of praise to the small plugs used on light tackle. They are extremely productive when fish aren't deep, and they are fun to use. Improvements in light spinning tackle and the greater strength of fine lines have made the use of the midget plugs very practical. We can take at least as many fish with small plugs as with bigger ones, and any fish with a small plug in his mouth is more fun to handle than one hooked with a bigger one.

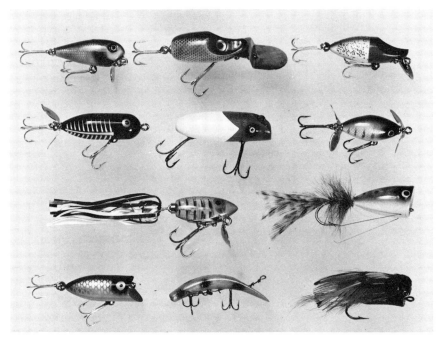

Midget plugs weighing from $\frac{1}{8}$ to $\frac{3}{8}$ ounce, replicas of larger models, are effective for small-mouthed fish that can't take big lures.

These midget lures in the $1/8$- to $3/8$-ounce class often are exact miniatures of popular larger ones which have stood the test of time. They land with a tiny "plop" instead of the heavier splash of their bigger brothers. They include darters, poppers, splashers, divers and wobblers for surface to medium-depth fishing for walleyes, trout, crappies, pickerel and bass. Remember that some fish, such as crappies and smallmouth bass, have mouths which are too small for some of the bigger lures. Also, miniature lures can be worked around pads and obstructions more easily than the bigger ones can.

If plugs are to be changed frequently, a small snap swivel may be helpful, but most small lures work better without one. Snap swivels rarely are used on surface lures.

Miniature plugs are not intended for use only on ponds and lakes. They can be deadly when worked properly on rivers and, when big fish are present, even in small streams. They often will take sophisticated big brown trout when nothing else will.

How to Vary Plug Action

Basically, there is only one best way to fish any plug, the way that makes it swim best or that gives it the action common to whatever it is supposed to represent. A plug imitating a baitfish usually should be made to swim like one. A plug imitating a frog would be allowed to sit on the water until the ripples of the cast have ceased, and then it would be made to act like a frog floating on the surface and occasionally making slight swimming motions.

But, when a plug doesn't attract takers by its natural movement, we have two choices. Either change to something else, or add unusual action to whatever is on the line. Sometimes fish, especially bass, react to a slow or to a medium retrieve, but, at other times, they respond only to a fast one.

When the proper action of a baitfish-imitating plug doesn't work, try fishing it more slowly and lazily. Then work it fast—perhaps so fast that it skips and splashes over the surface. There are times when bass will ignore slow plugs but will chase and attack something going unusually fast. A plug made for floating and diving doesn't always have to be fished that way. Let it lie on the surface for a minute and then give it a quick pop or two by jerking the rod tip.

Some plugs have little propellers fore and aft and commonly are used as splashers to create a commotion when fished along the surface. At rest, the tail probably will sink, with only the tip showing. This looks something like a frog, so it can be left lying motionless for a while and then made to bob and cause slight ripples. A bass may be eyeing it from down below, and may come up to take it then, or when it finally splashes away.

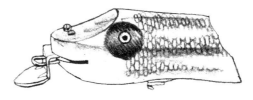

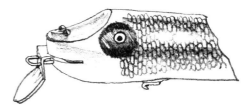

Plug action can be varied by adjusting the diving lip. Floating-diving
plug (*top*) will dive deeply on retrieve
with lip in normal position. To make
it dive less deeply, bend down lip
as shown in center drawing. To use
it as a surface splasher and popper,
bend the lip down completely, as in
the bottom drawing.

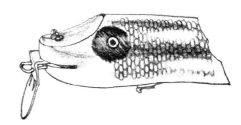

These instances illustrate that, when orthodox methods don't work, it
may be productive to try something else. Bass usually react to lures because
of hunger. Like other fish, they also react for different reasons. They may
attack a plug because its unusual action makes them angry; because they are
curious to find out what it is, or because the way it is being fished induces
them to grab it in the spirit of play.

JIGS

These are excellent bottom bumpers. They are cast and allowed to hit
bottom, slack line then is taken in and the rod is twitched upward, pulling
the jig a foot or more off bottom. It is allowed to sink again and the action
is repeated. Thus, in fishing a ledge or sloping bottom, the jig can be cast to
the shallower part and can be hopped down the incline to the deeper part
by a continuation of jerks until the lure is under the boat. From land, it can
be cast deep and fished up the incline. Variation in retrieve often gets results: quick twitches, pauses, slower and longer jerks—any action that
simulates a frantic baitfish.

Jigs don't look very baitlike, but when they are energetically fished the illusion fools gamefish consistently. Two jigs fished together often do better than one, probably because they simulate a small school of fish. Tie in a dropper 18 inches or so from the line's end, preferably by making a Blood Knot extension about 8 inches long (see Chapter 12). Tie the heavier jig to the line's end and a smaller one to the dropper.

Jigs are available in a wide range of weights or sizes and with various shapes of metal heads. These are so made that the hook's bend curves upward with the jig resting on its head to help prevent snagging. Oval-shaped jigs with vertically flat heads are used mainly in currents because the flat heads help the current to drift them. Some jigs are keeled more or less like the prow of a boat so they can be skidded along the bottom. Others for general use have roundish or bullet-shaped heads.

All jigs are dressed in one way or another, usually with a skirt of hair, nylon fibers or feathers. Those dressed with marabou feathers are very popular because of their greater fluffing action when fished. Undressed jigs can be baited, such as with a live worm, or can be fitted with a whole or part of a plastic worm. Pork strips or something similar often are added to the hook. It is economical to buy undressed jigs and to dress them as one pleases. This is simple and can be learned from Chapter 9 on fly-tying. It also is easy to paint or repaint them by dipping their heads in any color of enamel or plastic paint.

Sharpness of hook is very important in jig fishing. The triangulation method of hook sharpening is recommended, as described at the end of Chapter 11.

Jigs are obtainable in many color variations, but color seems to be less important than the size and type of the jig and the way it is fished. Colors such as white or yellow, or light colors in combination, can simulate those of baitfish. Darker colors, such as red or black, are used for visibility and contrast, such as contrast with the color of the bottom.

PLASTIC WORMS

Every experienced plastic-worm fisherman is a specialist who knows there are rules of the game, many of which can be broken. In other words, one goes by the rules until he develops his own system. Most experienced worm fishermen will agree that the method is more deadly, especially for taking big bass, than using any other kind of bait or any artificial lure.

Big worms 8½ or 9 inches long are preferred when going for the lunkers on the theory that fewer of the smaller fish will bother with them or that fewer smaller ones will be hooked. Hooks used for big bass usually are the Sproat pattern in sizes from 3/0 to 5/0. When fishing for crappies and similar smaller fish, sizes go as low as number 2, with the worms proportionately smaller.

Assortment of plastic worms rigged in various ways.

Each expert also has his favorite way of hooking his worm. Some of the favorite methods are shown in the accompanying illustrations.

Any tackle using monofilament line testing between 10 and 20 pounds can be used for fishing plastic worms if the reel is able to pay out line freely. Fishing without drag is necessary if the bass is allowed to run with the worm while swallowing it, which usually is the case.

First, let's get acquainted with how the worm acts by casting it nearby into shallow water where it can be watched. The lead will take it to the bottom but since the worm is a floater, its tail will rise and wave naturally in the current. Now pull the worm very slightly. The lead will kick up a little mud and the worm will actively appear to "walk" and to be grubbing along the bottom. That is how it should be fished—very, very slowly.

Now for a cast where the bass or crappies are supposed to be. If a fish hits the worm while it is sinking, the strike should be very hard and the hook should be set immediately. When the worm is on the bottom, fish it as previously described. In bringing it in slowly, with many pauses, a gentle

Largemouth Bass

Finned fury on a slender strand
of monofilament—the mighty
bass strikes like a thunderbolt.
Dredge the depths with a plug
or worm, fling a popper at a
glistening bed of lily pads . . .
and hold your breath!

Photos by Pete Czura

Beneath the placid surface of a Florida lake, a largemouth lurks in wait of food. Fooled by a yellow plug, he smashes the hooked morsel, blowing a shower of air bubbles . . . then bursts his watery confines in a head-shaking leap . . . plunges deep as angler pumps . . .

4

5

6

... brings him boatward,
grasps for the gaping jaw...
but bass foils man, leaps
beyond his reach and skulks
near weeds, the plug a sting
in his jaw. One weapon left—
the plunging net gets him....
a green-backed beauty
lying breathless on the
gunwale.

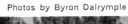
Photos by Byron Dalrymple

7

8

Slack line and a mass of surface weeds spell trouble for bass
fisherman as his almost-boated prize somersaults to throw the
steel. As netter readies his loop, inches from the quarry,
outcome of the contest is still in doubt.

Photos by Pete Czura

Smashing the surface or skulking below it, the largemouth's blend of pugnacity and wariness stirs respect. Bass addicts collect plugs by the dozens trying to solve the riddle of his foibles.

Photos by Pete Czura

1

2

3

Photos by Pete Czura

Thus did the early settlers taste the thrills of the American bass—in a slim canoe slicing fish-infested waters. They found him only in the East, those angling pioneers, but, tough and adaptable, he's taken hold in lakes and streams nationwide . . . and he waits, ready to match his cunning against any fisherman who invades his domain.

Pike

In a northern pine-fringed lake, the pike lies doggo in a sunken weed bed, his alligator jaws aquiver. A long cast, a solid hit . . . rod arcing in his hand, angler plays his fish with caution, never knowing if the erratic quarry will yield without a struggle . . .

Photos by Rex Gerlach

. . . or explode in a wild boatside rampage, a thrashing snake, his vicious teeth sawing the shock leader . . . until the net traps him and he's hoisted into alien air.

Photos by Pete Czura

Three types of hooks for rigging plastic worms. At left is special worm-holder hook; center, a bait-holder hook especially bent for weedless plastic-worm fishing; right, an ordinary long-shank hook.

nudging pressure or a few sharp taps may be felt. You must be able to distinguish the difference between when a fish mouths the worm and when it is pulled against some sort of obstruction. If in doubt, assume it is a fish. Point the rod toward the bait and let line run freely off the reel. If it's a fish it will make a run while mouthing and swallowing the worm. Let it go, with no drag from rod or reel; if it feels drag, it probably will drop the bait. Give it plenty of time to swim away; even as long as a minute or so. Then hold the line

RIGGING PLASTIC WORM
ON A WORM-HOLDER HOOK

1. Thread line through a slide sinker and tie to hook, preferably by snelling method. Worm should be a floater.

2. Start hook point in center of worm head at a 30-degree angle. Push hook point through worm about ½ inch from head.

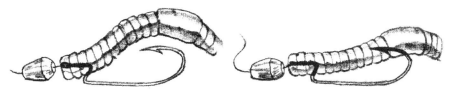

3. Revolve hook 180 degrees so point can stick into worm body. Bend worm slightly up hook so body will be straight when the point is embedded.

4. Push hook point almost through worm (1/16 inch from surface). This rig is weedless and will ride head up when fished.

PLASTIC WORM
RIGGED ON ORDINARY HOOK

1. With knife or cutting pliers, cut ¼ inch off worm's head.

2. Pass leader through sliding sinker and tie to hook. Push point of hook about ½ inch into center of cut-off head.

3. Bring the point of the hook out of worm ½ inch behind the head.

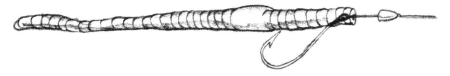

4. Pull the hook back through the worm until hook's eye disappears into the head. Revolve worm 180 degrees on the hook until point of hook is up.

5. Insert hook point into worm and, holding hook firmly, push forward on the worm until the point is embedded.

until tension is felt. When it is, put the line under control of the reel—and strike, hard.

Some fishermen strike immediately upon feeling a fish mouthing the bait. Others feel that the fish may take the bait by the tail and that it must be given time to swallow the whole thing before it can be hooked. The only way to learn is by experience. If underwater cover is thick, you should strike sooner. If the fish is heading for a brush pile or weeds or a stump bed, you should strike anyway. However, when a fish has the lure, it probably will head for open water.

Many fishermen think a double-hook rig is superior to a single. If a double is used, the lead hook is applied as described and the tail hook, snelled to it by 3 or 4 inches of strong monofilament, is hooked in near the middle of the worm. People who prefer single hooks think the tandem arrangement makes the worm act unnaturally, so fewer fish take it. People who like the tandem hook-up think it hooks more fish even though many will mouth it and drop it.

Many fishermen also use embellishments such as beads, skirts and spinners. Experts evidently agree that, as far as bottom fishing is concerned, they do more harm than good. Many plastic worms are sold with double hooks and other embellishments already affixed to them. If these are used they seem more adapted to near-surface fishing. Never discount the killing potential of a fancy plastic worm as it slithers through open spots amid lily pads or weeds!

Plastic worms are offered in almost every color and color scheme imaginable, and many are scented with preparations whose flavors seem to appeal to fish. While some experienced fishermen think that color makes little or no difference, most seem to prefer red or black. Purple and blue worms also are popular.

Finally, we should stress the importance of fishing plastic worms very slowly and naturally, but to *keep them working.* They won't catch fish all by themselves!

OTHER NATURAL IMITATIONS

Beginners in fishing often are tempted to purchase lifelike imitations of natural fish foods such as tiny plastic baitfish, frogs, grasshoppers, hellgrammites, crickets and so on. Since they are so realistic, how can fish refuse them? All these can be good lures at one time or another, but they may not prove as consistently efficient as you might think. If you want to present such lures to fish, why not use the real things, as discussed in the next chapter? Of course all of these fish foods also are reproduced artificially from hair and other substances for fly-rod use. Perhaps these are more productive because the substances they are made from provide a more pulsating and life-like effect than their counterparts in plastic.

PORK RIND LURES

Why do some fishermen fish pork baits almost to the exclusion of every-thing else, and why do they catch so many big fish with them so consistently? These baits, or lures, come pickled in jars of brine, in a wide variety of sizes, colors and shapes including pork frogs, wigglers, chunks, strips, skirts and imitations of eels. They have a firm, soft, muscular texture fish seem to like to chew on, and they often come scented, or flavored, to boot. They provide lifelike action in tough cover when fished knowledgeably with weedless hooks, and some of them can be added to other lures such as spinners, wobblers and plugs, often with better results. The skin strips or chunks are so tough that one can be used all day or until the hook is lost. They also are cheap.

Since these lures so often are fished in heavy cover such as pads, grasses and brush, we need a strong line to free the hangups which occur even with weedless hooks. The line should be 12- or 15-pound test, or perhaps even stronger, and can be used with any type of fairly strong casting tackle or

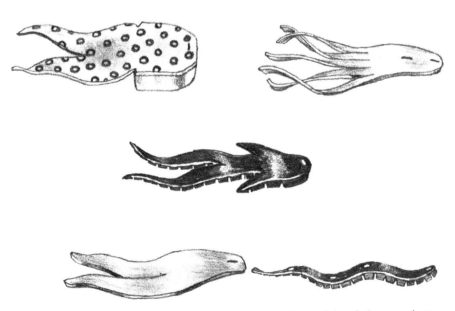

Pork rind lures provide lifelike action, come in variety of shapes, sizes.

even with the proverbial cane pole. In surface fishing the rod should be long enough to keep as much line off the water as possible. Big lures for big fish should have big hooks, as large as 3/0 or more.

Surface chunks which simulate frogs, pollywogs and lizards can be cast into avenues between clumps of grass, onto lily pads, or into open places between brush. Lily pad fishing can be especially exciting. Cast onto the pads; let the lure sit there for a few seconds, and then pull it off into the water. Leave it there for several seconds, and then give it a small twitch to start a few ripples. If nothing strikes, fish it in, over and between the pads in the same manner. One of two things sooner or later will happen. A fish will come up and smash it amid a geyser of water, or there'll be a wake from the side as one plows through the pad stems to reach the lure.

Eel-like strips as long as 9 inches can be fished like plastic worms. Since the rind is tough, perforations are stamped into the strips so weedless hooks can be inserted in the hole providing the desired length; the excess being trimmed off. If these can be cast without added weight for surface fishing, so much the better. Since an eel swims very slowly, make the lure slither along on or just under the surface amid the pads or weeds with a very slow crawling motion.

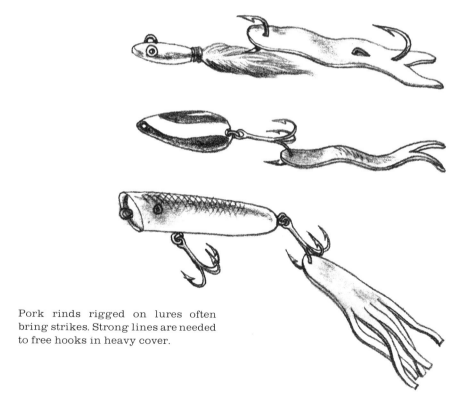

Pork rinds rigged on lures often bring strikes. Strong lines are needed to free hooks in heavy cover.

Weedless spoons can tempt smashing strikes when pork strips of any desired length are attached to them. A famous killer is a black spoon to which a black pork rind eel is hooked. If no spoons in the tacklebox are black, one can be sprayed with a pressure can of black automobile lacquer. Six inches is a good length for the eel. Sometimes bright spoons with white pork strips do extremely well, or a pork chunk could be used instead of the strip.

Smaller pork strips add to the efficiency of spinners of various kinds. If the hook is a treble one, try three very small strips, one on each hook, for an enticing fluttering action.

Pill-shaped pieces of rind are perforated in their centers to fit over a hook's barb. They stay on the barb indefinitely, but slide up the shank when a fish is hooked. They make lures more weedless and, on small wire hooks, or jigs or spoons, are favorites for fishing through the ice.

Pork rind skirts or strips on the tail hook often increase the efficiency of plugs. If they are too large or improperly connected they can interfere with the action of the lure.

Since these pork rinds are preserved in a brine solution, lures used with them should be rinsed afterward. If the brine is spilled in a tacklebox, everything should be washed to prevent rusting.

Addicts of this type of fishing often carry various jars of several shapes, colors and sizes of pork rinds in a special tacklebox. After experimenting with them on weedless hooks and on various kinds of lures they settle on lucky combinations they find most effective. They learn by experience whether they should fish on top or deeper down, and they learn the action that gets best results with each lure and method. Non-addicts often overlook pork rind because these lures aren't attractive and may be somewhat messy. Try them until you understand their many uses. Pork rind lures are famous for hooking the big ones!

HOW TO MAKE AND MEND SPINNERS

Fishing lures are easy to make or to repair. Plugs can be put together from a variety of materials, from ballpoint pens to broom handles. Jigs can be molded from low temperature metal alloys, dressed with hair or feathers, and enameled with bright colors. You can cut spinner blades from metal cans or pie plates and hammer them into shape. Teaspoons and other bits of metal are transformed easily into wobbling spoons. Discarded necklaces provide glass beads. Tools for these little jobs usually are found around the house, so there isn't much to buy.

Those who enjoy such things can make lures exactly as they want them, turning the useless into the useful while saving money and enjoying the pride of accomplishment. Fly fishermen in vast numbers dress their own artificial flies and think it more important to catch fish on what they make than whatever can be bought in stores. So why not do the same with artificial lures?

You will need the following items:

Small round-nosed pliers
Small wire-cutting nippers
Coil or two of #9 or #10 stainless-steel leader wire
Dozen clevises of various sizes
Dozen split rings of various sizes
Dozen assorted treble and single ringed-eye hooks

Cut apart or disassemble the unwanted lures. Discard the useless parts; polish and lacquer old blades; and separate everything worth saving in a compartmented box.

Following are illustrated directions for making three types of spinning lures from parts of old ones and the materials listed above. If you want to economize on lures, which often snag on underwater logs and are lost after a half-dozen casts, here is a way to do it and, at the same time, fill those winter evenings with a worthwhile activity.

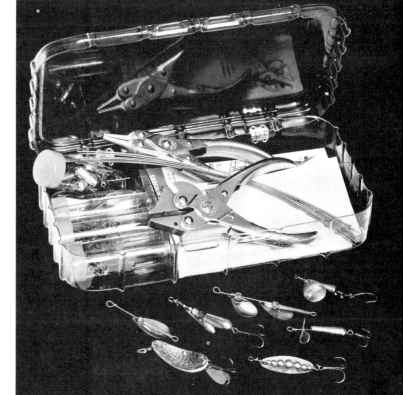

Basic lure-making and remodeling kit includes round-nosed and Sportmate pliers (with wirecutter), polishing and abrasive cloths, hooks, clevises, blades, bodies and some stainless-steel wire. All can be stowed neatly in a plastic box that fits in the pocket.

WEIGHTED SPINNER

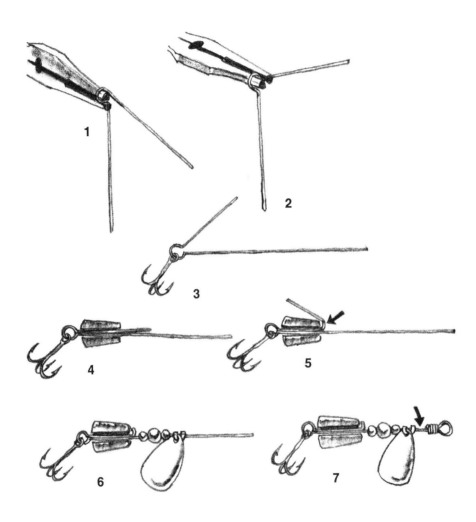

Bend a new piece of wire, as shown in Figs. 1 and 2, and string on a treble hook (Fig. 3). Slide weighted body over the ends (Fig. 4), bend short end out and cut off at arrow (Fig. 5). String on beads and clevised blade (Fig. 6). Turn a loop in end of wire, and cut off excess (Fig. 7).

UNWEIGHTED SPINNER

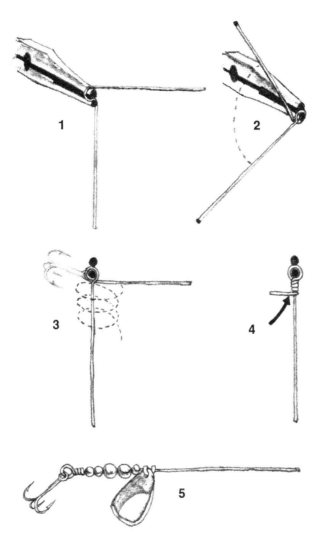

When forming the loop with pliers, begin as in Fig. 1, but then shift wire in pliers and bend until the end makes a 90-degree angle with the shank (Fig. 2). Slide on a treble hook (Fig. 3) and bend end around shank three times, maintaining the right angle in order to make close turns. Cut off end closely (Fig. 4) and string on beads and clevised spinner (Fig. 5). Then twist another loop in end of wire.

HOW TO MAKE A SNAP

1. Bend wire into shape of a hook.

2. Bend hook to a right angle.

3. Bend end of wire back.

4. Add loop.

5. Snap can be used for attaching flies, baited hook, etc.

5

Baits and Rigs

While it may not be intentional, fishermen often become amateur naturalists. In baitfishing, part of the fun is to relax while watching the line or bobber for signs of action. Meanwhile we observe the swimming of baitfish, and learn from them the kinds of action that should be given to streamer flies and bucktails to make them appear lifelike. We see pollywogs in dead water in the spring and perhaps bring a few home. We see salamanders emerging from under wet debris or dead leaves and we learn that they, too, can be used for bait. If we are very observant we see many kinds of underwater bugs and sometimes can watch their transformation from nymphs into flies.

THE FIRST STEP IN FISHING

When we were very young, we probably were fortunate enough to know an older fisherman who taught us the fundamentals of angling. Our instructor cut and trimmed a moderately whippy green branch from a tall bush and tied to its end a short length of line to which he then attached a yard or so of light monofilament and a small hook. Perhaps he put a split shot or two on the leader to sink the bait. We tossed this into the water from a dock, a boat, or from a rock jutting into a pool, and soon landed our first fish. It mattered little that it was a chub or some other undesirable species because it was our first one, and we probably were hooked on fishing from then on.

I exposed my own kids to fishing in this elementary manner and believe the fun of this first step should not be neglected. If interest is aroused, as it often is, the youngster later can be rewarded with an efficient fishing outfit, which he will treasure all the more because it is his graduation present from the "first step in angling."

Many adults never progress from baitfishing to using artificials with a fly rod. They realize that baitfishing can be a science in itself, and that even Izaak Walton evidently never went any farther. An important step in bait-fishing is to observe the development of nymphs into flying insects, not only because this is one of the wonders of nature, but also because the larger nymphs provide very good baits in themselves.

AQUATIC INSECTS

When the water of a stream becomes warmer in late spring and we turn over a few near-surface rocks, we find clinging to them various kinds of bug-like creatures known as nymphs. We may sit by a stream in late spring or summer and watch one climb from the water onto a stone or branch where it dries in the sun. Suddenly its body splits and it wriggles out of its drab covering, crawling away from the shuck as a large, shining and colorful insect. The insect quivers and seems to enlarge. The top of its body expands to form gauzelike wings. As body fluid is pumped into the wings, they ex-tend until suddenly it becomes a handsome fly—a dragonfly, an alderfly, a caddisfly, a cranefly or one of many other varieties. Its wings pulsate more rapidly, and it quickly flies away.

These flies make this transition from nymphs to flying insects on land near streamside or on the water. When some of them do it on the water anglers say that a hatch is occurring, and they know that fish feed on them avidly. More will be said about this in Chapter 21.

The flies that escape the feeding fish quickly mate and the females skim the water to lay their eggs in pond or stream. Many of the eggs will hatch, eventually to become larvae, which is the elementary stage of the nymph we saw emerging from the water.

Hellgrammites

The elementary stage of the dobsonfly is called a hellgrammite and, be-cause it is quite large, it is one of the very best baits for fish. Hellgrammites live under rocks or amid other debris in or near the water for a year or so, gradually developing until instinct tells them to come up into the air on a warm and sunny day to hatch into flies. About 2 inches long, hellgrammites are tasty tidbits for big fish, so fishermen often make a habit of turning over rocks and debris in shallow water to search for them. Their pincers can bite, but the nip is harmless.

During the summer many hellgrammites leave the water to crawl under logs, boards and flat stones near the bank before changing into flies. There they may be discovered in their small hollowed-out homes. They can be kept for several days in damp leaves or moss if not exposed to the sun, but ones taken from water will live longer than those found on land. Hellgrammites should be hooked through the tail, or under the collar, so they will be free to wriggle. Fish them *close* to the bottom; if they get *on* the bottom they will crawl under rocks where fish can't find them and they will be difficult to dislodge. They are excellent baits for all kinds of fish. A good way to use them is to drift them close to the bottom under a bobber.

How to Gather Nymphs

Fishermen who use live nymphs for bait often gather them with an old window screen. Have a friend help you. One person steps into rocky, shallow-flowing water and holds the screen against the bottom with its top above water and tilted downstream at about a 45-degree angle. The other person, working a few feet above the screen, turns over or dislodges rocks, thus freeing the nymphs and washing many of them downstream, where they are caught by the screen. A square yard or so of netting can be tacked on opposite sides to broomsticks so it can be rolled up for easy carrying. When unrolled, and the sticks spread apart, this serves the same purpose as a screen.

When you see several nymphs on the mesh of the screen, raise it from the water and pick off the large ones. Put these into a box containing damp

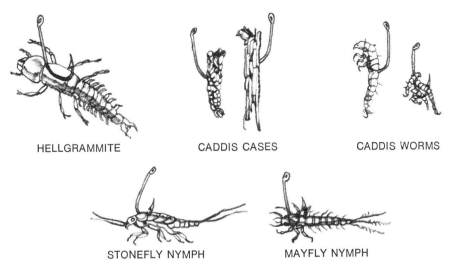

HELLGRAMMITE   CADDIS CASES   CADDIS WORMS

STONEFLY NYMPH   MAYFLY NYMPH

Typical nymphs and how to hook them.

moss or leaves. They make excellent baits when impaled on small, light-wire hooks. Some kinds of nymphs, such as caddis worms, live in protective cases that resemble inch-long rough cylinders of bark, or an encrusted layer of tiny bits of gravel held together by their mucous. The nymphs in their cases can be impaled on light-wire hooks, or the nymphs can be removed and one or more can be put on the same hook, as shown. Stonefly and may-fly nymphs are hairy, buglike creatures, the former being identified by two tails and the latter by three, forked like a prong. Dragonfly nymphs, some-times known as "perch bugs," are fat and somewhat resemble crickets.

WORMS: HOW TO KEEP AND RIG THEM

The common earthworm, which comprises more than a thousand varie-ties, is found almost everywhere, is easy to keep on hand, and is a favorite food for most species of fish. Since it is the most popular bait from coast to coast, too many fishermen think all one has to do is to put it on a hook and drop it into the water to get results. Fishermen who get the best results know there's a lot more to it than that, so let's see what successful ones know that the others don't.

Freshly dug worms are dark (because of the earth in them), soft and slimy. They should be prepared for fishing by scouring, which means leaving them in sandy, mossy soil or in a combination of sand and leaf mold for a few days. In such a preparation they expel the dark earth from their tracts and become a brighter shade of red. Their bodies toughen and are relatively free of slime. Thus they become more lively, easier to handle, and more attractive to fish.

The quick way to partially cleanse and scour them is to keep them in a can of damp moss or pulverized damp leaf mold for a few hours before going fishing. A better way is to have a scoured supply always on hand in a worm box sunk in damp (but not wet) ground, or perhaps kept in the barn, garage or cellar. A supply can be dug from fertile soil by using a spading fork (which is less inclined to cut the worms than a shovel is). Worms will propagate in a suitable box, from which a day's supply for fishing can be obtained quickly, so let's see how to make one.

Making a Worm Box

A fairly large and sturdy wooden packing crate, about 2 by 3 feet square and 2 feet deep, makes an excellent box if there are no holes or crevices through which worms can escape. A rectangle of wire screening can be laid on the bottom to cover small holes made for drainage. While the number of layers of material in the box, and their composition, can be varied, there should be a minimum of soil so the worms can scour themselves in alter-

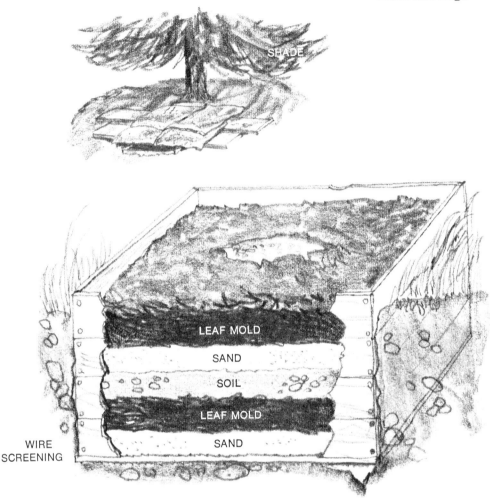

Packing crate serves as a box for keeping and scouring worms. Lined with wire screening, filled with leaf mold, sand and soil, the box is sunk into the ground in a cool place.

nate layers of sand and leaf mold or moss. Before filling, sink the box in cool, damp ground in a shady place, leaving a few inches of box above ground. The bottom layer should be of sand and the top layer of leaf mold or moss. Commercial bedding preparations, available at sporting goods stores, also can be used.

When the box has been prepared the worms are dropped on top so the lively ones can burrow in. The others should be picked out and discarded.

A quart or so of food also should be placed on top. This can be coffee grounds, vegetable cuttings, bread crumbs, cornmeal, chicken mash, etc., or a combination of such materials. Enough water should be added to dampen the contents. The box can be covered with canvas or burlap, held in place by boards. When a supply of worms is removed for fishing, the layers will be disturbed, but that is unimportant. If the box remains outdoors in freezing weather, leaves or other debris should be piled over it for protection. If small worms eventually are found it means that the box is functioning efficiently because a new crop is coming along.

Carrying Worms

A flat tobacco can makes a good container because it is handy to carry in the pocket. Air holes should be punched into the cover, and the can should be partially filled with damp moss or leaf mold. A difficulty with this is that the worms burrow to the bottom, so the contents may need to be dumped out to find a few. An alternative is to obtain a small round can which comes with a plastic cover; cocktail peanuts come in such cans. Cut out the bottom and put another plastic cover from a similar can on it. The worms can be seen through one cover or the other, and easily removed. To keep them lively they should be kept where it is shady and cool, out of the sun. Special cans for carrying worms can be purchased in tackle stores. These strap to the belt and keep the worms fresh.

Hooking Worms

Use small worms for small fish and large worms for large ones. If the worms are too big for the fish, the fish will steal the bait.

For trout, a single worm usually is best, hooked through the collar (Fig. 1, opposite). Trout like worms that wriggle naturally, and they rarely will take them when they are impaled on the hook more than once or twice. I like to have the worm cover the barb because often fish feel the barb and won't swallow the bait; also because this prevents the hook from catching in weeds.

When fishing for large fish, two small worms can be used (Fig. 2), or a single large worm can be strung up the hook's shank (Fig. 3).

Panfish are notorious bait stealers. If this happens, put half a worm, or a small end of one, on a small, light-wire hook (Fig. 4). In quiet water, let the worm sink slowly to the bottom under its own weight.

Large bass, catfish and some other species prefer several worms on a No. 2 or larger hook, strung up the shank and down onto the barb (Fig. 5).

In places where more than one hook is allowed, a tandem rig of two or three hooks keep the worm more securely on the hook for casting (Fig. 6). Such a rig also is used for slow trolling, usually with a spinner or two ahead of it. Worm rigs also are popular for bobber fishing, and there are some tricks to this which will be described later in this chapter.

Most important rules in worm fishing are that the worm(s) should be bright and lively; hooked so it can wriggle naturally; be allowed to drift with the current (instead of being towed through it); and fished where the fish are — which usually means on the bottom or very close to it. To get down there we may need to use a sinker, or one or two split shot. If lead is necessary, the smallest amount that will do the job is the best, and it should be placed

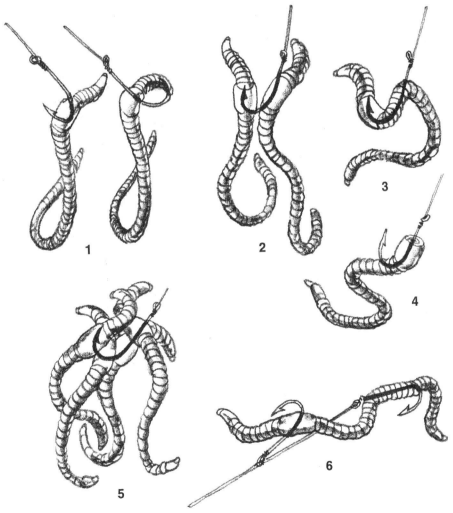

Ways to hook live worms.

well up on the monofilament, rather than too close to the hook. Many beginners use hooks that are too large, or too heavy. Smaller ones of light wire usually are better.

Catching Nightcrawlers

Beginners use nightcrawlers too often, evidently on the theory that, if a smaller worm will do well, a bigger one will do better. Nightcrawlers often are so big as to prevent hooking fish of reasonable size that could be caught readily with a worm or two. Favor nightcrawlers for big fish, or for smaller ones with bigger mouths, such as bullheads, large bass and catfish. They are hooked as worms are, and are fished in the same ways. The best time to use them is during a rise of water after a rain.

There are several ways of obtaining nightcrawlers (and worms) in addition to digging them with a spading fork. Some fishermen shock them to the surface with electrodes pushed into the ground; others by producing underground vibrations made by raking a driven stake with a board as one would use a bow on a violin, or by throwing solutions of one thing or another on the ground so the liquid will drain into their burrows and drive them up. The simplest way is to gather them on the lawn after dark just after a rain, or after heavily watering the lawn with a garden hose.

Some sort of illumination usually is needed to see the nightcrawlers but, since they are sensitive to light, it should not be shown on them directly. A piece of red balloon rubber stretched over a flashlight lens with a rubber band usually provides enough light to see the quarry without frightening it.

There's a trick to gathering nightcrawlers. While they lie on the surface in the grass, their tails are inside the neck of the burrow, so they can slip into it instantly. The trick is to crawl slowly and quietly over the lawn until you spot a crawler and grab its tail end. The crawler will hold on to its grasp in the burrow. Hold onto the rest of it until it relaxes enough to be pulled out. Some crawlers may be entirely out of their burrows, but it's hard to tell for sure. They can be dropped into a container they can't crawl out of, and then can be kept in the worm box with the worms.

MINNOWS

While minnows are considered the second most popular bait, many fishermen would give them first place if they weren't so expensive to buy, so hard to catch, or so difficult to keep for several hours in a lively condition. While all baitfish technically are not minnows, the term is commonly accepted. Those obtained at bait shops usually aren't as lively and won't stay alive as long as the ones fishermen catch themselves. Gathering enough for a day's fishing usually isn't very difficult.

Minnows often school in large numbers in quiet backwaters of streams and lakes, and they congregate around docks when scraps of bread and other foods made from flour are dropped to them. There they can be caught with a minnow drop net or a minnow trap baited with such scraps. Some fishermen carry a wide-mouthed thin-meshed net for the purpose. They set it in a foot or two of water on the bottom in a place where minnows are present and they throw a few scraps of bread into it; the long handle extending to shore. When things quiet down the minnows will return for the bread, and when enough are over the net it is scooped up.

The baitfish then are transferred to a pail or a bait bucket. When fishing from shore this can be left in the water. Lacking such a container, you can scoop a small depression in the sand or gravel close to the water and keep the bait in this shallow-water corral. When fishing from a boat, you can tether the bait bucket overboard. The important thing is to keep the water cool and well oxygenated so the bait will stay as lively as possible. One way to keep it oxygenated is by shaking the container occasionally, or by changing the water from time to time. Oxygen tablets or capsules and other mechanical aids also help, and some bait buckets come rigged with them. If ice is available—perhaps a couple of refrigerator trays wrapped in newspapers—a cube or two dropped in the container helps keep the bait alive when the water begins to become warm.

Minnow fishermen who live lakeside usually make a livebox in which to store their bait. This is a mesh-sided box about a foot deep and somewhat wider and longer, with a trapdoor on top. It is tethered in water deep enough to avoid wave action, and it will keep the bait almost indefinitely if a little food is added every few days.

Rigging Minnows

Different sizes of minnows should be used for various species of fish. The smallest ones that can be hooked properly (under 2 inches long) are best for panfish. These also are suitable for average-sized trout, but they could be slightly longer for the bigger ones; even as large as 4 or 5 inches for lake trout and very big browns and rainbows or steelhead. Sizes for bass vary depending on the probable size of the bass, the average being a length of 3 or 4 inches. Extremely large species such as pike and muskellunge might call for baitfish from 5 to 10 inches long.

Three ways to rig minnows for stillfishing are shown on the next page. Since they must be active, they must not be hooked through the vital organs. The barb can be passed through the tip of the lower jaw and out of the upper one, as shown in the top illustration. A popular way is to push the barb under the dorsal fin just above the backbone, as in the second sketch. A

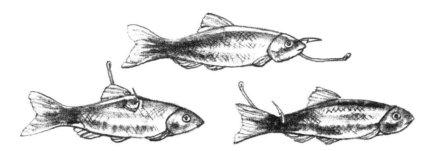

Minnows rigged for stillfishing.

Minnow rigged for casting.

Minnow rigged for trolling.

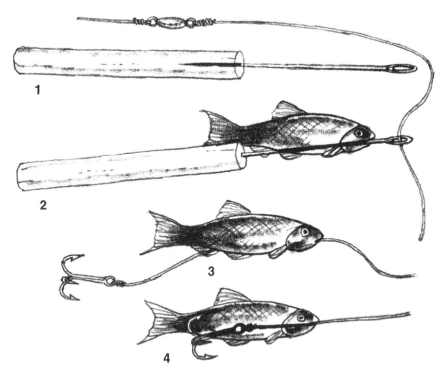

Threading tool, made from a dowel and needle (**1**) is handy for rigging minnow. Impale minnow on needle (**2**) and thread the leader through the needle's eye. Then pull the minnow off the needle onto the leader (**3**), attach the treble hook with a clinch knot, and pull the hook shank into the minnow (**4**).

third way is to put the hook through the rear of the body near the tail. Of these three methods the second one seems to allow minnows to swim most actively and, because the barb is in the midsection, it seems to hook more fish. These methods also are popular for fishing through the ice, and they are excellent for bobber fishing as discussed later in this chapter.

While these three methods, and especially the first one, can be used for casting, a cast that is less than very smooth probably will throw the bait. A more secure rig is shown in the center drawing. The barb is slipped into the mouth and out of either gill. Then a half-hitch of monofilament is made in front of the dorsal fin. The barb then is slipped into the skin of the body and curved out again, leaving enough skin behind the shank for a secure hold.

With the hook's barb and bend pointing outward, tighten the trace enough to put a very slight bend in the bait. Since the bait won't remain alive this slight bend helps to give it lifelike action. Too much bend would make it spin, which is undesirable. A favorite method is to cast up and across stream, retrieving fast enough to keep the minnow moving actively as the current carries it down. Since the hook is exposed one should strike immediately when a fish hits the bait.

A rig for trolling, as shown, must put a curve in the minnow so it will rotate slowly as the boat moves along. First pass the hook down through the lower lip and then through the whole head from top to bottom just back of the minnow's eyes. Pull some extra line (or leader) through so this can be done easily. Then hook the minnow through the rear of the side of the body, as in the third sketch. Holding the bait in the palm of the hand so it will be curved slightly, pull the leader back through the head and then back through the lip to tighten the rig. Now test the bait in the water at proper trolling speed (about as fast as a man can walk) to be sure it revolves slowly. The bait can be made to revolve faster by tightening the rig to give it more curve, or by loosening it a bit to give it less.

Since this rig will put a twist in the line, it is advisable to tie in a ball-bearing swivel or one or two link swivels between line and leader 4 or 5 feet ahead of the bait. If the line should become twisted it can be untwisted by rigging a bait curved in the opposite direction (with the hook coming out of the other side). By trolling this for about the same length of time the twist should be removed. If lead is necessary to fish the bait deeper, it should be put on the line just above the swivel(s), but not between swivels and bait.

If minnows are brought to a lake or stream from which they weren't caught, *never* dump the unused ones in the water. Many good fishing waters have been ruined by people introducing alien minnows which multiply and consume food which gamefish need. The result is fewer and smaller gamefish. It is better to take the unused minnows back where they came from, or to bury them far up on shore.

Almost everyone knows the black or dark-brown cricket which sometimes gets into houses and is supposed to bring good luck. The big black ones are best for fishing. Since they don't like dewy grass or rainy weather, look for them in cellars of old buildings; outdoors under boards, logs, stones or other refuse; in hay, wheat or corn stacks; and especially under strips of tarpaper. They can be caught by hand or in a fine-meshed net. One can be made by bending coathanger wire into a circle the size of the top of a stretched nylon stocking. Sew the stocking top to the wire, tie a knot a foot or so down on the stocking, and cut the rest off. Lash this to a wooden pole several feet long, and you're in business! Such a net also is good for catching grasshoppers because both kinds of insects have small spines on their feet which catch in the mesh. Ways to keep them for fishing uses are described in the next section. They are biggest in late summer and fall and can be caught more easily on cold mornings when they are partially dormant. Since their bodies are soft they must be hooked and handled carefully. Use fine-wire hooks of about size #6 and hook them as shown. Other information about them is the same as for grasshoppers.

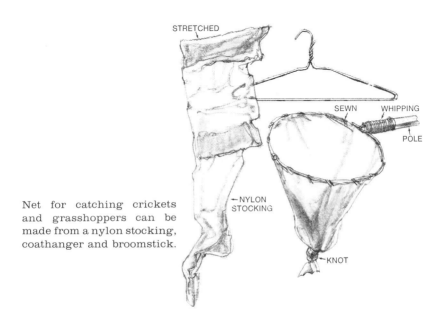

Net for catching crickets and grasshoppers can be made from a nylon stocking, coathanger and broomstick.

GRASSHOPPERS AND CRICKETS

When grasshoppers, locusts (cicada) and similar insects are buzzing over fields in summer, many of them land in the water and are favorite foods for fish. In early morning or during cool nights they are rather dormant and can be picked up easily. During the daytime a good method is to spread a woolly blanket on the grass and to chase the hoppers onto it. Their spurred feet catch in the wool, so they can be picked off easily. The nylon stocking net previously mentioned also can be used.

Some fishermen drop the insects into empty soda pop bottles from which they can't escape when the bottles are kept upright. It's easy to shake the hoppers from the bottle, one by one, as needed. Another way is to put them in plastic boxes, preferably the ones with sliding tops. A little grass keeps

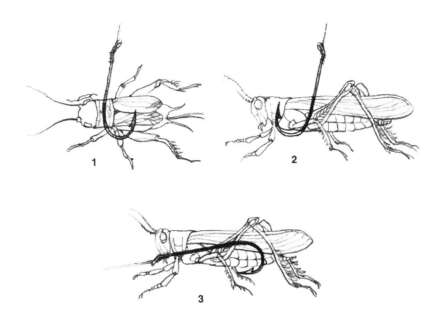

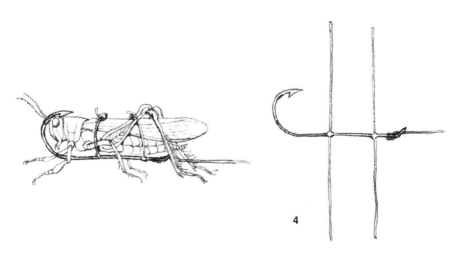

Ways to hook crickets and grasshoppers.

them from jumping out. A better way is to put part of a nylon stocking in the box. The spurs on the insects' feet catch in the mesh and prevent them from jumping out. A few holes should be punched in the box for ventilation.

The illustration shows four ways to hook such insects, using light-wire hooks. Fig. 1 shows the hook pushed down through a cricket's collar, with the barb then pulled up into the body. Fig. 2 shows a similar hookup in reverse. In Fig. 3 the hook is pushed into the insect's throat just below the head and then is turned downward to emerge from the body near the tail.

Many fishermen like to keep the insects alive on the hook, so they use the method shown in Fig. 4. Cut a few pieces of very fine wire $1\frac{1}{2}$ inches long. (The wire from an unraveled section of electrical cord is suitable.) With a small soldering outfit, solder the midsections of two wires to a hook at a right angle to its bend. A supply of these can be made for such fishing. The insect's head is placed inside the curve of the hook's bend with its body resting on the shank. The pair of wires are bent around the body and are lightly twisted to hold the insect. A hook thus rigged can be used many times, and various sizes from #6 to #4 can be made up for holding various sizes of insects. Of course other baits, such as caterpillars, large grubs and small frogs also can be rigged this way.

These baits can be cast up and across stream so they will drift naturally on the surface with the current. In fishing a lake, cast one close to weeds or stumps, allow it to lie quietly for a few seconds, then twitch it lightly. When using spinning or spincasting tackle, added casting weight — a plastic float is good — will be needed to get the lure out.

GRUBS AND CATERPILLARS

Nature provides an abundance of many kinds of grubs and grublike worms, many of which are large enough to use for bait. They are eagerly taken by most species of fish, including smaller pondfish. A badly decayed stump, when pulled apart, should yield a supply. Bark pulled from rotting trees will provide more. Keep such grubs and worms in a box like the one used for grasshoppers, but include in it some of the rotted material in which they were found.

In going through woods and fields we often notice large bulges on stalks such as goldenrod. These are gall worms of one sort or another and they are good baits, especially during the part of the season when it is hard to find others. Cut the stalk above and below the gall, or swelling, and take a quantity along. When needed, the stalk can be split to free the grub.

The best caterpillars are the kinds with no hairy fuzz, or with only a small amount of it. All these make good baits but, since their insides are very soft, they should be hooked through the head, or the Fig. 4 rig should be used. Cocoons contain caterpillar larvae, and they need not be taken from the cocoons until time to be used. Nests of tent caterpillars are common and often contain a day's supply. Cut the cobwebby nest from small growth or scrape it from large branches or trees. Take the whole thing along. If one collects a variety of grubs and caterpillars it is interesting to see which sorts the various species of fish like most, so the best can be selected for use on another trip. All these vary so much in kind from one part of the country to another that it is useless to try to mention them more specifically. Trees and bushes along streams and beside lakes drop them into the water in season and fish often collect there to gather them, so deep spots in such places can provide excellent fishing.

Even the more repulsive kinds of grubs and insects provide good baits, if one wants to use them. These include cockroaches, maggots, large meal-worms and so forth. There seems to be little reason to bother with them, because the others are at least as good.

CRAWFISH

Looking like miniature lobsters, crawfish (also called crayfish or craw-dads) are widely found in warm freshwater ponds, lakes and streams. They live there under rocks and logs on the bottom and often are in large colonies where they burrow into the peaty soil of undercut banks. They can be dug from the latter places and make excellent bait for bass, trout and other gamefish.

When you see crawfish in the water it is easy to catch them. Tie a rotting fish to a cord and throw it among them. When several crawfish collect to feast on the fish, raise it slowly by the cord and put a net under it as soon as possible to catch those that fall off. Some may hang on until they can be captured without a net, but using one adds to the catch.

Another way is to use a minnow drop net, baited similarly, and traps also are available for the purpose. Sometimes crawfish can be caught by hand, but one has to be quick, and not mind being pinched.

The best way to hook a crawfish is to embed all but the barb of the hook in the flesh of the tail just under the shell. Another way is to push the hook from under the tail out through the back. Since crawfish like to crawl under hiding places on the bottom, many fishermen break the claws off to prevent this. Some break off the body and use the tail part only, hooked as above. This is an excellent bait for catfish and other bottom feeders.

Similar to lobsters, crawfish shed their shells periodically as they grow bigger. Softshell crawfish, or "shedders," make the best bait. Being nocturnal creatures, most of them are out after dark.

Another way to fish crawfish is to drift the bait into riffles, runs and deep pools on a moderately slack line. A split shot or two may be necessary to get it down into the deeper places. The larger crawfish are heavy enough to be cast out to reasonable distances with spinning or spincasting tackle. Longer casts can be made by tying in a plastic-bubble float partly or wholly filled with water (or another type of float) 2 or 3 feet above the bait. Fish will mouth the bait before swallowing it, so let them do this for a short time before striking. Usually, the time to strike is when they start to swim away with it.

Crawfish hooked through the tail.   Frog hooked through lips or leg.

FROGS AND TOADS

Small frogs are one of the world's best baits for bass and big brown trout, as well as for other trout and many other species. Bigger ones also take the bigger bass, members of the pike family (which includes muskellunge), and many other gamefish. Some states have restrictions on frog hunting, so the fish and game laws should be checked.

Frogs can be caught with long-handled nets, and by other means, but my favorite method is this:

On a pleasant night paddle in a canoe around the edge of a weed-lined section of a pond or lake. The person in the bow does the hunting and directs the paddler in the stern. The bow man is equipped with a flashlight and an old fly rod. On the rod's short and fairly strong leader is a hook of size 4 or 6 or so to which is attached a very small piece of red flannel or red balloon rubber. If there's a breeze we may need a few split shot on the leader to prevent it from blowing excessively. By shining the light along and near the shore, frogs are spotted. Lower the red bait on the long rod close to their heads, and they usually will grab for it. Hoist each one around so the man in the stern can remove it from the hook and put it in a damp burlap bag, or some other suitable container. (Of course this can be done by one man from shore, but it's more fun with two in a boat!)

The frogs can be kept in the bag overnight if it is laid in shallow water, or they can be transferred to a wire screened livebox set partly in the water and with a board or some rocks in it so the frogs can emerge to rest and breathe. If the big ones aren't needed for fishing why not sauté them to make a delicious dish of frogs' legs?

I once took a big sack filled with frogs into the kitchen of a cottage where I was a guest so the frogs would be safe in the sink overnight. The cord tying the bag came loose and all the frogs escaped and hopped all over the place. The hostess discovered the frogs when she got up in the dark and stepped on one in her bare feet. Eventually calm was restored, but it became quite plain that it is much easier to catch frogs in the wild than to recatch them in a cottage. Everyone except the hostess thought all this was very funny, and it was a long time before I was invited back there again!

Frogs should be kept as lively as possible for maximum action while being fished. Two of the good ways to hook them are shown. The better way is to press the hook's barb upward through both lips. Another is to put the hook through a thigh, as shown. Others are to use one or another of the various harness arrangements to be found in tackle stores.

Spinning, spincasting or plugcasting tackle all provide excellent ways to fish with frogs, but spinning seems to be superior for the smaller ones. Cast to open spots amid lily pads or in the weeds and allow the frog to sit on the water for a minute or so before forcing him to swim in slow, short spurts. If a weedless hook is used, the frog can be cast onto the pads and then pulled off, or made to swim slowly between them. The commotion thus caused should bring a hard strike from a good bass. The same method can be used for members of the pike family. If big brown trout are in a stream, cast the frog into a run and let him drift downstream on a slack line. This often brings action.

Frogs can be fished deep, also, but some lead a foot or two above them on the line is necessary to get them to the bottom. A dead frog lying on the bottom is an excellent catfish bait, especially at night.

I remember having used toads for fishing only once, but without much success. Since toads are so helpful in eating bugs in the garden, perhaps they should be left alone in favor of better baits. Also, the smaller ones, which are best for bait, are hard to catch. A small, long-handled net usually will do it.

SALAMANDERS AND TADPOLES

Salamanders are the little "lizards" of various sizes and colors so often found when wet leaves and debris are disturbed along a stream or beside a lake. They can be caught by hand and kept in a can containing some damp moss or crumbled damp leaves. They are hooked either through both lips, through the base of the tail, or through a thigh. Grab the salamander near its head; otherwise you may pull off its tail. If one gets away without its tail it will grow another one. Salamanders are excellent baits for all kinds of sportfish, but they are especially good for trout in the spring.

Tadpoles, often called pollywogs, are embryonic frogs which are found swarming in dead-water parts of streams and lakes in the spring. When they reach sizes big enough for bait they can be scooped out with a finely meshed net. They are hooked through the base of the tail, and often are used for bobber fishing. While they may be good baits on occasion, the ones mentioned previously seem to be much better.

STRIP BAITS

After catching a few fish it's not unusual to run out of bait. But actually you haven't. You can cut strip bait from the fish. Clean one of the fish and cut off the lower fins and some of the belly. The drawing below shows three ways to cut and rig strip baits. Cut them in a long V and hook them as in Fig. 1. Or trim oval strips to a point and hook them as in Fig. 2. Use the fins also; their fluttering motion adds to the attraction of the bait. Fig. 3 shows both pectoral fins and the anal fin trimmed into one strip, but single fins can be used similarly. These should be given a mild bucktailing action to make them look alive, but, since they are actual baits, they often will take fish when being drifted, especially along the bottom. Such strips bring strikes by trolling when they are attached to streamer flies and bucktails. When plugs don't get results the addition of a strip bait on the tail hook can make a big difference.

Lacking an actual fish belly, similar strips can be cut from such things as discarded white kid gloves and balloon rubber, but of course action must be given to them. They are very similar to the pork strips or pork rind baits which were discussed in Chapter 4.

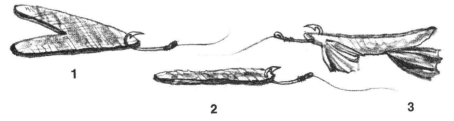

1   2   3

Three kinds of strip baits.

HOW TO RIG HOOKS WITH FISH ROE

Many kinds of fish, especially steelhead and other trout, are taken on salmon and steelhead roe and with the roe of other species. Preserved eggs can be purchased in jars in tackle stores, but the roe from fresh fish is better. When a fish is nearly ready for spawning the eggs may be large enough so a single one can be hidden in a very small hook.

Single salmon eggs are excellent bait for catching all species of trout in all but very large streams, especially those having spawning migrations. The best hook is a type made for the purpose: short-shanked, gold-plated (for less visibility), with a turned-down eye (so the eye will lock into the core of the egg more securely). Select the largest size—usually between 8 and 14—that can be concealed in the egg. Fasten this to the lightest practical leader tippet. Bait the hook as shown below.

To rig egg strips use a regular or shorter light-wire hook tied with a sliding snell (described in Chapter 12). Push the snell down the shank to form a loop. Loop the roe around the hook so the part where the two ends of the strip cross is under the snell. Slide the snell forward and pull the loop to tighten the connection.

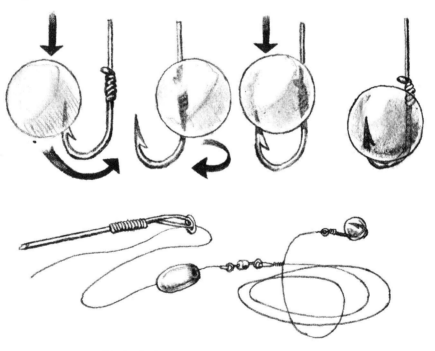

Method of rigging a single salmon egg.

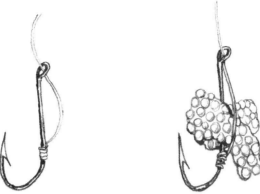

Egg strip rigged on hook with sliding snell.

Salmon egg clusters, often called "berries," are about the size of one's thumbnail. The eggs are pressed around a treble (sometimes a single) hook which is placed on a 3-inch square of red nylon mesh or gauze or a piece cut from a hairnet. A red fabric called "moline," similar to nylon stocking material, sold by dry-goods stores, is used for the purpose. A square is bagged around the hook and the roe and is secured with red thread. Fresh roe (when a female fish has been caught) is vastly superior to preserved roe because it milks in the water, thus attracting fish to it. These strawberry-like clusters are fished the same as single eggs. In rigging up, the sack's mouth is pushed down to expose the hook's eye so it can be tied to the leader. Then the sack's mouth is drawn over the eye.

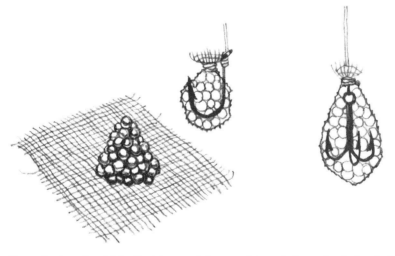

Egg cluster should be tied in mesh bag and impaled on single hook (*left*). Bag can be tied around treble hook (*right*).

Tie the hook to between 12 and 20 inches of the lightest leader that is practical. Before joining leader to line slip a small egg sinker onto the line. This should be only heavy enough to bounce the bait along the bottom, hitting it every foot or two. Tie the smallest swivel between line and leader that will prevent the sinker from sliding over it. The idea is to let the fish take the lure and to move off without feeling much drag from the sinker, which will be lying on the bottom with the line running through it. More information on fishing these baits will be found in Chapter 18.

DOUGHBALLS AND STINKBAITS

Doughballs are popular baits for such bottom feeders as carp, bullheads and catfish. There are many ways to make them, and some fishermen think that the worse they smell the better they work. A small piece of the dough is pinched off the big chunk (if the balls aren't made separately); worked into a ball, and put on the hook. When fishing for small fish a very small ball covering only the barb of the hook may be enough. In such cases, however, it seems better to use a smaller hook so the ball can conceal barb and bend, even also perhaps covering the shank. The size of hook used is consistent with the size of the fish. Usually the baited hook is allowed to lie on the bottom until a fish picks it up and starts to go off with it. If no strikes are obtained in one location, cast to another.

Addicts of this sort of fishing all have their favorite recipes, but beginners can try these examples and eventually settle on favorites of their own.

Peel and grate a large potato, or two or three smaller ones. Add two tablespoons of cornmeal, about half a teaspoon of salt, and enough flour and shredded cotton to make a stiff batter. Pinch off bits and roll them into balls between a half inch and an inch in diameter, depending on the probable size of the fish and the size of the hook to be used. Cook these in boiling water until they float. Dip them out onto absorbent paper to dry, and carry them in a bait box or plastic bag. As an alternative, add a grated onion to this, or two tablespoons of syrup, sugar or molasses, or both. Carp, especially, seem to like them sweet.

The use of shredded cotton as a binder helps to keep the bait on the hook. Cornstarch or white of egg can be substituted, but none of these is necessary if the dough is stiff enough. If doughballs are made well in advance they can be kept in a refrigerator.

Another recipe is to mix equal parts of bread, oatmeal, cereal and sugar with enough water to make a stiff dough. This can be carried as one ball and pieces can be pinched off and rolled into small balls as needed.

A simple recipe is to mix flour and any kind of cheese into a firm ball and to use it as above. One that may be tastier (to the fish) is to mix equal parts of hamburger steak and cheese with enough flour and water to make a stiff paste.

Plastic sponges in such colors as red, pink, yellow and white can be soaked with various preparations after being cut into cubes of whatever size is preferred. One recipe calls for working cheese spread into them; the smellier the better. Another is to soak the sponge cubes in blood and to let them dry. Liver of any kind can be cut up for use. Entrails of small animals (especially chicken) are used as bait, as well as the soft meat of clams or mussels. Almost anything goes!

Fishermen who don't want to bother to make their own dough and stink-baits, or who have wives who think they should draw the line somewhere, can buy them already prepared in tackle stores. However, addicts of this sort of fishing usually prefer their own formulas, of which these are only a few of the milder examples. Because lady anglers may read this and then refuse to cook the catch afterwards, it seems prudent to go no farther!

These baits of course are for certain varieties of bottom fish, and each variety has its preferences. Thus it may be helpful here to discuss some of these bottom feeders to see which baits they prefer and how best to catch them.

Carp

Carp are bottom feeders which frequent muddy places in ponds, lakes and sluggish rivers. Too often they thrive in such places to the detriment of more desirable fish because someone allowed Junior to empty his goldfish bowl there, thus doing serious and perhaps permanent damage to the fishery. Ponds in parks often contain carp for this reason, and they may provide easily accessible sport to young people.

Carp have small mouths and feed largely by smell, so small baits on small hooks are necessary, except for the very big ones. They should be fished on a loose line, preferably without a sinker, because they are wary and won't take a bait if they think something's wrong with it. A good time to fish for them is on dark, rainy days, although they will bite at other times. When one is hooked he should be drawn away from the others to avoid disturbing the school.

While carp eat snails, algae and various forms of vegetation, they also take small hooks baited with worms, peas, kernels of corn (several of both strung on the hook), partly cooked bits of potato, doughballs (as mentioned above), pellets of bread, small pieces of fish, shrimp, balls of moss scraped from underwater rocks, and even marshmallows. The doughballs can be sweetened. Other live baits, such as minnows, are not productive, and smelly baits are unnecessary.

Catfish and Bullheads

Bullheads are a species of catfish which inhabit the muddy bottoms of ponds, lakes, slow rivers and streams, canals and ditches, preferably in areas where there is protective vegetation. While they feed mainly at night, they will bite during the day. Both bullheads and catfish will take a wide variety of baits, including live minnows, frogs, a gob of worms, shrimp, crawfish tails, cut fresh bait (especially mossbunkers cut in pieces, because they are oily), pieces of rotted fish, stinkbaits and doughballs, chicken and animal entrails, liver of any kind, grapes, kernels of corn strung on a hook, nightcrawlers. Their diet includes the entire gamut from overripe cheese to laundry soap! Hooks of sizes 4 or 6, on line testing about 10 pounds, are good choices for bullheads, but the larger catfish may need something more substantial. Hooks often are of the baitholder type, with barbs on their shanks.

Catfish are found in both fresh and salt water. In fresh water they live in such places as protected holes in rivers, near brushpiles, fallen trees, and undercut banks. Fishing in tidal rivers is best when the tide is running, rather than at the high or the low. Bigger baits attract the bigger fish.

In addition to usual rod and reel fishing, catfish often are taken on trotlines, where such are allowed. These are long, heavy cords, perhaps extending across a stream, which are anchored at both ends, such as by tying them to brush. Middle sections may need to be kept near the surface by using plastic bottles as buoys. Short lines with hooks attached hang down from the main one, the hooks being baited with a choice of the stuff which has been described. Another way to catch catfish (where it is allowed) is by "jugging." Short lines with baited hooks are attached to handles of corked plastic jugs. Several of these are put overboard and allowed to drift in a slow current, being watched and guided by people in a boat. When a big catfish takes such a bait it may pull the jug under from time to time, or may tow it for a considerable distance.

Chubs

These are primarily river fish that often are taken by fly fishermen when fishing for trout. They like water between 2 and 6 feet deep with from slow to moderate flow, so they sometimes occupy the same habitat as smallmouth bass and trout. They like a gravel bottom and often collect near jetties, wharves and piers, under overhanging brush, or in beds of weeds. Tackle used can be the same as for smallmouth bass and trout. Chubs eat vegetable matter, small shellfish, insects, minnows, caterpillars, grubs, bread-balls, soft cheese, doughballs, etc. They also often take small spinners and dry or wet flies. Young people on their first fishing trips can have a lot of fun catching chubs, and older fishermen sometimes enjoy them, too, except when they interfere with the catching of species which are considered more desirable. Chubs are not fussy about water temperature and they feed more or less constantly. While lacking the challenge provided by more palatable species such as trout and bass, they can provide good sport.

Suckers

Although they're rated low as food fish, suckers can furnish fishing fun when not much else is going on. Neophyte fishermen often see several big ones lying clearly exposed in sandy pools, slow-water eddies, or backwaters and excitedly fish for them under the misapprehension that they are trout. Of course, they are not where any respectable trout would be, and a closer look at their snouts dispels the illusion.

Since these coarse fish don't fight much, any sort of light tackle will do. Their small mouths call for small hooks, which can be baited with a piece of mussel or one or more small worms. The bait is dropped to lie near them. Wait until one starts to go away with the bait before striking.

BAITFISHING WITH BOBBERS

While many kinds and sizes of floats or bobbers are available, it is important to select the right one for the kind of fishing that is to be done, because just any one won't do. When a bait is suspended from a bobber floating on the surface, the bobber must float just enough to prevent it from being pulled under by the weight of the bait. When a fish takes the bait he should feel almost no resistance. If he tugs at the bait, and the bait seems to tug back because of too much resistance from the bobber, the fish usually will leave the bait, unless his first approach happens to hook him. Since fish sometimes mouth the bait before taking it, this usually isn't the case.

British anglers have this very important bit of information reduced to sort of a science. They carry their bobbers (which are more like pencils, and which they call "controllers") in sets of various sizes or degrees of buoyancy, and they usually carry spares of more than one of each kind. In rigging a bait they put on a light bobber to see if it will hold the bait up. If it does, they try a smaller one, and if it doesn't they try a larger one until they find one that barely remains on the surface to support the pull of the bait, or the combination of it and the pull of the current on it. The result of this rather precise bit of experimenting is that, when the fish takes the bait, he feels almost no resistance at all. Feeling almost no resistance almost guarantees hooking him.

Other than that, it makes little or no difference what color or type of bobber one uses, but I like to use one which comes in only two sizes which

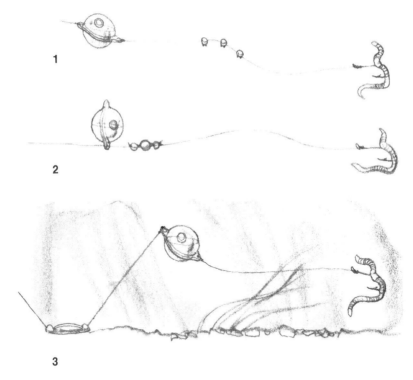

Three methods of rigging a plastic float.

cover all requirements. This is a colorless plastic ball float with a rim around it to which line and leader can be attached. A removable plug permits the float to be filled with just enough water or mineral oil. When entirely filled it is about the same specific gravity as water, so it will drift down in the current and yet provide an ample weight to cast tiny baits long distances with spinning or spincasting tackle. Since this float is colorless it resembles a bubble on the water, and thus attracts no attention from fish.

The main purpose of a bobber is to hold the bait off the bottom so it won't catch and so it will drift a bait naturally downstream without excess speed or drag. The leader (a piece of the spinning line) should be long enough to keep the bait as close to the bottom as possible without snagging it. Thus, with such a bobber, we have a suitable weight to cast a small lure long distances and we also have a means of keeping the bait off the bottom so it can cover a lot of ground as it drifts down in the current.

A second consideration is that the size of hook should be appropriate to the fish we are seeking. Most people use hooks that are too large, and probably too heavy in the iron. If in doubt, select the smallest and lightest hook that will do the job.

The illustration at left shows three ways to rig a plastic bobber. In Fig. 1, one side of the bobber is affixed to the spinning line and the other one to the leader. The bobber is filled with just enough water to allow it to hold up the bait. (An eyedropper is handy for this.) The leader is just long enough to keep the bait off the bottom. Two or three split may be needed to get the bait down, but use them only if necessary. Cast upstream, take in slack and then let out or take in enough line to guide the float where you want it to go. If the bobber is suddenly pulled under, strike hard.

In Fig. 2, a sliding float rig is shown. This rig permits the fish to mouth the bait without feeling tension on the line. String the float (through one eye only) on the line and tie on a barrel swivel. Tie a couple of feet of line to the swivel and tie the hook to the end.

The rig shown in Fig. 3 is for holding the bait off the bottom. Pinch a small lead on the line 2 or 3 feet behind the float, which may be partly filled with water. The lead holds bottom and the float seeks to rise, holding the bait off bottom. With this rig the bait can be cast out and left alone for a while. If there's no action in that spot the rod can be raised, thus raising the sinker to allow the rig to drift downstream a few feet more.

SINKERS AND OTHER ACCESSORIES

Sinkers come in many shapes and sizes from which specific ones are chosen for various reasons. Some of the more important types will be described and illustrated.

The old familiar *split shot* is available in a range of about ten sizes between #1 (.38 inch diameter) and "B" (.17 inch diameter), one or more being pinched on line or leader with pliers. These can be attached lightly to a short dropper so they will pull off if snagged. A more recent improvement is the pinch-on type designed for application without pliers.

Strip lead, also used where small amounts of weight are needed, is furnished in folders like matchbooks; the strips being torn off like matches and spirally wound around line or leader. If this isn't done neatly it can gather bits of weeds.

Dipsey sinkers are rounded in a teardrop design to help prevent them from catching on rocks. They are popular for fishing bait on the bottom in fresh water. They come in a range of sizes between 1/8 and 8 ounces.

Egg sinkers are oval, with a hole in the middle, allowing them to slide on the line. They sink a bait while allowing it to roll in a current, and also are used where there is little or no current action. An egg sinker can be cut in two parts for use as a bullet-shaped weight for plastic worm fishing.

SINKERS AND HOW TO RIG THEM

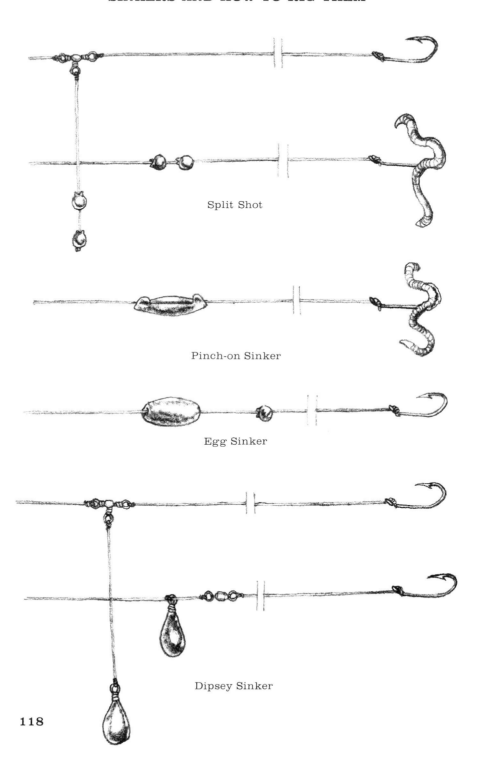

Split Shot

Pinch-on Sinker

Egg Sinker

Dipsey Sinker

118

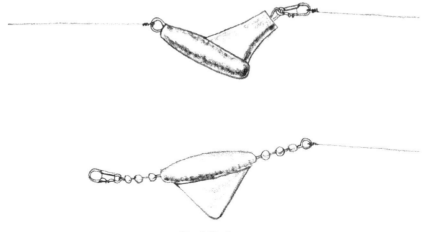

Keel Sinkers

Keel sinkers come in a great variety of shapes and sizes, all designed to prevent line twist (usually in trolling) and to provide weight. They normally are connected between line and leader. They can be made (or bought) for light lure or bait fishing by cutting lead sheeting into heart-shaped pieces which are crimped around line or leader to form small keels.

Diamond sinkers are of elongated diamond design with rings on both ends to provide a streamlined shape for minimum drag when trolling. A hook is added to one end for jigging.

Drails are more or less boomerang shaped, with rings at both ends, thus simulating keels. They usually are heavy to fish baits deep. Some have a clothespin-type snap at one end so the line can be clipped to it for deep trolling, allowing the line to be pulled free on a strike so the fish can be played without weight. They also are used in surf fishing with bait when casting from shore.

Several different types and sizes of *safety snaps, swivels* and *split rings* are shown in the illustration on page 120. Snaps and swivels are used only when necessary, and then only in the smallest sizes suitable for the tackle. Most anglers agree that black or bronzed finishes are superior to bright ones because they are less noticeable, although bright ones are commonly used in salt water, and in fresh water when the fish being sought are not presumed to be tackle-shy.

Split rings make handy connections and are easy to apply when one knows how. Slip a jackknife blade between the loops to raise one of the ends. Clip the hook eye or connecting loop around the raised end; withdraw the blade, and turn the ring until the connection(s) snap inside it.

Snaps and Swivels

Split Ring

HOW TO MAKE WIRE LEADERS

Because of its strength and abrasion resistance, wire has many uses in fresh- and saltwater fishing, but mainly to protect the terminal connection from being severed by the sharp teeth and other abrasive parts of many species of fish.

Although wire leaders are made in many ways for a diversity of purposes, most of them have a swivel on one end for connection to the line and a snap or snap swivel on the other for easy attachment of hooks or lures. The terminal end of some wire leaders is connected directly to the hook by snelling or by a loop which provides a loose hook for more natural swimming action of the bait.

Wire leaders vary in length from about 4 inches to 6 feet, the 4- to 12-inch ones are used in casting. The end of the leader which is connected to the line can be fitted with a ring, or with a swivel, which diminishes twisting when trolling or retrieving the lure.

Since each of several kinds of wire has its advantages and disadvantages for making leaders (or for trolling), it will be helpful to discuss them and how they should be connected to the tackle.

Solid Wire. Sometimes called "piano wire," but it isn't; true piano wire is carbon steel while that used for fishing is stainless steel. It offers extreme rigidity and highest density with the smallest ratio of diameter to strength. It is available in various diameters testing between 10 and 250 pounds. The disadvantage is that its stiffness inclines it to kink or break. It often is used in making very short leaders and is preferred by many anglers and boat skippers for longer ones for trolling. Connections at both ends are made with the Haywire Twist shown in the accompanying drawing.

Haywire Twist for making a loop in solid wire. For maximum strength make at least 3½ twists of the loop before winding several close coils. Bend excess back and forth until it breaks (*arrow*).

Stranded Wire. Usually consists of six strands of fine stainless-steel wire wound around a seventh wire which acts as a core, thus providing a Seven-strand (its trade name) miniature cable, as shown. The stranded wire is given a bronze camouflage finish by heat treating, which also provides more uniform strength and greater flexibility. This wire is very unobtrusive in the water and is amazingly fine for its strength which, in its many sizes, is from 18 to 600 pounds.

Nylon-coated Stranded Wire. Called Sevalon, this is the same as above except that it is covered by a thin coating of transparent nylon. This gives it a smooth surface with much less tendency to curl and kink. The nylon coating makes the wire more durable but it adds slightly to its diameter — a disadvantage so minor that its qualities far outweigh it.

Knots and Fastenings for Stranded Wire

Making loops in coated or uncoated stranded wire for looping it to the line or for attaching hooks, snaps, snap swivels or lures is easily and quickly done. An inexpensive crimping tool and several sizes of soft metal (usually brass) swaging sleeves are sold for the purpose, as illustrated on page 122. A sleeve is slipped onto the wire, the hook or other connection is threaded on, and the wire's end is pushed into the sleeve, whereupon wires and sleeve are crimped into a permanent connection. A stronger loop can be made by doubling the wire through the eye.

When a wire leader is needed that is so long that it must pass through rod guides, or when the crimping tool and metal sleeves are not available, the wire leader can be joined to the monofilament line by the Key Loop Knot, explained in Chapter 12. Other knots for joining stranded wire and mono-filament, such as the Figure-8 and Surgeon's Knot, are either unsafe or impractical.

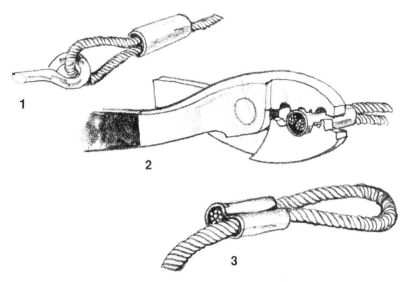

How to make a proper crimp: 1. Slide sleeve on stranded wire and make a loop by also threading end through sleeve, but don't allow end to protrude. **2.** Hold loop horizontally, being sure wires are not crossed inside sleeve. Apply crimping tool to sleeve and crimp tightly in one or more places, depending on length of sleeve. **3.** Proper crimp; wire should be flush with end of sleeve.

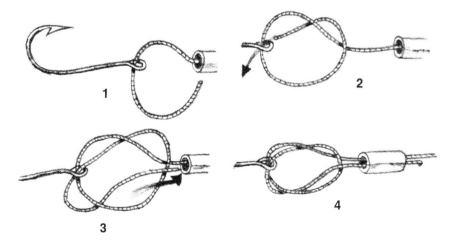

To make a stronger loop with nylon-coated wire: 1. Thread wire through sleeve and eye of hook, swivel or lure. **2.** Make an overhand knot. **3.** Pass wire through eye a second time. **4.** Make a second overhand knot; pass wire end through sleeve and crimp twice.

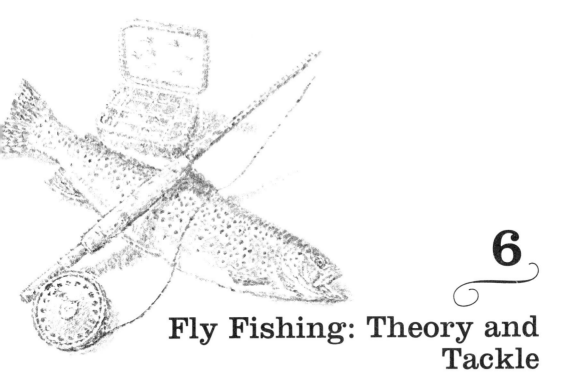

6

Fly Fishing: Theory and Tackle

In the strict sense, a "fly" is a combination of bits of fur, feathers, silk, tinsel and other materials tied on a hook to imitate one of the types of live or dead insects usually eaten by fish. In the general sense, the term includes many other imitations—insects in their larval stage (nymphs), grubs, grasshoppers, baitfish and even mice and frogs made of clipped deer hair.

Since artificial flies are weightless, or nearly so, the line which casts them must have weight so the flexing power of the rod can cast the line and thus carry the fly to its target. So fly fishing is the art of casting one of these nearly weightless artificial flies to spots wherever gamefish are presumed to be, tempting the fish to take the lure, and then handling him in such a manner as to tire him and bring him to the net.

Some flies are made to float; these are called dry flies. Others are made to sink; these are called wet flies, nymphs, streamers or bucktails. Some nymphs may be weighted slightly so they'll sink quicker. All, however, usually are given action when fished, to resemble the natural fish food they are supposed to represent.

HISTORY OF FLY FISHING

The art of fly fishing is one of the most ancient of modern sports; certainly more has been written about it than any other. In the second century of our era a Roman author told about using a fly called the false hippourous

123

for trout, apparently in a river in Macedonia. An hippourous evidently was a kind of wasp or bee and the false hippourous imitating it was made by tying wax-colored cock's hackles on a hook wound with red wool. This must have been the first streamer fly. Evidently nothing of any importance happened after that for well over a thousand years. In those days people fished for food rather than for sport.

The history of fly fishing begins late in the fifteenth century, when Dame Juliana Berners, supposedly a British abbess, was credited as being the author of a book entitled *Treatise of Fishing with an Angle*. The book, printed in 1496, probably was written long before that. It contains an amazing amount of fly-fishing information well worthy of our study today. This includes rod, line and hook manufacture and the dressings of a dozen artificial flies, one or more being recommended for each month of the season.

Much of the advice Dame Juliana gives is of value to us nearly five hundred years later: "Keep well off the water and out of sight, keep your shadow, too, off the water, and cast over rising fish. Strike neither too slow nor too quick nor too hard. When you hook a fish do not be in a hurry to land him, but tire him out and drown him." This fascinating little book has been reprinted several times, so it is available to modern readers.

While a few other ancient books stand out in the interim, the next solid impact on fly-fishing literature was made by Izaak Walton, "The Patron Saint of Angling," in England in 1653. His book *The Compleat Angler* went through five editions before it was combined with a book by Charles Cotton (1676) and one by Colonel Robert Venables (1662) to make up *The Compleat Angler* as we know it today. This combination of three books has gone through nearly two hundred editions, many so sumptuous and with so many notes and illustrations added that old Izaak hardly would recognize the small volume he started with.

Walton primarily was a baitfisherman. Cotton preferred using artificial flies, and Venables evidently was the originator of upstream fishing, so the combined writings of these three men provide an excellent insight into the general fishing methods of the latter part of the seventeenth century.

One of the great appeals of Walton's writing is his dialogue style, the teacher answering the questions of his pupil. Walton copied extensively from earlier authors and he contributed little to the actual knowledge of angling. Lately the originality of his prose style has been questioned because a single copy of a book written in 1577 has been found which was done in almost exactly the same style. This is *The Arte of Angling*. Only one copy of the book is known to exist. It was found in England in 1954 by my old friend, the celebrated angler and angling book collector C. Otto von Kienbusch, and was brought by him to the United States, where it now reposes in the angling collection of the Princeton University Library. A reprint of the book was made by Mr. von Kienbusch and was distributed to his friends. In Walton's day plagiarism was not considered unethical, and the newer writers were prone to copy whatever they wanted from the older ones, so many books of that era include material reprinted from older books without any expression of appreciation.

Books of the seventeenth century document four important steps in fly fishing. One is the imitation in artificial flies of the colors and shapes of the actual insects. Another is presentation of the fly, bringing it over the fish as the actual insect would travel on the water. Next is casting to individual rising fish. Finally, including both imitation and presentation, the old-timers learned to copy color, shape and motion in offering a floating fly to a fish.

Tackle of this era called either for single-handed rods as long as 18 feet or double-handed ones of 20 feet or more. The rod sections were spliced rather than jointed and were made from six to a dozen tapered lengths of various woods usually terminating with a whalebone tip, all joined together to provide an action resembling a switch. Tip sections sometimes fitted into hollow butt sections for easy transportation. Rods were long because reels were uncommon, although they are mentioned by Walton as early as 1655 for salmon fishing. (Evidently Walton never fished for salmon.)

Rods became shorter as the years went by and were made of hickory, lancewood, greenheart and bamboo, but the modern split-bamboo rod as we know it wasn't invented until 1845, when records point to Samuel Phillippe, of Easton, Pennsylvania, as its originator.

Lines were of twisted or braided horsehair, later sometimes combined with silk, tapering from as many as twelve to twenty hairs down sometimes to only one. The object was to make a heavy line to more easily cast the fly, a principle still in use today.

Fly lines were made of silkworm gut as early as 1724 but didn't become popular until fifty years or so later. Lines of braided silk, the forerunners of our modern synthetic ones, were developed about 1870. With their invention, silkworm gut was used only for leaders, and this was replaced by synthetic monofilament in the mid-1950s. The development of modern fly rods, fly lines, hooks and leaders will be discussed later.

The reels of the latter part of the seventeenth century were wooden winches. Gradually, as metal fabricating machinery developed, the reels were made of metal. In earliest times hooks were made of bone, stone, shell, thorns or what-have-you, and were hammered from metal before the fifteenth century. Modern hooks were born in Redditch, England, about year 1560, because Redditch was an important needle manufacturing region, and the father of the modern hook was the needle. Workmen of the day

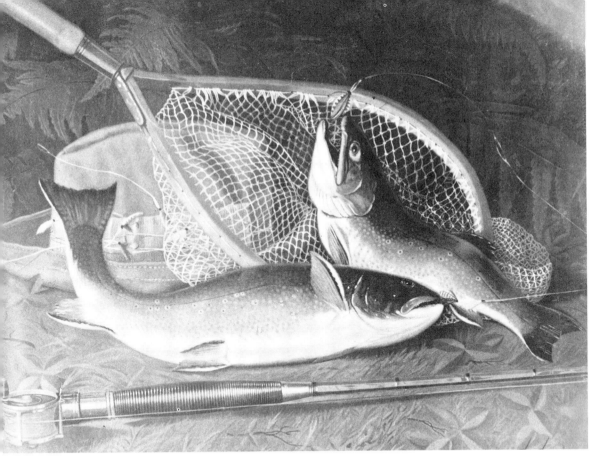

The fly fisherman casts a weighted line on a flexible, springy rod (*above left*). The flexing power of the rod carries the line, with its tapered monofilament leader and fly, through the air in a graceful loop which rolls out and lands lightly on the water. Playing a trout on a limber fly rod (*below left*) is one of the finest experiences of angling. Note how this angler plays his fish by a mere finger pressure on the line against the rod handle. "Two at a Cast," a lithograph by Thomas Sedgwick Steele (*above*), shows tackle used in the Rangely, Maine, area in 1895.

knew how to remove the temper from a needle, to bend and barb it, and then to restore the temper after a fashion. Since they didn't know how to bend an eye to the shank, eyes were made of single-strand or braided gut which was looped and lashed to the shank before dressing the fly. Examples of these old flies still exist in angling collections, and they were used even after 1890, when methods of bending the shank ends into metal eyes were invented.

About 1800 a few unknown fishermen learned that trout often would take a floating fly more readily than a sunken one. They would put on a fresh wet fly and present it until it was taken, or had sunk. Then they changed to another fresh, dry one. The first mention of actually drying the fly to make it float came about 1851, when the dry fly began to come into its own. In George P. R. Pulman's *Vade Mecum of Fly Fishing for Trout* (third edition), he says, "Let a *dry* fly be substituted for the wet one, the line switched a few times through the air to throw off its super abundant moisture, a judicious cast made just above the rising fish, and the fly allowed to float towards and over them, and the chances are ten to one that it will be seized as readily as the living insect."

After this, flies made specifically to float were developed. The historian of the dry fly was Frederic M. Halford, author of *Floating Flies and How to Dress Them* (London, 1886). Both artificial nymphs, and streamer flies and bucktails, are relatively modern developments.

THE FLY ROD

Older anglers who read this may be very fond of fly rods made of split bamboo. While these are works of art, usually cherished as collectors' items, they are expensive and delicate. No two are exactly alike. Fine split-bamboo rods are good investments, if we can afford them, because their increasing rareness is sure to make them appreciate in value. They are a pleasure to own and to use. But, from a practical standpoint, the sensible investment is one or more rods made of fiberglass—"glass rods," as they usually are called.

When one bought a split-bamboo rod he invariably tested its action to be sure it was what he wanted, because no two split-bamboo rods were exactly alike. The strips which were glued together to make the sticks (or rod sections) often came from different canes of bamboo, each of which varied in hardness and other characteristics. Rods of the same size and which looked identical could vary widely in power and action, particularly near the tips.

On the other hand, fiberglass rods are made by machinery from identical materials, so all rods of the same model number (made by the same manufacturer) are exactly alike. The average angler can buy the length or power of rod he wants. If it is made by one of the leading manufacturers it is sure to have the excellent casting characteristics preferred by the majority of anglers, because it was made for this purpose. Of course, each manufacturer incorporates individual differences in materials and processes but, in testing rods of the same power produced by several of the leading makers, the main differences seem to be those of appearance. Unless there is good reason to the contrary, we should avoid "bargains" sold under unfamiliar names. Famous nationally known brands are reasonably priced because they are made in tremendous quantities by firms possessing the intricate machinery and the skilled experts able to provide the best for the lowest price.

When one angler shows a rod to another, the frequently asked question is, "What does it weigh?" Weight is misleading and all but can be ignored in favor of the rod's power as given in the manufacturer's specifications. Rods of the same power in bamboo or fiberglass weigh differently, and even similarly powered fiberglass rods of different makes rarely weigh the same, partly due to varying weight in their fittings. The table given on page 136 covers this thoroughly. From it, select the type of fishing that most often will be done, and choose the power of rod indicated. Lengths and weights will vary slightly between tackle of various manufacturers, but the table provides good averages and gives line sizes that should fit any rod.

Proficient anglers may prefer somewhat lighter powered rods than the table gives for various purposes. This is a matter of choice tempered somewhat by the air resistance of lures to be used and the lengths of casts normally needed. When conditions permit, it always is more fun to use a lighter rod than a heavier one.

Rod action, or tapering, usually is what often is termed "parabolic"; that is, the action is slow in the butt and flexes noticeably down into the cork grip, yet it provides smooth power in the upper section, with sufficient backbone to provide long casts and to sink barbs into fish. Since manufacturers usually build the most acceptable action into rods designed for various purposes we do not need to become further involved with perplexing details of lengths, flexing, power, etc. here. Only a few experts will argue with the judgment of leading manufacturers, and even they usually are content with the beautifully and scientifically designed rods now available.

FLY LINES

All lures which are cast depend on weight to project them outward to the target. In spinning, spincasting and in bait- or plugcasting, we have seen that the weight of the lure does this, so the line merely acts as a connection. In fly fishing, however, since the lure is essentially weightless the line must have substance to carry the lure out. We are casting the line, and the lure merely goes along with it. Thus the fly line has bulk and is highly visible, requiring a length of much less obvious leader between line and lure to at least partially conceal from fish the fact that lure and line are connected.

The bulk or weight of the fly line used to be, and sometimes still is, produced by braiding many threads together, more being added, or some being cut out, to produce gradual and exact tapers. Old-fashioned braided silk lines then were oiled, but modern ones of braided synthetic fibers are coated with a plastic surface. Many lines no longer are tapered by braiding because the plastic coating can be applied and tapered over a level braided core. This coating is heavy or light, depending on whether the line is to be a sinking one or a floater. Fast-sinking lines have great density. Floating ones may have their coating filled with microscopic air cells to make them float permanently if kept free from algae and dirt.

Old-fashioned silk fly lines had to be dried after use to prevent rotting, and stored in loose loops to prevent them from setting in the coils which reel storage would induce. Modern plastic fly lines eliminate such bother. They can be stored on reels year-round. If coils occur they can be removed by stretching. They can't rot, but should be wiped occasionally with a damp soaped cloth or a felt pad to which a fly-line cleaning preparation has been applied. Suitable cleaning preparations often are supplied with the lines.

Fly lines differ in the type of taper, or lack of it, which they are given, and whether they float on the surface of the water or sink to the bottom. First, let's look at the various tapers and understand their purpose.

Level lines, as the name implies, have the same diameter throughout. The least expensive, they are used when fishing with baits and where precise and distant casts are not needed. Level lines can be used with flies for relatively short casts, but tapered lines are more desirable. Floating level lines are necessary with all floating lures. They are useful for shallow-water fishing when the floating line and a sinking leader will work the fly or other lure deep enough. For deeper fishing we need a sinking line—a slow-sinking, fast-sinking or very fast-sinking type.

Double-taper lines are of uniform diameter in the midsection, but they are tapered gradually smaller at both ends, the tapered sections usually being about 10 feet long and having level tips about 2 feet longer. The taper provides gentle delivery of the fly to the fish and is most useful for fish such as trout which are easily frightened. Tapered lines are available that float and sink. The floating type is most adaptable for fishing dry flies. Sinking tapered lines are ideal for very small sinking flies, such as artificial nymphs, but nymphs often are used on floating lines with sinking leaders in shallow streams where the leader will sink the lure deep enough.

Experts, after testing how well the tapered line acts (with leader and fly attached) on the rod, sometimes cut off a foot or so of the 2-foot level tip section to make the line and leader roll the fly out better. Beginners should avoid this unless they know what they are doing because of course the cut-off part can't be replaced.

While double-taper lines are rather expensive they are really two lines in one. Two anglers can divide the cost of a tapered line and can cut it into two lengths exactly in the middle. This provides two tapered sections, each about 45 feet long. The heavy end is attached to backing on the reel, using the Nail Knot described in Chapter 12. If you don't share a double-taper line, it can be reversed when one end becomes worn. But both halves are not needed. With the line cut in half, a considerable amount of backing can be used, even on small reels. Since you never know when you will hook into a large fish that might take out a hundred feet or more of line, the use of backing can be a wise precaution. Many of the smaller reels won't hold the complete double-taper line and enough backing to make the backing of any value.

Weight-forward lines make longer casts possible than do either level or double-taper lines. They are most useful for casting fairly bulky flies such as bugs, bucktails and streamers, because it is the weight of the line that casts the fly and the weightier forward taper will drive bulky flies greater distances.

The important part of a weight-forward line consists of about 20 feet of thick shooting line with about 10 feet of tapered line at the forward end of it (plus 2 feet or so of thin-diameter tip, which can be trimmed as mentioned previously). The rear end of the thick part is tapered backward steeply to over 50 feet of thin-diameter level line, providing about 90 feet in all. Backing can be substituted for the thin level section, if desired.

The following types of weight-forward lines are available: floating, slow sinking, fast sinking and very fast sinking.

Shooting-taper lines actually are the forward part of weight-forward lines without the backward taper and the level rear sections. A loop is attached to the rear end of the shooting taper. To this loop, as backing, is attached as much monofilament line or another sort of shooting line as can be accommodated on the reel. Shooting tapers are made for long-distance casting because the heavy shooting head will carry out a lot of the fine and light shooting line, or backing. As much of this as can be cast is coiled off the reel in one way or another. Some anglers lay it in large coils on the deck of a boat or on a dock. If wading, they may let it trail in the water or, preferably, may coil it in a "shooting basket" attached around the waist. In either case an alternative is to hold a few loose coils between the lips.

Quite obviously one must become used to handling this large amount of shooting line to avoid snarls in casting. Experts become very adept at this, and enjoy the extremely long casts the method makes possible for reaching fish long distances away. Beginners who want to become used to handling shooting tapers should allow enough time for practice to get used to the method. It is an excellent way to make very long casts when the tricks of line handling have been mastered.

Bass-bug-taper lines are weight-forward lines whose front tapers are shorter and heavier. Since it is the weight of the line which casts the lure, these shorter, heavier tapers are excellent for casting very bulky but relatively light objects such as big bass bugs, poppers and other small plugs suitable for a fly rod. Although there are *saltwater tapers* made specifically for the purpose, the similar bass-bug taper is excellent for casting the large and bulky wind-resistant bucktails so often used in salt water.

Variweight taper lines are fairly new as this is being written and are one of the innovations originated by Scientific Anglers, Inc. If we know the weight of line which fits a rod, presumably we can ignore them. If we aren't sure, they can offer an advantage. The idea is that, knowing the length of the rod, we can buy one of these floating lines to fit it. A variweight taper is a double-taper line wherein the two tapered sections are of unequal weight; one on each end of the line. A choice of two sizes of lines are provided. The size named Variweight I fits any rod less than $8\frac{1}{2}$ feet long; also $8\frac{1}{2}$-foot rods with light or medium action. The size named Variweight II fits any rod longer than $8\frac{1}{2}$ feet as well as $8\frac{1}{2}$-foot rods with medium or powerful action.

Thus, knowing the rod's length but not being sure what weight line will fit it, we can buy one Variweight line which we can be sure will fit the rod reasonably well. A guess of the rod's power should tell us which end of the line to try first. If the rod doesn't handle properly with this end, we can reverse the line on the reel and use the other one.

The density of the line is its floating or sinking properties, and our choice of line density depends on the kind of fishing we most often will want to do. As this is written, *floating lines* are most popular and are used for fishing dry flies, wet flies, nymphs, bass bugs or panfish bugs on or near the surface. *Sinking lines* are used less frequently but are essential for fishing streamers and bucktails, and any other lures we want to go deep. These are obtainable in various sinking densities, depending on how fast we want the line to sink. For example, I often fish a pond in Maine where one has to drag bottom, at a depth of 6 feet or so, to get strikes. In such a case a fast-sinking line is better because I don't have to wait too long for it to settle.

There also are *intermediate lines* which deserve attention. One of these is the floating line with about 10 feet of sinking tip. This type picks up for casting easier than a sinking line does. Another type of intermediate line is made to float when it is dressed with a floatant preparation or to sink slowly when used without such a dressing.

Obviously, then, no one line is appropriate for all situations. Weight is decided by the rod to be used. Ideally, we should have two extra reel spools to hold line of different kinds; for example, a double-taper floater, a weight-forward floater with a sinking tip, and a weight-forward sinking line. On a reel with easily interchangeable spools, such an assortment opens up a variety of possibilities for one rod.

Of course, color comes into the picture, but let's ignore it. The variety in colors usually is for the convenience of the manufacturer so he can tell one type of line from another. Line color, be it white, pink or pistachio,

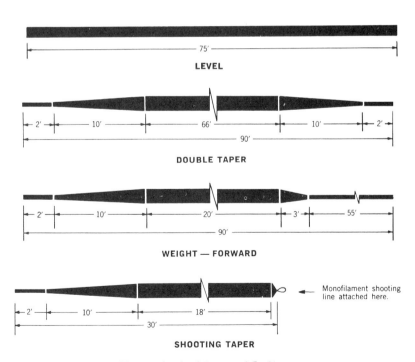

Four principal types of fly lines.

should make no difference to the angler because it is the degree of opaqueness the fish sees, not the color. Some fishermen won't use white lines, for example, because they think fish can see them too easily. Yet divers say that a boat's hull is most difficult to see underwater when it is white. A white line is easiest for the angler to see; so it has an advantage. When a long leader is used, the line's end is so far to the edge of a fish's window of vision that, presumably, the fish does not associate it with the lure at the other end of the leader.

Standardization of Fly Lines

Until a few years before this was written it was difficult to match a rod to a line, or vice versa, because we had little information to go by. Fly lines of different compositions varied widely in casting characteristics even if they were supposed to be of the same size. Line sizes were identified by letters, and the same identification by two or more manufacturers was no guarantee that the lines were identical.

This caused so much difficulty that the members of the American Fishing Tackle Manufacturers Association decided to give up letter designations and to identify all lines by the weights of their forward sections ranging from size 4 for the lightest to size 11 for the heaviest. These designations apply regardless of whether the line is level, double-taper, forward-taper, or whatever.

All one now needs to know is what size line is suitable for his rod. In fact, the recommended size usually is marked on it. If it isn't, Scientific Anglers, Inc. (Box 2001, Midland, Michigan 48640) will send without charge a table of fly-line size recommendations for every standard brand and model number of every fly rod currently sold in the United States.

Scientific Anglers, Inc. seems to have done more than any other manufacturer in translating the A.F.T.M.A. recommendations into charts the average angler can easily understand. They do not identify a rod's power by its length because rods of the same power can have different lengths, although there is a rough relationship between the two. One decides on the power or size of the rod he wants, depending on the kind of fishing he wants to do. If he buys one or more lines of the same power or size he can be reasonably sure that the lines will fit the rod, no matter what types of lines they are. Fly reels also can be purchased similarly, allowing ample capacity for the line, and for enough backing, if the power of the tackle calls for it. Scientific Anglers, Inc. designates their tackle by "Systems" (or power), rather than by rod length or weight, but the result is similar and much more significant. With their permission the author provides the table on the following page, and he has included Scientific Anglers rod lengths and weights merely for comparison. Meanings of the letter symbols are as follows:

Standard Symbols	**Author's Abbreviations**
L — level (same diameter from end to end)	**(BBT)** — bass-bug taper
DT — double taper	**FS** — fast sink
WF — weight forward	**EFS** — extra fast sink
ST — single taper (shooting taper)	**(SWT)** — saltwater taper
F — floating	
S — sinking	
F/S — wet tip (floating line with sinking tip)	

In consulting this chart we can find the kind of fishing we usually want to do, and can note the power of rod which is most appropriate for it. Then we can decide on the types of lines needed. Ideally, the reel should be purchased with two extra spools so lines for various purposes can be carried. On one occasion we may want a floating line; on another, a floating line with a sinking tip, or a sinking line. This versatility extends the uses of the tackle immeasurably, essentially giving us three reels in one.

One may say, don't I need a rod with a light tip for casting dry flies, or one with a stiff tip for streamers and bucktails, or some other type of action for something else? We used to be rather fussy about such things in the split-bamboo rod era, but it seems no longer necessary. Most rods are for all-round fishing, but specialists in one form of fishing or another can find specialized rod actions if they look for them. The answer to specialization is more in line selection than in the choice of the rod. Line selection is much more varied than it used to be. The same rod operates efficiently with a double-taper line for dry flies; with a forward-taper for streamers and bucktails, and with a bass-bug taper for bulky floaters that need a lot of weight forward in the line to carry them out. Thus, for any fly rod use, line selection is far more important than small differences in the action of the rod.

Rod Power or "System"	For this Kind of Fishing	Rod Length	Rod Weight	Fly Line Size (First Choice)	Second Choice	Third Choice
4 Extra light	Trout–small streams, tiny flies, fine leaders Panfish–sheltered ponds, tiny bugs, small flies	7'2"	3 oz.	DT-4-F	DT-4-F/S	
5 Very light	Trout–small streams, delicate casting, smooth water Panfish–ponds and small streams, tiny bugs, small flies	7'7"	3¼ oz.	DT-5-F	DT-5-F/S	DT-5-S
6 Light	Trout–medium size streams and ponds, larger flies Panfish, bass–sheltered waters, small bugs and flies	8'1"	3½ oz.	DT-6-F	DT-6-S DT-6-F/S	DT-6-F/S DT-6-S
7 Medium light	Trout–medium size streams and ponds, all flies Panfish, bass–sheltered waters, small bugs and flies	8'5"	4 oz.	DT-7-F	WF-7-FS	WF-7-F/S
8 Medium	Trout–large streams and lakes, all wet and dry flies, streamers Panfish–large streams and lakes, all panfish flies and bugs Bass, pike–open water, all flies, small bugs Atlantic salmon–smaller streams, short and medium casts	8'8"	4⅝ oz.	DT-8-F DT-8-F WF-8-F WF-8-F	WF-8-EFS WF-8-FS WF-8-FS WF-8-F/S	WF-8-F/S WF-8-F (BBT) WF-8-F/S WF-8-EFS
9 Medium powerful	Bass, pike–large water, all flies Atlantic salmon–medium-size rivers Steelhead, shad–medium-size rivers Bonefish, school stripers, snook, baby tarpon	8'11"	5 oz.	WF-9-F (BBT) WF-9-F WF-9-S or ST-9-S WF-9-F (SWT)	WF-9-FS WF-9-F/S ST-9-S or WF-9-EFS WF-9-EFS	WF-9-F/S WF-9-EFS WF-9-S or ST-9-S WF-9-F/S
10 Powerful	Steelhead, shad–largest rivers, long casts Striped bass–open water, all salt water use Salmon–open water, large flies, casting in wind	9'1"	5¼ oz.	ST-10-S or WF-10-EFS WF-10-F (SWT) WF-10-F	ST-10-S or WF-10-FS WF-10-EFS WF-10-F/S	WF-10-S or ST-10-S WF-10-F/S WF-10-EFS
11 Extra powerful	Tarpon, billfish, dolphin, etc.–heavy salt water use and any fishing requiring extremely long casts with big flies and bugs, casting in wind	9'3"	5½ oz.	WF-11-F (SWT)	WF-11-EFS	WF-11-I

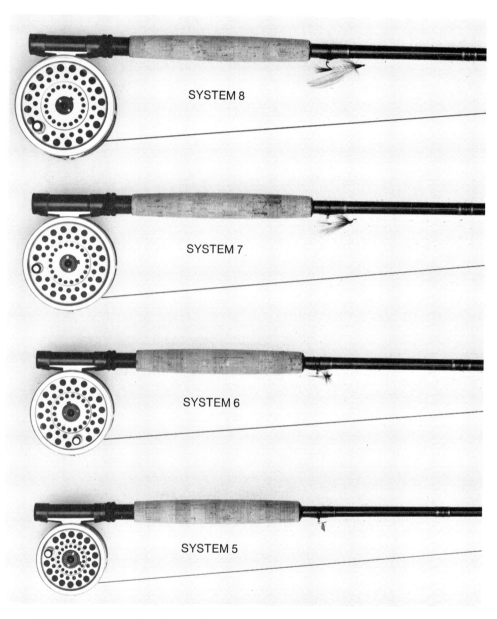

SYSTEM 8

SYSTEM 7

SYSTEM 6

SYSTEM 5

Fly fishing tackle is obtainable in matched sets of rods, reels and lines. These are Scientific Anglers' sets.

FLY REELS

One important manufacturer offers eight different sizes of fly reels, one to fit each of the eight sizes of rods as shown on the preceding chart. This merely indicates that there is an ideal weight and capacity of reel to balance every size of rod, but we don't need to be that fussy. The reel should feel comfortable on the rod, and it should have the capacity for whatever is required of it. One does not need a different reel for every size of rod but, if he uses several sizes of rods, he does need enough reels or extra reel-spools to hold the sizes and types of lines suitable for them.

For panfish, small bass and trout, and other fish unable to take much line, the reel acts merely as a storage winch. We needn't be concerned with drag and precision manufacturing. There is no need of backing. Any inexpensive fly reel will do.

Reel capacity and quality become important when there is a chance of hooking a fish strong enough to pull considerable line from the reel. Since such fish often can take out all the fly line and still keep going, we then need a high-quality reel with an adjustable drag, or brake, and capacity not only for the line but also for from 150 to 200 yards of braided backing with a breaking strength of about 20 pounds. Nearly all fly reels are sold with printed information on the sizes of lines and the amounts of backing they will hold. The backing is wound on tightly off the revolving line spool to avoid twist. The line can be tied to the backing with a Nail Knot (Chapter 12), and then the line is wound on, also without twist. We should guard against overfilling the spool because careless reeling under the stress of playing a big fish can overfill a spool which does not seem overfilled when its line is spooled on compactly.

We need the safety of at least 150 yards of backing for many species of fish which make long runs. If there ever is any chance of hooking such a fish it is wise to obtain a reel that will accommodate this backing. Even in handling fish that don't get us into the backing, the padding of the backing makes it possible to regain the fly line faster. Since the backing increases spool diameter, the line won't set into extremely small coils.

If backing is to be included, let's do the job right and make sure the reel is a high quality one which has a smoothly adjustable brake. This usually is a steel spring which provides click-drag tension adjustable to the desired amount by a lever or knob on the outside of the case of the reel. The click drag may be operated by friction discs or by some other means. The method isn't important if the drag is smooth and easily adjustable. Don't set the drag by pulling line from the reel, at least until you're used to it. The guides of the fly rod provide added tension, and it is dangerous to have too much. Hook the fly to something solid and walk backward, letting the reel pay out line. While doing so, adjust the drag to amply safe tension. A fish tires himself out by running, and he should be allowed to do so. Too much drag may cause the hook to pull out, or the leader to break.

Some modern reels are made with rims on the spools which make added temporary braking pressure possible by forefinger control or feathering the rim of the spool. Such reels offer a decided advantage. Other reels are so made that the reel handle doesn't revolve when a fish is taking out line.

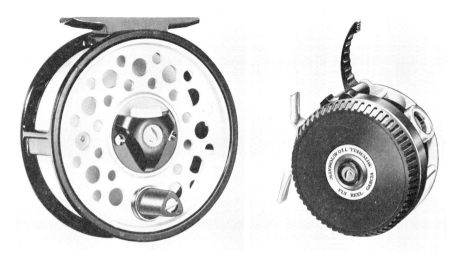

The fly reel serves as a holder for the line; it does not pay out line on a cast as do spinning and baitcasting reels. At left, a single-action reel that winds line onto the spool with a turn of the handle; at right, an automatic that actuates a spring-loaded spool by a finger lever.

The handle remains stationary and the spool revolves against a slipping disc clutch, but line can be regained by reeling.

Most fly reels are single action, the spool making one revolution with each turn of the handle. Some reels offer the multiplying action of two or more revolutions with each turn of the handle. Because of the added gears they are somewhat heavier and bulkier. Their selection is a matter of personal preference.

Automatic fly reels are operated by a coiled spring enclosed in a housing beside the reel spool. The spring can be wound manually, and it is wound automatically when line is stripped from the reel. Therefore, to regain line all one has to do is to press the retrieve lever.

There are two types of automatic reels: one clamps to the reel seat in the same position as a single-action reel; the other lies flat against the reel seat. Many fishermen like the ease and convenience of automatic line retrieve because it eliminates having to crank a reel handle. Such reels are made to accommodate level or tapered fly lines, but they are less efficient when backing on the reel is needed.

Fly Line Care

In the days before plastic, fly lines were made of braided silk threads which were treated with oil to provide a smooth finish. Wet lines had to be dried carefully, or they would rot. They also tended to become sticky and to set into almost irremovable coils when left very long on the reel. These troubles were eliminated with the development of fly lines made of plastic. Plastic lines can be left on reel spools from season to season without harm. If any coils develop over one winter they can be removed by stretching the line. Rotting and tackiness are eliminated. While it is better for both reel and line to dry a line before storage, this makes little or no difference unless the line has been used in salt water.

Modern plastic fly lines essentially need only two kinds of care. Avoid scuffing them by not stepping on them and by not pulling them against rocks and other rough objects. Since they eventually become dirty from algae and slime, they occasionally should be rubbed between a piece of cloth lightly coated with fly-line conditioner—a preparation often provided with the line itself. If the line is a floater it will float better when it is clean. It also will shoot out better between the rod guides, thus affording longer casts.

A Bit About Backing

We have seen that, on small reels, room for backing can be provided by halving a double-taper line or by removing part or all of the level part of a weight-forward line. Backing can be monofilament as used in spinning and spincasting, but this can become stiff and set in coils. It is more convenient to use softer and more permanent braided nylon or dacron (or a similar synthetic material) testing about 20 pounds. Anglers having backing on several reels usually stick to a single strength so they always know how strong their backing is. When stored on the reel, its strength deteriorates only slightly, if at all, although at the start of each season it should be checked for strength mainly because there may be a weak spot or two due to abrasion.

In adding backing to a fly line the two are connected by a Nail Knot (Chapter 12) and the backing is attached to the reel by a slip knot. But how much backing will the reel hold when the line has been added? We must not put on so much as to make the fly line bind in the reel housing if the line should become spooled on unevenly in the excitement of playing a fish.

One way to do it (the tedious way!) is to put the fly line on the reel spool first and then to add enough backing to comfortably fill the reel. Then remove both lines; spool on the backing compactly; tie it to the line, and spool on the line. This may, however, be the best way because you know exactly how much backing can be accommodated.

Some of the larger fly reels come with a chart telling how much backing the reel will hold when fitted with the various sizes of lines. If you lack this information, and don't want to bother with the previous method, do it by estimation. To be on the safe side when going for fish that make long runs, you should have between 150 and 200 yards of backing on a large-capacity reel. On such a reel you can add this much and usually have enough room for any size of fly line. In spooling on backing you can estimate the amount of space the fly line will require, and act accordingly. A few dozen yards, more or less, may not be critical.

One of the greatest thrills in fly fishing is to have a big fish make a run while we watch the fly line disappear and the backing peel off the reel down to what may be a dangerous remainder. At such times we are glad we fitted the reel with ample backing. Then, exhausted, the fish ceases his run and can be pumped in again. Finally, we see the fly line coming back, and we carefully ease the small knot through the rod guides. With some of the fly line regained we have confidence that, unless an accident happens, we are in control again.

LEADERS

Shortly after World War II a revolutionary improvement was made in fly-fishing tackle which marked a transition from split-bamboo rods to those of fiberglass; from silk lines to synthetic ones; and from leaders of silkworm gut to those made of synthetic monofilament. This was important because the new monofilaments were much cheaper, they didn't have to be soaked before using, and they deteriorated much less than did the old ones made of gut.

Now, monofilament can be obtained on inexpensive spools or small leader wheels in every size suitable for making every type of leader, even down to gossamer threads testing one pound, or less.

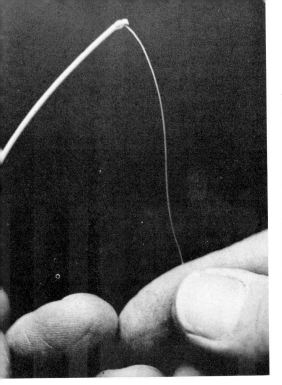
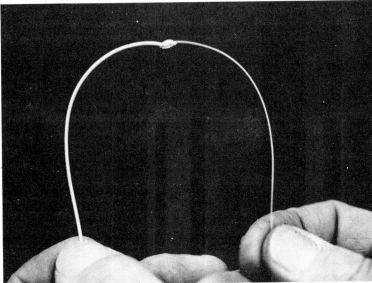

Leader butt must be of sufficient diameter and stiffness to cast properly. Butt that is too thin forms a "V" when bent between the fingers (*left*). Butt of correct size forms a "U" (*right*).

Leaders divide fishermen into two types: those who buy them, and those who make their own. Since there are details in leader making that some won't want to bother with, we'll discuss that in Chapter 8, where readers can ignore it, if they wish. This chapter is confined to ready-made leaders.

Tapered leaders are not necessary (but they are advisable) when using fly-fishing tackle and flies. A few feet of the appropriate strength of monofilament will do the job even though a properly tapered leader would do it much better.

Tapered leaders are made to roll the fly out as a continuation of the line and to make the leader fall to the water in a straight line rather than in coils. If the butt end of a leader is the wrong diameter for the end of the fly line, line end and leader butt will act as a hinge and thus land improperly instead of the leader acting as a continuation of the line. If the tip end of the leader is too stiff for the size of fly, the fly won't land and swim or float in a lifelike manner. If the tip is too light for the size of the fly, the fly may break off in being cast, or a fish may break it off. Thus, for efficient fly fishing, the right leader is essential. Knowing how to select the proper leader often separates successful from unsuccessful fishermen.

A micrometer or thickness gauge is very helpful in checking line and leader thickness. The butt of the leader should be smaller in diameter than the line's end; from six-tenths to two-thirds, depending on the stiffness of the monofilament. Correctness can be checked by holding the joined leader and fly line between thumb and forefinger of each hand, each about 6 inches from the knot. When bending this length the joined part should form a "U." If it forms a "V," or a hinge, the graduation in size between line end and leader butt is incorrect.

There are several ways of joining line and leader. I prefer the Leader Whip Knot given in Chapter 12.

Leader length is a matter of opinion, but the leader should be longer and more finely tapered for clear water than for discolored conditions. Usually it should be at least as long as the rod. A properly graduated tapered leader performs well in any length. Lefty Kreh, a noted Florida fly-fishing expert, demonstrated this by easily casting a 40-foot leader.

We will see in Chapter 8 that the rule for properly tapering a leader includes a heavy graduated butt section about two-thirds, or 60 percent of the leader's length. Half of the remaining one-third, or 40 percent, is a steep graduation from the heavy butt section to the light tip section. The front one-sixth, or 20 percent, consists of a final light graduation or two and the tippet.

The diameter of the tip section, or tippet, is decided by the size of fly being used. There is a bit of latitude in this. The tippet can be on the light side for open, clear-water conditions; on the heavier side for fishing near obstructions or in discolored water. See the table in Chapter 8, How to Tie Leaders, to match tippet and hook.

Another consideration in using the table is how leader shy the fish are for which we're fishing. Since trout usually are leader shy, this table is adaptable to them. With fish that are less leader shy, such as panfish or bass, we can use stronger tippets per hook size than recommended, especially when casting near snags, pads, weeds and such places.

Monofilament leaders are available in knotted and in knotless varieties. What's the difference? Knotted leaders are strands of graduated diameters, each tied to another. Knotless leaders are drawn through a die to provide similar graduations. Properly tied knots do no harm, and may help to sink the leader.

An excellent one-knot leader, available in various strengths and lengths, is Cortland's Twin-Tip, which comes with one butt section and two tip sections. Tie on one tip section, keeping the other in reserve. When the original tip section needs replacing, it can be removed and the other can be tied on, thus providing two leaders essentially for the price of one.

If leaders are stiff and set in coils the stiffness can be removed by stretching (pulling) them, or by drawing them between a doubled piece of rubber inner tube held between thumb and fingers. If you lack a piece of inner tube, use the doubled strap of your hip boot. Regardless of the type of fly, the leader should sink—at least the tip end. Various preparations are sold to sink leaders, but substitutes always are available. These include laundry soap, fish slime, and even mud.

No matter how expert the caster is, wind knots frequently appear in leaders. These simple overhand knots decrease leader strength by one-half, so check for them and promptly take them out. Usually you can loosen and remove them with the point of a safety pin. Stubborn wind knots may need to be cut out; the two ends then being joined by a Blood Knot.

What do we do about sharp-toothed fish which can bite through a leader tippet? Since these fish are not very leader shy, a short trace of wire, braided wire or plastic-coated braided wire can be used. Because these are apt to kink, and also are very conspicuous, many anglers prefer to tie a short length of much stronger monofilament to the leader's tip. Even such fish as pike and pickerel can't bite through it if it is heavy enough. When joining a leader's end to a piece of monofilament which is of much greater diameter, the usual Blood Knot won't be strong enough. Use the Double Strand Blood Knot described in Chapter 12.

FLIES AND OTHER LURES

Purists will say, and with good reason, that the only lure that should be put on the leader of a fly-rod outfit is an unweighted artificial fly. The fly line is the casting weight. The more weight or bulk tied to the leader, the more poorly the outfit will cast. The fun of using properly matched tackle is in making a smooth pickup, a high backcast, and in seeing the line shoot out straight with leader properly extended to drop the tiny fly exactly where we want to place it. Weighted lures, even very small ones, are more suitable to other types of tackle.

This doesn't mean that we can't use a hook with a worm or other bait on it; or add lead to the leader to make it sink, or use small spinner combinations or little plugs and so forth. It does mean that, when such lures are used, we take something away from the fun of fly fishing.

Purists also will say that such adulterations of fly fishing are unnecessary, because a properly selected and correctly presented fly can be just as successful as other lures. Sometimes it can be much more successful; occasionally less so. When less so, some other type of gear should be used.

A reason fly fishing is so popular is because so many types of artificial "flies" can be used with the tackle. Floating flies imitate any of scores of kinds of live insects landing on the water. Wet flies represent dead ones.

Trout

Dimpling rises on a smooth pool, cool water pulsing past your thighs, white line looping in the breeze . . . and afterward, two speckled beauties shimmering on a rock.

Photos by David Dale Dickey

1 **3** **4**

2

Early summer on Montana's
Flathead River . . . Dolly
Vardens moving upstream
toward fall spawning grounds . . .
the lightning strike, the
dogged underwater battle . . .
then the fish erupts, churning
the stream, and frantic angler
races for shore to save his prize . . .

. . . but the bull trout shakes the lure, turns toward open water . . . so angler beaches him with a booted foot . . . poses him with the deceiving blade back in his jaw.

Photos by Byron Dalrymple

Choose a wisp of feathers on
a slender hook, in shape and
hue a mimicry of nature . . .
cast it on a gossamer strand
and see the taking trout . . .
play him on a trembling wand . . .

. . . net him when he's almost
whipped, a wriggling crescent
in the dripping web . . . and then,
remove the barb and slide him
back to swim again.

Photos by David Dale Dickey

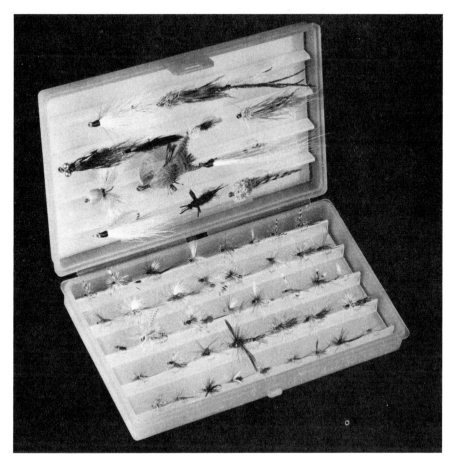

Fly box stocked with an assortment of dry flies, wets, nymphs, streamers, bucktails and terrestrials. Fly tyers have created hundreds of different artificials to match the myriad forms of aquatic and land insects.

Streamer flies and bucktails can be made to dart about exactly as baitfish swim, and specific baitfish can be duplicated faithfully in size, shape, flash and color. Many artificial representations accurately duplicate the various kinds of nymphs, which are the larval or nymphal stages of insects before they hatch. By the same token, beetles, bugs, caterpillars, ants, bees, crickets, grasshoppers, grubs and so on can be imitated with furs, feathers, silks and tinsels—and even mice, frogs and other things that various kinds of fish use for food. These can be used with lines made to cast each type properly and to fish selected lures at any desired depth, from the surface to way down under.

Obviously so versatile a method shouldn't be asked to do some of the things it's not suited for. Many people learn to fish by using spinning or spincasting tackle. If they are lucky, they eventually graduate to fly fishing, because those familiar with all the ways to enjoy angling usually agree that the fly rod and a small box of flies offer maximum pleasure and profit in fresh water or salt.

Too many fishermen shy away from fly fishing under the mistaken impression that it's rather difficult. Although it's a sport with infinite variations, the essentials for success are very easy to learn. We'll try to state them as simply as possible in the next chapter.

ACCESSORIES FOR FLY FISHING

Finally, what·do we need for fly fishing besides the basic tackle — rod, reel, line, leaders and a box of flies? A creel, if we want it, but a plastic bag will hold fish until we get to the cooler in the car. A net, if we want it, but tired fish can be drawn up on the bank or can be landed by hand in other ways. Some of these cumbersome items can be more bother than they are worth. In addition:

A safety pin or two to pick out wind knots; to remove varnish from hook eyes, and even to cut and bend into a line guide (fastened on with tape) if one gets pulled off going through the bushes.

A pair of small pliers of the parallel-jaw type to remove and straighten hooks, act as a wrench, clip off an embedded hook, and do various other jobs.

Finger-nail clippers, used mostly for cutting monofilament.

A small rectangle of inner-tube rubber to straighten coiled leaders.

A small sharpening stone to hone hook points sharp. (Many fish are lost because of dull hooks.)

A couple of plastic bags to carry fish, gather nuts and berries or (with one side slitted) to use as a hood over the head when it rains.

Bottles of solution to make dry flies float and leaders sink.

Felt soles on boots or waders to prevent slipping.

A good jackknife for many purposes, including promptly cleaning your catch. (A knife of the "Swiss Army Type" includes many tools in one.)

In addition to a fishing license, everyone will think of something else he wants to take along, but it's more pleasant to reduce to essentials than to be burdened with too much equipment.

7

Flycasting

The novice, sitting beside a pool on a wooded trout stream, lazily watched his little red and white bobber drift in the slight current, tethered by monofilament to a spincasting rod whose tip section rested on a forked stick stuck into the mud at the water's edge. There had been no action for the past hour, even though he had rebaited and recast his rig several times. He didn't realize that no trout would come near his worm-baited hook which dangled from the bobber because no one had told him that he was not fishing in trout water.

There must be more exciting ways to enjoy fishing, he thought, morosely.

The bushes parted below the tail of the pool downstream and a fisherman quietly emerged. He paused to light his pipe, studying the water. Two subsurface rocks near the tail of the pool claimed his attention. The novice didn't notice, but the fly fisherman did, that just below the rocks the pool's surface occasionally dimpled from the feeding of rising trout.

The fly fisherman stripped line from his reel and, with a casual swishing motion, let his rod feed it into the air. He stripped off more line and brought his right arm high. The novice watched in fascination as line and leader soared behind the angler, who then smartly swept his rod forward to snake the line smoothly over the pool to a spot over and above one of the rocks. When the line was fully extended, it and the leader and dry fly settled quietly upon the surface, leaving hardly a ripple. The novice watched the fly drift over the rock and, as it reached its downstream side, saw a swirl and heard a slight "plop" as a trout rose to suck it in.

As the trout did so the angler raised his rod slightly to tighten the line, thus hooking the trout. Feeling the prick of the barb, the fish cartwheeled and raced upstream, taking line from the lightly set drag of the reel. At the end of his run the trout swirled again and the angler reeled him nearer. After a few shorter runs the fish was brought to shore, and carefully released.

The angler cast a second time; this one over the other rock. The little dry fly danced down-current as before, and now a bigger trout took it. This fish put up a worthier fight, and it was several minutes before he could be seen, wobbling feebly on his side near the angler's waders. The man carefully reached down to clamp thumb and forefinger around the trout's back, just behind the gills. Thus stunning him, momentarily, the angler raised him high in admiration, and waded ashore to dispatch him and put him in a plastic bag, which the man then tucked into his game pocket. The novice noted that one or two other larger trout also were in the bag.

The fly fisherman didn't seem to notice the novice, as he sat quietly beside his resting rod, so he didn't observe the look of admiration and wonder directed at him. It all seemed so easy, the novice thought. The skillful handling of the rod was poetry in motion. The angler had known precisely where to drop his fly and exactly how to present it delicately so as not to disturb the feeding trout. Even if I were catching fish, the novice thought, what that man is doing is so much more fun, and so much more effective. I wonder if I could ever learn to do it? He reeled in his tackle, and went home.

IS IT AS EASY AS IT LOOKS?

Unfortunately, fly fishing has the reputation of being difficult mainly because it is a sport so comprehensive that one's whole lifetime can be spent learning the fine points, but this never-ceasing challenge is a reason for its fascination. We can make it easy by ignoring the fine points and confining ourselves, at first, only to the essentials. One can learn the essentials well enough to go out and catch fish after only a small amount of practice.

Among the essentials is obtaining one of the balanced fly-fishing outfits discussed in the previous chapter. For general freshwater fishing this could be an $8\frac{1}{2}$-foot rod fitted with a floating line with a sinking tip; a tapered leader no longer than the rod testing at the tip 3 or 4 pounds, and about half a dozen small, simple, sparsely dressed bucktail flies, perhaps about size 6 or 8 for trout, smallmouth bass or panfish.

The essentials include knowing how to knot the fly to the leader, and how to make only two very simple casts—the basic overhead cast and the roll cast. Of course we want to cast the bucktail where there are fish, and to impart to it (by twitching the rod tip) that darting motion which makes it act like a swimming baitfish. Those are the essentials, and they are easier to learn than to describe. Since the action of the current and that of the angler's rod always keeps the bucktail in motion, fish usually will hook themselves. Bringing small or moderate-sized fish to shore isn't much of a problem.

This chapter starts with the fundamentals of casting and proceeds to some of the more advanced methods.

BASIC OVERHEAD CAST

Practice this on a smooth lawn first, especially if no water is handy. Using a fly on the leader isn't absolutely necessary in practice, but if one is used cut off the barb for safety's sake and to keep the fly from catching in grass.

Stand with the feet comfortably apart, facing at about an angle of 45 degrees from the direction you want to cast. (The hand holding the rod should be rearmost in relation to stance.) We'll call the hand which holds the rod the "rod hand," the other one the "line hand." The line hand strips line from the reel when needed, retrieves it, and holds and releases it in casting. It keeps slack out of the line, keeps constant tension on the line while casting, and keeps the line under control at all times.

Holding the rod lightly and comfortably is important. The thumb should be on top of the rod grip to help keep the wrist stiff, thus transmitting the stroke to the forearm and elbow. Thumb pressure also aids in stopping the rod and in pushing it forward during the cast.

You now have a few feet of line and the leader extending from the rod's tiptop. Pull a few feet more from the reel with the line hand and, holding it, flip the rod upwards, or sideways and backward, pausing a second or more, and then flipping the rod forward, releasing the few feet of line as the rod is flipped forward. As line length extends, this pause must be increased. Notice that the forward flip of the rod takes this few feet of line and shoots it through the line guides, thus extending the cast.

150

1. Hold the rod lightly and comfortably, with the thumb resting on top of the rod grip to help keep the wrist firm during the backcast and to aid in pushing it forward.

2. Casting instructor Tom Stouffer assumes a relaxed position with the feet spread comfortably apart, his body turned about 45 degrees from the casting target. He has just pulled line from the reel and is holding the slack near the rod handle.

3. With a few feet of line extending from the tiptop, flip the rod upward and back . . .

Repeat this a few times until about three rod lengths of line extend from the tiptop: 25 or 30 feet or so, but no more. Since the weight of the line is what we are casting, this amount is necessary to cast properly. Don't try to use more until casting this amount has been mastered.

Now pull in a few feet of line with the line hand to straighten it. Don't let go of it while casting, for the time being.

The backcast part of the overhead cast is made with the rod pointing forward horizontally (at 9 o'clock). The rod is raised with a continuously accelerating motion almost to the vertical. At this point a smart kick, or flick, should be given to the rod, not to extend past 12 o'clock. It is this nearly imperceptible kick that makes the big difference between a mediocre and a good caster. The

4. . . . then forward, allowing line to work through the guides, repeating until 25 to 30 feet of line extend from the tiptop.

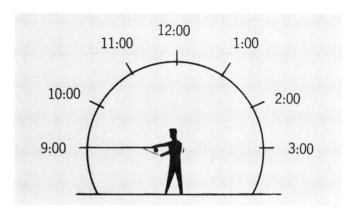

The clock positions referred to in casting instructions.

5. Ready to cast, with line extended on grass in front of you.

rod will drift back a little more; not beyond 1 o'clock. Here is where many
casters get into trouble because they
bring the rod back too far, thus allowing
the cast to drop behind them. In practice,
at least, never raise the rod beyond the
12 o'clock position.

With a castable length of line extending straight forward, raise the rod from
the horizontal with a continuously accelerating motion as above described.
The line should loop above and behind
the tip of the rod and should not pass by
its side in the same plane, whether vertical or at any angle. At the 12 o'clock
position, after the little kick, pause for
a second or two (actually stopping the
rod) to let the line straighten out behind,
but do not pause so long as to allow it
to drop. You can look over your shoulder to see how long this pause should
be but eventually this won't be necessary
because the timing will become instinctive. Of course the more line we are
casting, the longer the pause or stop will
be. The forward cast should be started

6. Rapidly accelerate the rod to 12
o'clock position, letting rod tip drift
back to 1 o'clock, but no farther. The
line should loop above and behind
the tip of the rod, and straighten out
behind you.

7. Start the forward cast the instant the line fully straightens out behind you. Look over your shoulder, at first, to get the timing.

8. Drive the rod forward with a movement somewhat akin to driving a nail into a wall with a hammer. Accelerate between 1 and 11 o'clock, and . . .

the very instant that the line has straightened out behind you.

The forward cast is started slowly by pushing the rod forward, also with a continuously accelerating motion, to the 11 o'clock position, where it is given a slight forward kick and stopped completely at 10 o'clock. This should make the line˙ shoot forward and drop to the grass or water.

This is the basic overhead cast, but there are some refinements to it which makes it more powerful and more useful. Before learning them, practice the elementary method until the backcast part and forward part can be done properly. All these are easy motions which utilize the flexing power of the rod. The rod should bend when making the backcast. The signal for making the forward part of the cast will be a slight tug on the rod, indicating that the line is fully extended behind.

9. . . . stop the rod tip abruptly at 10 o'clock. The line should roll forward in a smoothly flowing loop.

10. Line loop should drive forward to a point well over the target . . .

11. . . . and straighten out in the air before dropping to the ground. If the line slaps the ground (or water) before reaching the target, raise the visual point of aim.

SHOOTING LINE

So far we have been holding some line with the line hand. Now we'll learn to shoot it forward. At the completion of the forward part of the cast let go of the line, and the power of the cast will shoot it through the line guides, thus extending the cast.

With the castable length of line out, plus a leader of about 7 feet and 5 or 6 feet of line to shoot, we now will be casting to a distance of over 40 feet. This is far enough for average casting and, when we can do this properly, we are ready to start fishing. But how do we cast to twice that distance, or more?

The next step is to hold a somewhat larger loop of loose line, letting it touch the ground or water. As you raise the rod to make the backcast, also pull downward on the line with the line hand, thus drawing some of it back through the guides. As the forward cast is completed and stopped, let go of this line, letting it shoot out. This puts more bend in the rod; increases line speed; provides a more pronounced tug as the line begins to straighten out behind, and thus shoots the line forward with more force.

Additional line speed can be imparted to the backcast by pulling down sharply on the line with the line hand during the lifting movement of the backcast.

The line held in the line hand is released at the completion of the forward cast and allowed to shoot through the guides for greater distance.

LINE PICKUP AND RELEASE

When you want to hold a lot of fly line for shooting, or want to retrieve line for shooting out again, there are good and bad ways of handling it. A few coils on the ground or in the water may be all right for short casts, but too many are a nuisance and cut down casting distance.

Large-Coil Method

The large-coil method is a favorite for avoiding bothersome coils. The line hand strips in about two feet of line, which is held in a large coil on the fingers by the thumb. Another equal amount is stripped in to make a second coil, which is held the same way slightly ahead of the first coil. This is continued until as many coils have been retrieved as is necessary, each coil kept separated from

1. With the line hand, strip in two-foot coils and hold them on the fingers. Note that the forefinger of the rod hand holds line against the grip so the line can be stripped back against slight tension.

2. As you begin the backcast, release the line held by the rod hand's index finger but keep the coils firmly held in the line hand.

160

the others on the fingers, held by the thumb. In doing this, the forefinger of the rod hand holds the line against the rod grip, so the line hand can strip it back against slight tension to allow making the loose coils. When enough coils are being held, the forefinger of the rod hand releases the line from contact with the rod grip. When the rod hand completes the forward cast and a slight pull of the forward moving line is felt, the thumb of the line hand releases pressure on the coils, thus allowing as many to be pulled off the fingers as the power of the cast can take.

3. As the rod nears 10 o'clock on the forward cast, give the line a slight downward tug, imparting a kick to the cast.

4. At completion of forward cast, release the coils and allow the power of the cast to pull them off the fingers and line to shoot through guides.

Small-Coil Method

Another method, which we'll call the small-coil one, is handy in retrieving bucktails or streamers slowly, but it isn't practical for holding as much line as the former one. It isn't necessary to hold the line against the rod grip. The line hand grasps the line between thumb and forefinger and the other three fingers are extended to push down about three inches of line, extending under the little finger. The thumb and forefinger are doubled over the line and another coil is caught between them. This results in a bunch of coils in the line hand. When it is desired to shoot out this line the bunch of coils are tossed forward, where they usually uncoil in the air without entangling themselves during the shoot. Before starting this, a long loop of line can extend from the reel, if desired.

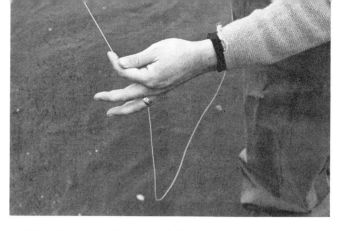

1. After the cast, when a wet fly or bucktail swings below you in the current, begin the retrieve by grasping the line between thumb and forefinger. Remaining three fingers are extended.

2. With the three extended fingers, push down about 3 inches of line. Then, with thumb and forefinger, catch another coil of line, and repeat previous action, bringing coils into the palm with the three fingers.

3. Small coils are held in hand, released at the completion of forward cast to shoot through guides.

162

Guide Bud Lilly demonstrates the tight loop, which is produced by keeping rod in narrow casting arc.

THE TIGHT LOOP

If we have been casting as has been described for the normal overhead cast, in the normal casting arc of between 11 and 1 o'clock, our backcast will form a tight, or shallow, loop. However, if we bring the rod back too far in the backcast, say, between 1 and 2 o'clock, the backcast will form a deep loop. This is mentioned because the deep loop is seldom desirable. A tight loop is more desirable and superior for long casts. A tight loop will foul easily in a crosswind, and a wider loop usually is preferable then. Any good fly fisherman can cast a wide or a tight loop, but he habitually uses a tight one for better accuracy and distance.

Widening the casting arc produces the seldom desirable deep loop during the backcast. Note how rod tip has dropped almost to the surface of the water behind the caster.

163

LINE AND DIRECTION CONTROL

Often one is casting in one direction and a fish rises somewhere else, or it is desirable to change direction for one reason or another. To do this, make the backcast as if you were going to cast again to the same position. On completion of the backcast, twist the body, or pivot, toward the new target, and make the forward cast in that direction. Do not try to change direction by sweeping the rod during the forward cast. If a radical change of direction is necessary it may need to be done in two steps, the first one being a false cast halfway to the new direction and the second one an actual cast to the new target. Experts can make a change of direction cast to an angle of as much as 45 degrees with only one backcast, but beginners may find it advisable to do it in two steps.

Another way to change direction is to use the roll cast. This cast, which is explained in this chapter, is especially useful when foliage behind you would interfere with a normal backcast.

1. In the midst of his backcast, Montana guide Gregg Lilly sights a fish rising to his left . . .

2. . . . so he twists his body toward new target during backcast . . .

3. . . . and makes his forward cast in the new direction.

THE ROLL CAST

Most fly fishermen couldn't get along without the roll cast. This cast is used to lay out a fly when obstructions are behind you, and to bring to the surface, for another cast, a deeply sunken fly. It is also handy for making changes of direction and is effective for casting 50 feet or more. One must practice it over water, because grass does not offer enough resistance.

To begin the roll cast, you should have at least three rod lengths of line on the water.

Bring the rod back over the shoulder of the reel hand to a position of about 1 o'clock, with the rod tipped slightly outward, meanwhile stripping in some line to shoot out. Notice that the line extending from the rod's tip hangs down a foot or two behind the rod. Now, with a brisk accelerating motion, forcefully switch the rod down to the 9 o'clock

1. With the line on the water in front of you, bring the rod tip over the shoulder to the 1 o'clock position. The rod should be tipped slightly outward, the left hand strips in line.

position. This will roll out the line onto the water. As the rod is switched down, release the line held by the line hand, and it also will shoot out ahead.

Notice that at no time during the roll cast does the line extend back any farther than the rod tip. Thus, with this cast, one could be standing directly in front of a cliff or high bushes, and cast

50 feet or more without touching them.

If the first roll doesn't cast line far enough, pull some more from the reel, pull in the slack, and do it again. To cast to the left, bring the rod back to the right and slap it down toward the target. A cast to the right is made by bringing the rod back to the left and casting to the desired position on the right. Loose line

2. Bring the rod forward with a brisk accelerating motion . . .

3. . . . and vigorously switch it down to the 9 o'clock position.

is always released at the instant of completion of the force of the cast. If the loose line is held lightly the power of the cast will take it away.

As in the overhead cast, the size of the loop of the roll depends on the arc through which the rod passes while power is being applied. A narrow arc makes a narrow loop, and a wider arc makes a wider loop. If the arc (the angle of power of the cast) is a bit forward, the line will unroll on the surface, but if the arc is tipped backward the line should unroll in the air and straighten out above the water.

In bringing in a deeply sunken fly one may not wish to tax the power of the rod by pulling the fly from the water to make

168

4. Line rolls out onto the water, the left hand releasing its line to allow slack to shoot through the guides.

an overhead cast. The fly may be too close for a good cast anyway. So bring the fly near the surface (even very close to the angler) and roll cast it out. Then it can be picked up easily for the usual cast. This also can be done as a false cast.

To switch direction, make a roll cast partly in the new direction and then make a usual cast or another roll cast in the new direction. While the roll cast is a good fishing cast in choppy water, it should be used with caution on a smooth surface because it can disturb the water. It does this less so, or not at all, when the casting arc is tipped backward, as noted above. It is a comfortably easy cast to use, and immensely handy in the angler's bag of tricks.

HORIZONTAL CAST

This one is recommended for relatively short casts into the wind or for putting a fly into a pocket where something overhangs from above. Hold some extra line for shooting and cast sideways with the rod pointed not over 45 degrees from the horizontal. Make the cast as a normal one in this position and, on its completion, when shooting the excess line, bring the rod tip down to only a foot or so above the water. The line should go flat, rather than in a rolling loop, to land the fly in the pocket.

12″—18″

BACKHAND CAST

This cast is especially useful in brushy situations or when a wind is driving down from the side of your casting arm. It is made by bringing the rod back and across your shoulder, at an angle of about 45 degrees. The forward cast follows the same diagonal plane, across the shoulder and chest to a point above the target. The photos show the backcast and forward cast being made.

LAZY-S CAST

This is used with dry flies to provide a longer natural float when fishing downstream or across and downstream. Strip off 6 feet or so more of line than will be needed for the casting distance. At the end of the forward part of the usual overhead cast, stop the rod high (at about 11 o'clock) and pull back on it a little. The line will jerk against the tackle and will jump back, thus causing it to drop in a snaky manner, as shown below. While the current is straightening out these curves, the fly will have enough time to float freely for several feet.

STOP ROD HIGH AND PULL BACK SLIGHTLY

CURVE CASTS

Curve casts to the right or to the left occasionally are useful, especially in dry-fly fishing, either to reach into difficult positions or, in casting upstream, to cast above a fish and allow a short free float down to him without putting line or leader directly over him. The principle is that whatever motion is imparted to the rod will result in a similar reaction in the placement of the fly. This cast could be called a "hook" cast, because it can make the fly curve or hook either right or left.

To curve cast to the right, let's

Expert Hardy Kruse demonstrates the curve to the right. Note how he has turned his forearm to the right after shooting the cast. The line must follow the same arc as that described by the rod tip.

assume that you want to reach a target upstream and to the right and that you want a few feet of free drift for the fly before the fish can see line or leader. Extend false casts and aim a few feet above the target. After shooting the cast, turn the forearm to the right. This causes the line to turn to the right; the signal being transmitted down the line to cause leader, fly and the forward part of the line to hook to the right.

A curve to the left is made similarly, except that the forearm (and sometimes part of the body) is turned to the left.

Curve to the left is accomplished by turning the forearm to the left as the cast is completed.

MENDING THE LINE

If you are fishing across a current to slower water beyond, the faster current will put a downstream bow in the line which will pull the fly downstream in an unnatural manner. Unless this is corrected, the excess speed of the fly usually repels fish rather than attracting them. To remove the bow you must "mend" the line.

First, keep the line on or near the surface. Then, flip the rod tip in the direction opposite to the bowed line, as in the photo. Thus you reverse, or partially reverse, the bow, regain control of the line from the current, and allow the fly to be fished in a normal manner. A natural, unimpeded drift is vital in dry-fly fishing, and correct fly speed is also necessary in wet-fly fishing. Hence it is important to learn this simple method of mending the line. Once mastered, it is a valuable tool of the fly fisherman.

INCREASING LINE SPEED
FOR GREATER DISTANCE

So far, we have discussed casting normal distances. In casting longer distances the rod hand and arm will be lifted higher and the line hand must be coordinated with it by also lifting it higher. If the line hand remains in its low position, the distance between hands will vary too much, resulting in jerking on the backcast and slack line on the forward cast. During the cast the line must be under tension, with accompanying severe flexing of the rod, to increase line speed. This is done with the single line-hand haul for casting average distances and with the double line-hand haul for greater distances.

Single line-hand haul begins with the backcast. Pull down on the line below the butt guide, starting the pull slowly, accelerating quickly as the rod comes up, and imparting a sharp final tug to the line as the final power kick is given to the rod as it is stopped at 12 o'clock.

The Single Line-Hand Haul

This affords a perfectly straight and more powerful backcast, which results in an improved and longer forward cast. It is the first part of the double line-hand haul and is done only on the backcast. It is made by grasping the line with thumb and forefinger below the butt guide and by pulling it down. The pull-down begins slowly and accelerates quickly as the rod is being raised in the same manner. The sharp final tug is imparted at the same time that the final power kick is given to the rod as it is stopped at the 12 o'clock position of the backcast. This pulls the line smoothly off the surface and provides increased initial speed to it. At the instant of completion of the forward cast, the line hand is raised and this line is released, allowing the amount stripped in and the slack to shoot out.

A less energetic modification of this is handy even in shorter casts because it slides the line easily from the water's surface, removes slack, and provides a better controlled backcast. It is done smoothly and without exertion, cutting the work usually done by the rod hand almost in half.

1. Double line-hand haul also begins with the backcast. Give the first power tug to the line, as in the single line-hand haul.

FIRST POWER TUG

2. As the backcast flows out behind you, allow the line hand to rise upward quickly a couple of feet toward the rod. Note how Gregg Lilly allows his rod to drift lower than 1 o'clock (after stopping at that point) without causing line to drop unduly low.

The Double Line-Hand Haul

This combines the single line-hand haul with an added sharp pull on the line when the rod is stopped on the forward cast. It is helpful in distance casting, in casting into the wind, and when using air-resistant bass bugs or big streamers or bucktails.

Make the single-haul cast by pulling down on the line as the rod is being raised. Then, as the backcast rolls out behind you, allow the line hand (still holding the line) to rise upward quickly about 2 feet toward the rod. Start the rod forward at the completion of the backcast with both hands close together, moving apart slowly during the forward acceleration, and traveling forward together as the forward cast is made. When the rod is stopped between 10 and 11 o'clock, *then* (at that precise moment) make a final, sharp, downward pull with the line hand and immediately let go of the line, which will shoot forward at very high speed.

If the final pull is made too soon or too late the cast will be ineffective. Remember to make the final power tug at the moment the rod is *stopped* on the backcast and the other at the moment the rod is *stopped* on the forward cast. The rod is being loaded during acceleration. The final pull unleashes all the power the rod can impart. In making very long casts the usual (about 2 feet) pull can be increased in length to provide even greater line speed.

In addition, *after* the backcast has been stopped at the 1 o'clock position, the rod can be allowed to drift even

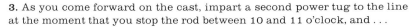

3. As you come forward on the cast, impart a second power tug to the line at the moment that you stop the rod between 10 and 11 o'clock, and . . .

SECOND POWER
TUG

SHOOT LINE

lower, and the line still will stay up high. *After* the forward cast has been stopped at the 11 o'clock position the rod should be lowered still more, as low as parallel to the water. This wide arc, if handled properly, affords even longer casts.

This description may seem simple, but the double line-hand haul requires a lot of practice to obtain the exact and instinctive timing which results in the very long casts it should provide.

4. . . . immediately release the line, which will shoot through guides at very high speed. The final pull unleashes all the power in the rod.

DID ANYTHING GO WRONG?

Scientific Anglers, Inc., manufacturers of fly-fishing tackle, has polled anglers about their casting problems and has made a list of the most common ones, together with their remedies. With their permission, I include them here with the hope that they will be helpful.

Low Backcast

CAUSE: Applying power too long on backcast, thereby driving the line down. Also, by permitting the line loop to straighten completely, at which time it drops.

CORRECTION: Make the backcast with a brisk movement up and back, holding the wrist stiff. Stop power application when rod is vertical.

Wind Knots

CAUSE: Tipping the rod forward first, then pushing it ahead; an instinctive fault when casting into the wind.

CORRECTION: Bring the rod forward in 1 o'clock position and tip it ahead *only* at conclusion of the forward movement.

Hooking Line

Hooking the line with the fly, or the fly dropping below the line on the way out are symptoms of the same casting fault, and the correction is the same as for wind knots. Hooking the line with the fly also is caused by casting a narrow loop in a crosswind.

Piling up Line and Leader at End of Cast

CAUSE: Releasing line too soon on the forward cast or continuing the application of power too far down on the forward cast, after the line is released. These faults are usually accompanied by waving the rod through a wide arc, rather than flicking it briskly.

CORRECTION: Release line after end of power application. Accelerate rod briskly at 1 o'clock position; tip it ahead sharply at end of forward movement, and stop it at 11 o'clock. Then release line held in the line hand.

Snapping off Fly

CAUSE: Snapping off flies and popping the line on the backcast are caused either by starting the forward cast too soon and too fast, before the backcast has had time to almost straighten, or else by failure to use sufficient force in the backcast. In this case it would never straighten, no matter how long you waited.

CORRECTION: Watch the backcast and start the forward cast when line and leader are almost straight out behind. Use sufficient force in making the backcast so they will straighten.

Hitting Rod with Fly

CAUSE: The same casting fault as tying wind knots in the leader.

CORRECTION: Bring the rod forward in 1 o'clock position; tip it ahead last, then release the line in your line hand. As a last resort, tip the rod slightly away from yourself while casting, though this merely prevents the fly from hitting the rod and doesn't correct the cause of the difficulty.

Slapping the Water

CAUSE: Aiming the forward cast too low.

CORRECTION: Tilt the arc of power application backward a little so the forward cast straightens 2 or 3 feet above the water, then settles gently. In other words, aim your forward cast higher.

Line Won't Go Out

CAUSE: When the line won't go out and straighten, even 30 feet of it, one or both of two casting faults committed by all beginners are nearly always to blame: (1) waving the rod through too large an arc, often from 3 o'clock to 9, instead of pushing it briskly through a narrow arc; (2) permitting the line to slip through the guides during the application of power.

CORRECTION: Have someone watch to make sure you keep the rod between 1 o'clock and 11 o'clock on the forward cast. Push the entire rod ahead with arm movement to lengthen power application if necessary, but keep the arc between 1 and 11. Accelerate rod rapidly (make it bend) and tip it ahead last. Make sure you stop power application on the backcast at 12 o'clock, then let rod drift back to 1 as the backcast straightens.

Never let line slip out through the guides while applying power. Instead, pull in a foot or so on both the back and forward casts. Release line only when you stop the rod at 12 o'clock on the backcast and at ten-thirty o'clock on the forward cast.

How To Tie Leaders

If your cast is good, but your leader drops on the water in coils, the taper probably is incorrect. If you cast occasional knots in your leader, or if it has the disconcerting habit of wrapping the fly around your line, the butt section may be too light, or you may be making one of the casting errors listed in the previous chapter. If fish break off too easily, or if they swirl up and don't take, perhaps the tippet is at fault. Since the leader is more important than most of us might think, let's see how to make or select the right ones.

Modern fly lines are scientifically tapered to transmit the power of the cast down the entire length of the line to make it lay out straight and true. Since the leader is an extension of the line, it also must be properly graduated, or tapered, to transmit to the fly the power given to it by the cast line, so it also will turn over properly and lay out straight and true. This is accomplished by using leaders whose butt sections are of proper diameter to suit the line; by a sufficiently long tapered butt section, and by a more sharply graduated taper of the shorter tip section all the way down to the leader's tippet.

So, first, use a leader whose butt diameter is about two-thirds the diameter of the tip of the line, thus continuing the line's taper properly into that of the leader. For example, if the end of the fly line measures .036 in diameter, the proper leader butt diameter is about two-thirds of this, or .024.

185

Thirty-pound-test leader material usually calipers from .021 to .025, and this is close enough. Generally speaking, we need leaders with only two butt diameters, or pound tests: 30 pound (about .021) for the big diameter lines used on powerful rods, and 25 pounds (about .019) for lighter tackle. If you want to make all your leader butts in 25-pound test, you can then tie on an additional 2- or 3-foot butt section of 30-pound test when using the leader with more powerful equipment. If it is necessary to err one way or the other, use the heavier butt section. When using powerful tackle for big fish, such as in saltwater fly fishing, you could go as high as 40- or 45-pound test (.026 to .028). The length of the butt section usually is between 18 inches and several feet, depending on how long the leader is to be. The butt section should be slightly more supple than the line itself, and should be of *hard* nylon, if obtainable. A leader's butt section transmits the power of the cast down into the rest of the leader. Butt sections which are too light (not stiff enough) act as a pivot, or hinge, which prevents the leader from straightening out during the cast. Conversely, if the butt section is too heavy for the line, the end of the line will act as a hinge, and the cast won't lay out properly. If the leaders you're using don't behave, this could be part of the trouble.

Next, the heavy butt section should gradually taper in the larger diameters for about two-thirds of the length of the leader. (The "Two-thirds Rule" again!) From this, it should taper much more quickly (with increasingly shorter sections) down the remaining one-third of the leader. Finally, tie on one or two quite long graduated tippets of approximately similar length to the quickly tapering sections. These help to straighten out the leader and to present the fly properly. They can be of more supple (limper) monofilament than the upper sections. This tip section (or sections) decreases visibility and allows the fly to float or swim more naturally. All adjustments in the leader for the size or wind resistance of the fly and for wind and water conditions are made in the tippets. Dry fly leaders should have longer tippets than wet fly leaders (even several feet long) to allow the fly a longer unimpeded float.

If the fly does not lay out properly with the length or size of tippet being used, try cutting back the tippet by degrees until it does lay out properly. Avoid too steep graduations in reducing leader diameters. For example, don't tie an .008 tippet directly to .012 monofilament, or larger, because the regular Blood Knot won't be strong enough. Use a short length of .010 in between. When sharp reductions (or increases) in monofilament sizes are necessary, use the Double Strand Blood Knot, which provides nearly 100 percent knot strength when tied properly.

This Two-thirds Rule is approximate because the relative stiffness of the leader material, and fishing conditions, enter into it somewhat. Some anglers express it as a 60-20-20 Rule, when the butt section is 60 percent of the leader's length; the quickly tapering section 20 percent, and the tippet section also about 20 percent. Use either, or a compromise. You can't go far wrong.

The size or wind resistance of your fly is important in deciding the diameter and length of the tippet. For example, if the fly size is between 12 and 14, an .008 tippet (5-pound test) should be about right. This has a diameter between 3X and 4X in the old silkworm gut ratings, which used to be considered fairly fine, but this diameter would have had a strength of only about 1½ pounds if the tippet were of gut. For flies smaller than size 14 you could cut the .008 tippet back a bit and tie on a foot or so of .007 (4 pounds) and .006, which would test about 3 pounds, and which should be strong enough for open-water fishing for small or average-sized fish. Conversely, if you're using medium or large streamers, bucktails or bass bugs, your tippet may need to be .010, or heavier, and probably it should be shorter. Making a cast or two will provide a clue to this.

Following is a table of *normal* tippet sizes for artificial flies in the hook sizes indicated:

Tippet Size	Pound Test	Hook Size Range
.013 (8/5)	12	2/0–2
.011 (0X)	10	1/0–4
.010 (1X)	8	4–8
.009 (2X)	6	6–10
.008 (3X)	5	10–14
.007 (4X)	4	12–16
.006 (5X)	3	14–18
.005 (6X)	2	16–22
.004 (7X)	1	14–25
.003 (8X)	½	18–28

Now, let's tie (or buy) a leader to these general specifications. Let's say that our tackle is medium or light, and that we want a 9-foot leader for using fly sizes between 10 and 14. The approximate two-thirds of the butt section could be tapered with 30 inches of .020 followed by 24 inches of .018 and 14 inches of .016. The quickly tapering middle section could have 8 inches of .014, 6 inches of .012 and 6 inches of .010. The tippet could be

18 inches of .008 (5 lbs.). This gives us a heavy butt section 68 inches long; a quickly tapered middle section 22 inches long, and a tippet 18 inches long.

A common fault in flycasting is to use leaders which are too short. Anything shorter than 9 feet usually is considered to be a short leader, but the shorter ones usually are necessary for short casts in such places as brushy streams, and are all right under cloudy water conditions. In general, however, longer leaders will catch more fish. Properly tapered, they will cast beautifully. When there's room to use them, I like leaders about 14 feet long. A good one for powerful rods could be tapered as follows: (36″−.022) (24″−.020) (24″−.018) (18″−.016) (12″−.014) (12″−.013) (18″−.012) and (24″−.010). It tapers to 8 pounds, which is strong enough for almost anything and which should be excellent for medium or large streamer flies. For salmon and some of the larger saltwater fish, we could increase the lengths of the heavier sizes a bit and end up with between 2 and 3 feet of .012 (10 pounds) tippet. A 14-foot leader may seem long to some people, but it is fairly common to use them much longer.

Leader lengths which generally are popular for trout fishing with small flies are:

Leader Length	Fishing Condition	Tippet Size
6′	Small brushy streams and slightly muddy water	.005 or .006 (2 or 3 lbs.)
7′ to 9′	Standard length for average fishing	.004 to .006 (1 to 3 lbs.)
11′ to 14′	Low, clear water under summer conditions	.003 to .006 (½ to 3 lbs.)

Some leader tyers skip a diameter or two here and there, but this usually should be avoided. In the larger diameters the differences between monofilament sizes being knotted are not critical. A good rule with leader strengths of 15 pounds or less is to taper with no greater difference in diameters than .002 down to size .010 (8 pounds). Smaller sizes than .010 should be tapered with no greater difference in diameters than .002, and .001 is better if these diameters are available.

Since leader diameters per pound test vary among various brands of leader material, checking them with a micrometer is advisable. Although small micrometers are expensive, every serious fly fisherman should use one, even if he has to borrow it to make a supply of leaders. A less accurate but very inexpensive thickness gauge can be obtained from tackle dealers, and is an expedient if no micrometer is handy. Remember that it is the diameter of the leader section that counts—not the pound test. Graduated stiffness is the secret of good leaders.

Since the monofilament produced by various makers varies in strength and stiffness as well as in diameter, if you go by pound test it is safer to use the material of only one manufacturer in order to be consistent.

From these simple rules it should be easy to plan and tie any length of leader for any size of fly rod, tapered to as fine or as strong a tippet as is desirable. Using these suggestions, it's easy to figure on paper the length and taper of the leader we want to tie and to have it terminate at the right length with the proper size of tippet.

Fly fishermen should learn to tie their own leaders, rather than being at the mercy of whatever dealers have to offer. We may be fishing in remote areas where the ability to tie flies and leaders, even if not a necessity, at least could provide exactly what is needed, while adding to the fun and success of angling. We must know how to tie a Blood Knot, because it is necessary to use one frequently to add on a butt or tippet section, or to repair damage. That's the only necessary knot, except for joining the leader to the line. If a loop is used, it is made with a Perfection Loop Knot. This can be attached to the line in two or three ways, the best one being to have a small loop made in the end of the line. Slide the leader loop over the line loop, and string the tippet through the line loop. This pulls tight to a smooth connection which is quick and easy to disassemble. Many anglers don't like this connection because the interlocking loops are bulky and can catch in the tip guide of the fly rod, as well as in weeds and algae.

If the line doesn't come with its tip already looped, it is unnecessary to whip a loop on it. Expert anglers usually dispense with the leader and line loops and join the leader to the line with a Nail Knot, or with the Pin Knot or the Leader Whip Knot, the latter being the author's favorite. The butt section can be affixed permanently this way, and the rest of the leader can be joined to it by a Blood Knot. The leader can be cut off or retied at this point whenever desired. The ways to tie these various knots are shown in Chapter 12.

Some anglers recommend that the butt of the leader should be tied with stiffer (hard) monofilament and that the final third should be of limper material. Both hard and soft monofilament can be obtained on spools or small leader wheels in all sizes or strengths. Those who tie their own leaders should assemble a kit of the necessary sizes, complete with the various simple tools which make the job easy.

The color of leader material also is a minor matter because all usual colors are almost uniformly translucent. This is of more interest to the fisherman than to the fish!

In addition to the leader formulas previously given, some others are included on the facing page. It's simple to plan whatever kind of leader is needed, and to tie it according to plan. We know from what has been said what diameter is needed for the butt and what is advisable for the tippet. We decide how long the leader should be and we figure out on paper how the graduations should be planned for the desired result.

Let's not ignore Chapter 12 on knots, even if we know how to tie most of them. It contains numerous suggestions I haven't seen published elsewhere. While discussing knots for fly-rod leaders we should mention a few tricks in tying them. Pulling some knots tight (such as the Blood Knot) causes friction, which makes heat, which weakens the knot. This is avoided by wetting the knot in the mouth before it is drawn tight. When drawing it tight, do it slowly and steadily, without pausing, because this will make the knot gather properly for maximum strength. Finally, check all completed knots both visually and by pulling to be sure they have gathered correctly. In the heavy butt sections, this isn't too important, but it becomes more and more so as we knot the leader toward the tippet. It's a good idea to test the completed leader by pulling it to be sure of proper strength, thus straightening it at the same time. When fishing with sinking lines it helps to use shorter leaders than normal, because monofilament sinks very slowly. When using bulky lures such as streamers, bucktails and bass bugs, the tippet should be fairly strong to prevent snapping off the fly on the backcast. In waters where algae is prominent it may collect on the knots of knotted tapered leaders. If it does, it will reduce fishing results. In such cases it is better to use knotless or level leaders.

When leaders are completed for later use they can be wound around a drinking glass which has a uniform flare. This evens all coils neatly, and the coiled leader can be slipped off the small end of the glass, with a few turns of the tippet made around the coils to hold them in place.

Most of us become so engrossed with the attractions of rod, reels, lines and flies that we too often neglect the essential and economical necessities of sharp hooks and efficient leaders. These two little elements of terminal tackle can separate the men from the boys, as far as catching fish is concerned. One of the greatest thrills in angling is to make a passable cast and to see the line stream out to roll the leader over correctly to drop the fly lightly—and then to see a lusty swirl as a fair fish rises to take the fly. If this doesn't happen to you as often as it should, perhaps you should look to your leader. Properly proportioned ones are extremely important in catching more and bigger fish.

LEADERS

#1 for Line Sizes 4 and 5

Length	Lb. Test	Diameter
18"	25	.019"
18	20	.018
18	15	.016
18	12	.015
7	10	.014
6	8	.012
5	6	.010
18	4	.008

#2 for Line Sizes 6 and 7

Length	Lb. Test	Diameter
18"	30	.021"
18	25	.019
18	20	.018
18	15	.016
7	12	.014
6	8	.012
5	6	.010
18	4	.008

#3 for Bucktails, Bugs and Flies Size 4 and Smaller

Length	Lb. Test	Diameter
18"	30	.021"
18	25	.019
18	20	.018
18	15	.016
12	12	.014
12	10	.013
12	8	.012

#4 for Large Flies, Salmon, Steelhead, Salt Water

Length	Lb. Test	Diameter
18"	30	.021"
18	25	.019
18	20	.018
18	17	.017
12	15	.016
12	13	.015
12	12	.014

#5 Simplified Version of Above

Length	Lb. Test	Diameter
30"	30	.021"
30	25	.019
24	20	.017
24	12	.014

#6 A Simplification for Line Sizes 4 and 5

Length	Lb. Test	Diameter
42"	25	.019"
42	20	.017
24	12	.014

#7 A Simplification for Line Sizes 6 and 7

Length	Lb. Test	Diameter
60"	30	.021"
24	20	.018
24	13	.015

9

Fly Tying Made Easy

After only a few minutes of instruction anyone can tie flies that will catch fish. Most of the basic tools and materials can be found around the house; others are available free, or at small cost. Fly tying can develop into a hobby (or business) providing a lifetime of pleasure and profit. Even so, why tie flies when we can buy them?

The pride of catching a fish on fly tackle is greatly enhanced when it is done with a fly you have made yourself. The accomplishment is even greater when you use a leader which you have tapered from inexpensive small wheels of monofilament. If you take a small fly-tying kit on fishing trips, it's easy to tie needed flies when you are far from a tackle store. This provides a fascinating and appropriate occupation when fish aren't biting. If you feel inclined to accept the challenge, dressing flies can develop into a form of art in which the pursuit of perfection never ends.

Fly tyers can originate new patterns or variations and can copy standard ones whenever desired. Clubs all over the country invite anyone to attend meetings where instruction is given and where materials can be bought or traded. Fly-tying addicts are a friendly group which recognizes no distinction of race, creed, education, affluence or age. Anyone interested is welcome to join after a visit or two.

Of course it's cheaper to tie flies than to buy them, but the fascination of acquiring materials for later use can add considerably to the investment.

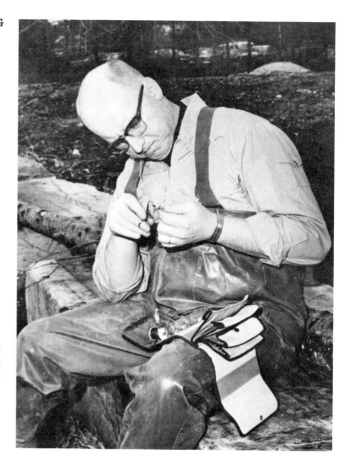

An angler matches the hatch by tying a fly at streamside with materials carried in a compact kit.

This, however, results very profitably in more flies made as the angler wants them, and in much more fun!

Before learning to tie simple flies beginners should decide on one type, such as bucktails or streamers, and become proficient in this before attempting others, such as dry flies and nymphs. It can become frustrating to try to learn too much all at once. The author recommends starting with bucktails, then streamers, because they are easier, showier, and always useful.

Should you start by buying one of the "complete" fly-tying kits sold in stores or by mail? These come in a wide range of sizes, prices and quality. It helps to ask an accomplished fly tyer to aid in the selection. Most tackle stores sell fly-tying materials. Why not let an expert help with a list, and buy needed items individually? Some of the ingredients of kits (such as small scissors) may be unnecessary because the same thing is available at home. Others (such as a fly-tying vise) may be of low quality and later should be replaced by something better.

ESSENTIAL MATERIALS

In this chapter we'll learn to tie three simple but very useful types of flies: a bucktail, a streamer and a wooly worm. These later can be varied to provide a range of color combinations and sizes. It is well to become fairly expert with these before going on to something else.

Tools needed:

A fly-tying vise
A bobbin, holding a spool of fine black thread
A pair of hackle pliers
A bodkin
A pair of small, sharp scissors
A small bottle of fly-tying cement

Materials needed to tie a simple bucktail fly: (**1**) fly-tying vise; (**2**) bodkin; (**3**) scissors; (**4**) flat silver tinsel; (**5**) streamer hooks; (**6**) thread in bobbin; (**7**) oval silver tinsel; (**8**) fly-tying cement; (**9**) bucktail dyed red; (**10**) natural white bucktail.

While some experts tie flies with their fingers, a good vise is a necessity for beginners. A high quality one will last a lifetime, so invest enough to get the best. The scissors and thread should be found in the sewing basket at home. Ladies' nail polish can be substituted for fly-tying cement. The illustration shows how to make a bodkin. It is better to buy a bobbin and some hackle pliers, but crude ones can be made, as shown.

HOMEMADE FLY-TYING TOOLS

Bobbin. Used to release thread as needed; also as a weight to keep windings tight while tying a fly. Make it of coat-hanger wire. Insert pipe cleaner in hole of spool to increase tension, if necessary.

Hackle pliers. For holding hackle tips when a hackle is being wound around a fly for a collar, etc. Also as a weight to keep thread and other materials taut. Whittle clamp of a spring-type wooden clothespin; wind a small rubber band around clamp for added tension.

Bodkin. For adjusting and picking out hackle barbules, picking varnish out of hook eyes, holding thread loop taut when making a whip finish. Make one by pushing the eye end of a large needle into a wooden dowel.

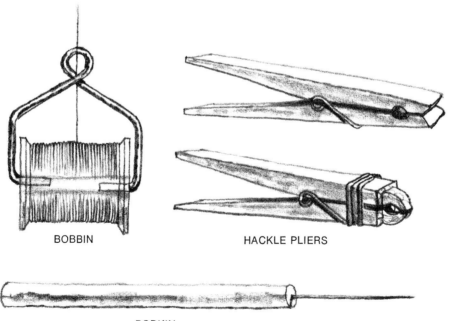

BOBBIN   HACKLE PLIERS

BODKIN

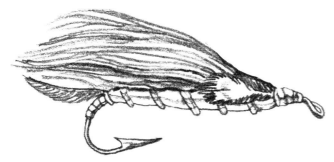

Above, a bucktail (hairwing fly); below, a streamer (featherwing fly).

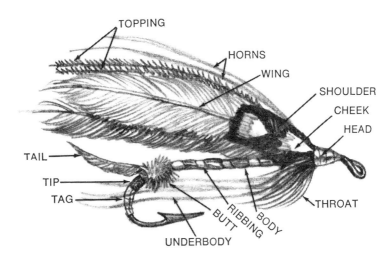

The basic fly consists of a dressed *body* and a *wing.* If more complicated patterns are desired the parts can be added about in this order of importance: *Ribbing* adds flash. The *tail* normally curves upward and extends only slightly beyond the hook's bend. It adds color and style. The *throat* may be a bunch of fibers tied underneath, or it may be applied as a collar, to provide more action to the fly. The *cheeks* are usually of jungle cock, or a substitute, to simulate the fish's eyes. The *shoulders* imitate a fish's head and gills. The *underbody,* usually of hair, is tied under the hook and about as long as it, to provide the lighter color of a fish's belly. The *tag* is of metal tinsel or thread, for added flash. The *topping* usually simulates a fish's back and often is of peacock herl. The *tip* is usually of silk, unnecessary except for appearance and perhaps to hold up the tail. The *butt,* originally simulating a fly's egg sack, is mainly for appearance. Like the tip, it rarely is used on streamers. *Horns,* uncommon on streamers, simulate a fly's "feelers," and are for appearance only. They usually are of macaw tail fibers.

197

Materials needed:

A few long-shanked hooks, about size #6
A small spool of oval silver tinsel, medium wide
A small spool of flat silver tinsel, medium wide
A piece of white bucktail
A piece of bucktail dyed red
A foot or so of red wool yarn
A yard or so of black chenille, medium wide
A few large grizzly neck or saddle hackle feathers

These inexpensive materials are available at most sporting goods stores. All tools and materials can be stored and carried conveniently in a small tacklebox.

SIMPLE BUCKTAIL

The method of tying a simple bucktail fly is shown in the accompanying drawings and photos. Once you have learned to tie it, you can tie several other similar varieties. By investing in other colors of bucktail, effective color combinations can be tied such as:

Brown over white   Black over white
Brown over yellow   Black over yellow
Red over yellow   Green over white (etc.)

A third color can be introduced by tying an extremely small (and perhaps shorter) bunch of bucktail under the hook and/or by adding half a dozen or so peacock herls as a topping. These embellishments can be continued indefinitely after proficiency has been obtained in the basics.

The instructions given are for a very secure and fairly thick body. This can be simplified, if desired. The ribbing can be eliminated, although it adds valuable glitter to the fly. This saves one application of windings. Oval tinsel is metal wound around a thread core. By picking apart an end of it, a quarter of an inch of thread is exposed, the metal which covered it being cut off. When the thread has been wound down the shank the first time this end can be tied in and the thread can be wound back to the head to tie in the oval tinsel there. This saves time and makes a slim body. Another method (without ribbing) is to make a few cemented windings of thread near the head to secure it to the hook. Then tie in the flat silver tinsel (or oval, if desired) and wind this down and back over the bare hook. It won't slip if it is tightly wound without any overlapping.

After applying the tinsel body, it can be made more secure and safe from tarnishing by painting it with cement. A tiny paint brush is useful for this. Like the baitfish they represent, bucktails should be darker on top.

TYING A BUCKTAIL

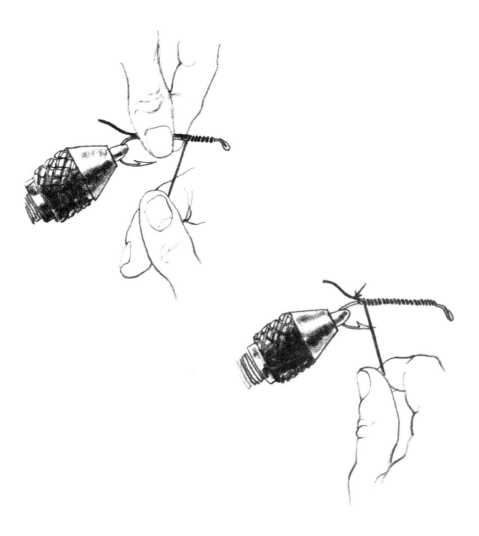

1. Affix the vise firmly to a table, with its jaw at a convenient height. Set the hook tightly in the vise. Lay an inch or so of thread over the hook, tip toward rear, and wind back over the thread, securing it to the hook. (All windings are made clockwise, unless otherwise noted). Continue the windings closely, but not overlapping, to a point on the shank over the hook's barb. Trim off the excess tip of thread, if any.

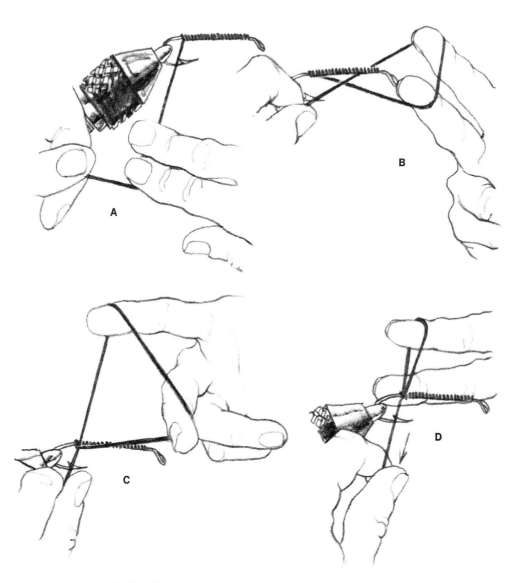

2. Tie the thread with a half-hitch, as shown in this sequence of drawings. Pulling the thread toward you with left hand (**A**), lay the first two fingers of the right hand over it and turn over the two fingers and the thread, forming a loop (**B**). Slip the loop over the eye of the hook and use the second finger to set the coil in the right position (**C**). Pull the thread, and the loop will be drawn off the first finger and tightly around the hook (**D**).

3. Cut off about 5 inches of oval silver tinsel and lay it on top of the shank, its end just behind the half-hitch. Bind this down by winding the thread around the shank and then wind over the original winding back to the binding behind the eye. Make another half-hitch at this point, and the dressing will look as at right.

4. Cut off about 8 inches of flat silver tinsel and trim one end on one side only to a fairly long point. Lay the tip of this point beside the shank just behind the half-hitches and secure it with two or three turns of thread. (The bobbin acts as a weight to hold the turns tight.) Wind the tinsel spirally around the shank to the rear so all turns are tight but not overlapping. This conceals the former windings.

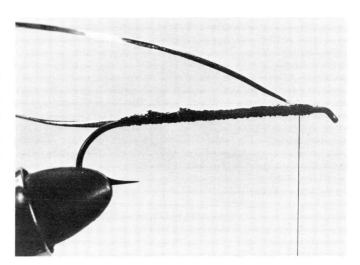

5. Continue spirally winding the tinsel until all the thread is covered, then wind back nearly to the eye. Holding the tinsel tightly, secure it with two or three turns of thread. Trim off excess tinsel; make two or three more windings of thread to bind in the cut end; and secure the thread with a half-hitch.

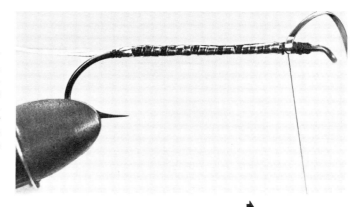

6. Wind the oval silver tinsel forward over the flat tinsel to evenly space it as a ribbing. Secure it with two or three turns of thread, cut off the excess, and secure the thread with a half-hitch. Put a drop of fly-tying cement on the half-hitch and spread it around with a toothpick or the point of the bodkin.

7. To add the wing to the completed body, cut a small bunch of bucktail close to the hide. Brush out short hairs and underfur and pull out overlong hairs. Set the bunch of bucktail on top of the hook, with the hairs extending slightly beyond the bend. Hold it in position and make two or three tight turns around it and the hook with the thread. Allow bobbin to hold thread taut, trim off hairs near the eye, and work drop of cement around hairs and windings.

8. Set the red bucktail on top of the white and bind it down in the same manner. Wind the thread tightly around the head, evenly without crisscrossing, until all the hair ends are concealed. Secure the thread with a whip finish and paint the head with cement.

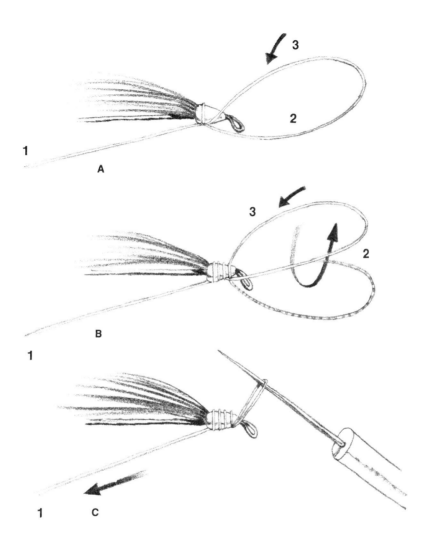

How to make a whip finish: (**A**) Make a loop with the thread by laying the end (1–2) beside the head and winding over it, always holding the winding part tightly at 3. (**B**) Make about four evenly spaced windings around the head, thus tying in the end (1–2). (**C**) Hold the loop upward tightly with the point of the bodkin and pull on the end of the thread (1) to pull the loop tightly closed. Remove the point of the bodkin when the loop has closed. Cut off the excess thread closely at the head.

Beginners usually make assembly windings too close to the hook's eye, leaving too little room for trimming and none for finishing the head. Windings on a long-shanked hook, such as a number 6, should be started about a quarter of an inch back of the eye. Beginners also make more windings than necessary, ending up with a bulky head instead of a stylish one. Use the finest thread that provides adequate strength. Broken threads can be mended by winding the new thread end back over them. This makes two thread ends which must be snipped off. Apply cement wherever it might be needed because a well cemented fly is a strong one affording longer fishing life. If early attempts prove too crude, take the flies apart by cutting the threads with a knife or a razor blade. The hooks, and perhaps other parts, can be salvaged. Bucktail is used mainly for large flies; finer hair is better for smaller ones. If a squirrel crosses the highway at the wrong time, his tail can provide excellent wings for small bucktails. Furriers always have scraps of mink, fox and other valuable pelts which they usually are glad to give to fly tyers. Pieces of bearskin in natural and dyed colors are especially useful.

Bucktails usually are considered more effective than streamers, mainly because the hairs of the wing pulsate more actively than feathers do. Feather-winged flies extend the range of baitfish simulators, and most anglers include them in their fly books.

TYING A STREAMER

Four matching neck hackles (two pairs) are used in most streamer flies. The feathers usually are of equal length and, to avoid short strikes, normally extend only to the end of the tail, or slightly beyond the hook's bend. The trick of applying them so all four lie closely together, without any "V" between them, is shown in the drawing.

To do this, make whatever sort of body is desired, such as one of those described in this chapter. It is important that the spot where the feathers will be tied in must be smooth, without any bunches or bulges of thread. The four feathers, pinched tightly together between the thumb and the forefinger of the left hand near their quill ends, are scored by resting the ends, side by side, on the inner surface of the forefinger of the right hand. Then the thumbnail of the right hand is pressed directly down upon them to score them at an angle of about 30 degrees. Still holding them this way, set the four parallel scored quill ends on top of the hook where they will be tied in. Make four or five tight turns of thread over the parallel and touching quill ends, but don't let the thread overlap the angle in the quills where it was scored by the thumb. Now the fingers can be removed to be sure the wing has been set properly, without any gap between the feathers. If they don't set correctly, unwind the thread and try it again. If they do, apply a drop of cement and let it dry before finishing the fly. Trim the four quill ends, all together, to the correct length (not over a quarter of an inch) before scoring them and setting them on the hook.

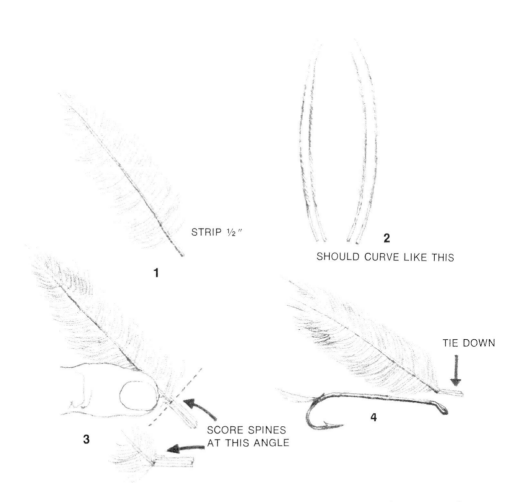

STRIP ½"

1

2

SHOULD CURVE LIKE THIS

3

SCORE SPINES
AT THIS ANGLE

TIE DOWN

4

How to set the wing of a streamer fly.

A good way to make a tail on a fly is to do it with feathers. The simplest method is to strip off a dozen or so barbules from a hackle, set their bunched butt ends on top of the hook where they are to be tied in, and wrap them down with two or three turns of thread. Tight windings will force them to cock up. After snipping off the excess, add a drop of cement so they won't pull out.

A fancier way of applying a tail is shown. Use fine scissors to snip out opposite sections not over a quarter of an inch wide of a large breast feather, such as a swan's. Match these two pieces with their concave sides facing each other. Holding them between thumb and forefinger of the left hand, set them on the hook, curved upward, where they are to be tied in. Bring the thread up between thumb and feathers and down between forefinger and feathers so a small loop of thread remains above. While tightly pinching the feathers in place, pull down on the thread to remove the loop. Still holding the feathers, work another tight turn over the first one, and then make a half-hitch over it. The downward pull of the thread to close the loop compresses the vertically held feather sections so they should remain absolutely vertical and cocked up after being tied in. This provides a very attractive tail. Many tails also are made with one or more small golden pheasant crest feathers. After trimming off the butts, they are tied in similarly, matched and curving upward in the reverse manner that the bend of the hook curves downward.

Streamer flies, and most bucktails, too, look better if a throat, or "beard," is tied in under the head. This is done after the body has been made but usually before the wing is applied. If it is done with feathers, a bunch of barbules of the right length are stripped from a saddle hackle, bunched between thumb and forefinger of the left hand, and set under the hook where they are to be tied in. After making two or three turns of thread to fasten them in place, the excess butt ends are trimmed off and a bit of cement is worked around the windings so they won't pull out. This also can be done with small bunches of hair in the same way, first removing the underfur, as described in applying a hair wing. After tying in throats it improves the fly to carefully work some of the hackle or hair outward on both sides fanwise, rather than letting it bunch below. Separating the throat in this manner adds to appearance and provides more of a breathing effect when the fly is being fished.

When a sparse throat is made from hair as long as the wing, it is called an "underbody"; in effect, putting a small part of the wing below the shank

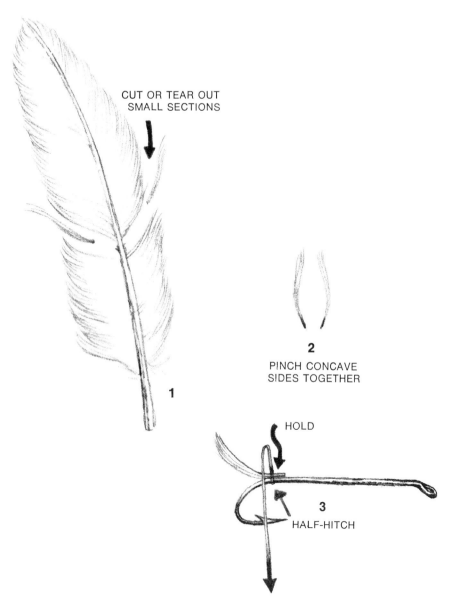

CUT OR TEAR OUT
SMALL SECTIONS

1

2

PINCH CONCAVE
SIDES TOGETHER

HOLD

3

HALF-HITCH

Tying on the tail of a streamer fly.

of the hook. Thus, on a silver-bodied bucktail, for example, three colors can be included, such as brown over yellow for the wing and white for the underbody. Underbodies also are used on streamers, adding considerably to their effectiveness as baitfish imitations.

TYING A WOOLY WORM

Wooly worms in many sizes are excellent takers because they evidently resemble different fish foods at various times, such as caterpillars, grubs and nymphs. We'll tie a black one and then suggest other color combinations. After adequate practice in making bucktails and streamers, this will be easy, and it will show how to enlarge the home-made fly collection by using chenille in various colors for bucktail bodies. The illustrations show the step-by-step procedure for tying a wooly worm.

Wooly worms are tied on regular length hooks in sizes between 4 and 12. Colors are black (with or without the red tail), yellow (R), gray (R), brown, orange, black and orange, green and peacock. The (R) means that the fly has a red wool tail. The grizzly hackle is used on all patterns in size appropriate to the size of the hook.

Long-shanked (3X) patterns also are very popular in sizes between 2 and 8. The most effective dressings for these are:

BODY	HACKLE	TAIL
Olive	Grizzly	None
Tan	Ginger	None
Black	Brown	Red
Black	Grizzly	Red
Brown	Grizzly	None
Yellow	Grizzly	Red
Black and orange	Grizzly	None
Black	Black	None

Chenille is available in many colors and in several widths wherever fly-tying materials are sold. Narrower widths make excellent bodies for bucktails, especially when tinsel ribbing is used. In the larger sizes these flies are excellent for pickerel, walleyed pike, and even for bass and trout.

WOOLY WORM

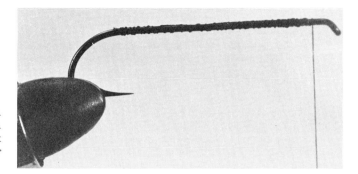

1. With the hook solidly fastened in the vise, wrap the tying thread from near the eye to the bend of the shank and back again, to make a base for materials to be added.

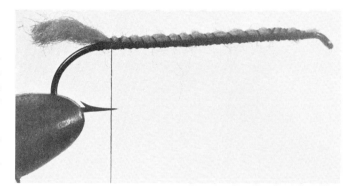

2. Tie in a piece of red wool yarn for the tail. This is tied in near the eye and the thread is wound tightly but in well-spaced coils to the bend, to hold the wool on top of the shank, thus avoiding the bulge near the tail. Make a half-hitch at the rear of the windings; trim the wool near the eye, and cut the other end off slightly behind the hook's bend.

3. Select a large grizzly neck or saddle hackle. Cut off the base part, and strip off enough barbules to expose about ⅛ inch of quill. Tie the stripped end in with about two tight turns of thread. Then tie in a piece of flat silver tinsel.

4. Prepare a piece of medium-width black chenille by scraping off about ¼ inch of fuzz to expose the thread core. Tie in the core only. Wind the thread forward to the eye and then wrap the chenille forward in tight coils to the beginning of the windings and tie it off with a half-hitch back of the hook's eye. Trim off the excess.

5. Grasp the unattached end of flat tinsel and wind it forward over the chenille, tying this off with a half-hitch back of the hook's eye. The space between the tinsel should be twice as wide as the tinsel itself.

6. Grasp the tip of the feather with hackle pliers so the inside of the feather faces forward and wind it around the body, each turn being made to follow each turn of the tinsel ribbing. Tie this off back of the hook's eye. Work a drop of cement into the materials at tie-off point, and complete the dressing with a neat, cemented head. The finished fly should look like the one at left.

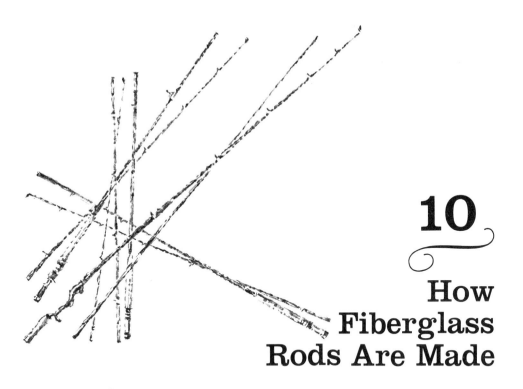

10

How Fiberglass Rods Are Made

Before World War II, there was only one quality material from which fine fishing rods were made—split bamboo. The names of fine rod producers such as Thomas, Payne, Leonard, Edwards, Winston, Granger, Orvis and others still are hallowed by connoisseurs of fine tackle. If you can acquire one of these at a fair price, you probably have located a prize.

A very few of the historic split-bamboo rod manufacturers still make rods just as fine as they always did, but their high prices put them more in the "pride of possession" category than in the realm of fiscal common sense.

About the time of World War II a change occurred in the rod business. The enamel-rich Tonkin cane from which the best bamboo rods were made came from that part of Indochina which eventually became Communist. In anticipation of a dwindling supply, a few of the historic rod makers hoarded as much as they could acquire. At least one of them (in Vermont) evidently still has enough on hand for years to come.

At the same time, the craftsmen who knew how to assemble fine bamboo rods gradually faded away. At this writing only a few are left. Labor costs of hand craftsmanship have escalated to the point that a fine split-bamboo rod now costs at least twice as much as it did a generation or so ago. But just as the future of the bamboo rod looked bleakest, modern fiberglass technology came into the picture.

When I handled my first fiberglass rod many years ago I didn't think much of it. But, year by year, the quality builders increased their skill to the extent that today many of the fussiest and most affluent anglers would as happily use a quality fiberglass rod as the most expensive one made of split bamboo. Many, in fact, now prefer fiberglass to anything else.

Why? Not particularly because fiberglass rods are cheaper, or because they can stand abuse, or because it hurts less in the pocketbook when loss or accidents happen. Mainly because modern technology can plan graduated tapers for superb actions much more precisely than ever could be done with the mitering plane, some glue and a file.

In either case, the hidden ingredient in fishing rods is quality, and quality rests on the reputation of the manufacturer. Since the great majority of rods today are made of fiberglass and since most of us don't realize the vast amount of scientific knowledge that goes into them, let's see how top-quality fiberglass rods are made.

PREPARING THE GLASS CLOTH

A tubular glass rod basically is a bonding of cloth-like woven glass fibers that are impregnated with a resin base and fabricated in such a way as to form a tube that is wide in diameter at the butt and gradually and scientifi-cally tapers to a much smaller tip. The kind of glass cloth and the method of converting it into a tube are very important to quality.

The cloth first is woven to the exacting specifications of the manu-facturer. These specifications can vary in diameter of thread, the count of threads per inch running in either direction, the width of the bolts of material, the number of imperfections allowed, and so on.

Added to all this is the type of resin-based material into which the finished cloth is dip-treated, and the method by which this is done. Since this is a plastic-based liquid resin, the process must be rigidly controlled to produce correct color, stiffness, final curing temperature and other factors.

All this may sound a bit complicated, but it indicates the great pains that top manufacturers take to produce quality fishing rods. Manufacturers of cheap rods (even cheap rods sold at too-high prices) find many ways to cut quality, thus producing equipment which looks much better than it really is.

After dipping, the cloth is run through drying towers and the viscous plastic resin that is left in the cloth after it has passed through squeegee-type rollers is allowed to dry and partially cure. At this time, when the cloth is rolled into bolts, it is separated by a layer of thin plastic sheeting to prevent the semi-tacky layers of cloth from sticking together.

Until used, these bolts are stored in humidity- and temperature-controlled rooms because, over a period of time, an aging process otherwise would take place which would make the cloth hard and unusable. The wide cylindrical rolls of bolts of cloth are hung for processing at the ends of large stainless-steel tables. Here, extreme care must be taken to keep dirt and other contaminants away from the cloth, because these would show in the finished rod sections.

BUILDING THE ROD TUBES

This cloth is unrolled and drawn over the tables in a small pile of multiple layers. A stainless-steel template, carefully engineered for each type of rod tube, is laid over the layers, which then are cut to the shape of the pattern. One side of the template is not straight. When cloth cut to this shape is rolled into a rod tube, the wall thickness of the tube will vary in diameter according to the number of thicknesses (or wraps) planned when the template was made.

The predetermined thickness of the rod tube helps to build proper action into the rod, so this step is very important. Hundreds of templates are made, each for a particular design of rod section, but there is only one which is correctly engineered for a specific rod tube.

When cut, these pieces of glass cloth are sent to another part of the factory where the straight edge of each piece is tacked with a hot iron to a steel rod called a mandrel. This is placed between high pressure rollers to wind the cloth evenly and under extreme pressure around the steel mandrel. This pressure also helps to determine the density and thickness of the finished rod tube.

Mandrels are designed with straight or stepped tapers. The combination of the design of the taper of the mandrel and the pattern of the glass cloth provides the predetermined action required in the finished rod tube, also called a "section," or a "blank."

This tube of glass cloth, compressed around the mandrel, then is machine-wrapped with strips of cellophane, applied under tension. It then is hung vertically in a curing oven controlled so that the temperature will rise gradually, level off, rise again, and so on until the final curing heat is reached. These curing steps serve to evaporate volatile materials from the plastic binders to assure that no bubbles or trapped air remains in the synthetic walls of the rod blanks.

After this curing, the mandrel is pulled from the glass, thus leaving a hollow tube covered with cellophane. The cellophane is lightly slit and is blasted away from the glass tube under extreme pressure.

STEPS IN BUILDING A FIBERGLASS ROD

1. Glass cloth is cut to shape using a sheet-metal template.

2. High-pressure rolling machine rolls glass cloth around a tapered steel mandrel to give rod final form.

3. Rod sections on mandrels are tightly wrapped in cellophane before going to an oven for heat curing.

4. Workman sands smooth the cured rod tubes before guides are wrapped on and rods are finished.

5. Guides are wrapped by hand with nylon thread, which is treated with a color preserver and lacquer.

6. Inspecting the completed rods is the final step in control of materials, quality and performance.

ASSEMBLY AND INSPECTION

Final processes of polishing and trimming to desired length complete the manufacture of the rod sections, or tubes. Identical bundles of these then go to the wrapping rooms where ferrules are applied and bonded with epoxy glue to the ends of the blanks. There is little or no grinding in fitting to prevent any possible weakening of the tubes.

Pre-assembled handles, or grips, on wooden dowels or aircraft aluminum tubes are fastened to the butt sections in the same manner. A catalytic finish is applied to the glass blanks by dipping and slowly withdrawing them from the liquid to prevent any runs or imperfections.

Line guides are positioned exactly by use of templates and the guides then are wound in place with nylon thread. The wraps then are treated with color preservative and lacquer, and the finished rods go to groups of inspectors for final examination and marking identification. Inspections go on through all of these various processes, and blanks or material containing even the slightest imperfections are discarded.

All this may seem rather complicated, but anglers should understand the vast amount of care, knowledge, equipment and skill necessary to produce rods that they will be proud to own. Of course, manufacturing processes vary somewhat with different manufacturers, so it should be stated that the method of rod construction we have been discussing is the one used by the Wright & McGill Company of Denver, Colorado, in the manufacture of its famous Eagle Claw fiberglass rods. We have not discussed several manufacturing refinements used by this company because they are more or less secret.

QUALITY COUNTS

Rods can be quickly and carelessly made by eliminating some of these intricate manufacturing steps. Such rods may look as good, and they may cost as much as high-quality ones, but the difference becomes obvious when the cheap rod fails to cast properly, or when it breaks or weakens in use.

The current perfection of quality glass rod construction has resulted in another revolutionary change, this time in selection of smaller and lighter rod sizes. In my collection of fly rods, for example, are some old split-bamboo specimens more than 9 feet long, weighing at least 6 ounces. They rarely are used.

Very long rods no longer are necessary except in certain cases, such as in bonefishing on the flats, where the line must be kept high to try to prevent its snagging on obstructions in shallow water. Long rods usually are heavy ones, and thus are tiresome to cast. The relative lightness of fiberglass rods in comparison to their greater strength makes their use a real pleasure.

Until mid-century, very long rods were obligatory for Atlantic salmon fishing. The toughness of fiberglass changed all this. Even novice anglers now rarely use rods longer than 8½ feet. Experts do well with even shorter and lighter sticks.

In modern rod selection it therefore seems sensible to choose from the shorter and lighter models, unless there is a reason to the contrary. In putting together a balanced outfit, line size is very important in bringing out proper fly-rod action. Too light a line won't bring it out. If one has to err one way or the other, it is best to use a line with a larger diameter.

Most fiberglass rods now are marked with recommended line size, but sizes vary a little between the various line makers so, even in this case, a specified size which doesn't bring out adequate rod action may indicate that a larger diameter or heavier line may do better.

Finally, in selecting a balanced fly-fishing outfit, don't ignore the importance of correct leader size. This book has stressed the fact that an incorrectly tapered leader won't roll the fly out properly.

With the proper leader and line, and the whole outfit matched to an angler's build and rod-handling habits, a modern glass rod comes pretty close to perfection. A fisherman can't ask for much more.

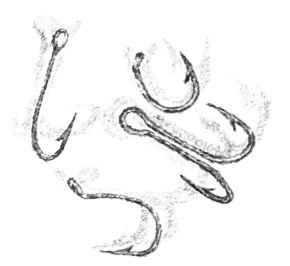

11

Facts About Fishhooks

Expert fishermen are fussier about selecting hooks than about any other tackle. Beginners learn the hard way that there are great differences in hook quality as well as in design.

When I was young and innocent I bought a box of imported salmon hooks. I tied fancy flies on some of them, only to find later that the brittle hooks snapped quicker than one can crumble a cracker. Of course, the opposite of this is when hooks are so soft they straighten out. These extremes are due mainly to improper heat treating. Large manufacturers temper hooks with such intricate and expensive equipment that it is out of reach of the small makers. The answer to quality is to buy from large and reputable manufacturers, and there are several world-famous brands from which to choose. Avoid "bargains" with obscure brand names, if you want your lures to hook and hold.

Sizes, finishes and designs of hooks run into the tens of thousands! Why risk missing strikes and losing "the big one" when the answer to hook selection is fairly easy.

Modern hooks are made from coils of wire alloyed to exact specifications; the specifications often varying with the type of hook to be made. The wire is fed into intricate automatic machines which cut, bend and eye it, also slice the barb. The soft hooks then go in metal boxes to heat-treating furnaces whose electronic controls provide the exact amount of rigidity required. Samples constantly are inspected, such as by bending tests and projecting their enlargements onto a picture screen. Each bin of hooks is tumbled for smoothness, and they may be plated, blued, bronzed or blackened, as required. Before packaging they are sprinkled on endless white canvas belts so eagle-eyed inspectors can remove imperfect ones and recheck the lot for quality. Of course there are many other steps in hook manufacture, but this provides the general idea.

Hooks for saltwater fishing differ from those used in fresh water in that they are plated with nickel, cadmium, gold or other metals to prevent corrosion. Some also are made of stainless steel. Saltwater fishermen sometimes use specialized designs, among which the short-shank, round-bend Siwash is very popular both for flies and for baitfishing, particularly in stainless steel. Bronzed or blued hooks will corrode when used in salt water, but this can be partially prevented by dropping the lures temporarily into a bucket of fresh water after use instead of returning them directly to the tackle box.

HOOK PATTERNS

What types of hooks should be selected for various purposes? Let's look at some of the well-known patterns to see how they differ from each other.

Sproat. A parabolic bend hook with a straight point. It is one of the best and strongest early designs for freshwater fishing and often is used for dressing wet flies. When made with light wire it is an excellent dry-fly hook.

Model Perfect. A perfectly round-bend all-purpose hook with a wide gap. It usually is made of light wire and is ideal for dressing both wet and dry flies. Many anglers maintain that the round bend reduces the hole in the jaw made when a fish is fighting the tackle.

Limerick. This hook has a half-round parabolic bend with a straight point designed for superior strength. It is excellent for dressing nymphs and wet flies when a heavier hook is needed. Its design in long-shanked sizes makes it very popular for dressing streamer flies and bucktails.

Carlisle. Round-bend hook with an extra-long shank and a straight offset point. It is especially designed for minnow and nightcrawler fishing because its length helps to prevent the fish from swallowing the hook.

Kirby. Round-bend hook, similar to the Sproat except that the point is offset or "kirbed" for better penetration. This directs penetration at an angle with the shank to help prevent fish from pulling loose. The Kirby is used mainly for bait fishing but advanced anglers now consider it excellent for fly fishing for the same reason of superior penetration. However, *double-*offset hooks are thought to be even better for reasons which we shall see.

O'Shaugnessy. Resembles the Sproat or Limerick except that its point is bent slightly outward. It usually is made of heavy wire for extra strength. Fishermen prefer it for dressing big wet flies and for bait fishing for heavy-mouthed slow-biting fish. It also is excellent for trotline fishing.

Aberdeen. This hook has a slightly squared round bend with extra width between point and shank so that, when baited with a minnow, its point will extend out of the fish rather than being imbedded in the bait. Its light wire avoids excessive puncturing, thus keeping the baitfish alive longer. It also is a good light-wire nymph hook. It is made to bend before breaking, and thus is easily retrieved from snags.

Eagle Claw. This American design correctly provides a direct line of pull because the point is curved inward in line with the eye. Varieties of this hook are double offset; that is, both kirbed and offset to the left and to the right to provide best penetration and balance. About two and a half million are made and sold every day.

Kirbed or double-offset hooks have become very popular for fly fishing as well as for baitfishing. An experiment provides the reason. Tie a piece of leader material to a straight hook and also to a kirbed or double offset one. Lay both side by side between pages of a thick catalog; place a hand on it for moderate weight, and try to pull out the hooks. The straight (flat) hook should pull out easily, perhaps without tearing a page. The other hook will dig in, probably making it impossible to pull it out. Fly fishermen reason that the straight hook in the mouth of a fish may pull out while the kirbed or double offset one should dig in for ideal penetration.

An example of this is in fly fishing for Atlantic salmon. Traditional hooks are straight, usually with a black enamel finish. Anglers in many areas break tradition by dressing flies on kirbed or double offset hooks, preferably the latter because they are better balanced. Their opinion is that traditional flat, black-enameled salmon hooks are "old hat" and that the other two types hook and hold fish better. Some anglers will object to this new concept in fly fishing, but a few experiments may make them change their minds. Those who do object will do so on traditional grounds or because they think straight (flat) hooks cause the fly to swim better. Those who use the offset hooks think the fly swims equally as well.

Baitholder Hooks. Available in some of the types just mentioned, baitholder hooks usually have two small forward-pointing barbs cut into the top of the shank. These prevent live or artificial worms and other lures from slipping down the hook toward its bend.

Weedless Hooks. Made in various ways, usually with a clamp of doubled light, springy wire. Since weedless hooks impair hooking ability slightly they should be used only when necessary.

Jig Hooks. The forward end of the shank is bent downward at a right

POPULAR FISHHOOK PATTERNS

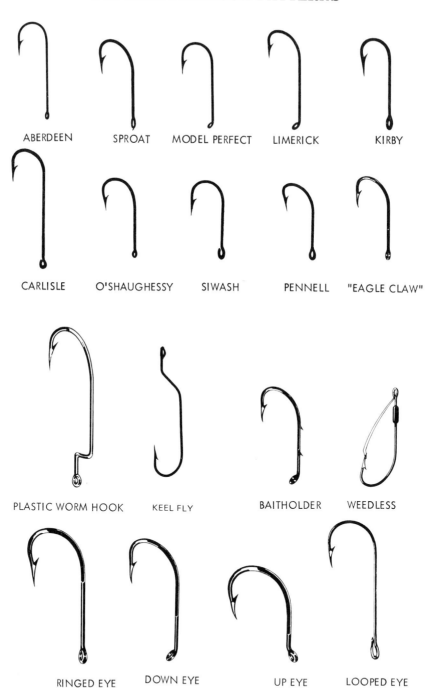

ABERDEEN   SPROAT   MODEL PERFECT   LIMERICK   KIRBY

CARLISLE   O'SHAUGHESSY   SIWASH   PENNELL   "EAGLE CLAW"

PLASTIC WORM HOOK   KEEL FLY   BAITHOLDER   WEEDLESS

RINGED EYE   DOWN EYE   UP EYE   LOOPED EYE

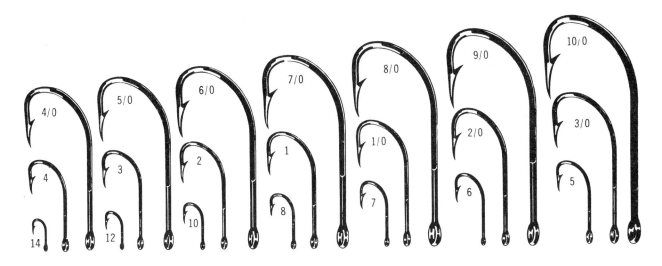

Weedless hook can be improvised with a rubber band. Slip a small, thin rubber band over the hook (*left*), push one end through the hook's eye (*center*), and stretch the end of the band over the barb. If the right size rubber band is not available, special ones are sold in tackle stores.

angle in the direction of the hook's barb so a lead head can be moulded onto the forward part of the hook without slipping.

Keel Hooks. Another development, particularly useful in fly fishing, is the keel hook. The shank behind the eye is bent downward and then straightened so the hook rides with its barb upward. Flies dressed on these hooks have been proved to be nearly weedless and snagless because, in addition to riding with the hook turned upward, the fly can be dressed to conceal its bend and barb. Thus they are very popular in weed- and root-infested waters where ordinary flies would become hung up. Fishermen who think this design impairs hooking ability will find an argument on their

223

hands. The design may cause a lost fish once in a while, but that means little or nothing when the alternative too often is to become hung up in areas frequented by big fish which are there because roots and snags provide protection.

Double, Treble Hooks. One perennial argument I would like to shy away from is the one about single, double and treble hooks. Double hooks are rather uncommon. Their proponents think the "keel" provided by the double hook makes the fly ride better, a point which may be well taken. Some also maintain that double-hooked flies sink quicker, but that is influenced primarily by the amount of dressing. They even may think that, if a single hook holds well, a double holds twice as well. Opponents say all this is hogwash; that a double hook provides leverage to make it pull out easier; that it sinks no more rapidly; and that it swims no better than a single one does. Proponents and opponents seem equally divided, and everyone is welcome to his own opinion.

Treble hooks are doubles with an added one welded to the double shank. In the early days of spinning we inherited out lure ideas from the British, who are very fond of using one or as many as several trebles on a single lure. Many Americans deplore this; some because they think it isn't very sporting; others because it is a nuisance to extract the hooks from a fish, particularly when it is enmeshed in a net. Fishermen often remove the trebles and substitute one or two singles. These believe that single hooks are fully as effective and much easier to use. Anglers fishing for records in some cases would be disqualified if treble hooks have been used on fish entered for recognition.

Snelled Hooks. These used to be popular, even for fly fishing, but nowadays they are not too common. They have certain advantages in "meat fishing" as opposed to angling. They are provided with a short leader already attached. It passes through the upturned eye and is tied securely around the shank. This holds the hook in direct line with the leader, giving it more positive hooking qualities. The opposite end is tied into a loop to make it easier and faster to change hooks. Snelled hooks usually are tied with the correct pound test of leader for the size of the hook, thus eliminating guesswork for the beginner. They are useful with heavy, nontransparent lines and with trotlines.

Sportfishermen avoid snelled hooks because they make the connection between hook and line so obvious that gamefish often refuse the lure. The idea is to reduce to the minimum the connection between monofilament line or leader and the hook or lure. Whenever possible, the monofilament line or leader is tied directly to the eye of the hook or lure.

KNOTS FOR HOOKS

We have mentioned that the hook should be in direct line with the leader in order to make the lure swim properly. This brings up a choice of knots, and beginners (plus many experienced anglers) often choose the wrong one. When the eye of the hook or lure is "ringed," or straight (turned neither up nor down), the Improved Clinch Knot is appropriate. When the eye is turned either up or down, this knot does not provide a direct line of pull. In such cases, I prefer the Turle Knot, which does provide a direct line of pull. But many anglers complain that the Turle Knot sometimes pulls out. After stringing the fly onto the leader, tie an overhand (wind) knot into the very end of the leader and cut off the excess. Then tie the Turle Knot as usual and work the common knot down to it so both are blended into what appears to be a single knot. I never have known this improvement to fail. An alternative is the Double Turle Knot. All important knots are shown in Chapter 12.

KEEPING HOOKS SHARP

No matter how efficient a hook is when you buy it, it can't do its best unless its point is kept needle sharp. Carry a small honing stone to touch up the point when it gets dull. A small flat file is even better if the hook is large. Inspect the hook often. A bent or broken hook can cause you to lose the best fish of the day.

Anglers who leave nothing to chance when fishing for record trophies long ago discarded the usual method of sharpening a hook to a rounded point. Dry- and wet-fly hooks of size 8 and smaller are too small for the new method, so the usual one still applies to them. Streamer-fly hooks, bait hooks and saltwater hooks larger than size 8 can be filed to three sharp cutting edges by the new triangulation method.

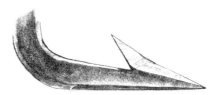

Side view of fishhook sharpened by the triangulation method. File both sides to a sharp cutting edge. Then file bottom to form flat cutting edge on either side.

Using a stone on small hooks and perhaps a jeweler's file on larger ones, the bottom of the point is filed flat. Each side then is sharpened on a slant from the point to the tip of the barb. With the rounded metal thus removed a cross section of the point then would somewhat resemble a triangle with three flat sides and three sharp cutting edges. When the hook strikes home these added edges usually will drive through bone and gristle, affording much greater penetration than a rounded point would. In addition, the hook's point is less inclined to curl when it drives into tough cartilage.

12

Knots for Fishing

More than twenty reliable and well-tested fishing knots are brought together in this chapter. Some are relatively new and unknown. Others are old standbys for which, in many cases, new information is provided which makes them stronger or easier to tie. You only need to learn a few, but you may want to refer to others from time to time, or to select from the alternatives described. Since tackle can be no stronger than the knots which join its parts together, knowing how to tie appropriate knots correctly is of major importance.

LEADER KNOTS

In Chapter 8, which describes how to make leaders, we noted that the Basic Blood Knot is preferred for joining strands of similar diameters. Those who have trouble with it may prefer the Surgeon's Knot, which follows. Use the Double Strand Blood Knot (also called the Stu Apte Improved Blood Knot) when joining strands of very unequal diameters. The Perfection Loop Knot often is used on the end of the leader so it can be joined to the line, although other connections are given which many anglers think are superior. Favorite methods for tying in droppers also are included in the next section.

Basic Blood Knot

This joins two lengths of monofilament together in making leaders and in mending monofilament lines. Since beginners often are bothered by the ends pulling out when drawing the knot together, start by lapping the two pieces to be joined so the ends above the crossing are a good 5 inches long and hold them between the right thumb and forefinger. Twist the leftward-pointing end around the other strand *five* times and place the end between the strands at point *X,* holding it there (Fig. 1). Transfer the knot to the left thumb and forefinger and wind the other end around the other strand *five* turns *in the opposite direction.* Pass the end through the knot beside the other end, but in the opposite direction from it (Fig. 2). The knot now can be released, and

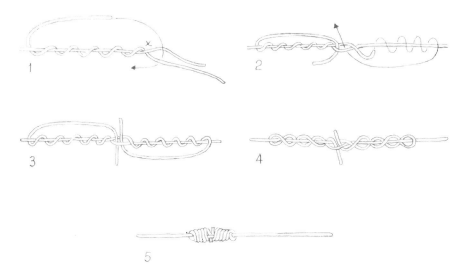

will look as in Fig. 3. Now pull on both strands of monofilament, being sure while doing so that the ends don't pull out. The knot will gather as in Fig. 4. Now pull the knot as tight as possible, to test it, and it will look like Fig. 5. Clip the ends close to the knot.

Five turns in each direction are correct. Six improves the strength very little, and are more trouble. Only four decreases strength by about 15 percent, and only three by 25 percent. When tied as above, the knot has nearly 100 percent of the unknotted line strength. Tightening a knot creates friction, which induces heat, which can weaken the knot. For this reason, expert anglers wet the knot between the lips before pulling it tight, to decrease friction.

Double-Strand Blood Knot

The Blood Knot is used for tying together monofilaments of the same or nearly the same diameters. If monofilaments are of greatly unequal diameters, such as when tying in a shock leader or a bumper line, this knot won't be strong enough. In such cases the Double-Strand Blood Knot should be used.

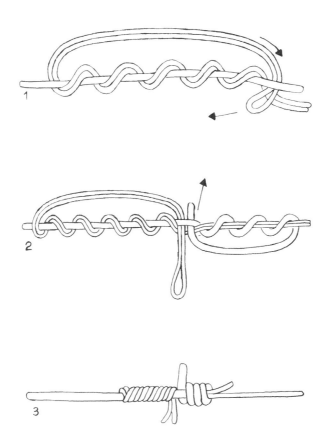

This is tied in the same manner as the Basic Blood Knot except that the end of the smaller monofilament is doubled. The doubled end is used as if it were a single one. Wrap the doubled end around the single strand at least five times. Do it six or seven times if the diameters vary very greatly. The single end is wrapped around the doubled end only three times. Cut off both single and doubled ends about 1/4 inch from the knot.

Basic Blood Knot (alternate method)

Beginners often have trouble tying the Basic Blood Knot because one of the ends pulls out when the knot is being drawn together. A gillie on the River Spey, in Scotland, showed me this alternate method, which prevents this and thus may be easier. Do it in these 4 simple steps, as shown in the sketches (one leader is shown black, for clarity): Tie the ends to be joined together by using a simple Overhand Knot (Fig. 1). Cross the monofilament above this knot to make a fairly wide loop. Wind the two looped strands around each other *five* times (Fig. 2). Pass the joined ends

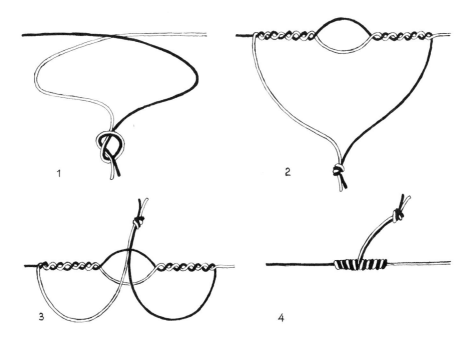

through the loop thus formed (Fig. 3). Pull each strand to draw the knot tight, wetting the partly-tightened knot between the lips before pulling it completely tight (Fig. 4). Clip off excess ends closely.

(In this case the two ends protrude from the same side of the Blood Knot, which seems to make little or no difference in strength. If it is desired to make the ends protrude from opposite sides, the Overhand Knot in Step 3 can be untied and one of the ends can be withdrawn and reinserted in the opposite direction.)

Surgeon's Knot

This also is used to join two strands of unequal diameter. It is easier to tie than the Blood Knot, but not used as extensively. A popular use is for tying a shock tippet to a leader point.

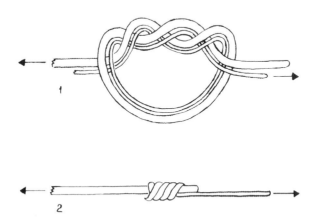

Lay the two strands together, with tips in opposite directions, with ample overlap. Treating the two as a single strand, tie a loose overhand knot in the two lines, and then repeat the overhand knot by pulling the two strands all the way through the loop again (Fig. 1). Holding both strands at both ends, pull the knot tight (Fig. 2). Clip the ends short.

Perfection Loop Knot

This knot is used to make the loop at the butt end of the leader. It provides a detachable leader which is tied to the line by using the Tucked Sheet Bend or the Jam Knot. When a loop is spliced into the end of the fly line, the two loops can be joined by threading the fly-line loop through the leader loop and pulling the leader end through.

To tie the Perfection Loop Knot, hold the end of the monofilament between left thumb and forefinger so that about 6 inches of it extend and point upward. Holding the end with right thumb and forefinger, throw a small loop to the left so it crosses behind the standing end (Fig. 1). Holding this loop between thumb and forefinger, bring the end toward you and pass it around the loop, clockwise, also grasping this between left thumb and forefinger (Fig. 2). You now are holding two loops, the second one in front of the first. Now take the short extending end of the monofilament and pass it between the two loops, also holding it between left thumb and forefinger.

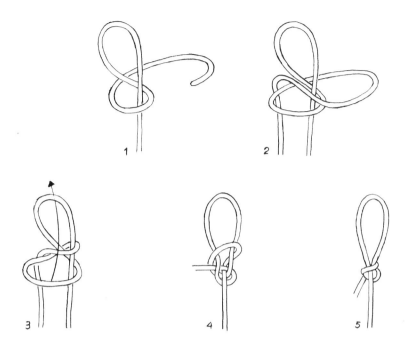

Now grasp the front loop and work it through the rear loop, at the same time pulling it out a little (Fig. 3). Still holding this tightly so the knot won't slip, pull on the lower extension of the monofilament, thus closing the smaller loop. If the remaining loop starts to twist, keep it from twisting and pull downward on the lower extension and upward on the remaining loop until the knot is tight. The knot can now be released from the fingers. Put a pencil or something similar through the loop and pull the loop as tight as possible. The short end of the monofilament will now extend at a right angle from the loop, and it can be clipped off closely.

Improved End Loop Knot

This knot is about 10 percent stronger than the one above, but is not quite as neat. It ties a loop in the end of either a line or a leader. First, double from 4 to 6 inches of the end, as in Fig. 1. Bend the doubled part backwards and around itself, making between three and five turns, depending on the thickness of the material, as shown in Fig. 2 and 3. Insert the doubled end through the first doubled loop made (Fig. 4), and pull the knot tight.

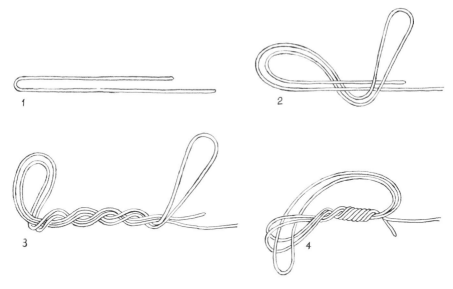

Making a Dropper

A dropper is a length of monofilament extending from a leader or mono-filament line. One can be tied in by making a Blood Knot, one end of which is left as long as is needed for the dropper. A fly, a hook or a lure is tied to the end of the dropper (Fig. 1).

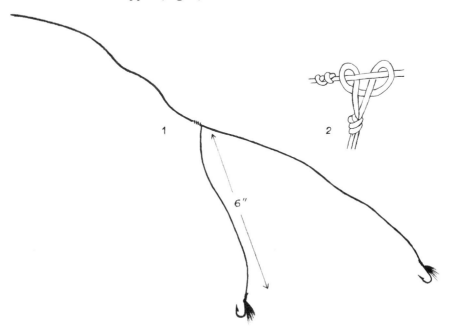

Another way to tie on a dropper is to make a Perfection Loop Knot in the end of a piece of monofilament of the desired length and strength. If the leader lacks a Blood Knot where the dropper is to be tied in, cut the leader and tie one there. Lay the Perfection Loop under the leader above the Blood Knot and put the dropper's end over the leader and through the loop (Fig. 2). Pull the connection tight and slip it against the Blood Knot. Tie a fly or hook on the end of the dropper.

Dropper Loop Knot

This is used to put a loop in a leader or monofilament line. A dropper can be attached to the loop for removal when desired. Usually this dropper, which is short, has a Perfection Loop Knot on one end, and a fly, hook or other lure attached to the other end. Put the Perfection Loop around the Dropper Loop and put the dropper end through the Dropper Loop, pulling the connection tight so both loops are connected in the same way.

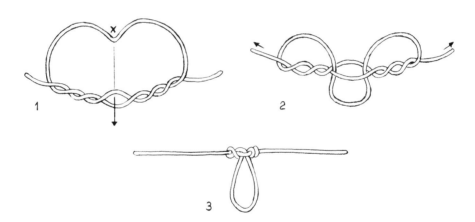

To make the Dropper Loop Knot make a loop in the line or leader and wrap the end overhand seven or nine times through the loop. Pinch a small loop at the point marked X in Fig. 1 and push it between the middle of the turns, as shown by the arrow. A pencil or pin, inserted in the middle turn, helps to keep the strands separated so this can be done easily. Pull on both ends of the line or leader, holding the loop with the third finger (Fig. 2). The Dropper Loop will gather and look like the finished knot shown in Fig. 3.

LEADER-TO-LINE KNOTS

There are several ways to connect leader to line, of which the important ones follow. Since each has good and bad points, these are discussed so the most appropriate one can be selected.

Jam Knot

This is a quick and easy way to attach a looped end leader to an unlooped line. It allows quick separation of the two, but the rough connection often catches in the tiptop and rod guides. The angler must watch this in handling the tackle.

As shown in Fig. 1, put the end of the line through the leader loop, completely around it, and under the line itself and then back through the loop between the leader and the line where it enters the loop. Work the knot tight, as in Fig. 2, not cutting the excess end too closely.

I always tie a simple overhand knot in the line's end, pulling this very tight and cutting it off closely. When the knot is snugged down, the overhand knot is worked as close to the connection as possible. This prevents the knot from pulling out. To untie the knot, loosen it by pushing the end of the line against it.

Tucked Sheet Bend

This has the same purpose as the Jam Knot. The line's end is passed through the leader loop, around it, then between line and loop, and down through the crossing that was made in the line. This is a simple figure-8. Be sure that the leader loop doesn't slip over the line before the knot is pulled tight. Since the clipped end of the line points toward the leader's tip, this is a neater knot than the previous one.

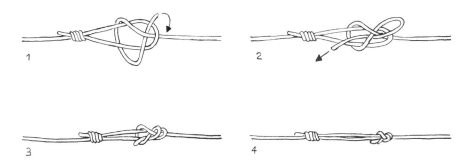

Making a Spliced Line-Loop

With a jackknife, scrape off the line's coating ³/₈ inch from the end, and fray the core with a pin. About an inch above this, carefully scrape another ³/₈-inch segment of coating off, trying not to damage the threads of the core. Lay the two scraped parts together to make a loop about ¹/₂ inch

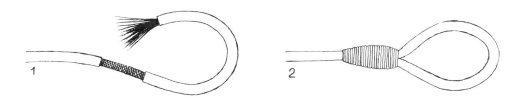

long. Lacquer the two scraped parts and whip them (wind them) with fine thread to make a smooth binding. This can be secured by two or three half-hitches, but preferably by a whip finish (which see). Apply two or three coats of lacquer to the joining to make it smooth. (Spar varnish, fly-dressing lacquer or Pliobond Cement can be used.)

Joining Looped Leader to Looped Line

Some anglers prefer this connection to any other because it is very secure and offers only slight resistance when passing through guides and tiptop. Many anglers prefer one of the following knots, thinking they pass through more smoothly. It takes time to make a good line splice, but it lasts for a long time. Since algae can collect in the knot, you may not want to use it under such water conditions.

Slide the leader loop over the line loop (Fig. 1) and thread the leader's tip through the line loop (Fig. 2). Draw the connection tight so both loops join (Fig. 3).

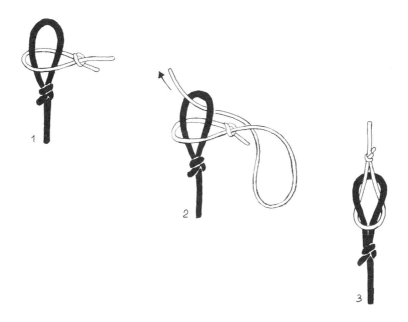

Key Loop Knot

This is also called the Line to Leader Knot, or the Albright Special, after Captain Jimmy Albright, famous Florida fishing guide.

Double the line's end and lay a similar reverse loop of leader over it, with the line's end through the leader's loop, as shown in Fig. 1. Make five or six turns of the leader's end around the line loop and then run the

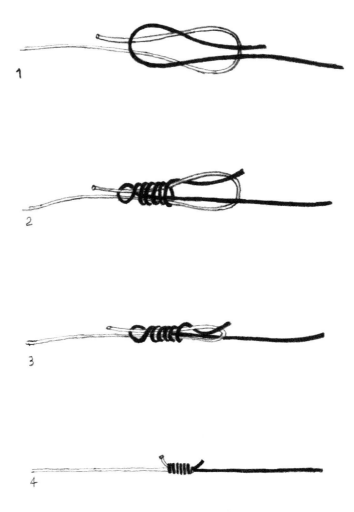

leader's end through the line loop (Fig. 2). Pull the turns tight (Fig. 3) and work them down to the end of the line loop, then pulling them very snug (Fig. 4). Cut off excess ends fairly closely and varnish the connection. (Two or three applications of Pliobond Cement, instead of varnish, are recommended.)

This is a jam knot which pulls even tighter under tension. It is not quite as strong as the Blood Knot, but is very good also for joining two strands of monofilament of widely different diameters. It is recommended for joining stranded wire to leader material.

Leader Whip Knot

The Nail Knot is very good for joining line to leader, and will be discussed later for use in joining a fly line to its backing. For joining a level leader section to a fly line I prefer the Leader Whip Knot. This is a new knot and my favorite for the purpose. It forms a semipermanent connection of 2 or 3 feet of leader-butt to the line to which a tapered leader can be tied by a Blood Knot if desired.

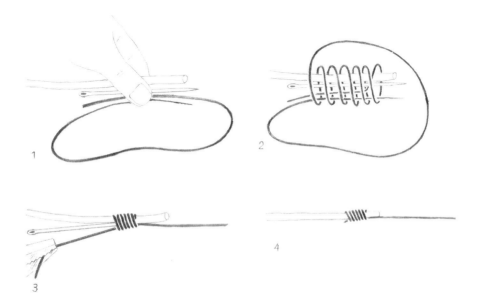

As shown in Fig. 1, hold the end of the line between left thumb and forefinger so it extends about an inch. Also hold the leader butt (leader extending to the right) so about an inch of it is between thumb and forefinger. Insert a heavy embroidery needle between leader and line, its point beside the line end. Take hold of the forward end of the leader and also put it between left thumb and forefinger, holding its tip so that it points to the right and lies beside the line end and the needle. (The rest of the leader hangs in a loop below the fingers. The loop is shown much smaller in the drawing than it actually is. You now have four items grasped between left thumb and forefinger: the line end, the needle, the leader butt and the leader tip.)

Grasp the part of the leader butt extending from thumb and forefinger and wind it clockwise to the left around the four items, making seven tight, close coils just in front of the thumbnail, as in Fig. 2. Holding these coils in place, between left thumb and forefinger, take hold of the leader tip with the right thumb and forefinger and pull it to the right so that all of the leader is pulled between the coils as far as it will go. (At this point be sure all seven coils lie closely together.) Now you can let go of the knot, pull out the needle, and grasp the rearward protruding end of the leader butt with a pair of pliers, as shown in Fig. 3. By also holding the leader which extends from the knot and pulling in both directions, the coils will bite into the line to form a rigid connection.

Now snip off the excess butt end of the leader and the excess tip end of the line, and test the connection to be sure it is tight, as in Fig. 4.

The rest is optional. The connection can be coated with Pliobond Cement to make it smooth. When partly dry, mold it around the connection for greatest smoothness. When very dry, add another coat or two, if you wish. In addition, you can leave about 1/4 inch of leader butt and line end and whip them and the knot for added smoothness, also coating the whipped knot with cement or varnish.

Pin Knot

This is very much like the previous knot but the leader comes out of the line's end instead of beside it, providing a slightly smoother connection.

Using a medium-sized common pin or needle, push it into the end of the line and out the side so that 1/4 inch of the line is strung on the pin. Pliers are needed for this and for holding the pin during the following operation.

Hold the pin's point with the pliers and apply heat from a match or cigarette lighter to the head until the part of the line nearest the heat begins to smoke *very slightly.* Push the line toward the pinhead and, holding the pin with pliers at this end, apply heat to the point until that end of the line which is strung on the pin also begins to smoke very slightly. (Avoid overheating so as not to impair the strength of the line. All that is needed is only enough heat to prevent the hole made by the pin from closing up when the pin is withdrawn.)

Now withdraw the pin and thread the end of the leader through the hole in the line's end (Fig. 1). It helps to do this if the end of the leader material is shaved to a point. Pull an ample amount through because excess can be recovered. Make five turns of this leader end around the line end fairly loosely and an inch or so up from where the leader comes out of the line. Place the leader end beside the line end, pointing away from it, as in Fig. 2. Now, holding the loop thus formed, wind the leader back around the line, starting the winding so the spot where the leader comes out of the line can be seen (Fig. 3). Wind tightly in close coils until all five coils

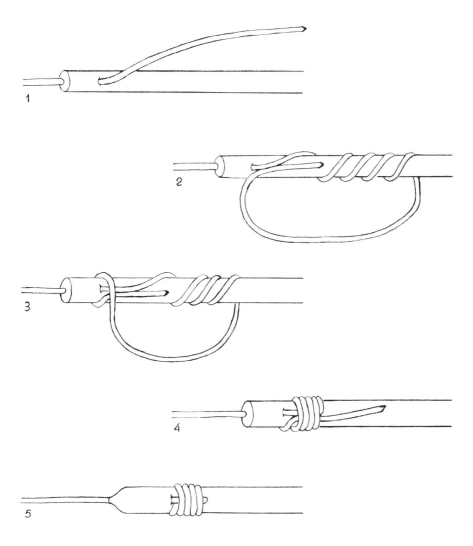

are used up (Fig. 4). Holding these coils in place, pull on the leader where it comes out of the line to take out all slack and to make a snug connection (Fig. 5). Pull on line and leader to be sure the coils cut into the line slightly. Snip off the excess leader tip and varnish the connection to complete the knot. Quite obviously, this is merely a five-turn whip finish.

JOINING LINE TO BACKING

Before somebody devised the Nail Knot, line was joined to backing by splicing it, a rather tedious process resulting in what is called a Rolling Splice. When the Nail Knot was devised almost nobody bothered with splicing line to backing any more because the new knot was nearly as good and could be done in a fraction of the time.

Nail Knot

Experienced anglers don't use a nail because a small tube of plastic or metal is much better. This should be as small in diameter as possible and yet allow the backing to be threaded through it, and not more than an inch long. These little tubes can be cut from tubing which is available in hobby shops where model aircraft parts are sold. They are also sold with Cortland leaders. Some fishermen use a sailmaker's needle with the point snipped off because its flat sides keep line and backing parallel. Find whatever object seems most useful for the purpose, and keep it for that. In tying this knot we'll use a small plastic tube.

With sufficient backing on the reel, pull out a comfortable length and lay the tube against it, allowing about 6 inches of the end to work with.

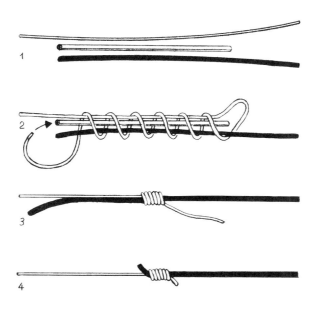

Lay the end of the fly line beside the tube, as in Fig. 1. Hold the three between left thumb and forefinger. Taking the protruding end of backing in the right hand, wind it in close and tight coils backward toward left thumb and forefinger and almost touching them. Wind at least five coils or as many as six or seven. With too many it is more difficult to draw the knot tight.

Holding these coils so they won't overlap, bring the end of the backing to the left and push it through the tube to the right (Fig. 2). Still holding the coils tightly, carefully pull out the tube, pulling the backing out as much as possible while this is being done. With the tube pulled out the coils will appear soft, but don't let go of them. Pull the backing from both ends alternately, as in Fig. 3, allowing thumb and forefinger to let the coils gather. When no more backing can be pulled from either end, let go of the coils and adjust them if necessary. Then pull hard again on both ends of backing to make the coils bite into the line. (If you use pliers to do this, be sure they don't injure the backing behind the knot. They can be used without harm on the excess end, because this will be removed.)

To be sure the knot is tight, now pull cautiously and then hard on fly line and backing. If the knot has gathered tightly the fly line won't slip, and further pulling will tighten it more. Clip off excess ends, as in Fig. 4, and coat the knot with two or three applications of Pliobond Cement or its equivalent. Let the knot dry thoroughly before winding the fly line on the reel.

KNOTS FOR TYING HOOKS AND LURES

WITH STRAIGHT EYES

The knots in this section are used mainly for joining lures to lines because such lures (unlike most flies), as well as swivels, have straight (ringed) eyes; that is, eyes with no bend in them. Don't use these knots on hooks or flies with upturned or downturned eyes.

Improved Clinch Knot

This is a basic knot everyone should learn for tying lines or leaders to hooks or lures with *straight* eyes, and for tying on swivels, snap swivels, etc. The knot is dependable, easy, and retains nearly 100 percent of line strength.

Stick the end of the monofilament line through the eye and make *at least five* twists around the line. Then push the end through the first loop (nearest the eye) and then back through the big loop, as shown in Fig. 1. Holding the lure or swivel and the line, pull the knot tight so it looks like the knot in Fig. 2. Cut off the end closely. Five turns around the line are essential for proper strength. If more than six turns are made, the knot can't be pulled tight enough. The knot must be pulled tight so the monofilament won't slip and cut itself. When using heavy monofilament, wind a handkerchief around your hand to protect it while pulling the knot tight. Three or four turns are enough for extremely heavy monofilament, such as 60-pound test and stronger.

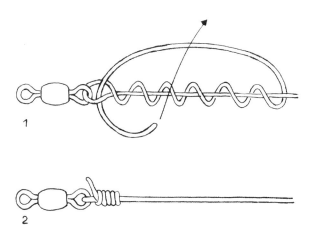

The regular Clinch Knot is the same except that the line end is not passed back through the big loop. The Improved Clinch Knot is usually considered better, but some anglers prefer the regular one.

Loose Loop Clinch Knot

This variation of the Improved Clinch Knot is useful for making a loose connection to a lure such as a jig to give it more action. Make an Improved Clinch Knot, but do not draw it tight. Insert something such as a pencil or pen into the loop and *then* pull the knot tight. Pull out the pencil and clip off the excess monofilament. This knot should not slip, but if it does, it probably would be due to the pull of a fish, which then would make little difference because it merely would revert to an Improved Clinch Knot.

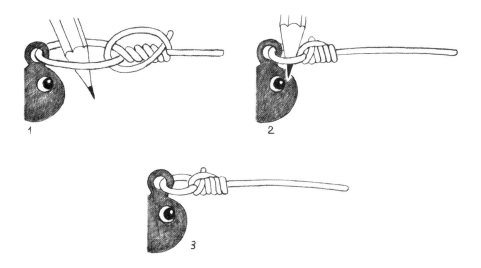

Lark's Head Knot

This isn't quite as strong as the previous knot, but is easier to tie. Being a looped knot, it is handy for attaching and detaching such things as swivels, eyed sinkers and short lures. Of course the loop can be made as long as desired, but the doubled part of the line makes it more obvious to fish.

Double the line for a loop as big as desired and tie a simple overhand knot in it. Clip off the excess end. Pass the loop through the ring or swivel (Fig. 1) and over (around) the lure (Fig. 2). Draw the loop back to the ring until it upsets the loop around it (Fig. 3).

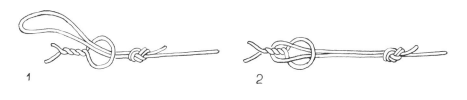

Palomar Knot

This one is a basic knot providing almost 100 percent of line strength. It is easy and fast to tie and handy for attaching hooks, swivels, eyed sinkers and small lures to lines or leaders.

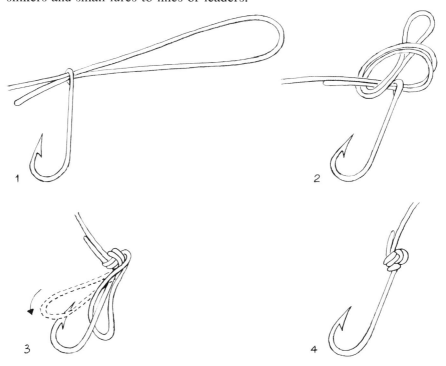

Put the line or leader through the eye and then return it through the eye to make a loop 3 or 4 inches long (Fig. 1). Holding line and eye between thumb and forefinger, use the other hand to bring the loop back over the doubled line, making an overhand knot around the eye (Fig. 2). Without tightening the knot, put the remaining loop over the hook or whatever is being tied on (Fig. 3). Then pull on the line to draw the knot to the top of the eye (Fig. 4). Pull either the line or the knot end to tighten the knot and cut off the excess end fairly short.

KNOTS FOR HOOKS WITH TURNED EYES

The knots in this section are for flies or hooks which have *upturned* or *downturned eyes*. The idea is to give the leader a direct line of pull to the fly or the hook, which can't be done properly when using the knots in the foregoing section.

Double Turle Knot

While this knot has only about 60 percent of the strength of the line or tippet it is tied on, it is used very successfully by fly fishermen everywhere.

String the fly on the leader and let it slide down, out of the way for the moment. Double the end of the line or leader and make a noose or slip knot in it, but put the end through the knot *twice,* as shown in Fig. 1. Pull

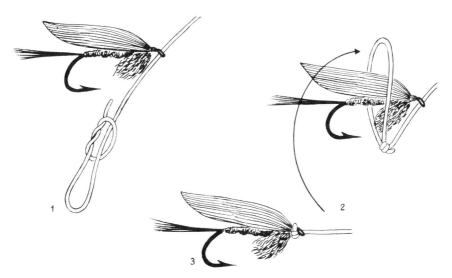

the knot tight and open the noose or slip knot enough so the fly can be passed through it (Fig. 2). Holding the noose in one hand, raise the leader so the fly slides down it into the noose. Gather the noose around the neck of the fly (*around the back of the eye* of the fly) so the knot is set against the back of the downturned or upturned eye to give the leader a direct line of pull when the leader pulls the knot tight (Fig. 3).

Single Turle Knot

This is the same as the Double Turle Knot except that the end is put through the knot only once. Anglers have found that this knot sometimes pulls out, which evidently was why the Double Turle Knot was developed. I use the Single Turle Knot with this improvement: Tie a common overhand knot in the end of the line or leader; make it very tight, and cut off the excess closely. Now tie the Single Turle Knot but work the noose up to the common overhand knot so the two knots are joined into what appears almost as a single knot. This never has been known to pull out, even when handling very big and very active fish.

Return Knot

The purpose is similar to the Turle Knots', and is somewhat stronger. However, it is better for use with hooks that will be baited than for artificial flies because the hackle of the fly gets in the way when tying the knot. Run the line or leader through the eye and pass it under the hook's shank (Fig. 1). Make a loop around the line in front of the eye, and return the end through the loop made around the shank (Figs. 2, 3). Pull the knot tight and clip off the excess end (Fig. 4).

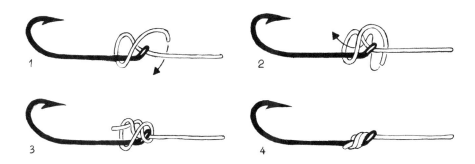

How to Snell a Hook

This isn't the way the professionals in the tackle companies do it, but it is good enough. After spending hours watching the pros at work, I still don't know exactly how they do it, which proves that the hand is quicker than the eye. But a snelled hook is a snelled hook, and here are two easy ways to do it.

Run 4 or 5 inches of leader material through the hook's eye and bend it in a loop under the shank, with the end of the material laying along the

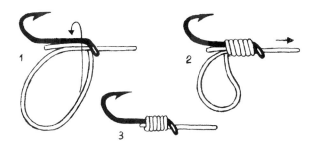

length of the shank (Fig. 1). Holding the loop, wind the forward part around the shank back of the eye, making as many tight and even coils as desired (Fig. 2). (The whole loop will wind around the hook each time.) When enough windings have been made, hold them tightly and pull on the line to remove the remainder of the loop and to make the snelling tight (Fig. 3). Clip off the excess end, and varnish the snelling, if desired.

A double or triple gang of hooks can be made by running a much longer amount of leader material through the eye to leave the free end about 6 inches long, or more. After snelling the leading hook, there should be enough material to snell the trailing hook in the same way. Be sure the trailing hook is properly aligned with the leading hook, and is at the desired distance from it, before snelling it in the same manner.

A Quick Snell Knot

A quicker way to snell a hook is similar to tying a Clinch Knot in a leader. As in Figure 1, run the line or leader through the eye and then wind it around the shank five (or more) times. Push the line or leader tip under the material just back of the hook's eye (between the material and

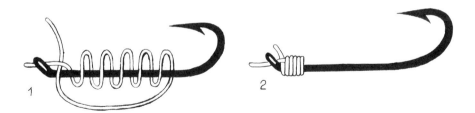

the shank). Pull the material tight from the line end and clip off the excess fairly closely. (It may be necessary to push the coils toward the eye to make them lay together.)

The quick snell is more suitable for use with monofilament of 10-pound test or over. If the end which is clipped off is not clipped too closely, it can be used as a bait holder.

The Steelheader's Looped Snell

This method of snelling provides an adjustable loop for holding attractors such as bits of yarn, foam plastic or, more particularly, a cluster of salmon eggs. First, slip the leader material through the eye and hold it near the bend of the hook (Fig. 1). Take hold of the forward end (Fig. 2)

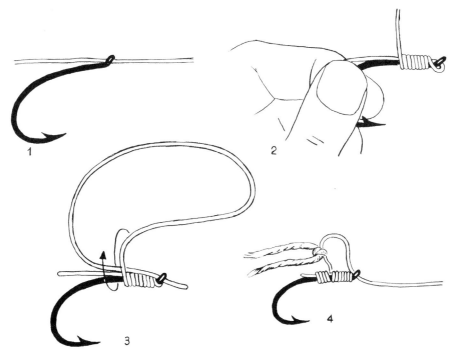

and make about eight tight turns down the hook shank. Pass the forward end of the leader through the hook's eye, leaving a fairly large loop over the shank. Grasp the end of the loop that was used to wind the coils, and make four more tight, close coils with it (Fig. 3). Pull the rest of the leader through the eye to tighten the connection.

As shown in Fig. 4, the leader can be pushed back through the eye to provide a loop which will hold an attractor or bait. The rig is used primarily on steelhead rivers for drifting a cluster of salmon eggs. These are held in place by pulling the leader forward, thus binding them in the tightened loop. Hooks with upturned eyes are necessary.

THE BIMINI TWIST

Although it appears difficult, this knot can be completed in not over a minute after a little practice. While a post or something similar can be used to hold the loop, it is easier to let another person do it. The "Bimini Twist," or "Bimini Roll," is the formerly preferred way to double a line and retain nearly 100 percent of the strength of the unknotted one. It is used both in fresh and saltwater fishing to attach leaders, make shock tippets and to strengthen terminal tackle.

The best description of tying this knot was prepared by the famous angler Stu Apte for the booklet "How to Use Du Pont Stren Monofilament Fishing Lines," and is reproduced here with permission. In the drawings the loop has been made small and the number of twists in the line has been reduced from the necessary twenty to keep the drawings from being too wide to fit the page.

250

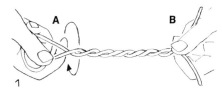

1

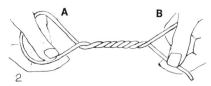

2

Double the line to form a loop some-what longer than what you intend to end up with. One person **(B)** should hold the end of the line. The other person **(A)**, holding the loop end, proceeds to twist the loop 20 times — by keeping his index finger in the loop and making circular motions with his wrist.

Once the 20 twists have been completed, separate the two strands of the loop (which will be much larger than illustrated) and work back toward the other end being held firmly by **(B)** to tighten the twist. Then **(B)** pulls the lines apart.

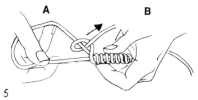

3

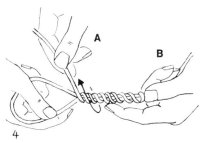

4

(B) Should place his forefinger on the twist and bring the running end of the line toward the loop. As **(A)** continues to open the loop, the twist begins to rotate.

As the twist rotates the running end is automatically wound around it. Care must be taken at this point not to let the running end wrap over itself. The wrap should continue until the end of the twist is reached.

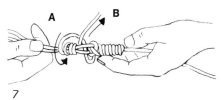

5

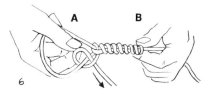

6

Now **(B)** must hold the wrap carefully to stop the rotation and at the same time execute a half hitch around the right base of the loop. **(A)** is still keeping the two lines of the loop separated.

Then another half hitch is tied about the left base of the loop. It is now safe to let go of the wrap; it can no longer get away from you.

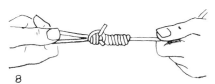

7

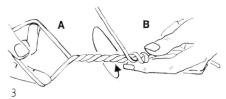

8

To finish the knot off, a little clinch knot is tied about both lines of the loop at the base.

With the clinch knot pulled tight and clipped, the Bimini twist is completed.

SPIDER HITCH

A new end loop which serves the same purpose as the Bimini Twist has been developed and is recommended by DuPont, the makers of Stren monofilament. Their tests prove that it is from 98 to 100 percent as strong as the unknotted line strength, and it is very easy to tie.

First, make a long loop in the line and hold the ends between thumb and first finger (Fig. 1), with the first joint of the thumb extending beyond the finger. Use your other hand to twist a smaller reverse loop in the doubled line (Fig. 2). Slide the fingers up the line to hold the loop securely, with most of it extending beyond the tip of the thumb (Fig. 3). Wind the line from *right* to *left* around *both* the thumb and the loop, taking five turns (Fig. 4). Then pass what remains of the large loop through the small one. Pull the large loop to make the five turns unwind off the thumb (Fig. 5). Use a fast, steady pull—not a quick jerk.

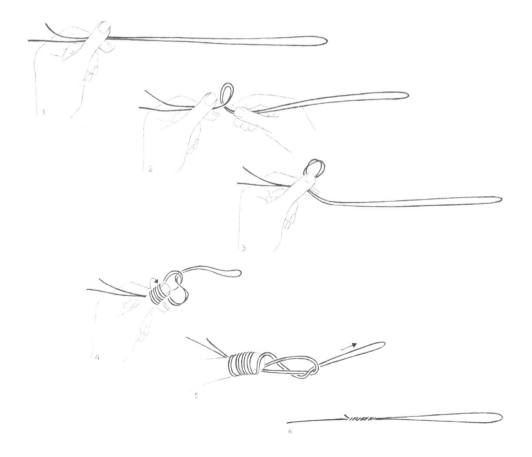

HOW TO TIE LINE OR BACKING
TO A REEL SPOOL

Run the line or backing around the arbor of any type of reel spool and tie an Overhand Knot, jammed tight and clipped closely, to the line's end. Tie another Overhand Knot around the line going into the reel spool. Pull the second Overhand Knot tight while working it close to the first one, thus forming a noose which can't pull out because of the first knot. Pull on the line to run the knot down snugly to the reel's arbor. If the knot is tied against the direction of reeling it will jam tight and will not slide when line is wound onto the reel.

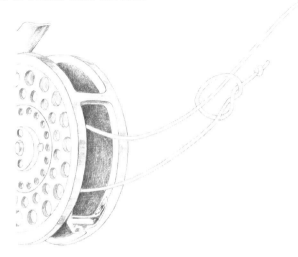

Successful fishermen take pride in tying knots carefully, and in selecting the right one for the job. This chapter describes knots for several purposes, including some variations and alternatives. Of course we don't need to learn them all, but it's handy to know they are available for use when needed.

While overhand (or wind) knots occasionally are used as "stoppers" to insure against other knots pulling out, even careful casters accidentally get them in monofilament lines or leaders occasionally. To avoid losing the "big one" it bears repeating that, since they decrease line or leader strength approximately by one-half, the line should be checked periodically to be sure none are there. If one is found it should be picked out immediately, perhaps using a pin carried for this purpose.

Fly fishermen get them most often on windy days, or when casting into the wind. Usually they are caused in casting by tipping the fly rod forward before pushing it ahead. The remedy in this case is to tip the rod ahead only at the conclusion of the forward cast.

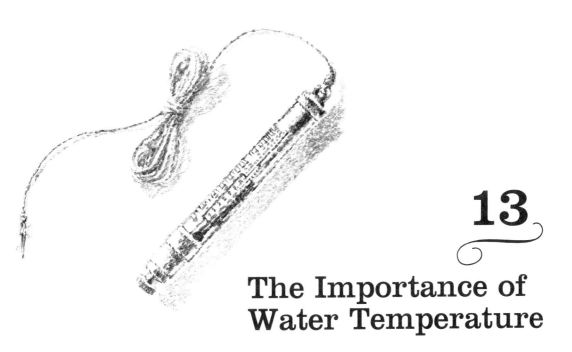

13

The Importance of
Water Temperature

The minority of fishermen who usually enjoy the best fishing are successful mainly because they understand that each species of fish prefers a very definite (and quite small) range of water temperature. They know they should confine their fishing to those places or to those depths where that proper temperature exists.

In addition, fish need well-oxygenated water; they want to be near a suitable food supply; and they usually are not far from places of protection which can be reached quickly to escape from enemies. The knack of finding fish, therefore, is to know their favorite temperature range and to fish where that range coincides with the other conditions. This chapter and the three that follow will explain why finding fish isn't as difficult as it might seem. We want to learn how to locate the fishy places without wasting time on the fishless ones.

Fish are like humans in determining where they want to live. Most of us prefer a temperature range close to 70 degrees, and we try to stay where it exists. Each species of fish has its own preferred temperature range, and it also tries to stay in it. People who live in the tropics or in Arctic regions may become used to a temperature range somewhat higher or lower, and various species of fish hereditarily become used to ranges which also vary somewhat. As we want protection from the elements and dangers, so do fish seek locations of agreeable water flow in or near places where they can hide. We want to live near a suitable food supply, and so do fish.

IDEAL TEMPERATURES

Every species of fish seeks an ideal temperature where it prefers to live, but there is an optimum and a tolerant range where it can live if it has to. In winter or under other adverse conditions fish may have to live in waters which are somewhat outside their tolerant range, but they are listless and perhaps in semi-hibernation, so they feed very little, if at all.

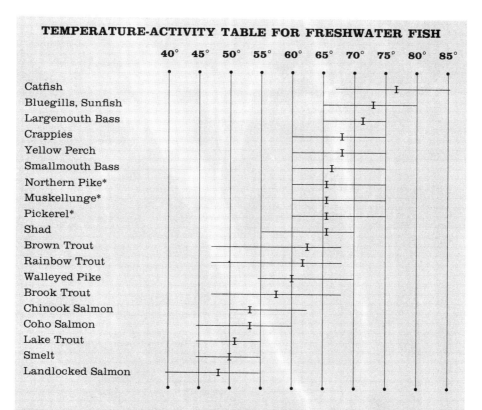

TEMPERATURE-ACTIVITY TABLE FOR FRESHWATER FISH

Note: "I" indicates ideal temperature. While this may vary somewhat in various regions, this chart should be followed unless regional data suggest variation. The horizontal line indicates tolerant temperature range. Fish usually will not take lures well outside of this range.

* Members of the pike family, which includes northern pike, muskellunge and the various pickerels, are much less fussy about water temperatures than other species. While the range shown for them is the optimum one, they usually will take lures when the water is slightly warmer or very much colder.

TEMPERATURE-ACTIVITY TABLE FOR TROUT

At Water Surface Temperatures	Water Is	Fish Are	Fishing Should Be	Fish Are Found	Suggested Lures	
FREEZING TO 40° F	MUCH TOO COLD	INACTIVE	VERY POOR	VERY DEEP (In lakes or pools)	BAIT FISHED DEEP	
40°–50° F	TOO COLD	PASSIVE	FAIR	DEEP (Or along shorelines or riffles where water is warmer)	LIVE BAIT SPOONS OR SPINNERS NYMPHS STREAMER FLIES	Tolerant Temperatures
50°–60° F	JUST RIGHT	ACTIVE	GOOD	NEAR SURFACE	WET FLIES STREAMER FLIES NYMPHS SPOONS OR SPINNERS	Tolerant Temperatures; Optimum Temperatures
60°–70° F	JUST RIGHT	VERY ACTIVE	EXCELLENT	NEAR SURFACE	DRY OR WET FLIES STREAMER FLIES NYMPHS SPOONS OR SPINNERS	Tolerant Temperatures; Optimum Temperatures
70°–80° F	TOO WARM*	ACTIVE TO PASSIVE*	FAIR	DEEP (Or in spring holes, brook mouths, shaded streams)	LIVE BAIT STREAMER FLIES NYMPHS SPOONS OR SPINNERS	Tolerant Temperatures
80° F AND UP	MUCH TOO WARM	INACTIVE	VERY POOR	VERY DEEP (Or in spring holes and cold water brooks)	BAIT FISHED DEEP	

* Temperatures very close to 60° are best for Brown and for Rainbow Trout. Brook Trout enjoy water a few degrees colder. While all anglers and scientists will not agree completely with these ranges, they are the most generally accepted. (Copyright 1949 and 1971 by Joseph D. Bates, Jr.)

The ideal temperature, or a little above or below it, should provide good fishing if the other conditions mentioned above are considered. The tolerant range may provide fair fishing, but outside this tolerant range the fishing should be very poor, if there is any at all.

Scientific study has established the ideal temperatures and the tolerant ranges, which are given in the table on page 256. While these temperatures are generally correct, they may vary slightly in various regions. We can go by the table unless local experience indicates the need for minor correction. The letter "I" indicates ideal temperature. The horizontal line shows the tolerant range. This tolerant range is quite specific for certain varieties of fish, such as trout. It is less specific for some other varieties. For example, members of the pike family, which includes northern pike, muskellunge and the various pickerels, are much less fussy about water temperatures than other species. While the range shown for them is the preferable one, they usually will take lures when the water is slightly warmer or very much colder. (It is helpful to write down the ideal temperature and the tolerant range of your favorite species and carry this information in the tacklebox.)

The other Temperature-Activity Table suggests (roughly) how deep we should fish for trout, and what kinds of lures to use. With the information given it should be easy to prepare similar tables for other species of fish. The habits of principal species are described in following chapters.

Since the ideal temperature is quite specific for all species of fish, and since the tolerant range varies more for some species than others, how are these ranges determined, especially if they are at considerable depth?

ESTIMATING WATER TEMPERATURE

Lacking a temperature-taking device, we could make a very rough estimation by dipping a hand in the water. In the case of smallmouth bass, for example, the ideal temperature is 67 degrees and the tolerant range is between 60 and 75 degrees. If the surface water feels cool but not cold, smallmouths should be in the shallows. If the surface water is very warm or very cold the shallows may be unproductive, so one should fish in deeper water nearer the bottom. When surface waters are too warm near midday, the best fishing in the shallows will be in the cool early morning or late evening when the fish come into the rich food-producing areas of grasses and pads to feed. Conversely, when surface water is cold in spring and fall, the best shallow-water fishing should be near the warmth of midday.

Winds blow warm surface water downwind, so cooler water will be on the upwind side of the pond or lake and the warmer water on the down-

WIND

SURFACE
FOOD

WARMER WATER

COOLER WATER

Fishing downwind side of lake is often productive if water temperature there is within preferred range of species present.

wind side. Winds also blow surface food downwind so, if the water temperature on the downwind side is within the acceptable range, bass and other fish, such as trout, may be feeding there. While bass are not avid feeders on insects, the baitfish they like to feed on do take insects, which is another point in favor of fishing the downwind side.

THERMOMETERS

A better way than estimating water temperature is to purchase a fish-finder thermometer or depthometer from a fishing-tackle store. Attach this to a length of fishing line in which knots have been tied at measured distances, such as every 5 or 10 feet. A sinker may have to be fastened to the rig to drop it down quickly. Ordinary thermometers are no good for deep measurements because the reading changes too quickly. Fish-finder thermometers may be of the shakedown type, or they may have a cup around the bulb for water entrapment. If you are going to any expense in buying a temperature probe, it is sensible to obtain one which is accurate.

An example of an accurate instrument is the Depth-O-Plug shown on the next page. This 5-inch-long device weighs about an ounce and can be tied to the end of the fishing line to be cast as a plug in order to locate drop-offs, ledges and the normal lake bottom. When valve D is closed the water enters through the hole in the bottom of the screw and overflows at the top of the tube at A, where it is trapped inside the transparent barrel,

The Depth-O-Plug tells depth and water temperature at the same time.

As depth increases, water pressure also increases, thus forcing more and more water inside the barrel. Thus the depth can be read directly on the scale, such as at *B*. The barrel also contains a thermometer on which the water temperature can be read of the depth indicated. The barrel is emptied before another use by unscrewing valve *D* and shaking the water out at hole *C*. This entrapped water also will indicate its degree of clearness. While this is a low-cost instrument in the five dollar range, it has a disadvantage in that it must be lowered, raised and emptied for each depth reading. More expensive instruments are available which give quicker and more accurate results.

ELECTRONIC TEMPERATURE DEVICES

In the area of about fifty dollars, various electronic depth thermometers are available with a probe that is lowered on the end of a wire so the temperature at whatever depth the probe is can be read directly on a dial held in the hand, without having to raise the probe and to clear it for another reading.

Fishermen who don't want to go to considerable expense for more sophisticated devices may find an instrument of this type to be ideal. An example is the Fish-N-Temp. This is about the bulk and weight of a three-cell flashlight, with the temperature-reading dial where the flashlight lens would be. The body of the unit pulls open in the middle to reveal a covered fine wire 100 feet long coiled around the enclosed body. Depth measurements are printed on the covered wire at 1-foot intervals. A small probe (sometimes called a sensory element or "thermistor") is attached to the wire's end and a 4-ounce bell sinker is fastened to a clip near the probe. By uncoiling the wire and gradually lowering the weighted probe the water temperature at the probe's depth can be read directly on the dial. All that's

Fisherman can instantly read bottom temperature of lake on the dial of the Fish-N-Temp, an electronic depth thermometer.

needed, therefore, is to keep lowering the probe until the battery-operated needle on the dial points to the desired temperature. The depth of this temperature is read on the wire. An instrument of this type saves time in temperature-probing and is more accurate than the thermometers previously mentioned.

In addition to locating ideal fishing depths the instrument is valuable in finding cooler underwater springs and warmer or cooler deep currents. In many cases we can drop the probe to the very bottom of a lake and still find the water not cold enough. In such cases springs and currents near the bottom may offer the ideal temperature, and the fish we seek may be concentrated there.

In using a probe like this, which has to be lowered, the boat should be stopped so the probe will go straight down. If the boat is in motion, even being blown very much by the wind, the reading on the dial will be less accurate.

Instruments like the Fish-N-Temp also are equally valuable in fishing through the ice if the water under the ice is deep enough to make their use practical. Information on this is given in the next chapter.

FISH-FINDER INSTRUMENTS

Finally, there are the flasher and beeper-type electronic thermometers and fish-locators of so many types that they must be mentioned only briefly. Being in the hundred dollar range, and up, they are of interest mainly to the chronic fisherman and to boat captains and guides. One finds them advertised in sporting magazines and they can be seen in tackle stores. Those interested in them should explore the offerings fully, collect information sheets on each, discuss their advantages with fishermen who have them, and perhaps see them in use before investing in any one.

One of these is a fish flasher which comes in a small portable case containing a probe which is placed overboard but which does not descend on a wire cable. This battery-operated electronic device transmits and receives sonar sound waves. These waves are projected by the transducer into the water in a cone-shaped pattern. When they hit an object within the pattern, they are reflected back to the transducer so the depth can be read on the dial. Thus, on the dial, we see a band which gives the depth of water under the boat. This band also tells us when we are passing over reefs or other underwater conformations which could be hot spots. From time to time, smaller flashing bands will be seen above the one which indicated the bottom. These are fish, and the dial tells how deep they are, and even whether or not they are a school of small fish or several larger ones. One has to learn to interpret the readings on the dial, but this information is provided with the instrument. Such units usually are effective to 120 feet of depth, and

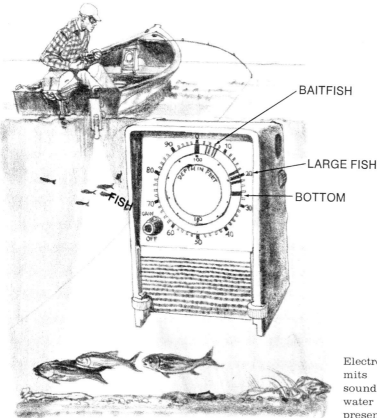

Electronic fish flasher transmits and receives sonar sound waves that register water depth, reefs, and the presence of fish.

under favorable conditions (such as sand, gravel or rocky bottoms) they can be read to twice that depth. They are effective in salty or muddy water, as well as for fishing through the ice.

Another similar unit includes a "beeper" which can be set to sound off at any predetermined depth, such as an ideal temperature level, to locate fish or to tell us when that level encounters reefs or the lake bottom. We may want to troll at a definite depth near the bottom, and this unit can tell us whether we are on course or in water that is too deep or too shallow. For example, if we know that the ideal temperature depth for coho salmon is at 75 feet in deeper water, the unit can be set at that depth and the beeper will tell us when we are over fish.

As a final example of the more elaborate models, there are those for big boats which are equipped with rolls of paper tape on which lines are marked for water depth. When the unit is turned on, a pen constantly traces a graph of the area below the boat, recording water depth as well as the locations of fish and their depths over the bottom or near reefs.

Some of these devices can be rented, which is helpful to people going on vacation who do not need such instruments year-round.

Those familiar with these temperature- and fish-finding devices can give countless examples of their effectiveness. One summer we were fishing a big lake for lake trout, whose preferred water temperature is about 42 degrees. We had to troll deep, using lead-cored lines. For protection and food, lake trout frequent reefs at depths where water is 42 degrees. The transducer finally found a reef and indicated that we were traveling along it.

Suddenly the man at the wheel said, "There are several large fish below. Let out two more colors (colored sections of line) and we should connect!" A minute later he announced, "The baits should be near the fish now, so be ready!" Almost instantly we had heavy strikes on both lines and soon afterward had two large lake trout in the boat.

Thus, among the things we should know are the ideal water temperatures of the fish we seek and (if not on the surface) how deep these temperatures are. Admitting that we can't always hit it accurately, we should try to hit the ideal temperature and more or less disregard the optimum and tolerant ranges because the farther off we are from the ideal temperature, the worse the fishing should be. When trolling, the effect of wind and currents has a resulting effect on trolling speed, and this has an effect on how deep the lures travel. We can try to troll at the ideal temperature depth but, since we may not be doing so, we may need to vary the speed of the boat or to let more line out or take some in until we connect with fish. Ways of determining proper trolling speed and depth are discussed in the chapter on trolling.

EXTREME CONDITIONS

We also know that, while fish will be at their ideal temperature depth if they can find it, they can't always find it. There are repeated instances of fish dying in streams in summer when the water becomes too warm (and therefore deficient in oxygen). Those that survive have found spring holes or the mouths of cold-water brooks where they can be reasonably comfortable; but, unless the water temperature is within their optimum range, they will feed very little, if at all. Conversely, in the icy waters of spring (here in New England, at least) the streams may be so cold that fish won't take lures at all except possibly when a small bait is dropped in front of their nose. Under such conditions, I have seen large trout in high-water grasses near the banks so cold and dormant that they wouldn't touch a lure, and even had to be prodded to make them move away. When surface waters are too cold in lakes, but the air is warm and perhaps the day is sunny, fish may be in the shallow warmer water on the downwind side of the lake, perhaps even in water almost too shallow to float them. If this surface water is warm enough, the fish may be active and feeding. I have often taken trout and landlocked salmon in shallow water under such conditions.

While we are involved here primarily with the importance of water temperatures in fishing, we know that whole lakes and ponds, and the deep pools and other parts of rivers and streams, may have an ideal temperature layer either on the surface or deeper. Ideal water temperature is the principal requirement for good fishing, but it's not the only one. Fish also want to be near a food supply, preferably where they can find protection. This means that, under ideal water conditions, fish will be near the shoreline or on or near reefs at the depth where ideal water conditions exist. An abundance of oxygen is another requirement, especially when water is warm. Thus, fish may seek places where it is oxygenated, such as near waterfalls or the mouths of tumbling streams.

Exceptions to the rule are fish that make migratory (or spawning) runs, such as steelhead and salmon. The desire to travel upstream transcends everything else. Years ago, I fished a famous stream during a spawning run of brook trout and landlocked salmon in the company of two accomplished anglers. Big fish were everywhere, even trying to swim between our legs. Yet no fly or method we tried would take even one fish.

There is a pattern of seasonal water temperatures in lakes and large ponds which has a distinct and interesting bearing on our ability to catch fish in them. Since this is a subject in itself, it will be discussed in the next chapter.

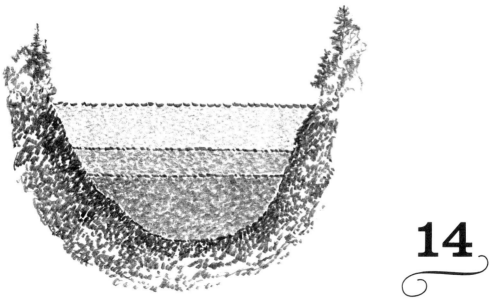

14

Lakes: How Seasonal Changes Affect Fishing

The famous author and hermit-naturalist Henry David Thoreau was the first to observe the peculiar phenomenon of "thermal stratification" which exists in certain types of lakes. Noting the warm surface waters and the coldness of the depths of Walden Pond, he observed, "How much this varied temperature must have to do with the distribution of fish in it! The few trout must oftenest go down in summer."

This comment preceded the birth of the science of limnology, or the study of lakes and other inland waters. Little was known of this subject prior to 1850, but since then a vast store of information has been accumulated. Much of this has a decided influence in assisting the angler to fish in the right places and at the right depths at the right time, and thus to catch more fish. Why is one of the best fishing times just after the ice goes out of the lakes—and how soon after it goes out? Why don't lakes freeze from top to bottom, or nearly so? Why is fishing poor near the surface in summer? If we want to troll, how deep should we fish, and how do we determine a trolling path for best results? These questions, and many others, are answered by knowledge of the seasonal changes peculiar to cold-water lakes. It pays rich dividends when anglers understand what happens, and why.

An annual red-letter period in the fisherman's calendar happens in early spring in our northern states when the ice leaves the lakes. One day their surfaces are great expanses of ice which have gradually thinned and become porous and rotten due to the increasing heat of the sun as the new year advances. The next day, seemingly without warning, the ice has completely disappeared and the clear, cold water dimples and boils with the action of fish newly freed from winter confinement under the ice and anxious to fatten themselves at the expense of smelt, shiners and other forage fish in the oxygen-saturated waters near the surface.

It is then that the northern sporting-camp owners send the word to their impatient clientele of sportsmen, who hastily assemble fishing gear and descend upon the reborn fishing grounds in great numbers. Now, the leaping landlocked salmon, the swirling squaretail and the tugging, boring lake trout are on the surface, insatiably hungry and avid for the artificial fly or the properly trolled bait. Where there is the salmon there is usually the smelt for his food. The smelt in vast schools assemble their ranks and begin their annual pilgrimage to the inlets and up the feeder streams to spawn. Daily, the salmon follow the smelt and the anglers follow the salmon. A fortunate boat locates a school and others collect in the vicinity as if by magic. Often trolling is unnecessary. Hunger induces the big fish to be less selective than usual, and almost any pattern of streamer fly or bucktail, or spinner or wobbler, or live or artificial bait, will get results.

During these few weeks after the ice goes out, the ascending sun warms the surface water more and more. Gradually, the salmon and the lake trout no longer come to the lure, and one has to search for other species of trout, and bass. Quite obviously something has happened to change their habits. Simply expressed, the lakes have "turned over"! What actually happens is less simple to describe, but the phenomenon is of utmost importance to fish life and therefore a knowledge of it is of corresponding value to the angler in deciding when, how and where to fish most logically.

The nub of what happens revolves around the fact that water is heaviest (of maximum density) when it is at a temperature of 39.2 degrees F. Thus, water at this temperature settles to the bottom and both warmer and colder waters (being lighter) rise and mix.

WINTER STAGNATION PERIOD

An insulating blanket of ice covers the lake, with the water just below it slightly above the freezing temperature of 32 degrees. Under this, as we go deeper, the water becomes gradually warmer, and therefore heavier, until the temperature of maximum density of 39.2 degrees is reached at the lake's bottom. The presence of this relatively warmer water explains why lakes don't freeze solid in winter. At this time there is relatively little movement in the water of any lake.

Plants which live in water harbor food for baitfish, and these, in turn,

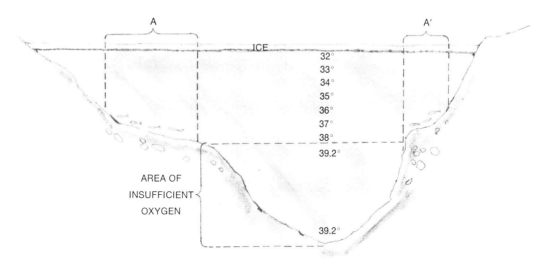

Winter stagnation. Temperature of ice-covered lake increases with depth, until it reaches 39.2 degrees at the bottom. Fish, in a state of semidormancy, remain at depth where there is sufficient oxygen and plant life.

provide food for larger fish. But water plants need sunlight, which helps them to absorb carbon dioxide and to give off oxygen, in order to grow. Fish need this oxygen, as well as food. There is a depth in deep lakes beyond which no sunlight, or an insufficient amount of it, penetrates. This depth depends on the degree of clearness of the water, which varies from lake to lake and from time to time. Because at and below this depth there is insufficient plant life and oxygen, very few fish will be found.

These facts provide suggestions on where to fish through the ice. We know that fish will seek the warmest water they can find, since all of it is below their tolerant ranges, but that they also need the proximity of plant life and the presence of sufficient oxygen in order to exist. These conditions are met at the greatest depth where there is plant life along the shoreline; out from islands, or over reefs, so fishing holes should be cut at positions such as *A* and *A'* in the illustration. These only can be found by trial and error but, when a productive hole is cut, the depth should be measured so you can try to cut other holes over the same depth.

Since all of this water is too cold, even for lake trout, fish are partially dormant; they eat very little, and wait out the winter for better conditions after the ice leaves. Underground springs and streams, as well as surface streams, may provide slightly warmer water. Since underground springs provide relatively warmer water in winter and relatively cooler water in summer, concentrations of fish should be found in and near them. Fishermen occasionally happen upon such conditions, mark down the bearings, and guard the locations as valuable secrets.

SPRING TURNOVER STAGE

After the ice has left the lakes, the sun heats up the surface water, which day by day becomes warmer and which mixes with the colder water below. This happens slowly in windless periods, but the mixing is more rapid with winds. Finally, a week or more after the ice goes out, depending on these conditions, all of the lake's water has mixed and blended until it all is at the maximum density of 39.2 degrees. Being all of the same weight, even a moderate wind actually can "turn the lake over." At this time the fish, having no choice in temperature, except that the surface water is somewhat warmer, with more food in it, come to the surface to feed, as was mentioned earlier.

Some fishermen say, "I went up right after the ice went out, but the fishing wasn't any good!" The reason is that the fact that the ice has gone out may not indicate that the spring turnover stage has occurred. Perhaps they

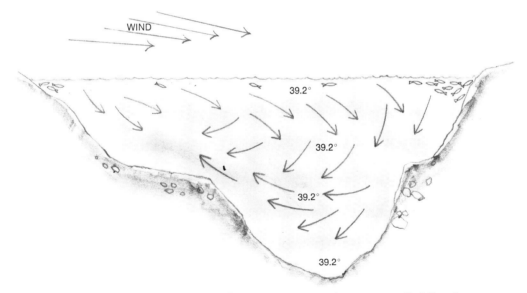

Spring turnover. The surface water warms to 39.2, or slightly above. Winds mix the water, causing the lake to "turn over." Fish come to the surface and feed hungrily.

should have postponed the trip for a few days, or even for a week or more. Many sporting-camp owners don't understand this phenomenon, and they want business anyway. If the few days following ice-out are warm ones, with good winds blowing, an early visit is indicated. If the days are cold and without wind, the spring turnover stage may not have been completed, so a later arrival may be preferable.

Even with surface water at 39.2 degrees, or slightly warmer, it still may not be warm enough for any species except lake trout. Remember that the sun warms surface water, that winds blow it from the upwind to the downwind shore, and that the winds blow surface food there also. Fishing the downwind shoreline should be best, either by trolling along it or by casting well into very shallow water.

SUMMER STRATIFICATION PERIOD

The summer stratification period begins at the ending of the spring turnover stage and it lasts as long as warm weather continues. As the air temperature rises the surface waters become gradually warmer, and therefore lighter. Being lighter, they do not mix with the colder waters below in lakes so deep that the action of winds cannot mix them. Thus, when the surface waters become increasingly warmer a period of thermal stratification sets in, known as the summer stratification period.

Deep lakes divide themselves into three definite temperature layers. The warm water remains on the surface, the cold water stays at the bottom, and, between the two, there is a transitional layer, where there is some mixing, in which the water temperature takes a very decided drop between the upper and lower layers.

Herein lies one of the most important reasons why fishing may be good in parts of a lake at certain times and poor at others. It clears up many of the so-called mysteries of the changes which take place in fishing conditions throughout the season. It helps anglers to know where the various species of fish may be expected to be, and it gives at least a partial reason why. It also influences the selection of lures and fishing methods which should be most successful and it immediately discourages methods which, once lake conditions are understood, are quite obviously of no value at all.

The upper thermal layer has the rather imposing technical name of *epilimnion*. In it the water is almost uniformly warm, varying only a few degrees between the surface temperature and that of the upper side of the middle layer. This upper layer normally has a depth of from 15 to 25 feet or more, depending largely upon the size and shape of the lake; the surface temperatures, and the extent and direction of the prevailing winds which cause the surface waters to mix. In ponds and shallow types of lakes, with

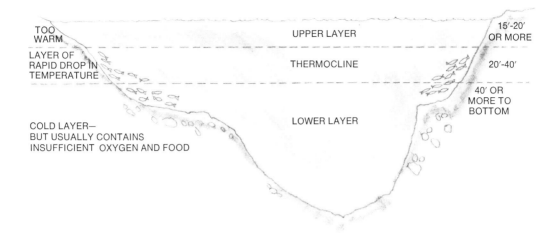

Summer stratification. Deep lakes divide themselves into three temperature layers. Best fishing is in the thermocline near sides of the lake or at that depth around islands and submerged reefs.

a depth of 25 feet or less, all of the water may be regarded as the epilimnion (we'll call it the "upper layer" from now on), since these lakes usually are too shallow to permit thermal stratification.

The middle layer, dividing the upper and lower ones, is the transitional area for the vastly divergent temperatures between the two. It is called the *thermocline* and we often hear it referred to in fishing magazines and books. It is usually between 20 and 40 feet in depth. The thermocline stratum is defined as the zone where the drop in temperature is at least 1 degree Centigrade per meter of depth. To those who are not used to thinking in terms of the decimal system it may be roughly considered that waters in the thermocline vary at least one-half a degree Fahrenheit per foot of depth. Since the thermocline separates the warm upper layer from the cold lower layer, it has a very sharp drop in temperature; perhaps, for example, as high as 76 degrees at its upper edge and 45 degrees at its lower one. The lower level, under the thermocline, is known as the *hypolimnion* and is, like the upper layer, fairly constant in temperature, rarely varying more than 5 or 6 degrees between its top and bottom. It usually is the deepest of the three layers, its thickness depending, of course, upon the depth of the lake and weather conditions.

Summer water currents and the action of wind and wave on the surface tend to make the warm surface water mix with the colder water below the thermocline. Since the colder water is heavier, it resists this mixing. This

270

results in layers nearly as well defined as oil or gasoline on water, with the cushioning effect of the thermocline in between.

Having seen that fish usually find both insufficient oxygen and food very deep in lakes, and knowing that the upper layer is too warm for many species, we can conclude that the best fishing for cold-water species will be down in the thermocline level in summer—usually where that level touches the lake's edge, reefs or islands. Its depth and its temperature range are easy to determine with one of the temperature probing devices previously discussed. "Thermocline fishing" becomes a way of life for many successful anglers in summer, and temperature probing tells them whether they should fish near the middle or nearer to the thermocline's bottom or top.

Incoming streams provide avenues of travel or escape for fish which don't want to venture into the warm top layer of the lake. We know that cool stream currents when entering lakes will flow more downward than outward because of their greater densities, so fishing in the areas of cool or cold incoming streams should be good. We know that springs and spring-holes, both in warm streams and in lakes, provide the cooler water which induces fish to seek them and to remain in them. Of course this refers more to cold-water species than to warmer-water ones.

FALL TURNOVER STAGE

With the coming of cold fall weather, the period of thermal stratification reaches its end, and the reverse of the spring turnover stage takes place. The cold days and nights gradually reduce the temperature of the surface water until it is colder than the water immediately below. As this water becomes colder it becomes heavier, sinking gradually to displace or mix with the warmer water underneath. This fall turnover stage continues until all of the water has again reached a temperature approaching that of maximum density, or 39.2 degrees.

It is at this time, with the breaking up of thermal stratification and the cooling of surface waters, that fall fishing is at its best, for the same reasons that it is good in the spring. Cold-water fish, such as lake trout and other trouts, landlocked, coho and other types of salmon, bass that have been bottom-feeders all summer, and others, come to the surface to revel in the highly oxygenated cold water and the abundant food it contains. They hit surface lures in wide variety, and lucky is the person who can enjoy taking them on flies.

With the advent of freezing weather the winter stagnation period begins again, and the annual cycle has been completed. As the surface waters approach the freezing point they become lighter, and therefore stay on top. Ice forms on the northern lakes often to a depth of three feet or more and the anglers who live in these areas have readied their ice-fishing equipment or have journeyed west or south to continue their sport in warmer regions.

In many lakes in northern states the water surface temperature in summer does not go above 70 degrees. Therefore, regardless of water stratification, cold-water fish such as trout may take lures on or near the surface. Many lakes in southern states remain stratified all year through.

We have gone into some detail to explain why lakes turn over, and their seasonal behavior, because all this is of major importance in understanding why we should be successful by fishing in certain ways and at certain depths, and unsuccessful by fishing in others. Many northern fishermen know that fishing in lakes is good in early spring or in late fall, but they don't know why. Knowing why can't help but add to one's success.

15

How to Find Fish in Lakes and Ponds

SPAWNING RUNS OF BAITFISH

Many lakes have migratory (or spawning) runs of baitfish or sportfish or both. It has been noted that in many northern lakes smelt run up feeder brooks and rivers in vast numbers in the early spring. Sportfish such as trout and landlocked salmon follow them to the brooks and rivers and are waiting there when they return.

Upstream, the hoards of smelt lay their brownish encrustations of eggs so abundantly that they completely cover all underwater rocks, sticks, stones and gravel, the eggs adhering thickly in gelatinous masses. Unfortunately, people who wade in to dip smelt trample large quantities of the eggs, and many more are consumed by predators. Smelt remain upstream for a week or so, or even much longer, and seem to return downstream more or less in a body rather than in occasional schools. However the downstream migration may take many days to complete.

On the return of the smelt the mouths of streams entering lakes should contain a concentration of sportfish not found at any other time except during the beginning of their own spawning periods. When sportfish concentrate to feed on baitfish the sportfish take lures much more actively than on their own spawning runs, so a knowledge of baitfish migratory habits is very valuable to fishermen.

Anglers who keep tabs on the migratory runs of baitfish usually can tell, almost to the day, when the baitfish will start coming out of the streams, and therefore when to start fishing for the "big ones." Dates will vary a bit if seasonal temperature conditions aren't normal, but the emergence of the baitfish and the concentration of the sportfish is certain. At such times anglers can take big trout, landlocked salmon, and other species on streamer flies or bucktails, or on almost anything else. Flies should imitate the coloration of the baitfish and should be similar in slimness and size. Since many "whoppers" not usually found near the surface are near the stream mouths at such times, this is something to remember.

After the schools of baitfish return to the lake the survivors travel down the lake to whatever destinations their instincts lead them. Sportfish follow these schools, which are not hard to locate by trolling and by noticing the activity of water birds which feed on dead or injured baitfish. Thus, after the flurry of good fishing when lakes "turn over," the migratory habits of baitfish provide keys to equally good or better fishing later on.

MIGRATORY RUNS OF SPORTFISH

Rainbow trout are spring spawners, but the anadromous rainbows called "steelheads" run up-river at other times, as will be discussed in Chapter 18. Landlocked salmon, brook trout and brown trout spawn in the fall, all running up entering rivers and feeder streams suitable for the purpose. These merely are examples; the habits of specific species will be described later. The point to be made here is that anglers should learn the habits of the fish they want to seek, because these habits help to tell when and where to fish for them. Migrating sportfish usually concentrate in stream mouths before going up-river, and they may be in or near the stream mouths for a considerable time, waiting for suitable water conditions before attempting the upstream journey. Other species, such as lake trout, bass and various other pondfish, usually don't go upstream for spawning, but each has individual habits that disclose the secrets of catching them.

HOW MAPS HELP ANGLERS

Nearly everyone has a few specific lakes and ponds where he enjoys going fishing. But too many fishermen fail to pin down the information that would make their fishing much more successful, especially on unfamiliar waters. Too many waste time on unlikely spots when a little experience in "reading the water" would suggest much better ones.

An excellent way to start is to obtain one of the topographic maps charted by the U. S. Geological Survey. These are available for almost every area in the United States and can be obtained for small cost at sporting goods stores, bookshops and other places. These stores can show customers large-scale key maps of a whole state, divided into named or numbered rectangles so the maps needed can be easily identified. The maps are printed in brown or green for land areas and in blue for water areas. Adjacent rectangles can be pasted together to show a larger area, if desired.

In the case of reservoirs and other man-made impoundments, perhaps we can do even better. An up-to-date map shows the reservoir or lake. A map of similar scale, made before construction of the impoundment, will show the land area before it was put underwater. By tracing the new water area and laying it over the old land area, rivers, brooks, roads, valleys and other details can be lined in on the tracing. River and brook beds may be productive far out into the lake. Ditches beside former roads can be hangouts for bass and other species, which also may lie in the protection of old culverts and bridges, some of which may not be far underwater. Depths marked by old land contours, related to present water height, should help in charting the path where the summer thermocline level touches submerged land masses. An evening or two spent in translating the most interesting parts of the "before" map onto the "after" map should suggest many definite places worth fishing, and some of these should turn out to be very valuable hot spots.

In the case of large man-made impoundments, this work already may have been done, so it pays to inquire at local sporting goods stores to see if such maps exist. They may not show all the hot spots, however. The person who made the map, and had it printed, may have chosen to keep some places to himself. Depth- and temperature-measuring devices previously discussed help to pinpoint actual locations, such as the usually productive deep ditches beside former roads.

WHAT DOES A MAP TELL US?

To illustrate what topographic maps can and can't do for fishermen, let's start at the north end of the lake in the map on page 277 and study the fishing spots around it. Just having the map gives an initial advantage in talking with camp owners and people who have been there. Instead of their vaguely describing a hot spot to us, we can produce the map and have them pinpoint exactly where it is.

The map says the brook at the northern end of the lake flows through a swamp, and, actually, if we didn't have the map we might not realize the brook is there because the area is overgrown with alders. The map helps by showing exactly where the brook emerges from the undergrowth. It doesn't tell us that the water in the lake where the brook comes out is very shallow because the stream spreads out rather than flowing narrowly like a ditch. It doesn't tell us that there is a very steep drop-off at least 25 feet out into the lake, and that the fish are down in the cooler water of the drop-off waiting for food to be washed down to them. If we scout the area before fishing it we know our boat must skirt the shore and anchor close to the brook mouth so we can fish outward over the drop-off.

This tells us that, while topographic maps may be very reliable for land contours, they are more or less unreliable for water contours, or depths. The map shows several islands, and we'll learn a lot from that, but evidently the water contour lines otherwise are just put in there to make the map look pretty.

Going toward the northeast we find the lake's outlet flowing into a pond and then over a waterfall. Actually, the waterfall is an old logging dam, and there is very good fishing there, especially in late fall when the brook trout and landlocked salmon run up-river from a lake below. The map shows a trail, if we want to walk to the falls. It doesn't show that the pond is very shallow, muddy, and only fit for trashfish such as chubs.

The map shows a large island and several small ones in the northern part of the lake. This implies that the northern end is shallow and that, if the lake has a thermocline in summer, it may be only in the southern part. Thus, the water of the northern part may be too warm in summer, with what fishing there is all being concentrated at the brook mouths. In spring and fall, however, fishing around the islands should be good.

Wide contour lines on the eastern shore indicate that the water off this shore is fairly shallow. Since, on good days, the wind or breeze will be blowing toward this shore, trolling along it may be better than trolling the opposite shoreline. The map shows no incoming brooks in this area, so we needn't waste time looking for any. However, when fishing in warm weather we could look for spring holes along the shore.

In the southeast corner the map shows a cove with several brooks merging into it. This should be a hot spot especially when the wind is from the northwest. This would be especially true in early spring soon after the ice goes out because we now know that a northwest wind will blow the warmer surface water toward the cove, thus making fishing better there. Without the map we might not realize that a brook comes into the cove because the whole area is overgrown with bushes.

The map shows a high southern bank, which indicates deeper water

Part of a U.S. Geological Survey Map. To learn how to read such a map for fishing information, see the accompanying text.

along the southern shore. Casting or trolling here should be good especially when the breeze is from the north or northwest.

The map shows two entering streams coming in from the south. Without the map we might guess that the one on the right is the larger one, but the map shows this is swamp drainage, so probably it has very little current. If this were a bass lake, it might be a hot spot for them. It should be obvious from the map that the stream on the left should be better for trout.

The stream on the left is the inlet to the lake — a fact we might not know if we didn't have the map. Since all this area is overgrown with bushes, we need the map to show that the stream is fairly wide and probably worth investigating. A canoe can travel up this stream at least as far as the entering brook. If this were a bass lake, the stream would be abundant with small-mouths. However, it is a trout lake, and this stream is a hot spot which most fishermen don't visit because they don't realize it is there.

The entering brook makes a trout hole which is especially productive in the summer. We can guess at this because we know that, when lake surface water is warm, trout spend the summer in cool-water brooks as well as going to the thermocline level in the lake. If the lake is too shallow for a thermocline they will have to go into the brooks anyway. We also can correctly assume that the stream and its entering brooks are the principal brook trout spawning areas for the lake, and that fishing should be excellent here in the fall.

Without the map we wouldn't know that this brook is the outlet for a pond, and that it might be worthwhile to push the canoe up the swampy and brushy brook to investigate it. The pond's outlet into the brook is dammed by beavers. A quick look will tell whether it is worth fishing, or not. If the beaver pond is a new one it will contain very little vegetation, and it will be "working"; that is, gas bubbles will be rising from it. This would indicate an oxygen deficiency which could not support either trout or bass. If the pond is an old one there may be no decay in it, and the absence of gas bubbles and the presence of green vegetation would indicate it could support fish. In this case we could have happened upon a real treasure — a hard-to-find pond containing dark-backed brilliantly colored brook trout, or perhaps a bonanza of bass!

Going back to the lake and up its western shore we pass two small brooks, and should try a few casts around their mouths, especially if the surface water is warm. The map doesn't show that, well offshore between these two brooks, there is a ledge which breaks the surface when the lake's water is low. This should be charted on the map because, under suitable water temperatures, this would be a hot spot for whatever types of sportfish live in the lake.

Finally, farther up the western shore a larger brook emerges from a swampy area. Since there is a gravel bar on its southern side we assume that the brook's current flows more northerly than outward. After fishing it we could drift over the outlet to familiarize ourselves with it. When we do so we note a deep channel extending to the northeast; a fact which should be sketched in our notes because it is a place that few anglers know how to fish properly.

This example may indicate that the best way to fish a small lake, or part of a larger one, is to start by obtaining a map of it. If necessary, the map can be blown up by making a drawing or by photographic enlargement. Whatever the map fails to show can be drawn in, or jotted down in supplemental notes. Many fishermen keep informational diaries from year to year. These are of special value if the same places are to be fished in years to come.

FISHING THE SURFACE IN SUMMER

While spring and fall northern lake fishing usually can be on or near the surface, water temperatures dictate that in summer most of it must be at predetermined depths deeper down in or near the thermocline level. However, even in summer cool and cold water temperatures suitable for trout and some of the other cold-water species can be on or near the surface.

Spring holes never should be ignored in summer. Look for lusher, brighter green foliage at the lake's edge, perhaps where water is trickling down. Every suspected spring hole should be fished carefully in warm weather, and an accurate first cast usually is the one that counts. Sometimes cold-water fish lie in the cool sanctuary of a spring hole as closely packed as cordwood.

Spring holes out in the lake may be harder to find, but they can be even better. A strike while trolling may indicate one if the spot is marked down and another fish is caught in the same place later. Evening or early morning activity of fish on the surface, with no activity anywhere else, can be the clue. Some deep-water spring holes are so large that countless fish, many of trophy size, summer in them and even can be taken with dry flies, especially very early or very late in the day. When such a hot spot is found a note should be made of it, such as by marking down landmarks at four compass points, as shown in the diagram on page 280.

Cold-water streams, especially where they enter lakes, can be havens for fish during warm-water conditions. Fishermen unused to such spots can spoil them by first casting in too close to the stream mouth. In the diagram of a stream mouth on page 281 it might seem logical to start casting in the area *A-A* and perhaps to have the boat as near as *B-B*, which is probably over the spot where most of the fish are! In this top and profile view of a

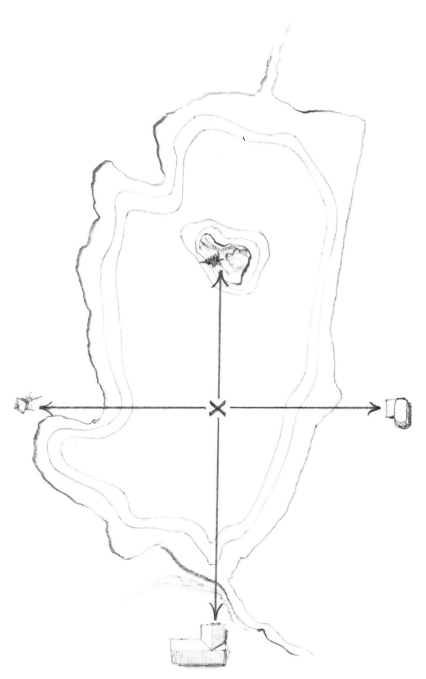

When a hot spot is located in a lake, mark it for future reference by lining up four landmarks and jot down the position in a notebook.

280

typical stream mouth note that, while area *A-A* seems to be the correct place to fish, actually the water flows too fast there, and the fish lie under the lip where they can rest in moderate flow in area *B-B*.

The suggestion therefore is to start fishing a stream mouth quite far out, and to let the lure sink deep; then gradually work in closer. When describing the northern brook in our Geological Survey Map, I noted that the fish lie under a very pronounced lip, or drop-off, quite far from shore. Such drop-offs are common in stream mouths and fish usually lie under them, especially when the lake's surface is broken by the current or when the current in the stream is swift.

The previous chapter explained how deep lakes become stratified in summer and why fish seek the coolest water they can find at or near the thermocline level where food also is present. While some species roam in schools at this level far out into the lake, most of them stay at this level where it meets the edge of the lake. In many cases this level may be part of the bottom of the lake, or on or near submerged ledges.

Top view and profile of stream mouth. Water at A-A is too fast and shallow to provide good holding places for fish; they would be at B-B, under the lip in moderate flow.

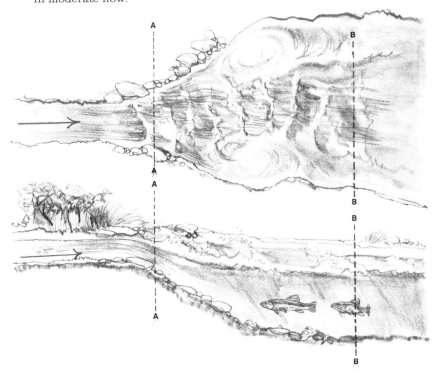

LEDGES AND POINTS

Underwater ledges nearly always are hangouts for fish; near the surface in spring and fall, and near the thermocline or the lake's bottom in summer. Some ledges show parts of themselves above water as a string of islands, or perhaps as an island or two outward from a point of land. Other ledges may be less obvious, and only may be found when a trolled lure becomes snagged in a place where the water is supposed to be deeper. Ledges should be charted and their underwater depths determined whenever possible because they are valuable fishing areas.

Rocky or weedy points extending into lakes usually provide good fishing especially when they shelve off deeply. When casting from shore, lures are cast out and allowed to sink, the object being to retrieve as close to the bottom as possible; fishing around the point until the area has been covered. In southern lakes these grassy or weedy points often harbor large bass, and probably panfish, which can be fished for more effectively from boats. The boat is anchored far enough off the point so the lure can be cast into the grass and allowed to sink to skirt the bottom. Weedless plastic worms often are used and made to "crawl" slowly along the bottom. The boat is moved from time to time until the area all around the point has been explored.

THE PATH OF MAXIMUM PRODUCTIVITY

In lakes having a thermocline the path of maximum productivity either in stillfishing or in trolling is at or near where the thermocline touches land of one sort or another. Note the copy of a state fish and game department map. The State of Massachusetts provides such maps for all its important ponds and lakes and, presumably, many other states do also. Anglers who can obtain them can use them to improve their fishing. For example, let's assume that a temperature probe shows the thermocline in this small lake to be at a depth of between 20 and 30 feet. I have marked areas of this depth range on the map. Trolling near bottom in summer along these "paths of maximum productivity" should be far more productive than fishing anywhere else. These also are the areas where baits or lures should be fished just off the bottom.

Typical map of a lake provided by some fish and game departments. Paths of best trolling in summer are indicated by shaded areas.

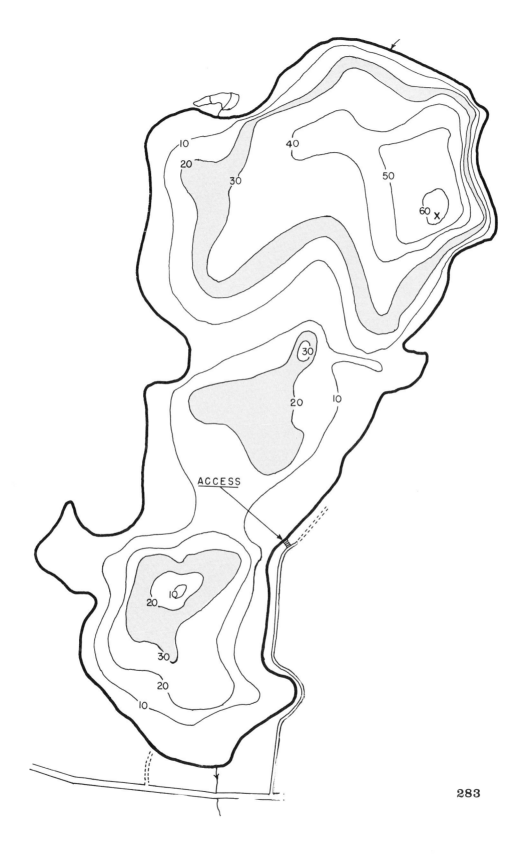

10
20
30
40
50
60 X

30
20
10

ACCESS

20 10
30
20
10

283

In addition, the map shows a deep hole at top right; a shallower hole near the center, and a ledge at the 10-foot level near the bottom. The two holes should be productive at other times, such as for ice fishing, and the ledge could be a hot spot for perch and other pondfish at any time of year. These hot spot areas only cover about 25 percent of this pond or lake, but we now are learning that they should be the productive areas and that it probably is a waste of time to fish anywhere else (except for pondfish) under summer conditions.

FISHING SOUTHERN LAKES

Since we know that cooler water sinks below warmer water under iceless conditions we have the key to fishing lakes which are too shallow to have a thermocline. The key is to fish the bottom, especially where brush piles or other protection exist, or where cooler water such as is provided by springs and entering streams can be found.

Many southern lakes are too warm for trout, but bass, crappies and other warm-water sportfish find that they provide ideal temperatures and vast areas of protection. Such places may be expanses of dead trees (where one

Cypress knees and grasses, as in this southern cove, provide ideal protection and feeding areas for many species of fish.

Edges of weed beds and grassy shorelines in southern lakes are best spots for finding largemouth bass.

should cast very closely to the roots of stumps), underwater brush piles, and the grassy points of land which have been discussed. Places offering shade also often are productive, such as is afforded by stone retaining walls, docks or swimming floats.

A great many southern lakes are man-made impoundments. While some are deep, generally they are shallow, often containing bayous, swamps, sloughs, potholes, stumps, vast reedy expanses, rafts of hyacinth and other growths. Often these lakes are drained by canals.

Anglers seeking largemouth bass find them most often in shallow, weedy lakes and river backwaters; places like the vast slowly flowing river of grass called the Everglades. Largemouths spawn in the late spring. In northern lakes they are in the 2- to 4-pound range, rarely exceeding 10 pounds, or so. The Florida bass is a subspecies which grows much bigger; usually in the 5- to 10-pound class but occasionally hefting as much as 15 pounds, or more. This relative of the largemouth spawns all during the year and has the same residential characteristics as the largemouth. In general, both are found along grassy shorelines or in or near the edges of weed beds.

Surface weedless lures are popular for fishing the weedy flats because there is more plant life under the surface than shows on top. During very hot weather the fish go to deeper water, only frequenting the weedy flats in late evening or early morning. These flats usually are shallow enough to be wadable but they often contain excessive algae growth, which can foul lures and lines.

Edges of hyacinth beds, which look like good places, usually are not as good as they look. They often grow so luxuriant that they have to be poisoned, and the resulting sludge on the bottom can ruin the fishing. It is well to check them, if convenient, but they are not as reliable as other forms of cover.

Thus, in southern fishing for largemouths, favorite areas are in and along the edges of weed beds. Potholes should be productive wherever they can be found. Other excellent places include fishing around stumps and cypress knees in the swamps and in oxbows or bayous offering protective places such as have been described.

SOUTHERN RIVERS AND CANALS

In these areas short rivers, which often are drainage canals, are so much a part of the shallow lakes that they should be included here. They often contain masses of lily pads, which are known as "bonnets," growing in clusters and bands of varying widths some distance from the shoreline. The open water between the shore and the bonnets usually is excellent for all kinds of gamefish. Inside the pad lines the water usually is not over 6 or 8 feet deep, but it may be deeper on the other side of the line. Bluegills (bream) are found in the pads or on the edges of them. Schooling bass often will chase baitfish close to the lines on either side.

Flood control or drainage canals connect many southern lakes; some being dammed where they flow into salt or brackish water. Thus saltwater fishing for baby tarpon, snook and other saltwater species can be enjoyed on one side of the dam and freshwater fishing for bass and pondfish can be had on the other. Some of these freshwater flood-control canals contain dense stands of cattails, sawgrass, lily pads and other forms of vegetation. The canal may be quite deep, but the water may be very shallow on the marsh side; this depending on the amount of water being held by the impoundment. Across the canal from the marsh side is the dike, which usually presents a steep drop-off. The marsh side of the dike usually contains an abundance of submerged growth, in addition to what is visible on top, so such areas usually are very productive.

Another type of southern canal is that which borders a cypress swamp. Since these also contain many varieties of vegetation, they are good places to catch panfish and bass. The ideal time to fish them is when the swamp has been almost drained, thus forcing the baitfish to leave the swamp and to come into the canal. One side of the canal usually is shallow because the dike is set well back from it. The depth of water on the other side will vary, often providing places where light skiffs and airboats can work into the swamp.

Although southern regions have cold spells, it isn't nearly as necessary to pay as much attention to water temperatures there as it is in the North. Temperatures in Gulf Coast states average between 65 and 70 degrees, which is about in the middle range for the freshwater fish which provide so much sport in areas such as northern Florida and Louisiana.

WHERE TO FIND FISH IN PONDS

Ponds differ widely in what they offer to fish, but the various species of fish do not vary in what they need in them. Many large lakes contain pondlike areas, which usually are coves and backwaters bordered and sprinkled with reeds, grasses, lily pads, floating plants, stumps, rocks and other things offering protection, shade and a food supply. Since these places are more pondlike than lakelike, they will be included here.

Perhaps ponds can be classified very roughly as cold-water ones such as are found in our northern states and warm-water ones as found in the South. In between the two regions there are cool-water ones which have some of the characteristics of both. Fishermen who have done their homework can make surprisingly accurate guesses as to the species of fish each type contains and also as to the places which should provide the best fishing. Since no book can provide more than a general solution for specific problems to be encountered, anglers fishing new areas should try to get more exact information from the local experts. Every region has its own peculiarities and its groups of indigenous specialists who think their own lures and methods are the best ones. Usually, they are the best ones, so visiting fishermen are lucky when they can learn about them.

Cold-Water Ponds

In northern regions all ponds ice-over in the winter but the summer temperatures of some may be colder than others, depending on such things as latitude, altitude, depth, and the presence or absence of springs and incoming cold-water brooks. Some may be relatively shallow, but with many underwater springs and an abundance of weeds which rarely grow very near to the surface. One such, which the author enjoys fishing, is a brook trout pond in Maine. It contains no characteristics suggesting where to fish, but many of the local anglers know the exact locations of underwater springs which are hot spots all summer. Visiting anglers usually must find these for themselves by random casting of small streamer flies or bucktails (or perhaps nymphs) on fast-sinking fly lines and long, light leaders. The trick is to lay out a long cast and to give it ample time to sink, then retrieve the fly at various speeds until the most successful method is found. If the hook doesn't pick up some weedy growth occasionally the fly isn't being fished deep enough. Many such trout ponds in Maine never are stocked, and the continued good fishing is due to the facts that only artificial flies are permitted and that motors are not allowed.

Generally, however, landmarks in such ponds suggest where to cast, such as along leeward rocky shorelines when the water is cold and near incoming brooks, or going deep, when it is warmer.

Cold-water ponds usually contain Eastern brook trout, but their clear, cold waters also are suitable for smallmouth bass. If both species ever have been in residence, one usually drives out the other, so such ponds may be either trout ponds or bass ponds, but rarely both. A distinction is that they ordinarily are relatively free from emerging weeds and lily pads and they usually do not contain an abundance of warmer-water fish such as pickerel and panfish. While surface or near-surface waters should be in the low sixties, they can be warmer when cold, deep holes, springs and incoming cold water provide areas of suitable temperatures.

Fishing a Cool-Water Pond

I make a distinction between cold-water ponds and cool-water ponds because, unlike the former, the latter have temperatures in the high sixties and into the seventies, with an abundance of shallow areas containing dense patches of emerging weeds such as cattails, grasses, lily pads and so forth. Being usually too warm for trout, they are ideal for smallmouth and large-mouth bass, pickerel and various kinds of panfish.

Since cool-water ponds, including farm ponds and many other man-made impoundments, are prevalent from our northern border down into southern regions, let's give them special attention. All have similar characteristics.

Look at the map on the opposite page. Starting from the dock at the camp on the eastern shore, we see no protection for fish around the sandy beach area, except that a bass or two may be in the shade of the swimming float. Beginning with the boat outside the 10-foot contour, the first casts are made as close to the lily pads as possible, and into the open water between their patches. Small floating-diving plugs should be good here, as well as spinners and wobbling lures. This looks primarily like pickerel water because there are no deep spots nearby where bass can rest when surface waters are warm.

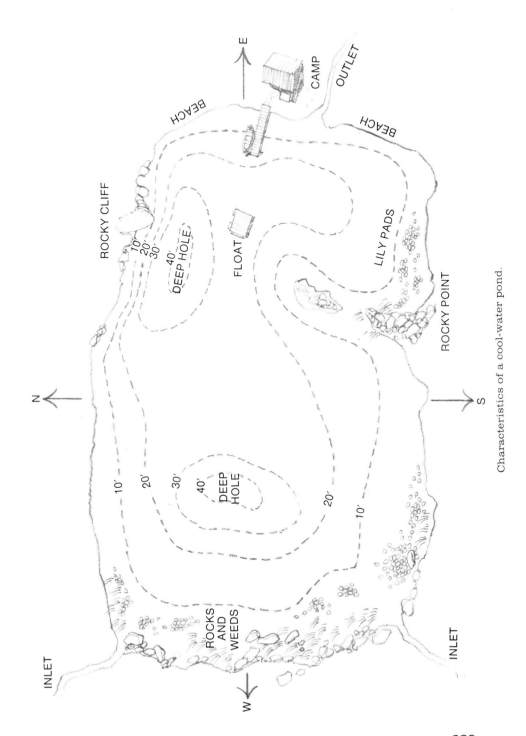

Characteristics of a cool-water pond.

The rocky point and the island suggest that a ledge runs between them. Grassy areas around the point should be carefully covered, and one rod could be rigged with a weighted plastic worm for fishing along the bottom. After touching bottom, and with slack line taken in, the worm should be retrieved with maximum slowness so it appears to "walk" down the ledge and along the bottom. When a bass strikes he should be given time to take the lure firmly but, when he decides to go away with it, it is time to strike.

After fishing around the point, the ledge, and the island, casts are made all along the pads and grasses of the western shore, and into them as far as possible. Weedless lures are good here, but it may be impractical to fish very deep on account of the weeds. Pickerel and other pondfish will strike on or near the surface all day long, and so will bass if surface waters are cool.

The brook's inlet area should be a hot spot, if it is deep enough. If no bass are taken during the daytime, most of them should be in the cooler water of the deep hole where they may be caught with lures fished deep. We may not know the deep hole is there, but we should be able to guess at it and to confirm the guess by lowering a temperature probe.

All this wide and deep weedy area should provide excellent fishing. If bass don't take here during the warmth of the day they are sure to come in to feed after sundown and to remain all night until the next day's sun warms the surface water and sends them back into the deep holes.

After fishing the northwestern inlet we note nothing of special interest until we come to the deep water under the rocky cliff. Dead trees have fallen from the cliff from time to time and are criss-crossed in a jumble in and around the deep hole. This is an example of excellent smallmouth bass water, and weedless lures fished deep should do the trick if the bass do not become frightened by noises in the boat and by careless casting. If we bungle the job we can drift over the spot and look down into the clear water to see what we have missed! Very probably fissures in the ledge drain cold water down from the land above, thus making a spot like this even better for summer fishing.

If dead trees and stumps are in shallow water the protection of their roots makes them favorite spots for bass. Bluegills (bream) and other panfish like quiet, weedy water and often are found in the shadow of docks and other places providing overhanging shade. Muddy and weedy bottom affords a haven for bullheads. Lures and baits for these were discussed in Chapters 4 and 5.

Cool-water ponds provide excellent fishing, sometimes on or near the surface, and sometimes down deep, in the parts where protection and suitable water temperatures exist. Rocks, stumps and aquatic growths also harbor food, so fishermen look for these places, to the exclusion of others, for the best fishing.

Warm-Water Ponds

Since warm-water ponds are in southern regions they usually do not freeze over in winter, and they maintain fairly constant temperatures of between 60 and 75 degrees all year round. Some ponds (and lakes) in the South are shallow, with great clumps of grasses; others are deep and sprinkled with stumps, cypress knees and brush piles. A favorite southern species is the crappie, or calico bass, which prefers the substantial protection of submerged logs, brush piles, wharfs and rock bars. In many southern ponds and lakes these brush piles are very obvious, distinguished by patches of dead brush appearing above water, with a jumble of their lower parts going down 10 feet deep, or so. Obviously this is a place for weedless lures, and a large supply should be taken along. Weighted plastic worms fished very slowly on the bottom are favorites. Crappies also frequent isolated patches of pads and weeds growing on a sandy bottom. The big ones usually are taken in deep water.

In Louisiana and other states bordering the Mississippi River we find a different kind of warm-water pond; shallow areas which receive backwaters from nearby rivers when they are in flood. Many of these are hard to locate from boats because access to them from the river may not be navigable, or may be imperceptible. However, these backwater ponds often are hot spots for largemouth bass and other fish.

16

Trolling

Previous chapters have described the characteristics of ponds and lakes, and where fish should be found in them. Now we'll learn various tricks for trolling, particularly in large lakes.

Knowing how deep to troll for different kinds of fish under various conditions, how do we get lures down there with reasonable accuracy? If we know how fast to troll, how do we determine the correct speed of the boat going with or against the wind? How can we troll deep and still handle fish on unweighted tackle? I shall repeat a few points I made in previous chapters as I explain effective methods of trolling large lakes.

MAPS: A KEY TO FISHING LARGE LAKES

When small lakes appear on maps, such as those provided by the United States Geological Survey, their depths usually are not charted, so boat owners and fishermen must learn their hazards and hot spots by experience or inquiry. Large lakes, requiring more complex navigational knowledge for boating safety, often are charted. Maps of these lakes show channels, depths and hazards. Depths are marked by a sprinkling of numbers indicating feet or fathoms. Anglers who fish a lake frequently should have a map of it that is large enough to contain the necessary information.

Lacking such a map, we can make an enlarged photograph of the best available outline map or copy a small map in a larger scale.

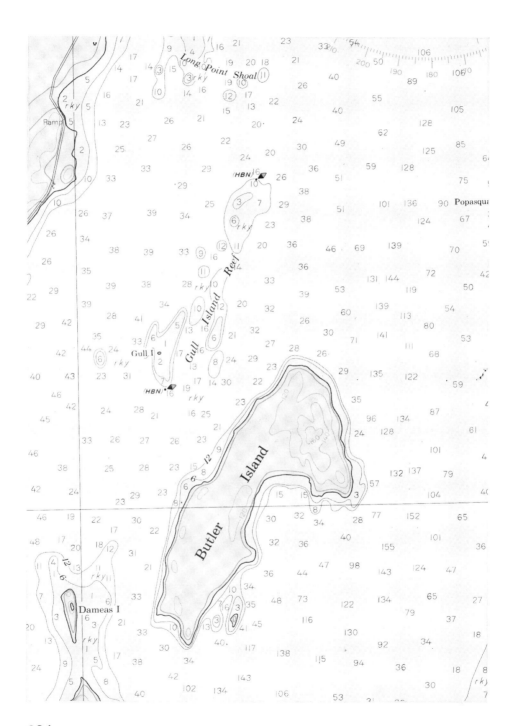

294

To enlarge a small map by copying, carefully rule in a checkerboard of grids which divide the map into small squares of a quarter inch. On a larger paper, rule in a similar checkerboard of grids which divide the paper into larger squares of an inch. Then, using the squares as a guide to accuracy, copy the outlines in the small squares onto the corresponding large squares. Thus we make a large map from a small one, with islands, points of land and all other available information carefully drawn in.

Now we need to go out in a boat and take soundings for depths, marking each on the map. While this takes a lot of time, it doesn't need to be done all at once, and friends or club members can combine to make a quicker job of it. We want to know, for example, how deep the thermocline (or "comfort zone" for fish) is. An electronic depth thermometer can locate this quickly. While thermocline levels may vary from time to time, the level in any lake stays about the same. If the level is 26 feet, for example, tie a heavy weight to a strong line of this length (plus another 3 feet or so for convenience) and move the boat slowly toward shore until the weight touches bottom. Mark this point on the map and add others until the 26-foot depth is charted wherever fishing is to be done. By connecting these 26-foot depth marks on the map we have outlined the path of good trolling.

All this is made much easier by a portable sonic instrument such as the Fish Lo-K-Tor. High-frequency sound waves penetrate the water and constantly show its depth on the dial of the instrument. Thus the device takes soundings constantly, and those we want can be marked on the map. In addition to outlining the path of good trolling, the location, depth and shape of ledges and underwater points of land should be charted. We are lucky if hydrographic or navigational maps are available, but the point to be made here is that a chart of lake depths is very important and that it's not very difficult to make our own.

If an electronic depth thermometer also is used, underwater springs and cold currents can be located and marked on the map because we know that these are hot spots in summer. While an electronic depth thermometer and a sonic depth indicating instrument add up to a considerable investment, both are valuable aids to good fishing. More uses for them will be described in this chapter.

Section of a navigational map of a large lake, with depths shown in feet. Note the depths of channels, bays and reefs—all good fishing spots. Areas of good trolling can be plotted by lines joining desired depths.

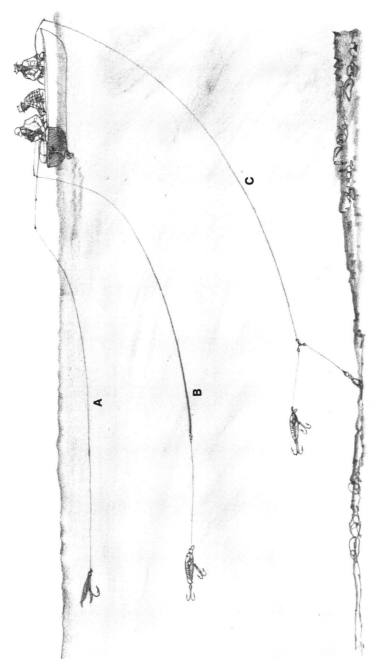

Three principal trolling methods: near surface with unweighted line (A); in the thermocline (comfort zone) with weighted line (B); bottom bumping with lead weight (C).

NEAR-SURFACE TROLLING

We have learned that when surface water temperatures are agreeable, fish should be cruising and feeding near the surface, probably along the windward shore, off stream mouths, near shallow ledges or bars, around points of land and around islands. They also may be following schools of baitfish, and concentrations of them can be located by trolling.

Whatever tackle one uses for casting generally is suitable for trolling just under the surface. When fly-fishing gear is used, the line should be a sinking one, either weight forward or level. This can be connected to between 12 and 15 feet of monofilament leader of about 8-pound test. Experts prefer dull colored leaders such as brown, and any swivels or snaps which are used also should be dull. Opinion varies as to whether the rod should be held by hand to work the lure or whether it can be put in a rod holder. If flies are used, I think constant action should be given to them, but often fish will strike anyway. If one doesn't wish to hold the rod, and has no rod holder, here's a useful trick:

Prop the rod safely and pull out some slack line. Make about two turns of this around a smooth oval stone, laying it on the deck. When a fish strikes he will upset the stone and hook himself while taking out this small amount of slack. This gives the angler time to pick up the rod.

If spinning or spincasting tackle is used, the antireverse mechanism is engaged and the brake is set lightly enough to avoid pull-out on a strike. If the lure tends to spin, one or two swivels (or a ball-bearing one) should be tied in 2 or 3 feet above the lure.

Many experts prefer baitcasting tackle for trolling, mainly because the reel allows faster retrieve and because the level-wind mechanism eliminates uneven line build-up

Streamer flies or bucktails are excellent for trolling, but what may be a hot taker one day can be a dud on another occasion. My friend Peter Sang, who makes a specialty of near-surface trolling, starts out by using three flies at once. He ties a very small, dull snap to the leader's end, and rigs three flies on 6- or 8-pound leader material, one on a 3-foot leader, one on a 2-foot leader, and the other on a 1-foot leader, each leader being looped at the end and all loops being attached to the snap. He says the rig doesn't tangle often and that fish invariably take one fly pattern to the exclusion of the others. When the best fly of the day is determined, he uses that one only; sometimes fishing two flies before deciding on one. His favorites are Governor Aiken, Gray Ghost, Nine-Three, Colonel Bates and Smelt. Trolling sizes of flies usually are No. 2 or 4 and often are dressed on long tandem hooks, the rear hook frequently being a double one.

Plastic keels to prevent line twist in light-tackle trolling: with snap-swivel
(*left*) and with plain swivel.

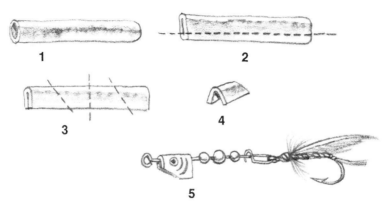

Pinch-on keels that add weight and prevent line twist can be made from
lead tubing (**1**). Flatten and cut (**2**), then cut into sections (**3**). Open for
crimping on line (**4**). Paint for use on lures (**5**).

Another type of keel that will add weight can be made from a piece of flat
lead cut to heart shape and scored down the middle (**1**), then crimped over
the line with its point toward rod (**2**).

Many wobblers and spinners will twist trolling lines, especially when they are being towed too fast. Plugs that are accurate imitations of baitfish, such as the Rapala, are very popular, particularly in small sizes not over 3 inches long. In New England the Mooselook Wobbler is hard to beat. This is a thin, elongated, fish-shaped fluttering spoon weighing a ¼ ounce or less. Rigged minnow baits are very successful, but many anglers think they are more of a bother than they are worth in comparison to the ability of selected artificials.

Trolling speed should be adjusted to suit the best action of the lure. Troll it beside the boat until this is determined, and then try to troll at that speed.

HOW TO MAINTAIN CORRECT TROLLING SPEED

Trollers often say that they catch fish when going in one direction, but none when trolling in the opposite one. If trolling speed is correct they should do well in both directions. It is nearly impossible even to approximate correct speed when going with or against the wind, or at an angle to it — impossible, that is, unless one has a speed indicator to go by.

The cheapest indicator is a 2-ounce dipsey sinker tied to a few feet of line and fastened to the side of the boat's stern where the operator can see it. To make it easier to see, dip it in a brightly colored paint such as fluorescent red or orange. See the drawings on page 300.

As the boat moves, the sinker will trail in the water at a certain distance beneath the surface, depending on the speed of the boat. When the speed giving best action to the lure is determined, notice how deep the sinker is trailing and maintain the speed which keeps the sinker at that depth. Trollers who have estimated speed by guesswork will be surprised at the variation an indicator will show when going with or against the wind or when trolling in currents. Maintaining proper speed is very important to fishing success.

Disadvantages of this cheap indicator are that it is bothersome to have to glance at it frequently, and it may be hard to see it under adverse light or wave conditions.

The bottom photo on page 300 shows a commercial speed indicator which is clamped to the side of the boat with the dial facing inboard. If you find the best speed is when the pointer points to 4, for example, troll at the speed which will keep it there.

Streamer flies are usually trolled at a speed a bit faster than a man can walk. Experiment with speed. On getting a strike, notice the speed at which the fish was hooked, and stay with it. Usually it is better to troll in a snakelike pattern than in a straight line. Speed will vary somewhat when going in a snakelike pattern, thus allowing the lure to vary in depth and allowing the boat to cover more ground.

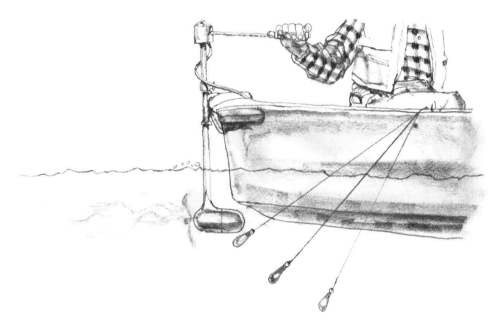

Dipsey sinker tied to a line attached to the boat's stern serves as a simple speed indicator to check correct trolling speed. Notice how deep the sinker is trailing, and maintain speed to keep it at that depth.

Commerical boat-speed indicator clamps to the side of the boat, registers actual speed on the dial regardless of currents and wind.

Weather has a pronounced effect on the success of near-surface trolling. An overcast sky, particularly before or after a weather front, is ideal; so is a steady drizzle. A mild wind is helpful because a choppy surface is better than a flat one. When the surface is glassy it pays to work the lures a bit deeper.

CORRECT ROD POSITIONS FOR TROLLING

A person trolling alone usually uses any rod position that suits his convenience. Fishing the lure just behind the boat's wake often is the most successful method. Most fish are not afraid of a motor or a wake; in fact, they often come up to see what's going on. When a second person is aboard, his rod should be held at a right angle to the boat's direction, mainly to keep the two lures as far apart as possible. He would take one of the outer positions, as shown in the illustration, and a third person would take the opposite one.

When three rods are trolling near the surface the middle lure travels just behind the boat's wake, partly because this is a good position, but also because the boat's operator should be able to get his line in quickly when someone has a strike so he can handle the boat to best advantage. The outer rods troll at longer distances, between 50 and 60 feet, one using a longer line than the other. One also should use a deeper trolling lure than the other. To start with, a variation in lures helps to decide which is the lucky one; for example, a streamer fly, a light wobbling spoon, and a small plug imitating a baitfish.

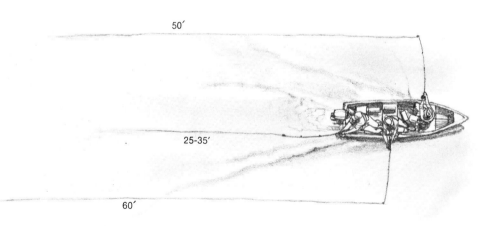

50′

25-35′

60′

Trolling near the surface with three rods.

When one rod hooks a fish, the other lines are taken in immediately to avoid tangles, unless the person who has hooked the fish suggests otherwise. When the lures get into a school of fish the first person to get a strike often asks the others to keep on fishing so they can share in the fun. Two or three fish on at the same time add to the excitement. The nearest fish should be brought aboard first and the others can be handled lightly until this is done to keep the action separated. These rod positions usually apply to trolling at any depth.

In letting out trolling line strip out 2- or 3-foot lengths, carefully at first to avoid overrunning the reel and because fish often strike close to the boat.

Birds such as hawks or gulls wheeling and diving in a group usually indicate that a school of baitfish is being driven up by big fish feeding below. Look for bird action as an indicator of fish action. If a school of fish is spotted near the surface the boat should circle it. Running directly into the school is sure to put the fish down.

MID-DEPTH TROLLING

When surface water is too warm, fish go deeper, to the level or comfort zone each species prefers. This probably is in or near the thermocline stratum; the exact depth can be determined by using an electronic depth thermometer. Although fish may be cruising away from places where this depth touches the sides of the lake and its reefs, bars and islands, these are the most likely places to find them. This may be termed "bottom fishing," but it is not really so. In bottom fishing we bump bottom intentionally because that's where the best fishing is supposed to be. In fishing the comfort zone (or ideal temperature level) for whatever species of fish we are seeking, it is accidental, because the fish are presumed to be at a higher level. Thus, even though we may snag lures occasionally, we aren't doing so on what actually is the lake's bottom. Mid-depth trolling is comfort zone trolling, and the closer we hit the level preferred by the kind of fish we seek, the better our luck will be.

Tackle and Rigging

The suggestions which follow are not for experts, each of whom is wedded to specific kinds of gear and favorite methods, but even these specialists may find something of interest. They are for fishermen more or less unacquainted with deep trolling who want a sensible way to start. After that, as they become more experienced, they can adopt variations of their own.

Fly rod. There is a way to use a fly rod and get light lures down deep which provides the enjoyment of playing fish on light tackle unencumbered by metal lines and heavy weights. It may be news, even to some of the experts. Lightweight lures are essential because those providing a lot of drag won't work.

The fiberglass fly rod should be between 8 and 9 feet long, with between stiff and medium action; the more backbone, the better. The fly reel need not be expensive, but it must have large capacity, such as the Pflueger Medalist Number 1498. This should hold about 100 yards of 20-pound test Dacron backing plus 100 yards of 18-pound-test nylon lead-cored deep-trolling line (10 colors of 10 yards each) to which is attached about 100 feet of about 15-pound-test monofilament spinning line. To the end of this attach a leader about 6 feet long of 10-pound-test monofilament (preferably dyed brown); the latter being mainly to protect the rest of the line in case one has to break loose.

Lures can be those mentioned for near-surface trolling, or a streamer fly and spinner combination, but the spinners (one or two) must be small enough to prevent excessive drag.

This combination gets the lure down as deep as necessary, but the idea is that, when the lead line has been reeled in, the fish can be played on the monofilament, unencumbered by weight. Many anglers use only 50 yards (5 colors) of the lead-cored line because this gets them down to 25 feet or so, which may be all that is necessary, and it allows them to use more backing. The drag on the reel is set as lightly as possible because the movement of the boat will set the hook and the tackle will not be damaged when the lure becomes snagged.

Multiplying reel. For deep trolling, a multiplying reel should have a capacity of at least 200 yards of line with a gear ratio of 3 to 1 or more for fast line recovery. It can be filled with lead-core line and backing as previously described, or with a wire line such as .016 or .022 monel or the Williams Gold Refining Company's stainless surgical steel line. While not always used, the 100 feet or so of terminal monofilament is very helpful and provides more fun when the fish is brought to the surface. Most anglers agree that, in any case, the final few feet should be a leader of slightly weaker brown monofilament and that, if any snaps or snap swivels are used, they should not be bright ones. There may be a few occasions when stronger line than that mentioned may be necessary, but the occasions would be unusual ones.

The colors on lead-core line, plus the length of the monofilament, indicate how much line is out. After a fish has been taken, the same amount

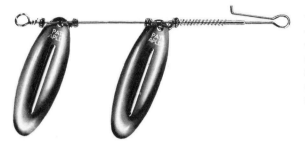

Williams Firefly spinner is note-worthy because it has flat, rather than concave, blades. A stabilizing crease causes the blade to revolve rapidly nearly at a right angle to the shank, providing a sonic buzz that attracts fish by sound as well as flash.

can be let out again. Monel lines can be equipped with length markings by adding a tiny drop of solder every 10 yards. These can be counted as the line slips between thumb and finger while being payed out.

Multiplying reels can be used on a medium-heavy spinning or bait-casting rod, but a boat rod may be required for large reels.

Loring Dodge, a Canadian friend, makes a specialty of deep trolling for lake trout and rarely returns without his limit of big ones. He has best luck on a fly and spinner combination. Anglers up there consider red, white and yellow the most productive color combination in streamer flies for lake trout. Here is his favorite pattern, which has been called the

DODGE LAKER
Hook size: 4/0 bronzed, long-shank
Tail: 3 neck hackles, 1 inch long, dyed fluorescent red
Body: Thick chenille, dyed fluorescent yellow
Wing: Fluorescent white bucktail, extra long
Topping: Fluorescent red bucktail, slightly shorter
Head: Well built-up, finished off with fluorescent red floss
Cheeks: Jungle cock (optional)

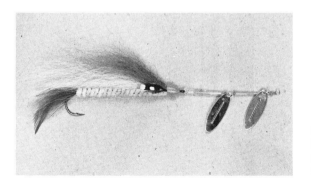

Williams Firefly spinner with the Dodge Laker bucktail fly (4/0 long shank) are an effective combination for trolling for lake trout.

While it has been noted that flies should not contain much fluorescent material, this amount seems to be successful in this case because the fly is fished very deep.

Loring trolls the fly on a large 2-bladed gold Williams Firefly spinner and says he and his friends know that the fast-revolving buzzing blades attract fish. He insists that leaders must be dyed brown and that the more energetically the rod is worked the more fish will be produced.

Downrigger trolling. Lures or bait can be trolled at an exact depth with this method without using metal lines or weights on the tackle. An outrigger is an extended pole allowing near-surface lures to be trolled outward from the wake of a boat. Owners of boats large enough for outriggers need no information on their uses. A downrigger is a heavy weight lowered by a rope or cable. The line is clipped to the weight, and the line can then be trolled at a predetermined depth. Downriggers can be homemade or can be purchased.

The drail-like or ball weight must be heavy enough to hang almost straight down while being trolled, and it sometimes is more or less jig shaped to prevent turning and line twist. Any roundish piece of iron or lead weighing 10 pounds or so can be used if two connections can be made to it. A rope or cable is attached at its top. This is marked in yards for lowering the device to the desired depth. A screw-eye, or something similar, is attached to the rear, and a strong, light cord is affixed to this. The other end of the cord is tied to an outrigger pin or some other kind of a quick-release device strong enough to hold the fisherman's line.

If the comfort zone of whatever fish we seek is at 25 feet of depth, for example, the rope or cable would measure 25 feet from waterline to weight and it would be fastened to the boat so that amount could be let out by hand or by a winch. The angler can use any kind of unweighted line with any tackle he desires. He pulls line from the reel and clips it to the snap 20 feet or so from the lure. With the boat in motion the weight is lowered over the side so the lure is being towed properly. The angler keeps releasing line while the weight is lowered. He then sets the reel's brake at moderate tension; rests the rod in a holder, or somewhere else, and relaxes until something happens.

When a fish strikes the lure he hooks himself and pulls the line from the release device, whereupon the angler handles his fish on tackle unencumbered by weight.

A big advantage of this is that the lure is being trolled at a predetermined depth all the time. Disadvantages are that the angler doesn't hook his fish himself, and that no added action can be given to the lure. Thus, lures should be used that make added action unnecessary.

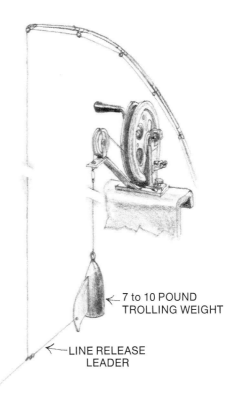

Downrigger trolling device lowers lure and line to the exact depth desired. The line is clipped to a quick-release trigger attached to a weight. A strike detaches the line from the weight, allowing the fish to be fought freely on unweighted tackle. *Below*, the device, made by Riviera, Inc., is shown in operation.

← 7 to 10 POUND TROLLING WEIGHT

← LINE RELEASE LEADER

 ← LURE

While a makeshift downrigger device may do to get acquainted with the method, a commercially made one is better, particularly when fishing very deep, as we may have to do for such fish as salmon and lake trout in the Great Lakes. The makeshift one may require too much rope or cable and too much weight for efficient and comfortable operation. For this reason, and mainly for use on big boats, downriggers available commercially usually include winches fastened to the boat. The reel or windlass of the device measures a known amount of monel line, such as 2 feet, with every turn. Thus, to lower the weight to 25 feet would require 12½ turns of the reel. Such devices are commonly used in saltwater fishing when catches can be made only by going deep.

TROLLING OVER THE BOTTOM

Fish often lie on or very near the lake's bottom because water is coldest there and as close as they can get to their comfort zone temperature. This calls for bottom bumping—perhaps not the most desirable method, but possibly the only one that will get results. Any suitable tackle can be used, but boat rods with multiplying-action service reels or 3/0 to 6/0 saltwater reels are preferable. Unweighted braided lines are satisfactory if the weight will get them down to bump bottom. Monel or stainless-steel lines (with or without 100 feet or so of strong monofilament) are popular. While care must be taken to prevent them from kinking they provide a minimum of water resistance. Lead-cored lines and backing with terminal monofilament are favored by many.

Regardless of choice of line, the terminal end is attached to a 3-way swivel. The weight—a bell or dipsey sinker of 2 ounces or heavier—is attached to the swivel with a foot or so of monofilament testing about half the breaking strength of the line. Thus, if the sinker becomes snagged, it can be broken off. (This suggests carrying plenty of sinkers in various weights.) The lure also is attached to the swivel by 6 feet or so of monofilament testing only slightly less than the line's breaking strength. For example, when using a 30-pound-test line, the leader to the lure could test about 20 pounds and the one to the sinker only about 6 pounds.

Lures for such a rig could include a 6-inch baitfish rigged to revolve slowly, the spinner and fly combination previously mentioned, or a plug. I like a floating plug of the Rapala type because it is a good baitfish imitator and because a floater will ride far enough above the bottom to prevent frequent snagging. The sinker holds it down, but its buoyancy keeps it off the bottom.

When the lure is out, you must feel the lead bouncing bottom. If you don't feel it, the lure may not be trolling deep enough, so a heavier lead should be used. Experiment with leads to select the lightest one that will bump bottom. When you feel the lead bump bottom, pull up on the rod to give the lure sort of a leapfrogging action. Thus the lead is made to bounce over the bottom, with added action being imparted to the lure. This kind of fishing necessitates getting snagged occasionally. Old hands at the game maintain that, if one doesn't get hung up often, he isn't fishing deep enough.

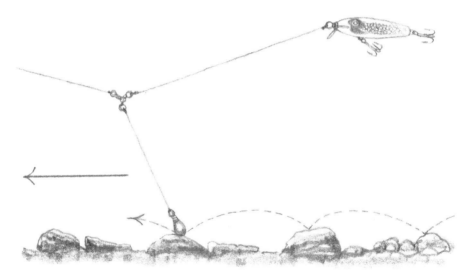

Bottom-bumping trolling rig to prevent losing lures. Dipsey sinker on a light 12-inch leader bumps bottom and keeps the lure down, but if sinker snags it can be broken off and the lure saved.

If the reel's brake isn't set too tightly, a suddenly snagged lure shouldn't strain or break the tackle. Stop the boat and *back it* over its former course. When you are over the lure or just back of it, steadily increasing tension should pull it free. If the boat circles, this only serves to wind the line around other obstructions, creating a bad mess. Jerking the lure rarely does any good. In the rare cases when backing over it won't pull it free, the answer is to lock the reel brake, regain all line possible, and then apply slowly increasing tension until something gives. Usually the lure will pull free, perhaps with a bent hook. This can be straightened with pliers and the barb can be touched up with a small file or a sharpening stone.

A NOTE ON LAKE TROUT

Lake trout may be near the bottom around midday, but they have a habit of working up into shoal water, in depths between 10 and 20 feet, toward evening to feed. Shoals and reefs can be hot spots for other fish, especially at that time. If contours of such places are known, it often is productive to circle them, first starting well out in deeper water and trolling in smaller circles as the shoal is approached. Conversely, early in the morning, fishing close to shoals should be good, but it usually is best to work into deeper water as noon approaches. We have noted that a way to locate shoals and sunken bars is to tie a 4-ounce sinker to about 25 feet of strong line and to hold this over the side while traveling at very slow speed. When the sinker hits a shoal the area can be probed for its size and shape. Then it can be sketched and lined up with four landmarks on shore so the exact spot can be found again.

HOW TO ESTIMATE LURE DEPTH WHEN TROLLING

If this were a talk before a club about fishing, instead of a book's chapter about it, someone in the back of the room now would get up and say, "All this about how deep to fish and how to locate paths of good trolling seems to make sense except for one thing. How do we know when the lure is down at the right level?"

We don't know, exactly, but let's look at a few rules and facts that should provide a fairly accurate answer. We don't know exactly because some lures troll shallower or deeper than others; because weighted and unweighted lines sink to different levels; because boat speeds vary; and perhaps because we've only guessed at how much line has been put out. Solving these various variables requires a computer.

A general rule, which isn't much good, but better than nothing, is that when a boat is going at normal trolling speed a weighted line will sink 1 foot for each 5 feet of its length. Thus, to get down to 50 feet, 250 feet of line must be out.

Everyone can solve the problem for himself by keeping a few notes, installing a speed indicator on the boat, going always the same speed, and using always the same tackle. The line should be marked for length. The length of the terminal leader is unimportant because it trolls fairly straight, but a foot of depth for every 20 feet of length could be included.

Now, let's say for example that we'd like to troll at 35 feet, which is about the average thermocline depth in medium-sized lakes. The "5 × 1 rule" just mentioned says 175 feet, or about 58 yards, or nearly 6 colors of line, should be put out. For the experiment we'll troll toward shallower water until the lure catches on bottom. Measure the depth with a marked plumb line or an electronic instrument. Let's say the depth is 30 feet. To get 5 feet more of depth we start again, but add (5 × 5) 25 more feet for a total of 200 feet, or about 67 yards, or about 6⅔ colors. We get hung up again, measure the depth, and find it is 34 feet. So we know that trolling with that line at that speed requires about 205 feet of line, or nearly 7 colors, to reach 35 feet of depth later on. With these 3 figures, and perhaps some others from time to time, we can plot a graph which will tell us how much line to put out to reach any desired depth.

Changing lures makes very little difference because fish won't all be exactly at the same depth, and they will go up or down a bit to take a lure. If we are correct to within a few feet, it should be enough. Speeding the boat will make the lure rise and slowing it down will make it drop, so maintaining the correct speed is important. At the instant of a strike the speed should be checked, because this is valuable to our calculations. Even if it is a bit high or low, it evidently is the correct one for the time being.

Since it's very easy to forget or confuse things worth remembering, carrying a fishing notebook helps save facts and is fun for later reference. When and where did we catch the big one? What were the weather conditions and what lure was used? What was the exact trolling speed, and how much line was out? A five-year diary is even better because it provides day-to-day comparisons of previous experiences with newer ones.

HOW INSTRUMENTS FIND FISH

Earlier in this chapter I mentioned the Fish Lo-K-Tor as a means for charting lake depths and locating underwater bars. (This and other electronic devices were described in Chapter 13.) Having now learned how to troll at various levels, you may be interested to know more about these modern instruments for finding fish. This is one of several instruments of the same type, but it is the one with which I am best acquainted. While there are models for fixed mounting on big boats, most of you will want the transportable one with a battery that can be recharged at home.

In operation, this portable sonic device sends high-frequency sound waves down in a cone-like path through the water to a depth as great as 300 feet. When these waves hit anything they bounce back, and the depth of what they hit is recorded on the dial in narrow or wider light bands, these varying in size according to whatever is being scanned. Since the bottom takes in the entire circle of the cone, it is indicated by a wide band. If there are fish cruising over the bottom their shapes take up less than the entire area of the cone, so these are indicated by a thinner band, or bands, on the place on the dial denoting their depth. A bit of experience with the instrument and the simple instructions for using it help to determine the sizes, quantity and depths of fish very accurately.

As we cruise along, a slowly moving band on the dial records the depth of the bottom, so this can be charted if desired. Suddenly the band of light says we are over an underwater bar, and a bit of circling tells how big and how deep it is. As we move off the bar small bands above the one which indicates bottom depth appear. This says that we are over fish. The size and position of the bands tell instantly whether this is a school of baitfish, or one or more big ones. Narrow bands over a wide one may say some big fish are under the school of bait, and perhaps feeding on them. The locations of the bands on the dial tell whether or not it is practical to stop and fish with spinning tackle or bait; where we should cast, and how deep the lures should go.

In trolling, even more valuable opportunities present themselves. Let's suppose we are trolling at 30 feet when the Lo-K-Tor's light band marks a few big fish at 40 feet. We promptly let out 50 more feet of line so the lures will troll at the level of the fish. The light band indicating the fish has disappeared from the dial but we know the lures are approaching them, so rods are picked up and we get prepared for strikes. If the strikes don't occur, at least we know the fish have seen the lures and that we ought to change them. We find fish electronically and can try for them, instead of fishing blind. While instruments like these are expensive, they pay for themselves in fish and in fun.

Well-equipped anglers own both the Fish Lo-K-Tor and the Fish-N-Temp. The latter is a temperature probe that measures depth and the temperature at that depth. Its most important use is to determine how far down the thermocline is, or the comfort level of specific kinds of fish. The Fish Lo-K-Tor can't take water temperatures, but it is a constant depth reader which makes lowering and raising a depth probe unnecessary. It is an amazingly accurate "bird dog" for finding fish.

TROLLING IN STREAMS

Casting is the favored method of fishing from a boat that is anchored or slowly drifting down a stream. Most streams have alternating deep holes and thin stretches, but some are uniformly deep, without obvious hot spots. In these the canny troller often finds big fish, partly because he can cover more ground while enjoying fishing the lazy way. Even when streams are narrow, the turbulence of outboard motors doesn't seem to bother fish; in fact, it may wake them up to see what's going on.

Sometimes surface trolling works well, but usually going as deep as possible is better, especially when streams are cold. Then, a small-diameter lead-cored line and a fairly long, dull-colored leader should be ideal, with a few split shot on the leader of an unweighted line a good substitute.

Streamer flies are favorites, and may do better with a worm on the hook. Try a small spinner or two trailed by a baited hook on 6 inches or so of monofilament. A universally popular lure is a very small red-and-white-striped Dardevle, or a small, narrow and thin wobbling spoon. Small surface-diving plugs often get results, and may be necessary on streams having frequent obstructions on the bottom.

Slow trolling, usually at a speed only slightly faster than the current, pays off best because the stream's currents add action to the lure. A fairly long rod can help to steer the lure through deep channels and pools, close to rocks, and into the shady protection of undercut banks.

The length of the trolling line must be adjusted to conditions — shortened when going around bends and let out enough on straight stretches to work the lure as deeply as seems prudent.

17

How to Find Fish in Streams and Brooks

A skill that distinguishes the expert angler from the novice is the ability to find fish in streams and brooks. We will start with the trouts because they are most prevalent in such places in most parts of the United States. Knowing the preferences of trout helps in catching many other species whose individual peculiarities will be dealt with as we go along.

EDGES, AND WHY FISH SEEK THEM

Trout usually lie near the edges of currents and in protected areas of relatively quiet water where there is moderate flow. While they *may* be in the very fast water or in the dead water of streams, this is so unusual that we can dismiss it as a probability. Although the various species of trout have slightly different water preferences they can be lumped together to start with. Rainbow trout like water a bit faster than brook trout, and brown trout generally prefer it a bit slower, but for all general purposes there isn't very much difference.

What are the edges of currents? A way to find out is to put on boots or waders and to stand knee-deep in fairly fast water, facing upstream. Trout usually lie facing that way. If you put a hand on either side of your boots, you'll notice that the water will be very fast. But if you put your hand in front of or behind a boot, the water will be much slower. There will be an area of quiet water just above and below the boot. Notice that between the

313

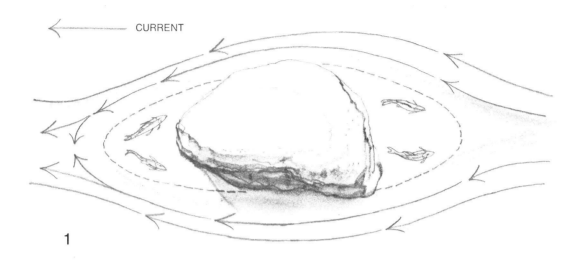

CURRENT

1

Quiet water above and below a midstream rock, just inside the edges formed by the current, is a favorite holding position for trout. Figure I, top view, shows fish lying near the edges (dashed lines). Figure 2, side view, shows how current is forced upward to pass over the rock, with quiet areas (inside dashed lines) above and below it.

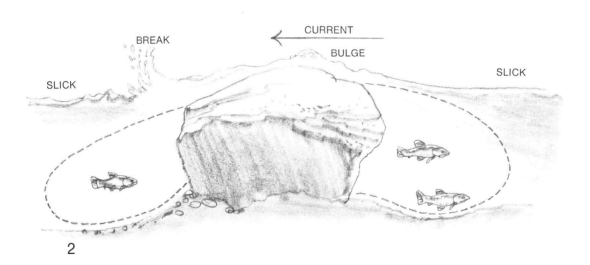

BREAK

CURRENT

BULGE

SLICK

SLICK

2

fast water and the quiet water the current makes sort of a streak, which separates the two. This is the *edge* of the current. Since it usually requires too much exertion to hold in the fast water, fish habitually lie just inside the edge, where they can rest and at the same time can see food drifting down to them. If they dash out to gather the food, they will return to the area just inside the edge.

The larger the rock or other obstruction, the longer is the edge, and the more quiet water there is between the two edges trailing downstream from the rock. A small obstruction, such as a football-sized boulder in a small stream, may have edges that can accommodate only one small trout, or perhaps none. A very large obstruction could accommodate several. If you catch a fish in such a place, try it again later on, because other fish will take the same position after it has been vacated. Desirable edges can harbor large fish because bigger ones will drive smaller ones from them.

The drawing shows such a position beside a rock in a fast stream. Looking down upon the rock, as in Fig. 1, we see that the current divides to flow around the rock. The dashed lines indicate the edges, and there are areas of quiet water in between them which provide resting places, or "holding positions" for fish.

Fig. 2 shows that the current not only divides to flow around the rock, but it also is forced upward to pass over it, if the rock doesn't extend much above water. Thus, the holding positions above and below the rock more or less resemble a cone of quieter water. Of the two, the one below the rock usually is the best one. Fast streams normally sweep out depressions on the upstream and downstream sides of the rock; these usually being deeper on the upstream side because the stream's force is greater there. Fish like to lie in the quiet flow of these depressions.

Edges are found in other places in streams also. The current of a fast brook entering a river will form an edge with that of the river itself. The edge will trail downstream and outward from the mouth of the brook, and it usually can be seen as a line marking the differences in current flow. Fish will lie just inside the edge, but the rest of the water inside the edge may be too slow for sportfish, and it may take the form of a quiet eddy.

A ledge or a big rock jutting out into a stream makes a very similar edge. When a river divides to pass around an island, an edge usually is formed on the downstream side. These are prominent examples, and all should be good holding positions for fish.

WHAT'S UNDER THE FAST CURRENT?

Fish seek areas where the current's flow is moderate, but these areas may be in water that appears faster than it really is. Rocks, both large and small on the stream bottom, act as brakes to the current, so the current near the bottom usually is much slower than that on the surface. There are many depressions in the gravel where the current is still slower. These provide good resting (or holding) positions for fish. As most of the available food is near the bottom, and deeper water provides more protection, fish usually lie very close to the bottoms of streams. They may rise up to take food on the surface, as when there is an insect hatch, but it is safe to presume that they are very near the bottom most of the time. They also may be near the banks because the braking effect of obstructions along the banks reduces the force of the current there.

In shallow streams, the surface and the bottom may be so close to each other that fish lying on the bottom can see food on the surface, and rise to it. In deeper streams it usually is one thing or the other. They rarely are on top, usually are on the bottom, and almost never are in the area in between. Yet fishermen who are using sinking lures or baits usually are fishing in the area in between, and they wonder why they don't catch fish! If there are indications that fish are rising for surface food, of course surface or near-surface fishing is indicated. If that isn't so, avoid the middle layer, which usually is fishless, and make sure your flies or other lures actually scrape the bottom. While this may result in occasional hangups and a few lost lures, it is the best way to catch the big ones.

AVOID USELESS WATER

Most water in a stream can be considered fishless. In deep runs and pools the useless water is everywhere except close to the bottom, unless fish are rising to surface insects. An exception in deep pools often is the shallower tail of the pool where the water gathers speed before passing over the pool's lip. The usually smooth surface of the pool becomes disturbed by the faster current as it approaches the lip. This rough surface provides a feeling of protection for fish and, since this area is narrower than the pool itself, surface-born food tends to concentrate there. The surface water may appear to be too swift, but, as the drawing indicates, water below the surface is more moderate, and this area usually is shallow enough so fish can lie in the slower water near the bottom and still see what food is being washed down near the top.

Very flat shallow stretches, where everything can be seen on the bottom, usually are useless, particularly when the flow is slower than moderate. An exception under conditions of moderate flow is when fish may be feeding in the riffles. Dead water usually is devoid of sportfish. Polluted areas should be avoided. For example, even in rural or wild regions sawmills which dump sawdust into the stream can ruin it for fishing.

MOUNTAIN AND MEADOW STREAMS

Many mountain streams, particularly in western regions, have long, swift, shallow stretches filled with small boulders as well as some bigger ones. Since this is not good holding water it should be passed by in favor of the occasional deeper, quieter stretches. If it is fished, the usual methods include drifting and bouncing salmon eggs, worms or other bait, or wobbling spoons, along the bottom. The deeper pools, which contain bigger fish, are suitable for flies. Large ones are used, such as streamers and bucktails, or Wooly Worms, and they are allowed to sink to the bottom before being retrieved. These fast, rocky streams often contain small pools, or pockets, which may contain small numbers of large trout. In general, though, the fast water only harbors small fish. This chapter attempts to explain where to find fish, rather than how to catch them. The characters of western rivers all are so different that many varied fishing methods are used, and visitors therefore are advised to go out with local experts who can show them how it is done there.

Western meadow streams (if one type can be differentiated from the other) may be deep and placid, since they often have been dammed by beavers. Mountain streams often become meadow streams when they reach lower country, and of course the latter have more insect life than the former, thus making the types of flies which imitate insects very popular. Favorite holding water includes deep pools and areas near undercut banks and ledges. Many of these meadow streams meander so much that a few miles of their length can be contained in about a square mile area. The outside of the sharp curves often contains a deep hole, perhaps with an undercut bank, and such places as well as the riffles, glides and runs, should be fished carefully. These are not places where careless anglers usually get results. A stealthy approach and a correct cast with a suitable fly is necessary.

On the following pages are diagrams of a typical stream, with suggestions on how to fish it.

HOW TO FISH
A TYPICAL STREAM

Nearly all streams harboring sport-fish (especially trout) contain stretches similar to those shown on the accompanying diagrams of a typical stream. Some should be hot spots while others are barren, or nearly so. The angler must be able to distinguish the hot spots from the fishless stretches. The following comments apply to situations designated by letters on the diagrams:

(**A**) In this deep run bordered by undergrowth, fish usually feed on bottom, but the bottom probably is muddy and brushy. Since paths and litter indicate overfishing, we should move downstream after a few quick casts along the bridge abutments.

(**B**) Except possibly in remote areas, spots near where cars can be parked are fished too often to be productive. Fish may be near or under the dam, but currents make them hard to reach unless they are out in the pool feeding on or near the surface.

(**C**) The deep run by the ledge and the edges below the three big rocks should be productive if lures are fished deep. The eddy on the left bank and the shallow water below it probably harbor only trash fish.

(**D**) The best bet is to start at the riffle and to fish upstream on the right-hand side. If trout are lying near the tail of the pool, this method may take some without disturbing others farther up.

(**E**) By wading down the riffle, an angler can cover the edges below the rocks. He can also cover them by fishing upstream and across from spots farther

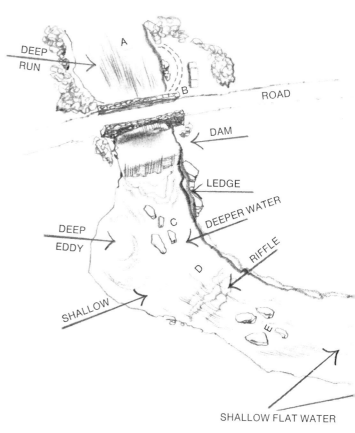

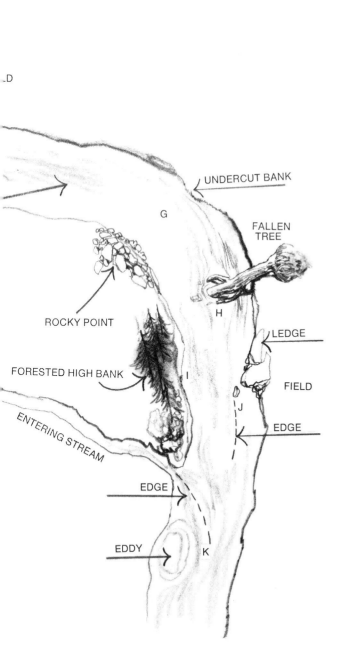

D

UNDERCUT BANK

G

FALLEN
TREE

ROCKY POINT

H

LEDGE

FORESTED HIGH BANK

I

FIELD

J

ENTERING STREAM

EDGE

EDGE

EDDY

K

down. If the water is deep, the fish usually will be lying near the bottom.

(**F**) This is shallow, flat water providing no protection. If the bottom is of gravel, fish could be feeding in the deeper stretch along the right bank.

(**G**) This deeply undercut bank provides moderate flow, shelter and food, so it should be a hot spot. When fish aren't showing, work lures deep and as far into the pocket as possible.

(**H**) Uprooted trees with branches and trunks in the water also offer ideal situations in moderate or swift flow. Trout often are under the submerged trunks and usually take lures only when they are fished within inches of the wood.

(**I**) This forested high bank provides afternoon shade. If water is reasonably deep, with a rocky or gravel bottom, fish should be in the shade near the bank. In shallow areas trout seek shady positions to the exclusion of sunny ones.

(**J**) The ledge across the stream should be productive. Fish should be lying just inside the edge, but they may be deep. The quiet water farther inside the edge is poor for sportfish.

(**K**) Since the entering stream brings food, its mouth may be a haven for trout all season long, but especially when the main stream is warm. Then, trout should run up the cooler tributary; and again, regardless of water temperature, during their spawning periods. In the river, look for them along the edge marked by the dashed line. The quiet eddy inside the edge looks unsuitable for trout, but it may harbor smallmouth bass, chain pickerel, suckers and chubs.

(**L**) Here the stream widens into shal-

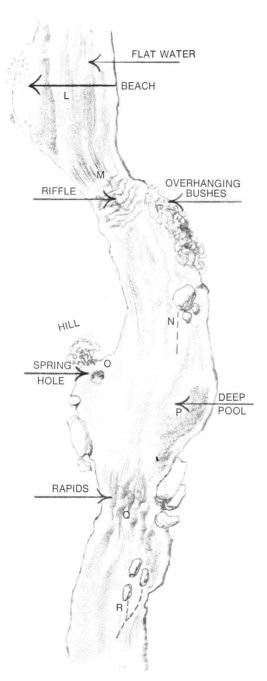

low, flat water which seems to contain no "trouty" spots. If the bottom is of gravel, trout may be feeding in the current lanes.

(M) The way to fish this riffle seems to be by wading down it, first being sure we can wade out at the lower end. Pay attention to the right bank where it is overhung with bushes, and cast as close under the bushes as possible. If current and depth on the western side are sufficient, casts can be alternated from one side to the other, covering all the water while wading down.

(N) The large rock should be fished thoroughly, perhaps by bumping bottom. The edge below the rock may be the best position, but the entire area should be productive.

(O) Just around the stream's bend, on the western shore, lush vegetation and trickling water indicate a spring hole. This should be a hot spot in warm weather. Start casts well out before working them in closer. Since cold spring water flows downstream, the short distance from the hole to the rock should be explored.

(P) Outward from the spring hole is a deep pool with many rocks, so the pool's bottom probably is rocky also. If there is no surface activity, fish lures near the bottom, using weedless ones, or weedless Keel Flies, if necessary.

(Q) Here, the deep pool's outlet is constricted by rocks. The rapids may be too fast for trout, or for effective fishing. By sinking the lure deep, the edges of the rocks here and at R could be productive.

BRUSHY BROOKS

In the Northeast we have many brooks flowing through woodlands and valleys which are so overgrown with bushes that few people bother to fish them. This is a pity because many are bonanzas for brook trout. Being a New Englander, I learned some of the secrets when very young. The first secret is not that they are there, but that they usually hold fish.

There's no sense in poking through the bushes, trying to make a cast or two, and then poking back out to see if it's any better somewhere else. The trick is to put on hip boots, get into the brook, and stay in it. Because of the bushes, a long rod is at a disadvantage. Use a short one, no longer than 6 feet. Use bait, if you wish, but tiny streamers or bucktails, or nymphs, or even dry flies in the summer, may be even better. Wear dark colored clothing that blends with the landscape. Fish slowly, quietly and deliberately.

In fishing small brooks, remember that a brook is a stream in miniature. On a big stream a rock of football size would be ignored. On a small brook a good-sized trout may be lying back of it.

Even careful wading will dislodge a stone or two, perhaps sending a small cloud of mud downstream. It may be a good idea to make this happen occasionally because trout may interpret it as a sign that part of a bank has caved in and go on the feed.

If the day is bright, fish the shadowy places. Trout often lie in the shade over a patch of dead leaves lying on the bottom. Stop often enough to read the water just ahead. Look for an undercut bank that could hold trout; a dislodged tree whose disturbed roots leave a watery hole under it; a big rock against the shore with a tiny pool behind; a little riffle making a larger pool; or any other place a sizable trout could hide.

If so, how does one get a fly or lure into the position without getting it tangled in the branches? With the short rod, a normal cast often can be made, or perhaps a miniature roll cast. If not, hold the rod out and let line through the guides, so the current can carry the lure downstream. If it sinks before getting to its target it can be pulled to the surface by raising the rod tip, thus letting the current take it down some more. When near enough to the target, a small twitch or two should start some action.

Another trick is to cut a green leaf with an inch or two of the branch connected to it. Nick the barb into the edge of the leaf and let this float the lure or bait downstream, trying to steer it to wherever it should go. If the place is a good lie for trout the current probably will take it there anyway. A twitch of the rod breaks the lure from the leaf, and another twitch or two (if it's a wet fly) should tempt a strike.

In using flies on such brooks there may not be enough room to operate small streamers and bucktails in a lifelike manner. Drifted nymphs work well, but summer favorites are natural imitations such as grasshoppers and caterpillars. My secret weapon at such times is a small, fat bee made of clipped bands of black and yellow deerhair, with brown deerhair wings.

MEADOW BROOKS

Another type of brook, too often ignored because it doesn't look like much, is the kind that flows through meadowlands. It may be well that such brooks are so often passed by in favor of larger streams, because they usually are nurseries and breeding grounds for trout.

Some meadow brooks appear to be so small that they would seem to be useless for fishing, but this often is far from the case. They can look like deep ditches, bordered perhaps by a few bushes and lusher vegetation left uncut by mowing machines, and one often can step or jump from bank to bank with ease.

Unseen below the narrow exterior may be deeply undercut banks where the stream perhaps is several times wider, and much deeper, than it would appear to be. This furnishes cool shade and protection, plus an abundance of small baitfish and quantities of caterpillars, grasshoppers, flies and other living things which fall from the foliage into the waters below. Fish live here year-round, and others come up from larger streams during spawning migrations to perpetuate their kind in the ideal and constant temperature of the gravel, unseen and unbothered except by the few adept anglers who understand this hidden secret.

Where the heavy turf of the topsoil becomes thin the banks may cave in, leaving slanted slabs of turf whose underwater nooks and crannies also are hiding places. Here and there may be a small riffle or waterfall emptying into a tiny pool, or perhaps even one quite large. But one specializes mostly on the undercut bank areas to find the biggest fish.

These places demand a quiet approach because an angler, thoughtlessly clumping along the bank, can send his echoing footfalls down to telegraph danger, thus forcing all fish to take cover. Such a man would leave the place in disgust, calling it fishless. These places demand a stealthy approach because, if the angler is seen, the fishing is done for. Experts, trying a new brook for the first time, make it a practice to stroll along it and map the good places, deciding how each cast should be made. They come back on another day and fish the brook efficiently because they know where and how to do it.

Such fishermen crawl when close to brookside, rather than walking directly to it, and they take their time. To the casual observer this may look rather silly, but it gets results. Their rods are long, rather than the short miniatures preferred for brushy streams, because some of the fishing is done by "dapping"; dropping the fly or other tiny bait time and time again onto

Undercut banks in narrow meadow brooks often conceal water that holds good-sized trout. A quiet and stealthy approach is necessary when fishing such places.

or into the brook's surface with little or no line out. Short casts also are in order, and the idea often is to flick the fly to grass overhanging the brook, and then to flick if off and into the brook as an insect would drop in. Needless to say, considerable accuracy is required. More than likely, however, a large trout, waiting below for such a tidbit, will grab it instantly.

Another way, instead of dapping or casting, is to lower the fly or bait into the brook, with the rod held high. By lowering the rod, several feet of drift can be obtained. After doing this two or three times the angler sneaks or crawls along a few feet more and repeats the process.

Meadow brooks, between one meadow and another, may turn into brushy brooks, and so can be fished a bit differently, as has been described. In general, however, a brook is either one kind or the other, and the techniques usually used on one are somewhat different from those used on the other.

Meadow brook fishing is at its best in the summer, when fish run up the cold-water brooks to escape the warmth of larger streams which are more exposed to the sun. Also, in summer, the bordering fields breed quantities of insects favored by fish for food. In flying or hopping from one place to another, these insects often land in the brook.

While some fishermen prefer to use small worms, perhaps impaled on hooks in the weedless manner, many find it more successful to use artificial flies that imitate these insects. These include imitation grasshoppers, ants, bees and caterpillars of one kind or another. The last two most often have spun deerhair bodies, clipped smooth and in natural shapes, sizes and colors.

In fishing brooks, particularly, one often has to be so close to his quarry that he wonders if fish can see him, whether or not he can see the fish. This is a question I never have seen answered satisfactorily in books.

WHEN CAN'T FISH SEE FISHERMEN?

Those who wade sandy flats to spear flounders, or who enjoy bowfishing, know that, when they aim the spear or the arrow directly at a fish, they don't hit it. They must estimate where the fish actually is in relation to where it appears to be. This is due to the principle of the refraction of light, explained by the fact that light rays bend at an angle when they pass from the air into water or from water into the air. Because of this, fish also can see fishermen even when fishermen think their silhouettes are so low they can't be seen. So when can and when can't fish see fishermen?

There are two points to consider, the first being a fish's "cone of vision." Light rays entering the water from the vertical are not refracted by the water, but all rays entering at an angle from the vertical are refracted, or bent. The greater the angle, the more they are bent until they reach about 48 degrees from the vertical. Then, light no longer is reflected back into the atmosphere, but is bent downward from the water's surface very much like the ricochet of a bullet when it is deflected by a solid object (and even by water).

Although the study of optics as it applies to refraction is complex, let's try to simplify it by referring to the accompanying diagram. Since light rays which are reflected back toward the atmosphere from below the water's surface are deflected downward at angles greater than 48 degrees from the vertical, the vision of fish is conical, the point of the cone being at the fish's eyes and extending upward and outward at a 48-degree angle to the surface. Thus the diameter of the cone at the surface is about 97 degrees, the circle of vision growing larger the deeper the fish is. The ratio is a little more than twice the diameter of the circle in proportion to the depth of the fish. Therefore, a fish at a depth of 3 feet, for example, can see through a circle on the surface which is about 6½ feet in diameter. Outside this circle, light rays are bent downward, so what a fish sees there is similar to a steely mirror reflecting the bottom, or the depths. This cone of vision is called the fish's "window."

The vision of fish is somewhat different from that of humans in that their eyes are on the sides of their heads, allowing them to see to the right, to the left, and above, at the same time. Their eyes protrude and can turn in their sockets, all this affording a very wide range of vision. Thus, unless the angler crouches down, out of sight, fish usually can see him before he sees them. An exception is when the surface is disturbed by wave or current action, but even then some vaguely seen surface motions may spook fish. Trout are particularly shy and usually won't strike if danger seems to threaten. Their blind spots are behind and below, which suggests an advantage in fishing upstream.

The second point is that when light rays enter water (in which the velocity is different) their direction is changed, or refracted. A pole driven

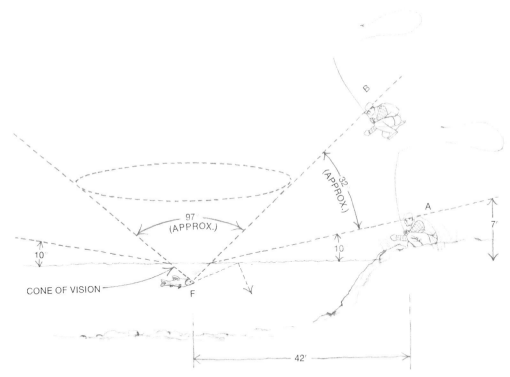

This diagram shows the limitations of a fish's vision due to the refraction of light waves on the water. The angler at *A* sees the fish at *F*, but due to light refraction the fish appears to be farther away and nearer the surface than it actually is. The fish cannot see the angler, but can see the motion of his rod. Again, due to light refraction, what the fish sees of the angler appears to be at *B* rather than at *A*.

into a lake bottom at an angle demonstrates this clearly. This refraction, or bending, forms an angle between two straight lines, the apex of which is the water's surface. The extent of refraction increases as the angle of entry or emission increases. In the diagram on page 325, we more or less correctly assume the angle of refraction to be about 32 degrees. The fish at *F*, looking upward through its window, can see far outside this cone of vision because of refraction, which widens its vision by an added 32 degrees or so, allowing it to see the rod of the angler at *A*, but not the angler himself, although he would be partly visible if he were standing. Because of refraction, the angler at *A* appears to the fish to be at *B*, but this is unimportant to us. The important thing is whether or not the angler can be seen.

Thus, if the angler is crouching below an angle of about 10 degrees from the point on the water's surface under where the fish is, he is hidden from the fish, or appears only as an indistinguishable object because he is outside the fish's window. An object 2½ feet tall at a distance of 15 feet, 5 feet at 30 feet, or 10 feet at 60 feet wouldn't be seen at water level. The simple fact is obvious: if you don't want fish to see you, you must lower your silhouette more and more as you draw closer to the water. While this is accepted as a fact, we have noted that it becomes less important when water is discolored or when its surface is broken by waves or current.

If an angler must move into a fish's vision in order to cast to it, he often can do so by approaching slowly and cautiously while keeping his silhouette as low as possible and wearing dull-colored clothes, at the same time making use of the concealment of rocks and other obstacles whenever possible. Since fish usually are concerned with feeding, they may not be spooked by a cautious approach.

When an angler does spook fish he should remember that their memories are short. After sitting quietly by streamside for several minutes, the fish may reappear and start feeding again. Then, a cautious cast without excess motion may attract them. Older fish usually are more cautious and remain spooked longer than younger ones. Of course, the angler's shadow should be kept off the water. Polarized glasses cut through surface glare and make fish and other underwater objects more visible.

WHAT DOES A FISHERMAN SEE?

Ordinarily, perhaps this isn't very important, but it may be worth mentioning. Due to the refraction of light rays entering the water, fish seen other than directly from overhead are not exactly where they appear to be and, the deeper they are, the farther they are from where they appear to be. The fisherman kneeling on the bank in the diagram on page 327 sees a fish at position *A*, but the fish actually is a bit nearer and deeper. This may not

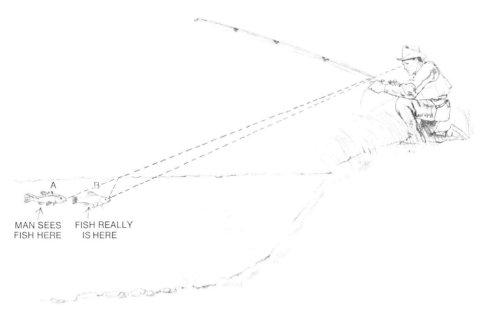

MAN SEES
FISH HERE

FISH REALLY
IS HERE

The fisherman, looking into the water from the bank, sees the fish at *A*. Actually, the fish is at *B*. Light refraction causes the fisherman to see the fish at *A*.

make much of any difference in how one casts to the fish, but it must be considered during activities such as spearing or bow-fishing.

By drawing a straight line from the angler *(A)* to the fish *(F),* we note that he can see the fish, but the fish can't see him. A standing angler, however, almost always is spotted by fish before he sees them. At best, as far as most gamefish are concerned, the most an uncautious angler can see is the flash of fish as they streak for cover. Spooked fish rarely take lures.

18

The Trouts

Whether the members of the two families called trout are more fun to catch than those of the bass families probably depends on what part of the country the opinion comes from. Anglers in the northern United States usually will opt for trout, and many of our southern friends look forward to northward trips to remote areas where they can cast for big ones on lures or artificial flies.

In the Northeast, the beautiful brook trout vies with the canny brown for being the most sought-after fish; that is, unless one has been so fortunate as to hook the true King of Fishes, the lordly Atlantic salmon. In the Northwest, the rainbow trout ranks supreme, especially when it returns to its river from the ocean as a steelhead. There, even the great steelhead is challenged by at least two species of Pacific salmon. These three, the "brookie," the "brownie" and the rainbow, are the aristocrats of the two families commonly combined and referred to as trout.

A glance at the chart on the next page will indicate that the brook trout really isn't a trout at all, but is a member of the small-scaled family of chars. This is a technical difference of small concern to the angler and so, for convenience, let's refer to all six principal species as trout. Each one of the six has very individual characteristics of appearance, size, habitat and what it prefers for food. Since understanding these characteristics is a great help in locating and in catching them, it may be interesting to learn the most important facts about each one.

CHARS AND TROUTS

CHARS[1]

BROOK TROUT	LAKE TROUT	DOLLY VARDEN
(Salvelinus fontinalis)	(Salvelinus namaycush)	(Salvelinus malma)
	also called	
Squaretail	Togue	Salmon Trout
Speckled Trout	Mackinaw Trout	Western Charr
Native Trout	Great Lakes Trout	Bull Trout
Red-spotted Trout	Forktail Trout	Sea Trout

TROUT

CUTTHROAT	RAINBOW	BROWN TROUT
or	or	or
BLACK SPOTTED TROUT	STEELHEAD (when sea-run)	LOCH LEVEN
(Salmo clarkii)	(Salmo gairdnerii)	(Salmo trutta)
	also called	
Salmon Trout	Kamloops Trout (in special cases)	
Harvest Trout	Shasta Rainbow, etc.	
Mountain Trout		
Blueback Trout		

[1] Either spelling, char or chars, charr or charrs, is correct. The derivation of the word is from the Gaelic, meaning "red or blood colored," with reference to the reddish color of the belly noted on many fish of this species.

BROOK TROUT

Called the brook trout because it is so often found in small streams, this northeastern favorite also frequents cold-water ponds, lakes and rivers, particularly in eastern Canada, where it grows to great size. The largest ever taken, which weighed 14 pounds, 8 ounces, was caught in Ontario's Nipigon River in 1916; a record which never may be surpassed. Brookies in the 10-pound range are found in remote waters such as Quebec's Broad-back and Rupert rivers and its Lake Assinica. There are so many lakes and river systems in Canada that some of the best spots probably still remain undiscovered. These trophy fish usually have to be hunted, with the right lure presented in the right way at the right time. Many such trophy fish, now reduced to wall decorations, were taken with little, if any, skill when they were over spawning beds in the fall.

In the United States, northern Maine used to be a brook trout hot spot. There are places there that still are pretty good, but a brookie of over 5 pounds is bragging size, and 2- or 3-pounders are considered very respectable. It may be interesting to note that when landlocked salmon were introduced into the Rangley Lakes and others in Maine at about the turn of the century the average size of the brook trout became greatly reduced. It takes up to ten years for a trout to reach trophy size and, in most trout waters nowadays, they are caught long before they grow that big. Large growth is dependent partly on heredity, but largely on the availability of an abundant food supply—and being left alone.

In many of these northern regions the usually white or yellowish flesh of brook trout is found to be pink, or even fairly bright red. This is due to their diet of crustacea such as copepods, daphnids (the so-called freshwater "shrimp," or scuds), crawfish and some other foods also containing red or orange-red pigments. The flesh of salmon becomes colored similarly but, for some strange reason, that of bass does not.

The brook trout quickly can be distinguished from its cousins by the brilliant red spots with blue aureoles on its sides; by the dark, wavy lines on its back and dorsal fin; by the pink or reddish lower fins with their pronounced white stripe, and by the "square" tail that lacks a distinguishable fork. As fall spawning time approaches, the bellies of the male trout are colored from orange to red, edged with black above the white. Nature gives brook trout a considerable amount of protective coloration; the backs of those which usually lie over greenish bottoms being similarly greenish, while those over muddy or gravel bottoms are correspondingly shaded from blackish to brown.

The fact that brook trout like colder water than browns or rainbows do indicates why they are native to the northeastern United States from the Arctic Circle no farther south than Georgia. However, they have been introduced to other areas with a suitable water temperature range, including parts of the Northwest. We have seen that they can't tolerate water over 68 or 70 degrees unless they have access there to cold-water streams or areas of spring seepage. Their favorite temperature is about 58 degrees. Knowing this, and that they like to be in protected areas near a food supply

Small headwater streams, clear and cold, are where the brook trout swims. Here an angler nets a splashing brookie he hooked in the shade of the overhanging bushes.

(as described in the two preceding chapters), anglers can fish in places where they should be found.

Increased fishing pressure has made it necessary to raise brook trout artificially and to plant them in streams and lakes on more or less of a "put and take" basis. Thus, those caught near heavily populated areas nearly always are stocked fish rather than the wild native trout of more remote regions. Even the wild natives are not very fussy about what they eat, and they will take a wide variety of flies, baits and lures unless they first see fishermen who have not taken the precautions of being quiet and of staying hidden outside the trouts' vision.

While brook trout are bottom feeders which usually stay on or near bottom when surface waters are warm, they are principally the game of fly fishermen. On feeding sprees they rise readily to a wide variety of nymphs and insects, as well as to earth-borne foods such as beetles, grubs, cater-pillars, ants and grasshoppers. Water-borne worms and nightcrawlers are favorite foods, especially when they appear in streams after rains. Minnows, and even the young of their own kind, are part of their steady diet.

The tip to fishermen who use natural baits is to use what they see over, on or in the water, because many natural baits vary in availability during the season. The tip to fly fishermen is to observe natural flies which are emerging at the time, and to "match the hatch" in drys or wets as closely as possible. While artificial nymphs should imitate actual ones, a reasonable representation of similar size, shape and color usually is sufficient. When in doubt, or when no aerial or terrestrial baits are in evidence, the streamer fly or bucktail should be effective. Those selected should approximate indigenous baitfish in size, shape and color, and should be fished in a lifelike manner, as we will see in Chapter 20.

Addicts of spinning or spincasting gear find that hardware works well on occasion, but let's not presume this to be a superior method for catching trout. One who understands his flies and his fly rod, or an expert in the use of natural baits, usually can beat the best in the hardware group. In using metal lures such as spinners, wobblers and spoons, favor the duller ones on brighter days and the shinier ones on dark days or when water is high and discolored. The tendency is to use lures that are too large. There are tricks of the trade in using all types of artificial lures, and these are of sufficient variety and importance to warrant separate discussion in the chapters which follow.

Brook trout spawn in the fall, beginning in September in far northern areas and as late as December in their southernmost range. At this time of year the lake fish may collect near stream mouths preparatory to running upstream when water temperatures are right. Lacking suitable streams for spawning, they will do this near the shores of lakes and ponds in protected areas of proper water temperature. At this time, when they often collect in vast numbers, they should be left alone to do what comes naturally. Too often this is not the case, and most of the spawning stock of entire lakes then can be decimated by thoughtless or greedy fishermen. Although fishing for brook trout should be good in feeder streams in the fall, the taking of a trophy male or two should be sufficient. The more drably colored females should be carefully released in the interest of maintaining the fishery.

Brook trout which have access to the ocean, or to brackish water, return upstream in the fall for spawning. Freshly in, they have a silvery appearance, and are called "salters." This sheen quickly disappears. Salters may be bigger than the average found in the area, but they may not reach the large sizes of some of the nonmigratory fish.

BROWN TROUT

The brown trout came to the United States from Europe. Contrary to general belief the first eggs brought here were from England, rather than from Germany. A gentleman named W. L. Gilbert, of Plymouth, Massachusetts, imported about 4,000 brown-trout eggs in 1882. A few hatched, and the fry were kept in a pond. While only three fish spawned successfully, this resulted in about as many eggs as were obtained originally. The hatched fish, the only brown trout in America at that time, started our brown-trout fishery.

Very shortly after the original importation a superintendent of the New York State Fish Commission arranged for an exchange which netted about 100,000 brown-trout eggs from Germany. This was followed by other importations and, after several failures and successes, the "German brown" was established in Michigan and elsewhere. (The brown trout is the common trout of the British Isles and of Europe, where it often is referred to as a "brook trout.") Other strains of brown trout were imported from Scotland, and were known as "Loch Levens." All during this time, between 1882 and about 1910, great controversy raged as to whether or not the introduction of brown trout to our waters was to be a boon to anglers or a piscatorial calamity. Proponents argued that the brown would thrive in waters which are too warm, and otherwise unsuitable, for brook trout and rainbows. Opponents called the brown trout a cannibal and said it would exterminate other species. After all this simmered down, and the various strains from England, Scotland and Germany merged essentially into one, considerable respect for the brown trout was established among American anglers. The brownie, they decided, grows satisfyingly large; he is a worthy contender on the end of a line; and he is fussier about lures and harder to catch than either of his principal cousins. They tempered this praise with the feeling, however, that big brown trout should be removed from the water whenever anyone can catch them. When brownies become too old to breed they feed almost entirely on baitfish, including the young of all species of trout. They become cannibals and, while they are trophies to catch, they do great harm to the fishery when left alone to die of old age.

We have noted that the brown trout can tolerate temperatures at least 5 degrees warmer than can the brook trout. This opens up to him a vast range of borderline waters in which the brook trout can not exist. He thus is becoming well established in many river systems formerly the domain of the brook trout, but which, due to deforestation, are suitable to the brook trout no longer. Because of this propensity for warmer waters, the brown trout does not migrate as far up little streams to lay eggs as the brook trout does. He (or she) prefers streams less swift and often can be found in flat

Classic brown trout stream, the Firehole River in Wyoming, is smooth-flowing and rich in insect life, the place for dry flies when a hatch is on.

meadow stretches not unlike the chalk streams so loved by his British cousins. When this is so, the brownie is more often in the deep, slow-running pools, while the brook trout is in the faster, colder stretches.

Brown trout usually are a golden brown, with large black or brown speckles, including a few of red or orange, surrounded by lighter aureoles on their sides, backs and dorsal fins. Their bellies are white, varying to yellow or tan as they mature. The fins are from brown to yellow, without the distinctively barred markings of the brook trout. Tails are slightly forked on young fish, but more nearly square on older ones. As with other trout, size varies with age, heredity and the amount of food available. While brown trout of between 30 and 40 pounds have been caught, the United States' average is well under 10 in the trophy class, and those of only a pound or less are more usual.

While large brown trout will eat almost anything, even including birds, frogs and mice, the brownie essentially is a fly-rod angler's fish. Those of less than trophy size rise steadily to emerging insects, and take nymphs on or near the surface. One usually casts dry flies to rises, using drab "match the hatch" imitations in sizes between 12 and 18. Flies must be presented properly, and the smaller ones often are more productive than the others. The "big fly for big fish" theory rarely works. Brownies of trophy size seldom are taken on small flies—more usually on bait, fished at night. When no rises are in evidence the fly-rod man normally reverts to streamers and bucktails, fished close to the bottom in deep, slow slicks and in pools. Hardware and live bait can be productive in such places—the same sorts as for brook trout.

Spawning habits of brown trout are so similar to those of brook trout that this need not be repeated.

Sea-run brown trout are called "sea trout" and, as far as I know, only run up rivers in the Northeast in a range extending from Newfoundland to Connecticut. They may spend only a few months in the brackish water of estuaries, or near them in the ocean, then return as bright, energetic fighting fish somewhat resembling young Atlantic salmon, or grilse. Even in salt water, they don't get very big, rarely reaching 10 pounds, and are usually much smaller. Their return up-river can be in the spring, or at other times and, since it can be of short duration, local anglers should be consulted to find out when runs in specific rivers, such as some of those on Cape Cod, can be expected. Silver-bodied streamer flies and bucktails with light bellies and darker backs are popular fly-rod lures, but wobbling spoons, spinners and jigs often are effective. Anglers in the Northeast should pay more attention to sea-trout runs. They can be the key to a wonderful day.

RAINBOW TROUT

Considered to be one of the greatest gamefishes of the world, the rainbow trout (which is native to America) is many fishes in one. In fresh water, for example, he may be small and brightly colored, usually with a pink or crimson lateral stripe, varying in intensity, on each side. Or he may come from a large lake, such as Idaho's Pend O'Reille, where he is silvered like a salmon and may grow to 30 pounds or more. When returning from the sea he is called a "steelhead." At first only experts can tell him from a salmon but after a few days in the river, his silvery sides grow duller and the familiar reddish stripe which distinguishes the rainbow, and which gives him his name, appears. One of the reasons the rainbow trout is so highly prized as a sportfish is because he usually is a leaper, like the salmon, putting on a display of aerial acrobatics that adds keener excitement to the battle when he is on the end of a line. All strains, the smaller rainbow of New England, the Kamloops of Pend O'Reille, the steelhead of northwestern rivers, and other varieties found in great abundance elsewhere, essentially are one and the same species of fish.

Contrary to the brown trout, and more so than the brook trout, the rainbow in rivers is a fast-water fish, living principally in the swift glides and riffles of big streams. His taste for water temperature, being in the "trouty range" of between about 50 and 70 degrees, is somewhat more tolerant of warmth than the brook trout's.

Undoubtedly one could write a lengthy book about the habits of rainbows, and their taste in baits and lures, in one place and another, and still

Fast water on a Rocky Mountain stream means rainbow trout, the leaping gamester whose aerial acrobatics always adds excitement to the battle.

not satisfy local experts who maintain that conditions in their areas are somewhat different. When there are pronounced insect hatches, rainbows will boil up for flies which imitate the naturals. In such places fly fishing is indicated, although other methods also usually are productive for those who want to use them. In other areas the insect hatches may be minimal, and the fish will be feeding on bait such as kokanee salmon and cisco. Here, spoons, plugs and spinners should do better, although imitations of shrimp or crawfish and large streamers or bucktails should take fish. Conditions vary so much that it is well for visiting anglers to pay more attention to the tackle and tactics of local experts than whatever can be garnered from books.

A tip on lake fishing may be appropriate. Since rainbow trout don't like temperatures much over 60 degrees, they will go deep when surface waters are warm in summer. It then is necessary to fish at depths where suitable water temperatures exist. Conversely, when fall arrives and water temperatures become cool, fish again will come up and feed on or near the surface for reasons which have been noted in Chapters 14 and 15. A knowledge of these requirements helped me in mid-October several years ago to hook on the surface, and to land, a 31-pound, 12-ounce rainbow trout in Idaho's Lake Pend O'Reille. All local experts maintained that the rainbows still were down deep, but a check on surface water temperatures indicated that the facts could be otherwise.

Trolling, or casting spoons and other hardware, on or near the surface is an excellent way to take rainbows when water surface conditions are cool and when no insect hatches are obvious. Deeper trolling at or just below the thermocline, at the depth of optimum water temperature, where this level touches land, is advisable during summer's warmth. When surface conditions are right, and a good insect hatch is on, the best sport can be had with the fly rod and the dry fly. Rainbows are the least selective of the big three of troutdom. While one lure may be better than another on occasion, almost anything goes.

Steelhead

Sometimes called the "steelhead trout" or "salmon trout," the steelhead is a true rainbow trout which has gone to sea and has returned to his river. Trout are called steelhead under other conditions, such as when they run up rivers from large lakes but, in such cases, the correctness of the term is questionable.

Steelhead country is the coastal area which extends from northern California north through British Columbia; the rivers increasing in number and productivity toward the north through Oregon and Washington. Depending more or less on their size, and obstructions, if any, most of the many rivers provide enviable steelhead fishing from their estuaries to many miles up-stream. While steelhead return from the ocean into their rivers during all months of the year, the runs vary from river to river, so there are not runs in all rivers at the same time. The runs are more or less divided into sum-mer, fall and winter types, and fishing for summer steelhead differs con-siderably from that for fall and winter steelhead, as we shall see. Summer fish are silvery-sheathed, immature early arrivals which enter rivers in spring and summer to mature in them for fall and winter spawning. Being in no hurry, they travel slowly, resting for long periods in the runs and pools.

Less ready to spawn than later arrivals, they are considered better fight-ers on light tackle. Fall fish are riper ones which eat less and travel more rapidly. The faint pink stripe of the rainbow usually is in evidence. Winter fish are ripe; heavy with roe or milt, and more brightly striped. They usu-ally wait in the estuaries of coastal streams, some of which are small and nearly dry in summer, until late-season rains cause freshets which impel the upstream journey during the winter for spawning between December and April or May. There are many more winter runs and rivers holding winter fish than there are summer runs and rivers holding summer fish.

Except for minor variations, such as the types of flies which are used, summer steelhead fishing is almost identical to that for Atlantic salmon. Fly-fishing tackle and methods are the same; the fish are similar in ap-pearance and more or less so in size; they jump spectacularly and fight similarly; and both species return to the ocean, if they can, after spawning.

The rainbow trout which is to become a steelhead enters the ocean to travel extensively in schools at least as far as the tip of the chain of the Aleutian Islands. After one or more years in the sea he returns to his river, as the Atlantic salmon does, perhaps pausing in its estuary for days or weeks until the flow and temperature of the water impels him to travel upstream. There, the spawning process is almost identical with that of the Atlantic salmon. The similarity between the two species extends to their appearance as fresh and stale fish. Newly arrived, both are similarly sheathed in silver, with dark greenish or brownish backs. As the steelhead stays in the river, and as he matures, he gradually reverts to the appearance of the rainbow trout. He loses his silvery sheen; becomes darker, and his lateral red stripe gradually intensifies, then earning for him the name of "redsides."

Summer Steelhead

Since steelhead rivers in summer usually are low and clear, this is the time for the fly rod and the fly. Other tackle, using spinners, spoons and other hardware, sometimes is used, but it is widely frowned upon in many areas as being not very sporty and much less fun. The splashing of heavy lures can ruin fishing for those using flies.

Fly rods in systems 8 and 9, from 8½ to 9½ feet long, emphasize power, with stiff tips and action extending down into the butt. The steelhead rod should have a screw-locking reel seat and large, correctly spaced guides. It should be fitted with a single-action reel with an adjustable brake, holding the line and between 100 and 150 yards of 20-pound-test braided Dacron backing. Lines usually are forward tapered, and many anglers prefer shooting heads because this method of rigging provides greater casting distance with less effort. Shooting heads, however, are more adaptable to big rivers and for experts familiar with this sort of line handling.

When steelhead seem interested in hatching insects, the dry fly in suitable imitation may be indicated. Otherwise, a sinking line, or a floating line with sinking tip, is better. Leaders are at least as long as the rod and are tapered to about 8-pound test. Flies vary in size from about 4 to 8 and usually are specially developed steelhead patterns; often duller ones for brighter days and brighter ones for duller days or high and/or discolored water. Since preferred patterns vary from year to year and from river to river, local experts should be consulted. Optic, Demon and Railbird patterns in various combinations, the Improved Governor, Thor, Royal Coachman, Queen Bess and Horner's Shrimp are old standbys, but more modern favorites are shown in one of the color plates.

In traveling upstream the steelhead follow definite routes and occupy the same holding positions from year to year unless the conformation of the river's bed has been changed. If a fish is taken from a certain place, another soon will come along to occupy it. The fish like water of moderate flow. That which is too swift to wade usually is too swift for them. Thus, obstructions like rocks in the stream are good holding positions. So are undercut banks, slicks above rapids, long channels with uniform flow, swirls and eddies near the main current, positions below reefs, and the tails of pools.

Fly fishermen usually start at the top of a pool and work down, gradually extending casts until all the good water is covered. The new arrival or the repeater in the pool starts behind the others and, in slowly wading down, is careful not to hold up the parade. On cross-stream casts, strikes usually occur between the time that the line straightens and the fly starts to hang downstream. At the latter point, the fly should be jigged during short retrieves before picking it up because a fish may have followed the swing and perhaps this unusual action can induce him to strike. Some anglers fish the fly on a dead drift, while others give it action. If one method doesn't work, try the other. The main point is to make it swim naturally rather than letting it whip in the current. Flies which start to whip can be slowed down by upstream mends. When a pool doesn't produce it's rarely worthwhile to spend much time on it, because another one not far away may be loaded. When a pool does produce, the steelhead will strike so hard that it rarely is necessary to set the hook.

Winter Steelhead

This fishing usually is quite different from what just has been discussed because late fall and winter rivers normally are high, dirty and fast. These conditions call for a different approach with different tackle. Of course, there are times in winter when rivers more or less duplicate summer conditions, so fly tackle then can be used. Such occasions, however, are exceptions.

Since winter steelhead lie practically *on* the bottom and since they rarely will move to take a lure, the lure must be fished or bounced on bottom, or at least within between a few inches and a foot of it. The tackle should be able to cast between 1 and 2 ounces of bait and lead 100 feet or more. Spinning outfits with reels holding from 150 to 200 yards of 10-pound-test line are used; also baitcasting outfits with level-wind reels and a retrieve ratio of at least 3 to 1. Rods are between 7½ and 9 feet long, with sensitive tips which can feel the light, nibbling "take" peculiar to this type of fishing. They also should have considerable power in the butt section to allow long casts and to set the hook into powerful fish.

A mighty winter steelhead taken from an Alaskan river.

The line is attached to the leader by a small swivel which allows the inclusion of a lead weight, as shown in the drawing. Leads usually are of the "pencil" type, which are less inclined to catch on bottom than bulkier varieties. As they weigh between a half ounce and an ounce, they are just heavy enough to make the rig bounce bottom. The stronger the current is, the heavier the lead must be.

Drawing *A* shows a special cinch for pencil leads which allows the lead's tip to be pressed into a constricting holder tied in between line and leader with Improved Clinch Knots. In drawing *B* a short piece of rubber tubing is strung onto the line just above the swivel, and the lead's end is pressed into it. Drawing *C* shows that the pencil lead is tied to a few inches of leader, which is tied to the line above the swivel. This leader is much lighter in strength than the one between line and lure so that it can be broken off in case of a severe hangup. A level section of leader material of about 10-pound test and between 1½ and 2 feet long connects the lure to the swivel on the end of the line. The lure usually is a gob of fish roe about as large as one's thumb to the base of the nail. This is enclosed in a bag of netting or veiling as described in Chapter 5. These sometimes are called "strawberries," and fishermen are very opinionated about their correct size. Anglers usually start with bottled roe, but use fresh roe when a female fish is obtained.

Steelhead lie in positions such as have been described, but they are on the bottom, usually in fairly deep water. Because of the coldness of the water they won't move to any extent to take a lure. Thus the lure must be bounced along, touching the bottom every foot or two. This calls for a combination of skill, experience and correct tackle. Also, since a steelhead takes the bait very softly, the angler must have the ability to feel the take in a manner very similar to nymph fishing. The fish usually will hold the bait for only a very few seconds. The slightest unusual feel of the bait therefore calls for a strike. If it's a steelhead, and he is hooked, be prepared for instant fireworks.

This method of bottom-bouncing the bait requires fishing with a tight line. Yet line must be payed out so the lure can bounce downstream on the bottom in the channel with the current. If one is standing at the head of a pool he can make a short cast and then release line to fish farther and farther down current, steering the lure to suspected holding positions.

The four most frequently used baits are jarred or oil-packed canned roe, fresh roe, single eggs and nightcrawlers, but other things are used on occasion, ranging all the way from crawfish to Velveeta cheese.

Wobblers, such as the Wobble-Rite and Dardevle are effective and usually need no added weight. Lighter lures, like spinners, cherry-bobbers and

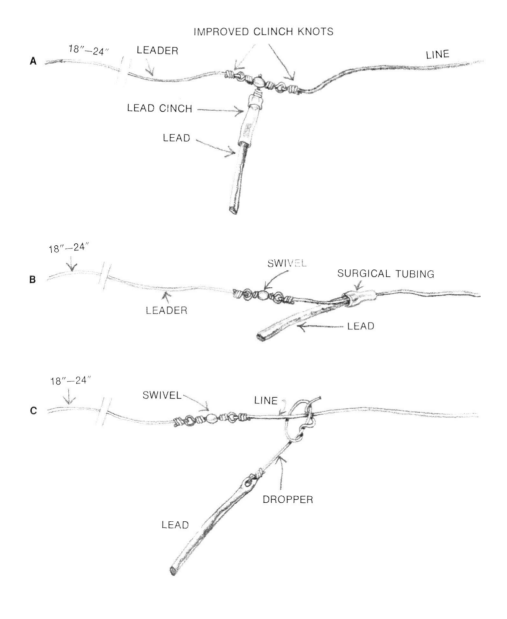

IMPROVED CLINCH KNOTS

A 18″—24″ LEADER LINE

LEAD CINCH

LEAD

B 18″—24″ SWIVEL SURGICAL TUBING

LEADER LEAD

C 18″—24″ SWIVEL LINE

DROPPER

LEAD

Three ways of rigging lead weight to bounce bottom for winter steelhead.

the popular Flatfish require enough lead, placed a foot or two above the lure, to get them down. Since muddy water is usual in winter, bright colors, including fluorescent ones, in red, pink and orange, help the fish to see the lures.

While wading or fishing from banks is customary up-river, trolling and casting from boats may be the only way to get to the fish in the lower, wider stretches. Winter steelhead fishing isn't easy. It can be a very cold sport, often with icy winds, heavy rains, dirty waters and swift currents. When steelhead first enter rivers they habitually leap into the air to shake off sea-lice—a sight that is sure to increase any angler's blood pressure. They often roll and jump on the way upstream, thus showing where they are. However, it isn't uncommon to fish for days without a touch when big, bright fish are showing all around.

A hooked steelhead will put on an aerial display that can last for half an hour, while making long, hard runs that test tackle to the extreme. With such strong and lively fish on, fishermen forget their discomfort while meeting the thrilling challenge of angling in one of its toughest forms.

CUTTHROAT TROUT

This is the beautiful native trout of the western United States and Canada. It includes several subspecies, some of which have become very rare. It is identified by a red V-shaped slash of color where the gills meet outside and below the lower jaw. There are numerous color variations, but all are more or less peppered with black speckles which give it a very trout-like appearance.

The cutthroat trout is a distant cousin of the rainbow, and frequently breeds with it to form a cross which has both the red slash of the cutthroat and the reddish lateral band of the rainbow.

As a challenge on fishing tackle the cutthroat is more on a par with the eastern brook trout, and less active than the rainbow and the brownie. It rarely jumps and, when its head can be pulled above water, the fight is about over. Nevertheless, it is a lovely fish, and excellent fare for the table.

The cutthroat trout is most prolific in spring-fed streams which rarely are fished. It is found in rivers and lakes, largely in the Wyoming-Yellowstone-Idaho area. Since it is shy, one should use fine leaders and small flies. It rises readily to dry flies, and will take spinners, spoons, wet flies, bucktails, streamers, nymphs and live bait. Anglers use either light flycasting or

Spring-fed streams in the high Rockies are havens for cutthroat trout, a distant cousin of the rainbow.

spinning tackle. The young fish feed mostly on insects and larvae; the older ones mainly on baitfish. It is a cold-water fish which is not adaptable to extremes of temperature. When both rainbows and cutthroats are in a stream the former will be in the riffles, and the latter in flowing pools and eddies. Fishing methods are the same as for other trout of relatively small size. Very big cutthroats no longer are common. A 5-pounder is a trophy fish, and usual ones rarely average over a pound.

Some cutthroats are anadromous, traveling downstream in late spring to estuaries in areas such as the Puget Sound and in the states of Oregon and Washington. Evidently they never go very far from the estuaries, and often are found in shallow water along rocky shores, where they take best when the tide is running. Since they feed there largely on shrimp and small bait-fish, shrimp imitations or streamer flies or bucktails are recommended with fly-fishing tackle. Small spinners or wobblers and, occasionally, small deep-running plugs do well on spinning or spincasting gear. Cutthroats also are caught by stillfishing and by trolling.

Sea-run fish usually go to the estuaries in their second or third year and return after a year or two there to spawn in tributary streams during the winter.

LAKE TROUT

Avidly sought by many because it is a "trout" usually running large and sometimes to trophy size, maligned by others on account of its relative lack of beauty and sportiness on the end of a line, the lake trout nevertheless in northern regions is one of North America's principal and most popular gamefish. While reports of a few not caught by rod and reel are in the 100-pound class, the all-tackle record is about 63 pounds and so-called trophy fish average between 20 and 30. Even "little" 10-pounders, when hooked near the surface, provide bragging stories long after the fish has been cut up into the chowder.

Compared to some of the less exotic species, the laker could be considered a good looker. It generally is light bellied, with back and sides from pale gray to brownish, well sprinkled with many orange, yellow or pink spots, somewhat resembling those of its kin. Unlike most of its relations, it has a rather deeply forked tail.

The togue, as the laker often is called, inhabits deep lakes which thermally stratify and which contain a reasonable abundance of oxygen. Since the depths of the lakes where togue can be comfortable must be in the 40- to 50-degree range, this fish rarely, if ever, is found in southern regions. Its range extends from the far North to a latitude bordered in the east by New England and New York State. It also is found occasionally in thoroughfares and in rivers flowing into cold lakes.

Pumping his rod steadily, fisherman brings a lake trout to the surface while his companion readies a net.

The key to the search for lake trout is the water thermometer, or depth temperature probe, because lakers will not feed (and usually will not thrive) in water colder than 40 degrees and warmer than 50 degrees. Thus, when surface water is warm in summer, lake trout may be in a stratum as deep as several hundred feet. When lake bottoms are at their density of 39.2 degrees the lakers will be above this, in the 40- to 50-degree range. Conversely, when surface waters are cold, as during a lake's spring and fall turnover period (see Chapter 14), lake trout should be on top, if the surface water is not over 50 degrees. Many lakes, even shallow ones, maintain such surface temperatures all during the year in far northern regions, so lake trout in such places consistently can be caught on or near the surface with all sorts of relatively light tackle.

Thus, there are two basic ways to fish for lake trout—on top if surface waters are compatible, and down deeper if they are not. The choice is decided by the thermometer. Let's take surface fishing first.

Lake trout large enough to bother with feed almost entirely on baitfish. The fly-rod angler therefore favors fairly large streamer flies or bucktails,

347

preferably in the colors of prevalent baitfish. Fishermen who prefer bait-casting, spinning or spincasting gear use spoons, spinners, plugs, or live or dead bait. In large lakes, lake trout are where you find them, which can be along the windward shore of the lake, in brushy coves, or along or over rocky reefs.

I have often fished a large lake in Canada which teemed with large brook trout. We never caught lake trout where the brook trout were. If we wanted fast sport with lake trout we would seek out one of several brushy coves where almost every cast brought a hard strike. There were no brook trout in the coves. The two species kept to themselves. This usually was in June, when most of the lake was the right temperature for brook trout, but a bit too warm for lake trout. In the coves the late snow water runoff made the surface water colder, which probably was why the lake trout were there.

While these observations may help a bit, they don't answer the question of how to find lake trout under cold surface-water conditions. One way to find them is by trolling, because where one or two are caught there should be many. We can use streamers or bucktails, but these may not be the best. Trolled baitfish could be the answer, but using bait may be inconvenient or bothersome. I have had my best luck with long, slim, silvery floating-diving plugs.

When surface waters are too warm for lake trout we'll have to go deeper for them. A temperature probe tells how deep to go to reach the 40- to 50-degree stratum, which probably will be below thermocline depth.

Finally, if trolling doesn't happen to be our cup of tea, we can try still-fishing. Select a spot near a rocky reef or near bottom where the temperature depth probe says the temperature is between 40 and 50 degrees. It's easy to find the depth, but it may be difficult to locate the right spot. If the line is marked with depth measurements, we know how much to put out. Fasten a lead to the end so it will go almost straight down. A short leader with a baited hook can be added below the lead. The boat can be allowed to drift until we feel the lead touching bottom. It may be necessary to experiment with several such places, but all needed for a good day's fishing is just one hot spot.

Under such conditions there are several ways to fish. One is by jigging with a wobbling spoon heavy enough to sink almost straight down. If we're fishing quite deep it helps to paint the back of the spoon with a luminous substance. Since the line is marked for the correct depth, it's easy to lower the spoon close to the bottom. Pull the spoon up quickly, 2 or 3 feet or so, and allow it to flutter down. Keep up the jigging action until something hits.

Another way is to select a lead barrel sinker just heavy enough to take a bait straight down. This sinker has a hole in it. String the sinker on a monofilament line of 10-pound test or so, and add a barrel swivel below it, so the lead can't pass the swivel. Tie a 2- or 3-foot monofilament leader to the other end of the swivel, and add a hook to its end. The hook should be the smallest and lightest that will do the job because a fish may not take the bait if he feels the hook. Put a fairly large live baitfish on the hook by one of the ways shown in Chapter 5. Here's what should happen:

Lower the rig so the sinker lies on bottom; then pay out 4 or 5 feet more of line. The baitfish will try to swim away, pulling out some of this extra line. The baitfish will be swimming fairly free, close to the bottom. When a lake trout picks up the bait, avoid striking until he starts to go away with it. When he begins to go off with the bait it's time to strike—hard! If the bottom is grassy, the baitfish could hide in the grass. Although a lake trout probably will find it anyway, it's helpful to raise the sinker a bit from time to time to be sure the bait is swimming free.

Another variation of this idea is to fasten a ball float to the lower swivel ring, or just below it. As the baitfish takes out some of the extra line the float will rise, thus helping to keep the bait off bottom. This doesn't seem necessary unless there is a difficult bottom to contend with.

Lake trout spawn between September and December (varying widely in various lakes and regions) over rocky or gravel bottoms, and often on or near rocky reefs. This may be in shallow water in fairly shallow lakes, but a hundred feet deep, or so, in deep ones. When spawning areas are found it is probable that the fish will return to them at about the same time, year after year, and that they will remain there for several weeks. At such times these places are hot spots.

DOLLY VARDEN

Nearly everyone would put this rapacious predator at the end of the list, as far as sportfishing for trout is concerned. Its yellowish flesh is poor eating, and it gives up quickly after being hooked. Since it dines largely on the young of more desirable trout species, many conservationist-anglers go for Dollies with pitchforks when they collect in vast numbers in small tributary brooks and streams in July and early fall to spawn.

Although some say the Dolly Varden reaches 40 pounds, the tackle record (if one bothers with it) seems to be about 32 pounds. Fish in the 10-pound range are fairly common in lakes and rivers. Dollies are considered to be ugly fish, having large mouths and snakelike heads. Their backs are greenish, with black, sparse brick-red, and pale yellow spots heavily sprinkled on back and sides. Sides vary from dark yellow through orange to pink or red, the color depending more or less on environment.

The fish ranges from northern California north to northwest Alaska and east to Idaho and Montana. It is considered a sportfish in some far northern regions, but usually not elsewhere. It does provide some sport when caught in cold headwater streams. Small Dollies will take flies, but larger ones are indifferent to them.

Some Dolly Vardens are anadromous, especially in the northern part of their range. They run to sea in the spring, returning between midsummer and fall for spawning in small tributary streams. Fresh from the sea, they have the usual silvery appearance of sea-run fish.

Small Dolly Vardens feed on insects, crustaceans, fish roe, and smaller fishes. Big ones dine mainly on other fish but, since they are scavengers, they eat whatever they can find, including small live or dead birds and animals. People who fish for them use bait, spinners or spoons. Trollers often attach large bladed spinners to baited hooks.

Rainbow and cutthroat trout often are in the deep pools and runs of streams infested with Dollies. Light-tackle anglers going for the more exotic species often get hard strikes from big Dollies which smash their equipment.

THE NORTHWESTERN FISHING SEASON

Easterners going to the Rocky Mountain areas of the northwest for fishing should remember that the season is short. Used to good northeastern fishing in May, I have found roads to remote Rocky Mountain lakes and streams unplowed in mid-June, and blocked by drifts of many feet of snow. Of course the well-traveled roads nearly always are kept open.

In the West, spring, summer and fall are compressed into weeks, as compared to months in the East. June in the Rockies is like April in New England. In June the sun quickly melts most of the snow, and the last two weeks of June usually are excellent for dry-fly fishing, with large hatches of mayflies and other insects in the early mornings and evenings. The warmth of midsummer tends to make fish logy and harder to catch. The first three weeks of September usually restore the best fishing because cooling waters make the fish more active. Many anglers consider the September dry-fly period to be the best of the year. However, spring and fall are rainy seasons, and this should be considered in estimating how many pleasant fishing days a vacation will provide.

In the spring the streams draining high mountain peaks usually are muddy torrents, or are milky due to melting glaciers. Streams draining from lower lands should be clearer and more moderate. Coastal areas are warmer than far inland ones because of the temperate effect of the Japanese Current.

19

Spinning for Trout

Many fishermen think that spinning or spincasting always is the best way to take trout. Others, more competent with the fly rod, while acknowledging that these two methods usually are very effective, also know that many situations come up where they can beat the weighted-lure addicts hands down. Since greatest success in fishing hinges on using the most appropriate method for the specific situation, let's delve into this in the next few chapters.

So far we have attempted to provide the background for spinning for trout in Chapters 1 and 2 on the tackle, 4 and 5 on lures and baits, and the four most recent ones on where to find fish under various conditions. Since these were rather general in scope, it may be helpful here to round things out by being more specific about trout, especially the brookies, brownies and rainbows which most of us seek so often. These can be grouped together if the slight differences in their characteristics, recently discussed, are remembered.

Anglers who fish near populated areas, as most of us do, primarily are confronted with "put and take" conditions where the trout are stocked and usually are small. Light spinning or spincasting tackle is preferable to heavier gear for two reasons; it is more fun to handle smaller fish on light equipment, and more of them can be hooked with it. But how light is light?

Light tackle is a relative term but it could be an outfit handling monofilament testing not over 4 pounds and using lures or baits weighing no more than ¼ ounce. When one becomes hung up and has to break loose he will realize that this really is pretty strong stuff. He may prefer to go toward ultralight gear with lines testing 2 or 3 pounds and lures of about ⅛ ounce. This really isn't "ultralight," but it is sensibly so. Real ultralight tackle runs quite a bit lighter, or finer. The whole idea behind going lighter is that it is more fun, more challenging, and perhaps more productive than merely pulling in fish with equipment that doesn't give them much of a chance.

On the other hand there are big, fast and deep waters holding big fish where 4-pound line may be too light, or where heavier lures are needed for longer casts. The strength of the tackle must be decided by existing situations.

Every rod performs best under a specific average lure weight which pulls the tip down only slightly. Use the weight best suited for the rod. If the lure doesn't depress the tip noticeably, the lure is too light to be cast properly. If it depresses the tip excessively, it is too heavy and may result in broken tackle.

To start with, only about a dozen artificial lures are needed for trout. These could be a shallow-running spinner and a deeper-running one in both flashy and duller finishes, plus the same of wobbling spoons, for a total of eight. About four midget plugs of various types can provide a set which can be deadly on trout when other lures are ineffective. They often take big brown trout when they will strike at nothing else! This initial dozen doesn't provide for spares. The favorite lure usually is the first one that is lost.

TROUT IN DEEP POOLS

Having suitable tackle and having learned how to use it in Chapters 1 and 2, let's apply this to some typical fishing situations. We might start with a fairly deep pool because, regardless of conditions, most fishermen seem to think that's where the big ones lie. This isn't always so, however.

Too many people waste too much time hopefully casting and retrieving lures 2 or 3 feet down when they should know there are no fish there. The cross-section of a deep pool in the accompanying drawing shows why, and it bears stressing.

In such a pool the trout feed on or near the surface only when there is surface food there. This usually means emerging nymphs or a hatch of insects. Even if the trout are feeding on top, they may not take spinning lures because they are selectively feeding. The only chance is along shallower edges of the pool, and this isn't a very good one. At such times the top is fly fishermen's water, and the spinning fisherman usually does better to leave it alone.

Beneath the top water of a deep pool is a barren area which extends

Landing a trout on a spinning outfit in early-season high water. When streams are high and insect hatches have not yet begun, spinning is the best way to take trout. Lures (or baits) can be fished deep, and long casts can cover all good water.

down nearly to the bottom. This is the area too many fishermen waste too much time with. Why should trout be in it? The food supply is better elsewhere; there are no places where they can rest without combating the current, and there is no protection near which they can hide.

So, in a deep pool, let's face the fact that trout most often are close to the bottom in protective places such as are indicated in the drawing. If surface water is very warm this is all the more the case, because the bottom water is much slower and much cooler. Trout lying on or near the bottom may rise up a foot or two to take a lure when the water is in the 50s, but they hardly will move for anything when it is too cold. Thus the answer to deep pools usually is to fish very close to the bottom. This may cost a lure occasionally, but it is the way to take trout when they are not actively feeding.

We can cast lures into a deep pool; wait for them to sink, and then fish them in under the illusion that they are scraping bottom. Actually, the current may take control of them and sweep them downstream far up from the bottom. It may be best to cast almost directly upstream and, by regaining line as the lure comes nearer, wait until we feel it touch bottom. Then, in fishing it in, an occasional pause should make it sink down again. This bottom-bumping technique is especially important in fishing for winter steelhead, but it works for other species of trout as well. Experienced anglers can sense or feel the lure bumping bottom, and they learn to fish it without getting snagged too often. It is a method which requires experimentation for complete success.

When actively feeding, which may be around noon when the water is cold, or in the very early morning or late evening when it is warmer, trout may leave their sanctuaries deep in pools and travel into the riffles and shallows to feed. Many trout, even big ones, do not lie deep in pools. They often are in more accessible places where the top water joins with the bottom water without the relatively barren middle stratum. This is water varying

Cross section of a typical trout pool showing good and poor water. Trout feed in surface water only when a hatch is on; otherwise they're on the bottom and lure or bait has to be fished deep. Middle water is usually barren.

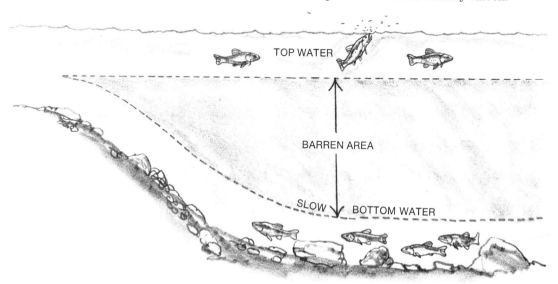

from shallow to only a few feet deep, with rocks and other obstructions which break the flow and provide places where fish can hide. When water temperatures are in the 50s, this water can be ideal for spinning.

THIN WATER

Spinning for trout in deep or moderately deep streams is one thing, but doing it in very shallow water is quite another. Trout in the riffles are feeding, sometimes in water so shallow it hardly can float them. This water usually is fairly flat and very pebbly, with occasional rocks. While the trout probably are feeding on nymphs they often can be taken on spinning lures. The idea here is to use the lightest lure that can be cast; probably a small unweighted spinner. With the rod held high and the line free, but released from time to time by forefinger pressure, the spinner (or light bait) can be worked downstream through small channels and around the larger rocks. While it must be fished far enough off to keep the fisherman out of the fish's cone of vision, it is easy to wade the stream and to steer the spinner into spots that could harbor trout. Under such conditions even the lightest spinners will get hung up occasionally but it is no problem to flip them off or to wade downstream to free them. The smallest hooks which will hold the fish should be used.

STREAM MOUTHS

Little needs to be added to spinning for trout in ponds and lakes in addition to what was provided in Chapter 15. There it was noted that fishing the shore toward which the wind is blowing should be best because winds blow surface foods such as spent insects in that direction. If surface water is too cold for trout they also will seek the shallows of that shore because winds blow the warmer top layer of lake or pond water in that direction.

In any event, when the weather is warm enough to hatch insects, which can be very early in the season at times, something happens that is of particular interest to trout fishermen.

Since water-borne foods for trout and for baitfish are washed down streams by their currents, stream mouths usually provide good fishing. When the wind, or even a slight breeze, blows toward the stream mouth, floating foods which have dropped into the water are wafted in that direction. The opposing forces of stream current and wind therefore concentrate surface food to confine it in a relatively small arc which usually is where the stream's current spends itself at the stream's drop-off. The stronger the wind, the nearer the stream mouth this concentration will be, but it will be seen as a scummy area which, on closer inspection, contains an abundance of fish food such as insects.

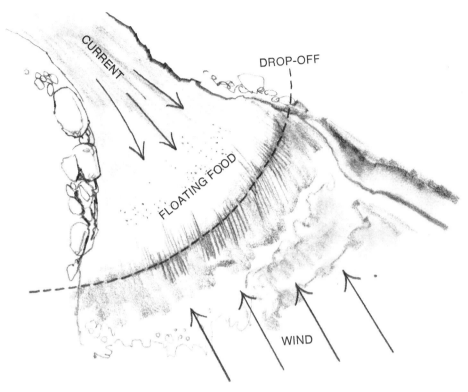

Opposing forces of wind and current can sometimes concentrate food near stream mouths. Food – usually in the form of insects – appears as a scummy area just before the drop-off.

At these times stream mouths provide a double bonanza because trout collect there for the surface food and also for the greater abundance of baitfish which are there for the same reason.

If trout are surface feeding this may be noticed by slight dimpling (made even by big trout) when they come up to sip in insects. One should not ignore such action under the impression that, because he can't see trout splashing and boiling on the surface, the dimpling is made only by baitfish. Regardless of surface commotion, or the lack of it, it can be assumed that trout are there.

If there is any evidence of surface activity, spinning lures (or flies) fished shallow should get results. Otherwise, the trout may be lying deeper, resting between feeding spreads in the slower water over the drop-off. This may be under the floating food concentration, but a fairly strong breeze may indicate that it is somewhat farther out.

If the area is fished from shore the lure could be cast more or less up-stream and allowed to sink to work near bottom over the drop-off. A fast current might require a compact wobbler rather than a bigger, thinner one, or a weighted spinner. If this isn't productive, an alternative is to make a high overhead cast with a compact wobbler as far beyond the food concentration as possible. The falling lure on the bellied line then will plummet down and can be fished in after it has sunk deep enough. Correctly done, this will let the lure drop to, or near, bottom, from where it should travel upward along the incline of the drop-off as it is being retrieved. Since trout may be concentrated in one area or another below the drop-off, numerous casts could be made.

If the area is fished from a boat, casting could start at a considerable distance from the food concentration because the trout may be schooled farther out than might be presumed. Fanwise casting can be tried at increasingly closer distances to cover the bottom area. In fishing the drop-off itself, a slowly fished compact wobbler should work downward as it is being slowly retrieved to travel as close to the incline as possible. While trout should be in the middle, there may be reasons for them to be in other holding positions even very close to shore. Admitting that every situation is a different one, a knowledge of probabilities should help when actual conditions are observed.

SPINNING WITH FLIES

Chapter 5 illustrated ways to use sunken baits with plastic floats. A question often asked is whether or not these little floats are practical for use with flies for trout. We could give the question a quick brushoff by saying that artificial flies should be used only with fly-fishing tackle, but this may not suit spinning and spincasting fishermen who want to try them. I did considerable experimenting on the subject when American spinning was in its infancy. While artificial flies of course are most suitable for fly fishing, they also are practical in a limited way for spinning when used in connection with the plastic float. Let's not say it is an ideal way to take fish but, under suitable conditions it can be a lot of fun!

In the top drawing at left, a float is tied to the end of the line. The float contains enough water to provide adequate casting weight. About a foot up on the line from the float we have tied in a dropper a foot or so long rigged with an artificial nymph, a sinking fly, or a bit of bait. A foot farther up on the line is a fairly short dropper to which is attached a dry fly. The droppers should be of the finest monofilament which is practical to use.

The fisherman casts this rig upstream and across and takes in enough line so the dry fly is above water. By raising and lowering the rod tip he

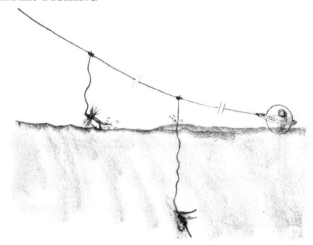

Rig for a dapping fly and a sinking fly (or bait).

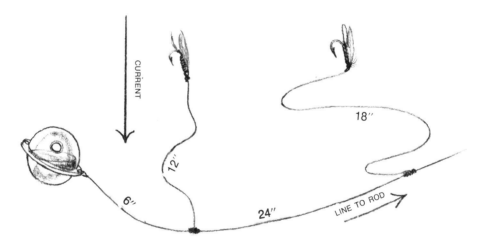

Method of rigging two wet flies with a plastic float.

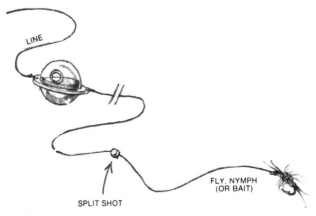

Surface-drifting rig for wet flies, nymphs or bait.

causes the dry fly to touch the water lightly and frequently as the float drifts downstream. Actually he is "dapping" the dry fly; a method as old as fly fishing itself. The fly dances on and just over the water, and trout very often rise up to take it. The fisherman usually must hook the fish, but that isn't difficult in this case.

Meanwhile the nymph or wet fly is drifting down in the current several inches below the surface, and it is being given very slight motion due to the dapping of the dry fly. This is exactly the motion a nymph should have as it evidently is struggling to reach the surface. If a fish takes the nymph, and the take can't be seen, it is signaled by unusual motion of the float. The fisherman should strike hard upon seeing any unusual motion of the float because it is difficult to hook a fish under these conditions. If a worm or a grasshopper is on the end dropper, the fish probably will take it in and will hook himself, but striking would do no harm anyway. On completion of the drift the float will swing with the current, but it can be left out there as long as it covers ground. Meanwhile the rig can be steered around rocks and other holding positions such as have been described.

I would be inclined to let the idea go at that, but there are two less efficient ways of rigging the float with flies (or bait). One is much like the former except that the two flies or nymphs are on longer droppers for underwater drift. A small split shot can be pinched on about halfway up each dropper if necessary. The trouble is that fish are very hard to hook with this rig when flies are used. Of course streamers and bucktails are unsuitable. Small baits provide a more sensible arrangement.

Lastly, for deeper fishing, a leader 2 or 3 feet long is attached to the float, with the float attached to the line on the other side as shown in the drawing at left. A nymph or bait is rigged to the end of the leader, perhaps with one or more small split shot clipped on midway up. This is a good rig for drifting down pools and runs but, as before, one has to be quick, clever and lucky to hook a fish on the nymph when any unusual motion of the float is seen. The rig can be cast long distances, sometimes under conditions where fly fishing isn't practical. Due to the difficulty in striking, the use of natural baits such as grubs, hellgrammites, worms, etc. would be better. Then, a trout takes in the bait and usually hooks himself.

Another question is about weighted flies, such as streamers and bucktails. Since a casting weight is needed, why not wrap the shank with plenty of wire before dressing the body? The idea has been tried in all its variations, but with insignificant success. The heavy body deadens the action of the fly to such an extent that only the most ignorant trout will bother with it. It can be tried for other kinds of fish, but even the poorest sort of plug would be better.

20

Streamers
and
Wet Flies
for Trout

Fly fishermen who understand the game know when to use each of the four basic types of flies: streamers, wet flies, dry flies or nymphs. These basic types are divided into various sub-types, each of which consists of a range of sizes all in a superabundance of patterns, most of which are productive at one time or another. We now are speaking only of flies for trout; although some of these also can be used for other species, some of the other species require specific patterns all their own.

Well-equipped fly fishermen gradually collect boxes of artificial flies of one type or another, the various types, sizes and patterns eventually running into the hundreds, even into the thousands. To keep costs down (or so they originally think!) many anglers tie their own flies, thus migrating into a sub-hobby with a fascination all its own. It is rather plain to see, however, that those who buy their flies must restrain themselves by applying certain rules of selection if they are going to collect a useful assortment for all purposes without having to mortgage the family homestead.

Leaving the last two basic types for future chapters, I will discuss in this chapter the selection of streamers and wet flies, and the elementary rules of where and how to use them.

STREAMERS AND BUCKTAILS

These are the flies that imitate baitfish and, at least in this author's opinion, they are the most important type because they are useful all the time, nearly everywhere, during the entire season. While trout may be so selective at one time or another that they want something special, they munch on baitfish regularly.

Although streamers differ from bucktails, they often collectively are called "streamer flies." Streamer flies have wings made all or predominantly of hackle feathers; usually two pairs, each from opposite sides of the bird, normally applied with the pairs of concave sides facing each other. Bucktails have wings all or mainly of one or more colors of hair, not necessarily from a deer. Both have the same purpose: to imitate baitfish. And both are used in identical ways. Bucktail wings may provide a more pulsating effect when fished, and they are more substantial if the quarry has sharp teeth (which trout do not). The choice, however, depends mainly on the effect desired. For example, the barred stripes of furnace or badger hackles imitate the dark medial lines of some baitfish, while grizzly hackles provide the vertical bars found in others.

When one sees a streamer fly, taken dry from the tackle box, it may not look much like a baitfish. When wet and being fished, however, the fibers and feathers gather and slim down into a very fishlike effect. The rest of the illusion depends on the lifelike action the angler gives to the fly.

Notes on Selection

The buyer must beware in selecting streamers or bucktails. Many are offered on the theory that, if a little dressing is good, a lot more is better. This isn't so. The fly should simulate the slim appearance of a baitfish, which it cannot do if ruined by excessive dressing. It is easy to overdress a fly; hard to underdress one. The buyer also must look for quality and question the value of bargains. No dealer should object if the buyer tries to twist a fly's head or to pull lightly on part of the wing because properly varnished flies should stand reasonable abuse. A well-made streamer or bucktail should survive the mouthings of over a hundred trout before coming apart.

Most buyers select flies that are too big. For average trout fishing in clear water, sizes between 8 and 12 are large enough, probably on 3X long hooks. Sizes 6 and 8 should be adequate for high or discolored water. Yet many fishermen collect sizes 2 and 4, which are harder to cast and mainly are of value for trolling. Wings should extend only to the end of the tail, not much beyond the bend of the hook. If they are too long, trout may strike short.

It is risky to recommend patterns in a book with wide distribution. Here in New England, for example, some of our favorite patterns are popular

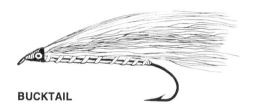

BUCKTAIL

STREAMER

Three basic types of streamers. When they are wet and
the fibers and feathers slim
down along the hook, these
flies imitate baitfish.

MARIBOU

nowhere else, and other regions have their own for one reason or another. Basically, streamer flies and bucktails are of two color types; the *imitators* and the *attractors*. The former imitate prevalent baitfish as closely as possible in form, flash and color. Examples are the Black Nosed Dace, which imitates the baitfish of the same name, and the famous Gray Ghost, which is made to look like a smelt. A national favorite is the Muddler Minnow, dressed to imitate the Cockatush minnow, commonly called the muddler. The attractor patterns are colorful: red and white or mostly yellow. These may be takers in high or discolored water but are of lesser value ordinarily. If a trout rises to one, and doesn't take, switch to an imitator pattern of a prevalent baitfish in the area. Only a very few attractor patterns are necessary.

Imitator patterns in general simulate three types of baitfish. There are the ones with pronounced medial stripes; those with dark backs, light bellies, and no stripe at all, and the ones with vertical bars, the last being imitated by wings of barred grizzly feathers.

Another important type of streamer is the one with a marabou wing. This is as fluffy as a powder puff when dry, but it slims down nicely when wet. It is noted for extreme pulsating action, an example of which will be described later.

In addition to color and form the two other important characteristics of streamers and bucktails are flash and action. Flash usually is provided by tinsel in the body. Some bodies are all tinsel and others are ribbed with it. Some bodies are made of mylar piping, which provides an excellent representation of a minnow's belly. Some wings contain extremely thin strips of mylar. Fluorescent silks and yarns, as tags or butts or a few strands mixed into wings, add to flash, and are especially valuable when water is high or dirty. Use fluorescent materials with restraint because only a very little is better than too much.

It is helpful to have flies with varying degrees of flash: only a little for bright weather and clear water; more for cloudy days or adverse water conditions. All baitfish have flash in varying amounts. Notice their glistening sides when they twist their bodies while gathering food.

A streamer fly or bucktail is a dead thing until put into action by the angler's rod. The action given should imitate the darting of the baitfish. It pays to watch them in the water and then to fish the fly similarly.

Why Fish Take Streamers

Fish take streamers because they are hungry and think they are baitfish. To a lesser degree they also take them out of anger, curiosity, or in the spirit of play.

Fish frequently strike streamers out of anger when they collect for spawning, as will be noticed by the immediate slashing hit of a bass when a fly is pulled over his nest. I have capitalized on this trait to take a big trout on several occasions. If I come to a hole below an undercut bank and know a good trout must lie there that won't come to a fly, I put on a marabou streamer, cast above his supposed position, and slowly work the fly down into it in the current. I stop the fly every 6 inches or so, but keep it fluffing. A whole minute each time isn't too long. I drop it down half a foot more and keep up the action. If the fly pulsates near the trout long enough, the chances are that he eventually will strike it. He isn't hungry, but its nearness bothers him and he wants to kill it to get it out of the way.

An excellent fly for this purpose is the white marabou, called the Ballou Special, when dressed correctly. It has a silver body with golden pheasant crest tail. The wing is a few hairs of red bucktail over which are two white marabou feathers tied on flat. There is a topping of about a dozen strands of peacock herl, and (usually) short jungle-cock cheeks. The wing should extend only to the end of the tail. Other popular marabou colors are blue and black, and they are necessities in every fly box.

Trout also strike flies because of curiosity or playfulness, but whether or not anger enters into it is a question only they can decide. These characteristics, however, may help to answer why trout so often strike at colorful attractor patterns which have so little resemblance to actual baitfish.

Fishing Streamers in Streams

When trout are rising they may take properly selected streamers as readily (or more so) than dry flies or nymphs. A rising trout falls back to his holding position a foot or more deep. The streamer should not be cast directly to him. It should be cast upstream and beyond his position so it will sink·and then, after drifting down sufficiently, be pulled actively in front of him. A floating line with a sinking tip is excellent for this. The leader should be long, with as fine a tippet as will work properly with the fly.

When trout are not rising, concentrate on the "trouty" spots which have been described: deep runs against undercut banks, fast glides and riffles, holding positions just above and below boulders, edges formed by obstructions, and so on. In directing streamers to such positions, cast across stream, or a little above and across, so they can drift fairly deep in the current. If the current is fast, little or no action may need to be given to the fly because the current will furnish it, but be sure that it maintains the darting action that has been described. Sometimes trout take when the fly is fished slowly but, at other times, they may want it fished faster and more actively. When trout take streamers that are fished fast they usually hook themselves, but tightening on them enough to set the hook is good insurance.

Strict attention should be paid to the fly when it completes its swing and starts to hang in the current. A trout may have followed it and often will take it during this change in its action. If nothing happens, the hung fly should be worked for several seconds before starting the retrieve.

Basically, there are three ways to fish streamers and bucktails. In fast water containing near-surface holding positions the fly can be retrieved rapidly by skittering it across the surface. In medium currents it can be allowed to swing and be fished with a jerky bucktailing motion, perhaps by moving the rod tip from side to side. In deep holes and quiet runs it can be sunk, twitched upward slightly, and allowed to sink again while being retrieved, in the manner of a wounded baitfish rolling, drifting and recovering.

In deep pools and runs, when there is no surface action, you may have to dredge bottom, especially when the water is cold early in the season. Therefore, streamer fishermen should carry a spare reel spool with a sinking or fast-sinking line. Upstream casts may be necessary to get the fly down in the current before taking in slack when the cross-stream position is reached. We need a tight enough line to feel a strike, but it shouldn't be so tight that it will pull the fly up. Extra line may need to be payed out as the drift progresses.

CURRENT

B

Basic method of fishing streamers or bucktails. Angler at *A* casts up and across stream, allows current to sweep the fly downstream while he guides it through good holding water. At completion of the float, he retrieves fly in short jerks, slow twitches, or a rapid topwater skitter. After covering all good water from first position, he moves upstream, to *B*, and works the next stretch.

Fishing Streamers in Ponds and Lakes

The positions to be covered are the same as when using spinning tackle because those are where trout should be: stream mouths, coves and spring holes when surface water is warm; around islands, rocky points and windward shores when it is not. Those who have read this far need no repetition.

In shallow ponds and small lakes with weedy bottoms the sunken streamer often pays off so well that it may be appropriate to touch upon it again. This is blind casting, fanwise around the boat, changing locations occasionally, until productive spots are found. In summer these usually are spring holes or seepages where colder underground water is forced upward. Fast-sinking lines are used to get flies down nearly to the weed level. After casting, give the fly time to sink, counting the seconds for it to do so. When a cast picks up weeds the count will be slightly shorter, but the idea is to get the fly down close to the weed level before fishing it in.

We know that baitfish such as smelt make spawning runs up the tributary streams of lakes, and that trout collect in and near the stream mouths to feed on them when they return. If streamers fished near the surface don't get results the deeply sunken fly, as just described, should do so. The fly used should imitate the baitfish as nearly as possible both in size and color. Even when there are hordes of baitfish milling around, and when the trout are so gorged with food that their gullets can't hold it all, they usually will strike at streamers. It is strange that under such conditions trout will pass by natural food to strike at imitations, but that very often is the case. It may be that the slightly different appearance and action of the artificial is what attracts them to it.

Trolling with Streamers

In addition to the information in the chapter on trolling, some added notes seem appropriate for streamer flies. Trolling usually is done to locate fish when they are widely scattered. Once located, casting from a drifting boat is preferable to disturbing near-surface fish by unnecessary boat action.

Trolling speed with streamers generally is agreed to be from 5 to 7 miles per hour, or a bit faster than a man can walk. If spinning gear is used, about 60 feet of line can be let out and the rod can be held by hand or set in a rod holder with the reel's antireverse engaged and the brake set only enough to keep line from paying out. Thus, when a fish strikes, it is hooked with minimum danger of pulling out, and it can start making a run while the fisherman picks up the tackle. Of course lead is undesirable, but a keel lead may be necessary to work the fly deeper. This is tied in 2 or 3 feet from the fly. When a boat is fishing two rods, lead can be used on one of the lines so the two flies will troll at different depths.

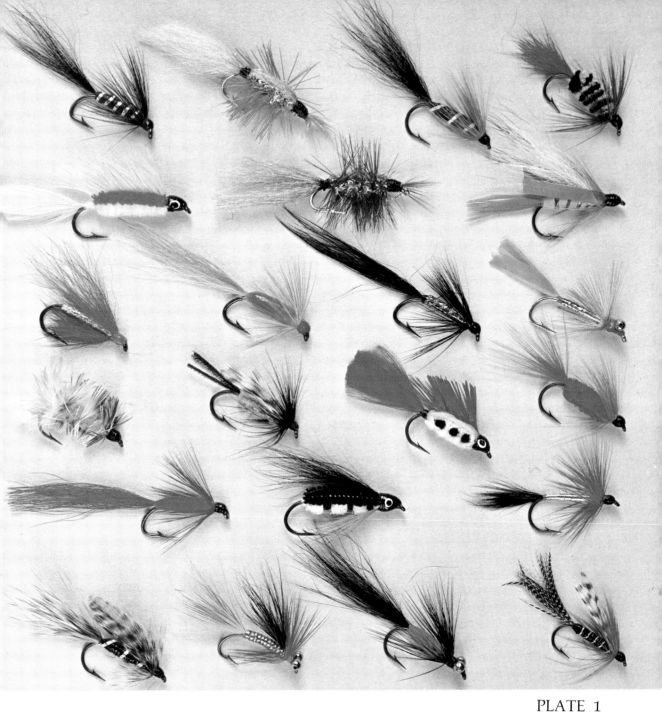

PACIFIC STEELHEAD FLIES

(Dressed by Irwin Thompson, Sebastopol, California)

PLATE 1

BLACK ANGUS	BLUE SHRIMP	BOSS	BRINDLE BUG
BUSTLE BACK	BROWN SHRIMP		THE CANADIAN
FALL FAVORITE	FLUORESCENT COMET	GOLDEN ANGUS	GOLDEN COMET
GOLDEN WOOLY WORM	KLAMATH RIVER SPECIAL	LITTLE JAK	THE OAKIE FLY
RED BARRON	SADDLE BACK		SILVER BOSS
SILVER HILTON	SYLVIOUS DEMON	THOMPSON'S RED COAT	WINGED BOSS

PLATE 2

FRESH WATER BUCKTAILS
(Dressed by Originators, or Exact Copies)

SHUSHAN POSTMASTER	EDSON DARK TIGER	GHOST SHINER
MUDDLER MINNOW	HERB JOHNSON SPECIAL	FULSHER'S SILVER MINNOW
MICKEY FINN	POLAR CHUB	ROYAL COACHMAN
LITTLE BROWN TROUT	LITTLE RAINBOW TROUT	LITTLE BROOK TROUT
GOVERNOR AIKEN	BLACK NOSED DACE	TRI-COLOR

PLATE 3

FRESH WATER STREAMERS

(Dressed by Originators, or Exact Copies)

COWEE SPECIAL	BLACK MARABOU	TROUT FIN
MILLER'S RIVER SPECIAL	BLACK GHOST	GOLDEN DARTER
RED FIN	GRAY GHOST	COLONEL BATES
SUPERVISOR		NINE-THREE
BLUE MARABOU		BALLOU SPECIAL

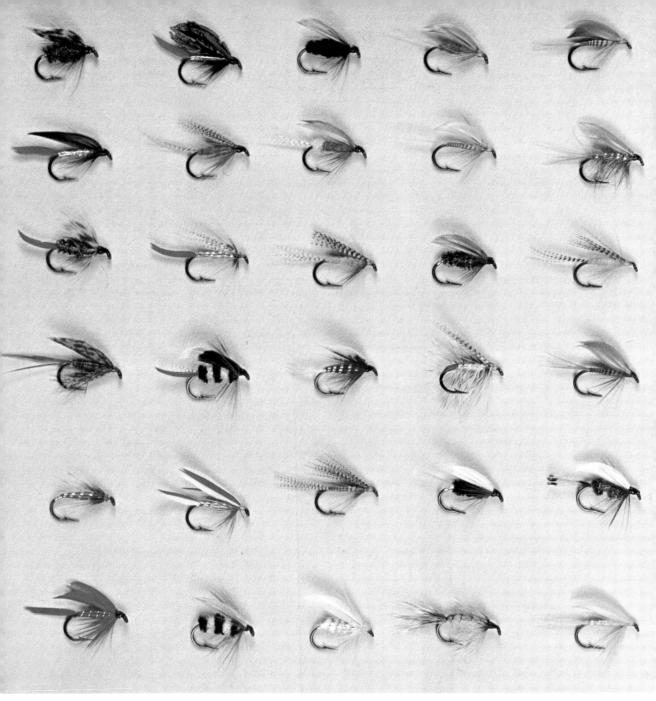

PLATE 4

WET FLIES

(Dressed by Robert V. Jacklin, Jr., Roselle, New Jersey)

ALDER	ALEXANDRA	BLACK GNAT	BLUE DUN	BLUE QUILL
BUTCHER	DARK CAHILL	FEMALE BEAVERKILL	GINGER QUILL	GOLD RIBBED HARE'S EAR
GRAY HACKLE PEACOCK	GRIZZLY KING	HENDRICKSON	LEADWING COACHMAN	LIGHT CAHILL
MARCH BROWN	McGINTY	MONTREAL	MORMON GIRL	OLIVE QUILL
ORANGE FISH HAWK	PARMACHEENE BELLE	QUILL GORDON	RIO GRAND KING	ROYAL COACHMAN
SCARLET IBIS	WESTERN BEE	WHITE MILLER	YELLOW BODIED GRAYBACK	YELLOW SALLY

With fly-fishing tackle, a long level leader—as much as 50 feet or more—is used. If two rods are used, they are held at right angles to the boat, one on each side, to keep the flies separated and away from the wake. This angle also allows the flexibility of the rod to hook the fish properly. A floating fly line with a sinking tip on one rod and a sinking or fast-sinking one on the other lets the flies fish at different depths. The lead-core line and long leader rig discussed in the chapter on trolling also is useful with streamers. If water temperatures are taken, the proper trolling depth can be presumed in advance.

Sometimes a fly which merely is being towed brings enough action. Bucktailing it usually is better. If the water's surface is rippled by wind and if surface temperatures are proper, near-surface trolling should get results. When the surface is flat and glassy it usually is more productive to go deeper. Erratic trolling—that is, steering a serpentine course—is better than going in a wide curve or a straight line. It covers more ground, and gives better action to the fly.

An angler friend who is supposed to be a purist has a trick he calls a "locator." He starts trolling by putting a worm on his fly, usually fishing it near the surface. If this doesn't get results he concludes that near-surface trolling with flies is useless under present conditions, so he adopts another tactic.

Flies used for trolling for trout (and landlocked salmon) on northeastern lakes average about 3 inches in over-all length because that seems to be the average length of the baitfish there. In early season, the flies may be shorter. Such flies need a tail hook to prevent fish from striking short.

Both single and double rear hooks are used since many anglers feel that doubles make the fly ride better. Monofilament and other plastic connectors aren't as popular because they tend to warp and throw the rear hook out of line. Twisted stainless-steel wire is less inclined to warp. Optionally, the rear hook can be attached to ride barb upward.

Small beads such as imitation pearls sometimes are strung on the wire, but this adds little, if anything, to the fly's effectiveness. Mylar piping often is slipped over the entire rig (except the bends and barbs of the hooks), adding greatly to the merit of the fly.

Slimness of line is a very important virtue in all streamers and bucktails. Test them by getting them wet, even in a glass of water. Regardless of how they look when dry, it's their soaking-wet slimness that counts.

WET-FLY FISHING

Wet flies were the first type of artificials used in fly-rod angling as we know it today. The first twelve named patterns are attributed to Dame

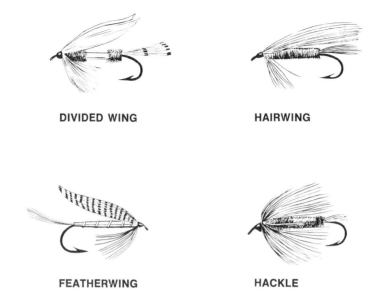

DIVIDED WING   **HAIRWING**

FEATHERWING   **HACKLE**

Basic types of wet flies. When drifting in the current, these flies imitate dead insects—for example, the spent mayfly after it has mated and fallen into the stream.

Juliana Berners, the English abbess who is thought to be the author of *Treatise of Fishing with an Angle*, published in 1496. She had a favorite pattern or two for each month of the season.

Anglers knew nothing about dry flies, streamer flies and nymphs until the mid or late nineteenth century. They used wet flies exclusively. Since no one knew how to bend an eye on a hook until about 1890, the eyeless hooks were lashed to snells of silkworm gut. Snelled flies were popular long after eyed flies became available and only went out of style when monofilament was perfected shortly after World War II.

Wet flies are dressed in four principal styles, as shown. The double quill wing is two sections of similar but opposite wing feathers of birds such as duck, turkey or swan. The feather wing is a bunch of fibers from a side or breast feather of any suitable bird. The hair wing of a wet fly is a bunch of hairs from an animal, such as the tail of a squirrel. Hackle flies have no wings, but have one or more hackles palmered around the body or wound on as a collar. Whichever style is used is the choice of the angler.

While wet-fly patterns run into the hundreds, only a few dozen are very popular for trout, but there are distinctive ones for certain varieties of trout such as steelhead. Every experienced wet-fly fisherman is loyal to his own choice of patterns, but a popular dozen might include:

Black Gnat (wing hugs body)	Professor
Blue Dun	Leadwing Coachman
Dark Cahill	Royal Coachman
Light Cahill	Quill Gordon
Gold Ribbed Hare's Ear	Montreal
March Brown	Silver Montreal

Sizes average about number 10 or 12 for clear water conditions, but there are situations which require sizes considerably smaller or somewhat larger. Selections should include a few dark ones, dull ones and bright ones. These include both attractor patterns and imitators. When insect hatches bring trout to the surface the wet flies used usually simulate the hatch in size and appearance.

Wet flies imitate dead or spent insects drifting with the current or floating on or sinking in the water. Trout may take them to be nymphs or minnows, or another desirable kind of food.

Since casting distances usually are short and a delicate presentation is necessary, a double-taper fly line is favored for wet-fly fishing, either a floater or a floater with a sinking tip.

The leader should be tapered, at least as long as the fly rod, and as fine at the tip as is considered safe. Trout may refuse flies presented on leaders that are too heavy. The practice of using more than one fly on a "cast" (a tapered leader with flies on droppers added) isn't as popular as it used to be, but there are some who think that, if one fly will do well, more than one will do better.

Chapter 12 described ways to add droppers to a leader. If two flies are desired, one of course is on the point, i. e., the leader's tip. The second one can be midway up on the leader. The dropper should be as fine as the tippet, or nearly so, and not more than 6 or 8 inches long. Ideally, the connection should tend to hold the dropper outward from the leader or pointing backwards toward the line to help prevent it from tangling with the leader. If a cast of more than two flies is desired, the droppers usually are equally spaced on the leader.

Since wet flies are presumed to imitate dead or dormant insects, no action usually is given to them on the drift, although they can be fished actively if the drifting method doesn't get results. After casting across and upstream as before, let the fly drift a bit and then quickly strip in a foot or two of line, alternating this procedure until the hung position is reached.

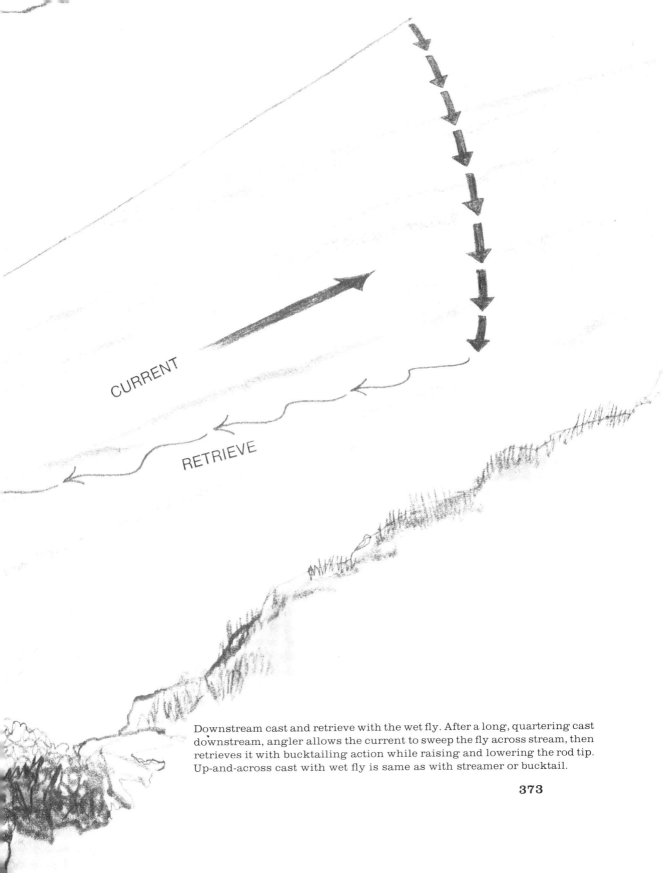

CURRENT

RETRIEVE

Downstream cast and retrieve with the wet fly. After a long, quartering cast downstream, angler allows the current to sweep the fly across stream, then retrieves it with bucktailing action while raising and lowering the rod tip. Up-and-across cast with wet fly is same as with streamer or bucktail.

Another method is a long quartering downstream cast, after which the fly is retrieved while alternately raising and lowering the rod tip to provide both faster and slower bucktailing action. What these two methods are supposed to represent is questionable, but it may be the action of tiny baitfish. Anyway, they work on occasion.

Wet flies do well early in the season probably because, when the water is cold and the trout are so logy they won't move far for food, they are more inclined to take the slowly drifting wet fly. At this time of year, it must be fished close to the bottom, so either a sinking line is necessary or a split-shot or two should be clamped a foot or so up the leader; perhaps both. Upstream casting also helps. When the fly gets down it will move upward as the current or the angler takes up slack line. Strikes often occur after the fly has scraped bottom and started to rise in a nymphlike manner.

While the wet fly seems most effective when fished in a current of some sort, it sometimes does well when there is none, such as in a pond or lake. Then the fly is allowed to sink and should be given various degrees of action. The take is very light, like a trout taking a nymph, so even the slightest resistance, or unusual motion of the line, should be considered as a take and the angler should strike lightly.

21

Fishing Nymphs

Let's explode the notion that fishing with artificial nymphs is difficult. Anyone able to handle a fly rod passably well can catch trout on nymphs all during the season—and big ones, too. He often can do it when trout won't take other artificials.

Nymph fishing is thought to be difficult because it can involve a great deal the beginner doesn't need to know. The expert delves into the science of entomology—the study of insects. Readers who prefer fishing to reading scientific theories about it can remain with the basics and have fun catching trout with nymphs.

Nymph fishing became popular partly due to the experiments and writings of an English gentleman named G. E. M. Skues during the first half of this century. In Chapter 6 we touched on how such insects as mayflies, caddis flies, stoneflies and others lay their eggs on the water. Some sink into the mud or gravel, eventually developing into the larvae or pupae of these insects, all of which are commonly referred to as "nymphs." We'll see that they are very small wormlike creatures, usually less than an inch long, which scurry amid bottom stones and debris or which cling to underwater rocks and other materials until they are ready to hatch into flies. When this time comes they rise to the surface; shuck their nymphal skins, and fly away as winged insects—unless they are eaten by trout.

Nymphs are of many kinds, each species emerging at certain times during the year, but mostly in spring and early summer. We must know how they act when they emerge in order to imitate their actions with artificials.

Before nymphs rise to the surface some varieties crawl slowly around the bottom, or quiver slightly. Thus, an artificial lying on the bottom, with even the slightest motion given to it by the current or by the rod, will imitate the live nymph and tempt trout to pick it up. In this case it takes experience and instinct to feel the delicate mouthings of a trout, and to hook him, during the few seconds he has the nymph in his mouth before he decides it isn't the real thing and spits it out. This is one reason why experts claim that nymph fishing is difficult.

In quiet pools, ponds and lakes, an emerging nymph will rise *very* slowly, gradually and steadily to the surface. Thus the sunken artificial can be drawn upward *very* slowly in a similar manner. It is plain that if an artificial should be fished faster it wouldn't imitate the natural and probably wouldn't be taken by trout. Artificials fished this way, off the bottom, can be drawn upward; allowed to drift backward and downward, and then can be fished upward again, more or less repeatedly. Since nymphs drift as well as rise, trout may take them at any time during this process. The take may be as delicate as before, or more like a strike, but the angler must be able to feel it and instantly to hook his fish.

If the pool is deep, a sinking line is needed, or a split shot or two or a twisted lead strip attached to the leader a foot or more above the lure. In currents, both the sinking line and the lead may be needed. Weighted nymphs are better than lead.

In faster water nymphs will be swept downstream by the current until they either are able to rise and hatch or until they are eaten by trout. Trout lie in or near eddies waiting for nymphs to be washed into the quieter water. Thus, in nymph fishing, look for eddies where debris collects. Since trout should be in the edges of the current near such places, artificials should be drifted into them too.

In faster water, therefore, nymphs can be fished exactly like wet flies. The fast-drifting nymph may be taken savagely, so hooking a trout under such conditions is less of a problem. The type of line used depends primarily on the water's depth and how deep we want to drift the nymph. We may need to find by experimentation whether trout want it near the surface or deeper down. If there is surface action, such as fish swirling, bulging or tailing, nymphs probably are being taken as they emerge, or as they are about to do so. A floating line with sinking leader is ideal for near-surface work. A floating line with a sinking tip takes the lure down deeper, the depth depending on the force of the current. A sinking line may be necessary for bottom-dredging, but it shouldn't be used unless necessary because it is more difficult to pick up for a new cast.

Only one nymph should be used. The leader's tippet should be as long and as fine as is considered safe. The nymph should be kept wet and should be fished on a leader that will sink immediately. This demands a minimum of false casting. You should not have to pull the nymph under the surface.

The nymph also should land lightly, without line or leader splash. To avoid splashing, cast to an imaginary point 2 or 3 feet above the water, so nymph, leader and line will drop lightly. Always keep the drifting nymph free from drag, except when it hangs downstream. A natural drift may require mending the line frequently.

When trout mouth the nymph so lightly that it is difficult to feel them, a bushy hard-to-sink dry fly can be used as an indicator. Tie the dry fly to a short dropper, and tie this to the leader a foot or more above the nymph. The nymph will drift down in the current, with the dry fly floating over it. When a trout mouths the nymph it will give action to the dry fly, perhaps pulling it under. This of course is a signal to strike.

When normal methods seem unsuccessful, remember that various nymphs have different ways of locomotion, so vary the fishing method until the most successful one is found. Try the natural drift at various levels, including very close to the bottom. Cast more nearly upstream in a slow current, but remove slack line during the drift in order to feel very light strikes. Upstream casting helps the nymph to sink deeper.

Some nymphs, like those of the stonefly, emerge so early they often crawl up on ice to transform themselves into adults. In early-season fishing, when water is below 45 degrees, it is impossible to fish nymphs too slowly or too deeply. Trout are on the bottom, and artificials must be fished there. Similar conditions exist when surface water is quite warm, when trout seek spring holes, brook mouths and other cooler places. Dragging bottom means getting snagged occasionally, but that's the chance one has to take. If the nymph's barb catches on anything one should strike lightly but instantly because it may be a big trout.

More moderate water conditions, in the 50- to 70-degree range, indicate that trout should be feeding on nymphs off the bottom. When there is no surface activity we should experiment to find how deep to fish, because correct fishing depth is very important to success.

TYPES AND HABITS OF NYMPHS

Although the nymph addict's fly box may contain more than a hundred varieties of nymphal imitations, he by no means would have them all. New ones are originated constantly. Some are so amazingly lifelike and so accurately constructed that entomologists could identify them by their Latin names. Others are merely crude representations, and these often do as well as the fancy ones. As in other kinds of artificial lures, anglers are bitten by

Fishing a nymph in quiet water, angler casts upstream and allows nymph to settle to the bottom, then strips in line as it floats downstream toward him, raising the rod tip to draw it upward. In this manner, the artificial is made to resemble an emerging nymph rising from the bottom of a stream. In faster water, the nymph can be fished in a manner similar to that of a wet fly—across or downstream.

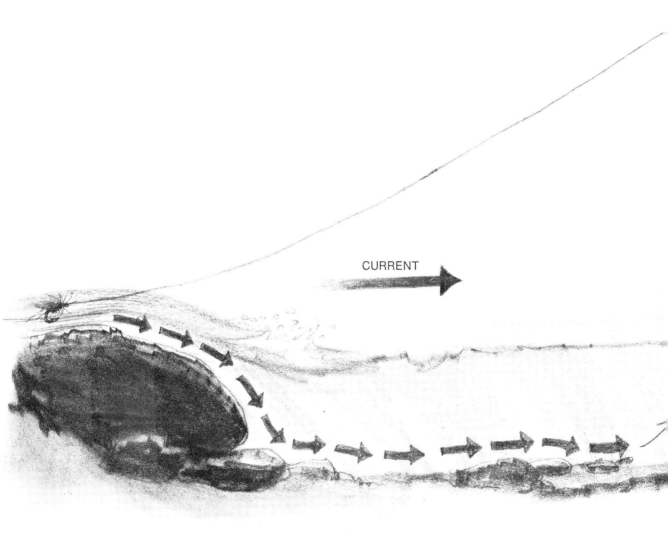

CURRENT

379

the "collectoritis bug," but the beginner doesn't need all this stuff. About a dozen patterns should suffice. Trout may be selective at times, and an accurate representation of whatever is emerging may be better than something else, but almost any nymph the angler presents may be taken as food at any time. Various kinds of nymphs may be emerging at one time in one place—so it is not always vital to "match the hatch."

Even so, those who want to fish with nymphs should become acquainted with them. In addition to reading books (several of which specialize on the subject) there are two good ways to do it:

When a trout is caught, open his stomach and put the contents into a plate containing a little water. Among various other things, you'll probably find nymphs. Probably one kind predominates, and that's the one to be imitated with an artificial. Fly dressers often drop a few into a little bottle of alcohol and take them home to go by in tying duplicates.

Another way is to pick up a few flat rocks in a stream to see what's clinging to them. Whatever is found may not be ready to emerge, but its undeveloped stage may provide a clue. Those who are more seriously inclined can make a net of screen or cheesecloth, as described in Chapter 5.

Since the next chapter describes how nymphs turn into flies, let's deal here with their nymphal stages briefly. There are three principal types, plus some others.

Mayfly Nymphs

These are the most prevalent and the most important. They are of many colors and sizes, some of which emerge successively all during the season, but especially between May and July. Some rise to the surface when hatching; others crawl up on rocks. The various kinds of mayfly nymphs and their flies, as well as their imitations, often go by the same names, such as March Brown, the Drakes, Hendricksons, Cahills and Coachmen. Being heavier than water they have little need to cling to objects, so they often are quite active, crawling about the bottom in search of food. Mayfly nymphs have hard shells and can not grow without shedding them, like crustaceans, which they do many times before finally emerging into flies. Thus the size of nymph imitations is of minor importance, but larger ones could be used at the start of the season, going smaller as it progresses. Shape is more important than color. Some anglers are more particular about color than others. One or two in light, dull and dark shades should suffice, the darker patterns giving way to lighter ones as the season goes on.

Caddis Fly Nymphs

Young fishermen, usually more inquisitive than their elders, become entranced upon noticing sticklike objects about an inch long lying in clear,

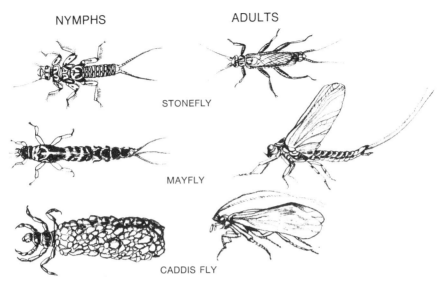

NYMPHS   ADULTS

STONEFLY

MAYFLY

CADDIS FLY

Three of the most prevalent aquatic insects found in our streams are the mayfly, caddis fly and stonefly, shown here in nymphal and adult forms.

rocky pools or eddies of mountain streams. They aren't sticks at all. They are caddis nymphs. Their cylindrical hard covering often resembles a stone-encrusted concrete pillar in miniature, or a collection of bark shreds cemented together. They may quiver, or even crawl short distances.

Picking one from the water, we notice that one end is open, with the head of a buglike creature looking out. There is a small opening in the other end, so water can flow through.

Caddis nymphs are second only to mayfly nymphs in importance to the fisherman. Commonly referred to as "stick worms," they can be imitated by dressing a hook with clipped deer hair. They are a favorite food of trout, case and all.

The caddis worm, or nymph, builds its protective house by secreting a sticky mucous-like substance to which tiny materials like sand, stones, bits of leaves, and bark adhere. When one opens a trout's stomach and finds tiny sticks and pebbles in it, they usually are the remnants of caddis cases.

When the caddis nymph is ready to hatch, it leaves its case and slowly swims to the surface, where it shucks its skin to become the small mothlike caddis fly we'll learn more about in the next chapter.

A caddis case probably could be imitated by lacquering the shank of a hook and rolling it in sand and leaves. Let this dry and then build it up to a cylinder about 3/8 inch in diameter by added applications. The result will be a caddis case (on a hook) much like the worm makes.

Artificial caddis cases could be used as lures more often than they are. Usually the emerging worm is imitated, such as the Breadcrust nymph. Some varieties of caddis nymphs do not build their own houses. Those that do usually inhabit rocky, flowing streams. Others, such as the green caddis, live in ponds and more slowly moving water. Cased worms obviously are fished very slowly on the bottom. Uncased nymphs are handled as has been described.

Stonefly Nymphs

Third in importance among the various families of nymphs are those of the stonefly, prevalent in many varieties throughout the United States. The nymphs are hard-shelled and abound in swift, rocky streams; hence their name. They are identified by two long tails, as distinguished from mayfly nymphs, which have three.

Stonefly nymphs emerge very early, often crawling up on ice bordering the stream to transform themselves from nymphs to adults. Later, they crawl up on rocks and logs, leaving their empty shells. Nymph or fly representations should be used to lure the trout which can be expected to be feeding nearby. Stonefly nymphs usually emerge at night, but if nighttime fishing isn't allowed or is impractical, the best time is early morning.

Stonefly nymphs are fished by drifting them deep, as was recommended for wet flies. The nymph should be steered close to banks and boulders where signs of emergence have been noticed. When it has swung and hangs in the current, it should be retrieved in short jerks. Strikes usually are more pronounced than the more delicate mouthings trout usually give to mayflies and caddis flies.

Since there are many varieties of stoneflies, some of which are regional, anglers should select their artificials from local favorites. Those who wish to dress their own stonefly nymphs will find detailed suggestions in *McClane's Standard Fishing Encyclopedia,* which contains seventeen authoritative pages on the subject of stoneflies, as well as formulas for dressing about three-dozen important nymph patterns, all of which are illustrated clearly in color.

Early-season stonefly nymph imitations should be in the larger sizes of numbers 14 to 6, and should be weighted for deep fishing. Artificials used later may be smaller, may not need to be weighted, and should be selected from those used regionally.

Other Nymphal Types

Anglers who have a dozen or so patterns of nymphs selected from the various ones imitating mayflies, caddis flies and stoneflies, should need few others for successful fishing. Other kinds of insects include dragonflies, damselflies, crane flies, alderflies, fish flies and midges, the nymphs of which can be imitated in fishing for trout. The smallest of these, the midges, bother fishermen in warm weather and also are called gnats, no-see-ums and other uncomplimentary names. Of course their nymphs are tiny, but not so much so that they cannot be dressed on very small shortshank hooks. Using them successfully is a specialized art requiring extremely light and sensitive tackle which the average angler neither owns nor needs.

One more type well worthy of mention is not a nymph, but it may as well be included here. This is the scud, erroneously called the freshwater shrimp. Very shrimplike in appearance, it is between $\frac{1}{4}$ and 1 inch long. Its smooth, arched body has numerous legs and leglike appendages imitated by clipped hackle. Dressing acceptable artificials is difficult, but I have seen examples that are extremely lifelike. Colors of the imitations run from pale green to brown to dirty yellow. Since scuds swim rapidly with a darting motion they can be fished in that manner. They are a favorite food for trout wherever they exist, which mainly is in western and southern states. Anglers fishing in such areas can increase their take by having some artificials ready for use.

SUGGESTED NYMPH PATTERNS

Any nymph angler who suggests a dozen useful patterns is sure to be faulted for some omissions. However, since everyone is entitled to his opinion, the following may provide sufficient variety for successful fishing almost anywhere. They are given more or less in order of emergence dates from May to the end of the season. Hook sizes or ranges are included.

Breadcrust (caddis nymph)	12, Reg.
Quill Gordon	14, Reg.
Hendrickson	12, 3XL
Iron Blue	14, Reg.
Green Drake	14–6, 3XL
Gray Fox	14–6, Reg.
Montana	8, 3XL
Zug Bug	14–6, 2XL
March Brown	10, Reg.
Leadwing Coachman	12, 2XL
Light Cahill	14–6, Reg.
Stonefly	14–6, 3XL

MARCH BROWN

DARK HENDRICKSON

Examples of artificial nymphs that imitate the naturals. The March Brown and Dark Hendrickson nymphs mimic two mayflies that hatch in mid-spring in the East; the stonefly nymph hatches in early spring. All hatch later in the West.

STONEFLY

The stonefly hatches late, usually from early July to the season's end. Its nymph also represents the tent caterpillar and the Dobson nymph. Part of the reason for this selection is to provide a range of coloration between very light and very dark. Many of these nymphs are useful during the entire season.

In addition, if anglers are in areas where they are prevalent, a few scud (freshwater shrimp) should be useful in sizes between 14 and 6. Hooks are regular length and usually are curved in the shank to simulate the hump-backed effect of the natural.

The Wooly Worm, more popular in the West than in the East, often is taken by nymphing trout. Wet flies probably also are taken for nymphs, and can be made more nymphlike by snipping off the wings to leave a bit of their bases to represent the nymph's thorax.

For early-season fishing and at other times when it is necessary to go down deep, a few weighted nymphs can be very valuable. Since some of these may be lightly weighted, and hard to distinguish from the unweighted ones, they should be carried separately. Nymphs usually are weighted by winding the hook with wire before applying the body.

No two fly dressers will tie any nymph pattern in exactly the same way. If you buy nymphs, obtain them from the most authoritative source available. Whoever does the work must be something of an entomologist as well as a good fly dresser. The Orvis Company, Inc. (Manchester, Vermont 05254) and Dan Bailey's Fly Shop (Livingston, Montana 59047) are two highly regarded firms which offer excellent nymphs. These are available by mail order and are shown in their catalogs. As previously stated, those who want to dress their own patterns will find instructions in *McClane's Standard Fishing Encyclopedia.*

NYMPHS OR DRY FLIES?

When trout are seen feeding on the surface their actions may indicate whether a nymph or a dry fly should be used. When they swirl with tails showing they usually are turning to take emerging nymphs. When they break the surface differently from this they probably are feeding on dry flies, so the prevalent type should be matched and used. Small trout often rise and splash more violently than the larger ones, thus giving the impression that they are big fish. The big ones rise more cautiously, even only dimpling the surface slightly as they sip in insects. Big trout often maintain a holding position and, when feeding, can be seen to rise periodically for surface food. Watchful, quiet anglers who stay out of sight often can see whether or not the trout are taking floating or skimming insects. Familiarity with the characteristics of various rises is important. You can use dry flies and not get results with them when trout are selectively feeding on emerging nymphs. If you observe large flies on the surface and elect to use nymphs, select large ones, especially early in the season.

Those planning to fish in one area from year to year would find it helpful to learn the emergence dates of the various insects. These dates are fairly consistent and definite. They may be published by local tackle stores, or can be assembled from information provided by other anglers. A year-to-year diary is helpful for reference. In it can be kept emergence data as well as the flies or nymphs which were used, the success obtained with each, and notes on successful and unsuccessful fishing methods.

I hope beginners won't shy away from nymph fishing under the impression that they don't know enough about it. Usually, various types of nymphs are developing or emerging at the same time in the same place, so there seems to be no need to be overly fussy about correct choice of pattern. How the nymph is fished is more important than what it looks like. Nymph fishing is one of the most fascinating types of angling, and it can be as simple or can become as complicated as we want it to be. The way to enjoy it is to learn the basics, and then to start right in.

22
Dry-Fly Fishing

Before the development of the dry fly, anglers found that they could take trout by fishing wet flies on the surface. The wet flies had to be false cast to dry them, after which they would float only momentarily. To improve their floatability various British anglers made several changes in wet flies, including winding them with collars of stiff hackles and adding tails that would make hooks ride properly. All this was reported in several classic books written by the great English angler, Frederic M. Halford, around the turn of the century.

An American angler named Theodore Gordon heard of this and made himself and his favorite trout streams, New York's Willowemoc and Beaver-kill, everlastingly famous by writing to Mr. Halford about it. On February 22, 1890, Mr. Halford sent to Mr. Gordon about three-dozen English dry flies—and dry-fly fishing in America was born.

Since British insects aren't exactly like American ones, Mr. Gordon used the English flies as models for American patterns, thus giving birth to the renowned Quill Gordon and perhaps the Light Cahill, among others. Thus started, in this area of New York State, the development of many of the classic dry-fly patterns as we know them today.

Most anglers who are familiar with all fishing methods consider dry-fly fishing to be the peak of the angling art. Fishing the dry fly requires a fairly close imitation of the actual insect, delicate tackle, and precise presentation. Unfortunately, too many anglers shy away from dry-fly fishing under the impression that it is difficult and complicated. As in nymph fishing, one can make dry-fly fishing extremely complex, but it doesn't need to be so. One can have fun fishing dry flies for trout with only the basic knowledge set forth in this chapter.

WHAT DO DRY FLIES IMITATE?

When the nymphs described in the last chapter rise to the water's surface or crawl up on rocks or logs, their nymphal skins split, allowing them to leave the skins and to transform themselves into flying insects. When this is done on the water's surface, the transformation can be almost instantaneous, in sort of a "pop, and away they go" manner—a hastening developed by nature to keep some of them from being eaten by trout. When it is done on land the process can be much slower. The skin splits and the insect crawls away from the shuck, still not looking very much like a fly. While one watches, however, the pulsating body pumps fluid into the almost invisible wings, which rapidly spread and become larger. Very soon, with wings fully extended, dried and hardened, the newly born insect flies away. We have seen that these flies are in many different species and subspecies, including mayflies, caddis flies and stoneflies, to mention only three.

Mayflies, the most important of all species to anglers, are water-born flies with folded upright wings like little sailboats. After emerging, the fly is called a *dun* because the wings are dun-colored; a dull grayish brown. The duns may spend hours or days perched in trees or on bushes before a final transformation takes place. When this happens they molt, thus becoming *spinners,* more brilliantly colored and somewhat different in size and shape, with three long tails. The spinners, often in dense multitudes, dip swiftly downward and glide more slowly upward in a dancing flight while they mate. The females then skim the water to lay their eggs. Then, evidently exhausted, their wings become spread and uncontrollable, and they fall to die as *spentwings*.

When this happens, usually just before dark in May, June and July, trout seem to indulge in a frenzy of gorging themselves, swirling and darting about to eat all they can while the supply lasts. Strangely enough during such times of abundance, trout take reasonable imitations in dry flies avidly. Anglers try to imitate not only these three phases of the mayflies' life, but also the many sizes and colors of the various subspecies which hatch from time to time during the season, thus giving birth to a bewildering complexity of fly patterns. Those most faithful to the "match the hatch" school of thinking go to great pains to do so. Less meticulous anglers feel that only a few general representations are sufficient, and this often is true if the selection is a reasonable one and is presented properly.

Rising from the stream bottom, aquatic nymph emerges at the water's surface as a winged mayfly. When a "hatch is on," hundreds of flies come off the water. As they flutter momentarily on the surface, trout feed on them and will strike a dry fly that is cast on the water, if it is a good imitation of the natural.

Caddis flies, second in importance to anglers, look like small moths, with long feelers and tentlike folded wings. Their various types emerge between April and July, flying over the water in erratic zig-zag swarms. They are called miller and sedge flies. After hatching and mating, the females swim or crawl down the branches of bushes and the stems of grasses and plants to lay their eggs in the water, after which they die. Trout are in the shallows of the grasses waiting with noses near the surface to sip them in. Anglers use flies of the sedge or miller type with heavy hackles so they won't be caught on the grasses. The idea is to cast to the grasses or to the bank and to pull the fly off into the water. Caddis flies also zig-zag over fast water stretches of streams, almost touching the surface. The idea then is to use heavily hackled flies of similar size and color and to skitter them on the top.

Stoneflies, perhaps third in importance to anglers, appear even before ice leaves northern lakes. In shades principally of gray, brown and black, they average about an inch in length and have two pairs of wings which are folded flat against the body when not in flight. They crawl beneath the water's surface or dip the ends of their abdomens into it while flying in order to lay their eggs. Imitations include flies such as those of the same name and the Adams, Brown Sedge and Grannom. The gray, brown or black Wooly Worm is presumed to be taken for a stonefly.

When I was fishing in northern Saskatchewan one year in June, I noticed a large, ragged black cloud, probably a few miles away. Changing shape rapidly, the cloud became denser as it approached and descended. When it arrived, the car was pelted with a hail-like storm of flies which were presumed to be stoneflies. The fly-storm lasted for many minutes and, when it was over, the ground in a vast area was covered with dead and dying insects. Vast hatches occur in many regions, and the insects often become lost and unable to find water. When hatches occur they can be very widespread. On another occasion, for example, we had to stop many times during a drive of a few hundred miles to clean the windshield of mayflies.

No list of the best dozen dry flies would be widely acceptable because (again) no two anglers would agree on it, and it also would vary with the area being fished. We can, however, start with one of which many anglers might partially approve and the reader can go on from there.

Black Gnat	12–16	Leadwing Coachman	10–14
Blue Dun	12–16	Quill Gordon	12 only
Cahill (Light)	14–18	Ginger Quill	14 only
Grannom	12 only	Royal Coachman	10–14
Hendrickson	12–16	Spentwing Adams	12–18
Irresistible	6–12	White Wulff	10–14

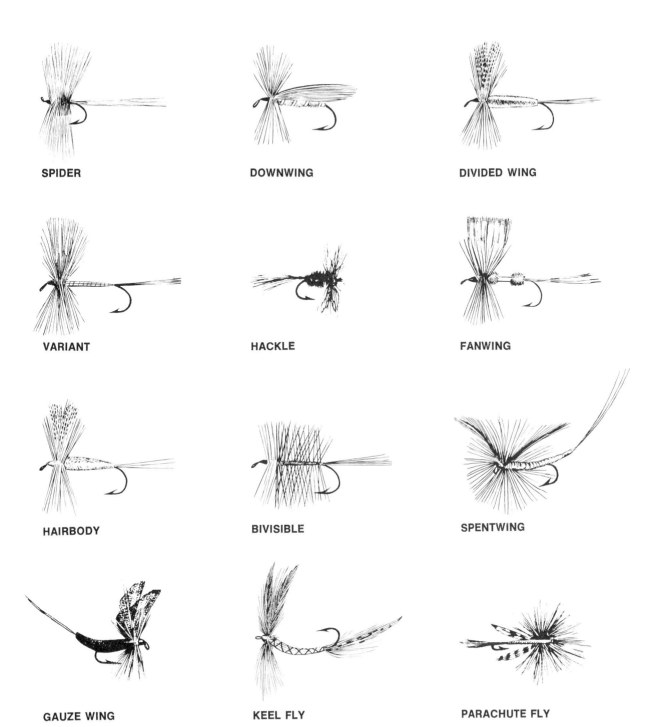

SPIDER

DOWNWING

DIVIDED WING

VARIANT

HACKLE

FANWING

HAIRBODY

BIVISIBLE

SPENTWING

GAUZE WING

KEEL FLY

PARACHUTE FLY

The basic types of dry flies are shown in this illustration. Each type is tied in many different patterns, or colors. For example, the divided-wing fly may be tied with blue, brown, or cream-colored hackles and matching wings. These flies usually imitate actual insects. Other types, such as the spider, bivisible, variant and fanwing, attract trout more by their color and shape than by their exact likeness to a specific insect.

About half of these flies are old classics, and seem to be perennials. In summer, when the naturals are around, good representations of the bumble-bee, the small green caterpillar and the grasshopper are very useful. Purists may frown on these being included as "dry flies," but there are many times when nothing can beat them. Tiny flies fished in the surface film often do well on long, fine leaders. These include midges, ants, grubs and a terrestrial called a Jassid. This is about the size of a house fly and often is winged with two jungle-cock tips tied on flat.

Part of the never ceasing argument about dry flies is how they should be constructed. Some like them collared with soft hackles, others with stiff ones, and a few with no hackles at all. Here, the stiff hackle advocates would win. I generally prefer high-riding flies for fast water and low-riding ones (such as the parachute type) that will settle in the surface film for use on ponds and lakes. Although stiffly hackled flies should have hackles no longer than the gape of the hook's shank, many are longer than that. If this causes the flies to cant over or otherwise to ride improperly, the lower hackles can be trimmed.

One could go on and on by discussing the pros and cons of heavily palmered bivisibles, fanwings, spiders, spentwings and many other types. Beginners can save money by staying with a few of the most popular patterns and trying the others only when it seems sure that they are needed.

These are the basic types of terrestrial flies that are tied to imitate insects that jump into the water from land or overhanging trees. After the hatches of aquatic insects have tapered off, terrestrials are extremely effective.

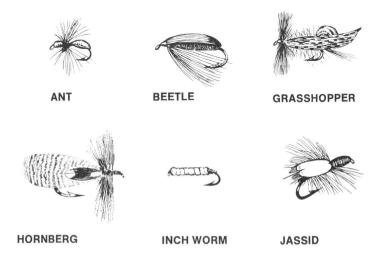

| ANT | BEETLE | GRASSHOPPER |

| HORNBERG | INCH WORM | JASSID |

DRY-FLY TACKLE

Since dry-fly fishing is more pleasant with light tackle, and since long casts rarely are needed, the most popular rods are in 7- to 8½-foot lengths. We have noted that makers of glass rods usually standardize on medium-action ones, and these all-purpose sticks handle dry flies very nicely. The dry-fly specialist, however, would prefer a rod with faster tip action (often called "dry-fly action") because it is superior for making the many false casts necessary to dry the fly in the air. By the same token, users of bushy flies such as streamers and bucktails would prefer a slower-action rod (often called "wet-fly action") because it takes more time for bushy flies to travel through the air during casts.

By gripping a rod with both hands and holding it extended forward, the tip can be oscillated from side to side and the extent of the deflection can be observed. Since it seems to be agreed that fast action is between medium and fast, and that slow action is between medium and slow, medium-action rods cover all requirements quite well. A slow-action rod obviously is not ideal for dry-fly work, but old rods passed down in the family often are of this type. Some may have been good dry-fly rods originally, but they may have softened through time. Another argument in favor of light rods for dry-fly fishing is that the lighter lines which fit them help to present flies more delicately.

Since light reels are appropriate with light rods, the single-action types are preferred over automatics and multipliers.

Delicate presentation of dry flies requires a floating line with a double taper rather than a level line or one with a heavy taper. We have seen that two can be had for the price of one by cutting the double-tapered line into two equal parts and putting half of the line on a reel with Dacron backing.

Although double-tapered floaters usually lie on the surface film without sinking, they handle better when kept clean. Put a little line dressing on a cloth and rub the line briskly with it. Then pull the line through the closed fist to remove excess dressing, which otherwise would scrape off to gum the rod guides. We need to dress only the part that will lie on the water. A clean line rides higher and will pick up better, with less drag, than one which has become stained by dried surface film.

The line can be picked up for recasting very smoothly and with almost no surface disturbance. Lower the rod tip while removing slack. Before making the backcast raise the rod tip quickly and smoothly until only the leader remains on the water. Then make the backcast using an upward and backward flick of the arm, as described in Chapter 7.

A properly balanced leader, as discussed in Chapter 8, is most important in presenting the dry fly delicately. It should be as long as can be handled

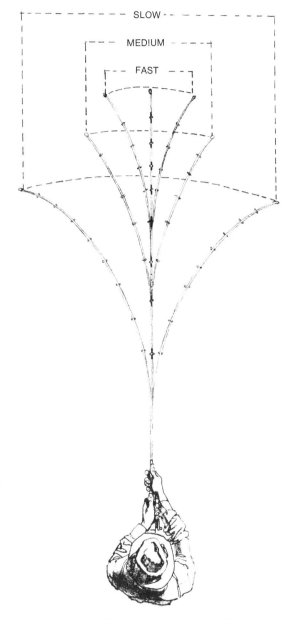

To determine the action of a fly rod, grip the rod with both hands and oscillate the tip from side to side. Fast- to medium-action rod, best for dry-fly fishing, will describe the shortest arc. Slow-action rod is better for casting wind-resistant streamers and bucktails.

394

properly, but need not be more than 12 feet. Shorter ones, at least as long as the rod, often are considered adequate, but specialists agree that longer ones increase the number of strikes. The leader, or at least the forward 6 feet or so, must sink. If it sinks the fly this can be corrected by false casting. The tippet must be as fine as will provide a secure connection; the general rule being "the smaller the fly, the finer the tippet." Many anglers like very long tippets of 3 feet or more. These probably will drop in coils, which is why some don't like them. However, the drifting fly will uncoil them and result in a longer free float.

Experienced anglers have a trick for hooking trout which is particularly useful when using dry flies and nymphs. Instead of raising the rod tip, they flick it *downward*. This provides a faster strike and, if the fish isn't hooked, the fly only has been moved a few inches and can continue its drift. We often miss by striking too soon as well as too late. This is a knack learned only by experience. Some wait until they feel the fish in the belief that he will turn and take the fly down before ejecting it.

Handling hooked trout on the dry fly is a delicate operation which usually requires only moderate tension while the fish tires himself out. When too much tension is applied, either the fine leader tippet will snap or the small hook will pull out. Pull-outs are caused either by faulty hooks or because the angler has been too heavy-handed with his fish.

Perhaps the most important maxim in dry-fly fishing is that the floating fly must be given an absolutely free float. We often think that the fly drifting in the current is floating freely when it isn't. This can be checked by watching other things, like bubbles, floating nearby. If the fly isn't traveling at the same speed, the drag must be corrected because the trout will know that something is wrong with it.

UPSTREAM CASTING

Casting upstream is the most important dry-fly method. Since trout lie facing into the current, the angler approaching from behind is less likely to be seen. The fly, drifting down over the fish, usually can be given a longer free float before drag sets in. Leader and line are less obtrusive, and probabilities of disturbing the water are less.

Upstream casting doesn't mean *directly* upstream, for line and leader then would pass over the fish, and the angler would have a problem taking in slack in fast currents without pulling the fly. Upstream casting means putting the fly partly upstream and partly across, on an angle that will provide the best float over the best water.

The position from which a cast is made is very important. Before casting, study the water to decide the best casting sequence. First, look for hold-

DRY FLY

TAPERED LEADER

Upstream cast and free downstream float is the basis of dry-fly fishing. The tapered line and leader (exaggerated for emphasis) provide the proper balance for casting and assure a light delivery of the fly ... (*continued*)

396

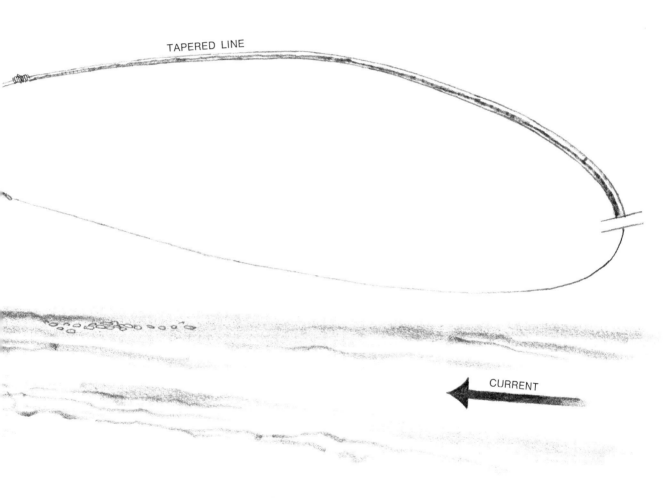

TAPERED LINE

CURRENT

397

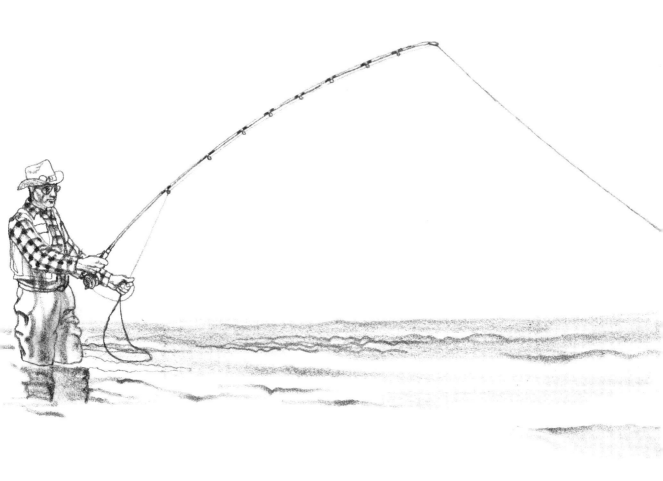

Since trout hold into the current, facing upstream, the aim of dry-fly fishing is to float the fly over the fish without drag. Note that the angler is not casting directly upstream, but slightly at an angle so the line and leader don't pass over the fish. As the fly floats downstream toward him, he strips in line to take up the slack.

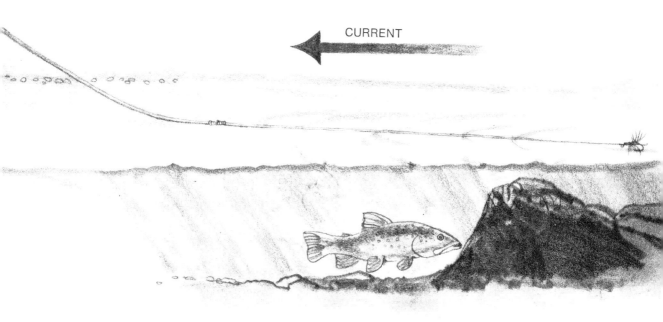

CURRENT

ing or feeding positions where trout should be: spots above and below big
rocks, deep holes in sharp bends of the stream, deep runs, obstructions such
as fallen trees, deep, shady places along brushy banks, bridge abutments,
and so forth. Bridge abutments are important because they break the flow
of water and provide shade. Trout invariably seek shady places in moderate
flow.

Having determined the trouty spots, you must then decide how casts
should be made to put the fly over them for the longest float that will be
free from drag. This demands a study of water currents. When you have
made these two determinations, you should know where to stand to make
each cast, the casting sequence necessary to cover the water, and the spot
to which each cast should be made. Old hands at the game can sum this up
almost at a glance. Newer ones should take the time to do so. A few minutes
invested in "reading the water" pays off in strikes. Inept fishermen ignore
most of this. They wade in where trout should be, flail the water with random
casts which send trout scurrying to safety, and then wonder why they don't
catch anything.

Figuring out the best casting positions and the best targets is important,
but two other things are equally so. The cast must be completed in the air
so that the fly will drop as lightly as an insect lands—with no splash from
leader or line. The cast must be delivered so the fly will drift at least within
a foot or so of where the fish is supposed to be.

It is greatest fun when trout can be seen, so one or more can be selected
as targets. When the fly goes over them, one of three things will happen.
The fish will rise and take the fly; it will frighten him away; or he will ignore
it. If he ignores it, you may have another chance, particularly if he showed
interest by rising to inspect the offering, or even quivering slightly. There
are several things that you can do: try a smaller fly, or a different fly, or
another method. Probably most experts would recommend resting the fish
for a few minutes while changing the fly and then using one of the first two
alternatives. Others, perhaps not wanting to bother with this, think other
methods work better. When the orthodox free float doesn't work, they give
a little motion to the fly. Remember that live flies don't always drift motionless. They often swim fast enough to take off. If a little motion doesn't work,
try skittering the fly, pulling it over the trout so it leaves a small wake.
Spiders are preferred for this tactic.

When trout can't be seen, of course blind casting is necessary. This
means floating the fly over all positions previously discussed, usually by
wading slowly upstream so good positions can be reached. On windy days
accurate casting may be difficult, but dapping may pay off. This means letting the wind handle the fly. Let enough line out so the fly blows in the wind,

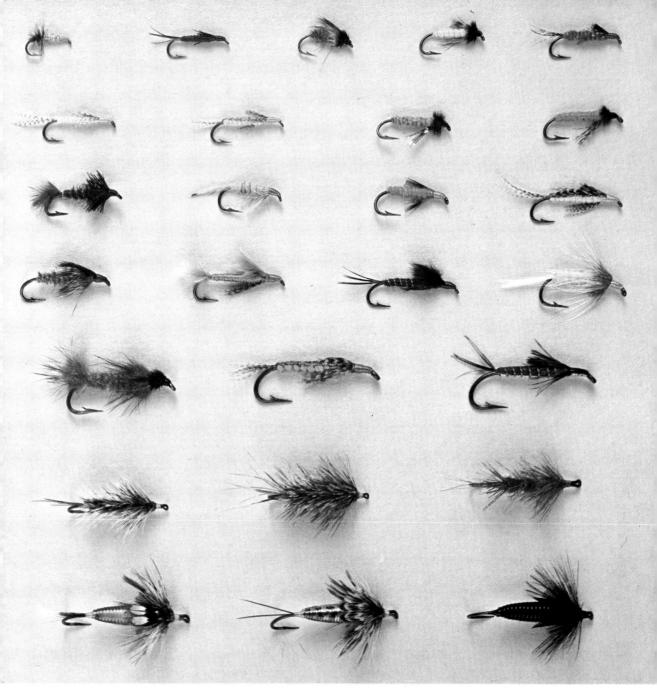

PLATE 5

TYPICAL NYMPHS

(Top 5 Rows by E. H. Rosborough, Chiloquin, Oregon)

(Bottom 2 Rows by George F. Grant, Butte, Montana)

BLACK MIDGE PUPA (12*)	LITTLE BROWN STONE (12)	HARE'S EAR (10)	LIGHT CADDIS PUPA (10) BLACK DRAKE (10)
YELLOW DRAKE (10)	LITTLE YELLOW STONE (10)	MUSKRAT (10)	GREEN ROCK WORM (10)
NONDESCRIPT (10)	SHRIMP (8)	DARK CADDIS PUPA (8)	YELLOW MAY (8)
FLEDERMAUSE (8)	GREEN DAMSEL (8)	BICOLOR WALKER (8)	BLONDE BURLAP (6)
CASUAL DRESS (6)	GOLDEN STONE (4)		DARK STONE (4)
BLACK CREEPER	ROUGH BADGER STONE		BRASS BUG
LIGHT HELLGRAMMITE	MOTTLED HELLGRAMMITE		BLACK HELLGRAMMITE

(* = Best Hook Size)

PLATE 6
STREAMERS AND BUCKTAILS FOR FRESH WATER TROLLING

STREAMER WITH UPTURNED SINGLE TRAIL HOOK   LONG SHANK SINGLE HOOK STREAMER
STREAMER WITH UPTURNED DOUBLE TRAIL HOOK   MYLAR BODY STREAMER WITH MYLAR STRIP THROAT
STREAMER WITH DOWNTURNED SINGLE TRAIL HOOK   BEADED BODY BUCKTAIL WITH DOWNTURNED SINGLE TRAIL HOOK
TANDEM HOOK MYLAR BODY MARABOU STREAMER
TANDEM STREAMER WITH MYLAR STRIPS   BUCKTAIL WITH UPTURNED SINGLE TRAIL HOOK

PLATE 7

UNUSUAL DRY FLIES AND TERRESTRIALS

GOOFUS BUG	PLASTIC-WINGED MAYFLY	FLYING BLACK ANT	"WONDER-WING" MAYFLY
PLASTIC-WINGED BEE	CATERPILLAR	DEER-HAIR BEE	GRUB	BLOW-FLY
LETORT HOPPER GREEN LEAFHOPPER	JASSID	PLASTIC-WING DRAGON FLY	ROCKWORM	COOPER BUG
GRASSHOPPER	PARACHUTE MAYFLY	BLACK ANT	PARACHUTE SPIDER
KING'S RIVER CADDIS		RUBBER LEGS	
DEER-HAIR BOMBER	BLACK AND ORANGE WOOLY WORM		JACKLIN'S BIG BLACK WOOLY

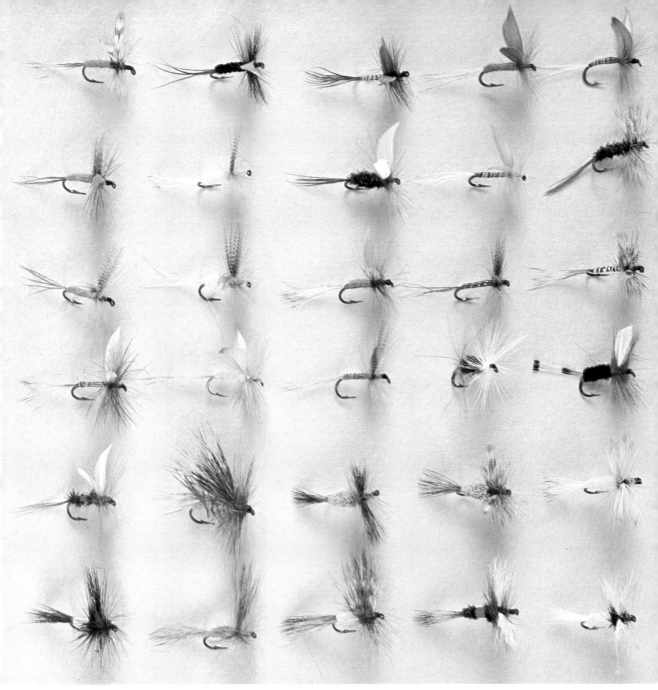

PLATE 8

DRY FLIES

(Dressed by Dan Bailey, Livingston, Montana)

ADAMS	BLACK GNAT	BLACK QUILL	BLUE DUN	BLUE QUILL
DARK CAHILL	LIGHT CAHILL	COACHMAN	GINGER QUILL	GRAY HACKLE PEACOCK
DARK HENDRICKSON	LIGHT HENDRICKSON	IRON BLUE DUN	MARCH BROWN	MOSQUITO
DARK OLIVE QUILL	LIGHT OLIVE DUN	QUILL GORDON	RENEGADE	RIO GRANDE KING
ROYAL COACHMAN	BUCKTAIL CADDIS	IRRESISTIBLE	RAT FACED McDOUGALL	BLONDE WULFF
BLACK WULFF	GRAY WULFF	GRIZZLY WULFF	ROYAL WULFF	WHITE WULFF

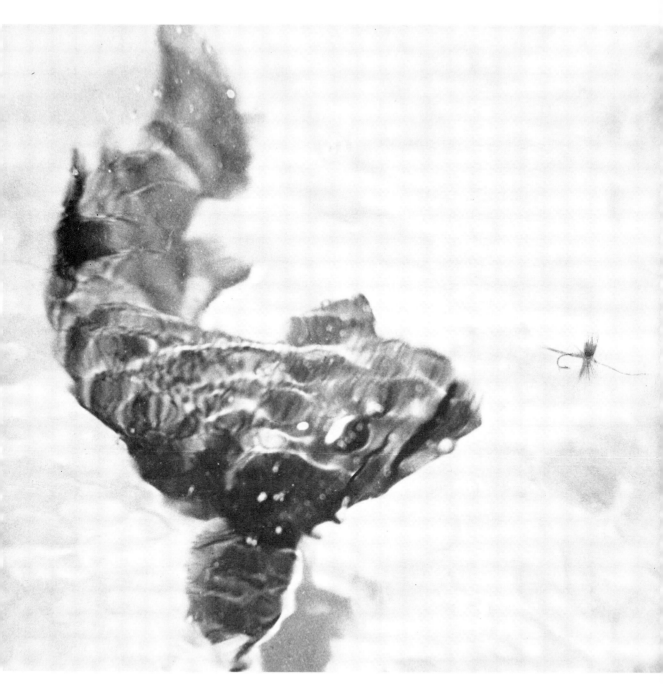

Free-floating dry fly brings a rise from a husky brook trout.

alternately being in the air and touching the water. This seems to simulate an insect skimming the water, and it takes but an instant for a trout to flash up and smash it.

Mending the line has been discussed, and it often is vital in obtaining a long, free float. When the current starts to put a belly in the line, this should be corrected before the belly gets too big by using the rod tip to flip the line into an upstream curve. Sometimes this may have to be done repeatedly, and it is a bit of a trick to know how much of a flip to give the line to remove the belly and yet not pull the fly. In casting to a good position, such as the moderate flow below a rock, a long float may not be necessary. You can drop the fly on target, let it float for only an instant, and perhaps repeat this several times, thus more or less simulating a hatch. This often pays off, and it often is the only way to reach a trouty target in fast water.

DOWNSTREAM CASTING

Many streams are too fast for comfortable or safe upstream wading. The dry fly can be fished downstream, but often broken water makes a free float impossible. However, a disturbed surface makes it difficult for fish to see you, so you don't need to be as concerned about a cautious approach. On this kind of water, any natural fly is buffeted about by wave and current action, so a tumbling or skittering artificial, or a fly that is being pulled, may appear natural if it isn't being towed too much. Obviously, good floaters are necessary. Heavily hackled Wulff patterns and flies with clipped deer-hair bodies are preferable. Padding the bodies of Wulff patterns with kapok before completing the dressings increases floatability. In fast water, it is easier for both fish and angler to see large patterns. Beyond a choice among light, medium and dark flies, the patterns are of minor importance. Trout must act instantly to take flies in fast water, and conditions are such that they don't see details clearly. By the same token, adding a little action to the fly usually helps to attract a trout's attention to it.

The slack-line cast helps to provide a good float in downstream casting, even if it is a short and quick one. Upon completing the forward part of the cast, aimed at the target, the rod is stopped quickly at 45 degrees and pulled back slightly. This causes the line to fall in S-shaped curves. While these are straightening out, the fly can get a free float to the position where a trout is presumed to be.

This slack-line cast can be extended with line that is off the reel by wiggling the rod tip from side to side, causing the extra line to pay out in curves. On completion of the float, action can be given to the fly as soon as it starts to drag. If the slack-line cast is made partially across stream it may pay to skitter the fly when the float has been completed. Thus, rough-water dry-fly fishing is done somewhat differently than upstream dry-fly fishing on more placid surfaces.

DRY-FLY FISHING IN LAKES

This rarely is the best method, and it only works when water temperatures are such that trout are feeding on top in lakes where insects are prevalent. These insects can be flies such as mayflies or caddis flies, or terrestrials such as ants, bees or grasshoppers.

The dry-fly leader must sink to eliminate too obvious a connection between fly and line. The fly can be given very slight motion to simulate the feeble action of a natural on the water, but this motion should be so little that it makes only the tiniest ripples.

Trout may be located cruising about or feeding in certain places on top, but this usually isn't the case. Other chapters in this book have attempted to describe where to find them. This may be in spring holes in summer. It usually is along the shore toward which the breeze is blowing, partly because drifting insects are blown there. It often is near stream mouths on the leeward shore where drifting food from the stream and from the lake collect together in a floating line or mass.

Dry-fly fishing for trout usually is done under warm-water conditions when terrestrial insects such as bees, ants and grasshoppers are prevalent. Although it is traditional to use imitations of water-born insects, the land-born ones often are more productive—so let's not be too traditional. Chapter 17 explains how to tie a bee with a black and yellow clipped deer-hair body, and the little lure is dynamite at times. Most tackle catalogs offer representations of grasshoppers, and most of them are very effective. Caterpillars usually work well. Artificial ants have many advocates, but this author hasn't had much success with them. Along the shorelines of lakes and ponds in the summer, representations of terrestrials such as these can do much better than imitations of water-born insects.

23
The Freshwater Basses

Largemouth bass, smallmouth bass and their less important cousins furnish year-round fishing sport in many regions, even under icy conditions. In big-bass country anglers rarely bother with anything else. These often are very successful specialists, so wedded to individual methods that some of what is written here may be considered rather basic. This chapter isn't for such experts, although the odds are that they'll glean a few ideas from it. It is for the casual bass fisherman who wants to improve his score.

Largemouths and smallmouths sometimes inhabit the same water, but not usually. Except for strength where needed, the tackle and lures for the one species are nearly identical to those for the other. Methods vary only with the type of water.

Anglers catching either of the two species, when both are found in the same place, often can't tell which is which. The most obvious difference between the two is that the largemouth's upper jaw extends well beyond a position under the eye, while that of the smallmouth's does not. Largemouth bass usually have blackish backs shaded to a greenish color below, and they often sport a variegated dark stripe along the medial line between head and tail. On the other hand, the smallmouth usually has a brown or bronze back shaded to yellowish green, and with variegated vertical dark markings on its sides.

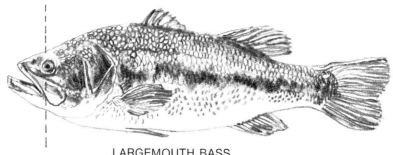

LARGEMOUTH BASS

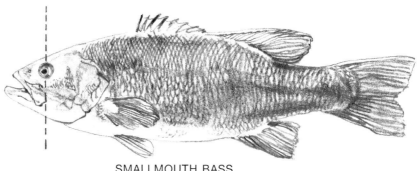

SMALLMOUTH BASS

Chief difference between largemouth and smallmouth bass is in the length of the upper jaw. The largemouth's jaw extends behind the eye, the small-mouth's doesn't. Also, the spiny front section of the large-mouth's dorsal fin is nearly separated from the softer section; the small-mouth's dorsal fin is continuous.

LARGEMOUTH BASS

Micropterus salmoides now inhabits nearly every state from coast to coast between southern Canada and northeastern Mexico. This increased distribution largely is due to the fact that (unlike the smallmouth) the fish is adaptable to farm ponds and man-made reservoirs, wherein it has been widely and successfully introduced. The rod and reel record is a 22-pound, 4-ounce whopper caught in Georgia in 1932.

The two principal keys to locating largemouths are water temperatures and protective cover. Ideal temperatures are between 68 and 72 degrees, which can be extended to a comfort zone of between 65 and 75 degrees, the ideal temperature being a bit on the higher side in the South, where the fish

Lunker Florida largemouth, and the tackle used to catch it.

have become acclimated to warmer water. At that temperature level, large-mouths should be found around points of land, dropoffs, steep banks near cover, submerged brush, trees and reefs, and in shallower water amid the protection of aquatic growths such as weeds, lily pads and grasses. Unlike smallmouths, largemouth bass seem to enjoy discolored water, if it is un-polluted, and they are more adaptable to warmer temperatures and tempera-ture changes.

Spawning habits also are a key to finding bass. They clean out large, circular nests near shore in water usually between 1 and 3 feet deep, this habit often causing loss of eggs and fry when reservoirs are drawn down. Spawning occurs in spring in northern regions when water temperatures reach 65 degrees, which usually is in April, May and June. It happens earlier as we go south, in late winter and very early spring. The male clears the nest by using his tail to fan silt and refuse from the gravel, also digging up and discarding plants and small roots which may interfere. After mating, the male guards the nest for two or three weeks, until the fry have absorbed their yolk sacs and school in the protection of grasses.

Nests are easy to see in the shallow water. If bass are on them they will strike at almost any lure, either through anger or to remove it from the nest. Fish thus caught should be freed to protect their young, and it is wise con-servation to leave them alone.

Largemouths in Deep Lakes

Under warm-water conditions, largemouths spend most of their time deep; as deep as from 25 to 35 feet, on or near the bottom where tempera-tures are about 68 degrees. The trick is to fish on bottom at this tempera-ture in areas providing protective cover. Deep trolling is a way to find the hot spots, and a good location always should be good under the same water temperature and light conditions.

Since bass have voracious appetites, the cover down deep may not pro-vide sufficient food. That usually being the case, they choose the colder surface temperatures between late afternoon and early morning to travel in schools to feed. This is a gradual journey toward the surface, rather than rapid transit. The schools usually will wander around, working higher, but frequently stopping at various "breaks" such as sunken brush piles, rock piles, ledges and drop-offs on the way to the shallows, where they feed as will be described when fishing in shallow lakes is discussed.

When largemouths are down deep they are inclined to be sluggish and hard to catch. The fishing is right on the bottom. If the lure isn't on the bot-tom, or very close to it, fishermen probably are wasting their time.

We have noted that trolling (which was discussed in Chapter 16 and to which more notes will be added later) is a way to locate deep hot spots.

These often are places where colder currents and springs exist. Depth thermometers and sonic bottom-scanning devices are helpful in locating them.

Many deep lakes are man-made impoundments such as the thirty-six reservoirs in seven states of the Tennessee Valley. These comprise about 600,000 acres of fishing water having about 11,000 miles of shoreline. In them the flooding of fields, woods and towns has left rotting brush piles and dead trees whose tops may emerge from the water, thus providing excellent havens and breeding grounds for bass as well as other species. These lakes are ice-free and can be fished all during the year. Navigation charts are available for most of them, as well as fishing maps provided by marinas and sporting goods stores. Good fishing usually is available by the fourth year after impoundment, and it normally improves at least until the eighth year. These lakes are so vast that visitors can't fish them effectively, but expert guides with boats can be hired to find the hot spots. Live lizards and minnows are favorite baits, and plastic worm rigs and plugs such as the Bomber and the Rebel are popular among the artificials.

Netting a largemouth in a typical bassy spot on a man-made lake. Flooded woods and brushy areas are the most ideal habitat to provide havens and breeding grounds for largemouths.

Largemouths in Shallow Lakes

When largemouths cruise deeply, because of more comfortable temperatures there, the inadequate food supply forces them into the shallows to feed. Feeding places in deep and shallow lakes essentially are the same — weedy coves, lily pad areas, and grassy spots wherever they may be. When shade is provided by rocks, stumps, etc., cast to the shady side, as close to the obstruction as possible. A foot can make the difference between a useless cast and a lunker.

Some weedy spots are better than others. In southern lakes they include sawgrass, pickerelweed, hyacinth expanses and other types of vegetation. Edges of hyacinth beds usually look more productive than they are. They often have been poisoned, which forms a sludge on the bottom, thus reducing fishing value. Pickerelweed provides excellent cover and shade, and these circular patches and rows can be hot spots, especially early in the season. This growth is identified by emerald-green bayonet-shaped leaves, with violet-colored flowers in season, growing in water only a few feet deep. The trick is to cast lures such as weedless spoons, plastic worm rigs or pork chunks beyond the patches, retrieving the lure as close to them as possible. When the lure is nearest the patch it can be slowed down. Popping plugs usually are reeled quite fast. If there is any open water inside the patch, cast right into it. A big one may be lying there! Horsing a big bass out of this kind of growth calls for strong tackle, but results often are well worth it.

Many shallow lakes are dotted with brush piles, their tips bunching above the surface. These present less of a problem than it might seem when weedless lures such as plastic worm rigs are used. Let the lure sink and work it in very slowly along the bottom and over whatever it may contact. No matter how slowly the worm rig is being fished, this probably is about twice as fast as it should be. In such cases the fish can't be allowed to run with the worm. Risk not hooking him by getting him out of the tangle as fast as possible.

Largemouths in Rivers and Canals

Southern areas have short rivers and drainage canals, many of which are part of the lake systems. They harbor bluegills, crappies and other species as well as bass. In them are masses of lily pads known as "bonnets" which grow in bands of varying width some distance from the shoreline in water

Floating silently through a Florida swamp, angler (*top*) looks for bassy spots among lily pads, in weedy coves, in the shade of submerged logs. *Below,* the weed bed in foreground looks like a hot spot to bass fisherman working a narrow southern canal.

as much as 6 feet deep. The water between the bonnets and the bank often contains many species of gamefish. On the far side of the pads it usually is deeper. Schooling bass often will be seen chasing bait very near to the bonnets on either side.

Flood control canals connect or drain many southern lakes, and often contain dense stands of sawgrass, cattails, lily pads and other vegetation. The canal may be quite deep and, if it was made to drain a marsh, may be shallow on the marsh side and much deeper on the dike side, with a steep drop-off along the dike. The shallower marsh side usually offers better fishing because it contains more submerged growth than what is visible on top. Depths vary, thus affecting the fishing, depending on how much water is being held back by the impoundment.

Another type of southern canal is that which borders a cypress swamp. The best time to fish this type is when the swamp has nearly been drained, thus forcing baitfish and bigger fish to leave the swamp for the deeper water of the canal.

Tackle and Tactics for Largemouths

In some areas, such as New England, largemouth bass don't run very big, and they often are caught in relatively open water. In other regions, such as Florida and some parts of the Southwest, the bass can be lunkers which have to be pulled out of brush piles and thickets of weeds. Since these extremes call for entirely different tackle, the range in between covers all freshwater methods in whatever strengths may seem appropriate. Selection is an individual choice depending on what will serve the purpose in the strength that seems sensible. Let's look at the various methods as they apply to largemouth bass.

Baitcasting. If a poll should be taken among largemouth bass addicts, baitcasting tackle undoubtedly would win, especially in regions where the bass are big and have to be hauled away from obstructions. Experts like this equipment because the free-spool baitcasting reel offers instant thumb control on the revolving spool. The reel is excellent for the short, accurate casts usually necessary. Modern refinements for easy, accurate adjustments make backlashes rare.

Baitcasting tackle has many advantages, some of which are shared by other kinds of gear. In addition to its suitability for handling big plugs it is especially useful for erratically retrieving lures where the resulting uneven spooling of line (as on spinning or spincasting reels) would be bothersome. In suitable strengths it is ideal tackle for quickly dragging big bass out of grasses and other tangles, and for fishing large lures through them. It is the favorite tackle for trolling.

Spinning and spincasting. This tackle, with lines of suitable strength, is excellent for largemouth bass when they are found in reasonably open water. The whippier rods and more complicated braking problems can present difficulties when bass are in the grass or in brush piles. Anglers preferring lighter lures may decide the advantages of the somewhat longer and more sensitive rods are in their favor.

Spinning offers longer casts with lighter lures, while spincasting has an advantage in erratic retrieving and in using baits and lures which are somewhat heavier. Bass fishermen who use small live baits such as minnows, lizards and frogs should prefer these methods to all but perhaps the lightest baitcasting gear. As this is being written, plastic worm rigs (discussed in Chapter 4) are highly favored. Smaller ones can be cast well and handled delicately on spinning tackle, while the spincasting method may have an edge when larger ones are used.

Either of the two methods are excellent for fishing jigs down deep. Jigging is very effective when bass are on the bottom, and often is even more so when an end of a plastic worm, a plastic skirt, or a fluttering piece of pork rind is added to the hook. In difficult spots a Johnson weedless spoon with pork rind attached often scores, especially when dropped into potholes.

Fly rods. These are for open-water fishing, but a long rod with stiff action in size 8 or 9 can offer real sport when lures are fished either wet or dry along the edges of lily pads, grasses, bonnets or stumps. A big bass hooked on fly tackle on or near the surface provides thrills when he erupts to smash a light and tiny lure and cartwheels above the surface with gills flaring.

In addition to the excitement provided, the fly rod enables you to make false casts, which help to land lures on target. It is an ideal weapon for wading, allowing you slowly and quietly to work an area, without the conspicuousness of a boat.

Wet-fly fishing calls for bucktails on size 2 hooks, or bigger. They can be dressed a bit bushier than is proper for trout. A good color combination is orange over yellow, but black over white, red over white or yellow, and green over white or yellow are among other combinations effective at times.

A level sinking line is satisfactory, but a weight-forward one is better. The choice between a sinking line and a floater with a sinking tip depends on how deep the water is, or how deep the fly should go. Level leaders about as long as the rod often are used in strengths of about 15 pounds; perhaps a bit more or less depending on conditions which will be encountered. Tapered leaders are better, but rarely are graduated to less than 12 pounds at the tip.

Bass bugging is an exciting way to fish for bass. Bass bugs are floating

Fly rod lures that are preferred by most fishermen for bass bugging. At top are four hair bugs; at bottom three poppers.

lures weighing $1/16$ of an ounce or less. Except for the floating line, the tackle is the same as for bucktails. Several types of lures are used, all of which are effective at one time or another.

Poppers have bullet-shaped solid bodies made of cork, wood or plastic, with flat or concave heads. Some have "wings" of hair, feathers or even cut rubber bands. They usually have bucktail or feathered tails, or rubber or plastic skirts. These may imitate frogs, grasshoppers, or perhaps nothing at all. Slow fishing is the key to success. Drop the lure lightly on the water, or pull it off a lily pad, and leave it there. When the little ripples have subsided, give it a very slight pop. Wait a bit, and do it again. Then make it pop and swim a foot or so. A bass may come for it the instant it hits the water—or he may be lying down there, eyeing it, and deciding whether or not he'll take it. If a minute or two of enticement doesn't draw a strike the lure should be picked up and placed somewhere else.

Hair bugs are made of deer body hair compactly massed by spinning it in small bunches around a hook and clipping it to whatever shape is desired. The bottom is clipped fairly flat and close to keep the dressing away from the gape of the hook. Some bugs have fan-shaped wings; others V-shaped tails, or are made in a wide variety of colors, designs and shapes to imitate frogs, moths, or other things. They are expensive because of the labor involved, but any amateur fly-tyer who can spin hair around a hook can make several in an evening. They are fished as described above.

A third type, less popular than the others, can be likened to a wounded minnow. This has a rounded head of clipped deer hair and a tail of hair or feathers. The feathered tail usually is split by tying in two hackles on each side, back to back to form a "V." This makes the tail open and close, scissors fashion, when being fished, an action that often is very effective. The same idea is frequently used on poppers and bugs.

Fly lines also are available in what is known as a "bass bug taper," which is a pronounced weight-forward taper. It is necessary only for casting big bass bugs which are very wind-resistant.

Trolling for largemouths. Although trolling was described in considerable detail in Chapter 16, it may be helpful to add some notes on three very effective methods of trolling plastic worms for largemouth bass. These are

Gliding from his hiding place in a mass of underwater weeds, a largemouth stalks a popping bug. When bass hit a topwater lure, the fun is fast and furious.

for hot-weather fishing when bass are down deep. The methods often are used as locators because a lot of water can be covered in a short time. On getting a strike it is usual to lower the anchor there for casting. Baitcasting tackle normally is used with monofilament lines testing about 15 pounds. Usually one starts trolling along the shallows over or around emerging grasses and weeds or underwater vegetation; then working deeper along drop-offs, ledges or other forms of cover.

One bottom-bumping rig is made as follows: Thread the line through a half-ounce slip sinker. Attach a black or brown #3 barrel swivel. To this attach a foot of leader material of the same (or slightly less) strength as the line. Attach to this a 3/0 offset hook or a hook made for plastic-worm fishing. Bait the hook with a 9-inch *floating* plastic worm, rigged weedlessly.

Letting out between 40 and 60 feet of line, run the boat as slowly as possible. Hold the reel in free-spool so line can be let out instantly. The lead will be felt dragging bottom and the rod then must be bucktailed continuously to give the lure a slow leapfrogging motion.

When a strike is felt, which usually will be a few gentle plucking tugs, stop the boat and let out line immediately so the fish can take the bait by pulling the line through the hole in the sinker. Reel in slowly until a connection is felt, and quickly set the hook. Some fishermen recommend doing this differently. On feeling the tugs, they reel in slack and strike hard immediately. Both methods get results.

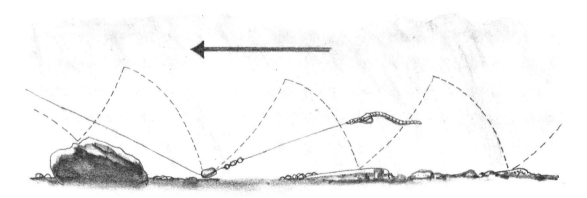

Proper action for bottom bumping a plastic worm. The rig should be trolled very slowly, and at the same time the worm is bucktailed to give it a continuous leap-frogging action.

Another bottom-bumping method is useful when the water is not over 10 feet deep and where the bottom is relatively weedless and free of obstructions. Put a 6-inch *sinking* worm on an undressed jig with a number 1 or 1/0 hook. Let out between 40 and 60 feet of line with the reel's drag engaged. Troll as slowly as possible. Work the rod as before, but set the hook immediately on feeling a strike.

All these methods can be used for casting. The third one calls for a *flat-headed* 6-inch sinking plastic worm and a regular number 1 or 1/0 offset hook. Thread the worm the entire length of the hook and push on a little more to make it bunch up on the hook and to give the worm as much of a bend of the hook as possible. Push the hook's barb partly out of the worm. Test the rig by pulling it beside the boat to be sure it has good action. For trolling (but not for casting) tie in a #3 black or brown barrel-swivel about a foot above the worm. The rig should be trolled very close to the bottom, but not bumping on it, with between 40 and 60 feet of line out. If it doesn't troll deep enough, run the boat slower and/or add a few split shot or a piece of striplead on the line above the swivel.

Keep the reel in free-spool, holding the line with forefinger (in spinning) or thumb (in baitcasting) pressure. When a hit is felt let out line and stop the boat. Take in slack, and strike hard when slight tension is felt. The barb must be driven into the fish.

Note that the various plastic-worm rigs this book describes have a single hook and that no embellishments such as spinners, skirts and beads are recommended. I prefer red worms, sometimes black ones. Purple and white also are effective. Devotees of the plastic worm all have their favorites, but the methods of rigging and of fishing seem more important than color.

Cane pole fishing. Every southerner is familiar with the sight of people placidly sitting on the banks of creeks and canals with long bamboo poles. The low cost of the rigs isn't the only reason for their popularity, because cane-pole fishing, poke-pole fishing, or jig fishing, as it is called, is a very productive way of obtaining food for the table. Here is a favorite rig for catching bass, although a crappie, a bluegill or something else may be on the hook when it is hoisted in.

You need a bamboo or fiberglass pole 10 or 12 feet long and fairly stiff, plus some line of 20-pound test or more. The line is tied to the pole near the grip and is taped to it so all won't be lost if the pole breaks. Only between 4 and 6 feet of line extend from the end. The line is put through a cork with a hole in it, the hole being plugged with a matchstick, toothpick or something similar so the cork can be pushed up and down the line to regulate fishing depth. A 4/0 or 5/0 hook is attached to the line's end, often being baited with nightcrawlers.

Thus rigged, one or more fishermen paddle slowly and quietly in a boat, looking for spots around stumps, grass clumps and elsewhere where bass may hide. The bait, dangling at the pole's end, is lowered into these places without letting the cork, a foot or two up on the line, touch water. If a bass sees the bait he probably will take it. If not, the bait is dipped somewhere else. Hits may be light ones but, when they happen, the pole is lowered to float the bobber, allowing the fish to go off with the bait while swallowing it. When the fish gets to the end of the line the fisherman strikes and jerks it into the boat. Fish are kept on stringers or in a sack fastened over the side.

This usually is early-season fishing when snows or rains have clouded the water. In addition to nightcrawlers, plastic worms, pork chunks or spoons with pork rind attached often are used—anything that will wiggle or that can be made to do so.

Fishing from banks is done in the same way, and the pole often is handled to let the floating bobber drift in a hole until something comes along to take the bait.

Since poles won't be mentioned very often, this might be a good place to comment on the difference between a fish pole and a fishing rod. Anglers, proud of their tackle, always cringe when a non-fisherman refers to a rod as a "pole"; thus proclaiming his ignorance of angling. A fishing rod, be it of split bamboo or glass fiber, is a carefully engineered instrument made to specific and exact measurements designed to provide maximum casting distance and accuracy. While some are of modest value, many cost a great deal of money because of the exacting workmanship required to make them properly. On the other hand, a fish pole is a crude stick, perhaps cut from a straight stem of a woody plant, or perhaps made without exacting specifications from fiberglass. The difference may be likened to that between a fine diamond and a cut glass bead, or between an expensive violin and a cheap fiddle.

SMALLMOUTH BASS

Going by the scientific name of *Micropterus dolomieui*, the spunky smallmouth is a member of the Sunfish family whose range principally includes all states east of the Rockies except those bordering the Gulf Coast. This little cousin of the largemouth inspired the original remark that "inch for inch and pound for pound (it) is the gamest fish that lives"—an accolade that may raise the eyebrows of trout and salmon fishermen and some of us who enjoy using light tackle in salt water. In any event, anglers who won't give the smallmouth top rating must agree that it belongs up there somewhere.

Smallmouths average only between ¾ and 2 pounds in weight. Four-

Handsome catch of smallmouths adorn stringer of satisfied fishermen.

pounders often are caught, and anything over 5 pounds is bragging size. The world record is about 11 pounds. The temperature range of the smallmouth is between 60 and 75 degrees, and one should probe for 67 or 68 degrees for best results. Spawning occurs when water temperatures rise above 60 degrees, which usually is between April and early June. Spawning habits are very similar to those of the largemouth. Open seasons for angling usually (or should) begin after spawning ceases.

The smallmouth seeks living conditions quite different from those of the largemouth. It wants clear water rather than turbid; deep rather than shallow; rocky rather than weedy; and somewhat colder. The habitat of the largemouth usually is currentless but, while smallmouths are happy in lakes, they also are found even in rapid waters of streams.

Fishing for Smallmouths in Lakes

The best smallmouth area in New England is the Belgrade Lakes region of southern Maine. These granite-bordered lakes abound with steep, rocky

419

drop-offs extending into clear, cool waters of moderate depth where the lakes' bottoms are strewn with gravel and boulders sometimes interlaced with waterlogged timber. Look for such places for smallmouths in lakes. Remember that winds blow insects and other foods toward the windward shore; that more baitfish concentrate there for that reason, and that wandering schools of smallmouths should be there, too. Rocky windward shores are excellent places to fish.

Another reason for rocky shore fishing is that, when available, the favorite food of bronzebacks is the crawfish, and crawfish like to live among rocks and boulders. Since the windward shore of a rocky lake can cover a lot of ground, the wandering schools of smallmouths must be located, particularly in summer when too warm surface waters send them down deep. Here's a locator rig using crawfish as a bait. (If they aren't available, try small shiners.)

Using a light baitcasting, spinning, or spincasting outfit with about 6-pound-test line, tie on a small three-way swivel. Attach a number 2 (or smaller) bait hook to about 3 feet of leader and tie it to the swivel. Also attach a half-ounce bell sinker to not over a foot of line and tie this to the remaining ring of the swivel. Bait the hook with a crawfish, hooked through the tail, bottom up. Drift or move the boat slowly over rocky areas, preferably where the 68-degree temperature is on the bottom. Let the sinker bounce bottom, the bait trailing behind. When a strike is obtained, there are two choices. Continue drifting the bait in the area, or anchor the boat and use artificial lures at that depth.

A breeze may drift the boat too fast. In that case use a dragging anchor, perhaps made by putting a rock in a mesh sack tied to a rope. There are two reasons for this. An anchor of the right weight will allow the boat to drift slowly. The anchor will bounce bottom, thus moving small rocks which then scatter crawfish hiding under them. This helps to attract bass to the bait.

In spring and early summer, and again in the fall, suitable water temperatures coax bass into shallow water. Bays bordered by rushes or lily pads then should be productive when lures are fished near the vegetation. On warm days in such places the best fishing should be early in the morning and late in the evening. At such times the edges of ledges and the rocky shores of islands also should be good. So should rocky or weedy points of land and other drop-offs.

When water depths are suitable, there is a very effective technique for fishing sinking lures for smallmouths. Using spinning or spincasting tackle, make a long cast and allow the lure to sink to bottom. Slowly pump it in by raising the rod, thus causing the lure to plane up a foot or two. Let it drop down again while reeling in slack, and continue this bottom-bouncing retrieve until the lure is nearly under the boat. A small wobbling spoon, weedless, if necessary, and perhaps with a flutterer attached to the hook, is a good lure for this; also a small, weighted, floating plastic worm. Fan-casting this way covers a lot of ground when bass are on bottom and won't rise more than a few feet for a lure.

While lure selection is important, more important is the way the lure is fished and that it is fished at the level of the comfort zone for bass. Readers may wonder why the importance of water temperatures is stressed so often in this book when it has been practically ignored in older ones. Accurate devices for taking deep-water temperatures and instruments to instantly measure bottom depths are of relatively recent development. They weren't available when older books were written.

Fishing for Smallmouths in Rivers

Unlike the largemouth, the smallmouth bass is also fond of flowing water, even water flowing as fast as that favored by trout. In fact, trout and smallmouths often are found in the same places.

As in trout fishing, take time to "read the water." Trout in trout rivers and bass in bass rivers occupy similar places offering protection and nearness to a food supply. That means ahead of or behind rocks in a stream, under undercut banks and ledges, in or near riffles, and in pools just below riffles. When river edges are rocky, bass may be amid the rocks close to shore. It is less effective to fish from the bank to rocks on the near side than to wade the stream and cast toward the rocks, drifting the working lure in the moving current in the same ways that have been recommended for trout.

One doesn't need to get up early to fish for bass in rivers. Mid-morning, mid-afternoon and early evening are better than the cold, gray dawn, fishing during the lunch and rest period, and late at night.

Bass fishing in rivers usually is best with subsurface lures. Small streamers and bucktails do well throughout the season. These include baitfish imitations, Muddlers and brighter marabou patterns, fished as for trout. Fish-shaped wobbling spoons and tear-drop wobblers in red and white, and small minnow-imitating plugs on a steady retrieve are favorites for spinning. Spinners should be fished slowly; only fast enough to make the blades revolve. Frog imitations are excellent when cast to the bank and retrieved in slow, short jerks.

Almost any bait will work, crawfish and small minnows being favorites. Also try hellgrammites, worms, grasshoppers, grubs, caterpillars and crickets. Bass lying in deep runs and pools can be taken by drifting the bait under a float only large enough to hold the bait up. Unless bass are seen feeding on top, bait should be fished deep.

Fly rods are preferred for top-water work, but this is best when there are insect hatches or during the cooler weather of early fall. Good floaters like the Wulff patterns do well. So do panfish poppers that can be made to pop and small bass bugs that can be made to wiggle.

Bass fishermen do poorly when they make too much noise and commotion—and any is too much! The slow and quiet approach, keeping as well out of sight as possible, is the one that helps to take bass. Fortunately, however, bass have short memories. If someone bangs a tacklebox in a boat, or throws out the anchor instead of lowering it, the solution is to relax for a few minutes. If the fish have been around and feeding, they'll be back on the job before long.

Tackle for Smallmouth Bass

What has been said about tackle for largemouths also applies to smallmouths except that it should be lighter, with finer lines and leaders and smaller lures. Baitcasting gear should be selected to handle lures in the quarter-ounce range except perhaps in cases where fish run larger than average or are found in congested places. Spinning and spincasting tackle should be similarly light. The fish usually average 3 pounds or less and are caught in fairly open water. Light tackle is sportier and more fun than heavier equipment, and it usually hooks more fish. By the same token, fly fishing equipment normally should be the same as is used for small or average-sized trout: size 7 or smaller, ordinarily, and perhaps size 8 when fishing near stumps or weeds.

WHITE BASS

This little fighter is no kin to the Sunfish family, but is a relative of the saltwater striped bass that comes into freshwater rivers to spawn. If one ignores his well-humped back, he is a striped bass in miniature. Scientists think that, like the landlocked salmon as compared to the Atlantic salmon, the white bass is a subspecies of the striped bass which became landlocked in early times. His back is light green, grayish, or brownish, depending on the type of water in which he lives, shaded to whitish yellow underneath. He is about the size of a crappie; usually between 1 and 3 pounds. White bass are spring spawners which lay eggs on the bottom, rather than building nests.

Small white bass are seen in schools roaming over the gravel bottoms of stream inlets and coves. They will take a wide variety of tiny lures. Larger bass mostly are lake dwellers, traveling in schools of fish of the same size, and often can be seen breaking the surface in pursuit of baitfish such as gizzard shad. They are very abundant in man-made lakes such as those in the Tennessee Valley.

Related to the saltwater striper, the white bass is a scrappy fighter that roams inlets and large lakes in schools. Anglers look for a flurry of white water—a sign that bass are feeding on baitfish.

The trick is to roam a lake trying to spot schools of feeding fish, because they may suddenly appear anywhere at any time, feed for a few minutes, and then go down again. Observant anglers will see a flurry of white water as a school of white bass chases a school of baitfish to the surface somewhere far out on the lake. Hurrying over, with light tackle ready, the boat is stopped within casting distance and long casts are made ahead of or into the school. Every cast should take a fish.

Baitcasting, spinning and spincasting fishermen use small baitfish-imitating plugs such as the Rebel, Rapala or Crippled Shad in sizes not over 2½ inches long, or mother-of-pearl wobblers. If the lure is a sinking one it is cast into the school, allowed to sink a foot or so, and then is retrieved fast, like a small baitfish trying to escape. Single hooked lures make it easier to unhook the fish than using multiple hooks—and there isn't much time. A fast fisherman may take half a dozen bass from the school before it goes down. The idea then is to keep cruising around until the same school, or another one, reappears. Fly rods are less efficient for this because of the long casts and the short time involved. If they are used, any small streamer fly or bucktail with some white on it should do the trick.

THE OTHER BASSES

The various basses are confused by having many names, most of which are regional. Both the largemouth and the smallmouth are referred to as *black bass*. The *spotted bass,* also known as the *Kentucky bass,* is more or less of an intermediate between the largemouth and the smallmouth. The *Florida bass* is a subspecies of the largemouth which also has been transplanted into California. Tackle and tactics for these are the same as for the largemouth. Although the *striped bass* has been introduced very successfully into fresh water, it principally is a saltwater fish.

24

Atlantic Salmon

Many anglers never have enjoyed the thrills of fishing for Atlantic salmon on the presumption that it is too expensive or too difficult. It can be very expensive, even to the tune of a few thousand dollars per person per week. On the other hand, licensed anglers can park their campers beside a remote salmon pool and enjoy miles of free (or small fee) fishing very economically.

While one is supposed to get what he pays for, based on the fame and productivity of the river and the quality of the accommodations, this isn't always so. For example, a friend of mine spent over two thousand dollars for a week's booking at a camp on a famous river and returned home, skunked. That same week two other friends camped at low cost on another river and, for a small daily rod fee (charged by the government for river upkeep), took their limit nearly every day. Both rivers are in the Province of Quebec.

That's the chance one has to take. The river may be "right," or it may be high and dirty. Runs of fish may or may not be in. Hooking one big salmon or two, or even a few grilse, seems to many to be ample recompense for occasional fruitless trips. The greedy and the unphilosophical would do better fishing for something else.

FROM RIVER TO OCEAN, AND BACK

Unlike the Pacific salmons, which die after spawning, the *Salmo salar* of the Atlantic (whose name means "the leaper") returns to the ocean (if he is lucky), perhaps again to come back to his river, bigger and lustier than before. His rivers include a few in Maine, many in New Brunswick, Quebec, Nova Scotia, Newfoundland, Labrador, Iceland, the British Isles, and others in the Scandinavian countries extending on the continent as far south as Spain. The world record is a 79-pound, 2-ounce fish taken in 1928 on the Tana (Teno) River, which separates Norway from Finland. The Canadian record is 55 pounds and the current record breaker in Maine is 26 pounds, 8 ounces. All fishing in North America is with the fly rod and artificial fly.

Atlantic salmon travel as far upriver as they can get, which often is to small, clear, gravel-bottomed tributary brooks many miles upstream. Their runs in spring, summer and fall vary from river to river, depending partly on water conditions. Anglers, knowing when these runs should occur, can visit various rivers at the appropriate time, thus extending the season and improving their luck. Salmon can find the river in which they were born, and usually return to it after spending between one and four years at sea. Fish returning after the first year are known as "grilse." They normally weigh between 2 and 8 pounds, although in some localities any over 5 pounds technically (or legally) are called salmon.

The fish spawn in late fall or early winter by laying eggs in a series of depressions they scour in the gravel. These beds are called "redds," the gravel scoured from one depression being used to cover the previous one. The warming water of early spring causes the eggs to hatch. When the baby fish have absorbed their yolk sacs, they wriggle between stones of the gravel to the surface and school amid whatever protection they can find. The fry which survive raids of birds and other fish exist on microorganisms of the river until they exceed finger length. They then develop vertical bars along their sides, are called "parr," and resemble small brook trout except for their deeply forked tails.

The parr, subsisting on nymphs, insects and smaller fish, live a year or more in the river, gradually drifting to sea. Reaching the estuary, their parr marks become concealed by a silvery sheen, at which stage they are called "smolts." The schools of smolts develop in the estuary until instinct sends them to sea. Their travels then take many of them to areas southwest of Greenland where, in recent years, far too many of the developing salmon have been caught in nets and on long lines, principally by fishermen from Denmark and its territory of Greenland. When this book reaches publication, it is hoped that the practice will have stopped. If not, this and other hazards to the survival of the species may doom this noble sportfish to extinction.

Atlantic salmon leaps a barrier on its spawning run upriver to the tributary stream where it was born.

After managing to struggle through an estuary net, this small salmon fell victim to an artificial fly.

When the survivors of these depredations return to their rivers, they must run the gauntlet of coastal and estuary nets and of pollution and poaching. The annually decreasing numbers that return diminish the sport of angling and of the tourist revenue it brings (or could bring) to the regions which for generations have been meccas for the sport.

Because of estuary netting, which, due to the size of the mesh, takes too many salmon while letting most of the grilse get through, some river systems, such as the once-famous Miramichi watershed in New Brunswick, are called "grilse rivers," meaning they contain far more grilse than salmon. Of course this unfortunate situation quickly could be cured by eliminating or drastically restricting estuary and river netting, an urgently needed remedy that would be a financial bonanza to all but a few commercial fishermen.

(After this was written we learn that the provinces of northeastern Canada have abolished commercial netting and that sport fishing for Atlantic salmon has greatly improved.)

Whether or not salmon feed after returning to their rivers is an oft debated question. It isn't a matter of whether or not they do, but of how much.

While the salmon's instinct at this stage of its development is toward spawning rather than eating, we do know they consume various tidbits from time
to time. Luckily, these include artificial flies. The smashing strike of a
salmon of 20 pounds or so when he slams a tiny fly and erupts cartwheeling
and gyrating high into the air will raise the hackles of even the most jaded
angler and should sell him on the sport for life.

ATLANTIC SALMON TACKLE

If your strongest trout rod has moderate stiffness and power, it should
be adequate for all but very big salmon in very fast rivers. Many a whopper
has been taken on lighter tackle. The choice of rod power depends on the
skill of the angler, how sporty he wants his fishing to be, and on the probable
size of the fish and the force of the water. Normally, this would be a choice
of size 8, 9 or 10, as tabulated on page 137. It is the custom in many other
countries to use much longer and stronger rods. We don't think we need
them, and we consider lighter gear to be more fun.

For North American Atlantic salmon fishing, I usually take about six
rods. These are a Scientific Anglers in size 7, a Cortland in size 8, a Scientific Anglers, an Orvis and a Fenwick in size 9, and a Fenwick in size 10.
The size 7 is a grilse rod, but salmon usually are no problem for it. If a few
salmon, along with the grilse, are expected, the size 8 might be used. When
rivers contain only (or mostly) salmon, the size 9 rods are selected. The
size 10 is for big fish and fast water. Of these, two usually are rigged for the
day's fishing—one with a floating line for dry-fly work; the other with a
floating line with sinking tip for wet-fly fishing. Sinking lines are avoided
because they are more difficult to pick up, but they may be necessary when
rivers are in flood or when fish are deep in pools. Well equipped anglers
have two extra spools for each reel, so a choice of the three types of line
can be used when needed. Leader butts are semipermanently tied to lines
with the Leader Whip Knot, to which tapered leaders are attached with the
usual Blood Knot. Since salmon are not very leader-shy, tippets can be
strong. Ten pounds is about average, but the tippet strength depends
mainly on the size of the fly. Use the strongest tippet that will fish the fly
correctly. The leader usually is about as long as the rod. It often is much
longer under low water conditions.

Reels for salmon fishing should hold the line and at least 150 yards of
about 20-pound-test backing. Line should not be packed on to full capacity
because fast reeling may spool it unevenly and jam the reel when the salmon
is brought in close. A smooth and easily adjustable drag is essential; never
set it so tight that it could cause a pull-out or a broken leader when a salmon
jerks the tackle suddenly. Multiplying fly reels are a bit bulkier and heavier

Fighting salmon on light fly tackle is one of the greatest fishing thrills.
Here Bob Zwirz brings leaper to net on Pinware River, Labrador.

than single-action reels, but they retrieve line much faster when fish are far out or making a run toward the angler.

ATLANTIC SALMON FLIES

In 1895 an English author named George M. Kelson wrote a book called *The Salmon Fly* which showed many of the then-popular patterns in color. Kelson had the peculiar notion that salmon rose most readily to butterflies, and he featured flies resembling them in his book. The error took hold and led to the popularity of hundreds of patterns of dreary sameness in style but of an excessive variety in color. Many of these old classics still are used occasionally. They include the Jock Scott, Durham Ranger, Black Dose, Thunder and Lightning, Green Highlander, Black, Silver, and Blue Doctors, and scores of others. If readers can locate any of these beautiful and complicated classics they should be preserved for museum pieces. Modern patterns are much better for fishing!

Most modern salmon flies are dressed with both featherwings and hairwings, the latter being more popular because they provide more action. I once obtained the records for several years on many rivers of the flies which had taken the most fish. In the vast Quebec area four patterns stood out so strongly that all the others were also-rans. These, in order of popularity, are the Rusty Rat, Green Highlander, Silver Rat and Black Dose. While the second and fourth are old classic patterns, the modern adaptations are dressed as hairwings.

While styles in flies vary from year to year, the present pets in New Brunswick include the "butt patterns." These are so simple that any amateur can tie them. The basic dressing calls for a fairly fat black silk body ribbed with fine silver tinsel, a sparse and short black throat (sometimes brown) and a wing of native Canadian red squirrel, for which black bear hair or some other dark fur often is substituted. These flies have a butt (but no tail) of yarn or silk of one color or another; usually red, yellow, orange or green, and often of fluorescent material. (The fluorescence, if sparse, is very important.) A fly of this type with a red butt is called a Red Butt, and so on. Other popular patterns are a splaywing called the Butterfly, and a hairwing named the Cosseboom. These few patterns, in various sizes, should be sufficient for all North American Atlantic salmon fishing, as far as wet flies are concerned. A few bucktails and nymphs are handy on occasion, but are unnecessary for casual anglers. Two types of almost unsinkable dry flies stand out. One comprises the various Wulff patterns, of which Black, White and Royal provide good variety, the Royal Wulff often having a fluorescent mid-body of one color or another. The other type is the Bomber. A Bomber resembles a Wooly Worm, but it has a closely clipped cigar-shaped deer-hair body and a

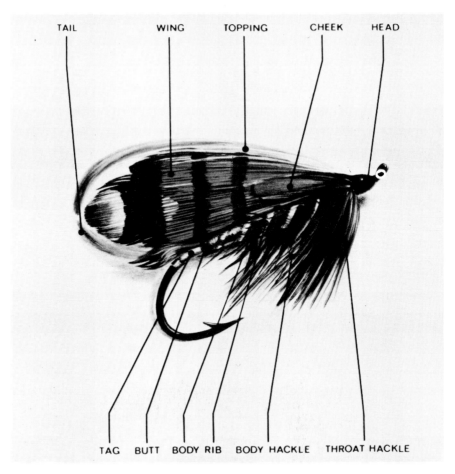

TAIL   WING   TOPPING   CHEEK   HEAD

TAG   BUTT   BODY RIB   BODY HACKLE   THROAT HACKLE

Parts of a salmon fly.

fairly short bunch of the same body hair extending forward at an angle of about 45 degrees to slant it upward over the eye of the hook. The Black Bomber is all black except for a white palmered hackle wound into the body from rear to front. The White Bomber is all white except for a red palmered hackle. These two quite different types are of primary importance.

Hook size 6 or 8 is a good average. Larger flies do well on big rivers, or on smaller ones during high water. Smaller sizes (which may be smaller flies dressed on larger light-wire hooks) may do better under very clear or low water conditions. While black salmon hooks are standard, many anglers think bronzed offset (kirbed) ones provide better penetration. Opinions differ on selecting color combinations of flies, but drab to dark ones should do better when days are bright and rivers are clear. Drab to bright ones could be selected for dull days or for high or discolored water.

432

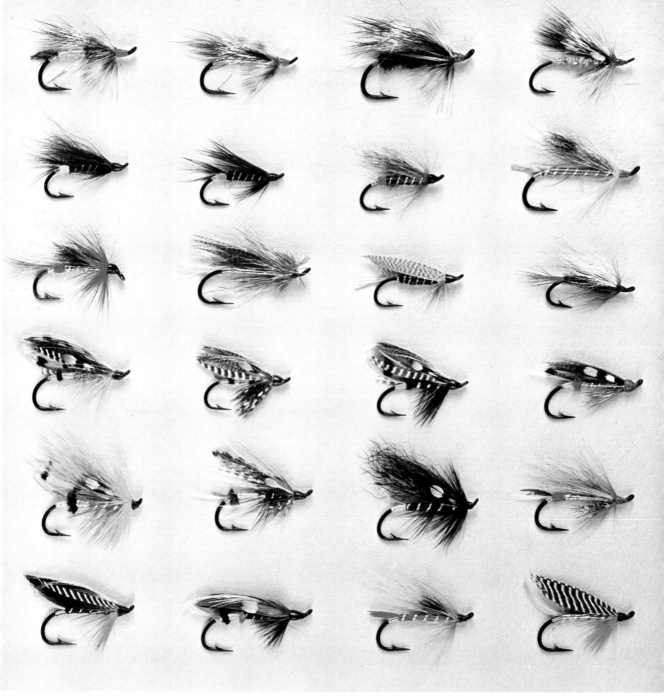

PLATE 9

ATLANTIC SALMON FLIES

(From Dressings in "Atlantic Salmon Flies & Fishing")

RUSTY RAT	SILVER RAT	BLACK RAT	GRAY RAT
BLACK BEAR GREEN BUTT	BLACK BEAR ORANGE BUTT	GRAY SQUIRREL RED BUTT	COSSEBOOM
COPPER KILLER	SALMON MUDDLER	ORIOLE	INGALLS' BUTTERFLY
GREEN HIGHLANDER	JOCK SCOTT	BLACK DOSE	SILVER DOCTOR

(The modern hair-wing version is below each of the four classic feather-wing patterns above.)

| BLUE CHARM | MITCHELL | RED ABBEY | SILVER BLUE |

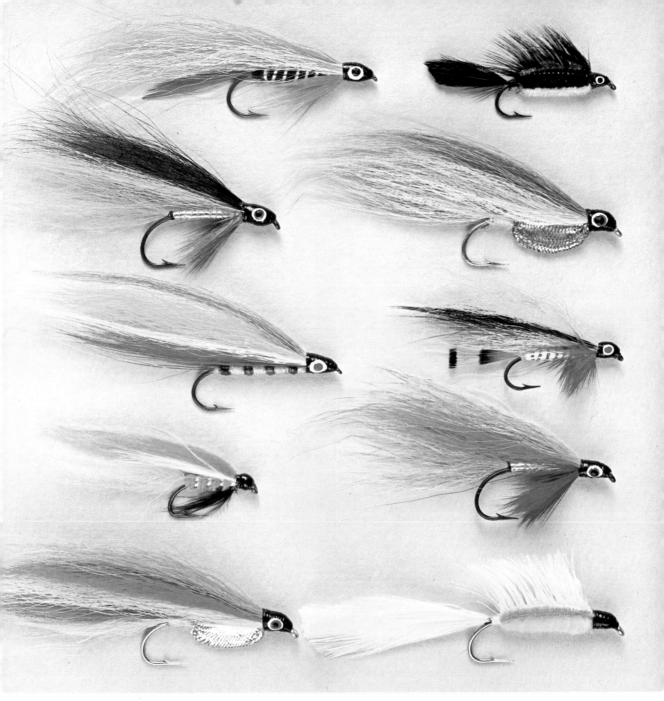

PLATE 10

PACIFIC SALT WATER FLIES

(Dressed by Irwin Thompson, Sebastopol, California)

APACHE
THE 49'ER
GYPSEY
SALMON CREEK SPECIAL
SILVER BEER BELLY

BLACK JACK
GOLDEN BEER BELLY
MOHAWK
SALMON KILLER
STRIPER SPECIAL

A featherwing fly is opaque and its action is rather stiff. This may be satisfactory in rapid streams, but not as much so in slower water. A correctly dressed hairwing pulsates under all conditions. It has translucence and mobility. The trend seems to be to the hairwing as the best modern type for salmon.

The reasons for selecting specific salmon flies for one purpose or another are involved ones on which much has been written. Readers wishing to pursue them further are referred to books specializing on the subject.

TIPS ON LOCATING SALMON

Knowledgeable guides are valuable to expert salmon anglers and almost indispensable to non-expert ones. Even old hands at the game, proficient at "reading the water" of salmon rivers, are helped by guides so familiar with specific pools that they know exactly where salmon lie in them under all water conditions. A good guide often becomes a valued friend who contributes immeasurably to the pleasure and success of a trip while sharing his knowledge of salmon fishing, handling the boat and helping to lug equipment.

We can't presume that all guides are that kind because some are non-professionals, guiding on a parttime basis, whose knowledge of salmon fishing leaves much to be desired. It pays to know the basics of locating salmon, rather than depending on someone else. Salmon fishing differs from trout fishing in many ways. For example, salmon make no attempt at concealment, and they do not lie near feed lanes in streams because they have little interest in food. In a nutshell, we find them not in slack water or in fast water, but in the "in between water" of moderate flow. Chapter 17 discussed the importance of "edges," the water in between the fast and the slow. It is helpful to review this because, under normal conditions, one should find salmon where he finds edges.

Normal conditions are when water is "right"; when streams are of average height, fairly clear, and not over 70 degrees in temperature. Salmon lie in different sorts of places when water is abnormal; that is, when it is too high and perhaps too cold, or when it is too low and too warm. Let's discuss normal conditions first, because they are most common during the fishing season, and most productive of good fishing.

When rivers are clear, moderately flowing, and under 70 degrees, the best places to find salmon are along the edges. A big rock in a stream forms two edges, the deeper one usually being the better one. Any obstruction along a stream's bank, such as a rock, a log or a ledge, forms an edge, even very close to shore. An edge is formed where water flowing over a bar merges with the main current. Salmon often rest in the deeper water just

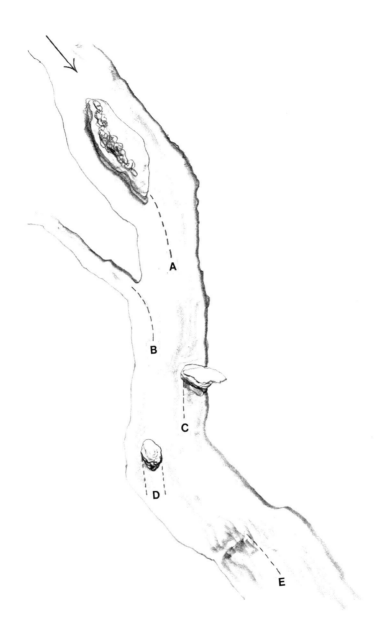

Typical edge water in a salmon stream: (A) where currents merge below an island; (B) an entering stream; (C) an obstruction jutting from the river-bank; (D) rock in the stream; (E) where water flowing over a bar meets the main current.

over the bar. Edges also are formed where a side channel meets the main channel, where a brook enters a stream, and where two parts of a stream merge just below an island. Salmon may lie in flat gravelly stretches if they contain potholes to break the flow. These stretches may contain fairly fast water, but the current is slower below the surface because of such depressions. These often are found in the narrowing tail of a pool. Wherever there is a major obstruction in the stream, such as a low dam or a waterfall, salmon should collect in the first good pool below it. They approach the obstruction and then return to the pool to rest before attempting to surmount it.

When rivers are high, and probably discolored, the problem becomes more complex. Larger and brighter flies are necessary for increased visibility. Fish should be in the "ponds," which is the flat water below pools, water that is too shallow ordinarily. The fish may be very near shore, where the flow is less swift; or they may be on bars which are too shallow when the flow is moderate.

Another problem is presented in the opposite situation, when water is low, clear, and over 70 degrees. Then, the salmon seek colder water with more oxygen, often in cold-water pools below entering brooks and streams. In fact, salmon may seek colder water by going up into the tributaries. These cold-water pools may be very shallow, but the fish have to put up with them. They often lie in plain sight — a tempting prey for poachers. Fishing for them is difficult because they usually ignore orthodox methods. A whipping fly, a rapidly retrieved fly, even a gaudy streamer or bucktail, may get results.

It is a maxim in salmon fishing that a fish can be caught if he rises to a fly or otherwise shows any interest in it, even so little as an increased quivering of his fins. The fish belongs to the person who attracted him, until the angler wishes to give up, or to offer the salmon to someone else. After resting the fish for a few minutes, the same fly, a smaller pattern, or a different fly may tempt a take. If that fails, a skated fly, dry or wet, or some other unusual method, may hook the fish.

WET FLY FISHING FOR SALMON

Under conditions of moderate flow the water in a salmon pool usually is only a few feet deep. Since the pool's bottom is rocky, salmon may be lying anywhere in it, and may not be seen. When we can't cast to individual fish, the usual custom is to cover all the good parts of the pool as shown in the accompanying drawing. In this stream, the current flows evenly; both sides are worth fishing. The stream can be covered from bank to bank by an angler in a boat in the middle. After fishing the head of the pool, the angler has moved to position *A*. The angler, standing if it is safe, makes quartering downstream casts, starting with short ones very near the boat. Salmon sometimes are hooked very close by.

It is of primary importance, regardless of the length of the cast, to make the fly swing on a tight line without any belly in it. A bellied line causes the fly to whip. Its speed usually should be moderate, which means that it is cast more nearly cross-stream in very slow currents and more nearly downstream in faster ones. When the swing is nearly completed, a few added feet can be obtained by transferring the rod to the other hand and moving it outward. At completion of the swing the fly can be bucktailed a bit in case a fish has followed it and may be reluctant to take. Some anglers bucktail the fly slightly during the swing; others use a dead drift. If one method doesn't work, try the other.

If the water looks good on both sides, alternate the casts from one to the other, extending each cast a foot or so for maximum water coverage. Of course, pay special attention to good lies, like the rock jutting into fairly deep water from the shore, the rock near midstream, and the edge formed by the current of the entering brook. When the casts have been extended as far as the angler wishes, he usually sits down, thus indicating to the guide that he wants to be moved to a new position where short casts can be resumed just below the previous longest one. By this means all the good water in the pool can be covered.

Salmon often can be seen lying in a pool. Select one and cast to the fish so the fly swings just above him or at the same depth. If he shows interest but doesn't take, he probably can be hooked by a smaller or different fly, or another method of presentation.

DRY-FLY FISHING FOR SALMON

Dry-fly fishing is not entirely a low-water method. It is very practical, and often superior to wet-fly fishing, under conditions of moderate flow. Seeing a salmon of any size rise to suck in a floating fly probably is the supreme thrill of angling. Using the dry fly for salmon isn't particularly difficult.

Salmon ordinarily take large and bushy dry flies, which fortunately are very good floaters. Being quite wind-resistant, they can be cast most effectively with a weight-forward floating line. Two efficient dry flies have been recommended: the Bomber in size 2 or 4 and the Wulffs in 4, 6 and 8. Trout patterns are acceptable in the rare cases when smaller dries are needed.

The dry fly usually is cast upstream and across, the rod being pulled back with a slight jerk to obtain a wavy line for a longer float. The rod usually is held parallel to the water, pointing at the fly.

Downstream or quartering downstream casts are used when needed. The rod is jerked back sharply just before the fly lands to provide the same snakelike effect for a long drift. Salmon often hook themselves, but the angler should tighten on feeling the fish.

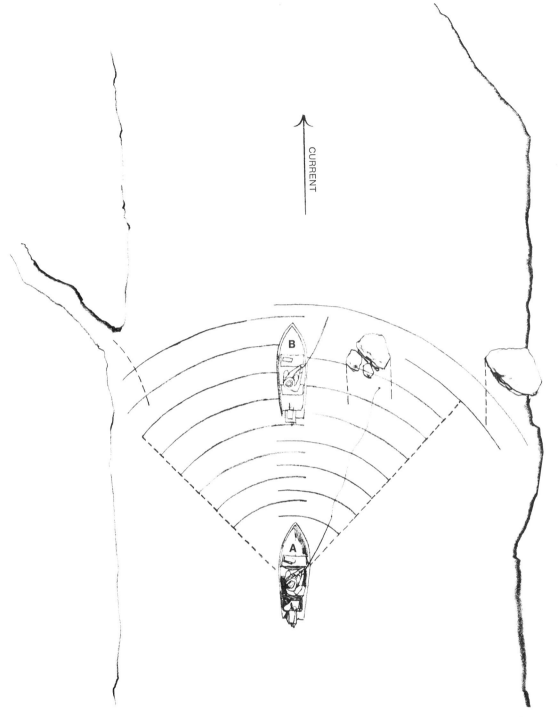

Basic method of covering a pool with a wet fly. After fishing the head of the pool, angler has moved to position A, from where he makes quartering downstream casts, starting close to the boat and working farther down. Then he moves to B, and continues to cover every foot of water. Edge water behind rocks and at stream mouth is especially good.

437

These large dry flies are effective in themselves, and they also are used as locators. If a salmon rises to one without taking it, at least we know where he lies. The trick then is to tempt him with a smaller dry fly, or perhaps with a wet one.

Another method is to cast above and beyond the fish and to deliberately pull the dry fly under, trying to move it directly in front of his nose. Skittering a large dry fly over a reluctant fish often works. Cast the fly on a tight line ahead of him, then skitter it past his nose.

HOOKING, PLAYING AND LANDING SALMON

Trout and bass fishermen talk about "striking" their fish when they feel a connection. A salmon angler never strikes because this could take the fly away from the fish or break the tackle. When the salmon rises to the fly he usually will turn with it and take it down before spitting it out. When this connection is felt the angler merely tightens up. Ideally, this will sink the hook into the angle between the jaws, which is the most secure place. Some salmon take with such a savage strike that they are well hooked in any event.

When the fish has been hooked there is scant time to put loose line, if any, back on the reel, but the salmon must be played off the reel. He'll make a fast run, probably followed by a spectacular jump. On the jump, the rod tip should be lowered to give slack line, thus diminishing the chance of the fish breaking the leader with his tail. As the fish reenters the water, tighten the line again. Hold the rod nearly vertically so its spring can be used to the fullest. Always try to keep a tight line with as much tension as safety permits.

After the first run the angler usually is put ashore so he can handle his fish from the beach. When the salmon seems ready to be led in, a suitable spot on the beach is selected. An angler fishing alone can use a tailing device, which is a wire-spring noose attached to a handle that is slipped over the tail and pulled tight. An alternative is to beach the fish by leading him into shallow water and pulling him on land. Only moderate tension is needed because his flopping aids the process. When the fish is partly ashore, the angler (still holding it by the spring of the rod) can get behind it, grab it by the tail, and push it to safety.

A guide or someone else with a net can make all this easier. A salmon net has a long handle, a wide hoop and a deep bag. The angler indicates where he wants the fish netted, and the net handler rests the hoop on the bottom in about a foot of water. The angler leads the tired fish over the hoop, and the guide raises the net. All this is done quietly, without any jabbing. Jabbing at a salmon with a net is an excellent way to lose it.

ARE BLACK SALMON SPORTING?

When Atlantic salmon spawn late in the fall they often are imprisoned for the winter in pools under the ice. These are called "black salmon" or "kelts"—thin, ugly creatures bearing scant resemblance to the noble fish they once were.

Freed in spring by the breaking up of the ice, the starving fish feed and slowly grow stronger, taking on a glimmering of their former silvery sheen. During the high and cold spring runoff, they can be caught on rod and reel in areas where fishing for them is allowed. Catching kelts is favored by some, violently opposed by others. The principal reason for permitting it seems to be the tourist revenue obtained.

Proponents of the practice think it is exciting to fish from boats in cold and swollen streams and to hook several big fish per day on large streamer flies and bucktails, even though patterns don't matter much and it only is necessary to drift the fly in the current to catch fish. These anglers maintain the salmon are edible—and that they release most of them, anyway.

Opponents scorn the practice, feeling that it is not sporting, that it requires no skill, and that it does great harm to the fishery. They say the slightly improved appearance of the fish mostly is an illusion because their bodies are highly liquid and deflate after being killed. They consider the flesh so unpalatable that even a dog wouldn't touch it.

These unfortunate fish have two strikes against them before they hit a hook. Exhausted by the long journey upstream, and by spawning, many starve and die in the pools under the ice. The survivors have a chance to return to the sea, but not if they expend their remaining energy fighting strong tackle. Released fish almost always die.

Statistics indicate that, of the black salmon which live to go back to sea, about 10 or 12 percent return to their rivers, fully mended, fat and vigorous, and much bigger than before. These are the trophy bright salmon we dream of catching. It seems that they, and we, should be given the chance.

RIVERS AND RESERVATIONS

Maine

The Atlantic salmon fishery is being restored in Maine and seems to be improving year by year. A license costs very little, and anglers need not hire guides. Fishing normally is good on the Dennys, East Machias and Narraguagus rivers from mid-May through the first two weeks of June. The best runs in the Machias usually are from late June through the first two weeks of

July, with smaller runs in the fall. The Sheepscott has a small run from early July through the season. When rivers hold fish, the banks of some of them may be crowded. Information can be obtained from Vacation Travel Dept., State House Annex, Augusta, Maine, 04330.

New Brunswick

The great Miramichi River system has many salmon streams. Parts of many of these are open to public fishing, and visitors can arrange to stay at various sporting camps to fish some of the private stretches. Guides are necessary, but the services of one can be shared by two anglers. Summer fish run the rivers from late June into July, with larger runs in September. For reasons previously mentioned, the runs in the Miramichi River system predominantly were grilse, but more salmon now are entering the streams due to the abolition of netting. Contact the Fish and Wildlife Branch, Dept. of Natural Resources, Fredericton, New Brunswick, for further information.

Quebec

The vast Province of Quebec offers an abundance of salmon rivers, many of which are available for fishing at small cost. Since various rivers have runs at different times, and since conditions frequently change, readers should write for up-to-date information. Quebec offers facilities for every pocketbook, from inexpensive camping on public waters to daily rod fee arrangements on restricted stretches of famous streams controlled by clubs or by the government. Fees range from cheap to expensive, and the employment of guides is not always necessary. Information can be obtained from Service des Parcs, P. O. Box 639, New Carlisle, P. Q.

Nova Scotia

While this province provides some of the most inexpensive salmon fishing, its productive rivers are few; notably the Medway, the Margaree and the St. Mary's. License fees are low, no guides are necessary, and waters are open to the public. There are spring and fall runs of salmon, with good fishing in June (unless the season is late) and usually better action in September. In June many of the rivers have runs of large seatrout, which increases the fun. The Margaree Salmon Association has a small angling museum near Margaree Harbor, on Cape Breton Island (connected to the mainland by a causeway), which is well worth a visit. Address inquiries to the Nova Scotia Travel Bureau, Halifax, Nova Scotia.

Newfoundland and Labrador

With the possible exception of Quebec, Newfoundland and Labrador offer the most remote (and sometimes the best) salmon fishing still available on the North American continent. Many rivers can be reached by road, others by float plane or railroad. Salmon enter some rivers in May, others as late as June or early July. The peak period usually is the first part of July. The nonresident season's fishing permit is inexpensive. While visitors must employ guides, one can serve two people. Lists of fishing camps and other information are available from the Newfoundland-Labrador Tourist Development Office, Confederation Building, St. John's, Newfoundland.

THE FUTURE

As this is being written, the future of Atlantic salmon fishing, in North America, at least, is in doubt. Indiscriminate netting and long lining of salmon on the high seas prevent too many from returning to their rivers. Large numbers of those that do return are poached in the rivers themselves or are prevented from spawning by dams and pollution. The good side of this glum situation (if there is one) is that alarmed anglers are beginning to force governments and politicians to remedy it before it is too late.

While governments include many a fisherman dedicated to the preservation and restoration of the salmon, they also include others who care only about which side their bread is being buttered. Even those short-sighted individuals are now being made to realize that salmon caught commercially are worth relatively little, while those taken on flies by sportsmen bring vast sums into regional economies.

With the new restrictions on commercial fishing, more and more Atlantic salmon are being allowed to return to their rivers. As this book goes to press the two past seasons have provided excellent fishing. Let's hope that this trend will continue to the extent that the King of Fishes no longer will be subjected to mass slaughter, but will be allowed to return home freely to propagate his kind and to provide, to a reasonable extent, peak sport to devotees of the fly rod and the artificial fly.

25

The Pacific Salmons

Although five species of salmon are common to northern Pacific waters, sport fishermen are mainly concerned with two. Mention either and watch their eyes light up! Then you'll hear tall tales of big ones landed by methods as diverse as trolling deep with "cannon balls" to laying an artificial fly across an estuarine pool.

The two featured actors in this annual angling bonanza are the spectacular chinook, or king salmon, and the smaller but no less sporty coho, or silver salmon. When the chinook reaches 30 pounds or more it is called a "tyee." These behemoths of the deep are sought in tidewaters and the lower reaches of great rivers such as the famous Campbell in British Columbia, where dedicated anglers try for them on light tackle with considerable ritual and frequent success.

The three others, more valuable commercially than for sport, are the sockeye (or blueback salmon), the pink (or humpback salmon) and the chum (or dog salmon). Although the sockeye has been ignored mainly because it is known as "the fish anglers can't catch," it is gaining the interest of a growing number of rodsmen who are learning how. This species has a non-migratory freshwater kin fish known as the kokanee, a landlocked miniature which is fun on tiny tackle and will be discussed later.

Since the tackle and tactics for the chinook and the coho are very varied and more or less interlocking, we'll discuss them together. Most anglers can't tell a small chinook from a large coho, and they fish for both species in about the same ways. While very similar in appearance, the coho, or silver salmon, has a grayish-white mouth and gums, while those of the chinook, or king salmon, are black around the base of the teeth.

THE CHINOOK (OR KING) SALMON

After birth and youth in a river (similar to Atlantic salmon), young chinooks travel over a thousand miles northward, spending up to five years at sea before returning home again. Adult chinooks average about 20 pounds, but those that have remained longer at sea may be double and triple that size. The rod and reel record is 92 pounds; a 126½-pounder was taken from a fish trap in Alaska in 1939.

From places as far away as the Aleutian Islands chinooks return southward along the Pacific coast to reach their rivers. Fish from these schools are caught by deep trolling at depths of from 50 to 150 feet. In estuaries and tidal pools they occasionally may be taken by near-surface methods and even on flies, particularly between dawn and daylight or when baitfish rise to the surface in the evening. Trolling depth, which is the cruising depth of the fish, depends largely on water temperatures. The favorite is about 54 degrees in a range between 50 and 65. Here again, a temperature-depth probe is useful, and schools of fish can be located by electronic devices.

Chinooks enter their rivers between early spring and late fall. Peaks vary with the rivers and water conditions, but good runs can be expected in April and May and in August and September. July is a hot month in some areas. Spawning takes place, usually far upstream, between summer and early winter. Before entering fresh water the fish are of a bright silvery color, with dark blue to greenish backs prominently marked by irregular black spots. They turn darker and gradually deteriorate as they move upstream, dying after spawning. While there is good fishing when schools are spotted along the coast, most of it is in the estuaries and tidewater because the fish mill around, in and out with the tides, while acclimating themselves to the transition between salt and fresh water.

Chinooks (and cohos) have been transplanted very successfully into some of the Great Lakes. Deprived of the greater bounty of the sea, these are smaller fish, but they are lively fighters which often tip the scales at 20 pounds.

Since chinooks evidently stop feeding on entering fresh water, the best fishing for them is in the salt. However, they do strike at a variety of spoons, spinners, plugs, baits and flies, perhaps because of instinct, or from anger or curiosity. Lures should be fished slowly.

This handsome chinook salmon was taken in a northern estuary on its way to its spawning run up a Pacific coastal river.

THE COHO (OR SILVER) SALMON

The appearance and habits of the coho are very similar to those of the chinook, but the coho is a favorite of light-tackle hardware heavers and fly fishermen because it often feeds near the surface and takes lures readily, sometimes accompanying this by spectacular jumps.

While coho grow to adulthood in the ocean they do not move far from their rivers, into which the schools begin to enter in early summer (earlier in northern California, and a bit later in Oregon and Washington). Entry time depends on water temperature; their favorite is between 45 and 60 degrees, with an optimum of 54. This being about the same as for the chinook, the schools of both species often are mixed. Average weights are between 10 and 15 pounds, with an occasional lunker going over 20.

Spawning takes place in the rivers between October and February, the fish dying thereafter, as all other Pacific salmons do. Like chinooks, the cohos drift in and out of the estuaries with the tides, becoming acclimated

A pair of coho salmon and the fly tackle used to catch them.

to fresh water and waiting for heavy rains to raise the rivers for the up-stream journey. The fish are bright and silvery in salt water, but start to put on their reddish spawning colors as soon as they enter the fresh, this due to bacteriological breakdown of their skin cells. They are easy to catch in salt water; much less so as they move upstream.

Cohos are taken with live and cut baits such as anchovies, smelt, herring, squid, prawns, cut sardines and mackerel. While it is necessary to get the baits down to the level of the fish, schools often are seen feeding on top, usually marked by the wheeling and diving of shearwaters, cormorants and other birds. In such cases trolling around schools or across their path (but not through them) can produce quick results. Casting into such schools with spinners, plugs and spoons can bring smashing strikes at nearly every cast. Fly fishing is popular, and growing more so, during periods when fish are showing on the surface.

PARTY BOAT FISHING

In the pitch black of pre-dawn the boats stream out from their harbors, seemingly in endless procession; lightless (to aid night vision), they chug and hum along precarious channels, over treacherous bars, bucking peeling swells to open water in search of schools of salmon in the sea. On commercial boats, party boats, private ones, big and small, crude and elaborate, murmuring crews are busily preparing gear while sportsmen are sipping coffee or rigging tackle as these invisible armadas plow out of scores of ports from San Francisco Bay northward to brave clashing tides and currents, some in hope of profit, others in search of sport.

Some of the paying guests are expert repeaters, but neophytes in Pacific salmon fishing can get their sea legs and learn the essentials by going along. Lacking the advice of old hands at the game, discuss your desires with proprietors of dockside tackle shops to obtain a list of skippers. Interview them and arrange with one for a booking. If the skipper is popular, the date may have to be made well in advance. Make sure he is agreeable to the kind of fishing you want to do. Discuss tackle; whether you will use that provided by the boat (which may be too strong to be very sporty) or whether you will bring your own. Discuss baits and lures, equipment and clothing, food and beverages. You want to be warm and comfortable, equipped with correct gear, but there's no sense in lugging things the boat carries for your use. It also may save later displeasure to agree in advance about who owns the fish you catch. Some skippers insist on a share.

Tackle and methods used on party boats vary so much under different fishing conditions that anything said here may be inappropriate, but an example or two may be helpful. In spring, salmon usually cruise deep, working shallower as the season progresses. August is the month for peak activity. The most active times are between first light and sunrise, the hours around dusk, and during tide changes. Let's assume here that the salmon are deep, because other conditions will be discussed later. Some anglers think deep fishing isn't very sporty, but it may be the only way to take fish.

Let's use a medium- to heavy-action two-handed boat rod about 8 feet long. On this put a metal-spooled star drag reel, such as a 3/0, loaded with between 275 and 350 yards of from 30- to 50-pound Dacron or monofilament, or perhaps metal line. This strong tackle is necessary because weights are used to slowly troll the lures at proper depths, which may be between 30 and 100 feet, or more, just above the bottom.

Newcomers to this form of fishing will find the weights and their rigging interesting. Called "bombs," or "salmon balls" or "cannon balls," these are from 1- to 3-pound balls of molded lead or scrap metal into which is set a brass screw-eye for attaching the tackle. On a strike, a spring-triggered device releases the bomb, allowing the fish to be handled weightlessly. These bombs are not very expensive, and many usually are used during a good day's fishing.

The connecting device is a metal tube about the size of a cigarette, with a swivel on both ends. In this is a spring-loaded slide-pin, or trigger, to which the bomb's eye-ring is clipped. This opens automatically to drop the weight when a fish strikes the lure.

The lure is connected to the swivel of the connecting device and its bomb by about 9 feet of strong monofilament. Baits usually are whole fish, such as an anchovy or a herring, carefully rigged on a special bait harness which runs through the body of the fish to keep it from spinning or rolling excessively while being trolled.

Artificial lures for chinooks for deep trolling usually are brightly finished metal spoons in brass and copper, brass and chrome or gold and bronze. Coho take the same lures, but also go for colored ones such as chartreuse with red dots, yellow-green, bright red, or cerise with black dots. They like brilliant colors, actively fished. Anglers on party boats usually ask the skipper to choose the lures.

Thus rigged, the rods are set in outrigger rod holders spaced along the boat's rail. A swift jerk of the rod tip signals a strike and a dropped bomb. While the angler handles his fish, one of the crew usually arrives with a yard-wide deeply bagged net. The action gets even more exciting when several men line the rail, all with fish on!

Another popular method of fishing for Pacific salmon is with a plastic or metal diving plane which keeps the bait at the desired depth. A strike levels the planer, which offers little resistance while the angler handles the

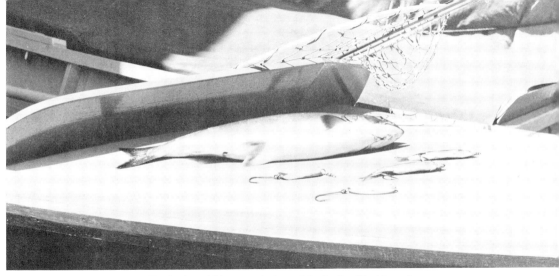

Typical wobblers and rigged baits for Pacific salmon.

Boat captain exhibits a Pink Lady plastic diving plane and a marker which is dropped to indicate where a fish was hooked, so the location of the school can be found again.

fish. Some planers are painted in bright colors which seem to attract salmon to the bait.

Another type of weight is crescent shaped with linkages at both ends for joining to line and leader. These are called drails, or keel leads, and are valuable in preventing line twist.

Party boats of different sizes offer varied facilities which newcomers may wish to consider. Large ones may be more stable, if one is inclined to sea-sickness. While they may be more comfortable, they also may be more crowded. Good skippers don't crowd their boats because many of their customers won't go out again after experiencing tangled lines and insufficient attention. Fish taken by each angler are strung on a ring or chain or something similar with his name or number on it. Crew members are careful to clean them and to see that everyone aboard gets what he catches. Sea birds, wheeling, screaming and diving for scraps tossed over the side, add to the fun of the return trip.

Smaller party boats offer more flexible facilities. One or more groups of fishermen, with the same or similar goals in mind, can agree to leave the dock when they wish, fish where and as they want to, and return whenever they desire, subject only to the captain's judgment of tidal and weather conditions.

PRIVATE BOAT FISHING

Small-skiff fishing is a growing sport along the northwestern coast. It offers excitement as well as solitude, but anglers unused to the capriciousness of the sea should be prepared for the worst. Dense fogs sweeping in from offshore can engulf small boats suddenly, and dangerous winds can come up. A compass, a chart and life preservers are basic necessities. Small boats are on their own, without radar, direction finder or radio. If prudent, however, the small-skiff salmon fisherman can enjoy the sport at its best.

Small-skiff anglers usually set up their tackle in the same manner that fishermen do aboard party boats, except that somewhat lighter gear is the rule. Knowing that salmon surface and enter shallow water more frequently as the season goes on, there may be no need for the deep equipment which has been discussed. In fact, schools of salmon may be in such shallow water that they could be reached from shore.

When fish are near the surface, medium-size spinning gear with lines testing between 10 and 20 pounds should be sufficient. One may need to get the lure down by using a keel type of trolling lead of from 1 to 3 ounces, to which is joined about 3 feet of 40-pound monofilament, used as a shock leader to prevent gill cuts. A good trolling speed is between 3 and 4 miles per hour, using rigged bait, diving plugs or spoons. Since cohos usually take flies readily, try double-hooked patterns about 4 inches long in colors as recommended on page 457. A spinner or two ahead of the fly usually adds greatly to its effectiveness. Varying trolling speed, or increasing it to 5 miles per hour, often helps.

A hooked salmon may take the boat far from the school, and it's difficult to find it again. It helps to drop a marker when a fish is hooked. This can be a plastic bottle or any other sort of small buoy with a flag attached to it, a line wound around it, and a small anchor. Without something of this sort to identify the general area, one could troll in circles for hours without finding the school.

When cohos are showing on top, some fishermen like to troll with fly rods, using a high-density line, or a front section with a lead core, to get the lure down to the fish.

TROLLING WITH FLASHERS AND DODGERS

Flashers and dodgers are slightly curved, nearly flat, rectangular polished metal attractors which are tied at both their ends into trolling tackle between lead and lure, thus providing added flash and action for attracting fish from long distances. The lure usually is bait, but it can be a wobbler, a plug, or something else. To provide best action, Luhr Jensen & Sons, Inc., whose flashers and dodgers are famous along the Pacific coast, recommends definite distances between the flasher or dodger and the lure and between the flasher or dodger and the lead. The method of rigging the tackle is shown in the drawing, and the distances for the various sizes are as follows:

	Size	Length	Width	Distance To Lure	Distance To Lead
Dodger					
	#000	4½"	1½"	12"	20"
	# 00	6	1⅞	14	24
	# 0	8	2⅝	18	26
	# 1	8¾	2¾	20	26
	# 2	10½	3	24	30
	# 3	11	3	30	36
Flasher					
	# 1	11¾"	2¾"	3'	4' (or more)
	# 2	14	2⅜	3	4 (or more)

These rigs usually are trolled with boat rods and conventional revolving-spool reels filled with line testing about 30 pounds. The line strength can vary according to the amount of lead used and the size of the dodger or flasher and the lure.

Trolling equipment for Pacific salmon. Dodger (*top*) is trolled slowly and dodges, or swings, from side to side. It should not rotate. Flasher (*center*) is bigger and is trolled faster. It should rotate. Both of these devices are attractors. The planer (*bottom*) pulls the lure down when it is in the cocked position, with the swivel against the apex of the "Y". Method of rigging flashers and dodgers is shown below.

HOW TO LOCATE SALMON IN SALT WATER

When salmon are not feeding deep (usually around August and later) they often drive bait to the surface, whitening and disturbing it in an acre or more of fine showers of spray. Sharp eyes, perhaps aided by binoculars, can spot this activity, and really sharp ones can see it from a long distance.

Birds look for such activity and spot it immediately, a few alerting others, all flocking to the scene. So if anglers don't notice the surface-driven bait, the birds will point it out. One by one and in flocks they fold their wings and plummet into the sea, usually emerging with small fish in their beaks. They adroitly turn these, head first, into their gullets, letting each fish slide down before immediately attacking another. Birds on a feeding spree often are so gluttonous that the food they have eaten prevents them from flying. They have to sit on the water to digest their meals until they are light enough to take off. Thus, a flock of birds resting on the water may mean that fish are in the vicinity and boats should troll there.

The color of the water also may indicate fish. Green often indicates a shoal area. Black water is best for salmon, although anglers aren't quite sure why. Some think the color is due to dense swarms of plankton, which baitfish feed on, thereby attracting the big ones.

When a school of surface-feeding fish is spotted, a boat never should run into it. Slow down as the school is approached and watch the frantic bait as the silvery salmon slash through it. One can drift with the school and fish into it, or troll around it, or spot its direction of travel and fish just ahead of it. A drifting boat usually won't disturb the fish, but the noise of a motor is sure to put them down.

SALMON IN THE GREAT LAKES

We have noted that both coho and chinook salmon have been transplanted successfully into some of the Great Lakes. This is largely due to the abundance of alewives there. Deep trolling is the usual method of fishing for them, although the fish can be taken on top at times, and even off piers and breakwaters. The downrigger, or undertroll, method seems to be common. I haven't seen this done along the Pacific, and haven't noted any introduction of Pacific "bomb" methods into the Great Lakes, but this may happen at any time. Of the two methods, the downrigger seems superior, but it is less adaptable to large party boats.

The secret of finding salmon in the Great Lakes is in water temperatures, because the fish should be at the 50- to 55-degree level in summer. This may be around 100 feet deep. It depends somewhat on the thermocline level, but wind action on big lakes causes thermoclines to vary in depth, and may disperse them entirely. Downriggers (readily available commercially) are used with 8 pounds or so of weight. The break-away snaps allow use of any tackle of reasonable strength; even fly tackle with between 500 and 750 yards of Dacron line on the spool and a monofilament leader about 40 feet in length.

Bait and fluorescent spoons (usually red) and plugs of various kinds are all productive. Burke's pale-green soft plastic ones seem to be current favorites, but "hot" lures change so frequently that popular ones one season are forgotten during another.

Salmon fishing in the Great Lakes may become a grab-bag of other species, including big rainbow, brown, brook and lake trout—substitutions anglers shouldn't mind at all! Flurries of surface and near-surface fishing sometimes occur in June and perhaps into the summer, but winds can change favorable surface temperatures quickly.

MOOCHING

"Mooching" means fishing near bottom in moderate depths, usually of not over 50 feet, while roving about in a skiff or other small boat in bays and estuaries where schools of salmon should be.

The usual tackle is an 8- or 9-foot medium-action boat rod equipped with a star-drag reel loaded with 250 yards or more of monofilament testing between 15 and 30 pounds. Spinning tackle of comparable strength also is popular. Lures can be spoons or plugs, but whole herring or anchovy hookups or plug cuts are popular.

Fishermen use various mooching techniques, the following being fairly typical. Stop the boat in a selected area and strip out line, letting the bait (usually unleaded) sink straight down. A "strip" is the amount of line that can be comfortably pulled from the reel by grasping the line near the reel and pulling it out to arm's length. This usually is about 2 feet; so 15 counted strips, for example, would let out about 30 feet of line.

Let's assume that bottom depth is somewhat over 50 feet and that two men are fishing. One might make 15 strips and the other 25 strips, to fish the two baits at about 30 and 50 feet. Counting the strips tells the amount of line out so that the proper amount can be put out again after a salmon has been taken.

With the lines down, the boat is started and the lines are trolled 25 feet or so. The boat is stopped to allow the lures to sink again, whereupon it again is started and run another 25 feet; this action being repeated constantly. The result is to provide an active "injured minnow" action to the bait while keeping it moving up and down and forward in a manner similar to exaggerated jigging.

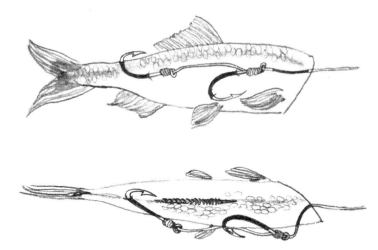

Plug-cut bait for mooching should be rigged as shown. Cut off head of baitfish at an angle, which will cause it to spin slowly when drifted, trolled or retrieved. Fish slowly to imitate injured baitfish. Use sinker if necessary to get bait down to the level of feeding salmon.

Stopping and starting the boat is unnecessary when tide or wind will drift it at a reasonable rate of speed, which should be between 2 and 4 miles an hour. Under such conditions, rods can be pumped slowly to keep the bait active. A sea anchor may be helpful in slowing a boat which is drifting too fast. A pail attached to the stern with 10 feet or so of rope will serve as a sea anchor.

Local anglers usually know good mooching areas, which of course change with seasonal and tidal conditions. It helps to watch the activity of other boats, the color of the water, and the actions of birds. We can guess that salmon may be deeper on bright days and nearer to the surface on dull ones, or around dawn and dusk, because baitfish seek these levels at such times. We know that changes of the tides are good fishing hours because bait is more active then.

When plug-cut baits are used they should be prepared with a sharp knife, and all innards should be removed. Monofilament should be checked constantly for abrasions, and knots should be examined and retied when they show any sign of weakness. Hooks must be kept needle-sharp. Big salmon

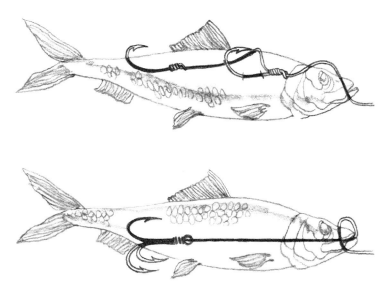

Whole herring hook-ups for mooching. For tandem single hooks (*top*), run
hooks up through both jaws and into near front and rear back of body.
For single treble hook, use needle to string leader through vent and out
of mouth. Loop the leader through both jaws to close mouth and pull tight.
Bury one of the hooks in bait, leaving two exposed. Pull leader tight
enough to give desired curve to the bait.

may mouth a bait very lightly, perhaps giving the impression that it's a small
fish. Let the fish take the bait until it pulls the rod tip down. Then strike —
very hard!

Artificials are made to resemble plug-cuts, and other fast-sinking plugs
often are useful. Local tackle shops may have up-to-date information. Bright
spoons in mother-of-pearl usually are effective.

A hooked salmon never should be horsed. When it feels the steel it will
run, and the reel's brake should have been adjusted properly to allow it to
do so. Green fish should not be brought to boat because a longer line provides more spring in the tackle. Fish shouldn't be netted until they have
given up and are lying on their sides. A salmon should be netted head first.
If it feels the net near its tail it will try to move away — fast.

Two fishermen mooching in a boat often hook fish at the same time. To
avoid tangled lines, they should decide who will bring his fish in first. The
other fish can be held, well out on a tight line, until this has been done.

FLY FISHING

Hooks used in salt water should be of noncorrosive metal or should be plated to avoid rusting, which ruins sharpness and strength and which discolors fur and feathers. Those for coho usually are between sizes 3/0 and 1 in patterns such as the Siwash, but those for chinooks can be as large as 6/0 or 7/0. Flies vary in length up to about 5 inches; smaller patterns of course being used for casting. When prevalent baitfish, such as candlefish, anchovies or smelt, are in evidence they are imitated in size and colors as closely as possible.

Flies for trolling usually are tandem rigged, the tail hook frequently pointing upward. Hook shanks and the connection often are encased in mylar tubing, or the body of the front hook is elongated and wound with silver tinsel or folded foil. Thin mylar strips can be added to wings for added flash. Flies for casting frequently are of the "Blonde" type, with the tail applied as a wing to prevent long wings from wrapping themselves around the hook shank when the fly is cast. Flies which are to be attached to spinners should have a straight ringed eye on the front hook. Some flies for Pacific salmon are well-known patterns; others are merely baitfish-imitating color combinations which anglers think should be lucky. Most are dressed with silver bodies, and usually with polar-bear hair, if it is obtainable. Here are a few popular color combinations (see others in Color Plate 10):

> Green over white
> Blue over white
> Orange over white
> Brown (bucktail) over white
> Green over yellow over white
> Blue over green over white
> Blue over red over white
> Green over red over white
> Gunmetal gray over medium green over fuchsia over white
> Blue over green over yellow over white
> Gray over green over peach over white

These flies usually are of hair for more pulsating action and because feathers are more perishable, although marabou often is used. Heads are built up, painted in an appropriate color with a large eye and pupil. Anglers think that a spinner (such as a number 3) ahead of the fly is an effective ruse. If the spinner causes line twist, a bead swivel 3 feet ahead of it should help.

In near-surface trolling best results are obtained when the fly is dropped back from 30 to 40 feet behind the wake of the motor. Trolling speed is important. Increase it until the fly bounces; then slow down until it is barely submerged. Run the motor at this speed. Cohos like a fast fly but chinooks want it trolled considerably slower.

When chinook and coho salmon are showing or are not very deep, fly-rodders can enjoy so much fun that other types of tackle are forgotten. Systems 9, 10 or 11 are most practical. As in Atlantic salmon fishing, reels (usually single action) should have smooth, adjustable drags, with about 150 yards of backing for the line. Leaders, about as long as the rod, are tapered to between 10 and 15 pounds.

Since much of this fishing calls for deeply and quickly sunken flies, even weight-forward fast-sinking lines may not get them down fast enough. Such lines are available in slow, fast and extra-fast sinking types, of which the latter should do nicely for most purposes. If it doesn't, the answer is to use a "lead-head," which is a shooting head of between 25 and 30 feet of lead-core line attached to monofilament backing.

Lead-core line, marked by a different color every 10 yards, comes in 100 yard lengths of 10 colors, so one color is 30 feet long, and one color should be enough for a shooting head. This line is available in strengths and weights as follows:

18-pound test weighs 13 grains per foot
25-   "   "   "   15   "   "   "
45-   "   "   "   16   "   "   "
60-   "   "   "   18   "   "   "

If we should decide on 25 feet of 25-pound-test line it would weigh 375 grains(*), which should be about right for average tackle in average water. A shorter length of heavier line could be substituted, and one weighing about 500 grains might be needed for fast, deep water. If a selected length and weight fails to suit the rod or fishing conditions it is easy to make adjustments.

(*) An avoirdupois ounce is 437.5 grains.

Salmon often hold in deep pools and runs. Cast up and across to give the line time to sink. A slow, jerky retrieve usually works best, but this can be determined by experimentation. In addition to the bucktails previously mentioned, flies imitating shrimps can be effective, but tackle dealers and other fishermen will offer more up-to-date opinions than any book can provide. The Blonde method of dressing is somewhat shrimp-like and prevents the wing from wrapping itself around the hook shank. The Pink Blonde, or a red one, should do well. Larry Green, a noted Pacific salmon expert, says that each of his salmon has been taken on a different pattern. Loring Dodge, who transplanted himself from eastern Canada to British Columbia, likes flies made with artificial hair, which comes in all colors and shades, including hot ones. Since this is very fine hair it is good for adding various blends of color, but I like some stiffer material, such as polar-bear hair, mixed in with it.

When a salmon is hooked on a fly from a boat which is near land, it is best for the angler to be put ashore so he can handle the fish from the bank.

SOCKEYES AND KOKANEE

These two closely related salmons are also-rans in the estimation of most anglers, but a few notes on them may be appropriate.

Anglers usually happen upon schools of sockeye salmon by accident, and may ignore them because of their reputation for failing to take bait or lures. Those who know how to catch them say that fresh-run sockeyes are better fighters than cohos, and even more delicious to eat. This is the fish which often is referred to as the "blueback," or in Alaska, the "red salmon." Although I have had no experience with them, those who have have reported that they can be taken on spinning tackle with ¼-ounce wobblers in fluorescent red, hot pink, or red and white, and jigs in similar colors. It seems to help to put three thin tails on the hook, such as those which can be cut from the rubber or plastic skirts sometimes used on small plugs. Unlike other salmons, sockeyes won't hit on the retrieve, and they want lures fished very slowly. The idea seems to be to cast out the lure and to let it flutter down, jerking it up and repeating, as one would fish a jig. While these fish are reported to be plankton feeders, they will, for some strange reason, hit a lure that looks and acts like a swimming shrimp.

The kokanee is a very small landlocked salmon which rarely grows longer than between 8 and 12 inches; the record catch being about 4 pounds. Native to the Northwest, it has been introduced widely, even as far away as New England, because it is fun to catch on tiny tackle and because it provides valuable food for larger fish. For example, the giant Kamloops (rainbow) trout of Idaho grow to such size because of the abundance of kokanee in lakes such as Pend O'Reille.

Kokanee can be caught on small lures by trolling, fly casting or still-fishing. Try a small hook baited with a small worm trolled behind a red-beaded flasher. Flies in size 12 or smaller do well, especially shrimp imitations and little bucktails or streamers in combinations of white and pink or red. The little fish also take worms, single salmon eggs and maggots.

SALMON OF SUICIDE ROW

One of my favorite steelhead streams is the famous and beautiful Klamath, of northern California, also renowned in season for coho and chinook salmon. I never have fished Suicide Row, but Larry Green has, and his account of it seems worth repeating:

The mouth of the river can be reached by boat. A short distance upstream from the little town of Requa is a place where the treacherous curling breakers of the Pacific smash into the outward-flowing Klamath, and it is here, in early September, that migrating hordes of salmon pour into the mouth of the river to acclimate themselves to the fresh water before proceeding upstream. Here, a strong cable has been stretched across the river, so small boat fishermen can tie up to it to fish their lures in the fast current. In season boats are moored closely together along the cable, this being referred to as Suicide Row.

Incoming or milling salmon eagerly strike at baited anchovies or flashing blades. When a fish is hooked the angler must quickly start his motor; untie his bow line, and drift free before becoming entangled in hundreds of lines. Then he must get to shore to battle his fish. If a motor doesn't start immediately, the boat will be swept to the mouth of the river into the dangerous breakers and undertow. In earlier days many anglers lost their lives, thus giving the place its name. More recently the Coast Guard has stationed a special rescue unit here, standing constantly by during the salmon season. Always alert for trouble, the Guardsmen swoop out in a fast boat and tow hapless anglers to shore. In spite of the danger and confusion, hundreds of brightly silvered chinook are taken here almost daily. Some of them weigh over 50 pounds!

26

Shad

Anglers living near coastal rivers think the Atlantic shad, or white shad, is everybody's sportfish and a toothsome table delicacy as well. A member of the herring family and related to the coveted tarpon and bonefish, it jumps like a small salmon, rips out line as if its tail was on fire, and frustrates heavy-handed rodsmen by sometimes breaking off because of its paper-like mouth.

Fancy tackle isn't needed for shad fishing; a cane pole often will do. Anglers use spinning, spincasting, baitcasting or fly fishing gear with equal success. Lures are simple. The mouths of shad are equipped with strainers, and they exist on a diet of plankton and algae; nevertheless, they hit artificials enthusiastically; even a bright, small hook with a couple of red or orange beads strung on ahead of it, or the same thing trimmed with a bit of foil from the wrapper of a chocolate bar.

The Atlantic hot spot for shad always has been the few hundred feet just below the low Enfield Dam on the Connecticut River near Connecticut's northern border with Massachusetts. Although there is no wide and deep pool here, the hordes of shad, running up-river from the sea to spawn, collect and mill around below the dam before attempting to swim over it. Since my home is only a few minutes drive from there, I have fished the area often. The best time is from late April to early June when the shad bush is in blossom, Peak fishing is about mid-May, this depending on water conditions.

Since anglers must show licenses before entering the area, they have the place to themselves. Walking down the short dirt road over the bridge of the ancient canal, they look down from the dam's abutment to see a line of fishermen – usually nearly elbow to elbow. A few anchored boats bob on the wide river, their occupants casting cross-stream or quartering downstream to allow lures to swing and sink. Strikes usually occur on completion of the swing. Men in a boat in the right place at the right time can hook shad on every cast, or nearly so. In spite of handling the fish delicately, with reel brakes set as lightly as practical, hooks sometimes pull out. Netting is a necessity.

Spinning tackle with 6- or 8-pound-test lines is usual. This is rigged with whatever type of shad fly, dart or spinner is fashionable, and with a sinker of between ¼ and ½ ounce (depending on the current, and distance needed) sometimes clipped to the line a foot above the lure. Since the sinkers often hang up amid rocks and moss on the bottom, smart fishermen have learned to put them on short droppers so they will pull off. Long casts are needed from shore to reach channels where the fish lie, although if the place isn't too busy, shad sometimes can be hooked close in. Most of the men are regulars who know each other, and the nearest always helps with a net. Strings of fish tethered to the bank indicate that some are much luckier than others. While the Enfield Dam and similar spots, such as Pennsylvania's Conowingo Dam, are traditional meccas in season, many anglers prefer more elbow room. These have located pools and runs in smaller tributaries where short casts produce quick results, plus ample space for the fly rod and the fly.

ATLANTIC COAST SHAD

Shad enter northern Florida's rivers for spawning before February; other schools migrate north at speeds coinciding with the warming water temperatures they prefer. These range between 55 and 70 degrees, 65 degrees making the fish most energetic. They reach North Carolina's waters during February and March, are in the Delaware Bay area in March, in New Jersey's rivers in April, Connecticut's in May and in the St. Lawrence River region (which is the northerly extent of their migrations) in June. They habitually return to regions where they were born, but are not as accurate in finding their own rivers as some of the other anadromous species.

Fresh from the sea, they are lusty, dark-backed, silversided fish dressed in large scales and somewhat resembling small tarpon. While they usually weigh between 3 and 6 pounds, occasional ones are bigger. These most often are females laden with eggs. The record is about 12 pounds. Females are called "roe shad," or "roes," and males are known as "bucks."

Several fish resemble the white shad, the principal one being the *hickory shad,* which is smaller. The former has lips of even length. The latter can be distinguished from it by a protruding lower jaw. Other herrings, such as *alewives,* are much smaller and often are noticed swimming between the legs of wading shad fishermen. These are of no particular interest to anglers.

PACIFIC COAST SHAD

In 1871 the great angler and conservationist Seth Green took several cans of shad fry from Rochester, New York, to California and planted the survivors in the Sacramento River. This started a prolific shad fishery that now flourishes all the way from southern California to Alaska. Shad enter many rivers along this vast coastline, but a few of those in the central and northern parts of the state are of special interest. Fishing peaks vary from river to river, starting in May on some and lasting as late as mid-August on others.

Although the great Sacramento River holds hordes of shad in season, most anglers consider it too big to bother with. They prefer its three smaller main tributaries, which are among the best in the state. Of these the Yuba is a great favorite, with peak fishing in June through July. The American is good at the same time, while the Feather's most productive season is the four weeks between mid-June and mid-July.

Next in popularity (as this is being written) is the Russian River, offering good fishing from mid-May through July.

The Klamath River, like the Sacramento, usually holds too much water during this season to offer good shad fishing, but its main tributary, the Trinity River, is popular from the first part of July to mid-August.

Last on California's list is the San Joaquin River, which holds a good shad run from late May to mid-June. However, it is a large river and usually is rather muddy because of the pumping and recirculation of water for irrigation projects.

TACKLE FOR SHAD FISHING

Although any tackle of light or moderate strength is suitable for catching shad in small rivers, big rivers requiring stronger tackle. Six-pound-test monofilament is about average for normal spinning and spincasting conditions, with 12-pound braided line for baitcasting gear.

Since lures are small and light, some lead is needed to carry them out and to get them down where the fish are, which often means bumping bottom. This may require about 1/2 ounce in fast, deep currents, plus stronger than average tackle to handle it. The trick is to use just enough weight to cast the lure far enough and to drift it deep enough without snagging often.

Since lead applied to the line itself can result in broken tackle when it becomes snagged, it should be put on a shorter and weaker dropper, or the pencil lead and surgical rubber tubing arrangement shown for steelhead on page 343 should be used. If clamped-on leads are not applied too firmly, they will pull off when snagged, making it easy to retrieve lures intact, after which the lead can be replaced. If tied-in droppers seem undesirable, a small 3-way swivel can be used with a short and light piece of monofilament and a dipsey or bank sinker fastened to one of the swivel's eyes. Lead is applied as far away from the lure as can be cast conveniently—which means a foot or more. Because of the distance between lead and lure, it is preferable to make casts with a sweeping swing rather than with the snappy motion commonly used with lures that don't require weight to carry them out.

Baitcasting tackle for shad is regaining some of the popularity it lost to spinning. Equipment that was recommended for bass also is appropriate for shad. This tackle commonly is used for trolling when the fish are in estuaries and wide rivers where schools need to be located. A long line—100 feet or more—diminishes the need for lead and seems to bring more strikes. Shad darts or small spinners in nickel finish are popular terminal tackle. Try to work them at moderate speed as near bottom as possible, raising the rod to pull up the lure slightly when bottom is felt.

FLY FISHING FOR SHAD

Most anglers agree that fly-fishing tackle is the top of the sport under conditions where it is practical. A bass-bugging rod is ideal with a sinking or fast-sinking line or with a lead-cored shooting head backed by monofilament —whatever is needed to get the fly down quickly. If the fly doesn't pick up a bit of moss occasionally it probably isn't being fished deep enough.

We have mentioned casting up and across, a method ideal for slow currents. In faster water it may be better to cast cross-stream, or down and across. The object is to get the fly very near bottom by the time it reaches the end of its swing, which is when most of the strikes occur.

What kind of fly to use? A taking shape or color combination popular in one region one season may be considered passé somewhere else or later on. Since we therefore only can indulge in generalities, it could be said the fly would be on a number 2, 4 or 6 gold or silver hook with a sparkling silver body and that it would be dressed in hair and hackle in white or red, or in combination, perhaps with a touch of yellow or orange. Small streamers and bucktails often are used. A white or a light-colored pattern is best in dark water. Try shad darts (which don't cast as well) when quartering downstream in enough current to keep them off bottom.

PLATE 11

SHAD FLIES AND LURES

Most of these flies and lures are unnamed regional favorites. The top row are wingless hackled flies popular in the Northeast. The second row are bead-eyed fluorescent lures most popular on Western rivers. The third row shows two other bead-head variations and two mylar-bodied bucktails. The third fly in the fourth row is the "Connecticut River Shad Fly" whose (red) wing and tail are common in other colors, such as orange and yellow, and often are clipped shorter. The fifth row shows a red and white "Fat Dart", a "Kast-master", a "Cherry Bomber" and a red and yellow "Fat Dart".

PLATE 12

PANFISH FLIES AND LURES

Many panfish flies and lures lack distinguishing names. In the top row the first and third flies are tiny bucktails; the second and fourth are tiny marabou streamers (sometimes weighted). The fifth one is a chenille-bodied bee. The second row shows a shrimp, two nymph patterns, a tiny plastic baitfish imitation and a beetle. The third row illustrates an inchworm, a deer-hair hopper, Fulsher's Silver Minnow, a brown ant and a grub. The fourth row features small surface poppers; the first two with plastic bodies and the last two with bodies of wood. The fifth row illustrates typical miniature jigs.

PLATE 13

JIGS FOR FRESH AND SALT WATER

Jigs vary in size and shape to suit specific fishing conditions, as explained in the text. Many, such as the two in the second row, are home-made. The pink one is the famous "Upperman Bucktail". The three nickel-plated jigs at lower left are a "Swedish Pimple" (red plastic tail), a light mackerel jig, and a feather-tailed one with a boat-shaped body. These are dressed both with hair (usually bucktail) or with syntheic fibers (such as the one at lower right).

PLATE 14

FLY-ROD BASS BUGS AND LURES

RED AND WHITE POPPER   BLACK POPPER

CLIPPED DEER-HAIR GREEN FROG   CLIPPED DEER-HAIR BROWN FROG   CLIPPED DEER-HAIR MOUSE

GREEN GRUB

PLASTIC DIVER   CLIPPED DEER-HAIR MOTH   RUBBER LEGGED POPPER

PLASTIC POPPER   FLAP-TAIL PLUG

CORK-BODIED MOTH   KEEL-FLY "ROYAL COACHMAN"   CORK-BODIED GRASSHOPPER

Baitcasting tackle is being seen again on shad rivers (*right*). Light spinning tackle (*below*) accounted for the full stringer of fish.

In this and other cases, the most popular fly of the season may not be the best one, and many others may be just as good, but it is the one fly anglers are talking about, and therefore the one most used.

For example, the hot producer for many years at Connecticut's famous Enfield Dam was what is called The Connecticut River Shad Fly. This simply is a nickel-plated hook with a body of silver tinsel and a wing of two sections of red goose or swan feathers. Some anglers clipped the wing at about mid-shank, and others liked it even shorter. It usually was fished with a red glass bead on the leader. Later on the wing and bead became orange.

Another simple pattern calls for a gold-plated Eagle Claw hook with three ball-like turns of pale orange chenille at the head and two turns of pale orange hackle *back of it*. Use red thread so it will show. This also could be done in red or white, and the addition of a glass bead on the leader wouldn't hurt.

A popular basic California pattern is tied on a weighted silver number 2 or 4 hook with a pair of bead-chain eyes on each side of the head. It has a

When boats are anchored in the right places, fly-rodders often hook fish on every cast.

silver tinsel body and two or three turns of a white hackle back of the eyes. (White seems to be the best color for western shad flies or lures.) From this simple pattern many variations have evolved. These include adding a fluorescent red tag with or without two or three turns of red or pink chenille (like a ball) behind the hackle. Sometimes the chenille is pale green, or another color. Neophyte fly tyers should have no trouble with these simple patterns, and they should be enough. The appearance of the fly is much less important than getting it to the fish.

WHERE TO FIND SHAD

During seasonal runs, shad along both coasts act in a very similar pattern. They enter rivers when the temperature suits them and hurry or tarry depending on it. Since the upstream runs occur mostly at night, they will spend daylight hours lying deep in eddies and pools, in main channels of moderate flow, and behind rocks. Channels and rips are hot spots. While most of them lie near the middle of big rivers, many may be near shore during high water. It is common for schools of shad to move upstream and then to return, and to mill around before resuming their journey. For this reason many anglers consider it practical to fish from one place on the bank or to wade out and keep on casting, waiting for a school to appear. When it does, and while it is there, a fish often is taken on every cast.

Fishermen near good shad areas have studied their river when it is low to locate its pools and channels. When the shad runs start, they know exactly where to fish. Otherwise two men can cast from an anchored boat, the man fishing on one side taking fish after fish, the one on the other side catching none. The reason is that the first lure, on the completion of its swing, lands in a little channel where a lane of shad are lying. The other lure ends up over a small ridge where there are none. In some waters a few feet can make a lot of difference. Another reason why one man may be taking fish is because his lure is getting down where the fish are while his partner's is drifting over the fish. The lure must get to the fish, because they won't move very far for it.

Thus, one casts up and across, cross-stream, or down and across, depending on the flow of the current. The object is to keep the lure near bottom on a slow swing, without letting it whip. The main thing is to have it near bottom when it stops its swing and hangs in the current. At this point let it hang for a few moments. If no strike occurs, jig it a bit, and let it drop back a few feet before bringing it in.

After making the cast, slack line should be taken in quickly. If the tackle signals that the lure is bumping bottom, the rod tip should be raised to raise the lure. The penalty for letting it drag bottom is to become snagged. The idea is to fish deep enough to let it touch bottom, but then to keep it just off

Delicate-mouthed shad must be played cautiously or else the hook will pull out. Striking the fish should be avoided.

the bottom so it will complete its swing without hanging up. Obviously the amount of lead used is very critical. It must be heavy enough to get the lure down, but light enough to prevent snagging. A cast or two quickly tells whether there is too little or too much, and this easily can be adjusted.

When a shad is hooked (they usually hook themselves, so striking should be avoided), he probably will run downstream, and the drag should have been set lightly enough to provide mild tension and still allow the fish to do so. At the end of the run he probably will jump, and then can be brought back cautiously. When wading or fishing from a bank, follow the fish and steer him into quiet water where there is less danger of him breaking off. While the fish have delicate mouths, break-offs are rare unless excessive tension is applied. This is part of the challenge of shad fishing, and one of the reasons why it is so much fun. Lead the fish over a wide-mouthed net and then raise the net carefully to avoid the final flop which could mean a break-off. Fresh shad can be the mainstay of a very fine dinner!

TIPS ON COOKING SHAD

Shad roe is a prized delicacy. The two roes can be lifted out and separated without breaking the membranes which enclose the eggs. Cook them very slowly in a covered skillet with two strips of bacon for each roe. Fast cooking burns the outside and makes the eggs pop, which doesn't help walls or clothing. When the roes are golden brown on one side, turn them over and lay the cooked bacon on top. Avoid overcooking, which toughens them. They are done when simmered to a golden-brown color. Serve a roe, with bacon, to each person. The roes are sliced through their wider parts and laid open on the plate. Sprinkle on a little lemon juice and add seasoning to taste.

Connoisseurs like the females for the roe but prefer the males for their flesh. The fillets have rows of Y-shaped bones which can be trimmed out in strips with a sharp knife. If boning the shad is too much trouble it can be broiled very slowly. Very slow cooking softens the bones so much that, if done slowly enough, they are no problem.

The time-honored way of baking a shad is as follows: Scale and clean the fish, cutting out dorsal and anal fins by slicing along both sides until they can be pulled out. Remove head and tail and the black blood under the spine. Wash the fish and set it in a roasting pan in about ½ inch of water (without salt). Bake in a very slow oven (225–250 degrees) for 5 or 6 hours. An hour before removing it from the oven lay a few strips of bacon over it. Serve with lemon, and condiments to taste. This slow cooking should dissolve the fine bones.

Another recipe calls for stuffing the fish and baking it (without water) in a greased paper bag. About 3 hours in a 225-degree oven should do it by this method. (Baking fish in greased paper bags seals in moisture and flavor. In New Orleans the best restaurants prepare pompano that way, and they charge a lot for it.)

27

The Pike Family

Regional opportunities influence fishermen to become specialists, perhaps favoring wet or dry flies for trout, plugging or bugging for bass, or learning the special tricks that catch other prizes that are available. In muskie or pike country, which covers a lot of ground, most of them specialize on the "tiger of fresh water," as the muskellunge is called, or his cousin the northern pike, which is nearly as big and ferocious. Except for the strength of the tackle, fishing methods for the pike family, including muskies, pike and pickerel, are similar enough to be discussed together. We'll begin with the biggest—the muskie—and add appropriate notes about the others. The walleyed pike also will be included here because many think it also belongs to the family. It doesn't. The walleye is the largest member of the perch family, and its habits are quite different from the pikes.

THE MUSKELLUNGE

When trout or bass fishermen argue the merits of their sports, the muskie specialist might say, "What would you rather do, stalk and shoot a big buck, or bag a bunch of rabbits?" Muskie mania could be compared to the lifetime pursuit of a big-game trophy, perhaps without ever getting it. Trophy muskies aren't very common. In many areas, landing even one good one in a season is considered quite an accomplishment. On the other hand there are places where those who know how can take big ones regularly.

Ferocious jaws opened wide, a muskie thrashes water frantically as it is brought to the boat. Called the "tiger of fresh water," the muskie is considered a prized trophy, mainly because hooking one is so uncommon.

A 30-inch muskie isn't even a keeper in most waters, even though one that long would weigh between 5 and 7½ pounds and be about 5 years old. The world's-record muskie (as this is written) weighed 69 pounds, 15 ounces. It was taken in 1957 from the St. Lawrence River on a Creek Chub Jointed Pikie plug. An average muskie weighs about 15 pounds.

The range of the muskie is wide, and expanding. Part of it extends from southern Canada through Wisconsin, Michigan, Minnesota, Ohio, New York, the Susquehanna, Potomac and Delaware river systems, and as far south as some of the waters in the Tennessee Valley states.

Muskies neither school together nor roam around very much. Big ones are solitary fish which need so much food that one will drive all others from an area as big as five acres. It will frequent a chosen place, such as a hole in the weeds, the water under a log jam or under the roots of a sunken tree. When a fish is seen to swirl, or follow, or to take a lure, the place should be marked because it will stay there until caught. If caught, another should move into the same spot.

Muskies inhabit the clear, cool water of lakes, rivers and flowages. In rivers look for them in weedy areas of quiet water near the swifter flow, or in the deep water near the banks of pools below waterfalls. In lakes they should be in hiding places such as those just mentioned in or near the edges of emerging or underwater weed beds, in lilypadded bays, near the mouths of rivers and brooks, near rocky ledges, or along shorelines laced by floating or sunken logs and tree roots.

Since muskies spawn between early May and late June, they should be in shallow water then. They usually go deeper in the warmth of summer and return to the relatively shallow areas in the fall. While members of the pike family aren't as fussy about water temperatures as most fish, they seek levels between 60 and 75 degrees, 65 degrees usually being best. They can become acclimated to water a bit colder in northern regions and a little warmer in southern ones. A temperature probe is helpful in knowing how deep to fish.

Tackle for Muskies

Most muskies are caught by casting or trolling with medium, heavy or extra-heavy baitcasting tackle. Rods need a lot of backbone to set sharp hooks into bony jaws and perhaps to coax big fish from weeds and roots. Some anglers prefer rods with extra-long butts for two-handed casting when heavy lures are used. Reels should be of high quality, with a level-wind mechanism and a star drag. Lines are monofilament or braided, testing between 20 and 50 pounds. Spools should hold about 100 yards of line, although not more than half of this usually will be needed because muskies don't run very much. The choice between the three strengths of tackle mentioned depends on the skill of the angler and whether fishing will be done in fairly open or more congested water.

Leaders which can't be cut by sharp teeth are vital. The choice is between single-strand stainless steel (which can kink), braided or twisted bronze wire (which can be weakened by revolving lures), and very heavy monofilament. These should test between 60 and 75 pounds. Some anglers prefer monofilament because it is less conspicuous, and they maintain that the sharp teeth of a muskie can't sever it if it is strong enough.

Tackle for muskies includes floating plugs with spinners fore or aft, jointed plugs, bucktail-dressed spinning lures and eels. Baitcasting tackle is preferred.

Leaders, usually fitted with strong snaps or snap swivels for quickly changing lures, are between 8 and 14 inches long for casting and considerably longer for trolling. Length has an advantage because fish sometimes roll up on them. If braided line is used, several feet of suitable strong monofilament is included between the metal leader or shock tippet and the line.

Lures in appropriate weights for the tackle are in great variety. While muskies may strike at anything that moves, they may prefer one type to another at various times, and fishermen often do. They include floating plugs, some with spinners fore and aft, poppers, solid or jointed floating-diving plugs, spinners and spoons, often with hooks dressed with bucktail, feathers or pork strips, and hooks baited in one way or another. Baited hooks are about 5/0 in size. Live bait, such as an 8- to 10-inch sucker, can be hooked under the dorsal fin or through both lips. Live bait can be kept at the desired level with a bobber, for slow trolling near weed beds. In this case the wake of the bobber acts as an attractor. Big plugs are not considered necessary. Those in the $^3/_8$- to $^5/_8$-ounce range are very popular. While big plugs take big fish, smaller ones take smaller fish as well as bigger ones. Black eel jigs, fished as was discussed with plastic worms for bass, are very productive. It can't be stressed too strongly that hooks must be kept as sharp as possible because the strike must drive them into bony jaws. Muskies will clamp down on a lure and hold it, thus giving the impression that they have been well hooked. They will be able to throw the lure less often when hooks are sharp enough to penetrate bone and gristle.

Spinning and spincasting tackle rate a poor second choice for muskies, mainly because the longer and whippier rods make it more difficult to solidly set the hooks. Those who prefer the tackle (and many do) solve the problem by using sturdier gear specially designed for saltwater fishing.

Fly-rod addicts sometimes use their equipment for muskies, occasionally with success. Systems 9, 10 or 11—that is, saltwater fly-rodding gear—are best for the purpose, with leaders between 9 and 12 feet long tapered not less than 12-pound test. A shock tippet between 1 and 2 feet long of 40- to 60-pound monofilament tied to the end of the leader is necessary. Lure choice is between saltwater poppers with large, strong hooks, and streamers or bucktails in lengths of 5 to 7 inches. Those in the Blonde series are very popular, tied on hooks ranging between 2/0 and 5/0.

Muskie guides will say that anglers using fly tackle should have their heads examined. Fly-rodders will retaliate that such tackle presents a challenge. I agree with the guides where muskies aren't plentiful, but with the fly-rodders in the few areas presenting good chances for a hook-up or two. The fun is in the fishing, but everyone wants a little action.

Trolling for Muskies

Opinions vary on the merits of trolling or casting for muskies, but the decision often is made for us. Some regions prohibit trolling. In other areas underwater vegetation and surface obstructions make it impractical. Some fishermen prefer the relaxation of trolling, while others like to search for probable lies and enjoy the challenge of casting to them to tempt a swirl, a follow, or a strike. On big lakes, trolling is an excellent way to cover a lot of ground. Fish that are found, but not boated, can be cast to later.

Muskie guide Homer Le Blanc, an old friend, has a method of trolling five lines when several fishermen are aboard his cruiser which is shown in the accompanying drawing. Rods are in holders, three pointed upward, and two down. Lines 1 and 2 are on rods pointing outward and downward, on opposite sides of the boat. The first is weighted with a heavy keel of 5 ounces or more, with only 10 feet of line out. The second has 20 feet out and a little less weight. Back of these are rods 3 and 4, pointed upward and outward on opposite sides. The first (on the same side as number 1) has 35 feet of line out on a 3-ounce keel. The second has 50 feet out on a 2-ounce keel, the lure trolling about 3 feet down. Rod 5 is off the center of the stern, with 60 feet out, and is leaded by only 1 ounce, fishing about 18 inches down. Since Lake Clair has a maximum depth of only 20 feet, most of this is covered. Depths are charted, and the deep lines can be taken in when necessary. This method can be varied for other lakes.

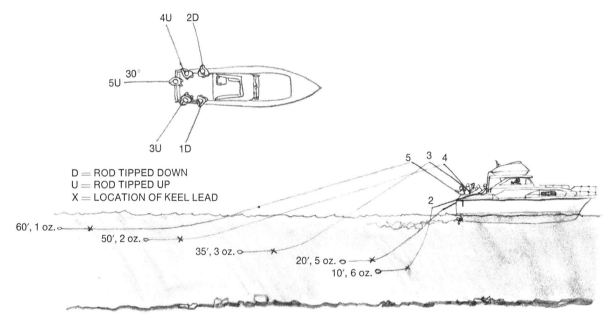

Trolling five lines for muskies.

In letting out line the trick is to release about 10 feet and to throw on the clutch while it tightens, repeating this until the desired amount is out. The lure sinks while line is let out and rises when it is tightened, thus adding to its action. One should be ready for a strike at any time, especially when the lure is near the boat. Muskies are attracted by the propellor and the wake to the extent that many have been hit by the blades.

The trick of landing muskies also applies to northern pike. It is important in preventing a violently thrashing fish from being brought aboard and in guarding against losing one at the last minute. When the fish has been hooked he will hold his ground rather than make a run. If line is leaving the reel, it is due more to the boat's motion than to the fish. The trick is to stop the boat and to circle back, instead of going to the fish. Keep him away from the boat, holding him under tension while circling. If he comes toward the boat, back it and keep circling to keep him out there, usually timing this to one minute per estimated pound. For example, keep a 25-pound muskie under tension for at least 25 minutes. Why?

Muskies and northerns have a habit of swirling for a short time and then coming in as docilely as a cow being led to the barn. Sometimes they even "play dead," and innocent anglers think they have them licked. Brought to boat, the fish may show he is as full of life as ever and perhaps run under the boat and smash tackle. Clubbing a fish too soon is dangerous, too. A non-lethal tap can goad him into furious thrashing that may cause him to throw the lure, which could strike an angler. Keep the fish at a safe distance until you are certain he's licked.

Displaying the skill and form of an expert, guide Dick Scheer, of Ghost Lake, Wisconsin, carefully brings in a muskie with a small gaff to protect himself against its vicious teeth.

These tips also may help:

● Trolling with or against the wind helps to keep a belly out of the line. A fisherman can't strike a muskie hard enough if the line has a belly in it.

● When a lure seems to be snagged, don't be sure it is. Set the hook hard anyway, because it may be held by a sulking muskie.

● Many anglers use a gaff, which makes the boat messy and prevents releasing unwanted fish. A big net is better, but have a stout club available, and use it. One made from the handle of a broken billiard cue is excellent.

● Lacking these, fish of from small to moderate size can be landed in two ways. Grasping one by the back of the neck, with thumb and forefinger pressing into the gill covers, seems to stun it temporarily. (This is a good way to land medium-sized trout.) Pressing and squeezing together the thumb and forefinger into the bony eye sockets also works, but beginners should practice on small fish first. A thrashing muskie or pike with a multiple-hook plug in his jaws can be dangerous when inexpertly handled.

Casting for Muskies

It is said that muskies are fished for by more people with less success than for any other species, but this rarely applies to experienced guides, who take trophies regularly. Perhaps hunting for muskies is like hunting for deer. The experienced hunter learns to think like his quarry, knowing where it should be under whatever conditions exist, and going there instead of wasting time somewhere else. Muskie hunting mainly is a matter of "reading the water": cruising around (perhaps while trolling) to locate the good lies.

Casting can be a waste of time until one knows how to concentrate on the hot spots. When these are found, avoid spoiling the cast by hooking weeds. Muskie lies often are in areas where thick weeds cover the bottom. A heavy wobbling spoon will sink and catch weeds, telling any fish nearby that it would be safer to postpone dinner for a while. Such fishing calls for surface plugs, or divers that won't go too deep. Choices include the Creek Chub Pikie Minnow, the Cisco Kid, and saltwater plugs like the Atom which are made for striped bass. Very large lures aren't necessary, but hooks should be 2/0 or larger, and sharp.

Many experts prefer to retrieve a lure very fast, with the rod held high, on the theory that it is impossible to retrieve too fast for a muskie, and that speed gives a lure more action while reducing the chances of a fish realizing that it's a fake.

Bright spoons are more visible under windy conditions when plugs would be less so. Diving plugs are more effective in choppy water. Surface lures do better when water is fairly flat.

Good fishing weather is unpleasant for fishermen. Choppy water, even with whitecaps, brings best results, perhaps because the fish can't see boats as well. The hours just before or after a storm front moves in seem to be unusually productive. If a muskie is seen to follow a lure without taking, retrieve it faster or change its action. He may take it right beside the boat. A swirl without a take suggests that the spot should be rested and fished again later, perhaps after offering a change of lures.

NORTHERN PIKE

Esox lucius, as scientists call the northern pike, has many friends among fishermen. His average weight is between 10 and 15 pounds. The record-breaker is a 46-pounder taken in 1940 from the Sacandaga Reservoir, in New York.

When this reservoir was built, thousands of pike were liberated from swamps and sloughs by rising water and were peddled by sackfuls in surrounding towns until the fish and game department put a stop to it. I was fishing for brook trout in a tributary river of the new reservoir at the time. While I was there several excellent pools suddenly became devoid of trout because pike had moved in.

On a much later occasion, I explored an unfished lake a little southeast of Canada's James Bay to investigate a report that "tremendous brook trout" were there. After a long trip by air from the end of the road, trout were found only in fast-water tributary streams because the lake was infested with pike. Keeping away from them was a problem, and they would strike at anything. After catching more than enough to last anyone a lifetime, we radioed for the aircraft and returned home. So, if I can't get very enthusiastic about pike, perhaps it is excusable.

Many people catch big pike and think they are muskies. The muskie has scales on only the upper halves of his cheeks and gill covers. The pike has scales that completely cover his cheeks, but only the upper halves of his gill covers. The pickerel's scales completely cover cheeks and gill covers. There also are other differences, such as in coloration, but the three species can't be identified by size. The wide range of pike covers most of Canada, and many areas of the northern United States as far west as the Continental Divide.

Since pike feed all winter (although they are logy then), they can be taken by fishing through the ice, usually over weed beds in water between 10 and 20 feet deep. When the ice breaks up and the water is 39 degrees, or warmer, they travel to weedy shallows and into the bays and coves of lakes to feed and to prepare for spawning. Spawning takes place when water is between 45 and 60 degrees. Pike strike best in water between 60 and 75 degrees; their

Northern pike leaps and thrashes just when angler thinks he has it licked. Pike and muskie often "play dead" as they come to boatside, then make a last-ditch fight for freedom.

Large plug enticed this pike to smash it sideways—as it would a baitfish—but it found hooks a deterrent to an apparently easy meal. The fish's powerful jaws exert a vise-like grip on whatever it grabs.

favorite temperature being about 65 (although this varies somewhat between northern and more southern latitudes). In this temperature range they should be in the weedy shallows.

For an unknown reason, pike seem to concentrate in some weedy areas to the exclusion of others. In the Canadian lake previously mentioned, I found great numbers in certain coves and few or none in other places that looked equally good. Presumably the extent of the food supply was the answer. When surface temperatures become too warm (75 degrees or more), pike will go to bars and reefs in deeper water near weedy shores. Except that they group together, their habits and habitats are very similar to those of the muskie. They feed in daylight, mostly on smaller fish, and early morning is a good time to catch them because they are hungrier then.

Pike in rivers and flowages usually are found near weedy banks and other cover outside swift water. They work up into pools, especially when they are below barriers such as waterfalls and dams. About 90 percent of them are taken in water less than 15 feet deep.

Tackle and Tactics for Pike

Baitcasting equipment is preferred for pike, but spinning or spincasting gear is adequate. Extra-heavy tackle isn't necessary. Pike usually can be handled effectively on gear suitable for big bass. Thus, one would choose between the light, medium and heavy matching sets discussed in Chapter 3, favoring lighter equipment unless there is reason to the contrary.

Spinning and spincasting tackle follow the same pattern. Outfits suitable for from 10- to 15-pound-test line should be adequate for most purposes, and perhaps too strong for experts. The answer lies in the kind of water being fished. If weeds, roots and lily pads are bothersome, one might choose medium or heavy baitcasting gear, and a similar strength for spincasting or spinning. For fishing in reasonably open water the lighter equipment is more fun.

Pike strike all kinds of lures very freely. Long spoons seem to work best when weed entanglement isn't a problem. Red and white stripes, with brass or nickel on the other side, are popular colors, but darker colors may do better when the water is very clear. Pork-rind strips or bucktail-dressed hooks often increase effectiveness. Weedless hooks are used only when necessary.

Plugs, as suggested for muskies but in smaller sizes, are equal to spoons in most areas. Jigs get excellent results when cast out and hopped in. Fluffy marabou dressings for these are popular. Spinners with dressed hooks do well, but usually are considered inferior to spoons, plugs and jigs. Pork chunks and weedless pork frogs like those used for largemouth bass score highly.

Unlike muskies, many pike usually inhabit the same area, giving fly-rodders ideal chances for sport. Fly tackle in System 8, 9 or 10 is suitable, System 9 being ideal in most situations. Unless the fish lie quite deep, a weight-forward floating line with a sinking tip would be suitable. Many anglers consider wire leaders (fastened to monofilament ones with tippets of from 12- to 15-pound test) to be a nuisance to handle and too conspicuous to the fish. They prefer 8 to 12 inches of monofilament shock leader in a strength of 30 pounds or more. This terminal part should be checked after every strike to be sure it hasn't been weakened by sharp teeth.

Fly hooks should be about 2/0 and usually are dressed with bucktail in a wide choice of colors. Of these, the Mickey Finn (yellow over red over yellow) is very popular. Lightweight popping plugs are effective and add to the fun because they make fish strike on the surface.

When several pike lie out there, casting to them is no problem because they will hit any lure they can see, even when it is splashed down clumsily. Try any speed of retrieve. Pike often like it slow, but fast, erratic ones also bring action.

Since pike hit artificials so well, it seems unnecessary to bother with bait, but drifting a live baitfish under a bobber in slowly flowing water, or even in a quiet cove, usually will take a fish. The best size and kind of baitfish is that which is most prevalent where it is being fished. Hook anything from 4 to 8 inches long through the lips or under the dorsal fin, and turn it loose.

PICKEREL

This smallest member of the pike family (called *Esox niger* by scientists) is more correctly named the Chain Pickerel because of his chainlike markings. The several varieties of pickerels don't concern anglers because fishing methods for them are the same. They inhabit streams, lakes and ponds in many parts of the eastern United States, with larger concentrations in New England, New Jersey and southern New York. A big one weighs about 3 pounds, although a few 8- or 9-pounders have been caught. People fishing for bass often catch pickerel. Since angling methods are so similar, the discussion of them can be short.

Tackle

Light bass equipment is ideal. When fishing for both bass and pickerel, light baitcasting gear is appropriate. Pickerel fishing is sportier when light tackle is used: spinning or spincasting gear using lines of between 3- and 6-pound test, or fly tackle in the System 5, 6 or 7 range. Here again, a stronger monofilament shock leader is better than a short wire trace. While pickerel have sharp teeth, they are small, and no great threat to a few terminal inches of 10-pound monofilament.

Small plugs of all types are good pickerel takers. Avoid those with many hooks because these small fish live longer and fight better on a single hook, or possibly a treble one. Small spinners and spoons do well, either with or without a strip of pork rind attached.

Pickerel furnish fun for fly-rodders. Favorite flies are bucktails in combinations of red, orange, yellow or white on hooks about size 4. Marabou dressings are very effective. Small popping plugs and clipped hair base bugs, including frog imitations, usually do equally well. Whatever is used should be fished in a lifelike manner. The method is more important than the lure.

Tactics

Favorite spots in streams for pickerel are eddies, pools and backwaters with considerable vegetation growing in the water along the edges. In lakes and ponds pickerel lie quietly under or amid the protection of grasses, lily pads and logs in the same kinds of places one finds bass.

Here is an effective trick: Make a short cast just outside a grass or weed line or near a lily-pad cluster. Fish in the lure parallel and as near to it as possible. Then make other casts to increasingly greater distances in about the same path. If one were to make the longer casts first, and should hook a fish, it would discourage those lying nearer.

While there is an ideal speed of retrieve for each type of lure—which is the one giving it the best action—pickerel usually respond best to lures that are fished fairly fast. If a fish is seen following the lure, fish it faster, or vary its action.

Since other methods are identical to those for bass, they need not be repeated. The skittering one, as described in Chapter 23, is worth remembering.

HOW GOOD ARE THEY TO EAT?

Too many members of the pike family (muskies, pike and pickerel) are wasted because anglers don't know how to cope with the row of Y-bones in each fillet. These little bones can be removed easily to make delicious *bone-free* fillets, as described in the Appendix. The fish can be baked whole or prepared by any other method. Bigger members of the pike family are highly prized after having been smoked.

WALLEYED PIKE

This so-called pike, actually the largest member of the perch family, usually is known as a "walleye" or, in Canada, as a *doré* because of its green-golden color. It has big eyes which appear clouded, and so it inhabits deep water to avoid bright sunlight, coming into the shallows to feed only between sunset and sunrise, or perhaps on cloudy days. A sluggish fighter when hooked, it makes up for this lack by its tastiness on the table.

The range of the walleye has extended from Canada and our northern states to most of the others. Average catches are between 2 and 5 pounds, with the biggest ever taken weighing in at over 22. Anything over 7 or 8 pounds is bragging size. Walleyes come from deep water into the shallow gravel of lakes and rivers to spawn after ice breaks up when water temperatures are between 45 and 50 degrees. There also may be large migrations up rivers at that time. After spawning, the fish return to deeper water, leaving the eggs to hatch without protection.

How to Locate Walleyes

Walleyes predominantly are deep-water bottom feeders whose depth can be located with reasonable accuracy by water temperatures. Their preferred temperature is about 60 degrees in a range between 55 and 70 degrees. Look for them where this temperature level touches rocky, sandy or gravel bars and submerged ridges, usually between 15 and 50 feet deep. Since the fish travel in schools, several should be hooked where one has been caught. Being chronic roamers, they prefer large bars or submerged ridges, but often are found where there are several smaller ones. These areas usually are well out in lakes, and their locations can be found by sonic instruments or by trolling.

When lakes are high, walleyes often migrate for food into weedy water off sandy or gravel points, especially when these points jut off into deep water.

I have taken many walleyes in rivers in Canada, where they often are the predominant fish. Favorite places seem to be deep runs, in which they school much like shad do, and in the drop-offs where streams flow into lakes. They also seek deep pools, river bends, and eddies, principally those below rapids, waterfalls or dams.

This might be called a bragging-size walleye—it weighed 8½ pounds. Erwin Bauer is the fisherman. Average catches are between 2 and 5 pounds. Though sluggish on a line, the walleye is tasty on the table.

Tackle and Tactics

Light spinning or spincasting gear is ideal for walleye fishing, with monofilament lines testing between 4 and 6 pounds for clear water and between 8 and 10 pounds for weedy places. Since their diet is primarily baitfish, deep-diving plugs that imitate them are excellent when they can get down to the fish. Light-colored ones usually are effective, between 3 and 5 inches long, with greenish backs and lighter bellies. Weighted spinners, often with fluttering pork rind fly-strips attached, do well, and so do wobbling spoons rigged the same way. Red-and-white-striped spoons are favorites.

Another top taker among artificials is the jig, if it is fished correctly. It is especially valuable when the schools are running deep. Marabou-dressed jigs, usually yellow, are excellent because they "breathe" in the water more actively than bucktail or hackles. Tie them on with a small loop, instead of a tight connection, for even greater activity. The trick is to cast them to the submerged ridge and to hop them down the incline by snapping the wrist.

Baits for walleyes usually are 3-inch shiners hooked under the dorsal fin (above the backbone) so that the hook's barb points somewhat forward, with the shank pointing upward. Enough lead, 10 inches or so above the hook, is needed to get the bait down quickly. A good method is to drift or move the boat slowly over or around a bar while raising and lowering the bait along the bottom. If the water is choppy enough to keep the bait in motion, it can be suspended from a small float. Although the bait is alive, this lazy up and down motion seems to help.

Poor seconds to shiners include crawfish, frogs (when fish are in shallow water) and worms or nightcrawlers. The last often are attached to a spinner rig having one or two small blades, perhaps with lead added, as above. This is fished in the same way, forgetting the spinner is there.

Fish all artificial lures at slow or medium speed for best results. It seems to do more good than harm to let the fish inspect them, and walleyes are slow takers.

Many fishermen use short wire leaders because the fish have small but sharp teeth, but I believe they are unnecessary. If a protective device seems to be required, a short shock tippet is much better. Try using neither. However, the line immediately above the lure should be checked for weakness frequently, cutting it back whenever necessary.

Like the true pikes, walleyes are active in winter and often are taken by fishing through the ice, using shiners baited as above. A fish called the sauger resembles the walleye and often is confused with it. While somewhat similar in appearance, the sauger is much slimmer, and is an inferior fish.

28

Panfish: Fun
For Everyone

The extremely abundant, easy-to-catch and delicious members of the panfish "family" are favorite year-round quarry for anglers of all ages. They are called "panfish" because their little fillets are so toothsome when delicately fried and also to distinguish them from the larger sportfishes. People who seek them for food can pull them in on baited hooks or artificial lures with almost any kind of gear. Those who fish for fun enjoy the maximum when using ultralight spinning tackle with lines as fine as 1- or 2-pound test, or wandlike fly rods not over 6 feet long, weighing about 2 ounces.

The panfishes, mostly members of the sunfish family, include bluegills (bream), crappies, rock bass, the common sunfish (or pumpkinseed) and the yellow perch. The bullhead sometimes is included but it isn't universally considered a panfish. All these little fishes go by many regional names, and there are allied species (such as black and white crappies and white and yellow perch), but confusion can be avoided by staying with the essentials because fishing methods for all of them are very similar.

Mostly caught for food, panfish swim everywhere in over a million ponds, and in lakes and reservoirs from coast to coast. Usually they are so prolific that their numbers exceed their food supplies, thus making them stunted. Excessive quantities of panfish often reduce populations of gamefish. For these reasons, fish and game departments encourage anglers to catch all they want, even to taking them off their nests during spawning time.

If populations are reduced in certain waters (a remote possibility regardless of fishing pressure) this would result in larger fish.

Those who want to catch lots of panfish for food or fun should realize there are a few tricks to it—not only in finding the big ones, but in using appropriate small baits or lures, and in fishing them very slowly.

PANFISH TACKLE

One of the simplest outfits is almost the same as the poke pole described for bass in Chapter 23. In this case it would be a cane or fiberglass pole about 12 feet long to the end of which is tied monofilament of about 10-pound test about as long as the rod. Hook sizes should range between 2 and 12, the larger ones for big bream and crappies. Using one of the baits which will be

Floating peacefully on a palm-fringed Florida lake abounding in panfish, a fisherman lifts his fly for another cast. Fly tackle offers maximum sport when angling for panfish.

mentioned, toss it out and let it sink slowly. If weight is needed, a split shot or two about 6 inches above the hook will get the bait down quickly. Add a sliding cork or bobber to drift bait over weed beds and around brush. The float should be only buoyant enough to hold the bait up, so fish will feel no more than imperceptible drag. Many anglers are quite fussy about this fine adjustment, using porcupine quills or what the British call "controllers" (which are cigar-shaped) in exact sizes to accomplish this.

When spinning or spincasting tackle is used it is more fun to go as light as possible. Ultralight spinning outfits are available with tiny reels suitable for 2-pound-test line, or less. While this gear isn't practical around brush piles and in weeds, it makes little fish feel more like big ones and is ideal for handling tiny spinners, jigs and wobblers weighing $\frac{1}{8}$ ounce or less, or for casting very small baits, perhaps with split shot and/or floats to match. Another argument for very light tackle is that lures must be fished slowly. Lures that are too heavy can't be handled slowly enough. The smallest baits or lures drifted down or fished at the slowest speeds are the secrets of catching most kinds of panfish.

When one watches smaller fish inspecting a bait the reason for this rule is obvious. Unlike gamefish, which usually attack, panfish swim up and hover nearby to gaze at the offering. Being timid, they will be frightened away if too much action is given to the lure. For this reason, poppers aren't very good for most panfish, although they often work—if small enough— when given almost imperceptible action.

Fly-rod addicts think their tackle provides maximum fun when the very lightest gear is used. The lightest ordinarily available is System 4, but midget equipment can be obtained which is even lighter. A floating line with a sinking tip is ideal, along with a leader tapered to the finest of tippets.

LURES FOR PANFISH

Small lures take smaller fish which may not be able to get larger ones into their mouths. Use smallest lures with numbers 10 or 12 hooks for little panfishes and usually nothing larger than 4 or 6 for the bigger ones. It should be stressed that all lures should be fished slowly because splashing and fast action will frighten panfish instead of attracting them. Within these limitations, jigs, spoons and spinners all do well on occasion, sometimes with slivers of pork rind attached. Small surface lures that swim slowly and quietly often get results when fish are not feeding deep. The larger panfish will hit small plugs and many other lures used for bass, including plastic worm rigs. For this reason, fishermen often return with a mixed bag of bass and crappies.

Trout flies in sizes 10 or 12 are productive with light fly-fishing equipment in patterns such as Black Gnat, White Miller, Gray Hackle, Coachman, McGinty and Black Ant. Small streamers and bucktails, nymphs and little freshwater shrimp imitations often do well. A very popular type of taker is a sponge-rubber spider or a chenille-bodied wet fly with legs made from rubber bands. If the bands seem quite long it helps to cut them back a little. Little floating bugs of various types usually do well; in fact, try anything very small that can be made to wiggle, but not much. Panfish can be very selective about lure colors, wanting one combination one day and a different one the next. Natural imitations usually are successful, but it may be necessary to experiment. Very tiny spinners and wobblers not larger than one's little fingernail can be handled with tiny fly tackle better than with other equipment. Since these surpass flies in sinking ability, they can be the answer when fish are fairly deep. It is important to get lures down to proper depth. If the seconds have been counted while the lure sinks to a strike, counting tells when that depth has been reached again. Then the lure should be fished with slow action.

BAITS FOR PANFISH

Since the best baits vary with the season, it helps to know which are available to the fish. In general, panfish will take anything very small that wiggles. This includes grasshoppers, crickets, roaches, garden worms, meal worms, catalpa worms, grubs, wasp larvae, nymphs, small crustaceans such as scuds (freshwater shrimp) and so on. Suit the bait and hook to the probable size of the fish; cast it out to sink slowly, or drift it under a bobber.

WHERE TO FIND PANFISH

Those who want to catch panfish, but don't particularly care what kind, should look for them near places of protection. These can be the edges of ponds and lakes near weed patches, pads and grasses. Small panfish school in the shade of boat docks and swimming floats. Submerged stumps and fallen trees can harbor many. Quiet coves offering such protection can be hot spots. In man-made lakes and impoundments there may be patches of brush, some of which can be seen above the surface, or masses of dead trees standing in the water. These are favored places for bigger fish. Big ones rarely are found near shore because they prefer the safety of deeper water where they are less often disturbed. Hot spots there are submerged ledges and underwater weed beds. If the bottom can be seen, look for sandy or gravelly openings in these masses of vegetation, and fish their edges. Maps showing depth contours help in locating them.

These general observations can be improved by becoming better acquainted with the principal species of panfishes because most of them have individual characteristics which may make certain baits or lures better than others, as well as specific fishing methods and types of locations.

BLUEGILLS

Called "bream," and usually pronounced "brim" in southern regions, the popular bluegill averages much larger there due to longer growing seasons made possible by milder weather. These bigger fish take bigger lures than their smaller northern cousins and are less shy of quietly fished ones such as small surface poppers.

Bluegills are very fussy about water temperatures. Schools of them will roam lakes in search of their favorite, which is about 73 degrees. They spawn in very shallow water when it is a few degrees below this temperature, sweeping out many roundish beds from 1½ to 2 feet in diameter near the shorelines of ponds and lakes. These clean gravel or sandy beds easily can be seen, and often overlap one another. Each male guards his nest and will strike at any small thing that comes near it, including wet flies, small wobblers, spinners and jigs. Nests guarded by bigger fish may be found in the deeper water of submerged bars farther offshore.

While many people think it isn't very sporting to catch male bluegills off their nests, conservationists and ichthyologists agree that this helps to reduce overpopulation, thus doing more good than harm because it results in bigger fish.

Bluegill stalks a floating spider, the type of surface lure that can be cast with a fly rod for this scrappy little fighter. Morning and evening are best times for surface fishing.

As surface water warms toward 80 degrees, the bluegills spend their days out deeper, returning to the shallows in the evening to feast on insects. Because shade then is on the water and more food is available, the fish are less timid and furnish excellent sport for fly fishermen casting little bass bugs and poppers, wet and dry flies, and sponge-rubber or chenille spiders with rubber-band legs. Small spinners and wobblers also work. Baits do, too, but they are unnecessary. Those who prefer them can let the cast bait sink naturally or can drift it, weighted by a split shot, under a float or spinning bubble. Thus, summer fishing for bluegills is best in the early morning or in the evening. While casting from shore is productive, fishermen run less chance of scaring bluegills when quietly wading or fishing toward shore from boats.

The traditional way to fish for these pretty little fighters is with a cane pole and small hook baited with a worm, a cricket, or one of the other baits noted earlier. The modern way is with ultralight fly rods or spinning tackle. Beginners usually make the error of fishing their lures too fast, or with too much commotion. As in nymph fishing, strikes on flies are very light, so anglers should respond by tightening up as soon as anything is felt.

Bluegills, or bream, are members of the sunfish family. The record, taken from a lake in Alabama in 1950, is 4 pounds and 12 ounces. Anything over a pound is considered large, especially in northern areas. Bluegills feed mainly on insects and small underwater crustaceans such as shrimps. In southern regions one of their favorite foods is the catalpa worm. In northern states it is the garden worm. They rarely take minnows.

THE CRAPPIES

Close competitors of the bluegills for fishing fun and delicious dinners are the crappies, members of the sunfish family which are found everywhere in two principal species—the black crappie and the white one. Both are so similar that they can be discussed together.

The white crappie, shaped like bass and other sunfishes, is silver-colored, with a sprinkling of black spots spaced in vague vertical bars. It inhabits the same types of places the black crappie does, but often is found in warmer, more turbid waters, perhaps with mud bottoms.

The black crappie's black spots are more numerous and sprinkled more haphazardly. It is more partial to cooler, clearer water, usually with a hard bottom. Its appearance gives it the common name of "calico bass." Except for these minor differences, both crappies are caught in the same places by the same methods and with the same tackle and lures used for bluegills. Crappies differ from bluegills, however, in their fondness for minnows. While 2- and 3-pound crappies often are caught in some southern areas, particularly in deeper water, the average good one weighs about 10 ounces.

A nice stringer of crappies taken from a Tennessee lake. Minnows are good bait for crappies—as opposed to bluegills—since they roam a lake in schools looking for baitfish.

The record white crappie, caught in Mississippi in 1957, weighed 5 pounds, 3 ounces.

Spring is the crappies' spawning time—earlier in the South and later in the North, when water temperatures are between 64 and 68 degrees. Their beds are much less obvious than those of bluegills, usually being in root clumps or weed patches in water between 1 and 10 feet deep.

The key to finding crappies is to look for deep cover—brush piles and flooded dead tree areas in man-made lakes, around timbers of docks, submerged roots and fallen trees, rock piles and boulders—anywhere baitfish collect that offers reasonable protection. Unlike some of the other panfishes, crappies do not prefer weed beds and lily pad or grassy areas.

493

This crappie fell for a small jig fished just off bottom. Small plastic worms on a jig are also productive.

The most popular method of catching crappies is to use small live minnows, hooked above the spine under the dorsal fin, or in other ways described in Chapter 5, because small baitfish native to its habitat are the crappies' principal food. These usually are drifted under a ball or pencil-type float. The hook should not be too small (number 2 or 4 usually is good). Very small hooks tend to tear out of the fishes' tender mouths. Minnows are used with cane or fiberglass poles.

I have had great success in southern waters with a plastic-worm rig, fished on the bottom amid brush piles. Small spoons, jigs, plugs or spinner and fly combinations are successful when properly used. These often do better when pork-rind skirts or fly strips are attached. The weedless Johnson spoon with a fly strip is a favorite. All lures should be fished slowly.

494

Crappies roam in schools, moving from deep into shallow water to feed, or traveling along the shoreline or far out in lakes and ponds to follow schools of baitfish. Thus trolling with small spinner and fly combinations, or with minnows, often is effective to find schools and then to cast into them. Like white bass, they often drive schools of minnows to the surface, then feed on them in a flurry of activity. This is the time to use small streamers and bucktails or floating bugs. Migrations to the shoreline often occur late in the day, and flies or poppers can be very productive then. When the fish are in shallow water any of the baits suggested for bluegills should be effective, including crickets and worms.

Thus, remembering that crappies like minnows, while bluegills don't, fishing for the two species is very much the same. Try brush piles and other protective spots during the day, trying to get baits or lures down to the depth level where the fish are feeding. Meanwhile, watch for surface activity. Cast or troll along the shoreline toward evening, fishing the side toward which the breeze is blowing, and paying particular attention to shaded areas.

ROCK BASS

This little panfish, often called the "goggle eye," or "red eye," has mottled sides, large red "goggle" eyes, a large mouth and a body of greenish-olive, with a dark dot on each scale. It can change colors from almost black to pale green. Big ones may be nearly 12 inches long, weighing about a pound, but the usual catch is not over 9 inches (usually between 6 and 7) and weighs less than half a pound.

Rock bass are fun on tiny tackle but they give up quickly when taken on anything but the smallest lures. They are delicious to eat when caught from clear water in spring and fall but the warm water of midsummer may make the flesh soft and less palatable. Since their favorite temperature is between 65 and 75 degrees, they seek shaded rocky riffles and pools in rivers where there are submerged hiding places in deeper water. Favorite hiding places are deep eddies against rocky banks. Thus their preferred stream locations are similar to those of smallmouth bass, for which they often are mistaken. Their preferred lake locations also are smallmouth bass water; usually deep, rocky coves offering plenty of protection.

Rock bass will take almost any small food which drops into the water or which can be found in it. This includes nymphs, worms, hellgrammites, crawfish, minnows, grasshoppers and other insects and grubs. These are fished as for other panfish, using hook sizes between numbers 2 and 6.

Since rock bass usually feed at night, the best fishing for them is in the evening when they leave their deep hideaways to roam in shallower water for food. Then, the lightest fly rod and small flies furnish the best sport.

Patterns with fat wool or chenille bodies, such as the McGinty or Western Bee, are favorites. Small streamer flies and bucktails which imitate baitfish may be as good, or better. Small spoons and spinners, often with a fly attached, do well, and so do tiny bass bugs and poppers. In smooth water the trick is to retrieve very slowly, with widely spaced twitches of the rod tip. Strikes usually occur during the pauses. Since rock bass commonly school together, anglers using the right methods in the right places often can fill a stringer in a short time.

SUNFISH

The common sunfish, or "pumpkinseed," is of interest principally to children because it is easy to catch and because its emerald-blue radial lines and orange-yellow belly make it the prettiest of the panfishes. Since its mouth is small, only tiny baits can be used. These include little jigs more commonly used in ice fishing.

Sunfish inhabit the same waters that bluegills do; mainly sandy bottoms well sprinkled or covered with weeds, and often around boathouses and docks. Any tackle will do if it is light enough, including a trimmed green whippy branch with a few feet of fine monofilament tied to its end. This can be rigged with a little jig or a very small hook baited with a small worm, or a part of one; perhaps under a cork bobber. While little worms probably are the best baits, sunfish will take grubs and other small foods, including a bit of bread balled around the point of a small hook.

All this is of little interest to anglers, although they can have fun with tiny wet or dry flies, nymphs and panfish bugs when there isn't much else to do. Sunfish mainly are children's fish, and many youngsters became interested in sportfishing because their parents taught them how to catch these jewel-like panfish from a dock on vacation when they were young.

YELLOW PERCH

Although not a member of the sunfish family, perch are favored panfish because they are fun to catch and delicious when freshly cooked. When nothing else will grab lures or baits this spunky and handsome little fighter is everyone's ace-in-the-hole. Longer and slimmer than the sunfishes, its dark-olive humped back blends into a yellowish midsection and a white belly, with orange-yellow pectoral and anal fins. Rarely very large, it averages half a pound, or smaller, although some lakes harbor one-pounders, or better. Lunkers may approach 4 pounds, but these rarely are found. The record is a 4-pound, 3½-ounce fish taken in New Jersey in 1865. Most lakes harbor perch in the 6-inch range because of overpopulation.

Yellow perch spawn in spring in feeder streams when water is above 45 degrees but they prefer to live in a range between 60 and 75, 68 degrees being most favorable. When spring spawning migrations begin, the streams draw thousands of anglers anxious for fast action and bountiful fillets for the skillet. After spawning, the fish return to the lakes and remain there in the shallow water of bays, over reefs, and around breakwaters, pilings and docks where they can find clean sandy bottoms and an abundance of vegetation. When summer shallow-water temperatures exceed 70 degrees they haunt weed beds between 20 and 70 feet deep or submerged weedy ledges far out in lakes. Although found in quiet waters of rivers, they primarily are pond and lake fish.

While perch will eat almost anything, including worms, crickets, grasshoppers, crawfish, grubs and insects, their favorite food is minnows about 2 inches long. They are notorious bait stealers and will mouth any offering until they have it off the hook. Therefore one has to learn by experience, and by keeping an eye on the bobber, when to set the hook. This (except for minnows) is when the float first begins to bob.

Minnow fishing—the favorite method—is a bit different than using worms and other baits because a perch attacks baitfish with a sharp yank, after which he makes a short run and stops in order to turn the minnow in his mouth so he can swallow it head first. This is the time to set the hook, which will be stripped if the strike is delayed.

The technique therefore is to carry a bait pail of small minnows and very slowly to troll one under a bobber (with a split shot about 6 inches above the hook to keep the bait down) set to fish the bait just over the top of the weeds. When a good-sized perch is hooked, the anchor is lowered so the spot can be covered by casting. Since perch run in schools of fish of about the same size, it is well to wait until a large one has been hooked before drifting the bait around the area. Best spots are weed beds, at whatever depths water temperatures dictate. Roughly speaking, this is fairly shallow in spring and fall and much deeper during the summer. If worms are used, the method is the same, but strikes should be made as soon as unusual motion of the bobber is noted.

Spoons, spinners and jigs in small sizes are productive when one can find a school of fish. The best bet is to locate them with minnows by the above method. Another is to drift over weed beds, letting the cast lure sink to the top of the weeds and retrieving it slowly. When a school is found it is fun to use a fly rod, with small streamers or bucktails on a sinking line that will get the fly down. Hooked fish should be kept above the weeds so they can't tangle in them. Flies should be of baitfish colors; those containing a little yellow being most productive.

When the supply of live minnows has been used, a few dead ones usually remain. These can be trolled behind small spinners, preferably of the willow-leaf type. The design of hook used for perch isn't important, but the best sizes are 2 or 4. Perch usually bite best around noon or toward evening, but they are daytime feeders and can be caught all during the day.

Except for noting a few differences such as that some panfish prefer minnows while others don't, and that some prefer slightly different habitats than others, we see that the same tackle and tactics can be used in fishing for all species. It is easy, and it is fun! These suggestions may make it more so. Half of the pleasure is in the fishing; the other half in the eating. Too many people think panfish are too small to bother with. This is a pity, because filleting and skinning a catch large enough for a big family can be done quickly, as explained in the Appendix of this book. Of the many methods of cooking panfish, the most popular one is to roll the little fillets in bread crumbs or corn meal and to fry them to a delicate brown, then serve them hot with Tartar Sauce.

29

Ice Fishing

Equipment for catching panfish and sportfish through the ice has blossomed since daddy was a boy. He froze in long johns, while our quilted, insulated clothing and thermal boots keep us snugly warm. He towed his gear in a wooden box on junior's Flexible Flyer sled while we streak out to the sets on snowmobiles, or perhaps in heated recreational vehicles. Spudding holes in thick ice was a time-consuming chore; now it's easy with power drills. Dad and his pals built bonfires on shore and crept back there periodically to thaw out. We have gasoline or propane heaters and stoves where hot beverages steam and bubble in tents, shacks, vehicles and windbreaks right where the action is, and on which complete hot meals can be prepared when needed. Dad's common sense in knowing where to spud holes has been superseded by electronic fish locators which can read through the ice to tell exactly how far down bottom is and what kinds of fish are cruising down there.

In spite of modern improvements such as these, knowledge still is required to hit the jackpot. Too many innocent ice fishermen merely drill a few holes somewhere, lower baited hooks, and try to keep warm while waiting for the action. No one knows all the answers, but there are rules and tricks which help to improve the score.

499

BASIC EQUIPMENT

Tip-ups can be homemade, but commercial ones are so cheap it isn't worth the effort. These have a reel spool and line held underwater (to prevent freezing) by a pair of cross braces set on the ice over the hole. The upright stick to which the reel is attached has a red or orange flag on a flexible trip wire which is hooked into a trigger so it can be released to pop up when a fish pulls line from the reel. "Tip up!" is the usual cry when this happens, whereupon the fisherman cautiously tests the pull on the line, attempts to hook the fish, and to pull it in. One fisherman can operate several tip-ups in as many holes, the number often being restricted by state or regional regulations.

Holes are cut by a spud (or ice chisel) or by an ice auger, which resembles a carpenter's brace, and which can be powered by a gasoline motor. Holes usually are about 6 or 8 inches in diameter and should have smooth edges to prevent chafing lines. The holes should flare outward toward the underside of the ice layer to diminish chances of fish being knocked off while being drawn through them. Since mush collects in the holes, a skimmer is needed to ladle it out.

Minnows are the favorite bait for most fish. Keep them alive in a minnow pail in which the water is oxygenated by oxygen pellets or other means, and kept from becoming cold by insulation or a source of warmth. Proper sizes of minnows vary with sizes of fish being sought: 1 inch for smelt; 2 inches for crappies and perch; 3-inch shiners for walleyes; 4- to 6-inch suckers for lake trout and pickerel; 12-inchers for pike. Since live bait is cold and slippery, it is more comfortable and does less damage to the fish to handle them with cloth work gloves. Have a few pairs so dry ones are always available. Use lively minnows for still sets. The dead ones can be fished with jigs.

Minnows usually are fished about a foot off bottom. This depth is found by attaching a sinker, such as a dipsey weighing 2 ounces or more, to the hook and lowering it until it touches bottom. Pull it up a foot or so and mark the line at water level. A good marker is a very small button strung on the line through two holes so it can be slid up and down for various depths. A piece of a pipe cleaner wound around the line also will do.

Falls on slippery ice can be avoided by wearing ice creepers strapped to soles of boots or shoes. These are rectangles of steel plate, slotted for straps, with corners bent down to form prongs. Sunglasses reduce glare and add to vision. A compass for use in snow squalls on large lakes and a coil of rope in case of accident are good insurance.

When a big fish is hooked on light line it can be lost while being pulled through the hole. A small gaff can be made from a 6/0 hook, or larger, and a wire coat hanger. Use wire-cutting pliers to remove the curved part.

Dangling a minnow over an ice hole, a cold-weather enthusiast is about to set his tip-up. Various kinds of tip-ups allow one fisherman to work several holes at the time; when a fish is on, the flag goes up.

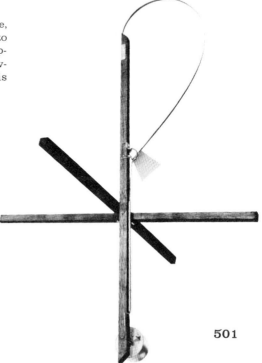

Holes in the ice can be drilled for fishing with special auger sold for the purpose (*above*), or chipped out with an ice chisel (*right*). Motor-driven augers (*left*) are available for fast, accurate cutting.

502

Straighten the rest of the wire and put an end through the hook's eye. Using strong pliers, to hold the hook, bend the wire around the shank for a secure connection, and clip excess wire closely. Bend a loop in the other end for a handle, and sharpen the hook's point, if necessary.

Every fisherman will want to add to these basics several other necessities and conveniences such as a Thermos of hot beverage, a lunch, and many other things of personal choice. If lightly equipped, a knapsack or packbasket should hold most of them.

Those who go out with only a few tip-ups are less than half prepared for good fishing because a jigging stick or rod, with some bait and lures, can more than double the catch and the fun. Jigging sticks are of many kinds. A typical one is a dowel, such as a broom handle, about 2 feet long with a screw eye under the tip for the line to go through. A cleat fastened under the dowel forward of the grip is used to wind on or release line. The cleat width is measured to indicate how much line is out. For example, if the cleat is 6 inches wide, each loop released from it would be a foot long. Jigging sticks can be made from rod tips, with handles and reels attached.

Many fishermen prefer complete spinning or spincasting outfits, and some like stronger baitcasting gear for the big ones. The strength of the tackle suits the size of the fish. For example, it's more fun to catch panfish on light monofilament of between 2- and 4-pound test, partly because such light lines give better action to small ice jigs and small baits like dead shiners. On the other hand, we may need a strong rod equipped with a reel holding 15- or 20-pound-test braided line for fish like lake trout down deep. Usually this terminates with about 6 feet of leader of suitable strength, with a split shot or two about a foot above the hook, if needed to get the bait down.

ICE FISHING LURES

Lures for panfish start with tiny jigs weighing less than $1/16$ ounce with hooks between sizes 10 and 14. One side often is nickel plated; the other is painted red, yellow, orange or green, often in fluorescent colors. Some jigs, usually called ice flies, are dressed with bits of marabou, like a wing, or are wound with small hackle. Other types, more like spinners, have tiny silver or gold blades and perhaps one or more small colored beads. These need not be baited, but they often are, with small grubs or worms.

Ice flies are easy to make. Pinch a small split shot back of the eye of a number 10 to 14 hook and dip it in paint. Tie on back of it a small, soft wing of marabou or hackle, or wind the shank with two or three turns of a small hackle.

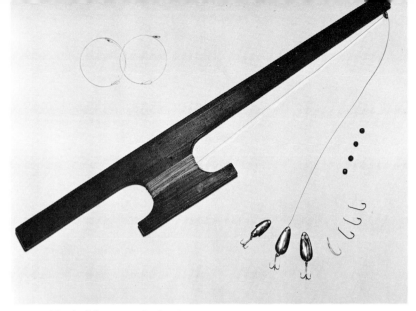

Typical homemade jigging stick with lures, hooks and split shot.

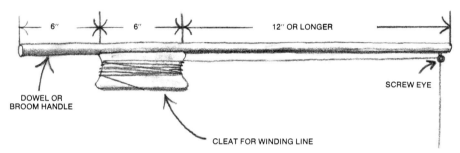

6″ 6″ 12″ OR LONGER

SCREW EYE

DOWEL OR
BROOM HANDLE

CLEAT FOR WINDING LINE

Jigging stick above is made of a dowel with a cleat attached for winding
on line. The one below is simply an oval reel cut from a 1-inch board and
grooved around its circumference to hold the line.

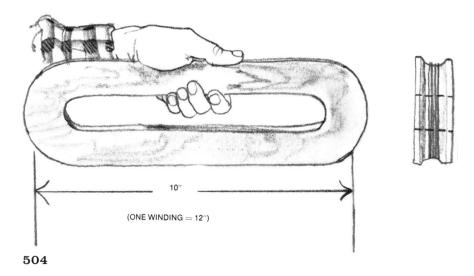

10″

(ONE WINDING = 12″)

504

Oval reel jigging stick in use on a Michigan lake. Windbreaks and shelters on the ice protect fishermen from freezing gales.

Normark double-tipped jigging outfit is 19 inches long and folds for carrying. Storage space for lures is in the hollow handle. Some models have a built-in depth meter which measures the amount of line out.

Spinning and baitcasting tackle, with rod holders, can be used for ice fishing. Holders allow fisherman to move about and avoid chills. The crossbar turns for carrying; the vertical support is hinged, with a latch to hold it upright.

ICE FISHING LURES FOR PANFISH

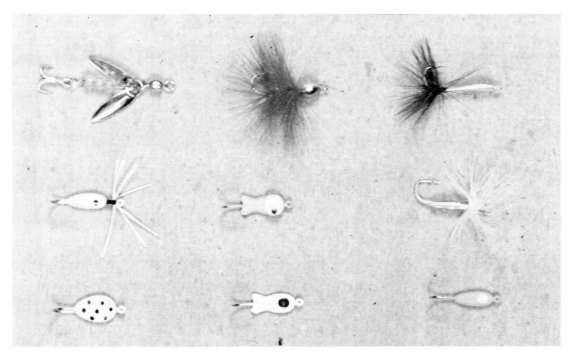

Worth Double Willowleaf	Worth Hackle Body	Worth Hackle Tail
Fin Rubber Collar	Fin Roving Eye	Fin Hackle Collar
Fin Indiana Body	Fin Fish Body	Fin Oval Body

Lures for medium-sized fish are similar but larger, including dartlike jigs with hair or feather tails. These vie in popularity with many shapes and sizes of wobbler blades of metal or pearl, either with fixed or loose hooks. For example, select an oval or fish-shaped wobbler weighing about $1/4$ ounce. Remove the hook and tie the line on the end where it was. Put a split ring in the other end, with a single hook on it and perhaps also an attractor such as a fishtailed piece of red plastic. Spinning lures with revolving blades also are used as jigs. Sometimes these are baited with any of the things to be mentioned, including a dead minnow impaled crosswise. A different vertical type is minnow-shaped, with the eye balanced in the middle of the back. Rigid single hooks point upward on each end and a loose treble one hangs below the eye. This type swims in a circle when jigged up and down.

JIGS FOR LARGER FISH

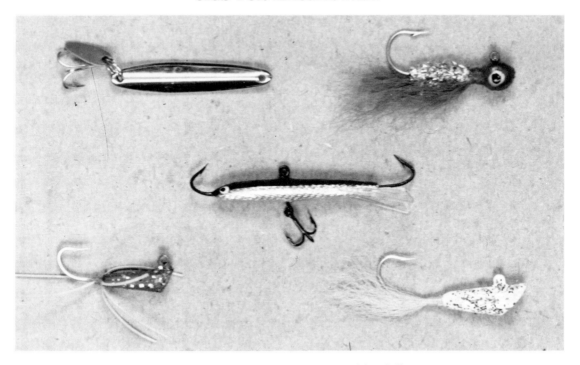

Swedish Pimple   Round-head Jig

Rapala

Rubber-tailed Dart   Bucktail Dart

Lures for big fish, such as lake trout, are similar, but even larger. These include jigs of the diamond type and other elongated ones like the popular Swedish Pimple.

BAITS

Baits for panfish comprise everything small enough to be edible—a range covering such a wide variety that a few examples should suffice. These include corn borers, grubs, meal worms, goldenrod gall worms and especially the larvae of the syrphus fly, called the rat-tailed maggot, or "mousie." Mousies are found in mud, or in decaying wood or vegetable matter and are so-called because they have "tails" which actually are breathing tubes. Two of these half-inch-long (not including "tail") tiny creatures usually are put on a single number 10 or 12 hook, the upper one being squashed in order to attract fish by scent. Preserved single salmon eggs are popular, as well as canned kernels of corn, presumably because they resemble fish eggs. Add roaches and crickets to the list, plus anything else that wiggles and many things that don't, including miniature marshmallows.

Garden worms are not very effective, probably because they are not in evidence in winter. Except for some of the smaller panfishes, the best baits are minnows and larger baitfish for everything else on up the scale, starting with crappies and perch. The proper way to hook a live minnow with either a single or a treble hook is just under and slightly to the rear of the dorsal fin, with the hook's barb angled toward the tail. This is because fish usually take minnows head first but, since larger fish may take the whole thing at a gulp, this point may not be very important. The important thing is to hook the bait above the spine because lower hooking will kill it. Dead minnows are hooked through both eyes or through the lips in order to provide maximum and more lifelike action when they are jigged.

Hook sizes 6 and 8 are excellent for crappies and perch, 6 for walleyes, 4 for pickerel, and size 2 or larger for pike, lake trout and other big ones. Short shock leaders of monofilament, or wire leaders, are necessary for sharp-toothed fish such as pickerel and pike.

Rig for small baits consists of a reversed wobbler as an attractor and two grubs on the hook. Split shot may not be needed to get bait down.

WHERE TO CUT ICE HOLES

Whenever possible, smart ice fishermen plan the locations of their ice holes during open-water months when they can probe the bottom, or see it. Many lakes have been mapped by fish and game departments or other sources, with depth contours included. Lacking these, sketch maps can be made to indicate submerged reefs, steep drop-offs, underwater brush piles, shallow or deep weed beds and other preferred feeding or hiding places for the species to be sought in winter. Since these hot spots will be hidden under the ice, the places should be identified on the map, using shore landmarks to line them up when necessary. Sonic fish-locating devices are ideal for this because they not only reveal exact depths but also the nature of the bottom, whether it is sandy, rocky or muddy and where there are weed beds, brush piles, and so on.

Although we know that every species of fish prefers its own favorite water temperature, it has to put up with the narrow one between freezing at 32 degrees and the maximum density of water at the lake bottom of 39.2 degrees unless it can find relatively warmer inlets or underwater springs. Since this range is only 7.2 degrees, water temperatures are not of major concern in winter. Fish seek food, protection and oxygen; three basic requirements as necessary in winter as in summer, even though the need for food is somewhat less when very cold water makes fish relatively dormant. It can be assumed that some species of fish, such as lake trout and smelt, will seek the slightly warmer water of the depths, but they won't be in the deepest water if protective and oxygen-generating plant growth doesn't exist there due to insufficient penetration of sunlight. Shallow-water species, such as panfish, pike and pickerel, seem unconcerned by water temperatures, and inhabit weedy areas of relatively shallow water at all seasons. Ice holes cut in coves or over weedy reefs should locate them.

Lacking more specific information to go on, and knowing that some species are roamers and that most of them cruise at definite depths, select a spot where travel must be concentrated. In the accompanying drawing, such a spot would be between the island and the point of land. Cut the first hole over about 10 feet of water on a line between the point of land and the island. Jig the hole for a few minutes. If nothing happens, put a still set there and cut another hole about 20 feet farther on, continuing this procedure as shown in Series 1. An alternative is to line up the holes toward the deepest water, as indicated by Series 2. In this case, which is an actual one, the best fishing was found at the 40-foot depth, so additional holes were cut there, as indicated by Series 3.

Some fish, such as perch and smelt, roam about in schools which remain in the same general location. When a hole has been productive and

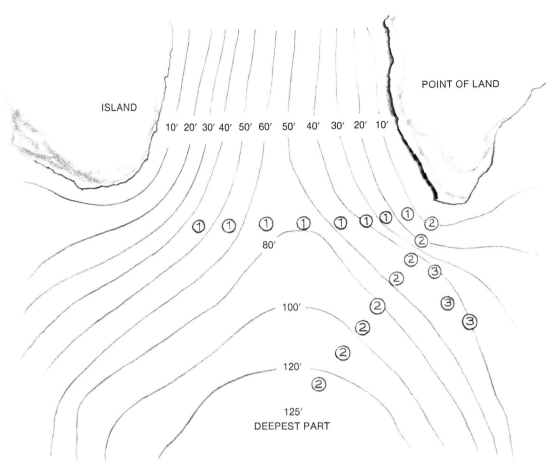

ISLAND

POINT OF LAND

10' 20' 30' 40' 50' 60' 50' 40' 30' 20' 10'

80'

100'

120'

125'
DEEPEST PART

Basic system of cutting ice holes for lake trout.
Series 1: Holes bored across channel between islands.
Series 2: Holes bored progressively into deeper water.
Series 3: Since best fishing was found at 40-foot depth,
          more holes were bored along this contour.

then becomes fishless, a few more can be cut in the same area, one or more
paying off as the school returns below it. Since a hooked fish tries to rejoin
its school, the direction in which it wants to swim indicates the one where
another hole should be dug. Like oil wells, some holes produce little or
nothing, and shouldn't be bothered with. On the other hand, a productive
hole or two can provide more fish than even the greediest fisherman desires.
Even the experts cut useless holes, but they do it less often than novices
do. Experts usually go out for a specific species and, knowing its habits,
can locate their holes with considerable accuracy.

510

HOW TO FISH ICE HOLES

Since lures or baits should be fished within about a foot of the bottom, or just over the weeds, put a sinker on the hook of a rod or a jigging stick and lower it until bottom is felt. Then raise it about a foot and mark the line at water level or wind it on the line holder so fishing at that depth can be maintained. A lure or bait or both is put on and lowered, using a split shot or two about 6 inches above it if necessary. The lure is jigged very slowly for panfish, more actively for other species. Just how the lure or bait should be jigged depends on water depth, the species being fished for, and the type of lure or bait used, so this must be found by experimentation. Tiny lures are jigged so slowly that they barely show motion. Larger ones, particularly when fished deeply, are given much more action. When lures weighing $1/4$ ounce or more are fished deeply, a proven method is to raise the rod or jig stick sharply to jerk the lure 3 feet or so upward, then allow it to flutter down. This is alternated by a slow twitch or two, imitating the action of a wounded minnow. Strikes often occur while the lure is settling.

Split shot or a sinker or two usually are needed to quickly take light baits or lures deep, but no more should be used than is needed to do this. A fish mouthing a bait will drop it if he feels too much resistance from leads. Diamond-type jigs, with hooks removed, often are tied into the leader or between leader and line to act as attractors as well as sinkers when baits are used. Sinkers can be scraped to brighten them.

After jigging a hole for a few minutes, this method is given up if no action results. The hole then is baited with a still set, probably using a minnow fished close to the bottom. A split shot or two usually will be needed to keep it down. After baiting the hole the fisherman goes on to the next one and jigs it, proceeding to new holes in the above manner.

Several tricks are helpful. One is to cut two holes fairly close together and to jig one while a still set remains in the other. The jigging often attracts fish to the bait in the nearby hole.

Another trick is to attract fish by chumming, or priming, a hole. This is especially useful when several holes are near each other. Chum includes salted shiners (one or two being dropped into the hole from time to time), crumbled egg shell, chopped fish bits, oatmeal, canned corn, split peas, cracker crumbs, rice, white beans, and fish scales or guts. Since most kinds of fish need to be scaled, this might as well be done over the holes so the scales can filter down to attract more of them. The sooner fish are cleaned, the better they will taste. If the weather isn't uncomfortably cold, why not do it on the lake and use the innards as priming? A taste of blood in the water often draws big fish to the bait.

Still sets should be given frequent attention. It helps to go from hole to hole and to raise each bait a few feet, then let it flutter down. This often

Spreader arrangement for jigging with a wobbler blade used as an attractor and sinker. The spreader is a curved spring wire, looped in the middle and at each end. Short leaders are attached to the end loops, with hooks baited with live minnows.

Nocturnal ice fisherman jigs two holes at the same time—and cleans up on crappies. Another trick is to jig one hole, rig a still set on one nearby. Jigging often attracts fish to the still set.

attracts strikes. Baits should be inspected periodically because a dead or nearly lifeless minnow won't interest fish.

Bobbers are helpful with still sets when rods and reels are used instead of tip-ups. Rod stands, which can be made or purchased, hold the rod angled upward with its tip over the hole. Bobbers are useless in very severe weather but, when holes freeze over very slowly or not at all, there are very small ones made of sponge rubber which can be squeezed to break off ice film. These are available in several sizes and, like sinkers, a variety should be carried so one can be used which is barely buoyant enough to support the bait. The little fish must be hooked when the slightest motion is noticed. There's a knack to it which, once learned, can quickly fill the skillet.

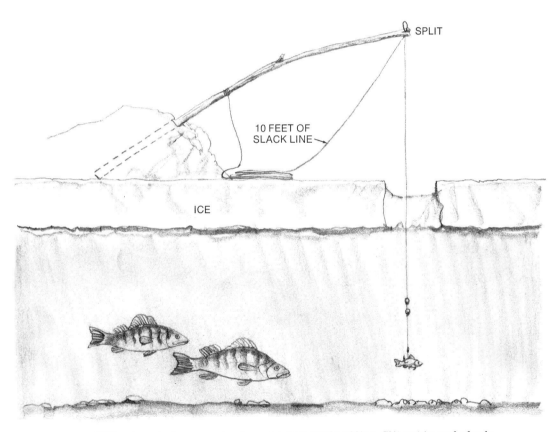

Still set made from a cut pole and a few yards of line. Slit cut in end of pole holds line, which is pulled off when fish takes the bait. Slack line gives the fish time to swallow the bait.

Fishermen who forget their tackle have no problem if they can borrow a few yards of line, a couple of split shot, and a hook. Cut and trim a limber green branch about 4 feet long and split the end so a loop of line can be pinched lightly into it. Tie the line to the pole with about 10 feet of slack extending to the loop. Support the pole by embedding its end in snow or mush ice, as shown in the drawing. Bait the hook, preferably with a small live shiner, adding one or two split shot on the line to keep the bait down. A fish which takes the bait will pull the loop from the pole's tip and the slack line should give it time to swallow the bait.

THEY DON'T HIT ALL THE TIME!

Successful ice fishermen have a combination of persistence, knowledge —and patience! Regardless of whether or not one believes in Solunar Tables and similar theories, there are major and minor periods when fish go on the feed. Bluegill fishermen know that when bluegills hit they do it all at once, the feeding period lasting for a certain time. Fishermen after lake trout and similar species know that they cruise deeply in winter, but that they also come up on the shoals and around the ledges about twice a day to feed. One period usually is early in the morning. Hours around noon probably will be dull. A second feeding period should occur in the afternoon, about 2 o'clock or later. No one can predict when these periods will occur, but be ready for them.

In mid-winter, as well as in summer, underwater springs can provide bonanzas most of the time. Subterranean water emptying into a lake can be in the 40's or 50's, while that in the rest of it is in the 30-degree range. This, to fish, is like our coming out of the cold into a warm kitchen for dinner, because baitfish also collect there, and the oxygenated water can be lush with grasses. Use a depth thermometer to locate such places in the summer, and mark them down for winter fishing.

Ice fishing methods for the various species are so varied from place to place that it is impossible for a chapter in a book to cover them all. Experts have their own ways of doing things, and don't need any help. The basic suggestions just covered may, however, be of value to novices and to casual fishermen who want to enjoy an exciting and exhilarating day outdoors when the ice is safely thick. Select a lee shore where the sun shines down. Take along a few congenial friends and something hot to eat and drink. Cut a few holes, set up the still sets, and try some jigging. It's sure to be an enjoyable day, and one thing is certain: the fish won't spoil.

Part II: Saltwater Fishing

30
Tackle
for Salt Water

Saltwater fishing can be as simple or as complex as we want to make it. We can use whatever freshwater gear we have and can enjoy action from shore, piers, bridges, breakwaters or small boats, casting, drifting or trolling for pan-sized fish or whatever else takes the bait or lure. On the other hand, experts can hook sailfish and other tackle busters on fly rods with flies, or can invest heavily in presenting trolled baits to marlin and other great billfish.

Saltwater fishing is complex only in the great variety of the fish and the types of fishing it offers. We can cast from shore with fixed or revolving-spool tackle, or even with fly rods. We can have fun fishing from piers, breakwaters and bridges. We can troll or cast inshore or offshore, and our methods will vary to suit the fish we're seeking and whatever conditions of tide, current and other factors exist at the place and the time. If ways of fishing from shore also are suitable for those on boats, this will be mentioned. For example, the benefits of using a chum line are equally valuable in a current regardless of whether the current passes a pier or breakwater, under a bridge, or by an anchored boat.

While readers will want to skip around a bit to locate methods and situations that most interest them, it will be advantageous to read these chapters at least superficially to learn the varied information they contain. After that, they can concentrate on whatever subjects seem most important. Those who want to learn how to catch the easiest fish on the simplest tackle while

517

on vacation may, for example, learn herein that something much more exciting may be available to them.

Vacationists who like to bask on the sand and swim in the surf may enjoy watching surfcasters throw baits or lures surprising distances and occasionally hook bottom fish or sportier varieties feeding within the range of their tackle. It's simple to be a participant, rather than merely an observer. The local tackle shop will rent or sell whatever is needed, and will gladly supply regional information. So let's start with that, and then go on to other methods which can be equally exciting, or perhaps more so.

TACKLE FOR SURF FISHING

Modern surf fishermen will be seen using fly rods, spinning rods or bait-casting rods such as have been described for fresh water. Although these can handle good-size fish, they are short-range implements incapable of heaving heavy terminal tackle the long distances so often needed in the surf, or even for handling big fish in the frothing combers and undertows usually whipping the beaches.

Two types of tackle principally are used for the surf: heavy spinning gear and conventional reels with revolving spools. The latter sometimes are called "squidding" outfits because their owners so often use squids as bait or their imitations as lures.

If a poll should be taken between the two methods, spinning would win by a wide margin. This is because the tackle is easier to use, mainly due to the fact that the reel won't backlash, as revolving-spool reels will when thumbed improperly. Both types will cast about equal distances—in the hands of experts, 500 feet or more. To do this, conventional tackle would need braided line testing about 36 pounds and a casting weight between 5 and 7 ounces, while spinning tackle would do as well with monofilament testing from 12 to 15 pounds (plus a shock leader) and a casting weight of only about 2 ounces.

In spite of the growth of spinning, there are many who prefer conventional revolving-spool reels, which can take stronger lines and heavier (larger) lures, or sinkers with baits. Revolving-spool proponents think such reels provide better control in casting and when playing fish. New anglers are advised to start with spinning, and few will ever want to change.

Rods used with both methods essentially are the same except that spinning rods have larger guides for reasons that will be discussed. While anglers in different areas vary in their preferences, we can settle on a set of specifications that should suit the majority.

A surf rod is a stiff and sturdy implement designed to cast weights between 2 and 7 ounces. Some are designed for lighter work, but let's discuss the more powerful equipment first.

When a school of fish invades the breaker line along North Carolina's Outer Banks, surfcasters have a heyday. Long rods are needed to get out long casts and hold the line above the waves on the retrieve. Surfcaster (*left*) has two stripers on his stringer, one on the line. Trend among surfmen is toward spinning, as can be seen here.

Backbone (stiffness or power) is more important than length, and does not depend on it. While some anglers like rods of 11 or 11½ feet, or even longer, these rods in average hands may be too cumbersome for frequent casting if they have adequate backbone. Dealers often sell extra-long rods with insufficient stiffness. When an angler finds he has purchased one, the trouble usually can be corrected by cutting it back and refitting the guides. The choice between a one-piece stick and a jointed one is minor; the one-piece being preferable when transportation isn't a problem.

The most generally acceptable surf rod for a conventional or spinning reel probably would be a 10½-footer that will handle weights up to 4 ounces. Such a rod would weigh close to 35 ounces and would have a carbide tip-top with an inside ring diameter of $^{28}/_{64}$ inch. Although this will handle a casting weight of about 4 ounces most conveniently, a range of from 2 to 7 ounces is practical with resulting shorter or longer casts.

Some experienced anglers will say that 4 ounces is heavier than average because many lures which are considered heavy don't weigh that much. In addition to artificial lures, the 10½-foot rod may be called upon to lob out 3- or 4-ounce sinkers. The addition of a swivel and a baited hook or two adds even more weight.

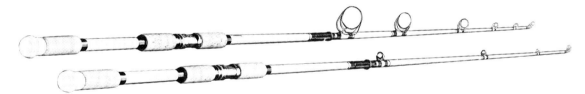

Rods for surf fishing are stiff and sturdy, between 10 and 11½ feet in length, to cast weights between 2 and 7 ounces. Spinning rod (*top*) is characterized by large guides; the rod below, with small guides, is for conventional, revolving-spool reel. Both break down into two pieces.

Those who want to test the backbone of a rod can fix its grip in a horizontal support and measure the deflection of the tip when a 3-pound weight is hung from it. If the deflection is 24 inches or more the rod may lack sufficient power for casting lures in the 4-ounce range. A deflection of 22 inches should be about right, and one of 20 inches may be even better when weights of 4 ounces or more are to be cast.

If this rod is used with a conventional reel, the rings should be of tungsten carbide. A braided line of 36-pound test should be most appropriate, although some anglers prefer 30-pound-test monofilament or lighter strengths as fine as 15-pound test when shock leaders are used.

High-quality conventional reels, like those offered by well-known manufacturers such as Penn, Garcia-Mitchell and Pflueger, are very similar in their features. They usually have a star-drag wheel (which sometimes is indexed so a favorite setting can be located quickly), a handy free-spool lever, and a retrieve ratio of at least 3 to 1. Some include antibacklash devices. These help beginners and are especially useful at night, but experts prefer thumb pressure because such devices reduce casting distance. The same is true of level-winding devices, which also require cleaning and care. These reels come in various sizes. Those commonly used in the surf have 250-yard capacity for heavy outfits, 200-yard capacity for medium ones, and 150-yard capacity for light gear when 36-pound-test braided line is used on them.

A conventional reel should have a lightweight spool of aluminum or plastic because heavy metal spools are more difficult to control, being harder to start and to stop, thus tempting backlashes. The reel spool should be wide so the line can peel off smoothly during the cast while the spool revolves at constant speed. Smooth respooling is important; allowing a hump of too much line on one part of the spool can cause a jam or weaken the line.

The typical revolving-spool squidding reel for surfcasting has a star drag, free-spool lever, retrieve ratio of 3 to 1, but no level-wind device, as this cuts down on casting distance.

If the rod we are discussing is used with a spinning reel the tiptop should be of tungsten carbide. This hard metal will not be scored by the line. The inside diameter of the ring should be larger than for conventional tackle—about ½ inch.

As with revolving-spool equipment, the placement of the first guide is about midway between the base of the rod butt and tip. This first guide (called a "gathering guide" in spinning) is uncommonly large—between 2 and 3 inches in diameter, preferably 3 inches if the reel spool is large. A good rule is that the gathering guide should be about the same diameter as the packed line on the spool. This allows the rapidly uncoiling line to pass through with minimum friction.

The other guides (usually four, not including butt guide and tiptop) are graduated about equally in diameter for the same reason. They should be chrome-plated to resist corrosion. Smooth passage of line through the guides, without line-slap against the rod, is a secret of long casts.

The owner of new spinning tackle should watch his casts to be sure they are being made without line-slap. If this isn't the case the positioning of the gathering guide may be wrong. A remedy (at least partly) is to put a wedge between the reel's front foot and the rod to cant the face of the reel down.

The larger the diameter the spinning reel's spool, the longer the cast that can be made. As the line peels off, it is being taken from deeper down in the spool, thus gradually setting up increasing drag. This happens less with a big spool than a smaller one. Distance also is increased by a fully filled spool—but we get into the troubles previously noted with an overfilled one.

Twenty-pound-test monofilament is light for revolving-reel surf tackle, but heavy for surf spinning. It is appropriate for fishing among rocks and weeds where long casts are unnecessary but its stiffness (especially in some brands) makes it rather difficult to use. Fifteen-pound test is better for more open work. Many anglers prefer lines between 10- and 15-pound test (usually used with shock leaders), but they run the risk of breakage when big fish could become tangled around rocks or kelp.

Terminal weight also is a factor because heavier lures and baits need stronger lines even though lighter ones will cast them farther. It would be well for novices to start on the strong side and then graduate to lighter lines for sportier fishing as they become more proficient. The average saltwater spinning reel should hold between 250 and 300 yards of monofilament in 15- to 20-pound strength.

Similarly, a 3-ounce terminal weight may be light for revolving-spool surf tackle, but heavy for surf spinning. Heavy plugs, squids and jigs aren't always necessary; many spinning anglers think smaller, lighter ones are as effective, or even more so. Since monofilament line presents less resistance to sea and surf than braided line of similar strength, we may not need extremely heavy sinkers to make them hold.

Some bottom fishermen set their rods in sand spikes when action is dull. After the cast, slack line is reeled in until the sinker can be felt. Then the drag is set lightly (with the antireverse engaged, if using a spinning reel) and the rod is set into the spike which is pushed firmly into the sand. If the drag or click is set too tightly it's possible for a big fish to upset the spike and make off with the tackle. Hand-holding it always is preferable, so a hit can be felt instantly. Baits should be changed before they become water-logged because chances of strikes are less when bait scent has been washed away.

Light Surf Tackle

While the strong equipment just described may be required to handle the heavy lures or weighted baits needed for maximum distances, or to hold big sinkers in the undertow of strong surf, such gear isn't always necessary. Many of us enjoy lighter tackle; when conditions permit, it is sportier and more fun to use. Conventional rods can be obtained with greater flexibility and perhaps somewhat shorter lengths which are correct for handling lures weighing between 1½ and 3 ounces, usually with proportionately lighter lines to go with them.

Anglers who prefer lighter tackle almost invariably select spinning gear for use in the surf, which even dedicated squidders will have to admit isn't always crashing. In this category I am one of many who has settled on lures in the 1½- to 2-ounce class, which covers a very wide and adequate range. My rod is a 9-footer, with a 6-foot tip and a 3-foot double-handed butt. My reel has a 3-inch spool and handles about 250 yards of 15-pound-test monofilament. I carry a couple of extra spools of other sizes. The reel has a manual pickup, and the rod's guides could be considered oversize. The gathering guide is about the same diameter as the reel spool.

This is an ideal all-purpose outfit except when fish are far out and a heavy surf is running, though at times it can be suitable even then. It lobs a stream-lined metal squid amazing distances and can drop an adequately large plug very accurately into likely-looking pockets amid the rocks. I prefer this tackle for casting from boats for stripers and bluefish, and it has accounted for several of the former in the 50-pound class. It is ideal for casting from rocks, with which much of the New England coast abounds, and is just the thing for long casts in tidal rivers and estuaries unless something even lighter is considered more fun. Lighter tackle is the same as freshwater gear, which has many uses in the salt.

Shock Leaders

Shock leaders, discussed in Chapter 1 for freshwater spinning, are at least as important for salt water. They prevent heavy lures from snapping off, and prevent big fish from breaking off at the last minute. They are also called "shock tippets" and "bumper lines." A shock leader is a length of stronger line (usually monofilament) tied to the end of the casting line to insure against breakage at this critical point of wear and strain.

On each cast a spinning lure is usually reeled in to about the same distance from the rod tip. Constant casting weakens that part of the line unless it frequently is cut back—a chore we don't want to bother with, especially when fish are hitting. Even without line weakness, it is easy to snap off a heavy lure on a cast, and it is rather embarrassing to watch it go sailing away without anything attached to it.

A good rule is to use a shock leader twice the strength of the line; perhaps even more. Thus, a 30-pound one could be tied to 15-pound line; a 40-pound one to 20-pound line, and so on. A second shocker length (usually shorter) can be added if need be. For example, tie some 60-pound monofilament to the 40-pound shock leader which is tied to 20-pound line.

When the lure is in casting position, the shock leader should be long enough so a few turns of it can be wrapped around the spool. The leader is tied to the line or to a stronger length of leader by a Double-Strand Blood Knot or by a Key Loop Knot sometimes tied after the line has been doubled by a Bimini Twist. These knots are shown in Chapter 12.

Casting with Surf Tackle

The methods of casting with conventional tackle and with spinning tackle are essentially the same. Let's use conventional tackle first, then discuss a few additional tips handy with spinning.

Reel in the lure or weighted bait to about 3 feet from the rod tip (some like it a bit longer or shorter, but this is a good length to start with). We'll discuss right-handed casting, so left-handers will have to reverse the procedure. The reel is in free-spool, properly adjusted for drag, and the right thumb keeps it from rotating.

Stand, with feet comfortably apart, at a right angle to the water, facing down the beach with the left shoulder pointing in the direction toward which the lure will be cast. Body weight is on the ball of the left foot, with the rod pointing nearly overhead.

Pivot the body to the right, at the same time lowering the rod and swinging it in the opposite direction to that of the cast. This puts body weight on the right foot and swings the lure backward. The caster's arms are now fully extended. Head and eyes face the lure as much as possible.

Always keeping an eye on the lure, gradually transfer body weight to the left foot as your arms apply power to the initial part of the forward swing of the rod. Increase power as the body pivots forward, the arms putting a deep bend in the rod.

In the above power stroke the right arm pushes the upper grip of the rod forward while the left arm pulls the lower part of the rod's grip backward. Body weight now is on the left foot. The right arm is pushing the rod overhead (a bit to the right) to point in the direction of the cast.

The cast is followed through (as in a golf swing) with the rod pointing in the direction of the cast to allow the line to run through the guides with minimum friction. In doing this, the right arm will be fully extended. The tip of the rod is pointed toward the lure through its complete trajectory until it drops into the water.

HOW TO CAST WITH
CONVENTIONAL TACKLE

1. If you are right-handed, stand with your left shoulder toward the water, at right angles to the line of cast.

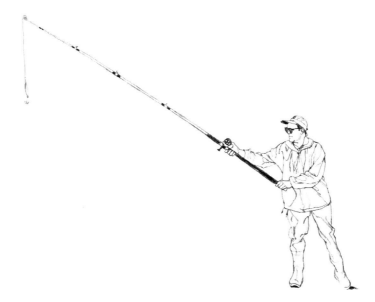

2. Turn body to right, lowering rod while extending it directly away from direction of cast. Body weight is on the right foot.

3. As cast begins, shift the body weight to the left foot, keeping eyes on the lure applying power with the arms.

4. Continue to shift body weight forward as full arm power puts a deep bend in the rod. Head rotates in the direction of cast.

5. In the full power stroke, the right arm pushes the rod forward while the left arm pulls the rod's butt back.

6. Follow through with the rod fully extended in the direction of the cast, to minimize friction of line being pulled through the guides.

In this cast the rod and lure are worked nearly overhead. This is safest, particularly when other people are nearby. It also is helpful when a strong wind is at the caster's back because an overhead cast with high trajectory will help the wind carry line and lure farther. The converse is true when a strong wind is blowing toward the caster. Then a side cast would help to drive lure and line under the wind's main force.

Releasing the lure by removing thumb pressure on the spool is a matter of timing and instinct that is perfected with practice. Since the idea is to get distance horizontally rather than vertically, the lure shouldn't be released too soon. At the time of release all thumb pressure is removed. But, as the lure speeds outward and gradually slows down, a slight thumb pressure is applied and gradually increased to prevent the reel from overrunning, or backlashing. Full pressure is applied the instant the lure hits the water.

The secrets of good casting are timing of the lure's release and thumbing of the spool. The secrets of good form are power and smoothness in casting. All this begins, of course, by having a suitable and properly rigged rod.

How close to the surf should one stand and when should he release the lure? If fish are near shore and long casts are unnecessary, the surf fisherman can stand anywhere. In some cases the fish may be so far out that the angler has to stand in the surf as deep as he can and still maintain a firm footing — always remembering that receding waves may be accompanied by a strong undertow. If he wants to cast from the beach, he should follow a receding wave, make his cast, and then return to the watermark while still paying out line.

There are a few special tips on casting with spinning tackle in the surf. Some anglers like quite a lot of line extending between lure and rod tip, which increases the pendulum power of the cast. The length is a matter of choice but often is about two-thirds of the rod's length. Accurate release of the line is an instinct that is aided by forefinger control. We noted that the line should be held over the tip of the forefinger, rather than in its cleft. This is of particular importance in surf fishing when heavy weights are being cast. Even so, the pull of these weights may bother some forefingers. In that case the protection of a glove forefinger, or something similar, may be of help.

THE GENERAL-PURPOSE OUTFIT

Saltwater fishing encompasses a wide variety of angling techniques ranging from big-game trolling to light-tackle casting, but any discussion of equipment for the marine world should rightfully include a general-purpose outfit. This rod and reel combination is extremely versatile and can be used for bottom fishing, drifting a bait in a chum slick, and even for light trolling.

The preferred rod for this assignment is made of fiberglass and is usually about 7 feet long including the butt. Depending on the section of waterfront you fish, it may be called a boat rod, bottom-fishing rod, light trolling rod, drift rod, or a dozen other names, but it is the same stick and does the job anywhere equally well.

The less expensive versions of the boat rod are made from solid fiberglass, while the better quality rods are fashioned from tubular fiberglass. Solid glass is more difficult to damage by accident, but it fails to provide the delicate action that makes fishing more enjoyable. The better choice would be a tubular glass boat rod with a detachable butt.

When you select a rod of this type, there are several areas that you should check out carefully. Hold the rod in your hand as if you were fishing with it and push the rod tip against the ceiling of the store or against the floor. Note the arc scribed by the rod under pressure. A well-designed rod has a progressive arc (called a taper) that seems to smoothly transmit power from tip to butt. If the tip is very soft, this will show up when you push it against the ceiling. Soft tips make it difficult to set the hook on a fish and also detract from the fighting qualities of the rod.

The detachable butt has a male ferrule on the rod portion and a female ferrule on the butt section. Inexpensive rods are made with a cheap ferrule that is pushed together and there is no locking device. Friction is supposed to hold the butt in place, but it doesn't always work this way. A better choice would be a detachable butt with a locking ring arrangement at the ferrule. Look closely and you'll see a groove on the male portion that fits a notch in the female section. This keeps the butt from turning under pressure. A locking nut screws down to hold the notch and groove in position.

Another key area to inspect is the number and quality of the guides. Better rods have at least five guides plus a tiptop. These ring guides should be made from corrosion-resistant material and should be spaced on the rod so that they distribute the strain under pressure. The easiest way to check this is to put a reel on the rod and string the line through the guides. Have someone pull down on the line while you lock the reel. The line should follow the curvature of the rod without touching the blank. If the line between the guides touches the blank or seems to run in a series of straight lines, the rod doesn't have enough guides or they are not placed properly.

Since you will be fighting fish with this rod, you want a comfortable foregrip in front of the reel seat that is 4 to 6 inches long. Put your hand around it and make sure it feels good. Then look at the reel seat. Better quality seats are made from chrome over brass or annodized aluminum. They also have a second locking nut to keep the tightening nut from loosening while you are fighting a fish.

Typical general-purpose saltwater rod.

Good reel for the general-purpose outfit would be this conventional model with star drag taking 450 yards of 20-pound-test mono.

Rod butts are made from wood, plastic, fiberglass, or metal. On boat rods, the butt would either be wood or fiberglass. Some of the expensive models boast the feature of the fiberglass blank running right through the rod with the butt of specie cork formed over the blank.

The bottom of the butt either has a rubber butt cap or is fitted with a gimbal designed to fit the slots in fighting chairs or rod holders on boats. One approach is to select a rod with the gimbal and then put a rubber butt cap over the gimbal. With the cap in place, you can hand-hold the rod easily, but if you wanted to use it with a fighting chair or place it in a rod holder, you could remove the butt cap and make use of the gimbal. Rod belts made from leather or plastic are available so that you can stand up and hold the rod without any discomfort from a gimbal or even a rubber butt cap.

There are any number of revolving-spool reels on the market that would match the general-purpose rod. The reel is the heart of any tackle system and it always makes sense to buy a well-made one even if you are a newcomer to fishing.

In choosing the reel, there are several factors that should be considered. The first is line capacity. Most general-purpose rods are tailored for either 20- or 30-pound-test fishing line. That means that the reel you pick should hold a minimum of 200 yards of line in the required breaking strength. Personal preference may dictate a somewhat narrow-spooled reel with

530

large diameter sideplates, or you may decide on something similar to a surf-casting reel with narrow diameter sideplates and a wide spool. Either type of reel will do the job for normal fishing situations.

Practically every saltwater reel today has a braking mechanism known as a star drag that permits you to preset a clutch arrangement. The setting is always under the breaking strength of the line, and the star drag will allow line to slip (giving more line to the fish) at that predetermined setting. When you buy a saltwater reel, look for the drag mechanism on the right sideplate of the reel just under the handle. Spool a little line on the reel and pull it against the drag to insure that the drag is relatively smooth.

On some reels, you have the option of metal or plastic spools. The plastic spools were originally designed for casting because they are lighter and are not as affected by centrifugal force as the heavier metal spools are. A number of reel models are of the quick take-down variety that have three knurled screws on the right sideplate that can be loosened quickly with a coin. The sideplate is then removed, exposing the spool. This feature enables the angler to use a different spool of different test line without taking the entire reel apart.

LIGHT TROLLING

Trolling has always been a favorite technique of the saltwater fisherman because it enables him to cover the maximum amount of area in the shortest possible time. Most fishermen are familiar with the blue-water trolling that is done for marlin, tuna, sailfish and a great variety of other pelagic species. However, even more anglers participate in light trolling.

The species would be smaller than big-game fish and they would be found in bays, estuaries, river mouths and inshore along the coast. For this type of fishing, there are a variety of tackle situations possible and they depend on the species you seek plus the conditions under which those fish are caught.

In bays and estuaries, the fish would usually be small, and the favorite outfit a popping rod or a light trolling rod. It is possible, of course, to use the general-purpose rod and reel we described above, and many anglers do this. Yet, if you are trying to maximize the sport by matching the outfit to the fish, lighter tackle is dictated.

A popping rod closely resembles a baitcasting outfit except that the handle is not offset like the freshwater models and the rod is generally about 7 feet in length. Again, it is made of tubular fiberglass, and the reel seat has a trigger or finger grip underneath for ease in casting or handling. The butt is also somewhat longer than those on baitcasting rods.

Along with the popping rod, there are also bay rods that are slightly lighter in weight than the all-purpose rod. These are designed for line tests between 12 and 20 pounds.

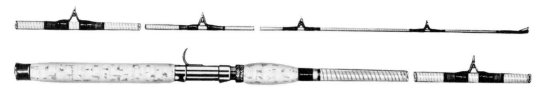

Popping rod for light trolling.

In choosing either of these rods, follow the same criteria we established earlier. They should have a minimum of five ring guides plus a tiptop made of noncorrosive material. Most important, remember to check the action by pushing the tip against the ceiling or the floor. If the tip is too soft, you'll lose fish on the strike and you'll have trouble landing them.

Reels for this type of outfit would either be the larger versions of level-wind, baitcasting reels or small bay reels. The level-wind feature is a good one, and there are also small bay reels made with the level-wind for this type of fishing. The reel should hold about 200 yards of the line test you select, and it should have a smooth drag that can be increased or decreased through a series of minor adjustments of the star wheel.

It is important to note that spinning tackle was never made for trolling and is not ideally suited to this type of fishing. A conventional outfit is a far better choice. And, this same outfit can be used for bottom fishing or chumming providing the species are not too large.

Light trolling is often done along the shoreline. In many sections of the country and the world, you can catch some large fish close to the beach. However, much of this trolling is done from small boats that are not equipped with outriggers and for that reason, many specialized types of rods have been developed. Some anglers, for example, take surf rod blanks and make trolling rods out of them. The finished rods are 10 to 11 feet in length. When mounted in rod holders that are angled on either side of the stern, these rods help to spread the lines much as outriggers would do.

REGULATION TROLLING TACKLE

Almost all rods made specifically for big-game, blue-water trolling follow the standards established by the International Game Fish Association (IGFA) many years ago. Unless he seeks a world record under IGFA rules, no angler is required to use this type of tackle, yet you would be hard pressed to find a trolling outfit that did not conform.

Trolling rods are normally rated by the breaking strength of the line they were designed to handle. The IGFA recognizes lines testing 6 pounds, 12, 20, 30, 50, 80, and 130 pounds. Following this example, anglers will talk about and use a "30-pound rod" or a "50-pound rod." What they really mean is that the rod has been tailored to withstand the pressures of fighting a fish with 30-pound line or 50-pound line or any other line class as the case may be. Within this system, there are variations. It is the manufacturer who determines the class that each rod fits into, and you may find that a rod rated 30 pounds by one maker will be identical in size and strength to another rod labeled 50-pound class by its maker.

For most offshore trolling, the angler must consider the size bait he will be trolling, the species he intends to catch, and the problems of setting the hook with a rod that has too light a tip. A 30-pound outfit is the standard for most offshore fishing with the exception of billfish, tuna, and other heavy-weights. It is always best to compare the trolling rods of a few manufacturers and then select the one that appears stout enough for its designated class. In the beginning, it is better to be a little overgunned than to use a rod that is too light. Again, use the flex test of pushing the tip against floor or ceiling to test the taper and the tip.

Keep in mind that the rod, reel and line should be in harmony. Veterans use the term "balanced" to describe components that go together. If you were to fish 50-pound-test line on a rod rated at 30 pounds, you couldn't gain any advantage from the heavier line because the rod would probably be too light. On the other hand, if you used a 50-pound rod with 30-pound line, the rod wouldn't flex enough and could cause the line to break simply because the rod was too stiff to absorb the shock of a surging fish.

The standard trolling rod is built with roller guides. Rollers are more expensive than the regular ring guides, but they reduce friction on a big fish and they help to keep the line from fraying providing the rollers are well lubricated and will roll under pressure. The first roller is usually higher than the others so that the line can be led in a straight line from the reel. A quality trolling rod usually has five roller guides and a roller tiptop. There are some rods made without roller guides and they are generally less expensive.

When you inspect a trolling rod, check the foregrip and make sure it is long enough to hold comfortably. Some foregrips are made of cork, others of neoprene, and a few are covered with felt. Felt or even leather foregrips indicate that the manufacturer is spending more money to make the rod since these components are relatively expensive.

On a quality rod, the hoods on the reel seat (the two holders for the foot of the reel) will be machined instead of stamped. If they look like an integral part of the reel seat, they are machined, but if the hoods are raised above the level of the reel seat just as they are on a spinning rod, they are stamped. Machined reel seats cost more money and demonstrate the willingness of the maker to use better components.

The gimbal butts on trolling rods are now made from a few different materials. The old standby is wood, but not just any wood. Better rods have hickory butts that are exceptionally strong. In recent years, butts are also being made out of fiberglass and others out of aluminum. Glass and metal butts are particularly strong and are not subject to expansion and contraction due to the amount of moisture dripping down the rod.

In general, simply look a trolling rod over carefully and compare it to other makes before you settle on the one you want. By inspecting the various components, you'll soon learn to recognize the little features that denote a quality rod.

Standard trolling rod with tiptop roller guide.

Two standard reels for offshore trolling: Heddon size 4/0 (*left*) and Ocean City size 9/0.

Reels made for offshore trolling have to be ruggedly constructed and capable of withstanding the strain of fighting some of the largest fish that swim. There are two basic designs: those with a star wheel to apply drag pressure and those with a drag lever that can be moved forward or backward to adjust the amount of drag.

Unlike rods and lines which are cataloged by breaking strength, reels have another system of designation called the "0" System. In this case, "0" indicates that it is an ocean reel and this is preceded by a number that represents size. A 4/0 reel, for example, is a size 4 ocean reel. The higher the number, the larger the reel. Recently, a few manufacturers are starting to designate some of the drag lever reels by breaking strength of lines so that there will be uniformity. An angler can then buy a 30-pound rod, put a 30-pound reel on it, and use 30-pound line.

As long as the ocean system of sizes continues, however, there will always be some confusion among anglers in matching the reel to the rod and line. If you can remember only two or possibly three sizes, you can easily figure out the others. The most popular size reel is a 4/0, which is the correct size for 30-pound tackle. Any rod and line combination lighter than 30 pound would take a smaller reel, such as a 3/0, 2½/0, etc.

A 50-pound outfit requires a 6/0 trolling reel and an 80-pound outfit requires a 9/0 trolling reel. These are the standards. A bit of subjective judgment is also required. If an angler is trying to land a big marlin on 50-pound tackle, he might use a slightly larger reel to get more line capacity. However, this is certainly the exception, and the best advice is to use a 4/0 reel for 30-pound class, a 6/0 for 50-pound class, and a 9/0 for 80-pound class.

CASTING TACKLE

More and more anglers are discovering the exciting world of saltwater casting in estuaries, along the coastline, and even in blue water. The type of tackle depends on the species and the conditions. Basically, fishermen are using spinning gear and baitcasting tackle, but occasionally, a surf rod with a revolving spool reel will be used along the beachfront when fishing from a boat.

For bays, rivers, and estuaries where the species may be relatively small, tackle would approximate the same type that is used in fresh water and discussed fully in the first part of this book. Since each situation must be analyzed on its own, simply use your judgment to select the casting tackle that is heavy enough to do the job.

One consideration is the distance you must cast. Normally, when you are fishing from a boat, you can reach the majority of fish with relatively short casts. However, the one exception is in working the rocks, jetties, and breakers along the shoreline. In this case, it is often necessary to hold the boat far enough away to insure personal safety and then use longer rods to cast into shore. This technique is a favorite along the rocky Northeast coast and is also practiced elsewhere where conditions warrant.

Author's light surf spinning outfit is also ideal for casting from boats and has accounted for stripers in the 50-pound class.

Saltwater casting tackle is usually designed to fight a fish first and then for its casting ability. Since most casts are reasonably short, distance isn't a problem when fishing from a boat. However, saltwater species can be large and you need a powerful rod to land those fish on casting tackle.

Generally, both spinning and plug rods for salt water are about 7 feet in length, built on tubular fiberglass blanks with a smooth arc. Soft tips have no place in this type of fishing except on the West Coast, where the light tip is helpful to toss small baits away from the boat. The saltwater plug rod or baitcasting outfit uses the larger sizes of baitcasting reels and does not have an offset handle. On a well-made rod, the blank runs right through to the butt for maximum power.

Spinning rods are similarly constructed and the average length is identical to the plug outfit. However, for smaller fish, some anglers will use a 6½-foot rod. For really big fish, specially constructed spinning rods of 7½ to 9 feet in length with reasonably long butts are preferred by veterans. The slightly longer length with spinning makes it easier to pump a large fish, providing, of course, the rod does not have a soft tip.

536

The only difference in reels for saltwater casting is in the size. Naturally, they would be larger because more line capacity is necessary for the longer running fish, and the angler would also be using heavier line which takes up more room on the spool.

In selecting saltwater casting tackle, check the components carefully to insure that they are made from noncorrosive materials. That applies to both rods and reels. And, make certain that the reels have adequate line capacity plus an exceptionally smooth drag system. Saltwater fish are tougher than their freshwater counterparts and it takes well-constructed tackle to stand up under the pressure.

LINES FOR SALT WATER

The history of saltwater fishing lines is an interesting one. Anglers fishing the seas were quick to adapt to the latest technological developments. Linen line was the mainstay for many years until the advent of nylon. Then, braided nylon took over and gained popularity. About this time, monofilament was extruded and anglers were torn between braided nylon or mono as their choice in lines. To complicate matters, someone figured out that if nylon were good, Dacron would be better and so they started to braid Dacron into fishing line. Now, the battle lines are drawn between monofilament and braided Dacron. Nylon has slipped out of the picture, although it is still used by some old-timers.

The area of contention centers around the properties of stretch and serviceability. Monofilament has a great deal of stretch, while Dacron boasts very little. This is good and bad. A great deal of stretch or even reasonable stretch makes it more difficult to set a hook and also frustrates the angler when he tries to pump a fish out of deep water. On the other hand, stretch is a forgiving factor in that it helps to compensate for the application of too much pressure. Very often, the stretch factor saves a fish for an angler and he isn't even aware of it.

On the question of serviceability, mono is less expensive than Dacron and can be changed frequently for little money. It is a single strand and therefore it is not affected by salt water, nor does it rot. Mono, however, does have a shelf life and deteriorates with time. Dacron is weakened by any type of tangle and it can also fray easily.

No one has satisfactorily resolved the question, but experts believe the best compromise at the moment is to use monofilament for most situations that require lines under 30-pound breaking strength and use Dacron for tests over 30 pounds.

Frequently, it becomes necessary to get a line very deep and the popular method is to use wire line. You can figure that 100 feet of wire line will take a lure to a depth of about 15 feet. A little over 200 feet of wire means the lure will troll 25 to 30 feet below the surface. The wire line, of course, is connected to braided Dacron backing.

Wire line is particularly hard on guides, and it will groove the ordinary types. Anglers using this method of fishing select rods with Carbaloy guides or the new Speed guides, because they can withstand the friction of wire running over them.

If you do decide to use wire, you must have a narrow spool reel. Otherwise, the wire will not spool properly and the resulting tangle will cost you a spool of wire. Once wire nests up, there's no way to salvage it. And the reel you choose should have a strong click mechanism on it, because you'll have it engaged while you stream the wire line.

SALTWATER FLY FISHING

Those who enjoy using fly rods in fresh water will find never-ending excitement with similar tackle in the salt. Nearly every species from panfish size to giants exceeding 100 pounds can be taken on wet flies or popping bugs, if one knows how. Some require extreme finesse in casting, presentation, hooking and handling, plus a benediction from Lady Luck. Others can be caught easily by even the clumsiest tyro drifting his fly in a current. Let's delve into the basics. The rest of it is so highly specialized that it is practiced only by a relative few.

The tackle used for fly fishing on freshwater lakes and streams should be adequate, if there is ample backing on the reel. However, a medium to slow-action fiberglass rod about 9 feet long would handle the greatest variety of saltwater species. This rod should take a size 9 or 10 line with a forward taper. If the reel has an extra spool, two lines are better than one — a floating line for fishing poppers and a sinking line for deep work. Deep means 6 feet or more.

The reel need not be expensive, as long as it has a smooth drag to handle long, fast runs. For this reason, at least 150 yards of backing, testing about 20 pounds, should be included. There are saltwater fish that can take all of this off the reel, and still keep going.

Leaders are less of a problem in salt water than in fresh, although in slack water they should roll out properly when presenting the fly. A leader no longer than the rod is excellent for surface and near-surface fishing, and a shorter one is adequate when going deeper. Fine tapers are undesirable because few species are leader shy, and tapers to about 10 or 12 pounds are more suitable to the relatively large hooks on which most saltwater flies are dressed. Short shock leaders or wire traces are used when sharp-teethed fish or those having cutting gill covers might be hooked.

Medium- to slow-action fiberglass rod about 9 feet long
suits most saltwater fly-
fishing requirements.

Saltwater fly fishermen use well-constructed reels with plenty of line
capacity. Streamers are popular flies for the salt.

539

Bucktail flies simulate baitfish and are useful for many saltwater species. Some, such as bonefish, may prefer shrimp imitations or something else; these exceptions will be mentioned in later chapters. In general, saltwater flies are simple unnamed bucktails or streamers of a size and general coloration simulating the bait on which the big ones seem to be feeding at the time. Stainless steel or plated hooks are better than freshwater hooks of carbon steel; the latter will rust or weaken quickly. Hooks vary in size or weight depending on the speed of sinking desired as well as on the size of fish being sought. All-white streamers or bucktails are very popular, and it helps to add a little glitter, such as thin strips of mylar. Red, blue, or yellow often are laid over the white, and a combination of red and yellow is also good. Many patterns are more or less heavily collared with hackles of these colors.

Anglers used to inland fishing (matching the hatch, delicate presentation, and all that) will find most saltwater situations easier. We just noted that saltwater flies are simple ones as compared with the complicated choices used in fresh water. They can be slapped down on the surface and often attract more strikes that way.

Visitors to new areas do better by employing guides, but working a fly or lure in any flowing water usually pays off in one way or another. Since most saltwater fishing—with flies and otherwise—is rather specialized, the next six chapters will try to clarify the types of places where specific varieties of fish are found, and tell how to catch them.

The main difference in methods is between those used in shallow water and in offshore (deep water) angling. In the former, one either wades or drifts or poles a skiff while hunting fish on the flats or in channels. In southern waters these include snappers, bonefish, permit, and channel bass.

In the latter, we are concerned with cruising deep water while trying to attract fish to the bait or lure. This is sometimes aided by chumming. Deep-water tackle is almost always revolving spool trolling equipment powerful enough to handle big fish. Casting tackle, including fly fishing, is fun to use when suitable fish have been spotted.

HANDLING BIG FISH

When an angler hooks a big fish, one of two things soon happens. Either the angler has control of his fish, or the fish does as it pleases. Time is wasted by applying tension which is inadequate for the strength of the tackle. This wasted time favors the fish because it gives it greater opportunity to rest or break loose. Anglers who understand their tackle know how much safe tension can be applied, and this should be utilized to the maximum. We must assume that the fish is solidly hooked. If it isn't, maximum safe tension still is the best bet, because the chances are that the fish will pull loose anyway.

Safe hooking is helped, not only by knowledge of tackle strength, but also by other factors. Did you remember to check the hook for sharpness? Are you sure the fish hooked itself securely, or should you strike to drive in the barb? Fish with bony mouths, such as tarpon, may need to be struck several times.

When the fish feels the bite of the iron and the tension of the tackle, it will often make a long run. Hold the rod tip high and let the fish run against the drag. This is an exhausting run for the fish, which will stop when fatigue forces it to, or perhaps when it reaches deep water. Here is when the angler takes over.

At this point the fish will roll, jump, sound or bulldog. Keep the rod high and bowed under maximum safe tension. Finding that these tactics have failed, the fish probably will try to ease tension by allowing itself to be reeled in, which means pumping the rod. This is done by raising the rod tip nearly vertical and reeling in as it is being lowered. In raising the rod we are pulling on the fish. To do this it probably will be necessary to keep the reel spool from turning by applying thumb or finger pressure. Of course this pressure must be released if the fish decides to run again. Some anglers screw down the reel's drag a bit at this point, but I consider it dangerous. It may even be advisable to decrease drag slightly, because the line which has been taken off the reel has decreased its depth on the spool and thus increased drag somewhat. Avoid fooling with the drag while handling a fish. Drag should have been set in advance.

After the various antics a fish displays on completion of its initial run, it often will swim toward the angler so quickly that he may fear it has become unhooked. Very fast reeling is necessary at this point to keep a tight line. Usually, line is regained by continuous pumping, but remember who is in charge. It is the angler, not the fish—so keep maximum tension on it.

If you're using spinning tackle, the pumping technique is more important. Watch the line spool. If it turns while reeling, this accomplishes nothing and puts a twist in the line. A badly twisted line can be fatal when the fish is brought near the angler.

Pumping and reeling brings the fish in, but it also presents another period of time when the angler must be careful. When the fish sees the boat (or the angler) it will make another run; usually a much shorter one. This repeats the earlier situation, and more than two runs can often be expected. So much the better, because they tire the fish.

Anglers (particularly those who fish for tarpon and salmon) often speak of "bowing to the fish" when it jumps. During the short period of the jump the rod is momentarily lowered and pushed forward to provide slack line. This is intended to prevent the fish from falling on a tight line and breaking it. Experienced anglers usually can tell when a jump is about to occur. It is hard to describe, but it is an instinct or signal, learned by practice.

So now, after a few runs and judicious reeling and pumping, the fish is near the boat. Keep the tension up and remember who is in charge! The battle isn't over until it is on the surface hopefully so tired that it is on its side, ready for net or gaff.

Now we decide whether we want to keep or release the fish. Many species, sailfish and tarpon included, are only caught for sport, and should not be killed unless one is to be kept for mounting. A gaff can be slipped between the gills or under the jaw so the hook can be removed, or, with smaller fish, this can be done after netting. A deeply embedded hook can be cut and left to disintegrate in the acidic juices of the mouth. This is a small sacrifice where important gamefish are concerned. Nothing is so disgusting as seeing important species left drying on a dock or hanging from hooks because those who caught them no longer want them.

When an angler is aboard a boat, regardless of its size, the boat handler plays an important part in subduing the fish. The skipper keeps the angler in the best position to handle the fish, and as near to it as is safe. He may back down toward it during a long run, and he may speed up to help the angler keep a tight line. The closer the boat is to the fish, the better the angler's chance of success. Some fish sound deeply. In this case the boat is kept as nearly over the fish as possible. Under proper tension, the fish will surface sooner or later. Be it a rowboat or a cruiser, the person handling the craft is part of the team, although he may get too little credit. Good anglers and efficient skippers know how to work together!

ADDITIONAL EQUIPMENT

Equipment for saltwater fishing ranges from simple to elaborate. Transportation, afloat and ashore, has a bearing on it. Addicts owning sleep-in beach vehicles can carry everything including the kitchen sink. Those roaming around afoot must cut the list down. Let's start with the latter, because his needs are rather basic.

While surf fishermen can wade wet in summer, in cotton pants and sneakers, surf fishing usually calls for waders, or boots and waterproof pants. The latter may be more comfortable, but you can't go in as deep. In cold weather this gear is rubber, with adequate insulation. Wet and weedy rocks are amazingly slippery. Felt soles help, but don't solve the problem entirely. The addition of wading sandals or ice creepers is better. The upper part of the clothing normally is a waterproof parka complete with hood and draw-

Properly equipped surf fisherman wears waders, parka, belt, musette bag and ice creepers. Short-handled gaff and stringer for fish are also standard gear.

string waist. Around this one usually wears a belt for warmth and water protection, and to hang things from. Army pistol belts rate high because they are of strong webbing, with plenty of eyelets.

A tacklebox is valuable when it can be carried conveniently. Since salt-water rusts metal boxes, preferred ones are of plastic or wood. Something smaller is needed when wading, and an army surplus canvas musette bag is about the right size. It can be slung over a shoulder or hung over one's back. Lunch and other things that shouldn't get wet can be stored in plastic bags. Anglers who consider this too cumbersome carry a few plugs, squids and jigs, plus pliers and small terminal equipment in a pouch strung on the belt.

Pliers are essential. Tackle stores carry sturdy parallel-jaw types equipped with wire cutters. A good stainless-steel knife is also important.

Surf fishermen who find it inconvenient to beach their fish usually need a gaff. This is a sharp barbless hook affixed to a handle. Wading fishermen do best with short handles. Those fishing from rocks and jetties may want them 6 feet long or so.

A wading fisherman also needs a stringer so he won't have to return to the beach with each catch. These are improvised from several feet of parachute cord or light chain. Tethered to this, fish can swim or drift behind the angler, who has one end of the stringer attached to his belt. A priest (a club, usually with a thong attached) may be necessary to make a fish permanently inactive.

Whether on the beach or in the surf, a butt belt with a leather cup is handy to rest the butt and take the strain off the arms when baitfishing. This is the counterpart of the vest harness used for heavy trolling on boats. Baitfishermen who don't want to hand-hold their rods can rest them in sand spikes. A towel, usually stuck into the belt, should not be forgotten for wiping hands and equipment.

Sunglasses prevent glare and make fishing more comfortable. Those which polarize light cut surface glare so anglers can see into the water more clearly. They are an important aid in spotting and handling fish. Sunglasses are almost mandatory in tropical or semitropical regions. Good head covering is also important, such as the lightweight fore-and-aft caps with visors and a skirt which can be turned down to cover the ears and neck and protect them from the sun.

Knowledgeable anglers dress conservatively. Clothing is on the drab, or tan, side mainly because this makes their presence less obvious to fish. Shirts usually have long sleeves for sunburn and insect protection. Insect repellent is necessary in some places and always should be carried. The mosquitoes or black flies that suddenly can swarm around when the breeze dies down can drive the hardiest unprotected fishermen off the water.

If these aren't all the essentials, they seem to be the most important ones. The kit probably includes a stone to sharpen hooks and knives. Night fishing usually requires a flashlight—a handy type is one that can be strapped around the cap or neck, with the battery (connected by a cord) carried in a pocket. Binoculars aren't essential but are useful in observing the actions of birds and in checking on how other anglers are doing.

The many types of fishing make various items essential to some that are useless to others. It is helpful to make a checklist and to go over it before starting out. You'll add and subtract from time to time but eventually will know exactly what you need to take along. Many a good trip has been spoiled by forgetting essentials.

CARE OF TACKLE

Some fishermen treat tackle carelessly, while others enjoy cleaning and assembling their gear to the point of obsession. Even if one has very little time for tackle maintenance, he must keep things in good enough condition so they will function efficiently. Let's go over some suggestions.

Reels are the vital element because sand and salt water can put them out of order quicker than one might think, as the following incident illustrates.

While fishing in rough weather along the edge of Florida's Gulf Stream, I noticed my spinning outfit had fallen on deck and that the reel was submerged in salt water that was sloshing around on board. I picked up the tackle, wiped it off, and planned to clean it on reaching port. Various things prevented this for several hours. By that time the reel spool had frozen to its spindle so solidly that it was difficult to remove even with a hammer. Salt water sets up a chemical reaction between the metals in a reel which can do this quickly. Regardless of immersion, reels should be rinsed under a tap of warm water, wiped dry, and all accessible parts oiled or greased. Reels should be protected from salt water but, in case of a ducking, they may have to be taken apart, the parts washed in gasoline, and reassembled while being oiled or greased.

The need to disassemble a revolving-spool reel is rare, and should be done only when necessary, unless one is familiar with the process. Most reels come with exploded parts diagrams which make it easier to do the job correctly. An open egg box can be used to hold parts in order of disassembly. In putting things back together again, just start from the other end. Some mechanically inclined anglers take new reels apart before using them on the theory that they were inadequately greased and oiled by the factory. This is rarely the case and the practice should be avoided. If a reel gets in serious trouble, let the factory fix it.

Spinning reels can be cleaned quite simply. Remove the spool and rinse out the parts inside the cup. Dry these parts, and add grease where needed. Salt water won't seep into the gear box except after long immersion. Instructions that came with the reel tell how to grease and oil it. Saltwater anglers should follow them carefully.

The worst thing that can happen is to drop a reel in sand. Rinse it off immediately; even in salt water. Sand is worse than salt for ruining a reel.

Rods may not need to be rinsed off, but good ones should be. Salt may only stain fiberglass, but it eventually will corrode the line guides. When freshwater tackle is used in the salt this is especially important. Saltwater rods should have corrosion-resistant fittings. Even these, and especially tiptops, will become grooved from constant casting. Examine tiptops from time to time to be sure they are not scored, because grooving or scoring rapidly cuts away line strength.

Salt won't harm braided or monofilament lines, but it makes the latter more wiry. A good rinsing under fresh water helps, and the equipment should be allowed to dry before storing.

Metal tackleboxes will corrode even after having been painted or varnished. Plastic boxes are better, and saltwater anglers usually like wooden ones best of all. Some of these, made of mahogany or other rare woods, are quite expensive, but they can be a lifetime investment.

No matter what kind of box is used, let's try to keep salt out of it. This applies especially to contents, such as flies, plugs, jigs and fittings. Anglers fishing from boats often have a pail of fresh water on board. They drop used items into it so salt will rinse off. Then they are dried and replaced. This is especially important for lures with feathers or hair, because even the slight corrosion of hooks can discolor them. Flies for fresh water usually have corrosive hooks and need special care when used in salt water. Even then they won't last very long and should be tested for sharpness and strength before each use.

Since lines gradually deteriorate and weaken, they should be replaced periodically depending on how much they have been used and how well they have been cared for. Protect them from bright sun as much as possible, especially monofilament lines. Braided and monofilament lines are relatively inexpensive. Why try to extend the life of old ones if this might mean losing a trophy fish?

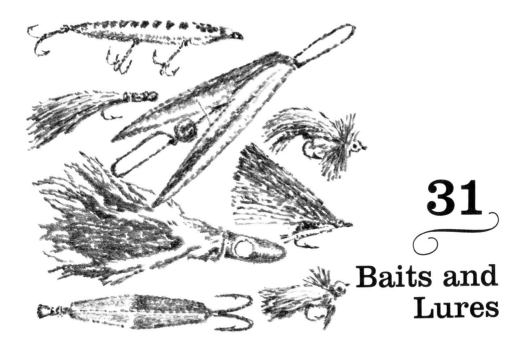

31

Baits and Lures

BAITS

Baits for salt water are rigged similarly to freshwater ones, but there are some variations important to successful fishing. Let's review a few basic ones.

The accompanying drawing shows three methods of rigging live baitfish. The top method is usually used when the bait can swim freely, such as under a drifting float. The middle one is preferred for light casts, for holding the bait in a current, or for trolling. The bottom method is an alternative which aids hooking in some instances. The leader of the trail hook is usually snelled around the upper one.

Two ways of hooking seaworms are also shown. The upper one will kill the worm but its actions and scent will attract strikes. If you want to keep the worm alive, the lower method could be used. Several worms are put on a hook for very large fish, but part of one on a small hook is better for fish with small mouths.

Shrimp can be kept alive by hooking them either behind the eye or through the tail. These can be attracted by a light and can be netted. The smaller grass shrimp can be netted in bays or creeks amid eel grass or similar vegetation. Two or three usually are impaled on a hook.

Sand fleas are the fat little bugs seen hopping along beaches behind receding waves. They can be caught by hand or in wire scoops and are excellent baits when several are impaled on a hook.

547

Three ways to hook live bait-fish (*from top*): through flesh behind head *above* the backbone; either through upper lip or both lips; with a double hook arrangement. Treble hooks may also be used with these rigs.

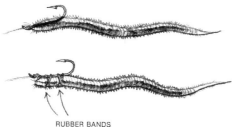

RUBBER BANDS

Two methods of hooking seaworm. *Top,* insert barb in mouth and bring it out about an inch behind the head. *Bottom,* to keep worm alive tie it to hook with two small rubber bands.

Shrimp may be hooked through shell behind eye (*top*) or through the tail with the barb up or down. Grass shrimp, which are smaller, usually require two or three hooked through the tail.

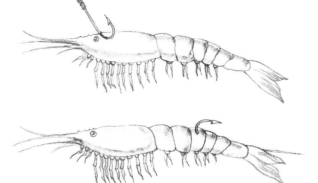

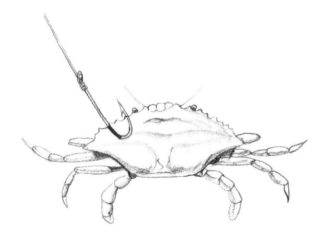

To hook a crab properly, remove large claws and insert hook through the edge of shell.

Rig for strip bait. One to three hooks can be used, depending on length of bait.

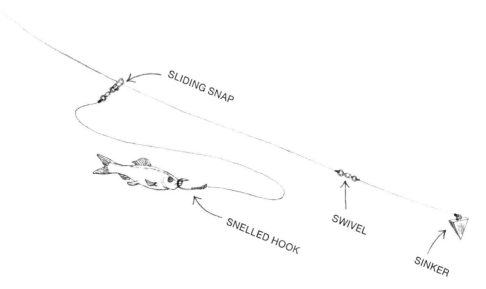

SLIDING SNAP

SNELLED HOOK

SWIVEL

SINKER

The "Dog Run Method" of rigging live baitfish for surf, pier and jetty fishing. Cast out the sinker; hook live baitfish through the lips on a 1-foot leader with a snap; snap leader on line, and let the baitfish slide and swim down the line to the swivel.

TYPICAL BAITS AND HOOK SIZES

	AVERAGE HOOK SIZE	SEA WORMS	CLAMS OR MUSSELS	SQUID	CRABS	SHRIMP	BAITFISH
Bass, Channel (Redfish) (Red Drum)	3/0	✔	✔		✔	✔	✔
Bass, Striped (Rockfish)	5/0	✔	✔	✔	✔	✔	✔
Bass, Sea	3/0		✔	✔	✔		
Bluefish	3/0						✔
Bonefish	1/0		✔		✔	✔	
Bonito	2/0						✔
Cobia (Ling)	3/0				✔	✔	✔
Cod, Atlantic	6/0		✔	✔			✔
Crevalle	2/0		✔			✔	
Croaker (Drum)	2/0		✔	✔	✔		
Flounder, Summer (Fluke)	2/0			✔	✔		✔
Flounder, Winter (Blackback)	8	✔	✔				
Grouper	8/0			✔			✔
Kingfish (King Mackerel)	3/0						✔
Permit, Atlantic (Great Pompano)	2/0				✔		
Pollock	3/0		✔	✔			✔
Scup (Porgy)	1/0	✔	✔		✔	✔	
Sheepshead	2/0		✔		✔	✔	
Snapper	3/0			✔			✔
Snook	3/0				✔	✔	✔
Tarpon	3/0				✔	✔	✔
Tautog (Blackfish)	1/0	✔	✔		✔	✔	
Weakfish (Sea Trout)	2/0	✔	✔	✔	✔	✔	✔

Note: Hook sizes given are a general average for medium-sized fish of the species. For example, while size 3/0 is a good average for tarpon in the 25–50 pound class, a hook as small as size 6 could be used in fly fishing for baby tarpon weighing about 5 pounds. Conversely, in going for record fish over 100 pounds, the hook size could be 5/0, or even bigger. While baits listed are principal ones for each species, others may be preferred in specific areas. Check this with local bait shops.

Clams and mussels are a problem because the soft meat often pulls off the hook. A way to prevent this is to tie a few inches of very fine monofilament or wire around the shank of the hook with an overhand knot so two ends extend. Wind these around the bait several times and tie them together. Smashed clams or mussels provide very good chum when stillfishing. Very large clams should be cut into smaller pieces for small-mouthed fish, such as flounders. The long, tough strip can provide several baits.

Crabs of all kinds are ideal baits for many gamefish including tautog, sheepshead, bonefish and permit. If they are very small, two or more crabs can be put on a hook. When using a larger one, remove the large claws and insert the hook through the shell near one of the points, as shown. Softshell crabs, or "shedders," in some varieties are better than hard-shell ones.

I enjoy casting for stripers and bluefish along the New England coast and I have always thought that live baitfish should be superior to baits without action. The trouble was that long casts prevented the baits from staying alive or even from staying on the hook. Anglers in New Jersey offered the solution shown in the accompanying drawing. It's fun to use, and it works!

Tie a swivel between the line and a 2 or 3 foot leader to which the sinker is attached and cast the sinker out. The rest of the rig is a foot or so of leader with a hook on one end and a snap on the other. Hook the bait through both lips and attach the snap around the line, letting this slide down it. The baitfish usually will head for deep water but the snap can't pass the swivel, so the bait has no place to hide and must swim around near the swivel until a gamefish comes along and takes it. This is called the "Dog Run Method" because it is similar to clipping Fido's leash to a wire between two trees in the backyard so he can go back and forth. The baitfish usually runs down the line as far as it can go. If it doesn't, raise and jerk the rod tip a few times. As far as the bait is concerned, it's a one-way trip!

The fluttering of a long and narrow strip bait makes an attracting enticer when it is fished in a current, trolled, or retrieved fairly fast. Size and shape usually depend on the live bait it is supposed to suggest, and upon the size of fish being sought. A baitfish can be filleted and the strips used, or strips can be cut from the belly of a fish already caught. A single hook may be enough, even for a fairly long strip, but two or three hooks snelled together may be better for added hooking ability and for keeping the bait on the hook.

ARTIFICIAL LURES

Since each variety of fish has favorites in lures and how they are fished, more will be said about this later. A few general observations will be helpful, however, before we get to specifics. What are the basic types? How do they work? What kinds of fishing are they best for?

The basic types of artificials are plugs, metal lures (including squids, jigs and spoons), and artificial flies.

Plugs

Saltwater plugs descend from the freshwater models discussed in Chapter 4, so little needs to be added here. Plugs weighing over 3 ounces are too heavy for spinning and should be used with conventional surf-casting equipment. Smaller ones should be used with spinning or plug-casting gear. When fish can be taken near the surface, poppers, swimmers or splutterers are chosen. For under-surface fishing, you can select from sinking poppers and deep runners designed either to float and pull under or to sink slowly or fast. Deep runners for salt water usually have no lips, but have flattened sloped foreheads. When fished in a jerky manner they can be productive in rips and fast currents.

As in freshwater fishing, plug size depends on the power of the tackle. Type depends on action desired and how deep we want to fish. Shape and color usually imitate baitfish.

POPPING PLUGS

Eppinger School Striper. Good on coastal waters, bays and rivers. For stripers, bluefish, snook, tarpon and other inshore species.

Pencil Popper. Heavy tail section makes it a good casting plug. Floats on the surface, should be retrieved in short jerks. Favorite in northeastern water for school stripers and bluefish.

Trouble Maker. Effective on stripers, bluefish, snook, tarpon and similar species. This type of plug is most productive in calm water.

Phillips "77". Used in northeastern coastal waters and on the Florida flats. Retrieved in sharp jerks, will bring strikes from topwater feeders.

DIVING PLUGS

Atom Plug. Cast or trolled, plug can be worked deep or shallow by adjusting metal lip. Favorite among northeastern surf and jetty fishermen.

Rebel. Large size for trolling and casting for all saltwater species in coastal waters—stripers, bluefish, permit, etc.

Creek Chub Darter. Floats at rest and darts side-to-side when retrieved. Good for coastal bays and flats.

Creek Chub Surfster. Surf-fishing favorite, this heavy plug can be cast beyond breakers for stripers.

Stan Gibbs Darter. Heavy tail section aids in distance casting. Floats at rest, darts side-to-side when retrieved. Favorite of striper fishermen.

SINKING PLUGS

Mirrolure. Big weighted lure that casts easily and sinks fast. Not much built-in action, so it must be worked with a jerk-and-crank retrieve. Effective for most inshore species.

Boone Needlefish. Good for bay, surf and jetty fishing, especially for stripers and blues. Must be retrieved in jerks since it has no action.

Boone T.D. Special. Can be worked at any depth and is equally good for New Jersey stripers or Florida tarpon and snook.

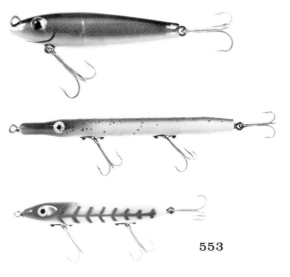

553

There are tricks in fishing saltwater plugs. Saltwater poppers must scoop water and "spit." A good way to bring out the action is to hold the rod a little above the horizontal, reel steady with one hand, and jerk the rod with the other. Surface swimmers are usually cigar-shaped, with lips to make them dig into the water and swim from side to side. Try varying the action. Most of these are molded of plastic, but many anglers still prefer old standard designs made of wood. These are often called "stick baits" because they can be made from broomsticks. Visitors to new areas should see what local experts are using. What was popular last season (perhaps for no very good reason) may be unpopular now.

Often a big fish will boil behind a plug and refuse it. The trick here is to quickly speed up the action. If that doesn't work, let the plug lie dead for a few seconds and then work it actively. Fish who don't like one plug or its action may smash at something else.

Metal Lures

Squids, or "tin-clads," are called "jigs" on the west coast, but we'll avoid confusion by using the former name because, to easterners, a jig is a different lure for a different purpose. A squid is an elongated, streamlined solid metal lure made to cast tremendous distances and to sink fast or slowly, depending on its design. Much earlier in this century, squids were made of expensive block-tin, valued because the metal could be burnished to a satiny silver sheen. Now they are molded from less expensive metals, usually chrome-plated, but sometimes in colors of prevalent baitfish, particularly on the west coast. Easterners usually prefer them naked, while westerners often want them dressed with skirts of hair or feathers.

In addition to their distant casting potential, squids work best in turbulent water, which is a reason why they are more popular in the North Atlantic than in the more protected waters farther south. In surf fishing they will reach beyond the combers. The trick is to drop a squid back of a wave and to instantly fish it in in the following white water where fish feed. The form, flash, and action simulates a frantic baitfish being pounded about in the lather. Another point is that squids can be retrieved instantly near the surface or allowed to sink and almost drag bottom. While plugs are bulky short-distance lures in the wind, a squid will cut through wind to much greater distances.

Since the sheen of squids reflects light, they are less productive after dusk, but they can be used effectively from bridges and piers at night where lights can make them shine.

All designs are favorites in one place or another, but an angler needs only a very few in various weights. One should be a very streamlined fast sinker

SQUIDS FOR SALT WATER

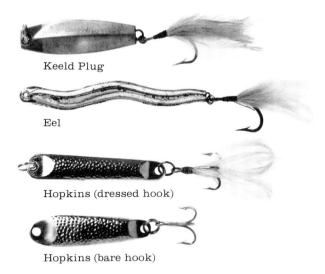

Keeld Plug

Eel

Hopkins (dressed hook)

Hopkins (bare hook)

and another a wider one that will sink more slowly. Retrieves are usually very fast and jerky. If a fish is given time to inspect a squid it will decide it's not what it wants.

Jigs

Jigs are quite different from squids, both in form and in the ways they are fished. Most of them are flat-headed, round-headed, bullet-headed or keeled, with the eye on top of the head and with the rearward protruding rigid hook curving upward (to diminish snagging), skirted immediately behind the head with hair, nylon or feathers.

The technique is to bounce them up and down off bottom or to jerk them, yo-yo fashion, to the surface and then repeat. The latter action can take bottom feeders as well as others cruising all the way up. Some saltwater jigs weigh several ounces and are used to work depths of 100 feet or more. Heads and trimmings are in various colors.

Diamond jigs, as previously discussed, fall into this category. So do the Scandinavian types, which are more curved, usually three-sided, and tinted various colors. The choice between these two is largely one of preference.

A different type, usually called a "Japanese jig," has a bullet-shaped head through which a wire is strung to a loose, closely trailing hook. The back of the head is grooved so it can be skirted with nylon or feathers. While this type can be cast, it principally is used for trolling, usually for offshore species of big fish.

JIGS AND JIG-AND-EEL RIGS

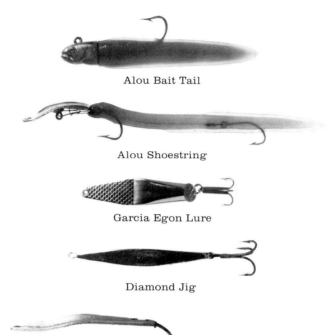

Alou Bait Tail

Alou Shoestring

Garcia Egon Lure

Diamond Jig

Block Tin Squid

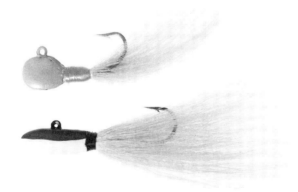

Upperman bucktail jig (*top*) and a bullet, or torpedo, bucktail jig.

Jigs for casting and deep fishing are available in many shapes. They are dressed with various colors of bucktail, feathers, straight or crimped artificial fibers, rubber or plastic skirts, etc., with or without mylar strips for added flash. Fluorescent colors are effective. Addition of pork rind, part of a plastic worm or a fish strip trailing on the hook often increases strikes. Jigs are designed to ride hook-up to prevent catching on grass and rocks. Hooks always should be needle-sharp for best penetration.

Upperman or lima bean jig sinks quickly. Flat sides make it swing with currents.

Bullet jig is for general use but especially favored for trolling.

Keeled jig is nearly flat on bottom and designed for shallow-water fishing. It is excellent for flounders and other bottom feeders.

Dart jig planes actively when being retrieved or fished downstream in currents. In small sizes it is favored as a shad lure.

"Japanese" Jig is used principally for trolling. Bottom drawing shows the undressed jig, with leader wire sliding through the head and attached flexibly to the hook. This allows head and dressing to slide up on the wire when a fish is on.

SALTWATER SPOONS

Eppinger Cop-E-Cat. Big mackerel-finish spoon designed for trolling and casting in coastal waters. Trolled deep on wire line for bluefish.

Eppinger Seadevle. Slimmer version of one above, for casting and trolling. Large sizes for stripers, bluefish, yellowtails; small sizes for mackerel.

Reed R.T. Flash. Well-designed spoon that can be cast, trolled or jigged. Effective for tinker mackerel, snappers, weakfish, kingfish.

Wob-L-Rite. Heavy brass spoon that casts great distances. Good for deep jigging reef species or surf and boat casting.

Tony Accetta Spoon. Comes in various sizes, usually rigged with a pork rind strip, as shown. For trolling or casting for inshore gamefish.

Spoons

Similar to those used in fresh water, but often of much larger size, saltwater spoons can be cast (in some designs), but in salt water are preferred for trolling. They are more or less concave, lightweight, and air-resistant. Hooks normally are rigidly affixed on the east coast and attached by split rings on the west. The motion is a flashing one produced by darting, diving and wobbling to simulate baitfish. When trolling for large fish, these spoons can be 6 inches long, or more, and equipped with hooks as large as 10/0.

When a spoon is being trolled, the angler notices a steady throbbing of the rod tip, which indicates that the lure is trolling correctly. When this throbbing ceases it usually is a signal that weeds have fouled the hook. Spoons which are trolled too fast will twist the line, often badly enough to make it useless. Ball-bearing swivels help prevent this. Of these three types of metal lures, the squids and jigs are of major importance to most anglers.

Another group of artificials is the saltwater "flies." In salt water this is a misnomer because these lures imitate baitfish and, to a lesser extent, shrimps and a few other items that saltwater fish feed on. Since patterns are quite specialized, they will be described in pertinent places in other chapters.

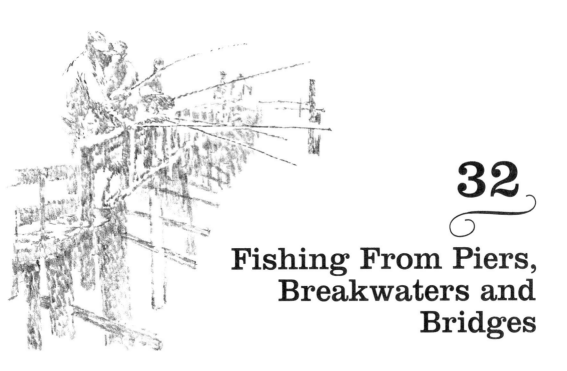

32

Fishing From Piers, Breakwaters and Bridges

People going on oceanside vacations or who live near salt water and want to try this kind of fishing for the first time usually start by casting from piers, breakwaters or bridges, because these are convenient and fish can be caught with the simplest equipment. First, we should understand tides and how they affect fishing. This knowledge is useful when deciding where to fish and what to do when we get there.

THE BEST TIDE

A tide is a periodic rise and fall of the ocean and the water of its inlets. This happens about every 12 hours and 26 minutes due to the gravitational attraction of the moon and the sun; principally the former because it is much closer to the earth. The moon revolves around the earth every 24 hours and 51 minutes. Hence the tide ebbs and flows twice each lunar day. High tide on one side of the earth is accompanied by a high tide on the other side. Generally speaking, high and low tides occur about one hour later each day.

Tides influence the movements of fish for many reasons. There are no absolute rules to follow, but there are general ones. Since fish like moving water, plus enough depth to allow them to roam and feel safe, the relatively slack water of high or low tide is least desirable for fishing. The high slack is the better of the two because the water is deeper.

559

After high slack the ebbing tide flushes water out of creeks, tidal rivers and salt ponds connected to the ocean. Since the current also takes baitfish and other foods with it, fish collect around the mouths of outlets in search of these morsels. Such outlets may provide good fishing all during the ebbing tide, if they are deep enough. The two hours or so just before and after high tide usually are best for surf fishing and for casting along rocky shores because the high water makes more food available.

As the tide nears its low point, action in the outlets usually diminishes. Then consider fishing tidal flats which were too deep before half tide. However, the flats, which are exposed or are too shallow after half tide, may be good when the water is higher. The low half of the tide makes outer bars accessible. When these bars are offshore their outside edges should provide good fishing; also the inside edges if the water is deep. Casts from shore to the inside edges should be productive. During the last of the ebb and the start of the flood, the channels which cut through sand bars are used by game-fish traveling through them before or after feasting on food found inside the bars.

Narrow entrances to coves or small bays should provide good fishing during the last of the ebb and the start of the flood because fish are moving and are more restricted by shallow water.

While low water slack is poorest for fishing, this tide also exposes channels, drop-offs and deep holes that may offer action. Since fish want moving water for food and deep water for safety, creeks and channels are less productive during this short period, but it may be the only time they can be reached.

The hour or so around low water slack can be used productively for bottom fishing because baits sink more easily when there is no current. Many reef areas are in open water where strong tidal currents prevent getting jigs or baits down at any other time. Since bottom fish collect in areas of best food supply, if you don't get strikes in one place, change position. Hot spots aren't hard to locate, and one good one can fill the freezer. Either high or low slack often affords productive fishing from piers and bridges, even though a running tide should be better.

Action begins to start up again with the incoming tide because baitfish and gamefish enter inlets in increasing numbers as water depth and speed of flow picks up. As this nears high tide the same conditions apply as were discussed for the first two hours or so of the ebb. The many different conditions which affect various areas take exceptions to the rules but, in general, these situations apply. It is helpful to find out what tide provided best fishing in a definite place and to be there at the same stage of the next tide.

When tides pour into a constricted opening between the mainland and a nearby island or between two points of land, a tide rip often occurs. The rushing current around mid-tide is so swift that hordes of baitfish can't combat it and are swept through. This is an ideal situation for schools of gamefish such as bluefish, weakfish, redfish and striped bass, which often can be seen slashing the surface to a froth as they rip through the helpless bait amid the screaming of wheeling and diving birds. Boats usually don't disturb the feeding, so anglers can hold sea-way and fish lures astern in the current, drift with it, or anchor. There may be acres of action, and any lure vaguely simulating the baitfish should bring fast strikes.

If there is any choice between fishing with lures or baits, a rule which is made often will be broken. Here is a rule: Use baits on the high half of the tide (the ebb and flood above half tide) because the increase of water makes baitfish harder to catch, so gamefish may be feeding on the bottom. Use lures on the low half of the tide because baitfish then are easier to catch, so gamefish may be feeding nearer the surface.

What do I think of this? Not much! I enjoy casting with lures, dislike the lack of action usually associated with baitfishing, and I'm too lazy to keep baiting up anyway. My rule is to stay with artificial lures. One of them usually works for the kind of fish I like to catch. If none of them proves productive, I find something else to do until action starts again. (That, too, is a rule to be broken!)

DOES THE MOON'S PHASE AFFECT FISHING?

We are familiar with fishing calendars that predict good, fair and poor fishing days depending on the phases of the moon. While the value of these may be debatable on inland lakes and streams, the moon does influence inshore saltwater fishing in a different way from that of the periodic rise and fall of the tides. A glance at the moon reveals its phase, making calendars unnecessary. Let's try to simplify what actually happens by referring to the accompanying diagram.

We have seen that the moon revolves around the earth every 24 hours and 51 minutes, thus providing approximately two full tide changes per day. The moon's relationship to the sun brings up a different situation of interest to saltwater anglers. Since the earth is moving in an inclined orbit around the sun, it requires 29.53 days for the moon to regain its same position relative to the sun's direction. This interval is called a lunar month or, to put it as simply as possible, the time elapsing between full moons.

The difference in distances from the earth to the moon and to the sun makes the gravitational attraction of the moon three times that of the sun. When the sun and moon are in line with the earth their gravitational forces are combined, as shown in phases 2 and 4 in the accompanying diagram.

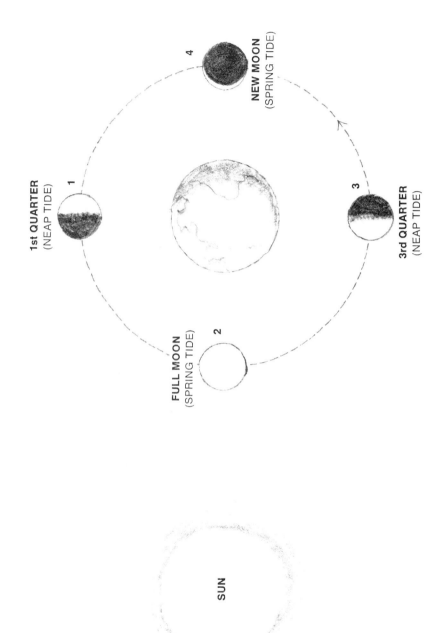

Phases of the moon that affect fishing.

These increased forces pull the tides more than ordinarily, thus making them abnormally high. These are called "spring tides," the word having no relationship to the season. Spring tides occur when the moon is full and when it is new. (Since we can't see the new moon, it is commonly called "new" when a thin crescent first appears.)

Conversely, when the sun and moon are not in line with the earth, the maximum gravitational attraction diminishes, reaching greatest impotence during the moon's first and third quarters, as shown by phases 1 and 3 of the same diagram. (This is when only half of the moon's disk is illuminated.) These times of minimum attraction cause abnormally low tides, which are known as "neap tides." Spring tides and neap tides each occur twice per lunar month, with about two weeks between them.

What does all this have to do with fishing? We now know that the full moon and the new moon bring abnormally high tides. This brings gamefish inshore to feed, particularly in rich, marshy backwaters they can't reach during ordinary high tides. Fish on spawning migrations seem to expect these tides, waiting near estuaries for them so they can pass over tidewater obstructions otherwise insurmountable. Fish see lures and baits easier during the full moon, and baitfish seem to travel more actively then. All this means that extra-good fishing can be expected during the high halves of tides when the moon is full and when the moon shows a thin crescent. Conversely, the neap tides during the moon's quarters may not be as good as average, but there may be holes and other hot spots such as outer bars which only can be reached then. Very low tides also may concentrate fish in channels.

High tides accompanied by winds result in crashing waves which uncover mollusks and other bottom foods and push them closer to shore, thus bringing gamefish into the surf. This means that a good time to fish the surf and from such places as breakwaters and rocks is soon after a storm when the weather has calmed down a bit.

TACKLE

When freshwater anglers visit the salt, their gear will be useful for a surprising variety of fishing. Let's assume it is a spinning, spincasting or plugcasting outfit in about the 8-pound line class. This is appropriate for everything from saltwater panfish to school stripers, bluefish, weakfish, redfish, snook, bonefish, small to medium-size tarpon and a host of other species. Of course ability plays a part in whether or not a real tackle-buster will be landed, but if one does latch on, take off for the horizon, and pop the line, the small loss is well worth the excitement.

Take along your largest freshwater fly rod, too, if its reel is well padded with backing. Dozens of kinds of small to average-size fish can be caught with it – the big tackle-busters, too, if they're handled properly.

What about freshwater flies and heavy lures? Many will do the job, but corrosive hooks will rust and may not be strong enough or large enough. Visit a bait shop where you'll be fishing. Find out what's going on, where the action is, and what tackle is recommended. Reserve freshwater terminal equipment for use as a last resort. Keep salt away from it if possible, and buy what the local saltwater experts recommend. Their advice usually is truthful and factual.

If line as light as 8 pounds is on the reel, remember that this is about minimum sensible strength for bridge and pier fishing. It's safer to go a few pounds stronger.

What's ideal equipment? My favorite is the same as that of many others – the 9-foot rod previously mentioned, fitted with a saltwater spinning reel filled with 12- or 15-pound-test monofilament. Conventional star-drag reels can be used with a similar rod, including monofilament in the 15- to 20-pound-test range or braided line going as strong as 30. This should handle lures or bait rigs in the 1- to 2-ounce class. If a fly rod is used (and it often should be) I previously suggested that it could be a 9-footer equipped with a weight-forward line – again with plenty of backing on the reel. Since terminal tackle is specialized, we'll come to it later.

FISHING FROM PIERS AND BRIDGES

Anglers should find out whether fishing is permitted from the bridge they want to use. It is not allowed in many places for the safety of fishermen and traffic. On the other hand, many regions encourage it to the extent of providing special walkways, and some old bridges have been left standing (after new ones have been built) for the exclusive use of fishermen. If signs prohibit fishing from a bridge, you can usually do it from the abutments.

Those without tackle can buy a dropline, a few hooks, and a sinker or two, mostly for use with bait, although jigging often gets results. Fish collect around piers and bridges because they are attracted by the shade, by currents made by the obstructions, and by growths on them that harbor food. When using droplines, try baits on the bottom when the tide slacks off, because getting baits to the bottom may not be possible when the current is strong.

Those with more complete tackle have the choice of up-current or down-current fishing. A method of up-current fishing with jigs and other sinking lures is shown in the accompanying drawing. The angler casts outward at an angle to the right or left so the lure will sink near bottom and can be retrieved as near the pilings as possible. Of course there is the possibility of tangling, but it is a chance worth taking, especially when strong lines are used.

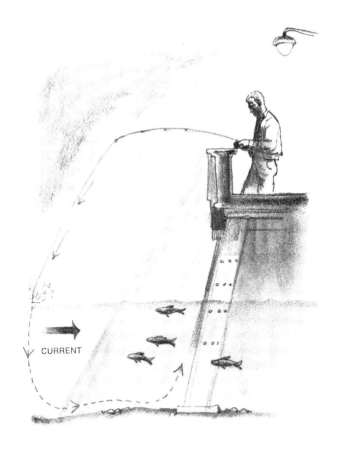

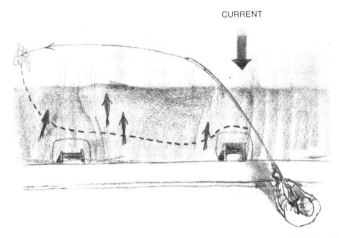

Up-current fishing from piers and bridges is most successful at night or in the shade. Cast up-current and to one side so the lure will sink and swing on a tight line as near to the pilings or bridge supports as possible. Fish usually lie facing up-current in the shaded water close to the supports. Since baitfish are attracted to light, a lantern should be used if the spot is not lighted.

It helps to inspect the area, particularly at low tide. You may see holes that should be productive, or submerged rocks that break the flow. Depths vary under bridges, and so do currents. Select the best looking spots.

Piers present somewhat different situations, especially when they are very long. A surf rod may be useful for longer casts or when big fish are following the shoreline. When tides are high fish may be feeding in the surf. The end of a pier may not be the best spot, and one side usually is easier to fish than the other.

A way to find hot spots is to fish down-current by walking the lure or bait. Start at one end of the bridge or pier (if other fishermen won't be disturbed) and troll the lure by walking. The line should be short enough to keep the lure near the pilings, and the lure's weight determines how deeply it is fished.

There are several methods for down-current fishing. A bait and sinker can be cast a short distance and left on bottom for the desired time. If there's no action, raise the rod tip and let out a little line so the current will take the lure farther away. This can be done several times. Baits or lures having weights appropriate to the current can be worked in it near bottom or nearer the surface. Rods usually are angled downward when being handled from a high position.

Floats, sometimes with small sinkers below them to keep the bait down, are very useful in fishing down-current. One idea is to use cork from a discarded life vest. Cut it into cubes of appropriate size. Slice each cube deeply enough to hold the line or leader so the bait will be between 3 and 6 feet (depending on water depth) from the cork. This usually pulls off when a fish is hooked. A bait with float attached can be worked down-current over a wide area. Another idea is to cast up or down current with a jig and to hop it in along the bottom.

When fishing from piers or bridges, landing the catch can be a problem. If possible, work toward shore and net, gaff or beach the fish there. Long-handled nets may be available on piers. Long-handled gaffs also can be used. A substitute is a 3-pronged grappling hook which can be lowered by a cord and jerked upward to impale the fish.

FISHING FROM BREAKWATERS

Jetties and breakwaters are barriers of very large rocks used to protect channels and harbors from erosion and waves. The former is connected to land and usually is relatively short. The latter may not be connected to land, and may be a mile or more long. The great rocks become encrusted with seaweeds, barnacles and other shellfish, and offer havens for shrimp, crabs and baitfish. Thus their nooks and crannies are protective spots and food sources for gamefish, some of which can be very large.

Some of these man-made barriers offer smooth walking, and others are so dangerous that one literally can break his neck. Use ice creepers or boot chains on the latter, and leave the family on the beach. Nothing can be more slippery than wet seaweed.

Since these barriers restrict the travels of fish, they remain close to them for food and protection, travel along them, and pass around the ends with the flow of the tides. These barriers can provide fabulous fishing at times, especially when they protect breachways, rivers and tidal creeks. Here again the smart angler inspects the place at low tide to locate big clefts in the rocks, deep holes and other hot spots. He usually fishes with the tides and, depending on conditions, may have better luck at the start of the flow or near the ebb or flow of high tide. When tidal creeks empty along a jetty the first part of the ebb may be best because more baitfish and other fish foods are washed outward then.

I usually fish the seaward side of breakwaters, looking for deep holes and places with white water. Casts can be made outward or along the barrier, but 180-degree fan-casting should decide this. Fish may be so far out that a surf stick is needed, but the 9-foot spinning rod with 12-pound-test line and lures in the 1½-ounce range can be ideal. The end of the obstruction usually is the hot spot when a good current rips by. Stripers, blues and weakfish can be taken on surface plugs in northern waters. Tarpon, snook and redfish can be hooked on similar equipment in southern waters. If this doesn't work, try metal squids such as the Hopkins, or jerk a jig near the bottom.

The insides of breakwaters and jetties lacking flowing water usually don't produce gamefish, but small sandsharks, rays and other less exciting species may be cruising there. Those who haven't dropped a bait before one of these should try it — at least once! If the bottom is sandy, cast a very small squid or jig outward and draw it in very slowly. If flounders are around, you may catch all you can carry. This also works off the beach, when the surf is quiet. The slowly retrieved lure sends up little spurts of sand with each tiny jerk, and any flattie within eyeing distance will grab it. Try a little diamond jig trailed with a small treble hook — about size 8.

SALTWATER PANFISH

When people go on seaside vacations the young ones often proposition their elders with the request, "Dad, let's go fishing." Dad may back away because he doesn't have the equipment, or doesn't know how. The first objection can be solved by investing only a few coins in a dropline or two, a few hooks in sizes between 8 and 1/0, some swivels and a few sinkers in weights between ¼ and 2 ounces. The tackle dealer will explain what's going on and where to find the action, usually from piers, breakwaters and bridges, but also perhaps from an anchored or drifting boat.

More people enjoy saltwater panfishing than any other kind available in the briny. As in fresh water, a "panfish" is small enough to be fried in a pan. Don't be surprised, however, if something much bigger tries to make off with the tackle!

While droplines furnish fun at minimum cost, the freshwater gear used on ponds and streams at home is also excellent for most saltwater panfishing purposes. Ways to rig it for baits or lures are described in this chapter.

You can find your own bait at low tide, usually shellfish with shells that can be cracked with a rock so the meat can be dug out. Push the hook through the fleshy or tougher parts, and cut the meat into smaller pieces if it is too large.

Clams and mussels provide good baits for most panfish, but tackle dealers may recommend something else for specific species. For example, small crabs are the best bait for tautog (blackfish), and in southern areas shrimps will catch almost anything. Other baits are seaworms, squid, sand eels and live baitfish or parts of dead ones. If bait runs out, cut a fish belly into strips and use it.

Leaving the bait on the bottom until something happens often tempts bait stealers. Lift it slowly every minute or two. If you feel a nibble, drop it back and wait half a minute, then repeat. A strong tug means a fish is on, and a quick, short jerk should hook him. Use small hooks and small baits for flounders and smaller panfishes. Many of them have such tiny mouths that large baits are useless.

Artificial lures may work better than baits, and they aren't as messy. Diamond jigs in small sizes are easy to use and productive. Drop the jig to the bottom, let it hang and wiggle for a few seconds, then raise it up smartly, repeating this at intervals. Raising it with a strong lift provides action and hooks the fish, if one is on. Small spoons and feathered jigs, such as those used in fresh water are useful.

RIGS FOR BOTTOM FISHING

Of the many rigs for bottom fishing, let's confine ourselves to the three basic ones shown. The first one is a basic bottom rig using a bank sinker heavy enough to just hold bottom. This is attached by a short length of monofilament to a 3-way swivel. The monofilament should be light enough to break if the sinker should become snagged. A baited hook snelled to a foot or so of monofilament is attached to the 3-way swivel for bottom fish such as flounders. Between 1 and 3 feet of monofilament connect the lower swivel

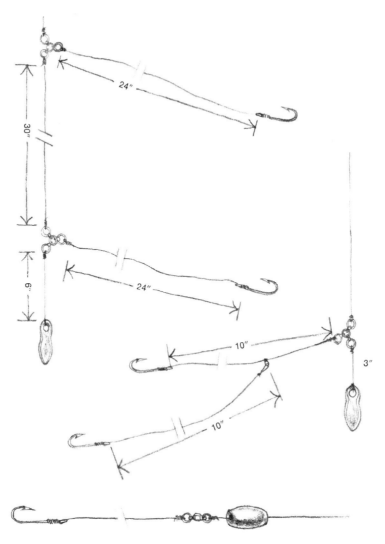

Bottom rigs for cod, fluke, flounder, pollock and other species caught from piers, breakwaters and bridges.

to the upper one, which is attached to the line. The leader of the upper hook is usually about the same length as the distance between the swivels; this part of the rig usually being intended for fish feeding off bottom.

A live baitfish can be attached to the upper hook by impaling it through the lips. Hook sizes and leader strengths vary, depending on the sizes of the fish being sought, such as 8- to 10-pound-test leaders and hooks between No. 8 and 2/0 for panfish and 15 to 20-pound-test line with hooks between No. 3/0 and 6/0 for big codfish.

Also shown is a hook-up with a lower rig only. This is for bottom feeders such as flounders. Either one or two hooks are used. The second hook is guarded against tangling with the first one by being connected midway of its leader by loops as described in Chapter 12 on knots. The drawing shows a dipsey sinker. Both of these types, being rounded, are less likely to catch between rocks than an angular one like the pyramid, which holds better than the others on a sandy bottom.

The third drawing shows a bottom rig using a sliding egg sinker, which can't slip through the swivel and so is kept away from the leader connected to the hook and bait. The idea of this rig is that a fish can take the bait without feeling the weight of the sinker because the line slides through it. Anglers lacking egg sinkers can make a similar rig by running the line through the loop of a dipsey sinker and attaching a swivel, which prevents the sinker from sliding down to the bait.

When current and tackle are light enough, other types of leading such as split shot and wrap-around sinkers can be used. However, strong currents and tides often require lead weighing about 6 ounces to keep the rig in place. All of these rigs can be cast to short distances without much trouble, but the egg sinker arrangement seems best for the purpose.

33

Eastern
Inshore Fishing

From the mid-Atlantic states northward saltwater anglers affectionately refer to their "favorite four"—the striped bass (or rockfish), the bluefish, the channel bass (or redfish) and the weakfish (or squiteague). In addition, this chapter will include notes on poor relatives which, although less exciting on the end of a line, are similarly delicious as table fare.

STRIPED BASS

"Stripers" school in a challenging variety of sizes along both coasts, in the brackish or fresh waters of rivers, and even are landlocked in a few large lakes. "Schoolies" up to 10 pounds or better are prime sport on any tackle; even the lighter gear used for trout. The "bull bass" and the "cow bass" which smash lures savagely in coastal waters require sturdier equipment because many are in the 40-, 50- and even 60-pound classes. Record stripers tip the scales at 70 pounds or better, but anything over 50 is bragging size. Even the smaller ones, sometimes so abundant that every cast brings a jolting strike, can test the mettle of expert anglers using light tackle, including fly rods with bucktail flies or poppers.

Roccus saxatilis, as scientists call this true member of the bass family, is known in its southern range as "rockfish" or "rock" because it so often frequents rocky waters. The name "striper" refers to about eight dark, longitudinal stripes running along its greenish to blackish back and silver

Joe Brooks lands his fly-rod record striped bass in Coos Bay, Oregon. The fish weighed 29 pounds, 12 ounces.

sides—these also giving it the nickname "linesides." The stripers along the northern Atlantic coast are similar in size and shape to the channel bass of the southern Atlantic, and both species are fished for quite similarly. Channel bass also are called "red drum" and "redfish."

Stripers in the Atlantic winter as far south as South Carolina, but predominantly in Chesapeake Bay. Warming spring waters cause them to migrate as far north as Maine and Nova Scotia, these migrations reversing themselves in the fall. Thus, excellent fishing is enjoyed along the New England coast in late spring; tapering off in summer, and reaching a peak in September and October. Some stripers spend the winter in tidal reaches of northern rivers, but they are semi-dormant, lying mostly in deep holes in bays.

In 1879 about 130 small stripers were transplanted from New Jersey to San Francisco Bay. This and later plantings started such a thriving fishery that vast schools of almost 2 million fish now cruise Pacific coastal waters from Los Angeles County to the Columbia River. Stripers legally are sportfish in the Pacific. It is illegal to catch them commercially, and many conservationists feel that more protection should be afforded to those in the Atlantic. In the Pacific the best spawning grounds include San Francisco Bay and the delta of the Sacramento River. The bass approach their spawning grounds between spring and early summer, the best fishing for them being from then until late fall.

Stripers migrate in schools in which all fish are of similar size. The schools of the big bulls and cows are small, perhaps including only a few fish. Expert anglers know this, and those seeking record fish ignore the schools and search for trophies elsewhere.

For example, in 1948 the late Joe Brooks, famous angler and author, and I made a fishing expedition to the Pacific, he with the goal of taking a world-record striped bass on a fly rod. Fishing in Oregon's Coos Bay in the rain, he ignored the boatman's suggestion that we should search for schools, and insisted on fishing along the rocky breakwater near the airport in spite of the fact that no bass were in evidence there. Joe's uncanny ability to "read the water" paid off by rewarding him with a 29-pound, 12-ounce trophy and the loss of another striper which appeared to be at least as big.

Tackle

Spinning, spincasting, baitcasting, trolling or fly tackle is suitable for stripers. The choice depends on whether one is fishing from shore or from a boat and whether the fish are on top or deep. The probable size of the fish and the presence of currents, rocks and weeds also affect choice of tackle.

When casting from beaches or rocks along the shore, you usually need a long and reasonably stiff rod which can send a heavy lure soaring beyond the breakers. The choice is between heavy spinning gear suitable for baits or lures in the 1½- to 2-ounce class, and a conventional star-drag revolving-spool reel with a long rod able to handle lures in this range or even larger.

When casting from boats the same tackle is suitable, although a somewhat shorter rod may be handier. One can troll near the surface with this gear or use it to go deeper by employing leads or downriggers. Boat rods with revolving-spool reels are more commonly used for trolling, with monofilament or braided line used for near-surface fishing and wire or lead-cored line for deeper fishing.

Lighter tackle is more fun when conditions make it practical, including the spinning, spincasting or baitcasting gear common to freshwater fishing. Big schools of smaller fish in the 5 to 15-pound class often are encountered in rivers, bays and estuaries. These can be taken with moderate casts using lines of between 4- and 8-pound test with lures weighing half an ounce or lighter.

Fly-fishing equipment provides peak sport when the fish are showing. Systems 8, 9 or 10 should be appropriate, the choice of these depending on the probable size of the fish and upon fishing conditions. Very light tackle may not be able to handle poppers or bucktails in the larger sizes usually needed, particularly on windy days or in currents. Weight-forward lines are customary, the choice between a floater with sinking tip and a sinking line depending on how deep the lure needs to be fished.

More specific notes on tackle will be given when various types of fishing are discussed.

Baits

Bass are finicky feeders which may boil into schools of baitfish and gorge themselves, then lie quietly while digesting their dinners, thus providing poor sport until they go back on the feed again. For various reasons they seem to do this all at the same time. During high tides they often work into shallow water to feast on seaworms, clams, crabs, small baitfish and other foods found among the rocks and in the sand and grasses.

One of the best baits is the seaworm, a long and flattish creature with so many legs that it looks fringed. It has nippers and will bite, but not badly. Seaworms can be dug, but usually are purchased from baitshops. Beginners buy too few and often run out. Old hands get them by the "flat" of ten dozen and frequently use more than a flat a day. They will stay alive if kept cool in a damp (but not wet) bed of rockweed or something similar. Seaworms probably are the most popular bait in New England, where they also are called "sandworms" or "clamworms." On the west coast they are known as "musselworms" or "pileworms." Another type, called the "bloodworm," is tougher and stays on the hook longer. It is less popular in New England than farther to the south. One or more seaworms or bloodworms are baited on a hook like freshwater ones and are drifted with currents and under floats, are cast on spinners and spoons, or are trolled behind spinners.

Another popular bait is the common sand eel, which is taken whole by big stripers even when it is over a foot long. Usual sizes for fishing are between 7 and 15 inches, the longer ones being used on hooks of size 8/0 to 10/0. For trolling, an eel is hooked barb upward through both lips. If kept wet, a baited eel stays alive for a long time, often after having been taken by several stripers. On boats they usually are kept in a pail of cool water. Since they are slippery to handle, an eel usually is rolled in a piece of cloth while being baited. Live eels should be trolled fairly slowly. They can be cast with an easy swing and need not be given bucktailing motion on the retrieve or when being trolled, although some anglers consider this more productive. Another way is to drift the boat in slow currents or with the wind around inlets and over weedy ledges. Since eels will try to swim down and hide, they should be raised up frequently.

Live baitfish, such as sardines, smelt, herring, anchovies and mackerel, make excellent bass baits when hooked through the lips, under the dorsal fin, or near the tail. Cut bait, such as parts of larger fish, do well in still-fishing or while being drifted. Other favorite baits include whole squid, or parts of them (especially in summer), shedder crabs (and other kinds), clams and shrimp. Selections from this bountiful array depend on what is available, how the bait will be fished, and what the bass are presumed to be taking at the time.

Lures

Bass can be fussy about lures, including their colors and the way they are fished. When convenient, such as on boats, anglers often have two rods rigged up, one perhaps with a surface plug and the other with a long-casting, deep-running metal squid or jig. On getting into a surfacing school one type of lure may do better than the other, and time would be wasted by changing lures on one rod. Also, a bass may boil at a lure, but not take it. A quick cast of the lure on the alternate rod may get a strike.

Popping plugs often are effective, and provide the thrill of seeing fish splash up to take them. Alternate reeling and jerking provides the surface commotion that brings lusty strikes. Swimming plugs are retrieved at a steady pace, letting the lure do the work. Darters are jerked to provide erratic action. Sometimes any plug and any action will do, but you often have to vary actions and to experiment. Bass venture into shallow water at night, and lures should be fished slower then.

Bucktail or feathered jigs often are killers when retrieved with the usual up and down jigging action. The Upperman Bucktail is a great favorite in red and white, all yellow, or all white. Another excellent distance caster for working all depths is an elongated flattish nickel or chrome squid such as the Hopkins, with a treble trailing bucktail-dressed hook. The best bet in a new location is to see what nearby tackle stores are selling the most of, because favorite styles and colors change frequently.

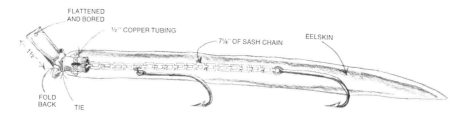

Homemade eelskin rig for big striped bass. The upturned flattened lip of copper tubing causes the lure to wriggle when being trolled or retrieved. Pull on the tail hook and trolling lip to be sure skin has no wrinkles.

A famous troller, which can be rigged with a lead head for casting, is an eelskin rig. It has many variations, some popular in one area, some in another. Many striped-bass addicts prefer to make their own, using eelskins which can be purchased in jars of brine. Whole eels can be rigged similarly by using a long needle to thread a cord, a piece of monofilament or a wire from vent to head, as shown in the accompanying diagram. Added weight usually isn't necessary. If it is needed, sever the eel's head, peel back an inch or so of skin, and remove that part of the body. Thread on a bullet-shaped sinker of the desired size, then tie the skin over it. This is called an "eel bob." These lures should be trolled or retrieved slowly and they should be checked for natural swimming appearance.

Where to Fish for Stripers

Let's presume that we are visiting a new coastal location and that no one is available to tell us where to fish for striped bass.

Owning a nautical chart is more than worth its low cost. Mark on it the sorts of places that will be discussed. Another name for the striper is the rockfish, which provides the clue to look for rocks—rocky shores where water is deep; big rocks, some of which may be submerged at high tide; the ends of jetties and breakwaters, and the ocean side along them.

Since many parts of the coast are entirely rockbound, we may have to pick the better rocky places from the poorer ones. Select those from which casts can be made near the water because it is difficult to cast and to handle fish when standing too high up. Select rocky places where water is a few feet deep at low tide. Look for white-water areas—white foam which offers concealment for fish. Look for breaks in the coastline where the tide pours into deep cuts and small coves along the shore. Look for rocks out deep where lures can be cast to their landward sides because these offer white water as well as milder currents in which fish can rest.

Stripers frequent rocky places because depth and white water provide concealment, because rocks break the flow of swift currents, and because food in the forms of baitfish and shellfish are there, too. Casts should be made very close to the rocks; stripers often lie in the crannies between them, and they may not travel very far out into the green water to hit a lure.

Underwater ledges are important hangouts for bass. Look for such places at low tide and fish them when it is running. Charts give their locations. Ledges shelving off deeply are best because big bass like deep water.

Saltwater ponds were made in years long gone when the ocean piled up sand to form a bar which eventually became a beach. These usually are connected with the sea by creeks or man-made breechways, and they are important nurseries for bait. When they flush on each ebbing tide, they empty hordes of baitfish into the sea, so bass gather near the mouths of creeks and breechways because of the food pouring from them.

When deep underwater ledges lie off the mouths of creeks or breechways, the area becomes a real hot spot in season. An excellent example is the famous Charlestown Breechway in Rhode Island. Big bass migrating north pause to feed there in late spring and early summer, and again in the fall while returning to the Chesapeake Bay area farther south. Then, during running tides, the rocks protecting the breechway entrance are covered with anglers casting into the edges of the current. They take small bass, and an occasional big one, but they can't reach the big bass lying around the ledges farther out. Small boats, trolling and drifting over the ledges, often fill their wells with bass in the 20- to 40-pound class. Using spinning tackle with 10- to 15-pound-test line, and lures in the 1½-ounce range, I often have taken a dozen or more big stripers while fishing a tide. My biggest one was 55 pounds. While these fish can be handled on 10-pound-test line there, 15 pounds is safer in case the first long run puts the fish around a rock or tangles the line in kelp.

Charts also point out deep holes, channels, tide rips where currents collide, underwater bars, drop-offs bordering bars, points jutting into a channel, bays, deltas and deep areas of estuaries; all good spots to prospect for bass.

These places in tidewaters of rivers are good, too. Bass enter rivers to spawn around April in the south and around June farther north. Bass (usually smaller ones) work into rivers with the incoming tide, grubbing in the shallow water of emerging grasses for mollusks, crabs, baitfish and other food found there. Submerged grassy areas provide great sport for wading fly fishermen, the best action usually being on an incoming tide during the night.

Surfcasters line parts of sandy beaches when the fishing is good. Newcomers notice where beach buggies collect and wander over to check on the action. There's always room for one or two more! These places, in addition to some of those already mentioned, are areas where there are deep holes and where the water shelves off sharply. Off the beaches, the pale water indicates a bar which may be dry at low tide. If the water on the inside is deep and foamy, stripers may be there. When one can wade out across the bar it may be productive to fish its outer side. Look for breaks in the bar, cuts leading to the inside water. Stripers use these like roads to reach the food-producing areas on the inside.

If one feels like walking a sandy beach he can roam it to look for the spots that have been described. Cast out over the crest of an incoming wave; first straight out; then to the right and to the left. A compact lure such as a metal squid or jig may be necessary for adequate distance. Look for dark water, which means deep water. Diving birds often point to where the action is.

When to Fish for Stripers

Bass usually are resting during high or low slack tides, and fishermen may as well do the same. The action is with a busy tide, and many of us work a busy tide regardless of what others think about it. Others may say that the first hour or two before and after a tide change is the best, meaning that mid-tides aren't as good. This may be true because more fish should be feeding then.

Calm days aren't usually very productive. A churning ocean with lots of white water is ideal. Watch the weather reports and try to hit the beach before and after a storm, and even during it. Daybreak and just before dark are favored hours when the tide is right. Bass feed mostly at night, so those who enjoy night fishing, and who have become familiar with a productive area in daylight hours, should do well. Beach buggy addicts sleep most of the day, unless something is going on. At night the running tides spur peak activity. Big bass may be cruising in the breakers and, being less afraid then, take lures and baits avidly. Some say no lights should show because lights spook bass; others maintain it doesn't make much difference. You can turn your back to the water and use a little pen-light to change lures, or a small spotlight attached by an elastic strap around your cap and connected by a wire to a battery in your pocket. Smart anglers try to get along without lights, mainly because they impair night vision.

Catching Bass from Beaches

Knowing these general guidelines about where and when bass fishing should be good, let's take our tackle, plus some food and beverages and other necessities and comforts, and spend a few hours at a selected spot. Spinning tackle has nearly supplanted conventional star-drag revolving-spool gear in many areas, but both methods are popular. This is usually heavy-duty equipment with monofilament lines of between 10- and 20-pound test on spinning reels and about 30-pound braided or 15- or 20-pound monofilament on revolving spools. While opinions vary, perhaps it can be said that monofilament casts and holds bottom better than braided line. Braids are more resistant in currents and surf.

Longer and stronger rods up to 12 feet or so may be necessary for distance casting with heavy lures in high surf. When bass are close to shore, lighter tackle is the rule, with rods about 7 feet long and lines in the 10- to 12-pound range.

Two popular rigs and a variation are shown in the drawings on page 580. To set up the standard rig, select a sinker (usually of the pyramid type because it holds bottom well) large enough to cast properly and to hold in the surf. Attach it to a 3-way swivel by a short, strong cord or metal link. Attach a hook of size 3/0 or larger to a foot or so of monofilament of the same strength as the line and attach this to the second ring. Attach the third swivel ring to the line. The hook can be baited with seaworms, cut bait or almost anything else.

Another rig is the popular fish-finder. This can be rigged with or without the glass beads and cork float. The swivel prevents the sinker from sliding too near the bait. With this rig the fish can mouth the bait and go off with it by pulling the line through the swivel-eye with minimum resistance from the sinker.

When they are used, the bait is lying on the bottom and may be stolen by flounders and other bottom feeders. If this becomes bothersome, the glass beads and cork are helpful. The cork can be of any size and shape which will support the bait, but it usually looks like a very short cigar

Standard bait rig for fishing striped bass from beaches.

Fish-finder striped-bass rig.

bored longitudinally so the line can slip through it easily. These floats often are painted in various color combinations, and double as attractors. The addition of two or three glass beads (usually red) aid in enticing fish. The cork holds the bait well off the bottom, keeping it away from bottom fish. Other little swimmers may steal the bait, however, so the only alternative is to use artificials.

The bait is cast *behind* an incoming wave. Casting in front of one would wash it toward the beach. When the incoming wave recedes the undertow takes the bait farther out.

The rod usually is set into a sand-spike and is left alone until action is noted or until the bait needs to be checked or changed. Be sure the spike is embedded solidly in the sand because otherwise a big bass could pull it over and make off with the tackle.

While any bait that can be cast may be effective if it stays on the hook, all experienced surfcasters have their preferences. Along the New England coast (where striped-bass fishing can be phenomenal in season) most anglers probably would opt for the rigged eel. This can be used with or without a front hook, and any suitably shaped metal squid or jig can replace the front hook for added casting weight and glitter.

Rigged eels should be flexible and the action given to them should be varied — slow and fast, jerky and smooth, rod held high and held low on the retrieve. The usual slow, snakelike, swimming motion of an eel changes to frantic flight when a big bass comes nearby. Numerous artificials are made to represent eels, and many of them can be cast satisfactorily, but it's pretty hard to beat the real thing!

Squid are molded from block tin or lead in boat-keel designs to ride keel down and hook upward. Some hooks are dressed with hair or feathers, usually in combinations of red, blue, yellow and/or white. They don't imitate anything in particular, but stripers evidently think their form, flash and action represents squids, sand eels or mullet. Sizes or weights for surfcasting vary between 1 and 3 ounces, depending on the strength of tackle used and how far one needs to cast with it. Being very compact, squids can be cast great distances. They ride well and can be retrieved at any depth, even in strong surf. They are especially useful on windy days.

A few plugs are a third necessity for surfcasting. In sizes appropriate to fishing conditions and tackle, they should include surface poppers and splashy swimmers (which fish both can hear and see), floating-diving varieties, and rigid or jointed deep swimmers. If one should want to buy only two of each type, a red-headed white one and a natural imitation would be good choices. I use the $1\frac{1}{2}$-ounce size and find it ideal for most conditions. Flash and action are more important than color.

Method of rigging an eel for striped bass. Attach a foot or more of strong braided line, wire or monofilament to a 5/0 to 8/0 hook. Using a long needle, inserted 3 to 5 inches from the tail, thread the line through the eel and out the mouth, firmly embedding shank of hook in the body of the eel. Insert a hook (one size smaller) upward under the eel's throat and out of top of head. Snell the connection from the tail hook to the front hook, first passing it through the hook's eye. Attach a swivel to the front hook with several small loops of fine wire bound in the middle to make a figure 8.

When bottom feeders steal the bait, surfcasters switch to plugs. Here Dick Kotis gaffs a 36-pound striper hooked on a plug off a Rhode Island beach.

Other types of lures are less essential or nonessential. They include heavy wobblers, with single or treble hooks usually dressed with feathers; Japanese feathered jigs, which are supposed to imitate squids (more useful for trolling), and several types of spinners connected to flies or baited hooks, which are not very useful in the surf.

All these usually are fastened to the tackle with a snap swivel so lures can be changed quickly, even in the dark. A fairly large snap swivel is easiest to handle, especially when hands are cold. Don't forget to keep hooks sharp and to check the line near the lure for weakness. Since constant casting can fray the terminal section a shock tippet is very useful.

Catching Bass from Boats

Let's assume that you rent a boat or take your own on a seaside vacation. You want to catch a few stripers, but have no one to guide you. Knowing the general locations and times of the tides for good fishing may be enough. The biggest boons to modern fishing are sonic depth-scanning instruments such as the Model LFP 300 Lowrance Fish Lo-K-Tor. While expensive, such a device pays for itself many times over in a lifetime of productive fishing. In water too deep to see bottom, an angler is blindfolded. He can't find deep holes, submerged reefs and channels—places where fish should be. Resident anglers know these hot spots and can locate them more or less accurately by lining up landmarks. Charts are a great help to visitors, but they surely can't show when and where fish lie down below. The Fish Lo-K-Tor removes the blindfold, instantly indicating bottom depth and even blipping the locations of fish. The nature of the blips on the dial tell how deep they are, how many there are, and even how big.

When hot spots are unproductive the alternative is trolling, usually with plugs, but often with live eels or eelskin rigs. Live eels are useless when bluefish are around because the choppers sever them behind the hook.

I'm not partial to trolling. It lacks action and challenge, although it's a pleasant way to relax after a period of activity. Trolling is the only alternative when fishing is poor; one may contact a school or find a few stray fish. Downriggers are a last resort. Those used along the New England coast usually are heavy drails with a clothespin attachment onto which the line is clipped. With the line clipped on, the drail is lowered on a cord which then is cleated to the rail.

Wading for Bass

Since the big bulls and cows found in occasional hot spots along the coast don't usually venture into rivers and estuaries, the fishing in such places normally is for school fish with spinning or spincasting tackle in the 6- to

8-pound-test line class and with lures (as have been described) weighing not over half an ounce. In big rivers, stronger tackle for longer casts with heavier lures may be necessary, but lighter gear is more fun and more usual. When fly-rodders run into schools that can be reached by wading, they can enjoy a field day.

Spinning and spincasting fishermen seek places in estuaries and rivers where they can cast from shore or wade out off points of land, to rocks, or into the current near drop-offs and bars. Stripers often lie in the edges of currents in rivers, and large, deep coves and backwaters also are productive. Fishing is best on running tides, usually on the ebbing one.

Those who prefer bait often use seaworms. I favor a 3/0 to 6/0 Eagle Claw baitholder hook rigged with two worms. This is cast out and allowed to drift, the bait being given a constant slow up and down motion. In a running tide a split shot or two may be necessary, and perhaps more as the current increases. All the artificials which have been mentioned do well in smaller sizes. A big favorite, and often the top producer, is one of Bob Pond's Atom plugs, made by the Atom Manufacturing Company in South Attleboro, Massachusetts.

Fly-rodders usually use System 8 or 9 rods, with plenty of backing on the reel. Floating lines with sinking tips are favored. Sinking ones may be more productive in the deeper spots. The big New England favorite in flies is the famous Gibbs Striper. The original pattern calls for a body of flat silver tinsel, but I prefer silver mylar piping. The throat is a small bunch of red hackle fibers, rather long. The wing is a bunch of capra (Asiatic goat) hair with some of the underfur left in. (White bucktail or polar bear may be substituted.) The shoulders are sections of dark blue Nazurias (swan wing feather) one-half as long as the wing. This should be tied in so it will lie midway of the wing, to make a stripe down the middle of it. The cheeks each are a short barred teal body feather, one-third as long as the shoulder. (Balli duck or guinea hen breast feathers may be substituted.) Lacquer the head black and decorate it with tiny yellow painted eyes with red pupils.

The (Imperial) Supervisor is an excellent back-up pattern, if one is needed. Color schemes such as those listed in Chapter 25 for coho salmon also do well. Shrimp imitators are used on occasion.

When stripers are on top, or can be coaxed there, little popping plugs are at least as productive as flies. These have round cork or balsa wood bodies about 3/4 inch in diameter and about an inch long, tapered toward the tail. The fairly long tail is dressed with bucktail or about half a dozen hackles. The face of the plug is flat or slightly concave, or angled a bit inward toward the humpback hook, which sets into a slit along the bottom. These little plugs are painted white and other colors, with large eyes and

When schools of bass are in rivers, wading fly-rodders can have a field day. Both streamers and popping plugs produce strikes.

pupils. All-white ones seem to do best except in creamy water. While the flies which have been mentioned are excellent producers, we shouldn't ignore the little poppers, which fish can hear as well as see. Drop one in a good spot; let it float a few seconds; give it a little gurgling "pop" and watch a bass come up and smash it! This doesn't apply only to saltwater stripers. The freshwater basses like them, too.

Stripers in Lakes

Stripers have been transplanted very successfully into inland lakes, and are thriving in many of them, sometimes growing to very respectable sizes of 30 pounds or so. In these lakes largemouth bass fishermen sometimes catch stripers, and vice versa, but this isn't common because the stripers usually are in or over deeper water than the largemouths prefer.

When lakes containing landlocked stripers have fairly large rivers flowing into them, as most do, schools of fish gradually will migrate up the rivers for spawning, which may start in spring or later, depending on latitude and water temperatures. Thus, knowing regional migratory habits is a key to finding the fish.

Since stripers otherwise are usually in deep water, the trolling is deep, using the tackle and tactics which have been described for lake trout. Deep-running plugs are productive, such as Mirro-lures and Countdown Rapalas, or other lures as used for bass.

Stripers must be located in lakes because the schools are constantly migrating in search of food. If baitfish migrations are known, this provides a key. Keep an eye out for surface feeding, because stripers frequently drive schools of bait to the top, churning the surface to a froth in a frenzy of feeding. Then, top-water baitlike lures are very good.

BLUEFISH

Admirers of bluefish say that, pound for pound, no scrappier adversary can be handled on any tackle of appropriate strength. This includes all the gear recommended for striped bass, ranging from stiff squidding sticks in the surf to fly rods and reasonable light spinning outfits in other places. Because bluefish are cannibalistic, they seek safety in schools of fish of the same size ranging from "snapper blues" less than a foot long to "choppers" pushing 20 pounds, or even larger. The appellation of choppers refers to their sharp doglike teeth, which make short work of smaller fish and which can bite into almost anything except solid metal. After viewing this formidable dental work one need not be warned to keep fingers away. The carnage bluefish can inflict on schools of bait is awesome. After consuming all they can hold they often regurgitate and start again. This spots schools of deep feeding bluefish because the oily remnants of bait and the plankton they have consumed form revealing slicks on the surface accompanied by a distinct odor variously described as cucumbers, watermelon or geraniums. The leaping, bulldogging, tailwalking fight hooked bluefish provide well earns their membership in the north Atlantic sportsmen's "favorite four."

Like weakfish and some other species, the abundance of bluefish (for no known reason) is cyclic and is reaching a maximum as this is being written in 1972. The current all-tackle record is a 31-pound, 12-ounce whopper caught off North Carolina in 1972. Anything over 15 pounds is bragging size.

Seasonal migrations of bluefish up and down the Atlantic coast are predictable. They provide good fishing in southern Florida from December to early April. Peak runs reach Georgia and the Carolinas in March and April; Virginia and Delaware in late April; and the New Jersey and New York region between late April and into May. Here, some schools become temporary residents, remaining into September. New England finds bluefish most abundant between June and October, their northerly migration rarely extending beyond the tip of Cape Cod. October gales start them southward (and eastward) again in a reverse migration which finds them along Florida's coast in early winter. Other schools range widely around the world.

Here is a tip on catching bluefish. Early schools appearing in an area probably have not spawned; are bottom feeders, and hard to catch. Use jigs fished off bottom or baits fished deep. Dead bait, such as cut bait, needs action to get action. If currents don't provide it, keep the rod-tip working. After spawning, bluefish become ravenous, striking at almost anything that moves. Best fishing is toward the end of their migrational sojourns.

How to Locate Bluefish

We have noted that deep-feeding fish slashing into schools of bait produce an oily slick on the surface accompanied by a distinct odor. When the fish are near the surface, schools often can be spotted by showers of leaping bait. Bird action often is indicative, but the birds usually will be taking bait in the air because of the instinctive danger of losing legs, heads and wings when diving. While schools of big fish prefer deep water, vast ones of 10 pounds or so often chase bait into bays where they can be caught with fly rods or other light tackle. The author has seen coves of bays in Rhode Island so slashed into flurries of white water by vast schools of herding bluefish that driven bait has been forced onto shore. One can wade amid this excitement and hook big blues between himself and land on almost every cast!

Tide rips and combatting currents can be hotspots. Bait often is helpless in such places, and bluefish should be feeding in the rips or just down-current of them. Anglers on shore or concentrations of boats usually indicate hot spots.

When fish aren't showing they may be deep in areas like those just noted. We may have to vary fishing depth to find them, using one or more of the following methods.

When bluefish aren't showing, as often is the case upon their migratory arrival in a region, let's assume they are bottom feeding and work baits or lures off bottom. A good way to do this is by jigging from a drifting boat.

The rod should have a stiff tip to work the jig actively. It can be a spinning, plug, or boat rod. The jig must be heavy enough to drop to bottom quickly. While it should be dropped rather than cast, an up-current cast may help to get it down in a strong flow. The trick of knowing when it hits bottom is learned by practice, and perhaps is merely indicated by a slowing down of line leaving the reel spool. Jerk the jig up and let it drop again, meanwhile regaining a few turns of line on the spool. Keep repeating until the lure can be seen; then drop it down; doing this again and again. Blue-fish may be concentrated near bottom or at a level farther up. A strike at any level, of course, indicates the proper depth to be fished.

Jigs may be less than an ounce in weight or may need to be as heavy as 4 ounces in order to hit bottom quickly. White ones, usually with mylar added, are very popular. All yellow or red and white are also good. Among the fast sinkers is the Upperman Bucktail, which has a roundish head flattened vertically. This type is very active in currents. Diamond jigs in plain silver finish are good alternatives.

Surf fishing for bluefish is top action. Light tackle can be used in some places. Squids, usually between $2\frac{1}{2}$ and $3\frac{1}{2}$ ounces, are very popular because they are excellent long-distance casters which are not harmed by sharp teeth. Plugs, including surface poppers, are used extensively by anglers who don't mind having them scratched. Experts often substitute very strong single hooks for trebles on the presumption that they hook and hold better. Live eels will be severed, nearly always without hooking the fish. Eelskin rigs don't last very long. Short wire traces or heavy monofilament tippets are necessary for bluefish.

When bluefish can be reached with fly tackle the excitement of the method transcends all others. Saltwater fly rodding began with a small cult of experts who have turned it into such a practical way of enjoying fishing that their numbers have expanded widely. A 9-foot fiberglass rod is ideal, rigged with a weight-forward (such as a saltwater taper) line on a quality reel with at least 150 yards of backing. Simple leaders are customary, such as 4 or 5 feet of 20- or 25-pound monofilament with a tippet of a foot of 45- or 50-pound mono. This is usually strong enough so the fish can't bite through it, and it's preferred to a wire trace.

Flies for average-size bluefish usually are on 2/0 or 3/0 hooks in buck-tail patterns roughly simulating baitfish in size and color, although hungry choppers rarely are fussy when flies are stripped in fairly fast. Some anglers like extra-long bright forged steel hooks with only a simple wing tied on near the bend on the theory that blues will bite on the shank instead of the leader. This isn't always the case but the idea helps. Keep all practical power on the fish, never allowing any slack. The usual custom of "bowing to the fish" on a jump is often ignored in favor of a strong pull to throw the fish off balance.

Bluefishing from boats provides better opportunities for exploring the depths by jigging or drifting baits when fish aren't showing, and for reaching schools by trolling or casting when they are on top. When schools are just out of reach from shore, boats often will be taking bluefish on every cast while the boys on the beach stand there, helplessly drooling!

Dead baitfish can be cast and retrieved or allowed to drift and tumble in currents. A good rig consists of running a short-shank hook through the mouth and out of one side of the gills, then impaling it back of the gills so very little of the shank shows. This, or cut bait, can be used in a chum line — a practical method of attracting bluefish to a boat and keeping them there. Let the fish run on slack line before striking so it will have time to swallow the bait. Artificial lures usually are more practical and more fun.

Trolling plugs, spoons or feathers often locate small schools or strays when casting isn't practical. "Feathers" are so-called Japanese jigs or bucktails (sometimes large) made of hair, feathers, nylon "whiskers," and so on, often embellished with mylar. These should be fished actively and may need lead for experimenting at various depths. Five boat-lengths is the usual trolling distance. Speed is moderately fast — between 5 and 6 knots. (A knot is one nautical mile per hour.) Due to the difficulty of estimating speed in currents, a speed indicator is almost a necessity.

Good fishermen avoid running boats into (or too close to) schools because this usually puts the fish down. The trick is to skirt a school, casting into the edge of it, or getting ahead of the school and drifting into it.

Anglers who can't arrange private transportation can enjoy a good day's fishing aboard a party or head boat. People going on such excursions represent all walks of life but they comprise sort of a fraternity famous for friendship and cooperation. Tackle can be rented at low cost and the crew explains procedures to newcomers. Good skippers want their customers to have fun and to catch fish, so usually only enough fishermen are taken aboard to line one rail. You are given a fish bag and can stake claim to a selected spot by tying it to the rail and putting your rod beside it. Some like to fish off or near the fantail while others think a spot near the chum buckets is better. Avoid taking light tackle because the idea is to bring fish in fast, thus helping to prevent tangled lines and giving the skipper enough fish to brag about when he returns to port. Even sturdy spinning gear usually is frowned upon.

A short-butt stiff-tip boat rod should be suitable, with a line strong enough to hoist big fish over the rail. Don't mind being a greenhorn on the first trip because from then on you'll know the ropes and be a member of a vast fraternity of addicts who enjoy happy days afloat and full freezers ashore!

CHANNEL BASS (RED DRUM, OR REDFISH)

What the striped bass is to saltwater anglers from Chesapeake Bay northward, the channel bass is to those from there southward. A valiant fighter, the channel bass tests the skill of fishermen and their tackle. The lairs of the big ones are the sloughs and surfs along the barrier islands from Virginia through the Carolinas, but smaller ones provide peak sport all around Florida and along the Gulf states southward to Panama. Let's discuss the two types separately because they vary in size, the tackle most suitable, and, to an extent, in the kinds of waters where channel bass are found.

Channel bass are known by many names, including red bass, drum and spottail, the last because they most easily can be identified by a round black spot on each side of the base of the tail (some have more than one). Shaped very much like a striped bass, the drum is a member of the croaker family which has a reddish copper-colored back shading to silvery-white along the lower sides and belly. It is not a true bass, and sometimes makes an audible croaking or drumming sound when feeding or when alarmed. The all-tackle record is an 83-pounder which was boated off Cape Charles in 1949. Those taken in the surf usually range between 20 and 50 pounds.

Redfish (a favorite name for channel bass in southern regions) primarily are bottom feeders and usually can be caught most easily with bait, although members of roaming schools often can be taken with artificials such as deep-running plugs, metal squids, spoons and jigs. Tackle for surf fishing is essentially the same as I recommended for striped bass, and angling methods are very much the same. While bait fishermen use terminal tackle with a 3-way swivel connected to line, bait, and a sinker, the most popular method is the fish-finder rig used for striped bass. Mullet is a favorite bait, either frozen, iced or salted; scaled and used whole if small, or cut into chunks if larger. It stays on the hook better than other baitfish, such as menhaden or mossbunker. Other popular baits are crustaceans, including peeler, shedder, or blue crabs (with top shell removed and the rest tied to the hook). Mollusks, bloodworms and squid are taken readily, and shrimps are a perennial favorite in Florida and Gulf waters. Hook sizes range between 5/0 and 9/0, with 7/0 a good average.

The Atlantic sides of the dozen or more barrier islands off Virginia and the Carolinas, such as Assateague and Chincoteague are hotspots for surf fishing in season but the lengths and remoteness of their shorelines require knowledge of where to fish. It pays to hire a guide who knows the best locations. These are usually sloughs—deep water along the shore protected by a sand barrier farther out. They have channels of access for fish, and these channels are preferred places on incoming tides or perhaps the first half of outgoing ones. Best times are between dusk and daybreak, especially after a storm when the water clears up.

In fishing bait we should remember that channel bass are cautious and that strikes should be delayed until the fish starts away with bait. Artificials should be fished slowly, and striking too soon will only serve to take the lure away from the fish. Jigs should be fished erratically, as most strikes happen as the lures are fluttering down. Baiting jigs with a strip often helps.

Surf fishing for channel bass (as with stripers) can be either a feast or a famine, but knowing where and when to try it improves the score. Big fish may move in in such great numbers that acres of water are colored by them into shades of bronzy pink. The fish are strong fighters which must be allowed to make their runs under drags not strong enough to cause pull-outs. Shock leaders usually are used with conventional tackle as well as with spinning gear. Nylon-covered braided wire traces are helpful when sharks are around.

Anglers fishing for redfish often catch black drum, which also are bottom feeders weighing up to 40 pounds or more. This is a deep-bodied hump-backed grayish fish with barbels under the chin and without the spotted tail which identifies the redfish. It may come bigger but isn't regarded as a good fighter.

Coastal redfish are more or less migratory but much less so than stripers and bluefish. There are spring runs along areas which have been mentioned, as well as fall runs which extend into winter. Presumably the schools disappear into deep water in summer and late winter.

Boat Fishing for Redfish

Private and charter boats provide an easier but perhaps less sporty method for catching redfish — the main advantage is that the anglers can hunt for schools. Since tackle and methods are similar to those for striped bass, most of the details need not be repeated. A popular method is to troll large spoons very slowly on long lines of 200 feet or more, fishing bays around high tide, along beaches on ebb tide and inlets during tide changes. This is blind fishing until a school is sighted.

Schools are located by noting contrasting color in the water; such as an area of bronzy pink. Since running a boat through a school will put it down, the idea is to troll beside it or just ahead of it. At this point casting tackle should be rigged and ready because metal squids, jigs or deep-running plugs dropped into the edge of the school are sure to bring all the action even the most greedy angler should expect. Big redfish often are released not only for conservation reasons but also because their flesh is coarse and much less palatable than that of "puppy drum," as the smaller ones are called.

Florida and Gulf Coast Redfishing

In bays, estuaries and sounds, especially on the grassy flats so abundant amid the myriad mangrove islands dotting Florida's coasts, the redfish are smaller, but no less challenging when taken on light spinning or on fly-fishing equipment. These small ones ("puppy drum") provide exciting sport and are excellent to eat. Big ones will go 15 pounds, but average weight is much less.

As in fishing for bonefish (to be discussed in the next chapter) a favorite method is to reach the flats by an outboard boat towing a skiff. The boat is anchored and anglers use the skiff to pole themselves over the flats on the rising tide. Experienced eyes, usually aided by polarized glasses, spot swirls or the wakes made by the fish as they work through shallow water searching for oysters, crabs, shrimp or small baitfish. Puppy drum may be selective at times, but usually they will eat most anything, including hard-shelled tidbits which they can crush.

Fishing is done by stalking—quietly poling the skiff until it is within casting range of one or more feeding fish. The idea is to cast slightly ahead of the fish, but close to it because drum are near-sighted. If the lure is an artificial it should be worked slowly because drum are bottom-feeders and take their time with their meals. If the lure is bait, such as a crab or shrimp, the fish will scent it and pick it up. Sometimes the fish can be brought to boat rather easily but an exciting run should be expected as soon as it realizes it is in trouble. Even small drum gain great respect from anglers because of their determined head-shaking fights.

I have found drum working up through small channels in grasses where the skiff could be poled only with difficulty. Oyster bars in shallow water are favorite feeding places, as are mangrove patches in bays and along creeks where casts must be accurate to avoid being caught in the branches. Go where the food supply is, and drum should be coming to it on the rising tide. While some times of year may be better than others, puppy drum inhabit Florida waters all year.

Spinning or plug-casting tackle suitable for freshwater bass is ideal for puppy drum. Favorite lures are feather, nylon or bucktail jigs or spoons in the ¼-ounce range, or surface plugs such as poppers. Color can make the difference between success and failure because drum are often selective. Red and white, red and yellow, all blue, or blue and white are good combinations.

Where conditions make it practical, peak sport is with the fly rod, using lures that simulate shrimp or feather or bucktail flies in the above colors, particularly those of the "blonde" design with a wing over the barb of the hook and another behind the eye. Fly rod poppers are also great favorites.

These tactics are used along the Gulf. I have fished near Pass Christian, Mississippi, with Billy Burkenroad and Lysle Aschaffenburg; the latter is the owner of the famous Pontchartrain Hotel in New Orleans. In this region low islands protect Mississippi Sound, a very shallow body of water which eventually extends into the Gulf. In an area within 10 or 12 miles

Salt Water

Out on the blue water, tossing gently in a sleek skiff, sport fishermen search the sea for her many prizes . . . a silver-blue permit, famed for the smashing strike and the stubborn fight, comes aboard tail-first and is released . . . a barracuda bares his fangs to the gaff.

Photos by Robert Stearns and Mark Sosin

Sentinels in the foaming surf, fishermen cast for the red-hued channel bass along the eastern coastline.

Photos by David Dale Dickey

The bonefisherman, stalker on the flats, sights the tailing quarry and casts his fly . . . reaches skyward as the fish's sizzling run rips line . . . then plays him in and gratefully returns him to the sea.

Photos by Robert Stearns

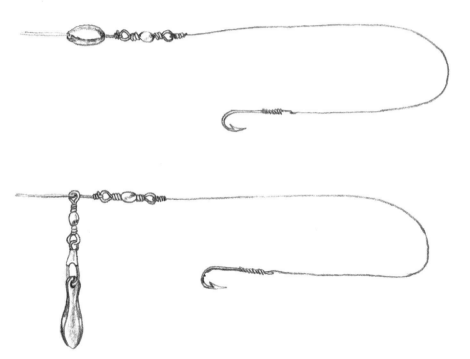

Two sliding sinker rigs. The upper one uses a sliding egg sinker. The lower one uses a snap swivel and a bank sinker.

of shore, reefs have built up in water 4 or 5 feet deep. While artificials are used there early in the season, live bait-fishing seems more productive after the end of May. Terminal tackle, usually used with spinning equipment, is a 6/0 or 7/0 hook attached to 12 to 15 inches of monofilament in the 30-pound range which is attached to a swivel. Above the swivel, which is attached to the line, is a ¼-ounce sliding egg sinker. Bait is usually a live croaker between 4 and 6 inches long. This rig is cast out and allowed to sit until something happens, which usually doesn't take long. Redfishing is best in the fall, beginning in September. "Trout" (spotted weakfish) and other gamefish also take bait. So do undesirable species such as catfish, sting rays and small sharks. Redfishing is good all along the Gulf Coast and is a favorite pastime in Texas channels and from beaches.

WEAKFISH

Last but perhaps no longer least of the North Atlantic anglers' favorite four is the gray or common weakfish which New Englanders also call "squiteague" or "squit." It should not be confused with its southern cousin, the spotted weakfish.

The northern weakfish is a member of the croaker family, troutlike in appearance and action—a gorgeous symphony of blending shades combining olive, green and blue on its back, blue, green, lavender, purple, copper and gold on its sides; a snowwhite belly, and fins tinged with yellow. Almost a vanishing species a few years ago, the schools now are staging a prolific comeback as this is being written.

The range of weakfish extends from Cape Cod to Florida's eastern coast, with major concentrations between Chesapeake Bay north to Long Island and Narragansett Bay. The fish usually run between 1 and 3 pounds but bigger ones of over 5 pounds (called "tiderunners") sometimes are encountered. The all-tackle record is a whopper of 19½ pounds caught off Trinidad, in the West Indies, in 1962. Weakfish are so named because they have soft mouths, and therefore should be handled with care. They are school fish which are migratory, seeking optimum water temperatures. They range in the Chesapeake Bay area between April and late fall and between May or June and early fall in waters farther north.

Weakfish are opportunists which adapt themselves to easiest obtainable food supplies of whatever is available, including seaworms, crabs, shrimp, squid, mollusks, and small fish. For this reason they may be feeding at various levels ranging from the bottom to the surface. The trick is to experiment with different depths and to concentrate on the one where a fish has been caught.

We quite often find weakfish over sandy flats where they are bottom-feeding, or in grassy areas where they probably are searching for shrimp. Small grass shrimp are a favorite food, 2 or 3 providing a good bait on a 1/0 to No. 4 hook. Sometimes they school near docks, piers and breakwaters. On one occasion I took all I could carry by casting a ¼-ounce bucktail jig into a sandy hole near the end of a breakwater in the vicinity of Barnegat Inlet. They also range the surf, sounds, inlets, channels, tide-rips, sloughs, creeks, shelving beaches and bays. When scaled and cleaned promptly, they provide delicious eating.

Trolling offers a good way to locate weakfish when they are near the surface or at intermediate depths. A spinner with a hook baited with seaworms is popular, but bucktails, spoons and small deep-running plugs are often used. When near-surface trolling doesn't pay off, try adding lead above the leader to fish increasingly deeper layers until action starts. Sandworms, bloodworms, strips of squid and small strip-baits are also used.

When in a known weakfishing area or when action is encountered we can fish on the bottom from an anchored boat or can try intermediate areas with the tide. If fishing near the surface use a baited 1/0 to No. 4 hook and let the bait drift naturally. When there is considerable current a sinker may be needed to keep the bait down. With little or no current a plastic ball or cork float is handy to hold the bait up. The float should be only large enough to do this.

Chumming is a very popular method from an anchored boat. All sorts of chum can be used, but grass shrimp are particularly effective. Mix about 3 quarts with an equal amount of sawdust to keep them alive and toss out a few handfuls at first; then cut down to a handful every few minutes. The hook can be baited with 2 or 3 grass shrimp or with seaworms. Let the bait drift naturally down the chum line; then reel it in and repeat. Strikes may be savage, but they are often light. In the latter case give the fish time to swallow the bait because a quick strike can take it away from him or cause the hook to pull out.

The bottom rigs which we have mentioned for surf fishing can also be used from a boat. Another very effective method is to cast out a bucktail jig in size not over 2/0 and to work it in near the bottom or at intermediate depths. Baiting it with seaworms, pork rind or strips of squid, or strip-bait often helps. These methods also are useful when fishing from piers or bridges in a tideway.

Driftfishing is an excellent method when fish can't be spotted. Use baits or jigs as above, or cast small metal squids or mackerel jigs. These often are baited. Bottom rigs also are effective for drift-fishing.

Incidentally, schools of weakfish don't usually make the surface commotion common to species such as stripers and bluefish, with the attendant bird action and all that. The fish may swirl or dimple the surface much like trout do, so one has to know what to look for.

Weakfish habitually feed on moving tides, and surf fishing can be good then, either by using bait on the bottom or by casting artificials near the surface or at intermediate depths. Specialize on the sloughs and shelving beaches unless there's reason to the contrary.

Surf fishing on the bottom is identical with the methods used for striped bass, and the two species occasionally are caught at the same time. Use a fish-finder rig, perhaps including a cork or wood float between hook and swivel to keep the bait off bottom. An alternative is the familiar 3-way swivel arrangement with one ring attached to the line, one to a pyramid sinker, and the other to a baited hook on between 1 and 2 feet of leader. The leader should be wire if sharks and bluefish are around.

Surf fishing off the bottom calls for artificial lures which must be smaller than for striped bass because, while stripers in the surf can run from 25 pounds up, weakfish usually scale in at under 5 pounds. Think in terms of 2 ounces or less, and the less the better. Tackle, therefore, is lighter, so it may not be practical in strong surf. If you're a revolving-spool addict, try the lightest conventional surfing equipment or whatever you use for fresh-water bass. Weakfish will make several long runs but more than moderate tension only will cause them to break off. Think in terms of trout! Six- or 8-pound test equipment should be strong enough.

When weakfish are finicky feeders they may not take plugs, but wigglers or splutterers on the surface or active deep-runners at intermediate depths often pay off. Metal squids or fish-shaped spoons (often baited) can be effective. Here, again, bucktail jigs are consistently the best producers, often with a small strip bait attached. Bounce them along the bottom or fish them higher. Favorite colors in all these lures which are not of shiny metal are combinations of yellow, red, blue and white.

Fly fishermen will think this reference to their favorite method should have been given premier billing in this chapter, and perhaps it should have been, although conditions rarely make it practical. When it is practical the troutlike appearance, size and behavior of weakfish recommend it highly as the sportiest way to take these relatively smaller but extremely active fish. It can be practical when schools are swirling and dimpling near the surface where they can be reached by wading or from such spots as points of land and breakwaters. Try it when the fish approach the boat while following a chum line. Try it blind or when schools can be spotted in small channels, sloughs and saltwater creeks.

Systems 6 or 7 outfits as used for trout usually are ideal, with leaders tapering to about 6 pounds, or a bit more if grasses and other obstructions make it necessary. Flies are bucktails, in about No. 2, which imitate shrimp or baitfish in size and coloration. Many of us prefer the "blonde" type in combinations as above. Bass bugs and other surface wigglers and poppers also contribute to results.

Finally, let's bear in mind that weakfish have the reputation of being shy and spooky. Avoid noise in boats and wade stealthily. Lower the anchor instead of dropping it, and net your fish.

Although the sportier northeastern inshore species command greatest interest among anglers, a few others also valuable for fun and food are worthy of note. Since catching them usually is less complicated, methods can be described more briefly.

ATLANTIC COD

The cod is a cold-water fish most numerous south of Long Island Sound between winter and late spring and north of there into the Maritimes throughout summer. Striped-bass fishermen, including myself, have hooked cod when a metal squid or jig scrapes bottom. Cod are bottom feeders which devour everything they think is edible. Due to their size, the weight of leads used, and the fact that two may be hooked at one time, heavy tackle is customary. This, in party boat and private boat fishing, often means conventional gear with lines and leaders testing 30 pounds or more. During a cod run, smaller fish of 10 pounds or so often are caught from surf, piers and jetties on conventional gear and sturdy spinning tackle.

Out deep, cod most frequently are found around ledges and wrecks. Inshore they cruise where the food is, which usually means a rocky or pebbly bottom inhabited by crabs and various kinds of shellfish. Here, even in shallow water, they can be taken by trolling baited spinners, deep-running spoons, metal squids and even bucktail flies.

A bait method, from an anchored or drifting boat, is to fasten a foot or two of strong monofilament to a bank sinker weighing enough to hold bottom, usually 4 ounces or more. A 3-way swivel is attached to this and to the upper part of the leader. A 5/0 to 8/0 hook on a foot or more of dropper is attached to the swivel's third ring. Optionally, a second dropper and hook can be tied in in the same manner high enough above the lower one so the hooks can't tangle. Hooks are baited with the necks of large clams, strips of fresh or frozen squid, conch, crabs, or most anything else. This rig is lowered to the bottom and, whether drifting or not, it is well to raise it periodically to give the bait action and because a codfish may have taken it without being felt. Strikes may be hard, or a series of light tugs. In the latter case wait until the fish moves off before striking.

An artificial-lure method is to use a heavy diamond jig with hook size usually between 5/0 and 8/0 tied to the line by 2 feet or so of strong swiveled leader. This is lowered to the bottom and raised fast by alternate reeling and jigging; then dropped back so the action can be repeated. Presumably this simulates the action of a herring or similar baitfish, and the method often is more successful than using bait. Cod usually are landed with a gaff. Pollock are often caught when one is fishing for cod.

FLOUNDER

Scores of flatfish come under this heading, including large halibut, many kinds of sole, winter and summer flounders, and other varieties ranging on both coasts, all of which are bottom fish and are caught similarly. Those of angling value enter shallow water during the warmer months, usually preferring sandy or sand-mud bottoms in bays, coves and the mouths of rivers and streams. They bury themselves lightly in sand with only their eyes showing. Their adaptive coloring making them nearly invisible.

When wading knee-deep, if one allows for the refraction of light into water, they can be taken with multiple barbed spears; lifted up by sliding a hand under them so they won't drop off, and deposited in a burlap bag slung by a loop of rope over the shoulder.

Despite their camouflage they are spotted by a faint lozenge-like outline in the sand. From such hiding places they instantly flap out to grab any food within sight. Bathers who buy fillets of sole at the corner grocery rarely realize they may almost have been stepping on them!

Although I haven't seen it done elsewhere, I have caught flounders in mild surf and in sandy coves on rising tides by casting out a small spoon and very slowly jerking it in over the sand. This mild action and the little spurts of sand it sends up cause flounders to pounce upon it and invariably become caught on the small treble hook. One can do this from a slowly drifting boat or even from bridges, piers, breakwaters and docks with small diamond jigs, lead-head jigs, small metal squids, or live or dead bait including crabs, shrimp, seaworms, and cut bait.

Fluke or flounders often strike hard but they may only mouth the bait, signalling this by light taps. In the latter case wait for a firm tug before striking lightly.

The accompanying drawing shows a spreader rig that, while less sporty, often results`in doubles. It can be purchased or made from coat-hanger wire. Spreader ends extend about 6 inches from the middle and are attached to swivels with about a foot of leader and a hook. Fluorescent red beads are optional but they add attraction, and the sinker can also be painted red or white. Lower the rig to the bottom and raise it periodically. Fish-finder and 3-way swivel rigs also are popular in the surf.

The giants of the fluke and flounder clan are the halibut. They often weigh over 40 pounds in inshore waters and perhaps much more out deeper.

Spreader rig for fluke and flounder.

Anglers on the West Coast consider them a gamefish and insist that they are underrated. Vast schools move into California's bays as the water warms up; usually between early June and October, preceding the arrival of king and silver salmon. Since they seek sweet or brackish water they are found near the mouths of streams as well as on the flats, usually in water less than 6 feet deep. In shallow water they often boil and jump while feeding on bait.

The old method (still used) was to drift with the tide and to drag a chunk of dead bait or a flashy jig on the bottom. Anglers later found that live bait was more productive, and this now is the accepted method.

They also found that halibut are cannibalistic aggressive gamefish that are very fond of multiple colored bucktails and streamers. Thus started a cult of California halibut fly-fishermen who cast for them using floating lines or floating lines with sinking tips; leaders between 9 and 12 feet long, and weighted flies. Catching one of these giant flapjacks in the 30- to 40-pound range on a fly rod with a fly is something any angler would like to see!

MACKEREL

The warming water of summer brings vast schools of mackerel close to beaches and into harbors where they easily are caught on light tackle with almost any sort of small baits or lures. Inshore visitors are of several species; the minor differences between them being of scant interest to most anglers, many of whom are vacationists cruising about in outboard boats in search of fun and a few tasty fillets for the broiler. Mackerel are their kind of fish; active little fighters which usually weigh about a pound (often less) and which can furnish excitement for the whole family when the boat drifts over a school.

Inquiries at bait shops provide information on whether mackerel are nearby and approximately where the schools are cruising. Owners of spinning or bait-casting equipment need little terminal tackle to load their coolers; even hand lines being useful in a pinch.

When schools are inshore, finding them isn't very difficult. Other boats usually are fishing over them and diving sea birds often mark their locations. Lacking these locators, look for oily slicks caused by the feeding fish. Professionals use electronic equipment to pinpoint schools and to tell how deep they are, and many amateurs now own these invaluable magic boxes. Schools often are so large and numerous that drifting boats or casters from shore can be successful when fishing blind.

Although seaworms, squid, or other cut bait catch mackerel readily, they take artificials so voraciously that we don't need to bother with bait. Any small lure will bring fast strikes especially if it is bright. Since schools

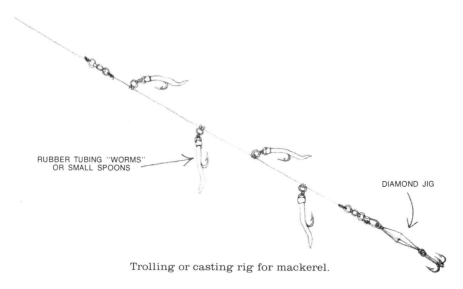

RUBBER TUBING "WORMS"
OR SMALL SPOONS

DIAMOND JIG

Trolling or casting rig for mackerel.

may be near the surface and perhaps visible, or may be deeper down, probing for the correct depth with metal squids or jigs may be necessary. Those
who want multiple action will find the following rig useful. Attach a diamond jig or something similar to the end of a leader 3 to 5 feet long, or so,
testing about 15 or 20 pounds. (This may need to be fairly heavy when a tide
is running.) Above this, at intervals of about 6 to 8 inches tie in one or more
small, light spoons on very short leaders.

A good alternative is the plastic or rubber tubing "worm" which can be
purchased at tackle shops. This is merely a section of tubing about 2 inches
long, the rear half of which is cut on a slant to form a tail. The hook shank
is slipped through this. The rig can be lowered to various depths and can be
jigged, or it can be cast or trolled. It works best when fished actively and one
often brings in a mackerel on every hook. Here again, we should avoid running a boat into the school. Cast into it from the side or get ahead of it and
drift into it.

An effective jig can be made by clamping a clinch-on sinker to a long-
shank hook and wrapping it with aluminum foil.

Take along a light fly rod and use any small streamer or bucktail. When
mackerel are near the surface this can provide the best sport of all!

POLLOCK

The pollock (often sold as "Boston bluefish") is a member of the cod
family which usually doesn't run as large but which is sportier and prettier.
Its olive or brownish-green back shades to yellow on its sides and silver-
white underneath. Offshore, where it is found around wrecks, it reaches a

maximum of about 35 pounds. Inshore, pollock usually weigh not over half that. Pollock range in schools along the Atlantic coast north of Chesapeake Bay and have similar habits to cod except that they are found at all levels, often coming into shallows and the surf on high tides, particularly between dusk and daybreak. They take the same baits as cod do, as well as jigs, metal squids, spoons, feathered lures and artificial flies. As in mackerel fishing, we may have to probe the depths to locate the level where they are feeding.

I remember several action-filled days when schools of pollock splashed in a small cove formed by a breakwater in Rhode Island. We caught several in the 10-pound range with an unusual rig. Round the ends of a section of broomstick about 4 inches long and put a screw eye in each end. Tie this to the line and to about 20 inches of monofilament. Tie a 2/0 to 6/0 lead-head bucktail jig to the monofilament; the size being appropriate to that of the fish. Cast this out with spinning or plug-casting tackle and work the wooden float like a popping plug. The result is that the float causes an at-tracting surface commotion and works the jig actively a foot or more deep. These floats usually are not painted and sometimes are egg or top-shaped.

Another good pollock rig consists of tying a 3-way swivel to the end of the line and tying a diamond jig on about 20 inches of leader to the swivel. Also tie a bucktail fly on about 6 inches of leader to the third ring of the swivel. This rig can be cast and retrieved fast, but it usually is used for jig-ging at various depths. Pollock may hit either or both lures.

When casting into a school of pollock, jigs of diamond-type are very effective. They should be retrieved fast but erratically. This is done by reeling fast while working the lure with the rod tip.

When pollock are in shoal water the fly-rod provides supreme sport. Use a large bucktail of any design, but probably one with baitfish coloration. The fly should be stripped in fairly fast.

TAUTOG (BLACKFISH)

Tautog sometimes are called "the bulldogs of the bottom" because they don't run very much, preferring to try to hold their ground and shake. Blackish in color, and not at all pretty, they are good fighters and con-sidered delicious to eat. Their range extends from Nova Scotia to South Carolina but they are most abundant between Cape Cod and Delaware. The waters in and around Long Island Sound are hot spots.

Tautog usually weigh under 5 pounds; "bragging size" being over 10 and occasional big ones perhaps going as high as 20, or even more when taken near wrecks and artificial reefs in deep water. They are bottom feeders which gorge themselves on mussels, barnacles, shrimp, crabs, snails and seaworms; having crushing teeth so strong that they can pull shellfish off rocks and eat them. Look for them any time of year in fairly shallow water where there is a rocky or pebbly bottom with plenty of shellfish growing on it. They congregate together, often in holes in such places and migrate little, if at all. Thus many may be found in a small area with few or none in likely-looking spots nearby. Once a hot spot is found it should be marked down because it should be productive year after year. Fishing on a running tide is best, with the flood usually superior to the ebb. Evidently tautog sleep at night and strike best on bright days.

Tackle for tautog is anything strong enough to pull them away from their hideways amid the rocks and barnacles. If they aren't pulled away quickly it may be very hard to dislodge them. Thus, 15 pounds test line is about a minimum, and many blackfish addicts won't use anything testing under 30. Bait is used to the exclusion of artificials.

An excellent blackfish rig is the one recommended for flounders, with stronger lines and leaders as above and with hooks not smaller than No. 4 and usually (in inland waters) not larger than 2/0. Some fishermen prefer the 2-hook rig; others only one. Fish-finder rigs also are used. I prefer as little as possible on the end of a line, having taken blackfish in shallow water with only a baited hook on the end of it. With light spinning tackle the bait can be cast out nicely and allowed to sink to the bottom. If nothing happens there, a cast is made in a new direction.

The favorite bait for tautog is fiddler crabs. The males have a large claw which should be broken off and thrown overboard (to act as chum); this to prevent the fish from grabbing it and stealing the bait from the hook. One of the middle legs also is broken off and the hook is inserted into the hole so the point (but not the barb) can barely be felt through the top shell. Green crabs are a second choice. Break off the top shell and discard it.

When a blackfish is felt mouthing the bait some fishermen strike instantly, while others wait until the fish has had time to swallow the bait. Those doing it the first way don't want to give the fish time to lodge itself amid the rocks. Those doing it the second way feel that too many fish are lost by the first method. If the bottom offers few hiding places the second way is probably best. Once the strike is made, however, it should be hard enough to pull the fish away from protection so it can be brought to the top.

Since blackfish have sharp spines and have a habit of disgorging whatever they have eaten, wearing a poncho or something similar is a badge of the veteran blackfisherman. Since blackfish can't be scaled they have to be skinned, but a pair of pliers makes this easy. One can remove the fillets and skin them afterward, as shown in the Appendix to this book. All agree that blackfish provide excellent eating. They should be kept moist while being cooked so the flesh won't dry out. A good way to do this is to baste them with white wine.

34
Southern
Inshore Fishing

Although Florida is many things to many people, it offers to fishermen some of the finest light-tackle angling in the world. The tendency seems to be to think of this in terms of the fabulous fishing found along the 130 miles of islands between Key Largo and Key West, but anglers on the northern section of the coast are far from neglected. Beaches, piers, bays and bridges all the way from Georgia to Miami's Biscayne Bay offer an abundance of food fish and gamefish which can be taken with whatever tackle one happens to have handy. Bonefish, spotted seatrout, snook, ladyfish, pompano, Spanish mackerel, bluefish, crevalle, tarpon, barracuda, redfish and snappers are only a few, and the short ride to the fringe of the Gulf Stream provides more species to be discussed later. Many of these are residents all year, but the greatest variety is taken when the water warms up and the weather improves between May and October.

Directly after World War II when I tested examples of the then-innovative spinning tackle in the Islamorada and Marathon areas of the Florida Keys, these sleepy little towns merely were wide places in the road. Every angler of any note knew which others were fishing there at the time, and they usually got together in quaint little seaside restaurants decorated with shells, nets and coconut carvings to compare notes on new developments in angling. We never changed from bleached tan cottons except to put on a fresh set. Turtle steaks and other indigenous viands were cheap and key-lime pie always was made with real key limes, piled with an island of snowy topping and washed down with a concoction of lime, rum and iced soda water. Those were the happy days before the burgeoning of neon signs, plush motels, too much traffic and the custom of wearing something fancy for dinner. Fishing was fabulous then from piers and bridges and in channels and on flats nearby. It still is good, although it may take a longer run in a fast outboard to reach spots where one has solitude and where fish aren't too spooky—so don't sell it short! Newcomers still can enjoy fabulous fishing in all these places.

Both tyros and experts, and all those in between, seem to look upon Florida fishing from the specialist's point of view. They may wish to take potluck by drifting or casting baits or lures from piers and bridges or they may want to go out for a specific kind of gamefish such as a bonefish, tarpon, snook or permit—which many think of as the Florida fishermen's "favorite four." So let's proceed in this chapter by dealing with each of the most important inshore species separately, because each one is caught most successfully by adopting a specific approach.

BONEFISH ON THE FLATS

Anglers who never have thrilled to the long, sizzling run of a bonefish on the Florida flats have missed a very important part of their education. Bonefish, found in all tropical seas, are silvery streamlined torpedos whose performance in shallow water is amazing for their relatively small size, which averages 6 pounds or so. Ten-pounders or better merit congratulations, and the all-tackle record is currently 19 pounds. Bonefish have strong crushers on their tongues and the roofs of their mouths, strong enough to mash shells—and even fingers. Bonefishing has been eulogized in books and articles which often give the impression that it is a sport for experts and quite difficult to master. To the contrary, anyone can catch bonefish on spinning tackle with bait, and those who are reasonably proficient can do it by casting small weighted lures. The method which separates the men from the boys is to hook and handle the "silvery fox of the flats" with a fly rod and artificial flies. Try it first by spinning with bait. The sportier methods can come later.

The medium 7-foot spinning outfit is excellent, but the light one is more fun for those who are adept with the tackle. Start with 8-pound-test line in areas where there are mangrove shoots and other obstructions such as coral, but work down to 6-pound and even 4-pound later, because the best sport is enjoyed by going light. I have taken bonefish of over 8 pounds on 2-pound-test line but this requires both care and luck. It is very important to use a quality reel holding a good 200 yards of line because the first fast

The timid bonefish, famous for its spectacular runs, is prime sport on a fly rod. Beginners can enjoy fishing for it with spinning tackle and bait.

run of a bonefish can exceed 150 yards. A smooth drag is vital. Hooks are short-shanked in sizes between 4 and 1/0, used with either live shrimp or crab bait. Polaroid sunglasses and protection from sunburn are necessities.

Let's take a typical trip to see what happens. The area near Islamorada is a good place to start from, and beginners should employ a guide to take them to productive flats and to point out the fish, which usually are difficult for the uninitiated to see. Fishing can be done anytime when the flats are a foot or so under water, but the best of it is on the incoming tide when fish move up onto areas which are above water when the tide is low.

The outboard, usually towing a skiff, threads its way along the channel and through a sprinkling of mangrove islands so numerous that a stranger easily could become lost. Near the selected flat (chosen because it is rich in crabs, shrimp and shellfish), the guide anchors the boat and the angler transfers to the skiff, which is pushed onto the flat with a pole. Scanning the edge of the flat, the guide soon calls attention to "mudding"—milky spots caused by bonefish disturbing the chalky marl of the bottom as they root in it for food. As the fish work closer he points to their dorsal fins and tails which wave as they move inward in the shallow water. There may be dozens of bonefish in the 2- to 6-pound class, but the trick is to locate a few big ones. These come in singly or in groups of a very few. Their size is identifiable by the distance between dorsal fin and forked tail. Their path onto the flat soon is indicated and the guide tells us to cast the shrimp or crab ahead of them and to let it lie on the bottom.

It is exciting to know where the bait is and to see the fish approach. One may go by it, waver as it scents it in the current, and turn to pick it up. He takes it casually and moves off as the line tightens. Strike! Feeling the bite of the hook and the pull of the line, the now frantic bonefish streaks for deep water, its alarmed companions also flashing away like underwater torpedoes. Hold the rod as high as possible to protect the line from obstructions and let the fish make its run on light drag. This first run is the sizzler that gives the fish its reputation. Line peels off the spool like magic, and one wonders if the fish will strip out all 200 yards, snap it, and keep on going, as bonefish sometimes do.

But it finally stops and swirls toward the horizon, too tired to run any more. The angler pumps it in and, once on the way, it comes quite easily —until it sees the boat! Then it is off again on another fast run, but shorter. Perhaps there is a third and fourth run, but now the exhausted bonefish circles the skiff—wide circles which grow increasingly smaller. The guide, wading beside the skiff, nets the fish and lifts it up to be admired. Unless it is a trophy to be mounted, the fish is released because bonefish are not very good to eat. To do this the guide holds the fish underwater by its tail and moves it back and forth until it has recovered enough to swim away.

Working the shallow flats for bonefish is a specialized game in which the angler only casts when he sees a "mudding" fish.

The next step in a bonefisherman's education is to wade by himself, to spot his fish, and to cast to them with bait. One must wade quietly because the fish are very shy, and any motion or noise that alarms one will flush the whole school. Cast bait at least 5 feet ahead of the fish, and try to make it land quietly. If a school is flushed one must look for another, which may mean returning to the skiff and going somewhere else. In good areas, the incoming schools can be so frequent that anglers can take several fish in a day.

Some fins or tails visible above the surface may be those of other species, such as small sharks, permit or barracuda. The permit is a prized gamefish. Barracuda often linger near wading anglers to see what's going on. Despite their baleful appearance they can be ignored, but they will attack a tired bonefish instantly. For this reason they should be avoided. If one seems about to attack a hooked bonefish the alternative is to try to break it loose or to open the reel's bail so it can try to escape. Even a tired bonefish usually can outrun a barracuda.

After catching a few bonefish on bait we can advance to using artificials. These usually are lead-head jigs weighing about ¼ ounce. Lighter ones are better, if the spinning tackle will cast them far enough, because they land more lightly. Cast as delicately as possible several feet ahead of and beyond the incoming fish so the lure can be pulled in front of it very slowly and with short jerks. This sends up slight puffs of marl and seems to give the impression of a moving shrimp or crab. Casting should be unalarmingly casual and fishermen should avoid wearing white or other bright colors that can be easily seen by the fish. This type of angling depends upon quiet stalking.

607

While lures or baits provide an introduction to bonefishing that satisfies anglers generally, no one can merit a master's degree in it until he has enjoyed the maximum in thrills and satisfaction by catching this gamefish with a fly rod and a fly. Usual equipment is a 9-foot rod handling a size 9 or 10 weight-forward floating line, but there's no reason why we can't go a bit lighter. Reels that can be palmed for added braking power have an advantage. The reel should accommodate about 200 yards of 20-pound Dacron backing. The leader, smoothly knotted to the line, should be about 12 feet long, tapered to 8-pounds test or so. Short-shanked bright wire hooks in sizes between 4 and 1/0 often are dressed to imitate shrimps or to simulate crabs in colors such as pink or brown. Since the most popular patterns vary from year to year, it helps to find out what the experts are currently using.

Probably the choice of fly is less important than the way it is fished. Some bonefish specialists insist that this should be by extremely short and slow strips of not over an inch at a time. The rod-tip can be in or very near the water to avoid line sag so this can be done more accurately. A fish then can be hooked merely by raising the rod tip. Distance is measured by a false cast to drop the fly lightly a few feet ahead of and beyond the fish so it can be worked directly in front of it. Bonefish disinterested in this tactic perhaps can be made to strike by jerking the fly a little faster. Flies tied on keel hooks prevent hangups when bonefish are in such places as mangroves. Some anglers think that opening the gape of a keel hook a little aids its hooking ability.

During the incoming tide bonefish flats often extend for miles, perhaps laced with channels also used by tarpon, permit and other species. Good ones are between 6 inches and knee-deep, and are very easy to wade with sturdy rubber-soled canvas shoes. While the flats provide ideal stalking areas for bonefish, many often are caught in deeper water when fishing for something else.

THE ELUSIVE PERMIT

When the tide covering the flats has risen to about knee-deep, bone-fishermen, back in the skiff again, may be fortunate enough to see one or more sharply pointed sicklelike blackish fins and tails that mark cruising permit—one of the sportiest light tackle trophies any angler could ever hope to catch. The permit is a slab-sided member of the pompano family which most anglers agree is spookier, more elusive, and a better battler than even the bonefish. The all-tackle record is a 50-pounder caught with a crab in Biscayne Bay in 1965. Fish in the 30-pound range are considered trophies, but much smaller ones are more common. Their favorite foods are crabs and shrimp.

Crabs, most often used for bait, are not much bigger than a silver dollar—between 2 and 2½ inches wide. There's a trick to baiting them properly. If one uses pliers to pinch the large claws near their tips, the crab will drop them, thus preventing it from clinging to the bottom. Specialists usually also break off the two points of the shell and hook the crab upward through the shell's edge, which keeps it alive. The favorite hook is a short-shanked 1/0 or 2/0 Eagle Claw.

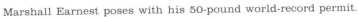

Marshall Earnest poses with his 50-pound world-record permit.

After a tough battle, angler boats a permit and weighs it, then releases it in the clear Florida sea.

Cast this bait well ahead of and beyond the fish, or the school of them, because a nearer cast (or any noise or startling motion) will cause the timid fish to flash away. Since they usually are moving fairly fast, there isn't much time. Hold the rod high and retrieve quite slowly to make the bait swim near the surface. If there's a boil without a take, drop the rod tip so the crab can swim toward the bottom. Pause only a second or two after a take, and set the hook as hard as the tackle will allow, because permit have tough mouths. Two or three strikes, with snappy wrist action, should drive the hook home, but a tight line always is necessary.

Permit make a sizzling run much like a bonefish does, and they will try to dislodge the hook by scraping on bottom. Several shorter runs can be expected, interspersed by the fish using his vertically flattened body to hold ground. Let it run when it wants to, but use all the power the tackle can safely stand by pumping it in whenever possible. There is a very tough battler on the other end!

Many anglers make a specialty of hunting permit on the flats. Others do it in a much easier but less sporty manner by fishing for them similarly where they often congregate in channels, deep holes, and around reefs and wrecks. Some prefer shrimp as bait, maintaining that it spooks the fish less often because it lands more lightly and thus can be cast a bit closer.

The Atlantic permit isn't an abundant fish and is so elusive that many can be nearby without being noticed. They frequent waters all around southern Florida, but are most common in the vicinity of Key West.

While baitfishing is the best way to catch permit, they often are taken with jigs in hook sizes between 2/0 and 4/0. Sometimes these are baited with shrimp, favorite colors being the shrimplike ones of brown, tan, pink or white. These are bounced in the usual manner. Small plugs are less effective, but they sometimes work. The best ones are about 3 inches long in colors that imitate baitfish, but red and white or red and yellow can prove useful. When using artificial lures one strikes immediately.

Accomplished anglers who read this know that permit can be taken on the same fly tackle used for bonefish, although it is rarely done and is much more difficult due to the necessity of accurate presentation without frightening the fish. They are prima donnas about flies, occasionally striking savagely, but usually ignoring the most expert casts. I have never taken a permit on a fly. The late Joe Brooks, world-famous writer and angler, had taken five over the years after probably casting to thousands. Lefty Kreh, another artist at flinging fur and feathers, says he had cast to over a thousand permit before hooking and landing even one. Other experts seem to have done no better.

LEAPING TARPON

A top contender for the "fightingest fish" is the tarpon, whose aerial acrobatics put even the Atlantic salmon to shame. Weighing as much as 300 pounds (but ordinarily much smaller), a hooked tarpon nearly always immediately jumps; a gleaming silver projectile erupting from the water to shake upward into the air amid showers of spray. With gills flaring widely, it clears the surface completely, cartwheeling at the crest to fall downward again with a thunderous splash, probably throwing the hook. Because of its bony mouth and ferocious fighting ability, perhaps less than one in ten hooked tarpon are brought to boat. The thrill is in the jumps.

Tarpon don't make the sizzling runs some other fish do, but they will leap again and again in almost endless succession. Unless wanted for mounting, the angler slips a short-handled gaff under the lower jaw while he extracts the hook with pliers so the fish can be harmlessly released. Tarpon aren't very good to eat, and the awesome show they perform well deserves their freedom.

Somewhat resembling a giant herring, the tarpon has a dark greenish-blue back with silver sides and belly, and very large scales. It inhabits Atlantic and Gulf tropical and semitropical shallow waters near shore — brackish and even fresh. Being a warm-water fish which prefers temperatures above 65 degrees, it is most abundant inshore between March and November, and especially between May and August. Its favorite foods include pinfish, mullet, crabs, shrimp and squid. It takes a wide variety of artificial lures, including flies.

Since tarpon range in size from a few ounces to around 300 pounds, it seems convenient to divide fishing information for them into three classes — the tiny tarpon (weighing under 5 pounds), the baby tarpon (between 5 and 50 pounds), and the big tarpon (50 pounds and over). Let's start with the "babies" because they are most popular and most often caught, realizing that these classifications are rough ones which can overlap.

The outboard boat, probably towing a skiff, wends its way along mangrove-bordered channels and amid mangrove islands to a location the guide has selected. Those not intimately familiar with the area should employ a guide to locate the hot spots and to avoid getting lost, because islands of mangroves all look alike. Tackle is a medium or heavy spinning outfit, or a plug rod of similar power. The tacklebox contains a selection of jigs, spoons, and plugs.

Those who prefer fly rods should take one along. It could be size 8 or 9 with plenty of backbone to set the hook. Flies for this slack-water fishing are splay-wing types which sink slowly and provide animated breathing action on retrieve (which should be very slow). Sizes are between 2 and

Expert Bob Zwirz plays a big tarpon from the beach on a fly rod.

5/0, depending on the size of the fish, and usually are in combinations of yellow, red, white and/or barred rock. The leader, about as long as the rod, should have a very strong shock tippet about 4 feet long of monofilament graduated up to 30- or 40-pound test, because anything finer can be cut by the sharp gill covers, fins and scales of the fish, and by contact with mangroves.

When we reach a pondlike opening in the mangroves the guide may call attention to surface bubbles near their edge. Bubbles indicate the presence of tarpon, which also sometimes can be seen rolling, or swimming with upper fins exposed. Poling very quietly, he pushes the boat nearer to get in position. The water is only a few feet deep and the dark forms of several tarpon can be seen, slowly cruising among the barnacle-encrusted finger-like roots.

613

We cast a surface plug ahead of the leading fish and as near to the roots as possible. There is a splashing boil where the plug was. We instinctively strike, feel the fish, and the plug comes sailing toward us.

"You struck too soon," the guide says. "You took it away from him. Wait 'til he clamps down on it."

After poling slowly for a short distance another pod of tarpon is located. This time we pause during the boil until we feel a solid take. "Hit him hard," the guide says. "Sock it to him, again and again."

The water erupts as a 25-pound tarpon leaps into the air. Shaking savagely, he jumps nearly twice his length—and he throws the plug!

"Par for the course," the guide says. "We'll try another."

The next strike is a secure hook-up. The big fish leaps, rolls, runs a bit, and leaps again and again. We lower the rod-tip during each jump to provide

Captain Cal Cochran gaffs a large tarpon caught on a fly rod. Since tarpon are not good to eat, this one will be killed for mounting.

enough slack so he won't break off by falling on a tight line. As he bull-dogs, we pump him in. After a few feebler antics he lies wavering beside the boat, completely exhausted—beautifully streamlined in shining silver.

We tell the guide to let him go. Holding the strong tippet near the plug with one hand, the guide uses pliers to extract it with the other. Thus freed, the tarpon slowly sinks and swims away.

While this situation is fairly typical, baby tarpon are found in varieties of places too numerous to mention; even occasionally coming up on the flats to feed, as bonefish do. They usually are visible, so individuals can be cast to, but they also are taken by drifting, stillfishing or trolling with crabs, shrimp, live baitfish or pieces of bait.

Tiny tarpon weighing between a few ounces and a few pounds are great fun on light spinning gear or the fly rods ordinarily used for trout, the same little lures and wet flies, also. Tiny tarpon grow with minimum interference in ditches, canals, ponds and backwaters; usually in secluded out-of-the-way places, but sometimes beside well-traveled roads such as the ditch near the Naples end of the Tamiami Trail. While driving to Flamingo, in the Everglades National Park, we found some. Noticing action similar to rises on the water, we parked the car to see what was going on. The spot abounded with tarpon not over a foot long!

My companion rigged a light spinning rod with 4-pound line fastened to a heavier shock leader and a $1/4$-ounce surface plug. I used a fly rod with size 6 line with a shock leader and popping bug, fishing so close to the road that roll casts were necessary to keep the lure out of trees and to prevent snagging a passing auto. Although we took fish on both lures, they were hard to hook on the popper, so it was changed to a No. 8 bucktail. Even though the place teemed with fish, only an occasional one was interested, and it was necessary to change lures often. One or the other of us, how-ever, usually had a tarpon on. The tiny fish ceaselessly jumping until they were beached and released.

"Makes trout fishing back home look sick," my companion exulted, as he carefully dispatched a little 7-incher to have mounted. (The smallest fish often are considered better trophies than the biggest ones.)

There is a growing cult of saltwater fly-rodders who set increasingly imposing records by catching increasingly bigger tarpon with the lightest of tippets (not including the strength of shock tippets used). Famous Miami angler Stu Apte holds most of the records as this is written, including that of a 151-pounder on a 12-pound tippet. Since this is a sport for experts who use custom-built tackle and who are exceedingly fussy about all its com-ponents, it won't interest casual anglers very much. One of the many tricks-of-the-trade is to locate big ones in shallow channels amid the flats where they have little choice about where to go, except up!

Since the fish may be cruising, one often has to make long casts quickly. A way to do this is to have the castable line trailing in the water and the shootable length coiled on deck, thus eliminating time for false casting. While stripping baskets are used when wading, or the shooting line is in long coils held between the lips, tangles often are prevented on board by using a large plastic trash can to hold the line. Expensive specialized fly-reels have super-smooth drags and extra capacity. Rods have plenty of backbone to drive the needle-sharp hooks home. The necessarily large flies of No. 6/0 or so, are powered out by specialized saltwater tapered lines.

Those with less experience who want to wrestle the big ones can try it with surf-type tackle and plugs, jigs or spoons to suit, or they can use bait. An example of many good places is from, or near, one of the many bridges on the Overseas Highway between Homestead and Key West; preferably at night on an ebbing tide. Many prefer to use a boat uptide of the bridge and to swing the cast as near as possible to the abutments. Since big tarpon are scavengers, bait-fishing often gets best results. Use surf tackle with the fish-finder rig described for striped bass, and any of the baits previously mentioned. Another way is to use a boat rod with a 2/0 or 3/0 star-drag reel filled with monofilament or braided Dacron of 50-pound test or so. Four feet or more of about 100-pound monofilament or braided wire is used for a leader, with an 8/0 to 10/0 O'Shaugnessy or Eagle Claw hook. If weight is needed it can be an egg-shaped slip-sinker on the leader below the swivel which attaches it to the line. Live baitfish 8 inches or longer are hooked under the dorsal fin, but almost any dead bait will work nearly as well. A favorite way to use dead bait is to cut the head off a fish, such as a mullet, and to thread the leader-wire from tail to neck along the spine, pulling the wire back into the bait until the hook's shank is concealed. This rig can be used without lead so it will hang in the current on at least 50 feet of line. When the bait is taken let the fish go off with it on free-spool or very light drag until it stops to swallow it. When it starts to move off again, that is the time to strike—several times, as hard as the tackle will allow.

By day or night, bridge fishing along the Florida Keys usually provides exciting sport because big tarpon are only one item in the grab-bag of prizes. Others include snappers, redfish, grunts, groupers, mackerel, jewfish, jacks, bonefish, permit, snook and panfish. Those who dislike to combat currents can reach bottom by fishing during the high slack tide. Heavy tackle helps to hold the big ones but lighter gear is more fun if one doesn't mind a tackle-buster occasionally popping a line and making off with some of it. Keys bridges have catwalks to separate fishermen from traffic. There are many fishing bridges, perhaps as good or even better, all around the Gulf.

HOOKING SNOOK

The snook is a bulldogging gamefish that acts much like a big freshwater bass and it (except for the big ones) can be taken on similar tackle. The all-tackle snook record is a 52-pound 6-ounce whopper taken in 1963 in La Paz, Mexico. The average in Florida and Gulf waters is between 5 and 20 pounds, the bigger ones usually being caught at night from Keys bridges with live bait. Snook look very much like walleyed pike, with brownish-gold backs shading to a yellowish-white belly, but distinguished by a distinct black stripe along the body from head to tail.

While snook can be taken year-round, a tip for finding them is to remember they are warm-water fish and prefer temperatures above 60 degrees. During winter months and cold snaps they usually lie in deep holes. At other times they frequent bays, estuaries, tidewater areas of rivers, bridges, piers, edges of mangrove clusters and canals. Their habitat is very similar to tarpon, and both species often are caught at the same time.

Prize-winning snook taken by the author on light spinning tackle.

A popular area is toward the Naples end of the Tamiami Trail (U.S. Highway 41) in the canal bordering the road. These drainage canals, of which there are many in southern Florida, are equipped with spillways and dams to conserve water, and the fishing in them is best after heavy rains when the spillways have been opened. At such times hordes of bait-fish are washed down, and schools of snook follow the flow until they are stopped by the obstructions. The canal along the trail connects with drainage ditches, resembling the teeth of a comb, which extend into the ocean. Many of these are hotspots, with locations marked by numbers on the bridges.

We went to one of these on a warm February day and found the water so muddy that nothing could be seen in it. Not then knowing that Floridians don't favor spinners for snook, I put on a flashy weighted brass one in the opinion that snook could see and hear it better under the circumstances. While my companions were doing little or nothing, the spinner took snook of between 4 and 8 pounds on nearly every cast; so many that I became tired of hooking and releasing them, and decided to go somewhere for lunch. This was delayed by a final cast which hooked the big one. The snook raced up and down the canal, with me following it as best I could amid the growths of jack-palms skirting the shore. Luckily the fish stayed in the channel, although he easily could have broken off by going into the obstructions on either side, because the tackle was a light spinning outfit with 6-pound-test line. The snook weighed in at 18 pounds 14 ounces and won a silver tray for first prize in its division of the Metropolitan Miami Fishing Tournament for that year. Experts in Florida, however, still maintain that spinners are rather useless for snook.

Since this is the type of snook fishing most readers will enjoy, let's discuss the tackle. Spinning gear (unless we want to go very light) should be the normal or heavy outfit described in Chapter 1, using line of about 12-pound test; this strength (or perhaps even stronger in some cases) because snook habitually head for protection of mangrove roots or whatever other cover they can find. For this reason and because they have knifelike gill covers, a shock leader of about 30-pound test is necessary. Braided wire often is used, but strong monofilament fishes lures better. Plug-casting outfits of about the same strength also are popular. These types of tackle are used with jigs, spinners, spoons and with plugs. Plugs are bait-fish imitators in natural colors, but also in combinations of the usual red, white and yellow. Poppers and splutterers are popular for surface fishing, and should be worked fast and erratically.

When conditions permit, a System 8 fly rod is even more fun, equipped with a saltwater forward-taper line, a leader about as long as the rod, and a 30-pound shock tippet. Flies or elongated popping bugs in size about 1/0 are used in color combinations usually of white and/or yellow and with mylar bodies or fine strips of mylar in the wings. Strip flies in quite fast, about a foot at a time.

Another type of snook fishing, such as in the Thousand Islands area near Marco and Naples, is along the edges of mangrove growths. Snook hide under the edges, waiting for food to appear. Since one must cast very close to the mangroves, and into pockets in them, casts often become hung up. Accurate ones often will tempt snook to flash out and slam the lure.

Many anglers like to locate fish by trolling in channels and along drop-offs, using tackle similar to that recommended for striped bass. The strength of the tackle in these various cases varies with conditions and how sporty anglers want to be. One can play it safe with sturdy gear or can chance broken lines by enjoying something lighter.

Baitfishermen use various rigs, such as a plugcasting or a boat rod with a level-wind reel equipped with about 200 yards of 20-pound-test monofila-ment or Dacron. The terminal end can be assembled as follows. Make a Bimini Twist to double 3 feet of line and tie a black barrel swivel to the end with a Clinch Knot. Loop this with a leader sleeve to a foot or more of about 30-pound (or stronger) wire leader and string an egg sinker on it. This is fastened to the hook, such as an Eagle Claw in No. 5/0 to 7/0. The sinker weighs between $1/2$-ounce and 3 ounces, depending on the current.

Bait for stillfishing is a live pinfish or mullet, usually hooked under the dorsal fin. For use in currents the bait can be alive or dead, hooked through both lips or through the eye sockets. Surf tackle or other heavy gear is used when fishing from or near bridges. Fishing is usually best in the deep edges of currents at night near bridges or around river mouths at high slack and during the first half of the ebbing tide. This is when and where the biggest snook are usually caught. It should be good anytime in canals and channels if the water is deep enough. Many anglers try not to miss the higher tides of the full moon, partly because visibility is better then.

When fishing for snook with any tackle it is important to check the ter-minal end of the line regularly for fraying because the gill covers of the fish and the barnacle-encrusted areas they like to frequent can ruin a line quickly.

SPOTTED SEATROUT

Northeastern freshwater fly-rodders, who use the sneaky approach to lay out a fly they hope "matches the hatch" on a fabled trout stream in search of a brookie that beats a pound, would lose their minds fishing for the kind of "trout" found in profusion in salt water bays down South. Never mind the stealthy approach because noise even attracts them. Don't bother trying to match the fly to anything, because any bright one will do. If the fish is under a pound, put it back, because the average is 5 pounds or so, and one can catch all he wants. Finally, the spotted seatrout, or spotted weakfish, or speckled trout, or just trout, or whatever you want to call him, is as sassy as the inland brook trout, and just as good to eat! Maybe catching southern "trout" isn't as challenging as hooking the northern varieties, but it provides a lot more action.

A member of the weakfish family, the subject of this section sports a back of gray-blue shaded to silver underneath, with a generous peppering of large black polka-dots on top from middle to tail. The record is (or was) a 15-pound, 6-ounce prize caught in Florida's St. Lucie River in 1969, but the average runs somewhere between 4 and 8 pounds, which is a nice range for light tackle. Spotted seatrout are found in bays and estuaries all the way from Maryland down around Florida and the Gulf to Mexico. Best times to catch them are from April or May into October when the water is calm and clear and when there is a moving tide but, preferably, a rising one. Best places are grassy areas where the water is between 3 and 5 feet deep or so because the fish find shrimp, crabs, seaworms and small fish there. One can drift over such areas or can wade if the water isn't too deep. The footing usually is firm, but experienced waders adopt a shuffling gait to avoid stepping on a stingray and being lashed by its lethal tail. Let's try it from a boat first.

Tackle can be whatever one uses inland for trout, or the light plugging outfit ordinarily used for bass. The line should test about 8 pounds and should be fitted with a stronger shock tippet in case fish burrow into grass, and also because they have teeth. Bait fishermen favor shrimps on 2/0 hooks. To keep the bait drifting at the right level over the grass they use a float with the hook far enough below to clear the weeds. Other baits are small live fishes, crabs, or cut mullet.

Artificial lures for casting are top-water and sinking plugs, usually silver to imitate baitfish. Quarter-ounce wobbling spoons also are popular, perhaps with the hook dressed with yellow or another color of bucktail or feathers. Jigs do well when the water is deep enough. Plugs are retrieved with various actions, usually fast, to see what works best at the time.

Here is a way to make a very popular lure: Remove the hooks from a surface plug and insert a screw-eye where the rear hook was. Tie a foot or so of about 20-pound monofilament to this and to it tie a jig with a 2/0 hook. (Short artificial worms also are used.) Cast this out and skitter it in on a fast retrieve. The trout usually hit the dangling and bouncing jig rather than the plug, which is used both as an attractor and to work the jig at the right level over the grass. The heavy monofilament keeps the rig from tangling. A plug-shaped cork can be used instead of the plug, but it may not cast as well. Boats usually carry an ice chest because spotted weakfish, while delicious to eat, are rather perishable.

Fly rods are used from boats, but more often while wading. Systems 7 or 8 are most appropriate, fitted with a weight-forward floating line or a floater with a sinking tip. The leader is about as long as the rod and tapered to about 8 pounds with a short shock tippet. Flies usually are in the No. 6 range and imitate baitfish or shrimps. They can be rather flashy, perhaps with some mylar added, but spotted seatrout aren't very fussy if the fly is fished with plenty of action. We haven't recommended sinking lines because they often drop into grass.

What does a wading fisherman do with his fish? Usually he puts them in a metal tub fitted into an inflated inner tube which is fastened to his belt by a short cord. Putting them on a stringer isn't recommended if sharks might be around!

In late fall spotted weakfish may leave the grassy areas of bays to come into brackish lagoons and rivers. If one area doesn't produce results, anglers move to another one. Fish travel in schools, sometimes very big ones, and often are located by the actions of birds, or by muddy areas made by feeding mullet. While these exist on vegetation, they root out shrimps, crabs and other bottom food, so the trout seek such areas. Sometimes trout make the "muds" themselves.

In traveling around the Gulf you'll find other species closely related to the spotted weakfish, for which fishing methods are quite similar. The corvinas of the west coast are also among these, and the same information applies to them. The southeastern spotted seatrout is said to provide the most fun for the most people of any kinds of fish. For this reason it has to survive such heavy pressure both from amateur and professional fishermen that many conservationists think its taking should be limited.

LITTLE LADYFISH, OR "CHIRO"

Those who'd like to hook a little leaper that jumps higher and more often than anything else of its size should try the ladyfish, which rarely exceeds 3 pounds and usually is much smaller. My introduction to them came late one night in Miami after a meeting at the Anglers' Club when my host parked the car by a bridge in the city. He assembled a light spinning rod and a light fly rod; a small silver-scale plug on the former and a bright streamer fly on the other. I selected the spinning outfit because in the blackness under the bridge my temporary night blindness caused by the bright lights above made effective fly casting seem impossible. My companion had fished there before and knew the hazards.

"We're after ladyfish," he announced, "and the idea is to cast the lure out into the current and to whip it in fast. Slow retrieves rarely produce anything."

I shot the lure into the blackness, saw a few swirls reflected by the lights above, and felt a nip or two. My partner made a roll cast across the current and let the fly whip around. His rod tip flicked up and a bright, silvery little fish cartwheeled into the air. Jumping and rolling continually, it put on an amazing show for its size. Although smaller and slimmer than a trout, and without any black spots, it looked somewhat the same. After a little practice, I also caught several. Fishing for these little leapers at night in the heart of the city on tiny tackle was an unusual experience and a lot of fun.

Ladyfish feed over sandy and muddy bottoms in bays and the flowing waters of estuaries and channels, often where tarpon do, all around southern Florida and in many places along the Gulf coast. Schools often work into the mild surf and are disliked because they are bait stealers which aren't very good to eat because of their many small bones. All that was said about tackle and tactics for the spotted seatrout applies to them with exceptions noted above. This includes the use of shock tippets because fine lines will be abraded by the rough bodies of the fish.

WHAT ABOUT BARRACUDA?

Anglers wading the flats for species such as bonefish often become nervous under the baleful scrutiny of a pikelike barracuda which just lies in the water nearby, evidently so fascinated by what's going on that it doesn't want to go away. Are these fish, with their long jaws and formidable teeth dangerous? Are they sporty? What should be done about them?

Barracuda seem smart enough to know that a wading angler will bring a tired fish within reach, and that's probably what it's waiting for. Once within reach, the loglike scavenger will flash into action and instantly sever any tired fish, even of larger size. Except for this, barracuda can be ignored because there are few valid accounts of their attacking humans. Such rare accounts may have been because the angler was bleeding after cutting a foot on coral or shells, or because he was dragging caught fish tethered by a cord.

One answer to getting rid of a curious barracuda is to catch him! Don't pass up such an opportunity because the barracuda is so exciting on the end of a line that it seems vastly underrated as a gamefish.

When fly fishing, carry a few extra large flies tied to wire leaders a foot long, or so. When spinning or bait-casting, carry a couple of surface plugs rigged the same way. To avoid flushing the fish (if that's what we want to do), the cast should be made far beyond it so the lure can be retrieved within its sight. If the retrieve isn't fast the fish only will follow the lure while inspecting it curiously. A fast retrieve should bring a savage strike, and what happens next is far more fun than bonefishing!

Feeling the prick of the barb, the 'cuda takes off like a jet, frequently leaping, tailwalking and twisting in the air as he goes. Although it gives up quicker than many sportfish, the initial run or two is a thrill every angler should experience. Needless to say, the hook should be extracted with pliers, and be very careful to keep fingers away from the barracuda's jaws.

Barracuda look menacing, but there are few valid accounts of their attacking humans. This one grabbed a tube lure cast on light tackle.

What one does after that is a matter of opinion. Some anglers release the fish, others give it a crack on the head and let it float away to become food for birds, or perhaps another barracuda.

The flesh of Atlantic barracuda generally is considered to be poisonous, probably due to some species of fish they eat. Pacific barracuda are favored for food. While small and medium-size ones infest warm inshore waters, the really big ones reaching 50 pounds or so usually are farther out. I have seen big ones lying like cordwood in shallow water around oil drilling platforms, probably hopefully waiting for someone to toss out a pail of garbage. On one occasion I cast spinners and plugs to them on foot-long wire leaders. They took lure, leader and all, biting through the monofilament shock tippet as if it was a piece of wet spaghetti!

THE DELICIOUS POMPANO

This little brother of the permit rarely exceeds 2 or 3 pounds but, because of its slab-sided body and lively, unpredictable fighting methods, it is a prized gamefish on light tackle. Gourmets consider it one of the best of all fish to eat. Schools of pompano often frequent tidal bays, river mouths and the surf of sandy beaches, coming in and going out with the tide. They are year-round residents of tropic waters all around Florida and the Gulf states but may be less plentiful inshore during the warmth of the summer.

Pompano can be taken by trolling or drifting while bouncing jigs off the bottom as well as by casting with light tackle, although heavier gear is used with lead to reach distance and to hold bait in the surf. They frequently are caught around drilling platforms while fishing on the bottom for grab-bag species, such as seatrout, red snapper, bluefish, spadefish, jewfish, cobia and some of the catfish family.

The most popular or effective way to catch pompano is to whip and jerk a small bucktail or nylon jig actively off bottom. This usually is baited with sand fleas. It may be necessary to trim the jig's dressing to expose the bait. Since pompano often root in sand or mud for foods, such as crustaceans and mollusks, these baits or pieces of them can be used, as well as very small fishes.

Since pompano strike swiftly, rather than nibbling or mouthing the bait, the strike should be immediate. When in shallow water, they are as timid as bonefish or permit. They sometimes can be taken on small spoons, spinners and pork-rind rigs, but rarely on flies. In some places, such as mild surf over sand, it may be possible to catch them by fishing small bucktails near the bottom.

PLATE 15

EASTERN SALT WATER FLIES

BUCKTAIL WITH GLASS FIBER WING
STRIPPER BUCKTAIL
RED AND WHITE BUCKTAIL WITH BODY OF MYLAR PIPING
WINGLESS BUCKTAIL
"KEEL-FLY" SHRIMP

RED AND WHITE "BLONDE" BUCKTAIL
CRIMPED NYLON BUCKTAIL WITH FRINGED MYLAR BODY

MARABOU WING BUCKTAIL WITH BODY OF MYLAR PIPING

WOOLNER'S SAND LAUNCE (with extended body of mylar piping)

PLATE 16

SOUTHERN SALT WATER FLIES

The three flies in the top row are typical bonefish patterns. Below these at upper left are a pink and a brown shrimp. The black and brown streamers to their right are splay-wings used for bonefish, snook, small tarpon and other species. Below them is a typical fly-rod popper with deer hair tail. The yellow splay-winged fly below this has a heavily hackled collar, used principally for tarpon. The three bead-head streamers are all-purpose flies often used for bonefish. They frequently are dressed on weedless hooks.

INSHORE AROUND THE GULF STATES

While Florida, with its chain of keys and thousands of other outlying islands, gleans peak publicity for its fabulous fishing, the other Gulf states also provide their share. Alabama's five great bays contain many good spots for tarpon, bluefish, spotted weakfish and redfish, while other areas inshore and offshore provide still more. Since this part of the coast is fairly shallow for many miles out, it has proved to be ideal for artificial reefs made by sinking automobile bodies, boats, and similar objects on which sea life can grow and which provide havens for fish.

While Mississippi has a short coastline, its bays and rivers extend it to over 200 miles and furnish excellent fishing for seatrout, redfish, bluefish, flounder, whiting and tripletail, among others. Tripletail, sometimes known as blackfish, are bottom dwellers which frequent such places as artificial reefs and wrecks. They are good fighters which often reach 30 or 40 pounds and are usually caught on bottom baits as well as with jigs and other deeply fished lures. This fish comes in various blendings of brown and yellow, as well as black, its appearance not unlike a crappie or a bass. Barrier islands protect Mississippi Sound, which provides vast areas of shallow flats fishing.

Louisiana offers over 600 miles of coast some of which consists of relatively inaccessible marshy areas and bayous which are ideal breeding grounds for fish. Grand Isle and similar spots provide fine surf fishing as well as boat access to offshore oil-drilling platforms around which congregate spotted weakfish, pompano, bluefish, red snapper, cobia, and other species. The wide expanse of brackish Lake Pontchartrain offers fishing for tarpon, redfish, spotted weakfish, croaker, sheepshead and flounder, among others. These are merely examples of Louisiana's excellent inshore fishing.

Texas, which boasts the biggest and best of most everything, proves it in inshore fishing by providing a dozen hundred miles of coastline much of which is protected by barrier islands such as Galveston and the 90 miles of the Padre Island National Seashore, plus broad expanses of lagoons, bays and other waterways. Here one finds nearly all of the southern species already described, and he can fish for them in the surf, on the bottom or by drifting, or trolling or casting along the shore.

Pier and jetty fishing is also very productive, especially for sharks. This is a specialized method of angling that requires heavy tackle. For this reason and because novices in the sport could find it rather risky, let's let local specialists provide the tackle and the experience.

35

Southern Offshore Fishing

The novice (usually a vacationer or a winter resident who has fled to the warmth of the South) becomes bored by landlubber activities and itches to try something new. He enviously eyes the sleek deep-water sportfishing cruisers moored at private docks or at marinas and gapes at their flying bridges, "tuna" towers, fighting chairs, or transom doors for boating the big ones, aluminum outriggers, electronic equipment, and tackle set up in rod-holders. Not knowing an owner of one of these exquisite and expensive fishing machines, he strolls the docks and inspects the fleet of charter boats. These are also efficiently equipped, although perhaps not as plush.

Our novice usually wants to catch a sailfish.

"No problem!" smiles the skipper of a cruiser he happens to contact. "Come aboard and look her over."

The deal made, Mr. Novice alerts his family or a few of his buddies, who come on board at the appointed time with box lunches and cartons of pop, but forgetting Polaroids, suntan lotion and a few other essentials, perhaps including hats that will stay on in the breeze and protect heads from the sun.

As the cruiser purrs out of the harbor, Mr. Novice watches the mate take balao from the bait well and prepare four of the little fish for action—beaked mouths sewed closed, and 8/0 hooks partly concealed in each. The mate rigs

627

one to each leader and line, clips each of the two outer lines to outrigger pins, and runs them up the poles. Two similar inner flat lines are also made ready and pinned to the transom instead of to the outriggers. The four baits skip and swim at varying distances astern. The rods to which they are attached are set in rod holders beside each chair, with drags on reels carefully set. Mr. Novice and his friends each are assigned to a chair and very briefly are told what to do when something happens. They are not told they are using tackle so strong that a break is nearly impossible. The reason is that the skipper dislikes losing any of his gear.

While the cruiser throbs along, the sports remark on the bluer water on one side and the amount of seaweed and floating debris on the other. They are told they are fishing the edge of the Gulf Stream. For an hour or so Mr. Novice is fascinated with all this, but then decides to go into the cabin for a cold drink. This is when it usually happens!

Responding to the mate's yell, Mr. Novice hurries on deck in time to see the mate grab his rod as the line flutters from the outrigger pin. The mate strikes when the line tightens, and Mr. Novice is startled to see a sailfish jump. The mate pushes Mr. Novice into his chair, hands him the rod, and tells him to reel. He does this furiously while watching with awe as the beautiful fish leaps again, twisting body and bill while extending and flapping his azure sail-like dorsal. The fish comes in quite easily, and this is because Mr. Novice doesn't realize the skipper is backing the boat to help him. Soon it is alongside. The mate, who has slipped on work gloves, reaches over to grab the leader with one hand and the fish's bill with the other. Then, using both hands on the bill, he raises the fish partly into view for his sport to see.

"Release it?" the mate asks, hopefully.

"Hell, no!" the sport replies. "That's a beauty, and I'm going to send it to have it mounted."

Leaving Mr. Novice's angling effort there, we wait several weeks until a big crate arrives at his home. The mounted sailfish, although only of average size, surely is a beauty. The fish now reposes on a great rectangular plaque of polished wood and a brass plate below it tells awed ogglers who caught it and when. It is hung up with considerable ceremony, and Mr. Novice likes to have people drop in for cocktails so that he can regale them with a play-by-play description of his angling skill.

Did Mr. Novice really catch the sailfish? No, he didn't. All he did was to winch it in. The mate and the skipper did everything else. Any kid old enough to pedal a bicycle could have done as well. In truth, however, Mr. Novice enjoyed a great day afloat and probably we shouldn't deflate him or the many others who have done so similarly. We do it only to stress the fact that there are much sportier ways to catch sailfish.

CHOOSING CHARTER BOATS

Offshore charter-boat skippers tend to run toward two extremes. Most of them use very heavy tackle and try to get the most fish aboard in the quickest way because that's how they and most of their customers want it. The niceties of angling are all but ignored. The mate will grab the tackle while the sport is handling a fish if he thinks it isn't being done right. He will hand-line the fish in as soon as possible and more or less treat his clients as his assistants in commercial fishing.

Such a skipper tries not to catch sailfish (which should be released if they aren't wanted for mounting) in favor of concentrating on a good haul of salable varieties. While this would turn the stomach of a true angler, most of the customers aren't anglers and don't know the difference. All they desire is a pleasant day afloat with a little action now and then. So don't blame the skipper, because his customers made him that way. The sport charters the boat and the skipper should provide the kind of fishing he wants. If there's any doubt about it, come to an agreement before leaving the dock.

The other (and much rarer) kind of skipper prefers tackle as light as is sensible and would rather catch one fish by true sporting methods than load his fishwell merely by hauling 'em in. While he likes to be chartered by experienced anglers, he is an excellent instructor for novices who ask for help. He welcomes his customers to bring their own tackle but gladly provides his own if need be. Even the most accomplished anglers can learn from him, because he pursues his specialties all the time.

A day or more with such a skipper usually provides thrills galore, while also making any angler a better one than before. Such men usually are booked far in advance, so make arrangements early. How do we find them? The best ones rarely advertise. Contact the outdoor editor of the newspaper where you're going or the local Chamber of Commerce. Be frank and specific about your abilities and your objectives. You need a good guide or skipper a lot more than he needs you, so you may need to sell him on taking you along.

ATLANTIC SAILFISH

The Atlantic sailfish is one of the sportiest and most beautiful species inhabiting tropical and semitropical waters. It ranges somewhat north of Florida's eastern boundary around its coast and the Gulf of Mexico, including Bermuda, Puerto Rico and other outlying islands. While sailfish are in Florida's offshore waters year-round some move somewhat northward as warm weather approaches, returning again in the fall. They average between 25 and 40 pounds in weight and around 7 or 8 feet in length. Fish smaller than 20 pounds or so, or bigger than 60, are considered trophies.

Sailfish hit trolled baits, such as rigged balao (pronounced "ballyhoo") and mullet, and occasionally strip baits, feathers (such as Japanese jigs), spoons and even large artificial flies. Sometimes they are taken on live baits fished deep. Their favorite foods are squid and smaller fishes. For all angling purposes, the Atlantic and Pacific sailfish are treated similarly, although the Pacific variety runs considerably larger. Since sailfish flesh is tough, those not needed for trophies or to establish records should be released.

Fortunately the days of using heavy tackle for sailfish are declining mainly because lighter gear is more fun. Fish which break off, or which are released by snipping the leader at the hook, evidently suffer only minor discomfort, if any, because the kinds of hooks used disintegrate quickly. Modern tackle favors revolving-spool trolling gear, heavy or extra-heavy spinning tackle, or even sturdy fly-fishing equipment.

Revolving-spool gear calls for a boat rod $5\frac{1}{2}$ or 6 feet long and a star-drag 3/0 reel loaded with about 500 yards of 20-pound-test Dacron line. (Dacron won't stretch, as will monofilament or nylon squidding line.) The terminal end is from 12 to 15 feet of number 7 leader wire connected to a swivel and 6 feet (more or less) of doubled line. Hooks for smaller baits are about 7/0. Baits usually are rigged balao, if obtainable, or rigged mullet. This gear can be a bit stronger or lighter, as the angler desires. It usually is stronger if bigger prizes such as marlin might be expected. Since as much as 500 yards of line almost never is needed, some padding of thicker backing with about 300 yards of line often is substituted.

Many anglers, including this one, enjoy using spinning tackle for reasons which will be noted. The tackle, as discussed in Chapter 1, offers a choice of monofilament lines between 10-pound test (or lighter) and 20-pound test on a sturdy reel holding at least 200 yards. The terminal end can be swiveled to wire or (preferably) can be tapered to about 15 feet of about 50-pound-test monofilament.

Since lighter tackle is more fun in sailfishing, how light can one go? I have mentioned that prior to 1947 and until after 1957 I did major pioneering on the development of spinning tackle and wrote three books and many magazine articles about it. In January, 1949, my wife Helen and I, fished aboard Captain Jimmy Albright's cruiser *Rebel* with the idea of taking a sailfish on spinning tackle, something that at that time was considered impossible because it never had been done.

Using my own tackle loaded with 8-pound-test monofilament, I trolled a small balao without the aid of an artificial drop-back. (Don't ask why the line was as light as 8-pound test, but old-timers will remember that monofilament then was in its infancy and was thicker and less limp than 8-pound test is now.)

Leaping in a rain of spray, a magnificent sailfish tries to shake the hook from his mouth. This sporty species is being taken on lighter gear these days, adding to the thrill of the fight.

The technique used then, and equally useful now, was to set a light drag on the reel and to troll the bait with the pickup open by holding the line against the tip of the forefinger. Fortunately it wasn't long before a small sailfish came up behind the bait and struck it. A quick drop-back was made by releasing the line from the forefinger, whereupon the bail was snapped closed. The fish was struck when the line tightened. The carefully pre-sharpened hook held and the fish made a long U-run, jumping several times.

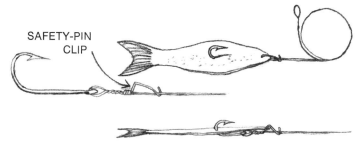

SAFETY-PIN CLIP

Strip-bait rig consists of hook attached to wire leader with a safety-pin clip. Bait is hooked through middle and secured at front by clip.

6" - 8"

Balao rig provides added security to keep trolled bait from coming off. Soft wire leader, 6 to 8 inches long, is attached to hook's eye and used to wrap the beak. Cut small hole in balao's ventral side to remove entrails and stitch hook through fish's eye to hold in place.

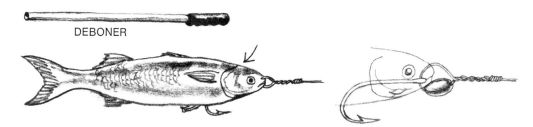

DEBONER

Deboner is used to rig a whole mullet. Cut hole in head (*arrow*), remove backbone with deboner, and stitch closed. Add lead (*right*) for deep trolling. For best swimming action, mash head flat after completing rig.

Probably the skipper helped a bit with the boat, but I was too busy to notice. This is the only sailfish I ever failed to release and it looks down from my wall as this is being written. It was 5½ feet long and weighed 17¼ pounds.

In this sort of fishing sailfish can be brought up behind a boat by trolling a teaser on a short line; a teaser being a large brightly painted plug-shaped piece of plastic or wood, often with a plastic skirt attached, that attracts attention by wiggling. When a fish is attracted by a teaser a bait is brought near the fish while the teaser is withdrawn. Sailfish that look the bait over but don't hit it often can be made to do so by pulling the bait up and dropping it back until something happens.

This sort of fishing requires a flat line rather than one held by an outrigger. The angler has to hook his own fish, teasing it into striking if necessary. Holding the rod makes instant response available, but we have to admit that it can become tiring after an hour or two of no action. The alternative is to hitch a clothespin (the same as an outrigger pin) by two cords to opposite sides of the transom. Set the rod in a holder and put the revolving-spool reel in free-spool with the click engaged or, if it is a spinning reel, set the drag so lightly that, when the line is pulled from the pin, the drag of the bait will take it out. Clip the line to the pin so the bait will troll without attention. One must be nearby and watchful enough to act immediately because the waving bill of a sailfish can appear at any instant and may not be noticed in the wake. It takes but a moment to make too long a drop-back. If the drag is light the angler must know exactly how many turns of the brake screw should be made to provide normal tension. Hand-holding the reel insures instant response and eliminates these details.

Trolling distance for a flat line varies with conditions but usually is just below the crest of the third wave behind the boat, where the skipping or swimming bait can be watched. An additional flat line should troll its bait 20 to 30 feet farther astern. Outrigger baits are trolled at somewhat greater distances, such as 75 and 125 feet.

While trolling for sailfish and other species such as dolphin and white marlin, which also may show, casting opportunities vary the sport and add to the fun. Have a favorite spinning, plugcasting or fly rod handy, rigged with line testing between 10 and 15 pounds (or a tippet of similar strength for the fly rod). The reel's drag should be very smooth and the rod should have adequate backbone to set the hook. Two or three rods are better than one to quickly provide a selection of lures such as a surface commotion plug and a jig. Fish can be attracted into the wake with a teaser, or others may accompany one hooked by trolling. Offshore anglers also happen upon schools of big fish herding bait or traveling near the surface. When an angler picks up a casting rod it signals the skipper to idle the engines so casts can be made. Offshore fish usually will take almost any lure.

The trend to light tackle is partly due to its improvement, making heavy gear less sporty and less necessary. Similar improvements in boat engines and designs reduce the need for big cruisers in offshore fishing. Fast smaller boats in the 25-foot range handled by experienced weather-wise owners can roostertail out to reefs, wrecks and nearby Gulf Stream areas quickly enough for a good day's fishing and can zip home safely when danger threatens. Thus, offshore fishing can be much less expensive than it used to be.

Fly Fishing for Sailfish

The growing sport of fly fishing for sailfish (and other big species) deserves special mention because some readers will want to try it. While they are advised to go out first with someone who has done it before, these notes may help as an introduction. Evidently no one ever caught, or tried to catch, a sailfish on a fly until about the early 1960s, but the sport is now well standardized. The angler must be able to cast a very large fly about 60 feet. Three people usually work as a team: the angler, the skipper, and someone to tease the fish sufficiently to strike the fly.

The angler is on his favorite side near the stern; the man doing the teasing on the other. The angler makes his longest practice cast and strips the shooting part and some of the casting part of the line on the deck, being sure it will remain free of tangles. He holds the fly so the convenient length of the casting part loops from the rod tip, ready to roll this out, pick it up, and make his cast to the target.

The man doing the teasing uses a casting or a boat rod with strong line attached to a wired bait without a hook, and he may troll a wooden teaser also. The bait is trolled in the usual manner until a sailfish comes for it. Then the person doing the teasing pulls the bait away and drops it back to frustrate the fish and make it angry and excited. When this happens to a sufficient extent the fish shows it by a more brilliant change in its coloration. (Anglers say that the fish "lights up.")

When the angler, nervously watching this, decides he wants to make his cast, he signals the man doing the teasing to pull in his equipment. As he makes his cast (hopefully, close to the fish's mouth) the skipper puts his engines out of gear. All this having been done properly, the sailfish should remain in the wake, angry or hungry enough to take the fly. When it does so, and the angler is sure of it, he strikes the fish several times to drive in the carefully sharpened hook. After the cast the angler may need to make several fast strips of the fly, and he may need to try again.

When the fish feels the steel the action starts, usually with an exciting jump and a run. The angler tries to let loose line pay out smoothly so he can handle the fish on the reel, letting it run as far as it wishes; providing a bit of slack during jumps, and pumping to nearly the maximum of the tackle's strength to regain line whenever possible. The skipper tries to keep the boat near the fish, or directly over it if it sounds.

Tackle is a powerful System 10 or 11 fly rod, a reel with ultra-smooth drag, a weight-forward floating line, and about 200 yards of 20-pound braided Dacron backing. Leaders, about as long as the rod, taper to about 18 inches of 12-pound-test tippet and a foot of about 80-pound-test shock leader. Anglers fishing for record are very careful to abide by the rules of the Salt Water Flyrodders of America and of the International Game Fishing Association, which are very specific. Those fishing for blue marlin or Pacific sailfish should use 30-pound backing or stronger, and leaders to suit.

Flies are as long and as fully dressed as can be cast properly; usually predominantly of white hackles 5 or 6 inches long and with thin strips of mylar and perhaps a darker topping. Many of them are dressed behind small popping bugs. Specialists in this sport are extremely fussy about their tackle, which often is custom-made and expensive. Each has his opinion on knots, but all agree they should be ones affording about 100 percent strength. Each also has his own ideas on all other details, none of which is too small to be overlooked.

MARLIN OF THE ATLANTIC

Of the five other principal billfishes (white marlin, blue marlin, striped marlin, black marlin and swordfish), only the white, the blue and the swordfish are found in the Atlantic. The white, being smaller and more prevalent, is of major interest. Whites and blues are taken by sportfishermen by trolling methods very similar to those for sailfish, except for variations in the strength of the tackle. Both exist almost exclusively on smaller fishes and are taken principally with baits such as balao, squid, mullet, flying fish and rigged eels. Strip baits and artificials such as feathered jigs and plastic imitations of the naturals also are used but many anglers consider the latter two inferior to the others.

White Marlin

This prized sportfish vies with the sailfish for popularity throughout its range, which extends from Cape Cod to Brazil, including the northern part of the Gulf of Mexico. Since sailfish are rare in North Atlantic areas, it takes their place there, hot spots being off Montauk Point, New York, and Ocean City, Maryland. We find them off Block Island, Rhode Island, in summer. Fishing tackle and methods are almost identical to those for sailfish. White marlin move northward in summer following water temperatures of about 70 degrees. Charter-boat skippers know their usual arrival dates and haunts so well that they usually can find schools easily, often being aided by working birds and feed slicks. White marlin are larger than Atlantic sailfish and are considered to be stronger fighters. The maximum size taken on rod and reel is about 60 pounds; those in the 40- to 60-pound range are most common. The fish has a low dorsal with a back of greenish-blue shading to silver-white below, marked by light blue vertical bars.

As in sailfishing, the charter boats equip their customers with tackle in the 50-pound-test range or greater — gear which many anglers consider much too strong. Thirty-pound test is about average, and sportsmen who won't bother their shipmates by doing so often go down to around 20-pound test, using Dacron or monofilament on revolving-spool trolling tackle and monofilament on spinning gear used for trolling. It is usual to terminate with about 12 feet of solid number 8 or 9 wire or a similar length of monofilament shock leader testing 80 pounds or more.

Handling a white marlin can be a dangerous job. This fish, taken on light line, is still putting up a struggle despite the efforts of three crew members to subdue it.

Favorites in baits and lures vary widely. In some areas experts swear by eels 12 to 14 inches long with a 7/0 hook, set in about a third of the way back and often with another loose one at the head. These swim under troll in a lifelike manner and are so durable that more than one fish are often taken with the same bait. Balao, squid, small fish, when and where obtainable, are popular in other areas. Strip baits, such as the belly of a fish, are often favored because they can be cut wide and trimmed narrower when the fish are window-shopping without buying anything. In such cases fish often can be teased into striking by pulling the bait away from them and dropping it back a few times.

Whole fish or strips rigged for baits should look fresh; promptly being changed at a sign of becoming soft. Colored plastic skirts are often slipped over the heads of baits, serving as attractors, making the baits easier to see, and helping to make them weedless. Colors are a matter of opinion which may not matter very much. Some anglers favor blue or green on bright days and white, yellow or blaze-orange on dull ones.

While anglers often think they should use larger baits for larger fish, this only is true to an extent because larger fish often take smaller baits better. When a fish shows, the bait is worked by pumping the rod. Presumably it takes the bait and pauses to turn it to swallow it headfirst, which is the reason for dropping it back. If one drops back so much that the fish drops the bait, pulling it quickly up to the surface and working it often tempts another take. On a hard strike some anglers, especially when they can see the angle of the take, strike instantly instead of dropping back—a choice learned only by experience. Some anglers, knowing their hooks are needle-sharp, strike only once on the theory that this embeds the barb, which will work deeper anyway, while repeated striking only serves to make a hole which helps the fish to throw the hook.

Trolling speeds are often varied, with baits usually trolled on much longer lines when seas are calm. Anglers sometimes leave their tackle to be better able to watch their baits from a higher elevation, such as the top of the ladder to the flying bridge, but they should be able to regain their stations almost instantly when a fish shows. This may be less perceptible than flashing fins and a waving beak on the surface; it may be only a darker shadow following beneath. One learns by experience what to look for, and skippers or mates often call our attention to action before we see it ourselves. When an angler leaves his tackle to visit the head or for some other reason, his rod can be taken over by anyone else if action starts, and that person has the right to handle the fish. Many prefer to do this by using a rod belt or gimbal belt and standing up.

Blue Marlin

Nearly all that has been said about baiting and handling sailfish and white marlin applies to blue marlin except that their larger size requires stronger equipment and usually bigger baits. The blue marlin, with steel-blue back shading to silver below, and with vertical bars, is a world-wide resident of warm and moderate seas. Its range in the Atlantic is between Massachusetts and northern South America; in the Pacific, usually south of the area near Acapulco, Mexico. Its size sometimes approaches or even exceeds a ton, but the all-tackle record is 1,153 pounds taken near Guam.

Very large reels and strong rods are used for blue marlin, with about 800 yards of Dacron line testing between 50 and 100 pounds. The fish are played from fighting chairs and a harness. The biggest ones are females; males usually do not exceed 400 pounds. Since few readers will fish for blue marlin, and most of these will be with experienced guides, these few comments should suffice.

SWORDFISH

Few, if any other angling skills call for more expertness than trying to bait a swordfish. The subject will be academic to most readers, but perhaps of sufficient interest for this brief note.

Swordfish are found world-wide in warm seas, migrating in summer in the Atlantic as far north as Newfoundland. While fishing for something else, I have seen one or two from time to time off Block Island, Rhode Island. In calm and warm weather they sun themselves on the surface, lying or cruising quietly with sickle-shaped dorsal and forked-tail tip showing. They usually are taken by harpooning. Grayish-blue to brown on back and shading to whitish below, their usual weight is about 200 pounds. The all-tackle record is a 1,182 pounder taken off the coast of Chile. Their food is squid and fishes, usually of the tuna family.

Experts who try to bait broadbills aren't always successful because the fish are spooky and may show no interest, even after repeated attempts. The bait is made up with two 14/0 hooks and must be trolled without a wake. This is attached to about 30 feet of about 500-pound-test stainless-steel cable, as the fish may roll on the line. The idea is to present the bait on about 200 feet of line by pulling it before the fish while the boat arcs slowly. Extra line is off the spool for a drop-back, this usually being held by the mate while the angler's reel is in free-spool. The fish usually dives to come up on the bait and the angler, after line has been dropped back, strikes repeatedly on contact. Then, if the hook holds, follows one of the greatest contests in all angling!

DOLPHIN

The subject of this section isn't the "dolphin" one sees doing tricks in seaquariums. That one is a mammal, more properly called a porpoise. This one is a fish—one of the most beautiful and most explosive fighters of the seas, and it swims in warm parts of most of them.

Between the greenish inshore water and the cobalt blue of the Gulf Stream, where we were trolling for sailfish, the variation in current catches patches of weeds and floating debris which offer havens for dolphin, which like to lie in the shady protection of such things, partly because forage fish also collect there. Thus, when one trolls for sailfish he also often catches dolphin, sometimes big bulls or cows in the 50-pound class. The fish hits the bait with such an explosive strike that no drop-back is necessary. It makes as lusty a run as a bonefish, jumps nearly as often as a tarpon, and uses its flat sides to put on the dogged fight of a big permit. All the angler can do is to let it run, drop the rod tip to provide slack when it jumps, and pump the fish in whenever possible.

Finally exhausted near the boat, it shimmers below in a gorgeous spectrum of greens, blues, orange and yellow remindful of a gleaming opal. Once the fish is boated, however, these brilliant colors quickly fade to a silver gray, and we only can remember the valiant fight it provided and how excellent its fillets will taste when broiled. The world's seas offer no more succulent food fish.

Those who troll for sailfish don't like to have their carefully prepared baits mashed by dolphin, but the fact remains that, pound for pound, the dolphin puts up as good a fight as anything and that one can catch dozens when schools are around. Excluding the fairly rare big bulls and cows, which travel in pairs or only of a few, school dolphin in the 2- to 15-pound class, or even bigger, are prime targets for light tackle of all sorts, and especially for the fly rod.

Dolphin roam the warm seas of the world, coming as far north as Maryland in the Atlantic in summer. Although they provide prime sport in spring and fall off Florida and along the Gulf coast they are found to some extent there year-round. They are numerous in warm waters of the Pacific coast, especially in the Sea of Cortez and along Panama, where they are known by the Spanish name of "dorado." The all-tackle record is a 76-pounder caught off Acapulco, Mexico. The bigger the school, the smaller the fish. Schools average between 2 and 30 pounds.

Dolphin are usually located by trolling offshore along weed lines, but not always. Their keen eyesight spots lures 50 feet or more away, whereupon they flash from cover, racing for the lure in waves of brilliant colors.

Exploding from the sea, a dolphin shows the fight that has earned it a reputation as one of the sportiest gamefish that swims in the salt.

Trolled lures can be baits or large artificials such as Japanese jigs, plugs or spoons. The fish usually go for any lure viciously, but sometimes one has to experiment. Trolling speed should be fairly fast.

When a dolphin is hooked the trick is to keep it in the water away from the boat while getting out casting tackle, because others rarely leave a tethered school-mate. Any casting tackle will do; its power being matched to the size of the fish. Long casts may not be needed because dolphin often will lie in the shade of the drifting boat. They will strike almost any lure so hard it is unnecessary to set the hook. Occasionally they are selective, making it advisable to try different offerings, different types of retrieve, and different lure actions on the surface or deeper. When using plugs, anglers normally remove all hooks except the rear one to minimize danger from thrashing fish on deck. Shock leaders are necessary, partly because dolphin have sharp teeth. The sport is to use the lightest tackle that seems practical, including fly-fishing gear.

Here again, the peak of the sport is with the fly. A 9-foot rod is a good choice, with a sinking line or a floater with sinking tip. Leaders about as long as the rod are tapered to about 10-pound test, with a foot or so of about 40-pound shock tippet. Fly sizes vary between 1/0 and 5/0 in the usual combinations of white, yellow and/or red, preferably with a flash of mylar. When the fish are small a lighter outfit would be more fun.

In addition to the usual practice of keeping a hooked fish near the boat, the school also can be kept nearby by chumming. If one school offers fish too small in size, a little more trolling should reveal a better one.

AMBERJACK

While seeking sailfish near the Gulf Stream's edge I once hooked something big and totally unlike any of the species previously described. Failing to show above water, the fish's runs were mostly straight down, so it was necessary to stay over it. This tactic, also the best in reef and wreck fishing, makes the line as short as possible and seems to tire fish faster. Eventually, whatever it was came up to the gaff, and it proved to be an amberjack of about 40 pounds.

To distinguish this species from the many others called "jacks," it is called the "greater amberjack," and the biggest taken with tackle weighed about 149 pounds. With a back of blue-black shading downward to silver with shades of yellow and a deeply forked tail, this powerful fighter resembles an immense bluefish. Although it is a deep-water denizen often frequenting outer reefs near the edge of the Gulf Stream (as well as oil drilling platforms, wrecks and other such places), it often comes to the top to feed around patches of weeds. Its Atlantic range is from the Carolinas around Florida and the Gulf. The vast families of jacks include the crevalle, yellowtail, roosterfish, pompano and permit, among over fifty others.

While normally a deep-water resident, amberjacks evidently move into relatively shallow inshore areas in spring for spawning and then can be taken with heavy fly-fishing tackle. They can be brought up by chumming and often by making a surface commotion such as by gunning the engines of a boat. They are tough fighters which strike at almost anything. Deep fishing is done by jigging or using bait, and they also are often taken when drift fishing with live bait. Greater amberjack average about 30 pounds. Other members of the family come in various sizes.

Amberjack is a deep-water fish that comes to the top to feed and spawn. Two scales were needed to weigh this mammoth.

KING MACKEREL

The king mackerel (or *"kingfish"* or "king") is a fast and vicious fighter found during warm-water months all around Florida and along the Gulf to and south of Mexico. Tourists hiring charter boats who just want to go fishing probably will catch kingfish because skippers find them easily and know they'll provide plenty of action. This often happens when the boat is (or is presumed to be) sailfishing.

A smaller relative, the Spanish mackerel, is often caught in the same locations by the same methods. Peak fishing is enjoyed in Gulf state areas in July and until late fall; a bit earlier and later if and where the water re-

Using heavy trolling tackle on a sailfishing trip, this fisherman tied into a kingfish—and he wasn't displeased.

mains warm. Best locations are offshore where the green water meets the blue; around natural or artificial reefs, and near oil rig platforms. Many angling methods are successful and tackle of various sorts varies with the methods and, in strength, with the size of the fish and how sporty the angler wants to be.

People fishing from charter boats who don't insist on using their own gear usually will be handed conventional equipment including star-drag reel and line of about 50-pound·test. This terminates with a wire leader 5 feet or longer and the mullet, balao or strip baits usually used for sailfish. While this is in the heavy class, such trolling often connects with bigger game. For example, my wife hooked a large kingfish which a shark attacked, cutting it in three sections. It came back for the drifting tail part and then swallowed the head. Thus, she was fast to the shark and battled it to exhaustion. The shark was several times her weight of 100 pounds or so and had to be cut loose because we had nothing on board to kill it with. Regardless of the justification for heavy tackle, the smashing strike and long runs of big kingfish provide a lot of fun and often snap line or leader if drags are set too tight. When kingfish are abundant, charter-boat captains often troll feathers or plugs, which help to make the action even more interesting. A good day afloat often loads the fish well.

When kingfish are plentiful, drift fishing is productive. Live or dead baits such as croakers, sand trout or any other small fish are used either free-fished or with lead. Revolving-spool equipment as used for casting for freshwater bass (with a foot or two of wire leader) is popular. Surface or deep-running plugs, weighted spoons (usually with dressed hooks), and baited or unbaited jigs lead among artificials. When fish lie deep one casts ahead of the drift of the boat to get the jig or spoon down. Fast retrieves are essential. Lures can't be fished in too fast. Lines testing as low as 10 pounds are practical if the reel's drag is set light enough to protect against smashing strikes. The fun is in letting the fish make their runs. If this is done, even big kingfish can be handled on light gear. School fish weigh between 5 and 30 pounds, but some of the others are considerably bigger.

Kingfish used to be regarded more as commercial catches than for sport, but the development of spinning tackle established them as prized sportfish. This now seems to be the favorite method. Line strength is a matter of judgment. In fishing around oil rigs, lines are stronger than average because they may be rubbed against the barnacle-encrusted structures and also because such fishing can be a grab-bag of red snappers, groupers, bluefish, cobia, bonito, dolphin, and even large sharks. (When sharks are encountered, fishermen usually move to another rig.) Thus, tackle may be in the 30- to 50-pound-test class.

In fishing near oil drilling platforms (where water can be 50 feet deep or so) one usually starts with a baited jig, dropping it down and working it fast at various levels. Then one may change his tackle to suit the predominant fish, going heavier or lighter and varying lures. This also is true when working natural or artificial reefs. Big fish congregate in these places because forage fish collect there to feast on smaller foods which cling to the structures.

In the Gulf of Mexico excellent kingfishing is found off Freeport and Port Aransas, Texas. These are among the shrimp-boat ports, and shrimp boats are keys to kingfishing.

Shrimpers operate far out in the Gulf. They put down their trawls during the night, usually pulling in the nets at daybreak. Crews then anchor and cull what has been taken on board to separate the shrimps from the trash fish. Around daybreak the trash is put overboard, providing colossal chum lines for hoards of big fish of every description, but particularly for kingfish. The trick is to leave port early enough to be on hand near the anchored boats to enjoy good fishing before the kingfish have eaten their fill. Sportfishermen drift, troll and cast from the boats using their favorites of the various methods previously described.

If this doesn't provide a bonanza of fishing in the morning because somebody got up too late, you can fish deep with jigs or deep-running plugs and wait until the fish become hungry again later in the afternoon. The shrimpers still will be anchored because the crews are sleeping after a long night's work, and the fish will be in the vicinity, ready to feed again. Deep baits often take sailfish and other exotic species. Countless shrimp boats offer this fringe benefit all during the warm-weather months. Lacking it, of course, fishermen can start chum lines of their own.

DEEP JIGGING

If anyone's favorite southeastern offshore fish hasn't been mentioned in this chapter it is because it is of lesser importance or because one or more of the methods described will take it. For example, the fast-running wahoo, a relative of the kingfish and the Spanish mackerel, doesn't occur in schools but occasionally is taken when trolling for sailfish. It is a prize often in the 50-pound range.

When one wants to take pot-luck with whatever is around, undoubtedly the best method is by jigging over such locations as wrecks and natural or artificial reefs, so a few added notes may be appropriate.

Tackle can be of any sort that will work a jig. Usually it is in the 20- to 30-pound-test range for working jigs in size about 7/0. This varies with the depth of jigging and with whatever is down there, which could be a grouper or something else in the 50-pound range or better which has its heart set on burrowing into a cleft in the coral and shearing the leader or popping the line. It also could be a mixture of panfish, which deserve much lighter tackle.

The tackle is important. Regardless of the power of the rod, it should be a stiff one because soft tips don't work jigs actively enough and don't have the lifting power to derrick fish quickly away from their holes. The terminal end of the line usually is doubled and fastened to a yard or so of wire leader at least double the strength of the line. Jigs should be fastened with a loose loop knot, and swivels and snaps should be avoided.

The choice in jigs can be narrowed down to two types: the flattened Upperman string bean and one of the bullet models. Color is of minor importance, but remember that a few thin strips of mylar help the flash, particularly down deep. Weight, of course, must be enough to reach bottom quickly.

"Sweetening" the jig's hook with half a plastic worm, a strip of pork rind, or bait usually helps. The best of these is a strip cut from the belly of a fish, and about the length of the jig.

The usual practice over reefs is to drift toward deeper water and to drop the jig to bottom, then to jerk it up very actively. This can be done continuously near bottom or all the way to the top—a method which we have already described for freshwater fishing. One soon learns whether the fish are on the bottom or at a higher level.

To keep fish from wedging themselves in the coral or kelp it is important to strike immediately and then to keep the fish coming up at least to a level where it can't find protection. A stiff rod is necessary to do this.

Deep jigging under a great variety of circumstances is one of the best— if not the best—ways to take fish down deep. Thus this reminder bears repeating. Never underestimate the value of a jig!

36

Pacific Offshore Fishing

Extending from southern California's boundary about a thousand miles into Mexico, the peninsula of Baja California encloses a vast gulf containing the best and most varied sportfishing in the world. Called either the Gulf of California or the Sea of Cortez, this relatively unexplored expanse of in-shore and offshore angling offers over 300 species of gamefish in a total of at least 600 different varieties. The gulf is the world's greatest fish trap, about a hundred miles wide at its narrowest place; sprinkled with islands both large and small, and holding tackle-busters of every description from black marlin up to 2,000 pounds down to panfish suitable for the very lightest of tackle. Black marlin, striped marlin, sailfish, roosterfish, dolphin, amberjack, yellowtail, Sierra mackerel, snappers, groupers, bonito and cabrilla include only a very few found in the Gulf.

HOW TO GET THERE

Although Baja California is remote by modern standards, and in some areas with too many miles between services of supply for recreational vehicles, it does offer several towns and cities complete with comfortable air-conditioned resorts which should satisfy the most fastidious anglers and their families. Chief of these is La Paz, near the southern tip of the penin-sula and reachable not only by road but also by commercial air services from several points in the United States and by an excellent ferry from

647

Mazatlan. Farther to the north the towns of Loreto and Santa Rosalia have similar air connections and the latter is available by ferry steamer from Guaymas on the Mexican mainland. Long-range charter boats from San Diego and other parts fish the western coast and offer two-week trips around the peninsula to La Paz and other areas. Since facilities constantly are being improved and expanded, people planning trips should contact the Mexican Tourist Council (300 Wilshire Boulevard, Los Angeles, California 90005) for up-to-date information.

Recreational vehicles can reach the tip of the peninsula by road from San Diego but, as this is being written, parts of the route are rough, making the mainland trip to Guaymas or Mazatlan, and to Baja by ferry, an easier selection. Air travel is by far the most practical way. However, a friend of mine drove to La Paz this year (1972) with his family and reported that the trip was comfortable and that the fishing was "out of this world!" I might add that, as far as angling ability is concerned, he is more or less of a novice, so Baja isn't only for experts.

Tackle for Baja California

Anglers fishing Baja's waters should bring their own equipment because very little is available there. This includes extra rods and reels, plus extra spools of lines and terminal gear.

While few may be interested in chartering a cruiser for offshore fishing for marlin and other big ones such as tuna and grouper, those that do will need heavy tackle. A favorite boat rod down there is Fenwick's Model PT 809, affectionately known as the "Baja Workhorse." With this and a 9/0 reel loaded with 80- to 100-pound-test line and a vest harness, even giant black marlin shouldn't be a great problem. A 6/0 reel with 60-pound-test line provides a good runner-up for the light-heavyweights.

More than half of the fishing inshore and offshore around Baja calls for lighter tackle in the angler's choice of fixed and revolving-spool outfits. We would find uses for the light, normal, heavy and extra-heavy spinning outfits described in Chapter 1 but, if a selection must be made from these, the heavy rig, using 10- to 15-pound-test line and lures or baits in the ½- to 1½-ounce range, should be most useful. Include extra spools, one or two perhaps being a bit overgunned with lines between 15- and 25-pound test for trolling or deep jigging. Include wire traces and/or shock leader material; an ample selection of hooks in various sizes, and whatever lures suit the outfit.

All lures previously described will do well from time to time but some always are better than others for various purposes. All reel spools should be of metal because the constriction effected by handling strong fish on

Lures for Pacific fishing range from ½-ounce jigs and spoons to 1½-ounce (or heavier) metal squids and wooden plugs; also feathered trolling lures.

monofilament will expand plastic spools, making them bind and probably break, thus causing the line to pop. Since bait may be in short supply in Baja, a light outfit is handy for catching it. Since tackle stores may be inadequately equipped for visiting anglers, it is well to bring plenty of everything.

Of the hundreds of species of fish found in Baja waters, only a few dozen are of primary interest. Most of these are bottom species or top-water travelers which we now know how to catch because they fall into patterns previously discussed. Eliminating these, we find a few deserving special attention.

THE UNIQUE ROOSTERFISH

Big-game fishermen who troll baits in front of black or striped marlin and sailfish find new challenge and excitement when they tangle with roosterfish on lighter tackle. The roosterfish (*pez de gallo,* in Spanish) is a member of the jack family which averages offshore between 30 and 100 pounds. An I.G.F.A. all-tackle record of 114 pounds was established near La Paz on 30-pound-test line. Fish between average size and only a pound or two are caught in sandy-bottomed surf. The little ones are highly prized as trophies. Size is of minor importance because the roosterfish is a champion fighter in every class.

So-named because its first dorsal extends into seven elongated spines about half the length of its body (longer for its size than any other fish), this characteristic reminds one of the long, curving tail of a game cock. The fish is greenish-black on its back, with tinges of blue, pink, lavender, silver and gold. This shades to yellowish-white below, marked with four curving greenish-black stripes, the rear two going downward and backward from the first dorsal. Otherwise, the roosterfish resembles an amberjack.

Its range, only on the western coast of the United States, extends from northern Peru around the Gulf of California and into the southern part of the state. In the Gulf the best areas are from Mulege to the south and the best season is between April and November. Between Loreto and the peninsula's tip a lesser number of roosterfish are caught year-round.

Average roosterfish tackle is 20-pound test, using 6/0 short-shanked hooks. Many anglers, particularly when using artificials in the mild surf, go as light as 8 pound. Artificials include small spoons, feathers and plugs, or live bait. Since bait is difficult to purchase (or has been), many anglers catch their own by snagging it on large cast treble hooks. In the surf the bait is hooked ahead of the dorsal and lobbed out, whereupon it usually swims toward deeper water. When schools of roosterfish are concentrated offshore, one may hit an artificial, but most of the strikes are on bait. This usually is a live baitfish, such as a bonefish or grunt, hooked through both lips or through the back so it can be drifted. Strip baits also are used for trolling.

Since roosterfish have relatively small mouths, considerable slack line is given, or dropped back, after a strike. The fish needs time to turn the bait and to swallow it. The strike is made when it starts to move off. Many stories are told about the battle that follows, but all agree the fish never gives up while it can swim. The first run is a long and sizzling one in which it makes several leaps like a dolphin. After a few such runs, sometimes as long as the first one, the fish may stop fighting on top and will sound and continue down below.

Roosterfish migrate northward to some extent in summer and are found farther up the Gulf. Stories told about such migrations include one of anglers seeing what looked like a tidal wave; a wide rolling crest of white water made by hundreds of big roosterfish as they leap-frogged over one another while advancing. As with other species, schools of big ones are very few in number. They often are spotted in the usually calm and clear water of the Gulf while cruising on the surface with large dorsal fins extended to make wakes. Anglers call this "flashing the comb," and these fish are usually taken by trolled baits. Reports are that they are excellent when baked, barbecued or smoked, but that the meat becomes dry when fried.

PACIFIC BILLFISH

Pacific waters boast four prized billfish, of which two (the broadbill swordfish and the blue marlin) were discussed in the preceding chapter. The other two are the black marlin and the striped marlin. The former is so big that even the most experienced anglers seek it with boat captains who are specialists and in command of cruisers large enough and with suitable equipment for handling fish that can tip the scales at over 1,000 pounds. Thus we'll mention the black marlin only briefly and leave it to the few who wish to seek it to obtain more authoritative information from skippers when they go on board. The striped marlin, smaller and more prevalent, is more suitable to anglers on cruisers who see tails cutting the surface while fishing for it or something else. Being a more practical quarry for the non-specialist, it deserves greater attention here.

Black Marlin

Found only in the Pacific, the black marlin is second only to the broadbill swordfish as a prize for the big-game angler. It averages larger even than the blue marlin, the all-tackle record being a 1,560-pounder caught off Capo Blanco, Peru—a noted hot spot for the species. Fishing methods usually consist of trolling whole fish (such as bonito) on heavy tackle as was discussed for swordfish and blue marlin. Heavy tackle can be as much as a 12/0 big-game reel holding about 600 yards of about 100-pound-test line with the end doubled long enough to put a few turns on the reel. To this is fastened a 25-foot leader testing over 200 pounds and a 12/0 hook. Black marlin usually hit baits hard. Small ones often take trolled feathers or other artificial lures.

Striped Marlin

The striped marlin cruises the Pacific coast from southern California to Chile. A hot spot for it is near the mouth of the Gulf of California between Mazatlan and the tip of the peninsula—an area where combating currents are ideal for the species. Striped marlin enter the Gulf in summer seeking water temperatures of over 60 degrees. Thus they are most abundant between June and December, the month of September usually being best. Several often can be seen at one time, their tails cutting the smooth surface of the sea. Their dorsals, typical of marlins, usually are cased in their backs unless they are aroused. Big fish usually are loners or in very small groups. Smaller ones may be in larger groups, often widely scattered.

Striped marlin are credited with putting on the best fight of all the marlins, often making long runs and as many as 25 spectacular jumps. They are distinguished by their vertical bars, or stripes, but these are not always brilliant. Their average weight is between 175 and 250 pounds; the all-tackle record being a 483-pounder caught off Chile. In addition to their almost continuous leaps, they thrill anglers by fighting on or near the surface.

Sporty tackle for striped marlin is a 3/0 or 4/0 trolling reel fitted with from 400 to 500 yards of between 30- and 50-pound-test braided Dacron line. The line's end usually is doubled enough so several turns can be wrapped around the reel. This is swiveled to a stainless-steel wire leader, usually not longer than 15 feet, to which is attached a short-shanked 9/0 hook.

Whole fish or strip baits are presented to the fish by arcing them on about 75 feet of line. When trolled in an arc in front of the fish the bait tracks much closer to it than does the boat. Whole fish usually are preferred, rigged by a choice of two methods. The usual one along the Mexican and California coast merely is to insert the hook upward through both lips. The so-called New Zealand rig consists of sewing lips and gills closed with twine or wire, a few turns of which are made around the bend of the hook. Artificials such as feathered lures often are successful.

When a fish is baited in this usual manner it normally will slash at the lure. This signals the angler to lower his rod and to drop back some line. Seeing the bait evidently stunned and drifting, the marlin usually will return to pick it up, swallowing it while moving off. The time to strike is when the weight of the fish is felt. Several strikes may be needed to set the hook solidly. If the fish hasn't taken the bait the angler may interest it in it by reeling in fast. Upon connection the skipper usually speeds the boat momentarily to aid the angler in setting the hook. While the fish is allowed to make its runs the skipper often handles the boat to keep it nearby. If this is overdone a green fish can be boated in minutes. Many anglers consider it more sporting to handle the fish from a dead boat, thus taking credit for winning the battle with minimum assistance and also having a more exciting time of it. Marlin should be released unless desired for trophies. Trophies rarely are taken, one reason being that they need so much wall space.

CALIFORNIA YELLOWTAIL

Several fish are called yellowtail that shouldn't be. This one (correctly named) is a popular member of the jack family similar to the amberjack discussed earlier. Handsome and husky, it has a metallic blue-green back and silver belly separated by a brassy medial stripe. Its fins and forked tail are of a pronounced greenish-yellow, from which it gets its name. Yellowtail weighing over 100 pounds have been caught but, in Pacific coastal waters, most of them are between 5 and 25 pounds, with a few lunkers reaching 50 or even more.

Yellowtail range from the Mexican coast into the Gulf of California and up the Pacific as far as Oregon. San Diego calls itself the yellowtail capital of California and promotes popular fishing derbies for them in season. From there a vast fleet of charter boats offers daily trips to favorite haunts around islands and over kelp beds and rocky banks; others offer excursions of between one and two weeks duration down the Baja coast and into the Sea of Cortez itself. Private boats seek yellowtail with equal enthusiasm. California fishing licenses are required in its waters. Boats entering Mexican waters must be registered by Mexican officials, and Mexican licenses are required for all on board fishing craft.

Like most other species, yellowtail are more or less migratory, seeking water temperatures between 58 and 65 degrees. These bring them into Baja waters in early spring and concentrate vast schools off southern California between May and mid-October, after which most of them return southward again.

Yellowtail are hard-hitters and strong, fast swimmers that never want to give up. When caught over kelp beds they will high-tail for the grass, making strong tackle necessary. Tackle strength varies between 20 and 50 pounds, depending on size of the fish in the schools, where and how deep one is fishing, and whether or not it is from a party boat with many other anglers. Those on private boats can go lighter.

Usual rods (varied as above) are 8- to 9-foot sticks with fast taper and plenty of backbone. These are equipped with conventional or fixed-spool reels holding about 250 yards of monofilament testing between 20 and 50 pounds. Live bait normally is used on party boats; often anchovies, sardines or small mackerel, usually hooked through the forward part of the back. The bait is allowed to swim out and down until a yellowtail takes it. If the take is light the strike is delayed while some slack is given. If it is hard the angler usually strikes immediately.

A trick in casting live bait is to "lob" it with a swinging motion to avoid snapping it off the hook.

Party boat fishing usually is done by chumming—in this case with live bait such as anchovies—from an anchored boat. Skippers always know exact locations and move from one hot spot to another. Since boats may leave at 3 A. M. or so, fishermen go aboard early and enjoy comfortable berths until the fishing grounds are reached. Most boats are well equipped with all comforts, including good meals and music. Fishing for yellowtail also is done by drifting, trolling or by casting artificials such as squids, jigs and plugs, the latter usually being baitfish imitations.

Jigs, especially when used from party boats, usually call for heavy equipment because one doesn't know what will take hold. Lines average in the 40-pound monofilament range and may be swiveled to a wire or monofilament leader which is stronger and more abrasion resistant. Jigs vary in size and weight up to about 3 ounces, depending on tackle, depth, current and whatever is expected to take hold down below. They are connected to line or leader with a split ring or loose loop and usually are chromed and dressed in blue and white or all-white; fished in the conventional manner. One doesn't always hook yellowtail. He more often may connect with bonito, kelp bass, bluefin tuna, halibut, whitefish, grouper, jewfish, sea bass, or something else. The last three can weigh over 100 pounds and can dash out from rocky hideaways for the lure, returning to the safety of their lairs in seconds. Strong gear is needed to bring such fish up and to prevent shearing lines or leaders on shells and rocks. Although books record general experiences, only judgment can recommend whether or not stronger or lighter equipment should be used in individual situations. With more time to handle fish without bothering others, anglers on private boats have more fun fishing jigs and baits off bottom with lighter tackle.

TUNA AND OTHER MACKERELS

The tackle-smashing mackerel family, big and small, ranging far and wide, is so extensive that only a few typical members can be mentioned in any comprehensive book of reasonable length. That's just as well because, except for size and tackle to suit, the traits of all the mackerels from half-ton bluefins to tiny tinkers are quite similar. Having discussed some of the others previously, let's end this chapter with notes on four more: the bluefin tuna, the yellowfin tuna, the albacore (or longfin tuna) and the bonito (or false albacore). Another family member, the Sierra mackerel, is considered identical to the king mackerel (or Florida kingfish), which was discussed earlier. It also is known as the cero. It is very much like the Spanish mackerel (also called the Sierra mackerel) and seems to be a distant relative of the wahoo, all of which are more or less similar in size and in habits and are fished for in about the same ways.

(I must note here that confusion reigns in proper and regional names of many specific fishes, of which the above is a good example. Species and fishing methods for some are so much like others that discussions of them would be pointless. This book tries to use the most generally accepted names and to mention only the others which seem important.)

Bluefin Tuna (Horse Mackerel)

This hard-striking and deep-fighting whopper not only is the largest of the mackerel family but also one of the biggest and most prized of all game-fish. In summer vast schools which have wintered off South America follow warm currents northward as far as Oregon on the Pacific coast and as far as Labrador in the Atlantic. Runs are predictable and often come close inshore, such as into Long Island Sound and around the tip of Cape Cod. The big ones reach 1,000 pounds, or more, and are sought with large, elaborate specially rigged boats and heavy tackle. Some of these also are hooked and beaten by anglers in small boats, who get the excitement of what whalers called a "Nantucket sleigh-ride" and then wonder what to do with the tremendous fish in the event that it has been licked. Other bluefin schools consists of smaller and younger fish between 10 and 100 pounds, which provide prime sport on lighter tackle and which are more practical for anglers lacking complicated equipment and a knowledge of equally complicated methods. These methods, both complex and simple, are many and varied, so we'll mention only a few.

A favorite one is to attract bluefins by chumming from an anchored or drifting boat, or one perhaps tied to a buoy. In recent years anglers found that their chumming could be done better and easier for them by the simple expedient of cruising around draggers, which periodically haul their nets. Many fish are discarded after being culled, and many other dead or exhausted ones slip through the nets to form a giant chum line.

One of the tricks here is to rig a big reel (such as 12/0) with Dacron line testing in the 100- to 130-pound range and the usual doubled terminal length, plus about 15 feet of number 12 to 15 stainless-steel wire or similar strength braided cable leader and a strong hook in size about 12/0. A cork cut to size is sometimes rigged into or with the whole fish used as a bait to neutralize the sinking of the wire so the bait can drift down the chum line naturally. Big bluefins are not boat shy and often can be seen feeding down below or breaking the surface. One flashes to the bait and takes it solidly. The hook is set immediately, and the fight is on!

The bluefin, probably weighing a few hundred pounds, will make a fast run and will sound to fight below; perhaps a few hundred feet below, if the water is deep enough. The angler counteracts this by pumping and planing on a heavy drag. In the latter the boat runs forward for several hundred feet, pulling the fish, and then backs up while the angler regains line. It is important to use maximum power and to give the fish no rest.

Some rigs are made by attaching a quickly removable float far enough above the bait so it will drift at the desired depth; the bait usually being a live fish which can be hooked under the back or through the lips. Baits are herring, mullet, menhaden, mackerel, flying fish, squid and other species; whatever is available and regionally popular. When bluefins can't be located, these often are trolled fairly fast.

Baiting big bluefins has an army of proponents, as well as some detractors who call it "a job for a strong back and a weak mind." While the latter may not realize the skill and stamina involved, they usually belong to the cult which enjoys seeing fish fight and jump on top rather than be dragged up from the bottom.

Many anglers prefer to fish for school tuna in the 10- to 100-pound range. These usually are taken by trolled feathers on a line short enough to work the lure just behind the prop-wash. Teasers often are used to increase surface commotion, and skippers often polish their propellers for added attraction. Not being boat shy, the bluefins come close into the wake to investigate all this and hit the lures solidly; then fighting in the same manner as their older and bigger brothers. From Maryland to Cape Cod this usually happens between June and October; in other places, such as in Pacific waters, during warm-weather months.

The power of tackle for school tuna obviously is relative to their size, each school being made up of similarly sized fish. An average outfit is a 4/0 reel with about 500 yards of 30-pound-test Dacron. In addition to Japanese feathered jigs, other successful lures include metal squids and spoons. We often use heavy or extra-heavy spinning tackle for trolling, or for casting when tuna are in the wake. Even the little fellows put up a strong argument by fighting deep and sideways to resist the tension of the tackle.

Yellowfin Tuna (Allison Tuna)

One of the best and most beautiful of gamefishes, the yellowfin is a typical tuna distinguished mainly by a yellowish medial stripe and pronounced golden-yellow in its fins. The all-tackle record is, or was, a 266½-pounder taken off the Hawaiian Islands, but evidently others up to 400 pounds have been taken by commercial means. From the average angler's standpoint, fish not exceeding 100 pounds can be expected, and most are much smaller.

Yellowfins, like bluefins, follow deep warm-water currents northward in summer and southward in winter. In the Atlantic they are found in the Gulf of Mexico, and they follow the Gulf Stream usually as far as Maryland and New Jersey. They are more common in the Pacific as far north as mid-California, where they reach the peak of migration in early fall.

Once considered to be different fish, the yellowfin tuna and the Allison tuna now usually are listed as the same species, this being made more confusing by also calling them "albacore."

Fishing methods and tackle are the same as for school tuna. In addition, commercial fishermen who chum up schools fill their boats quickly by using bait or feathered jigs attached by short and strong lines to sturdy bamboo poles, two poles, held by two men, often being attached to the same bait or lure. On the strike (which usually is immediate) the fish are swung inboard without allowing them to fight. Sport fishermen who give them a chance find that yellowfin tuna are fully as active as bluefins of similar size, and they are a favorite big-game fish along Baja's and southern California's coasts.

Albacore (Longfin Tuna)

This one of the "little tunas," also called the "white-meat tuna" is the kind that brings premium price in cans. It is also a member of the mackerel family. Rarely found along the Atlantic coast north of Florida, during warm months it is common on the Pacific coast from Chile into southern California. Schools migrate into the San Diego area in late June or early July, the runs continuing northward into October. Albacore migrate counterclockwise around the Northern Pacific. For example, a fish which was tagged off southern California was recovered 196 days later near Tokyo, Japan, after having covered more than 4,600 miles to average $23\frac{1}{2}$ miles per day.

Albacore are distinguished by their pectoral fins, which are so long they almost look like wings. While they reach 100 pounds, those usually caught by anglers are in the 10- to 40-pound range, with 20 pounds being a good average. Atlantic and Pacific albacore are considered to be the same species. Their diet is small fishes, squid and crustaceans.

Albacore are found traveling in large, loose schools in deep blue offshore near-surface waters having temperatures between 62 and 68 degrees. Anglers locate schools by trolling in such waters, particularly over ledges or undersea mountains. Working birds often pinpoint schools, some of which may be seen feeding on the surface. Trolling usually is done fairly fast (about 8 knots) with whole or strip baits or with artificials such as feathered or plastic-tailed jigs and sometimes with plugs or squid. The lures are trolled about 75 feet behind the boat. When bait is used the reel is in free-spool (or, in spinning, with bail open) so a drop-back of a few seconds can be allowed before striking. Such trolling often is done with hand-lines. As in dolphin fishing, a hooked fish can be kept out because the school probably will stay with it. When a school is located the boat is allowed to drift for casting, and the school usually is kept nearby by chumming.

Bait (and chum, also) in southern California usually is live anchovies

Deep-sea predators such as the bonito often herd baitfish into a compact mass—called "balling the bait"—then strike the prey on the fringe of the school. They'll strike a lure cast on the fringe, mistaking it for an isolated or disabled baitfish.

between 3 and 6 inches long. Hooks are ringed straight bronze between numbers 4 and 1/0, size 2 usually being best. Baits are hooked either upward through both lips or in the back forward of the dorsal in the usual manner. It may be necessary to use small sinkers of between 1/4 and 1/2 ounce to cast to desired distances. Heavier sinkers are used when one wishes to go deep.

Tackle includes heavy or extra-heavy spinning gear with lines in the 15- to 20-pound-test range, but anglers on private boats probably will want to go lighter. It also includes conventional tackle with lines testing between 20 and 40 pounds; in other words, the same gear as for yellowtail and many other species. Since action may be fast but of short duration, many anglers have more than one outfit handy. If wire leaders aren't used, the line should be inspected and probably cut back after each catch.

Albacore fishing is a way of life with many anglers in southern California, who leave everything else to go fishing when the news comes out that "they're in!" Excellently appointed and uncrowded party boats leave docks in areas such as San Diego and Southgate daily for short offshore trips or excursions of a week or more along the Baja coast. Anglers' catches are kept refrigerated and can be traded at the docks for canned or smoked tuna, but the flesh of these fish is so delicious that many are taken home for immediate enjoyment or for the freezer.

On the end of a line albacore fight in the same manner that other tunas do. They make a fast run and then go straight down, putting up dogged resistance while being pumped up. Casts from a drifting boat usually are made to windward to get the bait or lure out farther and to prevent fish from breaking off by going under the boat.

Bonito (False Albacore)

Several species of bonito or similar fish are found along Atlantic and Pacific coasts; the Atlantic or "common" bonito, the Pacific or "California" bonito, the striped or "Oceanic" bonito, and other "little tunas," such as the false albacore (also called "bonito") and various others known as "skipjacks." They all are members of the mackerel family and are so similar that a nonscientific book such as this need make no distinctions between them. They are often caught in the same ways when we're fishing for other little tunas. They range most warm seas—in the Atlantic from Florida to Cape Cod between late spring and early fall, in the Pacific usually in southern areas, but some species travel as far north as Vancouver Island. Their sizes average in the 10-pound range. Because of their abundance they are popular sportfishes, and often are used as bait for much bigger varieties such as big tunas and billfishes.

37

Pacific
Inshore Fishing

From shore and from boats near shore all around the Sea of Cortez; up the Baja coast, and along California into Canada the varied wealth of inshore fishing covers so many species and methods that it defies description. The Sea of Cortez, for example, abounds with a myriad of species which are caught along the coast as well as offshore. These include mackerel, corvina, snappers, black snook, whitefish, groupers, flounder, triggerfish, several species known as cabrilla, plus other rockfishes, and occasionally migratory prizes such as yellowtail, roosterfish, amberjack and jack crevalle, with which we now are familiar.

Although many of these inshore fishes may prefer a definite sort of abode, they also may be found in others. In spite of this, perhaps they best can be described by separating them into their most usual living or feeding places such as rocks along or near shore, in and around deep and shallow banks, amid and over kelp forests, and over sand in the surf.

ROCKFISHING

Rockfishing pertains more to the kind of place than to what's in it. What's in it may be swarms of small snappers and other fish of various kinds and colors, or perhaps a giant black sea bass that could tip the scales at a few hundred pounds. Rockfishing includes many species of bottom fish of which the cods, croakers and snappers constitute a majority in many places along the coast. Some of these regionally are known as rockfish rather than by their proper names. Black rockfish are called "sea bass," or vice versa, but there are several kinds of true sea bass we'll discuss later. One group of fishes on the southern Pacific coast is called "cabrilla"; composed of many kinds of small groupers and kelp bass. A lingcod is a rockfish worthy of separate mention. All this can get confusing, so let's more or less ignore the names of the many species and just have fun catching them. All are delicious to eat and more to be regarded as table fish than sportfish—even if some can be very sporty.

The kind of place for rockfishing is along the coast where there are rocky shorelines, reefs, breakwaters, jetties, tidal pools, kelp beds and calm inlets. Rockfishing is done by casting from shore or by casting or jigging from anchored or drifting small boats, usually in places where big ones can't go. Since most rockfish are not migratory they furnish food and fun year-round. The best time is low, slack tide when little or no current is running.

Tackle for rockfishing basically is anything one can cast with or jig with. In various parts of the thousands of miles of coast fishermen will be a lot more specific because they seek certain species in definite kinds of places. As an average, try any outfit using monofilament testing between 8 and 15 pounds, such as a heavy spinning rig—we can go light if we don't mind losing terminal gear occasionally. A shock leader helps to prevent breaks by sharp-teethed fish or abrasions from rocks. Stronger lines are needed where there is kelp or when fish make runs for cover amid rocks. A little judgment on location helps to decide such matters as this.

Since rockfish aren't fussy one can use any bait which can be kept moving, such as live or dead or cut anchovies, sardines, mackerel, squid or prawns (shrimp). Deep-running plugs and shiny spoons do well when they can be fished close to bottom without hanging up. One of the best artificials is a jig, often considered better than anything else. This includes diamond jigs and lead-heads with feathered or plastic skirts. Where possible, cast out and whip the jig in 2 or 3 feet over the bottom. From a drifting boat, let the jig touch bottom, take in 2 or 3 feet of line, then bounce it over the area. From a jetty or breakwater casts can be made fanwise, but the best spots are close to the obstruction, so casting along it may do better.

While enjoying rockfishing, don't neglect the fly rod! Use a high-density fast-sinking line and a short leader testing between 12 and 15 pounds—this usually being necessary to pull fish away from caves and tangles of floating kelp. Any streamer fly or bucktail should be effective, regardless of size or color. Shrimp patterns also work well. No matter what tackle is used, one often catches a small rockfish and finds that something much bigger has taken it. This may be a lingcod, which is highly prized and worthy of special mention.

Lingcod, and Homemade Lures

The lingcod is a rockfish that sometimes exceeds 50 pounds but more often is in the 10- to 25-pound range. Usual baits for it are small baitfish such as live sea trout or herring. It also takes artificials, principally jigs. Larry Green, one of California's most prominent anglers, says that the favorite bait for lingcod is small octopus, and he makes an artificial that he says is as good as, and easier to use than, the real thing.

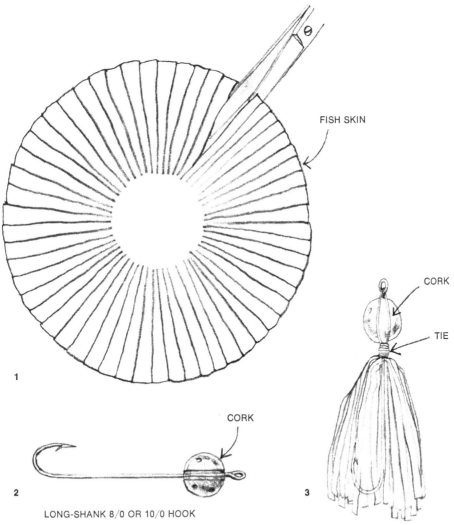

FISH SKIN

CORK

TIE

CORK

1

2

3

LONG-SHANK 8/0 OR 10/0 HOOK

How to make an artificial octopus rig for lingcod. See text on following page for full details.

When preparing a lingcod for the table, save the skin, or any other large scaled skin. Use shears to cut a circle about 10 inches in diameter from it and punch a small hole in the center. Cut narrow tapered strips toward the middle to about 1½ or 2 inches from it. Round a small cork (such as from a wine bottle) and drill a ⅛-inch hole through it. Push a long-shanked single 8/0 or 10/0 hook through the hole and lay the circular fringed skin (outside of skin outward) over it so the hook's eye protrudes through the hole in the skin. String a piece of strong monofilament through the hook's eye to hold the cork forward on the hook and then wrap it around the skin and the base of the cork to bunch the skin together. Tie this tightly. This is an excellent representation of a small octopus or squid, and requires only a few minutes to make. Experts on the California coast say it is the most effective lingcod rig ever developed.

A similar rig is made with a jig and one or two children's cylindrical rubber balloons. Cut off the ends opposite the necks and cut strips toward the necks. Slip the necks around the jig and tie them where jigs usually are dressed. Squids change color to red, pink, yellow, blue and brown, so any balloon colors should be effective at one time or another.

KELP FISHING

Inshore and offshore along the southern Pacific coast vast kelp beds grow like forests in shallow parts of the sea. The rubbery pipelike trunks extend into waving fronds covering the surface to remind eastern freshwater anglers of lily pad areas where big bass lurk back home. These kelp forests harbor counterparts of the eastern bronzeback; kelp bass, sand bass and spotted bass in size and shape very much like the smallmouths and large-mouths of fresh water.

Kelp Bass

Of these, the kelp bass is the best fighter and more inclined to take lures and baits near the top. With the bass, in season, one often hooks other fishes such as barracuda, bonito, yellowtail, rockfish, lingcod, white sea bass and sheepshead. When any one of these species is predominant, tackle and lures are used to suit. Kelp bass fishing is good in the Baja area all year but is more or less concentrated between April and October farther north, with peak fishing around August. Since it is warm-water fishing, the best of it is south of Los Angeles.

Tackle for kelp bass fishing (with exceptions as above) is whatever one would use for freshwater bass in eastern regions: spinning, spincasting, plugcasting or fly-fishing gear. Because other and bigger fish may be en-countered, and to prevent bass tangling in the kelp, lines of between 15- and 30-pound test are used; 20 being about average. A No. 1 hook is preferred for bait, which is live anchovy, herring, mackerel, squid or other baitfish, hooked as previously described. Squid is excellent when available.

The best fishing usually is on the seaward side of a kelp bed. While one can troll or drift-fish, it is more usual to anchor off the seaward side and to let out anchor line to within easy casting distance of the edge of the kelp. Bass usually are brought out by chumming, using small live anchovies if possible. In night fishing (which is most productive) a light is used to lure baitfish, and thus the bass, near the boat.

Casts are made to the edge of the kelp. If bait is used the spinning reel bail is left open, or the conventional reel is left in free-spool, so the bass can have time to run and to swallow the bait before striking. The strike must be made before the fish reaches the kelp. Getting tangled in the kelp usually costs the fish and probably the hook or lure. Lures are what would be used for freshwater bass, principally plugs and feathered jigs. Jigging is a favorite method.

Kelp bass may take almost anything in a frenzy of feeding, but at times they are hard to catch. If surface and near-surface fishing doesn't get results, one tries it deeper, using a rubber-core sinker weighing an ounce or so placed about 3 feet above the baited hook. Deep jigging also often pays off.

I don't know that this idea has been used in kelp bass fishing, but it is a useful one for all purposes where a bait should be drifted at definite depth. It also is a lot of fun!

Buy a package of children's round rubber balloons, preferably in very visible colors such as red, yellow and orange. Blow one up, knot the neck, and tie it to the swivel above the leader of a baited hook, or at any other desired place on leader or line. Pay out line from the reel to let the balloon float downwind, taking the bait with it. If the fish that strikes is big enough it will pop the balloon as it takes the bait deeper. If the fish isn't large a strike is signaled when the balloon suddenly starts to bob and skitter. When the breeze is right the balloon can take the bait beyond casting distances, at the same time drifting the lure over submerged grass patches or over the bottom.

Among various fishes encountered in the kelp, two which have not yet been mentioned seem worthy of note. These are the sheepshead and the white sea bass.

Sheepshead

Somewhat debatable as a sportfish, sheepshead often appear in great numbers along the Baja coast and into southern California, where they are prized as table fish. They reach 20 pounds or more in weight and offer a dogged fight on light tackle. In their southern range they are taken year-round, but are more numerous during winter months. They frequent inshore rocky waters and kelp beds, thus are often taken when fishing for rockfish or kelp bass.

Although sheepshead occasionally are caught on artificials such as streamer flies and jigs, most are caught with bait—usually sand crabs, shrimp or squid. When a school is around it can be chummed up with crushed sand or fiddler crabs. The preferred rig, used with light or normal casting tackle, is a 1/0 hook on the end of a monofilament line with a 1- or 2-ounce rubber-core pinch-on sinker about 3 feet above it. Impale the hook through the middle of the sand crab so the barb protrudes. The bait often is taken while it sinks. Some anglers use shock leaders while others don't. They are recommended because sheepshead have canine-like teeth.

White Sea Bass

Another denizen of the kelp beds is the white sea bass, improperly named because it is a member of the weakfish family. It is an excellent surface fighter and regarded as one of the best medium-weight gamefishes on the Pacific coast. While it reaches 50 pounds or more in size, those normally caught are in the 15-pound range. Many are taken by fishermen on party boats. Shape and color are not unlike those of bluefish.

Many white sea bass are found following migrations of squid and, at such times, squid about 6 inches long are the best bait. Use a hook about 2/0 (between 1/0 and 4/0) in size to hook the squid between its fins through the tip of the tail. If the squid is alive, avoid being pinched by its beak by holding it behind the eyes. Point the tentacles (feelers) away to prevent being squirted by ink. The artificial lures recommended for lingcod in this chapter are useful. Others are white jigs or metal squids painted white. These are cast and retrieved or are yo-yo'd off the bottom. In California most white sea bass are caught between May and September but they are taken in winter farther to the south. Any rod and reel combination handling monofilament of between 10- and 25-pound test can be used. When jigging off bottom the line strength often is increased to as much as 40 pounds.

BOTTOM FISHING

Since most of the surface-feeding fish have migrated from California's coast between November and March, fishermen look to other ways for food and fun. The always popular party boats are even more so then, and private craft also make excursions to deep and shallow inshore and offshore banks for bottom fishing. This includes many of the species already discussed, plus halibut up to 40 pounds and giant black sea bass that can weigh 500 pounds or more. Goals of the boats also include coastal kelp beds, old wrecks and the sides of reefs, some of these places being many miles offshore. Party boat skippers know from long experience what locations pay off and when fishing is best there. Running on a compass bearing for a known length of time, they arrive at the general location and pinpoint it with fathometers. Less experienced boatmen depend on contour charts to find reefs, water depths, drop-offs and deep holes.

While fishermen on private boats may use any of the tackle previously discussed, using their judgment as to strengths and methods, those on party boats usually stay with heavy gear because the number of anglers and the lines they have out make it impractical to waste more time than necessary in boating fish.

For this reason a typical outfit is a stiff boat rod with roller guides and tip. The conventional reel has a metal spool holding 250 yards or more of about 45-pound-test line which can be Dacron but is usually monel or lead-core to get down deep quickly. Monofilament is rarely used for deep bottom fishing because it has too much stretch. The leader, as long as the rod, is 60-pound test, or more, with a ball-bearing swivel at its upper end and a snap-swivel at its lower end to which is attached a sinker weighing up to 10 ounces. Equally spaced on the leader are four or more loops to each of which is attached a snelled long-shank hook, size 6/0 or 8/0. The snells are of slightly lesser strength than the leader so hooks can be broken off if necessary. These rigs are baited with cut or live bait, sometimes varied with pork rind or plastic attractors if bait-stealing fish are prevalent.

This rig is lowered to bottom and then raised just above it while the boat drifts over the area. If the area is a small one a marker buoy often is dropped to mark it for later drifts. On feeling a strike, the angler usually doesn't pull up the rig. He wants to wait until all or most of the baits have been taken.

When fishing for big fish such as lingcod and large sea bass, anglers use a similar rig with only one 8/0 or 9/0 hook and a larger bait. Some deep holes in kelp beds or amid rocks or near wrecks are known to contain black sea bass. Such spots are pinpointed because after one of these big fish has been taken another one or more usually move in.

Black Sea Bass

The behemoth of the bottom is the black sea bass which, unlike the Atlantic variety, averages nearly 200 pounds and can be 500 pounds or more; somewhat like the *Atlantic jewfish,* which is caught similarly. Black sea bass frequent rocky bottoms offshore or inshore at various depths and sometimes are hooked while people are rockfishing or kelp fishing. Unless the tackle is extremely strong or the fish is smaller than average, the only alternative is to break loose. Those who deliberately go out for black sea bass use lines testing between 75 and 100 pounds, with tuna-type hooks in the 8/0 to 10/0 range and other tackle to match. Leaders usually are about 6 feet of nylon-coated braided wire of about 100-pound strength. Bait is a large live or dead fish weighing 5 pounds or so with a heavy sinker sometimes concealed in the dead bait. The initial strike usually is light, after which the fish makes a slow run of less than 100 feet. After this run one sets the hook. The bass fights with slow but powerful runs and by jerking the tackle. The angler retaliates by pumping it up. If brought up from considerable depth the bass probably will be dead because its air bladder has ruptured from the change of pressure.

Anglers in small boats sometimes hook large black sea bass and bring them to the surface. Since they are too big to take aboard, the alternative is to pass a heavy line through mouth and gills and to tow the fish home. Smaller bass are taken occasionally on feathered jigs, spoons and plugs. They are edible but not excellent. Whether one should deliberately bother to fish for them, regardless of size, is a matter of opinion.

Halibut

The California halibut is a flatfish which usually weighs between 5 and 35 pounds, although it can exceed 60. (A deep-water variety called the Pacific halibut is similar but runs larger.) Often caught near kelp beds, halibut also frequent bays and sloughs on sandy and muddy bottoms and brackish estuaries of rivers.

Halibut take live or dead bait drifted near or fished on the bottom. The sliding sinker rig or the fish-finder one (using a bank sinker) with about 20-pound-test line and a stronger monofilament or wire leader can be used for this. Halibut take shiny metal lures, jigs and underwater plugs readily.

If the bottom is sandy and clear, drag a metal squid or jig from a slowly drifting boat. Also try casting the lure and retrieving it slowly in short spurts so it will throw up small puffs of sand while being fished on the bottom. Halibut hit artificials readily and should be struck immediately. They take baits slowly and cautiously, so strikes should be delayed.

A Homemade Jig

Jigs of various types are so effective and have been mentioned so often that readers should be reminded that they're simple to make at home. Lead-heads can be cast from molds obtainable from tackle mail-order houses. They can be dipped in enamel, dressed with hair, feathers, artificial bristles, rubber or plastic skirts and/or mylar strips in whatever colors and combinations anyone desires. Some of the long metal sand eel or Hopkins types can be fashioned from copper tubing obtainable from plumbing-supply stores.

For example, cut a section of $\frac{1}{2}$-inch copper tubing so both ends are slanted as shown in accompanying step-by-step drawings. Make a loop of wire and string a split-ring and a swivel on it. Insert this in the tube and

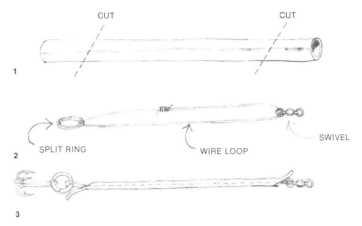

Jig from copper tubing can be made by threading wire loop, with split ring and swivel attached, through tube, which is then flattened and rigged with treble hook.

squeeze the tube flat in a vise (and/or hammer it) to make the jig. Bend up the front lip and bend down the rear lip if desired. Add a hook to the split-ring at the rear. Jigs like this can be bent for added action, but none should be needed.

Use of the wire is optional. One can hammer the tubing flat without it and can drill holes at both ends. Insert a split ring in the rear hole for the hook and attach a snap-swivel to the front hole. In this case the lips should not be bent, but the lure can be curved.

Another way to use tubing is to make unslanted cuts to desired length (4 or 5 inches for a ½-inch tube) and to squeeze the rear half inch or so flat in a vise. Round the flattened part and drill a hole in it for a split ring and a hook. Fill the tube with melted lead or white metal and insert a small screw-eye into it before the metal hardens, as shown in accompanying sketch. (White metal is an alloy with a very low melting point.)

These suggestions can be varied in several ways. Hooks can be dressed if desired. The jigs can be dipped in enamel of any color. To keep the tubing bright, rub it with steel wool and dip it in lacquer, or polish it before each use.

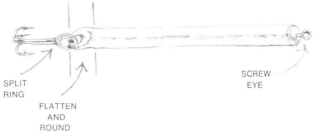

Alternate method of making a tubing jig. Flatten tube at one end and drill hole; attach split ring and treble hook. Pour hot lead or white metal into tube and insert screw eye before metal hardens.

SURF FISHING

Anglers who vacation in recreational vehicles on the shores of the Sea of Cortez sometimes remark that if they camp too near the water the noises made by splashing and feeding fish keep them awake. While varieties and quantities are large, most of the fish are suitable for sporty, light casting tackle, so heavier gear need not be used unless larger visitors make it necessary. Having discussed this fabulous fishing previously, let's go on to a few surf species which are of special note up the Baja coast and into California.

In the surf the white sea bass takes spoons, metal squids, and feathered jigs. It also takes whole baitfish and cut bait using the fish-finder rig and others recommended for striped bass with surf fishing or other casting tackle in normal to heavy ranges. Many of the corvinas or corbinas won't take artificials, or are difficult to catch with them. They are bottom feeders very fond of crustaceans and mollusks, particularly crabs. Here is a method very productive for anglers who know about it.

These fish and many others such as surfperch come into the surf to feast on sand crabs. They come in very close, usually feeding in the first breaker because this is the one that disturbs the sand and washes crabs from it until the wave recedes and they can bury themselves again. The large crabs (large enough to molt) are in the sand very close to the surf, the smaller and less useful ones being farther up. The idea therefore is to dig them out as close to the surf as possible and to select the softshell ones (which are molting) in preference to those with hard shells. These big ones will be about 2 inches in diameter.

Being shedders, they are hard to keep on a hook, a matter solved by using long-shanked ones of the bait-holder type, size 4. A normal spinning outfit is ideal for this, with a sinker of an ounce or so to get the bait out. Sometimes a dropper with another crab-baited hook is included in the rig. The best time of course is on the incoming tide, and casts are made behind the first breaker. This sort of rig is very productive for most species of surf feeders all along the coast, including surfperch.

The barred surfperch is reported to be the most important fish taken in the surf by California anglers. It is one of several dozen varieties of oceanic perch, most of which feed in the surf. Those living far out are called "seaperch." Those in the surf are called "surfperch," and those roaming in both places, merely "perch." They vary in size between varieties too small to bother with and bigger ones, such as the barred surfperch and the redtail surfperch, which are husky fighters weighing as much as 6 pounds. In the spring some of the varieties bear live young.

Baits for these fish include clam necks, cut fish and crabs. While they take hardshell crabs, softshell ones are considered much better. Some varieties, such as the rainbow seaperch (a surfperch) inhabit areas near piers, docks and wharfs. Reports are that they take baits best during a rain. Fishing methods in the surf are the same as for corvinas. Most fun is enjoyed by using the lightest tackle that seems practical.

Appendix

1

HOW TO KEEP, PREPARE
AND COOK THE CATCH

The fun of fishing pays extra dividends by providing the principal ingredient for delicious meals. Too many sportsmen shy away from cooking what they catch either because first attempts didn't reach family expectations or because inexperience made preparation and cooking too much trouble. Being an old hand at the game and having written a popular book about it, I'll try to show how easy it really is.

Little panfish fillets are delicious when crisply fried into golden-brown nuggets or combined into a flavorful steaming casserole. Each little fish can be prepared for cooking in less than a minute. The larger gamefish can be served whole, or if too large, transformed into succulent fillets or steaks, then fried, broiled, baked or poached.

KEEP THE CATCH COOL

Fish are more perishable than is generally presumed, principally because they begin to lose flavor slowly soon after they die. Usually they should be killed as soon as caught. When kept alive on a stringer, tethered to boat or shore, the time should be short if the water is warm. Don't blame the cook if they have been allowed to lie in the bottom of a boat in the sun! For best results, clean them as soon as possible and store them in a portable refrigerator.

Wading fishermen often carry their catches in creels. Covering the fish with damp leaves or moss helps because evaporation of moisture enhances

675

coolness. Since I dislike creels because of their bulkiness, I carry small fish, such as trout, in a plastic bag tucked in the game pocket of my jacket. However, this is a bad practice in warm weather. A quick transfer to the portable ice chest is advisable.

When you carry fish on long trips, pack them in ice. Shaved or cubed ice is preferred to block ice because fish can be packed in it more tightly. Open the refrigerator's drain often to let the water out; soaking in water causes fish to deteriorate quickly.

BASIC FISH CLEANING

The basic way to clean a fish is to slit the underside of the body from the anal opening to the gills with a sharp knife, as shown in the accompanying drawing. Also make a crosscut at the head to sever the lower junction of the gills. Open the body cavity and pull the innards out. Also pull out all the gills. If this proves difficult with large fish, it will be noted that the upper and lower parts of the gills are connected to the head by cartilage, which can be cut. Some dark matter will be left under a membrane beneath the backbone. This membrane should be cut so all of the dark matter can be scraped away. If the fish isn't very large, this can be done by pushing the thumbnail along the cavity, although some people use an instrument such as a spoon. Finally, cut off the pectoral fins (the two lower ones in front) and the small bones at their bases. Then wipe the fish dry, washing it as little as possible.

Large scales should be removed, preferably before fish are cleaned. The backs of the blades of many fishing knives are serrated for this purpose. The scales can be quickly scraped off by holding the fish by its head on a table or board and by stroking the serrated edge of the scaling tool toward the head.

Wrapping fish in a few layers of newspaper is a good way to keep them cool. Fish will stick to newspapers unless they are protected by plastic bags, waxed paper or foil. Damp sawdust also insulates well.

The above method is standard for preparing small fish that will be cooked whole, such as trout, or for preparing larger ones that will be baked. Here are some other important ones:

CLEANING PANFISH

It takes only a minute or so to clean or to extract the meat from a perch or a bluegill. Some like to cook panfish with the skin on, others want the meat only. In either case, when there is a mess of fish to prepare, you may as well do it as easily and efficiently as possible.

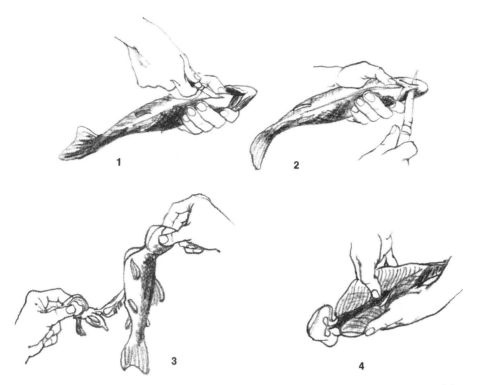

Basic method of cleaning a fish: (1) Slit belly from anal vent to gills. (2) Sever lower junction of gills. (3) Pull out inards and gills. (4) Run thumbnail along cavity to clean out dark matter.

First, dump the fish in the sink. Have a supply of newspapers handy, to keep the fish from sliding and slipping, and to dispose of unwanted material. Use a sharp knife with a blade about 6 inches long, preferably one of carbon steel with a wooden handle. A scaler (on the knife or separate) is necessary, and a pair of lightweight cotton gloves protects hands from sharp spines.

The accompanying drawing shows the "skin on method." Scrape off the scales (preferably under running water to keep them from flying around). A V-cut on front and back of the anal opening removes it and severs it from its canal. Now set the fish on its belly on a cutting board or on newspapers. Holding it by its back with one hand, slice downward with the knife to sever the head just behind the gill plates. This slice should cut through the backbone, but not through the belly flesh. By pulling upward on the body

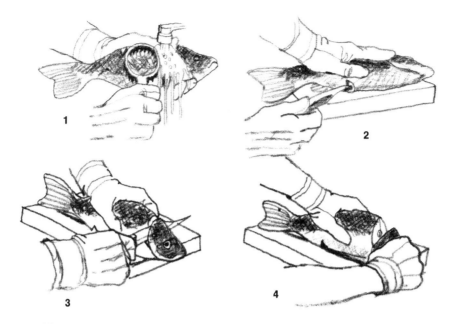

"Skin on method" of cleaning a panfish: (1) Scrape off scales. (2) Sever and remove anus. (3) Sever head behind gill plates; don't cut through belly flesh. (4) Pull head away, taking entrails with it.

and downward on the head, the head will break loose and can be pulled away, the entrails pulling away with it. Some cooks also cut off the tail.

Scaling isn't necessary when the "meat only method" is used. Holding the fish as above, cut down through the backbone behind the head. Slice down along both sides of the dorsal fin so it and all fin bones can be pulled out. Remove the anal fin and bones in the same way. Use knife and fingers to pry the skin away from the points where the dorsal cut met the head cut. Holding these two flaps of skin, peel them down and back, below the rib cage. Grasping the meat in one hand and the head in the other, pull them apart. The clean meat, with the backbone, is in one hand, and the head, skin and other material to be discarded is in the other. The ribs can be trimmed, if desired. Wash the meat under cold water, also scraping away the dark matter under the spine. Wipe the meat dry. It is now ready for cooking or freezing.

I enjoy little panfish fillets without the bones. While filleting fish is described later in this chapter, it may be helpful to discuss handling the little ones here. Make the head cut and the dorsal cuts as above, without bothering to remove the dorsal fin. The dorsal cuts open the flesh down to the rib cage. Laying the knife blade in one of these cuts, use a rolling slice to

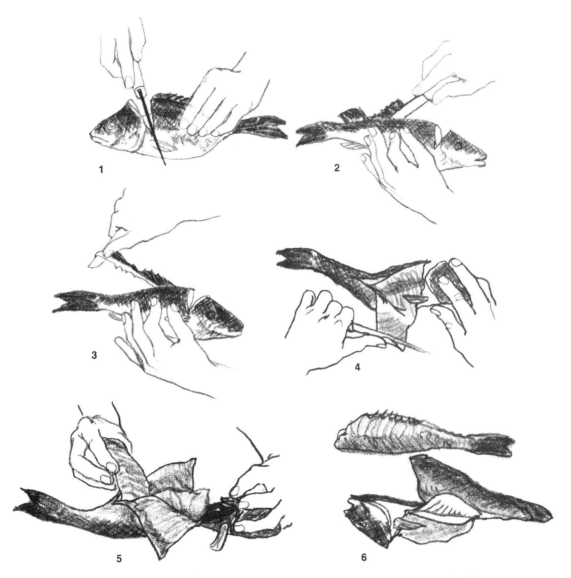

"**Meat only method**" **of cleaning a panfish: (1)** Cut down through backbone behind head. **(2)** Cut on both sides of dorsal fin and anal fin. **(3)** Remove dorsal fin and bones, also anals fin and bone. **(4)** Pry skin from body, peel both flaps below rib cage. **(5)** Pull meat and head apart. **(6)** Head and skin are discarded, leaving clean meat.

sever all the meat from the rib cage, thus cutting the fillet from the body with as little loss as possible. Doing the same with the other fillet results in two pieces of meat with skin on them, but without any bones.

Lay the fillet, skin-side down, on a cutting board and hold the tail end of the skin down with the thumbnail. Setting the knife against the thumbnail, slice between meat and skin (with the knife nearly flat against the board) to remove the skin. In these quick operations no meat should be left on the skin, and nearly none on the bones. After rinsing and drying the little fillets, they are ready to be cooked or frozen. It may take a minute or two to prepare the first fish but, after a very little practice, the fillets can be cut loose and skinned in seconds.

BONE-FREE FILLETS FROM PIKE

My old friend Robert Candy, of the Vermont Fish and Game Department, thinks that too many fish of the pike family (pickerel, pike and muskie) are wasted because anglers don't know how to cope with the Y-bones. Since many gourmets think these fillets are delicious, Bob explains how to do it in the accompanying drawings.

To bake fish whole, they should be scaled. Follow Steps 1 through 4, but leave the fillets attached to the skin. Skewer or sew the skin together, if desired, to form a pocket for the stuffing, recipes for which will follow.

When pan-frying or baking, it isn't necessary to scale the fish. Merely wet the body and work, scale-side down, on dry newspapers to prevent slipping. After following Steps 1 through 4, remove the fillets from the skin. This provides four bone-free sections of fillets which can be prepared in ways described later in this chapter.

After you have removed the strips of Y-bones (Step 4), the filleting is completed. Each fillet has a separated narrow strip along each side of the back. These can be rolled up, pinwheel fashion, and held together with toothpicks or skewers. When cooked, these are delicious dipped in a sauce. Those who like this method can cut and coil the rest of the fillets similarly.

Steps 1 through 4 are illustrated here.

HOW TO FILLET FISH

When fish are filleted promptly after being caught, it isn't necessary to clean them before removing the fillets. This is the usual method:

Wipe the fish fairly dry and lay it on a few sheets of flat newspaper on a dry board to prevent slipping. Using a sharp knife with a pointed blade, cut behind the bony gill covers on a slanting line as shown in *A-B* in accompanying drawings. The cut should slice the flesh down to the backbone.

HOW TO CLEAN PIKE

1. Remove the head and clean the body. With a sharp knife, cut along both sides of the dorsal fin so it can be lifted out. Cut the back of each fillet away from the spine and along the anal fin, thus freeing the ends of the fillet.

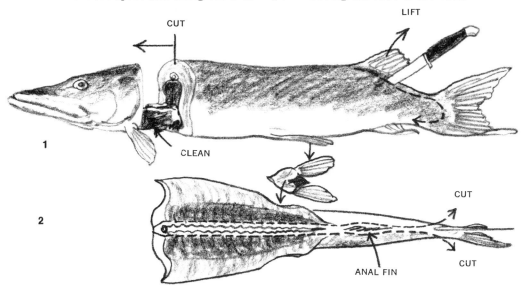

2. Remove the remaining pair of fins and their bones. Lay the fish on its back. Cut along each side of the backbone (dotted lines), severing the ribs. Pull out the backbone. This leaves a pair of attached fillets which still contain rib bones and a line of Y-bones.

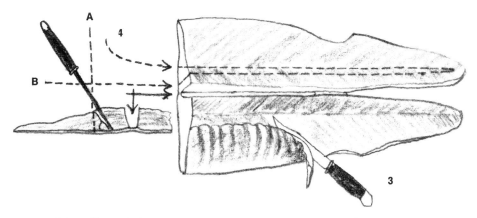

3. Slice off the rib bones, retaining as much meat as possible.
4. To cut out the Y-bones from each fillet, run the tip of an index finger along the flesh to locate the line of butts. Ease the knife along the sides of this line, slightly twisting the blade's edge away from the bones and tilting it, as shown by lines A and B, and the end view. Push the knife through, and it will easily follow the bone line. Both the Y-bone strip and the backbone strip can then be pulled free, leaving two boneless fillets.

Insert the knife point at *A* and slice closely along the upper side of the fin bones down to the backbone from *A* to *C*. Then push the knife blade from *C* through the fish to the vent and slice along the backbone until the flesh is severed near the tail. (This cut should not remove the anal fin, but should be close to it.) The end of the fillet now is free, and the fingers can be used to lift the top of the fillet away from the fin bones. Place the knife blade in this opening and make several strokes along the ribs, thus gradually raising the fillet and slicing until it can be freed. The belly is cut through when the point is reached that no flesh remains on it. This should leave almost no meat along the fin bones, the backbone and the ribs. When properly done, the body cavity is not opened.

Turn the fish over, and remove the other fillet in the same manner.

If the fish has been cleaned, you can use a second method of filleting. Make cut *A-B*, cut down to the backbone, and make the cut at *C* through the fish. Then cut from *A* to *C* through the ribs.

After a little practice, the whole fillet can be removed in one quick cut by slicing from *A* to *C*, then turning the blade toward the tail and slicing off the fillet. Those who lack experience in this quicker method may waste some flesh along the fin bones unless they are careful to slice very close to them.

The second method can be followed *without* cleaning the fish, but some people consider it rather messy. Either way, it makes a more attractive

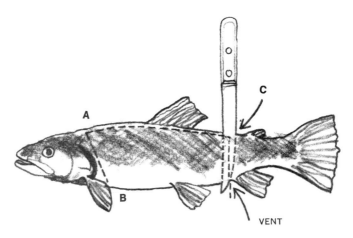

To fillet a fish, cut at *A–B*, slicing to backbone, to point *C*. Push point of blade at *C* through vent and continue cut until flesh is severed at tail. Turn fish and remove other fillet.

fillet because the belly skin stays on. However, there isn't enough edible material along the belly to bother with. The rib bones can be sliced off in one thin strip, if desired. Many chefs prefer to cook the fillets without removing them because they can be pulled off so easily afterwards.

If the fillets have been prepared by the second method the belly skin (and fins, if any) should be removed to leave only firm flesh, as in the first

To remove skin from fillet, hold end of skin and cut with a sawing motion along the skin until it comes free of the meat.

method. To do this, lay the fillet on a flat board, skin-side down, and slice some of the skin of the tail end away from the flesh. Holding this small end of free skin, lay the knife flat along the inside of the skin and push it forward with a slight sawing motion. A flat cut will make the knife follow along the skin to slice it free with no meat left on it. (Some people use pliers to hold

How to fillet a flounder. Lay the flounder belly-side down on a cutting board. **(1)** Holding it by thumb and forefinger in gills, use a very sharp knife to slice inward halfway back on the body, cutting along the upper side of the bones. **(2)** Holding cut flesh upward with thumb, continue to slice above the bones to the tail: then near the head until the fillet has been detached. **(3)** Turn the fish over and make a downward cut behind the gills. **(4)** Guiding the knife along the spine, slice backward to the tail to free the fillet. This provides two fillets with the skin on.

the end of the skin, or they use tools made to skin fish, but these are unnecessary.)

Anyone who has watched professionals on party boats or on docks quickly observes that it is quicker to fillet a fish, and to skin a fillet, than it is to explain how to do it. The pros do either or both in a matter of seconds. The methods apply to fish of any size, from panfish to tacklebusters. If fillets are to be skinned, it isn't necessary to scale the fish.

684

ON COOKING FISH

Fresh fish taste sweet (although not sweet like sugar). They remain sweet if they are kept cold and are not immersed in water for a long period. The warmer it is, the more quickly they acquire a fishy or rancid taste. Oily species, such as bluefish, mackerel and shad, lose flavor quicker than non-oily ones, so should be stored for shorter periods and eaten as soon as possible. Fish that are caught in warm, muddy water are less palatable than those taken from cold, clear water. Proper storage and preparation are essential to peak flavor.

Fish that are overcooked, lose flavor and become either tough or mushy, depending on the cooking method used. They are done as soon as the flesh becomes opaque and can be flaked away. A few notes on cooking methods may help.

Baking without sauces or liquids, usually is done with the skin left on to help prevent the fish from drying out. Baked fish are excellent when stuffed and cooked whole. After the fish has baked, the skin can be peeled off easily, and parts of the meat can be lifted from the bones. Sauces are delicious when added to baked fish, and pieces can be mixed with a sauce covered with bread crumbs, and cooked in a deep dish to brown on top.

Frying is an excellent method when a few essential points are remembered. Bacon fat often is used, but vegetable or peanut oils frequently are preferred. If butter is used, some oil should be mixed with it to prevent burning. The temperature of the oil or fat is of primary importance. It should be very hot, but not smoking—about 425 degrees. An easy way to test temperature is to drop a piece of bread into the fat. If the bread bubbles actively and starts to brown quickly, it is time to put the fish in. Deep fat isn't necessary, but it must be kept hot. Enough to cover the bottom of the pan should be sufficient. Fish, either fillets or whole, should be wiped dry before cooking. They can be dredged in flour, corn meal, bread crumbs or rolled potato chips. They can also be dipped in milk or cream, then in flour; or they can be dipped in a batter of flour and beaten eggs, then rolled in corn meal or crumbs. Pan-frying is an excellent way to cook small fish, fillets or parts of fillets. Pans should not be covered if maximum crispness is desired. The fish (or fillets) should be done when they are golden brown. If in doubt, flake a small piece off with a fork. They are done when they flake. Don't overcook. Remove excess fat by letting the hot fish drain for a few moments on absorbent paper.

Broiling or outdoor grilling is an excellent way to cook small whole fish, or fillets with the skin on, especially the fatty species such as bluefish and mackerel. Basting with sauces isn't necessary because flavor is at its peak when salt and pepper are added, plus a little lemon juice. When a wing broiler is used in outdoor cooking, it helps to raise the wings once or twice to prevent the fish from sticking to them. Strips of bacon can be laid over the flesh during the broiling, but they may have to be removed if put on initially to avoid their becoming blackened.

Poaching means simmering, rather than boiling. It is an ideal way to serve large, firm-fleshed fish — particularly salmon. Clean the fish and scale it if necessary. Remove the head and tail, if desired. Wrap the fish in cheesecloth so it won't break apart when being lifted from the stock. If it can be set on a perforated rack which fits the pan, it can be lifted out more easily. After the stock has been brought to a boil, set the fish into it and turn the heat down to a simmer as soon as boiling is regained. The stock should cover the fish. Poaching takes between 8 and 10 minutes per pound, depending on thickness. When it is presumed to be done it can be removed from the broth, unwrapped, and tested for doneness by being sure it flakes at the thickest part near the backbone.

When done, most of the skin will adhere to the cheesecloth. Remove the rest and allow the fish to cool. Serve warm or after having been refrigerated, with a choice of sauce. Whole fish, fillets or steaks all are poached in a similar manner.

A simple stock can be made by combining a quart of water, a cup of milk, a tablespoon of salt and the juice of half a lemon. Another simple one calls for equal quantities of water and white wine. If fish heads, bones and tails are on hand, simmer them about three-quarters of an hour in a mixture of equal parts of white wine and water, plus other seasonings (if available) such as bay leaf, a sprinkling of thyme, chopped onions, celery, carrots and/or parsley and a little salt and pepper. After cooking, this is strained and the liquid is used as stock. A vegetable stock can be made by combining 2 quarts of water with half a cup of vinegar, plus the above vegetables. It is prepared in the same way. The amounts of vegetables which are used depend on taste and whatever is available.

Poached fish, served either hot or cold, should be accompanied by an appropriate sauce. These, in great variety, are described in cook books and include Black Butter Sauce, White Butter Sauce, Tartare Sauce, Mustard Butter Sauce, Hollandaise Sauce, White Sauce (a hot cream sauce) and Cucumber Sauce. The latter is ideal with salmon when it is served cold. Here are the recipes for three of them:

Tartare Sauce, served cold, is excellent with fried fish. There are simple and fancy recipes for it. An easy way is to chop fine a dill pickle, some stuffed olives, and a slice of onion. Include a strip or two of anchovy and a teaspoon of capers, if available. Stir this with about twice its volume of mayonnaise, and add a few drops of lemon juice and salt and pepper to taste. A little parsley and tarragon also add flavor, if they are available. This sauce can be thinned with heavy cream, but it isn't necessary

White Sauce, served hot, is a favorite for pouring over hot poached fish. Blend 2 tablespoons of flour in a saucepan or skillet with 2 tablespoons of melted butter. Remove from the low heat and slowly blend in a cup of milk. Return to heat and cook slowly, stirring constantly, until the sauce is thickened and smooth. Add salt and pepper to taste. If desired, the cup of liquid can contain some cream and/or fish stock with some of the milk. For added embellishments over the fish, sprinkle on slices of hard-boiled egg, chopped egg, and/or a few capers and/or parsley.

There are many variations to this basic white sauce. For example, add mustard to taste, or two or three tablespoons of grated cheese and perhaps some heavy cream, or some drained horseradish, or some chopped or dried dill, or curry powder.

Cucumber Sauce, served cold, is ideal with cold poached fish—especially salmon. Beat half a cup of heavy cream until thick and then beat in 2 tablespoons of vinegar. Add salt and pepper to taste, and then fold in a cucumber which has been pared, chopped and thoroughly drained. Before chopping, cut out the seed portion, if desired. Another recipe is to add some vinegar and salt and pepper to two cucumbers, prepared as above.

Since this isn't a cook book, we'll have to let sauce recipes go at that, but other simple ones can be found easily. For example, butter sauce is very popular with hot fish. Merely melt some butter and add lemon juice to taste, or parsley, or chives, or any other herbs that go well with fish.

Even a basic chapter on the trips of fish from pond to plate wouldn't be complete without a few recipes, so here are some of my favorites:

Fish Cakes

2 cups cooked fish, shredded	¼ teaspoon curry powder
4 medium-sized potatoes,	(optional)
freshly boiled and hot, put	3 eggs
through a ricer, or chopped	1 cup dry bread or cracker
very fine	crumbs
Salt and pepper to taste	½ cup butter, margarine, or
1 small onion, minced	bacon fat
(optional)	

Combine the fish, potatoes, onion and seasoning. Stir in the eggs (stirring as little as possible). Shape into cakes and dip in the crumbs. Sauté in the butter or fat until brown. (Remember that if butter is used it won't blacken if about an equal amount of vegetable oil is combined with it.)

The fat should be hot, as for any other kind of fat frying. If a food grinder is available, the fish, potatoes and onion can be put through it, rather than preparing them separately. When the cakes are nicely browned, drain them on absorbent paper. They often are served with tomato sauce or catsup, but some people prefer Tartare Sauce.

FISH CHOWDER

In this recipe, as in many others, the experienced cook "cooks by the soul," instead of following directions too closely. We can combine more or less fish with more or less vegetables, and we can use vegetables of many sorts, including leftovers. A pinch or two of herbs, such as sage, marjoram or thyme, always adds to fish dishes, whether the recipe calls for them or not. Either bacon or salt pork can be used in which to sauté the onions. Milk and/or cream always is added last, and never should be allowed to boil. Just heat it. The substitution of canned, condensed soups, such as cream of celery, cream of mushroom or creamed pea soup is even better. The chowder should be quite thick, but can be thinned with a little water, milk or stock, if desirable. It helps to blend the flavors if the chowder is allowed to set for a few hours, or overnight, in the refrigerator.

Every fall we go to the New England coast for the striped bass fishing, and bring home a few to fillet for the freezer. In doing the filleting, some tidbits of flesh are left, and these are carefully cut off to store in the freezer for chowder. Some people make fish chowder the easy way, by using just these bits and pieces. Others do it the tastier way, by cooking fish heads, fins and the larger bones, along with whatever meat is left on them. These are boiled in a quart or so of water which is strained to make stock. Stock makes a much more flavorful chowder than water does. Here are the ingredients for building an excellent chowder:

6–8 strips of bacon, cut in small pieces, or a similar amount of diced salt pork

2 large or 3 medium-sized onions, chopped fairly fine

2 pounds or so of fish fillets or pieces, cut small

3 large or 4 or 5 medium-sized potatoes, diced

1 teaspoon salt

1/2 teaspoon pepper

1 teaspoon dried herbs (marjoram and/or thyme, or herb blend)

3 cups water (or stock, if you have made any)

1/2 cup cream, or canned milk

1 can condensed cream of celery soup (or other creamed soup)

In a skillet, fry the bacon pieces or cubes of salt pork until crisp. Remove from fat, and drain. In the fat, sauté the chopped onions until translucent, but not very browned. Put the fat and onions into a fairly large kettle and add the fish, potatoes, salt, pepper, herbs and water or stock. Let this simmer until potatoes and fish are cooked. Then add the cream or milk and the cream soup. Let this simmer a while longer before serving, but don't let it come to a boil. Correct seasoning, if necessary.

Serve the chowder in big bowls, with crackers. Sprinkle some of the crisp bacon pieces on top of the chowder in each bowl. Remember that flavor is improved if the chowder is allowed to stand in a cool place overnight.

One of my favorite dishes is trout chowder, made with small fish. Merely clean them and drop them into a pot of water. Let them simmer slowly until the flesh can be pulled off the bones. Then remove them from the broth and peel off the meat when they are cool enough. Put the skins, heads and bones back into the pot. Let this boil a while and then strain off the liquid for stock. Since the fish has been cooked, don't add it to the chowder until it is nearly ready to be served. Such a chowder can be made from panfish, if they are scaled before being cooked.

Fish Casserole

This is a good way to use leftover fish, but the dish can be made from any cooked ones.

2 cups fish chunks (small) and/or flakes	½ cup parsley, chopped
1½ cups cracker crumbs, rolled coarsely	1 green pepper, seeded and chopped
1 cup diced celery	½ cup melted butter
2 large onions, chopped	2 eggs, beaten lightly
	Salt and pepper to taste

Combine fish, crumbs and chopped vegetables. Add seasoning and mix with the butter and eggs. Pour the mixture into a buttered casserole. Sprinkle with bits of butter and extra crumbs, if desired. Bake for half an hour at 375°.

Baked Fish Fillets I

2-3 pounds skinned fillets	1 tablespoon flour
1½ tablespoons melted butter	1 medium-sized onion, minced

½ bay leaf

1 cup chicken stock *or* 1
chicken bouillon cube
dissolved in 1 cup water

Salt and pepper to taste

½ tablespoon lemon juice

½ cup bread crumbs

Cut the fillets into serving-size pieces and set them into a greased baking dish. Melt the butter and add flour and onion, blending thoroughly. Add the bay leaf and chicken stock, and simmer for 15 minutes, stirring until the mixture has thickened. Remove the bay leaf. Season with salt and pepper, and stir in the lemon juice. Pour this over the fish, and sprinkle the bread crumbs on top. Bake in a 425° pre-heated oven for about 20 minutes.

Some people like to sprinkle a little Parmesan cheese over the bread crumbs. This makes Baked Fish Fillets au Gratin. Others want a very easy recipe. In this case, try the following:

Baked Fish Fillets II

2 pounds fish fillets or steaks

4 tablespoons melted butter

1 cup potato chip crumbs
(chips rolled to crumbs)

Salt and pepper to taste

Cut the fillets into serving-size pieces and dip them in butter; then roll them in the potato chip crumbs until they are thoroughly coated. Set the coated fillets into a baking dish and add salt and pepper to taste. Pour the remaining butter over them. Bake at 350° for about 20 minutes, until golden brown. Test for doneness with a fork. Chopped parsley or chives or other suitable herbs add to the flavor and appearance of fish dishes such as this, so don't be afraid to "spice things up a bit!" However, the flavor of fish usually shouldn't be hidden by too much seasoning.

Baked Stuffed Fish

Once in a while we get a "bragging-size" fish and want to serve it whole. Here is a recipe with a choice of two kinds of stuffing. Following it is one for people who don't want to bother with stuffing.

1 dressed fish, about 5
pounds

1 rounded teaspoon salt

4 tablespoons melted butter,
margarine, or other fat

3–4 slices bacon

Stuffing

Clean and dry the fish, and rub it outside and inside with salt. Stuff the fish loosely, and fasten the opening with skewers, or sew it closed. Lay the fish on greased foil in a baking pan, and brush it with melted fat. Drape bacon over the fish. (Bacon is optional and shouldn't be used with fatty fish such as bluefish.) Bake in a preheated moderate oven at about 375° for about 12 minutes to the pound. Baste occasionally with the drippings. When cooked, remove the skewers or thread and serve on a hot platter, with your choice of sauce.

BREAD STUFFING

1 cup chopped celery stalks
3 tablespoons chopped onion
6 tablespoons melted butter,
   margarine, or fat
1 teaspoon salt

4 cups bread crumbs
1 teaspoon herbs (thyme,
   savory, sage or herb blend)
Dash of pepper

Sauté the celery and onion in the fat until translucent and tender. Mix all ingredients. Add a little milk or water to the dressing if it seems too dry, but keep it on the dry side. Stuff the fish loosely with the dressing, and bake, as above.

VEGETABLE STUFFING

3 medium-sized onions, sliced
   thin
1 small green pepper, seeded,
   sliced thin

1 tomato, sliced thin
2 sprigs parsley, chopped

Salt and pepper to taste. Combine the above ingredients and stuff the fish.

BAKED BASS

1 fresh or salt water bass (or
   other fish) of 4 to 10 pounds
2 bay leaves

2 slices bacon
2 slices onion

Line a pan with foil and put the bay leaves, bacon and onion on the foil so that the fish will be on top of them. (This helps to flavor the fish, and prevents sticking.) Lay the fish (cleaned and wiped dry) on the above ingredients, adding seasoning, if desired. Bake in a preheated oven at 400°

to 425° for not over 12 minutes per pound. Baste the fish occasionally with whatever juice is in the pan. Test to be sure the fish is not overcooked.

This is an easy recipe and is one of my favorites for striped bass from 8 to 10 pounds.

HOW TO FREEZE FISH

Modern freezing units are so efficient that it is difficult to distinguish frozen fish from fresh ones when the packaging and freezing have been done properly.

Among numerous suitable materials for packaging are plastic containers, waterproof rolls of plastic sheeting or plastic laminated paper, aluminum foil, and plastic bags. Select the one for the job into which the fish can be sealed with a minimum of air space (none, preferably) inside the package and also a material that locks moisture in and prevents outside air and moisture from entering. Cardboard containers, for example, don't do this. The result soon is that the food nearest the container dries out and becomes fiberous and discolored—a deterioration referred to as "freezer burn."

Plastic containers with lids are excellent for small bits and pieces of fish and shelled shellfish. Fill them only to the proper level (usually marked) so the expansion of freezing fills the container, but not so much that the lid is forced off.

Plastic sheeting or plastic laminated paper usually comes in rolls, so the right amount can be torn off. These materials are excellent for packaging fish

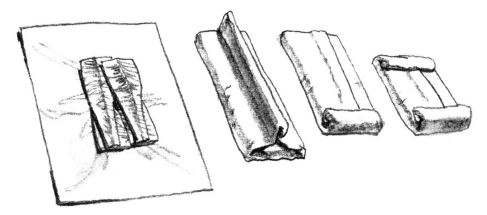

The Drugstore Fold packages fish tightly for freezing, or for cooking in the coals of a fire. Use freezer paper or foil for freezing; foil for cooking. Lay fish in center; gather opposite ends and fold over together at least twice. Do the same with both sides to make a tight package. When using freezer paper, seal with adhesive tape to secure folds.

fillets, steaks and other nonrigid cuts. An airtight seal can be made by using the Drugstore Fold shown in the accompanying drawing. If the seal tends to unfold (which it usually does except with aluminum foil) it can be secured with an adhesive tape such as masking tape. The lengthwise folds should be made tightly enough to squeeze the contents slightly. Before making the folds at the ends, all air should be stroked out. Contents and date should be marked on all packages.

Aluminum foil can be used for packaging fillets but it is especially useful for odd-shaped foods such as whole fish or fish chunks because the foil can be pressed into depressions in the food to exclude air. Use the Drugstore Fold and be sure the foil is not ruptured. Heavy foil is preferred for this reason.

Plastic bags are also useful for odd-shaped pieces, such as fish roe, which can be compacted by pressing air out of the bag. If lightweight bags are used, an outer bag can be sealed around the inner bag.

When whole fish are frozen in ice they will keep for many months. A way to do this is to fit small fish, such as trout, into a milk carton whose top has been cut off. Then fill the container with water, being sure all body cavities are filled. Cap the container with foil, which can be held in place by tape or rubber bands.

Proper packaging is the first step in successful freezing. Quick freezing is the second one. Most freezers have a space for quick freezing, but the coldest place should be used. After a successful fishing day we may want to freeze many packages at once. Only about 5 percent of the freezer's capacity should be used at one time, and packages to be frozen shouldn't be piled one on another. When it is desired to freeze larger quantities the excess should be kept in the refrigerator and not added to the freezer until the first batch has become firmly frozen. To freeze foods quickly, do them in small enough quantities so the machine can do its job efficiently.

When fish have been packaged and frozen correctly they will keep longer than most people presume, but any fish will deteriorate slowly in storage, gradually losing flavor. Enjoy the catch while it is fresh. Fatty fish, such as bluefish and mackerel, deteriorate more quickly and taste best when eaten within a month or so. Nonfatty species will retain reasonable flavor for several months. After that, they still may be tasty when transformed into casseroles or chowder.

SMOKING FISH

There are more ways to smoke fish than to make a palatable martini. These include hot smoking and cold smoking, using a wide variety of ingredients considered ideal by some and abominations by others. All sorts of smokers are employed, including commercial ones and those improvised from such items as discarded refrigerators, garbage cans and even corrugated paper cartons.

Although a book could be written about the various ways to smoke fish and other foods, I'll describe a method I use with an inexpensive commercial smoker. My favorite is called the Little Chief, made by Luhr Jenson & Sons, of Hood River, Oregon. This is a rectangular aluminum lidded box, 1 foot square and 2 feet high, which is easily transportable for use near an electrical outlet. A small pan of hickory shavings is put over an electric coil in the bottom of the unit to provide smoke and mild heat. The fish are put on three racks of a strong wire liner that can be lifted in or out of the box. While this little smoker is easy to operate, it will handle only between six and nine medium-sized fish or fillets at a time. However, it can be reloaded once a day as often as desired. Those who prefer mass production may want to build something larger, but commercial smokers like the Little Chief should be the ideal solution for most people.

Gourmets who have turned up their noses at smoked fish sold in jars or cans, or falsely "smoked" fillets cured by using vinegar, should not ignore the easy procedure that follows. The whole process takes about twenty-four hours, but only an hour or so of actual work is involved—if such productive fun can be called work.

Let's say that we come in about sundown with two or three fish weighing 2 or 3 pounds each, plus a few smaller ones. Prepare the large ones as fillets, with the skins on. Clean the small ones, but leave them whole, scaling all if necessary.

The only other evening job is to coat the fish with a mixture of equal parts of salt and sugar. While table salt and white sugar can be used, it is better to have pickling salt (pure salt, without the ingredients that make it "pour when it rains") and brown sugar. Mix enough to coat the fish (about a pint of each).

Throw a handful or two in a large plastic bag and drop in a fish or fillet. Turn this over to coat it thoroughly. Add more mixture and another fish, and continue until all are coated. Be generous with the salt and sugar mixture. Close the bag to exclude air and leave it in a cool place overnight. Next morning the fish will have released enough moisture to provide a thick brine.

After breakfast the next day, rinse the fish in water to remove all salt and sugar except what has been absorbed. Lay the fish on racks or anything else that will let them dry, preferably where there is a cool breeze. (Don't let the family cat get involved in this.) The surfaces of the fish and fillets will dry enough to form sort of a glaze.

While the fish are drying, start the smoker, because one pan of hickory chips should be burned to get it ready. This takes about an hour. Merely plug the smoker into an outdoor or porch outlet, fill the pan with the hickory, and put it on the electric coil. It is safe because there is no flame. The wood will smolder and give off a fragrant smoke.

After this preliminary run, lay the fish on the racks so the pieces are separated as much as possible. The skinsides of fillets should be down. Lower the racks into the smoker, put on the lid, and add more chips to fill the pan. If animals are around, it may be well to put a heavy rock on top of the unit.

It takes less than an hour for the pan of chips to be consumed, but the pan should be replenished hourly. Dump the pan if there are too many ashes, but merely add wood to it otherwise. Proper smoking takes at least six hours, perhaps as long as ten when thick pieces are involved. Except for this hourly restoking of the smoker, there isn't anything else to do.

After about six hours the fish should be inspected because racks may need to be interchanged so all contents will be smoked evenly. Break off a piece and sample it. The fillets should flake apart easily and be a dark golden brown. The job should be done in time for the "Happy Hour," and everybody should use reasonable restraint, or no one will want any dinner!

The firm that sells the smoker also provides boxes of hickory chips. Of course, anyone can make his own chips. Use hardwoods, such as apple, hickory or maple. Never use evergreen wood, because it gives off a distasteful pitchy odor. If an apple orchard with dead trees or branches can be located, this is ideal wood for smoking.

Smoked fish can be kept in a refrigerator for a month or so (if they last that long), and can be packaged and frozen for storage for several months.

Any non-oily fish can be smoked, including trout, salmon, bass, crappie and bluegills, if they are big enough to bother with. Some say that carp is the best of all, so doughball addicts and bowfishermen can have their fun and eat what they catch!

Smoked fish could be refrigerated and served cold. Some people think they are best without any condiments. If any are used, the vote probably is for merely a sprinkling of freshly ground pepper and lemon juice.

2

BOOKS FOR THE FISHERMAN

More books have been printed about fishing, or angling, than about any other sport. Having the money, the time and the luck, one could assemble an angling library of over ten thousand volumes, although some would be different editions of the same work. Izaak Walton's *The Compleat Angler* for example, has been reprinted in various sizes and degrees of elaborateness about three hundred times. There may be very few collectors who own every edition, one or two of the earliest being valued into four figures. Back in 1653, when he wrote the (now) most expensive first edition it could have been bought for pennies. Books offer another confirmation that anglers are afflicted with "collectoritis," whether it be acquiring excessive quantities of flies, plugs or rods, shelves lined with trophies, or other forms of piscatorial playthings. Inquisitive fishermen also invariably collect books.

But why collect books about fishing when the sporting magazines publish so much up-to-date material? An answer seems to be that all valid facts eventually are distilled, subject by subject, into books where the information can be located for reference whenever desired. Angling books are convenient sources of solid information, but that is only one reason for starting a private library, or borrowing from a public one.

Another reason, fascinating to some and of little or no interest to others, is that old books depict the history of angling as it developed over past centuries — particularly the history of fly fishing. For example, my modest library contains a copy of Charles Cotton's *Instructions On How to Angle For a Trout or Grayling in a Clear Stream,* printed in London in 1676. (This is one of the three books which now are combined into Walton's *The Compleat Angler.*) One can read in it exactly how the old-timers went fishing three hundred years ago, how they traveled, what they caught, and what they used for tackle. *The Compleat Angler,* comprising three little books, is fascinating reading, and an even older one, Dame Juliana Berners' *Fishing with a Hook,* published in 1496, is at least as rewarding. Luckily it also can be obtained in low-priced modern editions. These are only two examples of many ancient books describing the tackle and tactics of early times, but they are the two most important ones for an angling library.

While modern fishing books are in great abundance, anyone starting a library needs only to specialize on the titles of greatest interest to him. There are books which can answer every angling question, be it how to tie a Gray Ghost properly, how to rig plastic worms for various purposes, or what bait or lure should be used to catch a snook. Fishermen who own books on their favorite methods don't have to flounder around for the information they want. They merely look it up in the index!

Collecting books about fishing can become a very profitable hobby, an investment that can appreciate over the years. In the meantime, one has the books to look at, to refer to, and to help settle friendly arguments. Pride of possession is only a fringe benefit. Luckily, we can inspect books before we buy them. Whether the authors are famous or unknown makes little difference. Is the book larded with too many words, or is it packed with clear, concise information? Is it complete and authoritative? Is it the best one on the subject? Does it contain material to which we'll want to refer from time to time? Look for the gems, and ignore the costume jewelry!

A wisely selected library should never decline in value because prospective buyers increase in number, and older books often become scarce after they go out of print. When older books are reprinted, the original editions can be worth even more. Dealers' catalogs of old angling books list current values and are well worth watching. Although new information is always appearing, older books generally retain their value and interest to a greater extent than those in most other fields of endeavor.

HOW TO START A LIBRARY

Let's assume that we want to start in a small way, investing only a few dollars from time to time as convenient, but that we'd like to gradually acquire an angling library we can be proud of; perhaps one that will turn out to be a good investment. An angling library may not consist only of books. Manufacturers' catalogs are worthy of reference, and old ones can become valuable. These and booklets on fish and fishing either are free or cost very little. Angling and fly-tying periodicals are mines of information, and complete sets often command high prices. Hardcover bindings usually can be obtained for magazines, and important articles can be tab-indexed for quick reference.

In collecting angling books, the best are acquired by following a plan, rather than by haphazard buying. For example, do we want to assemble old classics, or new books, or both? Is the library to be based on fly-fishing and fly-tying books, on saltwater subjects, on bass fishing, or what else? Of course, we'll deviate when new books on other angling subjects strike our fancy, but there should be a basic plan of acquisition.

Collectors of modern books can save money and shopping time, and can avoid unrecommended purchases, by joining a book club specializing in outdoor titles, from which desired angling ones can be selected. Book clubs have to offer the most popular best sellers because their low prices depend on volume sales. Various mail-order houses also sell contemporary books at discount, and often offer good titles not obtainable by club membership. These sometimes feature reprints of old classics.

Old classics and valuable books which are out of print for one reason or another can be obtained by selecting from the mail-order lists of dealers in old angling books. Such dealers often offer second-hand contemporary books and new titles. Since these lists give current values, they are helpful for inventory purposes. Ask other collectors for the addresses of such dealers because they are usually regional. Printed price lists normally are free, but one must buy a book or two occasionally to receive new lists as they are issued. Experience is required to distinguish worthwhile titles from undesirable ones, of which there are many. Prices usually are fair, and many are low, but new collectors should know what they are buying to avoid cluttering libraries with titles purchased on impulse.

Collectors or their families sometimes want to sell their angling books for one reason or another. This often offers opportunities for bulk buying at low prices. While many "gems" can be uncovered this way, it pays to be selective. Some collectors buy entire libraries to obtain a few coveted titles. Undesirable volumes then can be sold to, or traded with, other collectors and dealers.

What about second-hand bookstores? Since nearly all of them know angling book values, finding bargains is like picking up crystals on a beach. Worthwhile books may be overpriced. It pays to look, if one has the time. It also pays to be careful.

Old books containing good color plates often go up in value, particularly the very old ones having fine color plates of flies. Before color printing became practical many angling books were illustrated with steel engravings which were hand-colored. Some had actual flies bound into them. In good condition, these usually appreciate in value, but most are now rare and expensive.

Limited editions often offer excellent investment possibilities if the prices are right. They can become valuable because of having been printed in small quantities. Values of books appreciate only because the supply is less than the demand. It pays to look for limited editions, but try to evaluate their importance before buying. Many of the best ones are sold by pre-publication subscription, and are offered to known collectors—collectors known, that is, to whomever is offering the books. Write to authors and publishers who produce limited editions and tell them you'd like to be informed of new offers. Mailing lists often are sold or traded, and producers of older limited editions might be willing to sell copies if any have been retained. When issues have been oversubscribed, perhaps copies can be obtained from mail-order dealers, who usually get them when estates are settled.

Since many collectors find it pleasant and profitable to specialize in books on fly-fishing subjects, a few words about them may be helpful. This is the category in angling book collecting that appreciates fastest in value.

When I was a budding collector I visited a rare book dealer and selected a few books for purchase. The dealer—a fine old gentleman, now deceased—refused to sell them.

"You don't know what you're buying," the man said, "but I'll make a bargain with you. I'll loan you this book (*). When you've read it, come back to see me, and we'll talk about book collecting."

The book was *A History of Fly Fishing for Trout,* by John Waller Hills, published by Philip Allan & Co., London (1921). This fascinating book describes British fly fishing and the important books about it, from recorded history to its date of publication. Its bibiliography provides a list of well over a hundred of the leading British angling works up to that time. After thorough study, I visited the dealer again.

"I've decided to try to collect the books on Hills' list," I announced.

"I hoped you would," the old gentleman replied, with a broad smile. "Some are expensive; some unobtainable, but I'll do what I can."

Over the years books and bills arrived from time to time from the old man, until most of the volumes Hills recommended had been acquired. To these, of course, many more by both British and American authors later were added, including the works of Bergman, Brooks, McClane and others. Since these acquisitions have proved to be a great source of pleasure, a valuable aid to research, and an excellent investment, it seems appropriate to pass on the old gentleman's suggestion.

John Waller Hills was a barrister, an angling book researcher and a collector who authored several books of his own. His famous work, *A History of Fly Fishing for Trout*, provides the complete British background of the sport—a background American anglers will find basic and fascinating, and a necessary introduction to the great strides we have taken on this side of the pond. The book has been reprinted in the United States and is currently available.

What books should fishermen start with for maximum information without spending a lot of money? Following are twenty from which those desired can be selected for the basis of a comprehensive library:

GENERAL FISHING

TROUT, by Ray Bergman
Penn Publishing Company, Philadelphia (1938) $12.50
This 500-page classic by the former fishing editor of *Outdoor Life* magazine provides the complete course on tackle and tactics for all species of trout. It includes fifteen color plates of trout flies and basic instructions for tying them. Reprinted in a revised and enlarged edition.

TRICKS THAT TAKE FISH, by Harold F. Blaisdell
Henry Holt & Company, New York (1954) $3.95
This 299-page book, written by a reliable authority, is filled with excellent ideas that do what the title says. It includes all freshwater gamefish and panfish, and is illustrated with explanatory drawings.

HOW TO FISH IN SALT WATER, by Vlad Evanoff
A. S. Barnes & Company, New York (1962) $5.95
One of America's leading saltwater fisherman describes in 208 highly informative pages all the basic lures, rigs, tackle and methods for catching principal species of saltwater fish, including both large and small varieties.

COMPLETE BOOK OF BASS FISHING, by Grits Gresham
Outdoor Life—Harper & Row, New York (1966) $6.95
A southern expert discusses in authoritative detail how to deal with all habits and habitats of the various species of bass, including all methods of lure, bait and fly fishing.

STRIPED BASS FISHING, by Henry Lyman and Frank Woolner
Salt Water Sportsman, Boston, $5.00
Since the striped bass is of paramount importance along both coasts and
(to an extent) inland, it deserves this authoritative 250-page book by two
noted experts. Filled with how-to-do-it information on selecting and using
lures and tackle, the book also explains where to find stripers and proven
methods for catching them.

MCCLANE'S STANDARD FISHING ENCYCLOPEDIA, by A. J. McClane
Holt, Rinehart & Winston, New York (1965) $19.95
Recently revised, this big 1,088-page book is an authoritative encyclopedia describing over 1,000 species of fish, angling methods, fish biology,
fly-tying, casting, rod-making, etc. Many of its hundreds of subjects are
illustrated in accurate color.

SALT WATER FISHING FROM BOATS, by Milt Roskoe
The Macmillan Company, New York (1922) $6.95
This acknowledged saltwater expert provides excellent information on
the various types and uses of boats; how to select tackle; trolling, chumming,
casting and bottom fishing from boats; data on handling and boating fish,
and notes on where to find and catch about 50 most popular species.

FLY FISHING

ATLANTIC SALMON FLIES & FISHING, by Joseph D. Bates, Jr.
Stackpole Books, Harrisburg, (1970) $14.95
This up-to-date 362-page book provides complete information on the
tackle and methods of fly fishing for Atlantic salmon, including how to
locate them in streams and new ways to make them strike. Eight accurate
color plates show over 100 most popular flies, with detailed instructions for
dressing about 200 of the most accepted patterns used all around the
Atlantic.

STREAMER FLY TYING & FISHING, by Joseph D. Bates, Jr.
Stackpole Books, Harrisburg (1966) $7.95
This 368-page book is the world authority on streamer fly and bucktail
patterns, providing detailed tying instructions for over 300 exactly as done
by their originators. It contains instructions on how and why to select
specific patterns for all conditions and how to fish them for all fresh- and
saltwater gamefish. Eight full-page plates show 119 famous patterns in full
and accurate color.

COMPLETE BOOK OF FLY FISHING, by Joe Brooks
Outdoor Life: A. S. Barnes & Company, New York (1958) $4.95
Considered by many to be the greatest fly fisherman of all time, the late Joe Brooks, former fishing editor of *Outdoor Life*, explains the details of fly fishing for beginner and expert: fly choice and presentation, selection of tackle for fresh- and saltwater species, and suggestions for improving casting and fishing success. The 352 pages are fully illustrated.

TROUT FISHING, by Joe Brooks
Outdoor Life: Harper & Row, New York (1972) $8.95
This modern master of the fly rod takes his readers all over the world in search of trophy trout of all species, accurately describing all fly-casting methods, tackle selection, and favorite flies for every trouting purpose. The 302-page book is profusely illustrated in accurate color.

NEW STREAMSIDE GUIDE, by Art Flick
C. P. Putnam's Sons, New York (1947) $4.95
Again revised, this pocket-sized 110-page book on dry-fly fishing answers the question of what fly to use by explaining the selectivity of trout and how to match natural insects and nymphs with the proper imitations. Insects and flies are illustrated in color, with identification and emergence tables of principal ones.

SPORTS ILLUSTRATED BOOK OF FLY FISHING, by Vernon S. Hidy
J. B. Lippincott Company, Philadelphia (1972) $1.50
This pocket-sized 94-page paperback is an elementary presentation of all aspects of dry, wet, nymph and streamer fly fishing, with helpful sections on trout stream insects, strategy, casting and fly selection. It is sponsored by the editors of *Sports Illustrated* magazine and also is available ($3.95) in hard cover.

A MODERN DRY FLY CODE, by Vincent C. Marinaro
Crown Publishers, Inc., New York (1970) $10.00
This is a revised 269-page edition of an important classic on dry-fly fishing with aquatic and terrestrial artificials including the popular Jassids, Ants and Grasshoppers. The new edition contains color photographs of flies originated and tied by the author, plus pictures of trout rising to natural insects.

MODERN FRESH & SALT WATER FLY FISHING, by Charles F. Waterman
Winchester Press, New York (1972) $8.95

This basic book on fly fishing by an expert angler and prominent angling writer emphasizes methods for catching fish other authors seldom write about, in addition to the trouts and salmon. It contains chapters on large and smallmouth bass, panfish and various saltwater species; also an excellent section on southern brackish water fishing.

FLY TYING AND TACKLE MAKING

FISHING FLIES AND FLY TYING, by William F. Blades
Stackpole Books, Harrisburg, Pennsylvania (1962) $8.50
This 320-page book describes and illustrates the tying of all types of wet and dry flies and nymphs, bass and salmon flies, and jigs, etc., together with the dressing formulas for hundreds of patterns. It contains entomological information on imitating specific flies and nymphs with artificials.

HOW TO MAKE FISHING LURES, by Vlad Evanoff
Ronald Press Company, New York City (1959) $3.50
Illustrated with how-to-do-it drawings, this 108-page book tells how to make plugs, bugs, spoons, spinners, jigs and other lures for both fresh and salt water.

PROFESSIONAL FLY TYING AND TACKLE MAKING, by George L. Herter
Herter's, Waseca, Minnesota (1949) $1.50
Here is a big 416-page soft-bound book at a very low price describing fly-tying and equipment, tackle making, and how to make many other types of lures, including considerable information unavailable elsewhere.

FLY TYING, by Helen Shaw
Ronald Press Company, New York City (1963) $7.00
Over 250 clear, life-size photos, with specific instructions, in this 282-page book take the fly dresser through all details of fly dressing and the uses of materials, as done by a noted professional. As a how-to-do-it book this is the very best, but it lacks dressing formulas for specific patterns.

I previously mentioned that twenty angling books of general interest would be listed in this chapter. Those who count them will find only nineteen. We hope that the book you now are holding will be a worthy addition to the list!

Photo Credits

A. I. ALEXANDER: pages 195, 201, 202, 209, 210

FRED ARBOGAST COMPANY: page 582

ERWIN A. BAUER: pages 2, 34, 35, 48, 126, 332, 335, 341, 347, 411, 415, 423, 445, 472, 474, 477, 480, 481, 485, 488, 491, 493, 494, 512, 640, 643, 649

ART BILSTEN, NATIONAL AUDUBON SOCIETY: page 337

BRADFORD LaRIVIERE, INC: page 145

COBIA BOATS, INC: page 285

CONNECTICUT DEPARTMENT OF ENVIRONMENTAL PROTECTION: pages 465, 466

PETE ELKINS: pages 465, 468

THE GARCIA CORPORATION: pages 52, 139

REX GERLACH: pages 20–32, 41–45, 55–61, 150–181

LARRY GREEN: pages 446, 449

HARDY BROTHERS, LONDON: page 432

BRYAN HITCHCOCK: page 126

LUHR JENSEN & SONS: page 449

BING McCLELLAN (BURKE FISHING LURES): page 409

WERNER MEINEL: pages 401, 428

CHARLES R. MEYER: page 585

MICHIGAN DEPARTMENT OF CONSERVATION: pages 505, 512

MONTANA FISH & GAME DEPARTMENT: page 345

THE ORVIS COMPANY: pages 194, 414, 605

ART OURANGEAU: page 502

PENNSYLVANIA FISH COMMISSION: page 501

SCIENTIFIC ANGLERS, INC: page 137

SHAKESPEARE TACKLE COMPANY: pages 8, 37, 530, 532, 534

DON SHINER: pages 502, 504, 508

MARK J. SOSIN: pages 6, 9, 10, 11, 13, 15, 38, 51, 142, 353, 539, 607, 623, 636

ROBERT STEARNS: pages 609, 610, 614, 642

TRUE TEMPER TACKLE COMPANY: page 530

CHARLES F. WATERMAN: page 407

WRIGHT & McGILL COMPANY: page 5, 214, 215

LEE WULFF: page 427

BOB ZWIRZ: pages 17, 284, 419, 430, 519, 613

Index